The Design and Implementation of the

4.4BSD
Operating System

The Design and Implementation of the

4.4BSD
Operating System

Marshall Kirk McKusick
Consultant

Keith Bostic
Berkeley Software Design, Inc.

Michael J. Karels
Berkeley Software Design, Inc.

John S. Quarterman
Texas Internet Consulting

Addison-Wesley Publishing Company

Reading, Massachusetts • Menlo Park, California • New York
Don Mills, Ontario • Harlow, United Kingdom • Amsterdam • Bonn
Sydney • Singapore • Tokyo • Madrid • San Juan • Milan • Paris

This book is in the **Addison-Wesley UNIX and Open Systems Series**

Series Editors: *Marshall Kirk McKusick* and *John S. Quarterman*
Publishing Partner: *Peter S. Gordon*
Associate Editor: *Deborah R. Lafferty*
Associate Production Supervisor: *Patricia A. Oduor*
Marketing Manager: *Bob Donegan*
Senior Manufacturing Manager: *Roy E. Logan*
Cover Designer: *Barbara Atkinson*
Troff Macro Designer: *Jaap Akkerhuis*
Copy Editor: *Lyn Dupré*
Cover Art: *John Lasseter*

UNIX is a registered trademark of X/Open in the United States and other countries. Many of the designations used by manufacturers and sellers to distinguish their products are claimed as trademarks. Where those designations appear in this book, and Addison-Wesley was aware of a trademark claim, the designations have been printed in initial caps or all caps.

The programs and applications presented in this book have been included for their instructional value. They have been tested with care, but are not guaranteed for any particular purpose. The publisher offers no warranties or representations, nor does it accept any liabilities with respect to the programs or applications.

Library of Congress Cataloging-in-Publication Data

```
The design and implementation of the 4.4BSD operating system /
  Marshall Kirk McKusick ... [et al.].
    p. cm.
    Includes bibliographical references and index.
    ISBN 0-201-54979-4
    1. UNIX (Computer file) 2. Operating systems (Computers)
    I. McKusick, Marshall Kirk.
QA76.76.063D4743 1996                    96-2433
005.4'3--dc20                            CIP
```

1 2 3 4 5 6 7 8 9 10-MA-99989796

Dedication

This book is dedicated to the BSD community.
Without the contributions of that community's members,
there would be nothing about which to write.

Preface

This book is an extensive revision of the first authoritative and full-length description of the design and implementation of the research versions of the UNIX system developed at the University of California at Berkeley. Most detail is given about 4.4BSD, which incorporates the improvements of the previous Berkeley versions. Although 4.4BSD includes nearly 500 utility programs in addition to the kernel, this book concentrates almost exclusively on the kernel.

The UNIX System

The UNIX system runs on computers ranging from personal home systems to the largest supercomputers. It is the operating system of choice for most multiprocessor, graphics, and vector-processing systems, and is widely used for its original purpose of timesharing. It is the most common platform for providing network services (from FTP to WWW) on the Internet. It is the most portable operating system ever developed. This portability is due partly to its implementation language, C [Kernighan & Ritchie, 1978] (which is itself one of the most widely ported languages), and partly to the elegant design of the system. Many of the system's features are imitated in other systems [O'Dell, 1987].

Since its inception in 1969 [Ritchie & Thompson, 1978], the UNIX system has developed in a number of divergent and rejoining streams. The original developers continued to advance the state of the art with their Ninth and Tenth Edition UNIX inside AT&T Bell Laboratories, and then their Plan 9 successor to UNIX. Meanwhile, AT&T licensed UNIX System V as a product, before selling it to Novell. Novell passed the UNIX trademark to X/OPEN and sold the source code and distribution rights to Santa Cruz Operation (SCO). Both System V and Ninth Edition UNIX were strongly influenced by the Berkeley Software Distributions produced by the Computer Systems Research Group (CSRG) of the University of California at Berkeley.

Berkeley Software Distributions

These Berkeley systems have introduced several useful programs and facilities to the UNIX community:

- 2BSD (the Berkeley PDP-11 system): the text editor **vi**

- 3BSD (the first Berkeley VAX system): demand-paged virtual-memory support

- 4.0BSD: performance improvements

- 4.1BSD: job control, autoconfiguration, and long C identifiers

- 4.2BSD and 4.3BSD: reliable signals; a fast filesystem; improved networking, including a reference implementation of TCP/IP; sophisticated interprocess-communication (IPC) primitives; and more performance improvements

- 4.4BSD: a new virtual memory system; a stackable and extensible vnode interface; a network filesystem (NFS); a log-structured filesystem, numerous filesystem types, including loopback, union, and uid/gid mapping layers; an ISO9660 filesystem (e.g., CD-ROM); ISO networking protocols; support for 68K, SPARC, MIPS, and PC architectures; POSIX support, including termios, sessions, and most utilities; multiple IP addresses per interface; disk labels; and improved booting

4.2BSD, 4.3BSD, and 4.4BSD are the bases for the UNIX systems of many vendors, and are used internally by the development groups of many other vendors. Many of these developments have also been incorporated by System V, or have been added by vendors whose products are otherwise based on System V.

The implementation of the TCP/IP networking protocol suite in 4.2BSD and 4.3BSD, and the availability of those systems, explain why the TCP/IP networking protocol suite is implemented so widely throughout the world. Numerous vendors have adapted the Berkeley networking implementations, whether their base system is 4.2BSD, 4.3BSD, 4.4BSD, System V, or even Digital Equipment Corporation's VMS or Microsoft's Winsock interface in Windows '95 and Windows/NT.

4BSD has also been a strong influence on the POSIX (IEEE Std 1003.1) operating-system interface standard, and on related standards. Several features—such as reliable signals, job control, multiple access groups per process, and the routines for directory operations—have been adapted from 4.3BSD for POSIX.

Material Covered in this Book

This book is about the *internal* structure of 4.4BSD [Quarterman et al, 1985], and about the concepts, data structures, and algorithms used in implementing 4.4BSD's system facilities. Its level of detail is similar to that of Bach's book about UNIX System V [Bach, 1986]; however, this text focuses on the facilities, data structures, and algorithms used in the Berkeley variant of the UNIX operating system. The book covers 4.4BSD from the system-call level down—from the interface to the kernel to the hardware itself. The kernel includes system facilities, such as process management, virtual memory, the I/O system, filesystems, the *socket* IPC mechanism, and network protocol implementations. Material above the system-call level—such as libraries, shells, commands, programming languages, and other user interfaces—is excluded, except for some material related to the terminal interface and to system startup. Like Organick's book about Multics [Organick, 1975], this book is an in-depth study of a contemporary operating system.

Where particular hardware is relevant, the book refers to the Hewlett-Packard HP300 (Motorola 68000-based) architecture. Because 4.4BSD was developed on the HP300, that is the architecture with the most complete support, so it provides a convenient point of reference.

Readers who will benefit from this book include operating-system implementors, system programmers, UNIX application developers, administrators, and curious users. The book can be read as a companion to the source code of the system, falling as it does between the manual [CSRG, 1994] and the code in detail of treatment. But this book is specifically neither a UNIX programming manual nor a user tutorial (for a tutorial, see [Libes & Ressler, 1988]). Familiarity with the use of some version of the UNIX system (see, for example, [Kernighan & Pike, 1984]), and with the C programming language (see, for example, [Kernighan & Ritchie, 1988]) would be extremely useful.

Use in Courses on Operating Systems

This book is suitable for use as a reference text to provide background for a primary textbook in a second-level course on operating systems. It is not intended for use as an introductory operating-system textbook; the reader should have already encountered terminology such as *memory management*, *process scheduling*, and *I/O systems* [Silberschatz & Galvin, 1994]. Familiarity with the concepts of network protocols [Tanenbaum, 1988; Stallings, 1993; Schwartz, 1987] will be useful for understanding some of the later chapters.

Exercises are provided at the end of each chapter. The exercises are graded into three categories indicated by zero, one, or two asterisks. The answers to exercises that carry no asterisks can be found in the text. Exercises with a single asterisk require a step of reasoning or intuition beyond a concept presented in the text. Exercises with two asterisks present major design projects or open research questions.

Organization

This text discusses both philosophical and design issues, as well as details of the actual implementation. Often, the discussion starts at the system-call level and descends into the kernel. Tables and figures are used to clarify data structures and control flow. Pseudocode similar to the C language is used to display algorithms. Boldface font identifies program names and filesystem pathnames. Italics font introduces terms that appear in the glossary and identifies the names of system calls, variables, routines, and structure names. Routine names (other than system calls) are further identified by the name followed by a pair of parenthesis (e.g., *malloc*() is the name of a routine, whereas *argv* is the name of a variable).

The book is divided into five parts, organized as follows:

• **Part 1, Overview**   Three introductory chapters provide the context for the complete operating system and for the rest of the book. Chapter 1, *History and Goals*, sketches the historical development of the system, emphasizing the system's research orientation. Chapter 2, *Design Overview of 4.4BSD*, describes the services offered by the system, and outlines the internal organization of the kernel. It also discusses the design decisions that were made as the system was developed. Sections 2.3 through 2.14 in Chapter 2 give an overview of their corresponding chapter. Chapter 3, *Kernel Services*, explains how system calls are done, and describes in detail several of the basic services of the kernel.

• **Part 2, Processes**   The first chapter in this part—Chapter 4, *Process Management*—lays the foundation for later chapters by describing the structure of a process, the algorithms used for scheduling the execution of processes, and the synchronization mechanisms used by the system to ensure consistent access to kernel-resident data structures. In Chapter 5, *Memory Management*, the virtual-memory–management system is discussed in detail.

• **Part 3, I/O System**   First, Chapter 6, *I/O System Overview*, explains the system interface to I/O and describes the structure of the facilities that support this interface. Following this introduction are four chapters that give the details of the main parts of the I/O system. Chapter 7, *Local Filesystems*, details the data structures and algorithms that implement filesystems as seen by application programs. Chapter 8, *Local Filestores*, describes how local filesystems are interfaced with local media. Chapter 9, *The Network Filesystem*, explains the network filesystem from both the server and client perspectives. Chapter 10, *Terminal Handling*, discusses support for character terminals, and provides a description of a character-oriented device driver.

• **Part 4, Interprocess Communication**   Chapter 11, *Interprocess Communication*, describes the mechanism for providing communication between related or unrelated processes. Chapters 12 and 13, *Network Communication* and *Network Protocols*, are closely related, as the facilities explained in the former are implemented by specific protocols, such as the TCP/IP protocol suite, explained in the latter.

• **Part 5, System Operation**   Chapter 14, *System Startup*, discusses system startup, shutdown, and configuration, and explains system initialization at the process level, from kernel initialization to user login.

The book is intended to be read in the order that the chapters are presented, but the parts other than Part 1 are independent of one another and can be read separately. Chapter 14 should be read after all the others, but knowledgeable readers may find it useful independently.

At the end of the book are a *Glossary* with brief definitions of major terms and an *Index*. Each chapter contains a *Reference* section with citations of related material.

Getting 4.4BSD

Current information about the availability of 4.4BSD source code can be found at Addison-Wesley's web site: http://www.aw.com/cseng/authors/mckusick. See the catalog listing for this book. At press time, the source code for the 4.4BSD-Lite Release 2 system, as well as that for the FreeBSD version of 4.4BSD, which is compiled and ready to run on PC-compatible hardware, are available from Walnut Creek CDROM. Contact Walnut Creek for more information at 1-800-786-9907, or use orders@cdrom.com, or http://www.cdrom.com/. The NetBSD distribution is compiled and ready to run on most workstation architectures. For more information, contact the NetBSD Project at majordomo@NetBSD.ORG (send a message body of "lists"), or http://www.NetBSD.ORG/. A fully supported commercial release, BSD/OS, is available from Berkeley Software Design, Inc., at 1-800-800-4273, bsdi-info@bsdi.com, or http://www.bsdi.com/. The 4.4BSD manuals are jointly published by Usenix and O'Reilly. O'Reilly sells the five volumes individually or in a set (ISDN 1-56592-082-1): 1-800-889-8969, order@ora.com, or http://www.ora.com/.

For you diehards who actually read to the end of the preface, your reward is finding out that you can get T-shirts that are a reproduction of the the the original artwork drawn by John Lasseter for the cover of this book (yes, he is the John Lasseter of Walt Disney/Pixar fame who masterminded the production of "Toy Story"). These shirts were made available to the people who helped with the creation, reviewing, and editing of the book and to those folks who first reported errors in the book. A variation on these shirts that is clearly different from the originals (so as not to diminish the rarity of the ones that people had to work to get) is now available. For further information on purchasing a shirt, send a self-addressed envelope (United States residents please include return postage) to

> M. K. McKusick
> 1614 Oxford St.
> Berkeley, CA 94709-1608
> USA

Alternatively, you can send mail to mckusick@McKusick.COM with subject line "T-shirt Information Request" or visit the "History of BSD T-shirts" web page at http://www.zilker.net/users/beastie/index.html.

Acknowledgments

We extend special thanks to Mike Hibler (University of Utah) who coauthored Chapter 5 on memory management, and to Rick Macklem (University of Guelph), whose NFS papers provided much of the material on NFS for Chapter 9.

We also thank the following people who read and commented on nearly the entire book: Paul Abrahams (Consultant), Susan LoVerso (Orca Systems), George Neville-Neil (Wind River Systems), and Steve Stepanek (California State University, Northbridge).

We thank the following people, all of whom read and commented on early drafts of the book: Eric Allman (Pangaea Reference Systems), Eric Anderson

(University of California at Berkeley), Mark Andrews (Alias Research), Mike Beede (Secure Computing Corporation), Paul Borman (Berkeley Software Design), Peter Collinson (Hillside Systems), Ben Cottrell (NetBSD user), Patrick Cua (De La Salle University, Philippines), John Dyson (The FreeBSD Project), Sean Eric Fagan (BSD developer), Mike Fester (Medieus Systems Corporation), David Greenman (The FreeBSD Project), Wayne Hathaway (Auspex Systems), John Heidemann (University of California at Los Angeles), Jeff Honig (Berkeley Software Design), Gordon Irlam (Cygnus Support), Alan Langerman (Orca Systems), Sam Leffler (Silicon Graphics), Casimir Lesiak (NASA/Ames Research Center), Gavin Lim (De La Salle University, Philippines), Steve Lucco (Carnegie Mellon University), Jan-Simon Pendry (Sequent, UK), Arnold Robbins (Georgia Institute of Technology), Peter Salus (UNIX historian), Wayne Sawdon (Carnegie Mellon University), Margo Seltzer (Harvard University), Keith Sklower (University of California at Berkeley), Keith Smith (Harvard University), and Humprey C. Sy (De La Salle University, Philippines).

This book was produced using James Clark's implementations of **pic**, **tbl**, **eqn**, and **groff**. The index was generated by **awk** scripts derived from indexing programs written by Jon Bentley and Brian Kernighan [Bentley & Kernighan, 1986]. Most of the art was created with **xfig**. Figure placement and widow elimination were handled by the **groff** macros, but orphan elimination and production of even page bottoms had to be done by hand.

We encourage readers to send us suggested improvements or comments about typographical or other errors found in the book; please send electronic mail to **bsdbook-bugs@McKusick.COM**.

References

Bach, 1986.
> M. J. Bach, *The Design of the UNIX Operating System*, Prentice-Hall, Englewood Cliffs, NJ, 1986.

Bentley & Kernighan, 1986.
> J. Bentley & B. Kernighan, "Tools for Printing Indexes," Computing Science Technical Report 128, AT&T Bell Laboratories, Murray Hill, NJ, 1986.

CSRG, 1994.
> CSRG, in *4.4 Berkeley Software Distribution*, O'Reilly & Associates, Inc., Sebastopol, CA, 1994.

Kernighan & Pike, 1984.
> B. W. Kernighan & R. Pike, *The UNIX Programming Environment*, Prentice-Hall, Englewood Cliffs, NJ, 1984.

Kernighan & Ritchie, 1978.
> B. W. Kernighan & D. M. Ritchie, *The C Programming Language*, Prentice-Hall, Englewood Cliffs, NJ, 1978.

Kernighan & Ritchie, 1988.
> B. W. Kernighan & D. M. Ritchie, *The C Programming Language,* 2nd ed, Prentice-Hall, Englewood Cliffs, NJ, 1988.

Libes & Ressler, 1988.
> D. Libes & S. Ressler, *Life with UNIX,* Prentice-Hall, Englewood Cliffs, NJ, 1988.

O'Dell, 1987.
> M. O'Dell, "UNIX: The World View," *Proceedings of the 1987 Winter USENIX Conference*, pp. 35–45, January 1987.

Organick, 1975.
> E. I. Organick, *The Multics System: An Examination of Its Structure,* MIT Press, Cambridge, MA, 1975.

Quarterman et al, 1985.
> J. S. Quarterman, A. Silberschatz, & J. L. Peterson, "4.2BSD and 4.3BSD as Examples of the UNIX System," *ACM Computing Surveys*, vol. 17, no. 4, pp. 379–418, December 1985.

Ritchie & Thompson, 1978.
> D. M. Ritchie & K. Thompson, "The UNIX Time-Sharing System," *Bell System Technical Journal*, vol. 57, no. 6, Part 2, pp. 1905–1929, July–August 1978. *The original version [Comm. ACM vol. 7, no. 7, pp. 365–375 (July 1974)] described the 6th edition; this citation describes the 7th edition.*

Schwartz, 1987.
> M. Schwartz, *Telecommunication Networks,* Series in Electrical and Computer Engineering, Addison-Wesley, Reading, MA, 1987.

Silberschatz & Galvin, 1994.
> A. Silberschatz & P. Galvin, *Operating System Concepts,* 4th Edition, Addison-Wesley, Reading, MA, 1994.

Stallings, 1993.
> R. Stallings, *Data and Computer Communications,* 4th Edition, Macmillan, New York, NY, 1993.

Tanenbaum, 1988.
> A. S. Tanenbaum, *Computer Networks,* 2nd ed, Prentice-Hall, Englewood Cliffs, NJ, 1988.

About the Authors

Left to right: Mike Karels, Keith Bostic, Kirk McKusick, and John Quarterman together for the first time at a Usenix Conference in San Diego.

Marshall Kirk McKusick writes books and articles, consults, and teaches classes on UNIX- and BSD-related subjects. While at the University of California at Berkeley, he implemented the 4.2BSD fast file system, and was the Research Computer Scientist at the Berkeley Computer Systems Research Group (CSRG) overseeing the development and release of 4.3BSD and 4.4BSD. His particular areas of interest are the virtual-memory system and the filesystem. One day, he hopes to see them merged seamlessly. He earned his undergraduate degree in Electrical Engineering from Cornell University, and did his graduate work at the University of California at Berkeley, where he received Masters degrees in Computer Science and Business Administration, and a doctoral degree in Computer Science. He is a past president of the Usenix Association, and is a member of ACM and IEEE. In his spare time, he enjoys swimming, scuba diving, and wine collecting. The wine is stored in a specially constructed wine cellar (accessible from the net using the command ``telnet McKusick.COM 451'') in the basement of the house that he shares with Eric Allman, his domestic partner of 17-and-some-odd years.

Keith Bostic is a member of the technical staff at Berkeley Software Design, Inc. He spent 8 years as a member of the CSRG, overseeing the development of over 400 freely redistributable UNIX-compatible utilities, and is the recipient of the 1991 Distinguished Achievement Award from the University of California, Berkeley, for his work to make 4.4BSD freely redistributable. Concurrently, he was the principle architect of the 2.10BSD release of the Berkeley Software Distribution for PDP-11s, and the coauthor of the Berkeley Log Structured Filesystem and the Berkeley database package (*DB*). He is also the author of the widely used **vi** implementation, **nvi**. He received his undergraduate degree in Statistics and his Masters degree in Electrical Engineering from George Washington University. He is a member of the ACM, the IEEE, and several POSIX working groups. In his spare time, he enjoys scuba diving in the South Pacific, mountain biking, and working on a tunnel into Kirk and Eric's specially constructed wine cellar. He lives in Massachusetts with his wife, Margo Seltzer, and their cats.

Michael J. Karels is the System Architect and Vice President of Engineering at Berkeley Software Design, Inc. He spent 8 years as the Principal Programmer of the CSRG at the University of California, Berkeley as the system architect for 4.3BSD. Karels received his Bachelor's degree in Microbiology from the University of Notre Dame. While a graduate student in Molecular Biology at the University of California, he was the principal developer of the 2.9BSD UNIX release of the Berkeley Software Distribution for the PDP-11. He is a member of the ACM, the IEEE, and several POSIX working groups. He lives with his wife Teri Karels in the backwoods of Minnesota.

John S. Quarterman is a partner in Texas Internet Consulting (TIC), which consults in networks and open systems with particular emphasis on TCP/IP networks, UNIX systems, and standards. He is the author of *The Matrix: Computer Networks and Conferencing Systems Worldwide* (Digital Press, 1990), and is a coauthor of *UNIX, POSIX, and Open Systems: The Open Standards Puzzle* (1993), *Practical Internetworking with TCP/IP and UNIX* (1993), *The Internet Connection: System Connectivity and Configuration* (1994), and *The E-Mail Companion: Communicating Effectively via the Internet and Other Global Networks* (1994), all published by Addison-Wesley. He is editor of *Matrix News*, a monthly newsletter about issues that cross network, geographic, and political boundaries, and of *Matrix Maps Quarterly*; both are published by Matrix Information and Directory Services, Inc. (MIDS) of Austin, Texas. He is a partner in Zilker Internet Park, which provides Internet access from Austin. He and his wife, Gretchen Quarterman, split their time among his home in Austin, hers in Buffalo, New York, and various other locations.

Contents

Chapter 3 Kernel Services   **49**

Part 3 I/O System   191

Chapter 12   Network Communication   395

Chapter 13   Network Protocols   435

PART 1

Overview

CHAPTER 1

History and Goals

1.1 History of the UNIX System

The UNIX system has been in wide use for over 20 years, and has helped to define many areas of computing. Although numerous organizations have contributed (and still contribute) to the development of the UNIX system, this book will primarily concentrate the BSD thread of development:

- Bell Laboratories, which invented UNIX

- The Computer Systems Research Group (CSRG) at the University of California at Berkeley, which gave UNIX virtual memory and the reference implementation of TCP/IP

- Berkeley Software Design, Incorporated (BSDI), The FreeBSD Project, and The NetBSD Project, which continue the work started by the CSRG

Origins

The first version of the UNIX system was developed at Bell Laboratories in 1969 by Ken Thompson as a private research project to use an otherwise idle PDP-7. Thompson was joined shortly thereafter by Dennis Ritchie, who not only contributed to the design and implementation of the system, but also invented the C programming language. The system was completely rewritten into C, leaving almost no assembly language. The original elegant design of the system [Ritchie, 1978] and developments of the past 15 years [Ritchie, 1984a; Compton, 1985] have made the UNIX system an important and powerful operating system [Ritchie, 1987].

Ritchie, Thompson, and other early UNIX developers at Bell Laboratories had worked previously on the Multics project [Peirce, 1985; Organick, 1975], which had a strong influence on the newer operating system. Even the name *UNIX* is merely a pun on *Multics*; in areas where Multics attempted to do many tasks, UNIX tried to do one task well. The basic organization of the UNIX filesystem, the idea of using a user process for the command interpreter, the general organization of the filesystem interface, and many other system characteristics, come directly from Multics.

Ideas from various other operating systems, such as the Massachusetts Institute of Technology's (MIT's) CTSS, also have been incorporated. The *fork* operation to create new processes comes from Berkeley's GENIE (SDS-940, later XDS-940) operating system. Allowing a user to create processes inexpensively led to using one process per command, rather than to commands being run as procedure calls, as is done in Multics.

There are at least three major streams of development of the UNIX system. Figure 1.1 sketches their early evolution; Figure 1.2 (shown on page 6) sketches their more recent developments, especially for those branches leading to 4.4BSD and to System V [Chambers & Quarterman, 1983; Uniejewski, 1985]. The dates given are approximate, and we have made no attempt to show all influences. Some of the systems named in the figure are not mentioned in the text, but are included to show more clearly the relations among the ones that we shall examine.

Research UNIX

The first major editions of UNIX were the Research systems from Bell Laboratories. In addition to the earliest versions of the system, these systems include the **UNIX Time-Sharing System, Sixth Edition**, commonly known as **V6**, which, in 1976, was the first version widely available outside of Bell Laboratories. Systems are identified by the edition numbers of the *UNIX Programmer's Manual* that were current when the distributions were made.

The UNIX system was distinguished from other operating systems in three important ways:

1. The UNIX system was written in a high-level language.

2. The UNIX system was distributed in source form.

3. The UNIX system provided powerful primitives normally found in only those operating systems that ran on much more expensive hardware.

Most of the system source code was written in C, rather than in assembly language. The prevailing belief at the time was that an operating system had to be written in assembly language to provide reasonable efficiency and to get access to the hardware. The C language itself was at a sufficiently high level to allow it to be compiled easily for a wide range of computer hardware, without its being so complex or restrictive that systems programmers had to revert to assembly language to get reasonable efficiency or functionality. Access to the hardware was provided through assembly-language stubs for the 3 percent of the operating-system functions—such as context switching—that needed them. Although the success of UNIX does not stem solely from its being written in a high-level

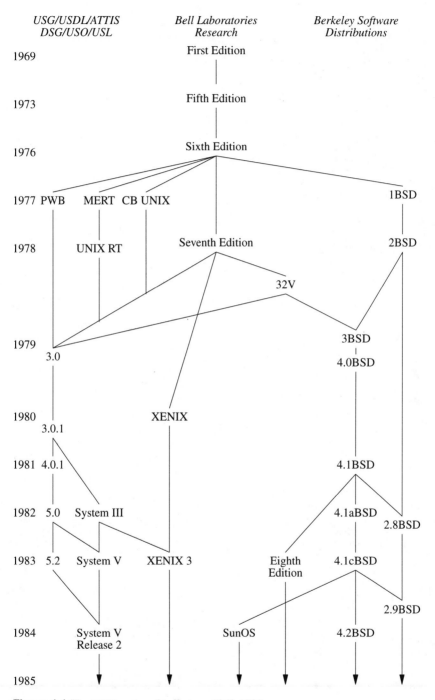

Figure 1.1 The UNIX system family tree, 1969-1985.

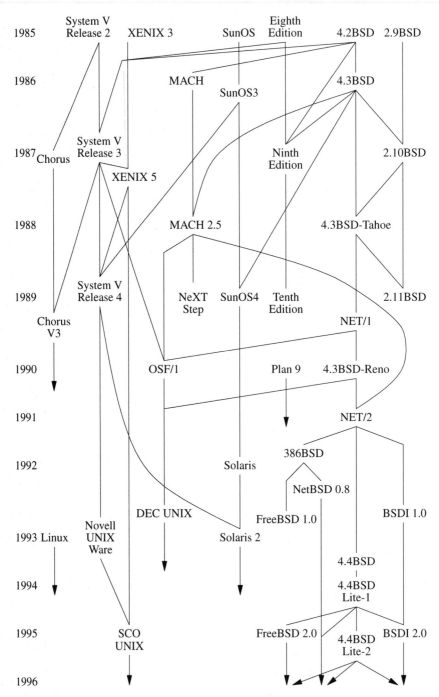

Figure 1.2 The UNIX system family tree, 1986-1996.

language, the use of C was a critical first step [Ritchie et al, 1978; Kernighan & Ritchie, 1978; Kernighan & Ritchie, 1988]. Ritchie's C language is descended [Rosler, 1984] from Thompson's B language, which was itself descended from BCPL [Richards & Whitby-Strevens, 1980]. C continues to evolve [Tuthill, 1985; X3J11, 1988], and there is a variant—C++—that more readily permits data abstraction [Stroustrup, 1984; USENIX, 1987].

The second important distinction of UNIX was its early release from Bell Laboratories to other research environments in source form. By providing source, the system's founders ensured that other organizations would be able not only to use the system, but also to tinker with its inner workings. The ease with which new ideas could be adopted into the system always has been key to the changes that have been made to it. Whenever a new system that tried to upstage UNIX came along, somebody would dissect the newcomer and clone its central ideas into UNIX. The unique ability to use a small, comprehensible system, written in a high-level language, in an environment swimming in new ideas led to a UNIX system that evolved far beyond its humble beginnings.

The third important distinction of UNIX was that it provided individual users with the ability to run multiple processes concurrently and to connect these processes into pipelines of commands. At the time, only operating systems running on large and expensive machines had the ability to run multiple processes, and the number of concurrent processes usually was controlled tightly by a system administrator.

Most early UNIX systems ran on the PDP-11, which was inexpensive and powerful for its time. Nonetheless, there was at least one early port of Sixth Edition UNIX to a machine with a different architecture, the Interdata 7/32 [Miller, 1978]. The PDP-11 also had an inconveniently small address space. The introduction of machines with 32-bit address spaces, especially the VAX-11/780, provided an opportunity for UNIX to expand its services to include virtual memory and networking. Earlier experiments by the Research group in providing UNIX-like facilities on different hardware had led to the conclusion that it was as easy to move the entire operating system as it was to duplicate UNIX's services under another operating system. The first UNIX system with portability as a specific goal was **UNIX Time-Sharing System, Seventh Edition** (**V7**), which ran on the PDP-11 and the Interdata 8/32, and had a VAX variety called **UNIX/32V Time-Sharing, System Version 1.0** (**32V**). The Research group at Bell Laboratories has also developed **UNIX Time-Sharing System, Eighth Edition** (**V8**), **UNIX Time-Sharing System, Ninth Edition** (**V9**), and **UNIX Time-Sharing System, Tenth Edition** (**V10**). Their 1996 system is **Plan 9**.

AT&T UNIX System III and System V

After the distribution of Seventh Edition in 1978, the Research group turned over external distributions to the UNIX Support Group (USG). USG had previously distributed internally such systems as the **UNIX Programmer's Work Bench** (**PWB**), and had sometimes distributed them externally as well [Mohr, 1985].

USG's first external distribution after Seventh Edition was **UNIX System III (System III)**, in 1982, which incorporated features of Seventh Edition, of 32V, and also of several UNIX systems developed by groups other than the Research group. Features of UNIX /RT (a real-time UNIX system) were included, as were many features from PWB. USG released **UNIX System V (System V)** in 1983; that system is largely derived from System III. The court-ordered divestiture of the Bell Operating Companies from AT&T permitted AT&T to market System V aggressively [Wilson, 1985; Bach, 1986].

USG metamorphosed into the UNIX System Development Laboratory (USDL), which released **UNIX System V, Release 2** in 1984. System V, Release 2, Version 4 introduced paging [Miller, 1984; Jung, 1985], including copy-on-write and shared memory, to System V. The System V implementation was not based on the Berkeley paging system. USDL was succeeded by AT&T Information Systems (ATTIS), which distributed **UNIX System V, Release 3** in 1987. That system included STREAMS, an IPC mechanism adopted from V8 [Presotto & Ritchie, 1985]. ATTIS was succeeded by UNIX System Laboratories (USL), which was sold to Novell in 1993. Novell passed the UNIX trademark to the X/OPEN consortium, giving the latter sole rights to set up certification standards for using the UNIX name on products. Two years later, Novell sold UNIX to The Santa Cruz Operation (SCO).

Other Organizations

The ease with which the UNIX system can be modified has led to development work at numerous organizations, including the Rand Corporation, which is responsible for the Rand ports mentioned in Chapter 11; Bolt Beranek and Newman (BBN), who produced the direct ancestor of the 4.2BSD networking implementation discussed in Chapter 13; the University of Illinois, which did earlier networking work; Harvard; Purdue; and Digital Equipment Corporation (DEC).

Probably the most widespread version of the UNIX operating system, according to the number of machines on which it runs, is XENIX by Microsoft Corporation and The Santa Cruz Operation. XENIX was originally based on Seventh Edition, but later on System V. More recently, SCO purchased UNIX from Novell and announced plans to merge the two systems.

Systems prominently *not* based on UNIX include IBM's OS/2 and Microsoft's Windows 95 and Windows/NT. All these systems have been touted as UNIX killers, but none have done the deed.

Berkeley Software Distributions

The most influential of the non-Bell Laboratories and non-AT&T UNIX development groups was the University of California at Berkeley [McKusick, 1985]. Software from Berkeley is released in **Berkeley Software Distributions (BSD)**—for example, as 4.3BSD. The first Berkeley VAX UNIX work was the addition to 32V of virtual memory, demand paging, and page replacement in 1979 by William Joy and Ozalp Babaoğlu, to produce **3BSD** [Babaoğlu & Joy, 1981].

The reason for the large virtual-memory space of 3BSD was the development of what at the time were large programs, such as Berkeley's *Franz* LISP. This memory-management work convinced the Defense Advanced Research Projects Agency (DARPA) to fund the Berkeley team for the later development of a standard system (4BSD) for DARPA's contractors to use.

A goal of the 4BSD project was to provide support for the DARPA Internet networking protocols, TCP/IP [Cerf & Cain, 1983]. The networking implementation was general enough to communicate among diverse network facilities, ranging from local networks, such as Ethernets and token rings, to long-haul networks, such as DARPA's ARPANET.

We refer to all the Berkeley VAX UNIX systems following 3BSD as 4BSD, although there were really several releases—4.0BSD, 4.1BSD, 4.2BSD, 4.3BSD, 4.3BSD Tahoe, and 4.3BSD Reno. 4BSD was the UNIX operating system of choice for VAXes from the time that the VAX first became available in 1977 until the release of System V in 1983. Most organizations would purchase a 32V license, but would order 4BSD from Berkeley. Many installations inside the Bell System ran 4.1BSD (and replaced it with 4.3BSD when the latter became available). A new virtual-memory system was released with 4.4BSD. The VAX was reaching the end of its useful lifetime, so 4.4BSD was not ported to that machine. Instead, 4.4BSD ran on the newer 68000, SPARC, MIPS, and Intel PC architectures.

The 4BSD work for DARPA was guided by a steering committee that included many notable people from both commercial and academic institutions. The culmination of the original Berkeley DARPA UNIX project was the release of **4.2BSD** in 1983; further research at Berkeley produced **4.3BSD** in mid-1986. The next releases included the **4.3BSD Tahoe** release of June 1988 and the **4.3BSD Reno** release of June 1990. These releases were primarily ports to the Computer Consoles Incorporated hardware platform. Interleaved with these releases were two unencumbered networking releases: the **4.3BSD Net1** release of March 1989 and the **4.3BSD Net2** release of June 1991. These releases extracted nonproprietary code from 4.3BSD; they could be redistributed freely in source and binary form to companies that and individuals who were not covered by a UNIX source license. The final CSRG release was to have been two versions of 4.4BSD, to be released in June 1993. One was to have been a traditional full source and binary distribution, called 4.4BSD-Encumbered, that required the recipient to have a UNIX source license. The other was to have been a subset of the source, called 4.4BSD-Lite, that contained no licensed code and did not require the recipient to have a UNIX source license. Following these distributions, the CSRG would be dissolved. The 4.4BSD-Encumbered was released as scheduled, but legal action by USL prevented the distribution of 4.4BSD-Lite. The legal action was resolved about 1 year later, and 4.4BSD-Lite was released in April 1994. The last of the money in the CSRG coffers was used to produce a bug-fixed version 4.4BSD-Lite, release 2, that was distributed in June 1995. This release was the true final distribution from the CSRG.

Nonetheless, 4BSD still lives on in all modern implementations of UNIX, and in many other operating systems.

UNIX in the World

Dozens of computer manufacturers, including almost all the ones usually considered major by market share, have introduced computers that run the UNIX system or close derivatives, and numerous other companies sell related peripherals, software packages, support, training, and documentation. The hardware packages involved range from micros through minis, multis, and mainframes to supercomputers. Most of these manufacturers use ports of System V, 4.2BSD, 4.3BSD, 4.4BSD, or mixtures. We expect that, by now, there are probably no more machines running software based on System III, 4.1BSD, or Seventh Edition, although there may well still be PDP-11s running 2BSD and other UNIX variants. If there are any Sixth Edition systems still in regular operation, we would be amused to hear about them (our contact information is given at the end of the Preface).

The UNIX system is also a fertile field for academic endeavor. Thompson and Ritchie were given the Association for Computing Machinery Turing award for the design of the system [Ritchie, 1984b]. The UNIX system and related, specially designed teaching systems—such as Tunis [Ewens et al, 1985; Holt, 1983], XINU [Comer, 1984], and MINIX [Tanenbaum, 1987]—are widely used in courses on operating systems. Linus Torvalds reimplemented the UNIX interface in his freely redistributable LINUX operating system. The UNIX system is ubiquitous in universities and research facilities throughout the world, and is ever more widely used in industry and commerce.

Even with the demise of the CSRG, the 4.4BSD system continues to flourish. In the free software world, the FreeBSD and NetBSD groups continue to develop and distribute systems based on 4.4BSD. The FreeBSD project concentrates on developing distributions primarily for the personal-computer (PC) platform. The NetBSD project concentrates on providing ports of 4.4BSD to as many platforms as possible. Both groups based their first releases on the Net2 release, but switched over to the 4.4BSD-Lite release when the latter became available.

The commercial variant most closely related to 4.4BSD is BSD/OS, produced by Berkeley Software Design, Inc. (BSDI). Early BSDI software releases were based on the Net2 release; the current BSDI release is based on 4.4BSD-Lite.

1.2   BSD and Other Systems

The CSRG incorporated features not only from UNIX systems, but also from other operating systems. Many of the features of the 4BSD terminal drivers are from TENEX/TOPS-20. Job control (in concept—not in implementation) is derived from that of TOPS-20 and from that of the MIT Incompatible Timesharing System (ITS). The virtual-memory interface first proposed for 4.2BSD, and since implemented by the CSRG and by several commercial vendors, was based on the file-mapping and page-level interfaces that first appeared in TENEX/TOPS-20. The current 4.4BSD virtual-memory system (see Chapter 5) was adapted from MACH, which was itself an offshoot of 4.3BSD. Multics has often been a reference point in the design of new facilities.

The quest for efficiency has been a major factor in much of the CSRG's work. Some efficiency improvements have been made because of comparisons with the proprietary operating system for the VAX, VMS [Kashtan, 1980; Joy, 1980].

Other UNIX variants have adopted many 4BSD features. AT&T UNIX System V [AT&T, 1987], the IEEE POSIX.1 standard [P1003.1, 1988], and the related National Bureau of Standards (NBS) Federal Information Processing Standard (FIPS) have adopted

• Job control (Chapter 2)

• Reliable signals (Chapter 4)

• Multiple file-access permission groups (Chapter 6)

• Filesystem interfaces (Chapter 7)

The X/OPEN Group, originally comprising solely European vendors, but now including most U.S. UNIX vendors, produced the *X/OPEN Portability Guide* [X/OPEN, 1987] and, more recently, the *Spec 1170 Guide*. These documents specify both the kernel interface and many of the utility programs available to UNIX system users. When Novell purchased UNIX from AT&T in 1993, it transferred exclusive ownership of the UNIX name to X/OPEN. Thus, all systems that want to brand themselves as UNIX must meet the X/OPEN interface specifications. The X/OPEN guides have adopted many of the POSIX facilities. The POSIX.1 standard is also an ISO International Standard, named SC22 WG15. Thus, the POSIX facilities have been accepted in most UNIX-like systems worldwide.

The 4BSD *socket* interprocess-communication mechanism (see Chapter 11) was designed for portability, and was immediately ported to AT&T System III, although it was never distributed with that system. The 4BSD implementation of the TCP/IP networking protocol suite (see Chapter 13) is widely used as the basis for further implementations on systems ranging from AT&T 3B machines running System V to VMS to IBM PCs.

The CSRG cooperated closely with vendors whose systems are based on 4.2BSD and 4.3BSD. This simultaneous development contributed to the ease of further ports of 4.3BSD, and to ongoing development of the system.

The Influence of the User Community

Much of the Berkeley development work was done in response to the user community. Ideas and expectations came not only from DARPA, the principal direct-funding organization, but also from users of the system at companies and universities worldwide.

The Berkeley researchers accepted not only ideas from the user community, but also actual software. Contributions to 4BSD came from universities and other organizations in Australia, Canada, Europe, and the United States. These contributions included major features, such as autoconfiguration and disk quotas. A few ideas, such as the *fcntl* system call, were taken from System V, although licensing and pricing considerations prevented the use of any actual code from System III or System V in 4BSD. In addition to contributions that were included in the distributions proper, the CSRG also distributed a set of user-contributed software.

An example of a community-developed facility is the public-domain time-zone–handling package that was adopted with the 4.3BSD Tahoe release. It was designed and implemented by an international group, including Arthur Olson, Robert Elz, and Guy Harris, partly because of discussions in the USENET newsgroup **comp.std.unix**. This package takes time-zone–conversion rules completely out of the C library, putting them in files that require no system-code changes to change time-zone rules; this change is especially useful with binary-only distributions of UNIX. The method also allows individual processes to choose rules, rather than keeping one ruleset specification systemwide. The distribution includes a large database of rules used in many areas throughout the world, from China to Australia to Europe. Distributions of the 4.4BSD system are thus simplified because it is not necessary to have the software set up differently for different destinations, as long as the whole database is included. The adoption of the time-zone package into BSD brought the technology to the attention of commercial vendors, such as Sun Microsystems, causing them to incorporate it into their systems.

Berkeley solicited electronic mail about bugs and the proposed fixes. The UNIX software house MT XINU distributed a bug list compiled from such submissions. Many of the bug fixes were incorporated in later distributions. There is constant discussion of UNIX in general (including 4.4BSD) in the USENET **comp.unix** newsgroups, which are distributed on the Internet; both the Internet and USENET are international in scope. There was another USENET newsgroup dedicated to 4BSD bugs: **comp.bugs.4bsd**. Few ideas were accepted by Berkeley directly from these newsgroups' associated mailing lists because of the difficulty of sifting through the voluminous submissions. Later, a moderated newsgroup dedicated to the CSRG-sanctioned fixes to such bugs, called **comp.bugs.4bsd.bugfixes**, was created. Discussions in these newsgroups sometimes led to new facilities being written that were later incorporated into the system.

1.3   Design Goals of 4BSD

4BSD is a research system developed for and partly by a research community, and, more recently, a commercial community. The developers considered many design issues as they wrote the system. There were nontraditional considerations and inputs into the design, which nevertheless yielded results with commercial importance.

The early systems were technology driven. They took advantage of current hardware that was unavailable in other UNIX systems. This new technology included

• Virtual-memory support

• Device drivers for third-party (non-DEC) peripherals

• Terminal-independent support libraries for screen-based applications; numerous applications were developed that used these libraries, including the screen-based editor **vi**

4BSD's support of numerous popular third-party peripherals, compared to the AT&T distribution's meager offerings in 32V, was an important factor in 4BSD popularity. Until other vendors began providing their own support of 4.2BSD-based systems, there was no alternative for universities that had to minimize hardware costs.

Terminal-independent screen support, although it may now seem rather pedestrian, was at the time important to the Berkeley software's popularity.

4.2BSD Design Goals

DARPA wanted Berkeley to develop 4.2BSD as a standard research operating system for the VAX. Many new facilities were designed for inclusion in 4.2BSD. These facilities included a completely revised virtual-memory system to support processes with large sparse address space, a much higher-speed filesystem, interprocess-communication facilities, and networking support. The high-speed filesystem and revised virtual-memory system were needed by researchers doing computer-aided design and manufacturing (CAD/CAM), image processing, and artificial intelligence (AI). The interprocess-communication facilities were needed by sites doing research in distributed systems. The motivation for providing networking support was primarily DARPA's interest in connecting their researchers through the 56-Kbit-per-second ARPA Internet (although Berkeley was also interested in getting good performance over higher-speed local-area networks).

No attempt was made to provide a true distributed operating system [Popek, 1981]. Instead, the traditional ARPANET goal of resource sharing was used. There were three reasons that a resource-sharing design was chosen:

1. The systems were widely distributed and demanded administrative autonomy. At the time, a true distributed operating system required a central administrative authority.

2. The known algorithms for tightly coupled systems did not scale well.

3. Berkeley's charter was to incorporate current, proven software technology, rather than to develop new, unproven technology.

Therefore, easy means were provided for remote login (*rlogin*, *telnet*), file transfer (*rcp*, *ftp*), and remote command execution (*rsh*), but all host machines retained separate identities that were not hidden from the users.

Because of time constraints, the system that was released as 4.2BSD did not include all the facilities that were originally intended to be included. In particular, the revised virtual-memory system was not part of the 4.2BSD release. The CSRG did, however, continue its ongoing work to track fast-developing hardware technology in several areas. The networking system supported a wide range of hardware devices, including multiple interfaces to 10-Mbit-per-second Ethernet, token ring networks, and to NSC's Hyperchannel. The kernel sources were modularized and rearranged to ease portability to new architectures, including to microprocessors and to larger machines.

4.3BSD Design Goals

Problems with 4.2BSD were among the reasons for the development of 4.3BSD. Because 4.2BSD included many new facilities, it suffered a loss of performance compared to 4.1BSD, partly because of the introduction of symbolic links. Some pernicious bugs had been introduced, particularly in the TCP protocol implementation. Some facilities had not been included due to lack of time. Others, such as TCP/IP subnet and routing support, had not been specified soon enough by outside parties for them to be incorporated in the 4.2BSD release.

Commercial systems usually maintain backward compatibility for many releases, so as not to make existing applications obsolete. Maintaining compatibility is increasingly difficult, however, so most research systems maintain little or no backward compatibility. As a compromise for other researchers, the BSD releases were usually backward compatible for one release, but had the deprecated facilities clearly marked. This approach allowed for an orderly transition to the new interfaces without constraining the system from evolving smoothly. In particular, backward compatibility of 4.3BSD with 4.2BSD was considered highly desirable for application portability.

The C language interface to 4.3BSD differs from that of 4.2BSD in only a few commands to the terminal interface and in the use of one argument to one IPC system call (*select*; see Section 6.4). A flag was added in 4.3BSD to the system call that establishes a signal handler to allow a process to request the 4.1BSD semantics for signals, rather than the 4.2BSD semantics (see Section 4.7). The sole purpose of the flag was to allow existing applications that depended on the old semantics to continue working without being rewritten.

The implementation changes between 4.2BSD and 4.3BSD generally were not visible to users, but they were numerous. For example, the developers made changes to improve support for multiple network-protocol families, such as XEROX NS, in addition to TCP/IP.

The second release of 4.3BSD, hereafter referred to as 4.3BSD Tahoe, added support for the Computer Consoles, Inc. (CCI) Power 6 (Tahoe) series of minicomputers in addition to the VAX. Although generally similar to the original release of 4.3BSD for the VAX, it included many modifications and new features.

The third release of 4.3BSD, hereafter referred to as **4.3BSD-Reno**, added ISO/OSI networking support, a freely redistributable implementation of NFS, and the conversion to and addition of the POSIX.1 facilities.

4.4BSD Design Goals

4.4BSD broadened the 4.3BSD hardware base, and now supports numerous architectures, including Motorola 68K, Sun SPARC, MIPS, and Intel PCs.

The 4.4BSD release remedies several deficiencies in 4.3BSD. In particular, the virtual-memory system needed to be and was completely replaced. The new virtual-memory system provides algorithms that are better suited to the large memories currently available, and is much less dependent on the VAX architecture. The 4.4BSD release also added an implementation of networking protocols in the International Organization for Standardization (ISO) suite, and further TCP/IP performance improvements and enhancements.

The terminal driver had been carefully kept compatible not only with Seventh Edition, but even with Sixth Edition. This feature had been useful, but is increasingly less so now, especially considering the lack of orthogonality of its commands and options. In 4.4BSD, the CSRG replaced it with a POSIX-compatible terminal driver; since System V is compliant with POSIX, the terminal driver is compatible with System V. POSIX compatibility in general was a goal. POSIX support is not limited to kernel facilities such as termios and sessions, but rather also includes most POSIX utilities.

The most critical shortcoming of 4.3BSD was the lack of support for multiple filesystems. As is true of the networking protocols, there is no single filesystem that provides enough speed and functionality for all situations. It is frequently necessary to support several different filesystem protocols, just as it is necessary to run several different network protocols. Thus, 4.4BSD includes an object-oriented interface to filesystems similar to Sun Microsystems' vnode framework. This framework supports multiple local and remote filesystems, much as multiple networking protocols are supported by 4.3BSD [Sandberg et al, 1985]. The vnode interface has been generalized to make the operation set dynamically extensible and to allow filesystems to be stacked. With this structure, 4.4BSD supports numerous filesystem types, including loopback, union, and uid/gid mapping layers, plus an ISO9660 filesystem, which is particularly useful for CD-ROMs. It also supports Sun's Network filesystem (NFS) Versions 2 and 3 and a new local disk-based log-structured filesystem.

Original work on the flexible configuration of IPC processing modules was done at Bell Laboratories in UNIX Eighth Edition [Presotto & Ritchie, 1985]. This *stream I/O system* was based on the UNIX character I/O system. It allowed a user process to open a raw terminal port and then to insert appropriate kernel-processing modules, such as one to do normal terminal line editing. Modules to process network protocols also could be inserted. Stacking a terminal-processing module on top of a network-processing module allowed flexible and efficient implementation of *network virtual terminals* within the kernel. A problem with stream modules, however, is that they are inherently linear in nature, and thus they do not adequately handle the fan-in and fan-out associated with multiplexing in datagram-based networks; such multiplexing is done in device drivers, below the modules proper. The Eighth Edition stream I/O system was adopted in System V, Release 3 as the STREAMS system.

The design of the networking facilities for 4.2BSD took a different approach, based on the *socket* interface and a flexible multilayer network architecture. This design allows a single system to support multiple sets of networking protocols with stream, datagram, and other types of access. Protocol modules may deal with multiplexing of data from different connections onto a single transport medium, as well as with demultiplexing of data for different protocols and connections received from each network device. The 4.4BSD release made small extensions to the socket interface to allow the implementation of the ISO networking protocols.

1.4   Release Engineering

The CSRG was always a small group of software developers. This resource limitation required careful software-engineering management. Careful coordination was needed not only of the CSRG personnel, but also of members of the general community who contributed to the development of the system. Even though the CSRG is no more, the community still exists; it continues the BSD traditions with FreeBSD, NetBSD, and BSDI.

Major CSRG distributions usually alternated between

• Major new facilities: 3BSD, 4.0BSD, 4.2BSD, 4.4BSD

• Bug fixes and efficiency improvements: 4.1BSD, 4.3BSD

This alternation allowed timely release, while providing for refinement and correction of the new facilities and for elimination of performance problems produced by the new facilities. The timely follow-up of releases that included new facilities reflected the importance that the CSRG placed on providing a reliable and robust system on which its user community could depend.

Developments from the CSRG were released in three steps: alpha, beta, and final, as shown in Table 1.1. Alpha and beta releases were not true distributions— they were test systems. Alpha releases were normally available to only a few sites, most of those within the University. More sites got beta releases, but they did not get these releases directly; a tree structure was imposed to allow bug reports, fixes, and new software to be collected, evaluated, and checked for

Table 1.1 Test steps for the release of 4.2BSD.

	Release steps			
Description	**alpha**	**internal**	**beta**	**final**
name:	4.1aBSD	4.1bBSD	4.1cBSD	4.2BSD
major new facility:	networking	fast filesystem	IPC	revised signals

redundancies by first-level sites before forwarding to the CSRG. For example, 4.1aBSD ran at more than 100 sites, but there were only about 15 primary beta sites. The beta-test tree allowed the developers at the CSRG to concentrate on actual development, rather than sifting through details from every beta-test site. This book was reviewed for technical accuracy by a similar process.

Many of the primary beta-test personnel not only had copies of the release running on their own machines, but also had login accounts on the development machine at Berkeley. Such users were commonly found logged in at Berkeley over the Internet, or sometimes via telephone dialup, from places far away, such as Australia, England, Massachusetts, Utah, Maryland, Texas, and Illinois, and from closer places, such as Stanford. For the 4.3BSD and 4.4BSD releases, certain accounts and users had permission to modify the master copy of the system source directly. Several facilities, such as the Fortran and C compilers, as well as important system programs, such as *telnet* and *ftp*, include significant contributions from people who did not work for the CSRG. One important exception to this approach was that changes to the kernel were made by only the CSRG personnel, although the changes often were suggested by the larger community.

People given access to the master sources were carefully screened beforehand, but were not closely supervised. Their work was checked at the end of the beta-test period by the CSRG personnel, who did a complete comparison of the source of the previous release with the current master sources—for example, of 4.3BSD with 4.2BSD. Facilities deemed inappropriate, such as new options to the directory-listing command or a changed return value for the *fseek*() library routine, were removed from the source before final distribution.

This process illustrates an *advantage* of having only a few principal developers: The developers all knew the whole system thoroughly enough to be able to coordinate their own work with that of other people to produce a coherent final system. Companies with large development organizations find this result difficult to duplicate.

There was no CSRG marketing division. Thus, technical decisions were made largely for technical reasons, and were not driven by marketing promises. The Berkeley developers were fanatical about this position, and were well known for never promising delivery on a specific date.

References

AT&T, 1987.
> AT&T, *The System V Interface Definition (SVID)*, Issue 2, American Telephone and Telegraph, Murray Hill, NJ, January 1987.

Babaoğlu & Joy, 1981.
> O. Babaoğlu & W. N. Joy, "Converting a Swap-Based System to Do Paging in an Architecture Lacking Page-Referenced Bits," *Proceedings of the Eighth Symposium on Operating Systems Principles*, pp. 78–86, December 1981.

Bach, 1986.
  M. J. Bach, *The Design of the UNIX Operating System,* Prentice-Hall, Englewood Cliffs, NJ, 1986.
Cerf & Cain, 1983.
  V. Cerf & E. Cain, *The DoD Internet Architecture Model,* pp. 307–318, Elsevier Science, Amsterdam, Netherlands, 1983.
Chambers & Quarterman, 1983.
  J. B. Chambers & J. S. Quarterman, "UNIX System V and 4.1C BSD," *USENIX Association Conference Proceedings*, pp. 267–291, June 1983.
Comer, 1984.
  D. Comer, *Operating System Design: The Xinu Approach,* Prentice-Hall, Englewood Cliffs, NJ, 1984.
Compton, 1985.
  M. Compton, editor, "The Evolution of UNIX," *UNIX Review*, vol. 3, no. 1, January 1985.
Ewens et al, 1985.
  P. Ewens, D. R. Blythe, M. Funkenhauser, & R. C. Holt, "Tunis: A Distributed Multiprocessor Operating System," *USENIX Association Conference Proceedings*, pp. 247–254, June 1985.
Holt, 1983.
  R. C. Holt, *Concurrent Euclid, the UNIX System, and Tunis,* Addison-Wesley, Reading, MA, 1983.
Joy, 1980.
  W. N. Joy, "Comments on the Performance of UNIX on the VAX," Technical Report, University of California Computer System Research Group, Berkeley, CA, April 1980.
Jung, 1985.
  R. S. Jung, "Porting the AT&T Demand Paged UNIX Implementation to Microcomputers," *USENIX Association Conference Proceedings*, pp. 361–370, June 1985.
Kashtan, 1980.
  D. L. Kashtan, "UNIX and VMS: Some Performance Comparisons," Technical Report, SRI International, Menlo Park, CA, February 1980.
Kernighan & Ritchie, 1978.
  B. W. Kernighan & D. M. Ritchie, *The C Programming Language,* Prentice-Hall, Englewood Cliffs, NJ, 1978.
Kernighan & Ritchie, 1988.
  B. W. Kernighan & D. M. Ritchie, *The C Programming Language,* 2nd ed, Prentice-Hall, Englewood Cliffs, NJ, 1988.
McKusick, 1985.
  M. K. McKusick, "A Berkeley Odyssey," *UNIX Review*, vol. 3, no. 1, p. 30, January 1985.
Miller, 1978.
  R. Miller, "UNIX—A Portable Operating System," *ACM Operating System Review*, vol. 12, no. 3, pp. 32–37, July 1978.

Miller, 1984.
R. Miller, "A Demand Paging Virtual Memory Manager for System V,"
USENIX Association Conference Proceedings, pp. 178–182, June 1984.

Mohr, 1985.
A. Mohr, "The Genesis Story," *UNIX Review*, vol. 3, no. 1, p. 18, January
1985.

Organick, 1975.
E. I. Organick, *The Multics System: An Examination of Its Structure,* MIT
Press, Cambridge, MA, 1975.

P1003.1, 1988.
P1003.1, *IEEE P1003.1 Portable Operating System Interface for Computer
Environments (POSIX),* Institute of Electrical and Electronic Engineers, Pis-
cataway, NJ, 1988.

Peirce, 1985.
N. Peirce, "Putting UNIX In Perspective: An Interview with Victor Vyssot-
sky," *UNIX Review*, vol. 3, no. 1, p. 58, January 1985.

Popek, 1981.
B. Popek, "Locus: A Network Transparent, High Reliability Distributed
System," *Proceedings of the Eighth Symposium on Operating Systems Prin-
ciples*, pp. 169–177, December 1981.

Presotto & Ritchie, 1985.
D. L. Presotto & D. M. Ritchie, "Interprocess Communication in the Eighth
Edition UNIX System," *USENIX Association Conference Proceedings*, pp.
309–316, June 1985.

Richards & Whitby-Strevens, 1980.
M. Richards & C. Whitby-Strevens, *BCPL: The Language and Its Compiler,*
Cambridge University Press, Cambridge, U.K., 1980, 1982.

Ritchie, 1978.
D. M. Ritchie, "A Retrospective," *Bell System Technical Journal*, vol. 57,
no. 6, pp. 1947–1969, July–August 1978.

Ritchie, 1984a.
D. M. Ritchie, "The Evolution of the UNIX Time-Sharing System," *AT&T
Bell Laboratories Technical Journal*, vol. 63, no. 8, pp. 1577–1593, October
1984.

Ritchie, 1987.
D. M. Ritchie, "Unix: A Dialectic," *USENIX Association Conference Proceedings*, pp. 29–34, January 1987.

Ritchie, 1984b.
D. M. Ritchie, "Reflections on Software Research," *Comm ACM*, vol. 27,
no. 8, pp. 758–760, 1984.

Ritchie et al, 1978.
D. M. Ritchie, S. C. Johnson, M. E. Lesk, & B. W. Kernighan, "The C Programming Language," *Bell System Technical Journal*, vol. 57, no. 6, pp.
1991–2019, July–August 1978.

Rosler, 1984.

L. Rosler, "The Evolution of C—Past and Future," *AT&T Bell Laboratories Technical Journal*, vol. 63, no. 8, pp. 1685–1699, October 1984.

Sandberg et al, 1985.

R. Sandberg, D. Goldberg, S. Kleiman, D. Walsh, & B. Lyon, "Design and Implementation of the Sun Network Filesystem," *USENIX Association Conference Proceedings*, pp. 119–130, June 1985.

Stroustrup, 1984.

B. Stroustrup, "Data Abstraction in C," *AT&T Bell Laboratories Technical Journal*, vol. 63, no. 8, pp. 1701–1732, October 1984.

Tanenbaum, 1987.

A. S. Tanenbaum, *Operating Systems: Design and Implementation,* Prentice-Hall, Englewood Cliffs, NJ, 1987.

Tuthill, 1985.

B. Tuthill, "The Evolution of C: Heresy and Prophecy," *UNIX Review*, vol. 3, no. 1, p. 80, January 1985.

Uniejewski, 1985.

J. Uniejewski, *UNIX System V and BSD4.2 Compatibility Study,* Apollo Computer, Chelmsford, MA, March 1985.

USENIX, 1987.

USENIX, *Proceedings of the C++ Workshop,* USENIX Association, Berkeley, CA, November 1987.

Wilson, 1985.

O. Wilson, "The Business Evolution of the UNIX System," *UNIX Review*, vol. 3, no. 1, p. 46, January 1985.

X3J11, 1988.

X3J11, *X3.159 Programming Language C Standard,* Global Press, Santa Ana, CA, 1988.

X/OPEN, 1987.

X/OPEN, *The X/OPEN Portability Guide (XPG),* Issue 2, Elsevier Science, Amsterdam, Netherlands, 1987.

CHAPTER 2

Design Overview of 4.4BSD

2.1   4.4BSD Facilities and the Kernel

The 4.4BSD kernel provides four basic facilities: processes, a filesystem, communications, and system startup. This section outlines where each of these four basic services is described in this book.

1. Processes constitute a thread of control in an address space. Mechanisms for creating, terminating, and otherwise controlling processes are described in Chapter 4. The system multiplexes separate virtual-address spaces for each process; this memory management is discussed in Chapter 5.

2. The user interface to the filesystem and devices is similar; common aspects are discussed in Chapter 6. The filesystem is a set of named files, organized in a tree-structured hierarchy of directories, and of operations to manipulate them, as presented in Chapter 7. Files reside on physical media such as disks. 4.4BSD supports several organizations of data on the disk, as set forth in Chapter 8. Access to files on remote machines is the subject of Chapter 9. Terminals are used to access the system; their operation is the subject of Chapter 10.

3. Communication mechanisms provided by traditional UNIX systems include simplex reliable byte streams between related processes (see pipes, Section 11.1), and notification of exceptional events (see signals, Section 4.7). 4.4BSD also has a general interprocess-communication facility. This facility, described in Chapter 11, uses access mechanisms distinct from those of the filesystem, but, once a connection is set up, a process can access it as though it were a pipe. There is a general networking framework, discussed in Chapter 12, that is normally used as a layer underlying the IPC facility. Chapter 13 describes a particular networking implementation in detail.

4. Any real operating system has operational issues, such as how to start it running. Startup and operational issues are described in Chapter 14.

Sections 2.3 through 2.14 present introductory material related to Chapters 3
through 14. We shall define terms, mention basic system calls, and explore historical developments. Finally, we shall give the reasons for many major design decisions.

The Kernel

The *kernel* is the part of the system that runs in protected mode and mediates
access by all user programs to the underlying hardware (e.g., CPU, disks, terminals, network links) and software constructs (e.g., filesystem, network protocols).
The kernel provides the basic system facilities; it creates and manages processes,
and provides functions to access the filesystem and communication facilities.
These functions, called *system calls*, appear to user processes as library subroutines. These system calls are the only interface that processes have to these facilities. Details of the system-call mechanism are given in Chapter 3, as are
descriptions of several kernel mechanisms that do not execute as the direct result
of a process doing a system call.

A *kernel*, in traditional operating-system terminology, is a small nucleus of
software that provides only the minimal facilities necessary for implementing
additional operating-system services. In contemporary research operating systems—such as Chorus [Rozier et al, 1988], Mach [Accetta et al, 1986], Tunis
[Ewens et al, 1985], and the V Kernel [Cheriton, 1988]—this division of functionality is more than just a logical one. Services such as filesystems and networking
protocols are implemented as client application processes of the nucleus or kernel.

The 4.4BSD kernel is not partitioned into multiple processes. This basic
design decision was made in the earliest versions of UNIX. The first two implementations by Ken Thompson had no memory mapping, and thus made no hard-
ware-enforced distinction between user and kernel space [Ritchie, 1988]. A
message-passing system could have been implemented as readily as the actually
implemented model of kernel and user processes. The monolithic kernel was
chosen for simplicity and performance. And the early kernels were small; the
inclusion of facilities such as networking into the kernel has increased its size.
The current trend in operating-systems research is to reduce the kernel size by
placing such services in user space.

Users ordinarily interact with the system through a command-language interpreter, called a *shell*, and perhaps through additional user application programs.
Such programs and the shell are implemented with processes. Details of such programs are beyond the scope of this book, which instead concentrates almost exclusively on the kernel.

Sections 2.3 and 2.4 describe the services provided by the 4.4BSD kernel, and
give an overview of the latter's design. Later chapters describe the detailed design
and implementation of these services as they appear in 4.4BSD.

2.2   Kernel Organization

In this section, we view the organization of the 4.4BSD kernel in two ways:

1. As a static body of software, categorized by the functionality offered by the modules that make up the kernel

2. By its dynamic operation, categorized according to the services provided to users

The largest part of the kernel implements the system services that applications access through system calls. In 4.4BSD, this software has been organized according to the following:

- Basic kernel facilities: timer and system-clock handling, descriptor management, and process management

- Memory-management support: paging and swapping

- Generic system interfaces: the I/O, control, and multiplexing operations performed on descriptors

- The filesystem: files, directories, pathname translation, file locking, and I/O buffer management

- Terminal-handling support: the terminal-interface driver and terminal line disciplines

- Interprocess-communication facilities: sockets

- Support for network communication: communication protocols and generic network facilities, such as routing

Most of the software in these categories is machine independent and is portable across different hardware architectures.

The machine-dependent aspects of the kernel are isolated from the mainstream code. In particular, none of the machine-independent code contains conditional code for specific architecture. When an architecture-dependent action is needed, the machine-independent code calls an architecture-dependent function that is located in the machine-dependent code. The software that is machine dependent includes

- Low-level system-startup actions

- Trap and fault handling

- Low-level manipulation of the run-time context of a process

- Configuration and initialization of hardware devices

- Run-time support for I/O devices

Table 2.1 Machine-independent software in the 4.4BSD kernel.

Category	Lines of code	Percentage of kernel
headers	9,393	4.6
initialization	1,107	0.6
kernel facilities	8,793	4.4
generic interfaces	4,782	2.4
interprocess communication	4,540	2.2
terminal handling	3,911	1.9
virtual memory	11,813	5.8
vnode management	7,954	3.9
filesystem naming	6,550	3.2
fast filestore	4,365	2.2
log-structure filestore	4,337	2.1
memory-based filestore	645	0.3
cd9660 filesystem	4,177	2.1
miscellaneous filesystems (10)	12,695	6.3
network filesystem	17,199	8.5
network communication	8,630	4.3
internet protocols	11,984	5.9
ISO protocols	23,924	11.8
X.25 protocols	10,626	5.3
XNS protocols	5,192	2.6
total machine independent	162,617	80.4

Table 2.1 summarizes the machine-independent software that constitutes the 4.4BSD kernel for the HP300. The numbers in column 2 are for lines of C source code, header files, and assembly language. Virtually all the software in the kernel is written in the C programming language; less than 2 percent is written in assembly language. As the statistics in Table 2.2 show, the machine-dependent software, excluding HP/UX and device support, accounts for a minuscule 6.9 percent of the kernel.

Only a small part of the kernel is devoted to initializing the system. This code is used when the system is *bootstrapped* into operation and is responsible for setting up the kernel hardware and software environment (see Chapter 14). Some operating systems (especially those with limited physical memory) discard or *overlay* the software that performs these functions after that software has been executed. The 4.4BSD kernel does not reclaim the memory used by the startup code because that memory space is barely 0.5 percent of the kernel resources used

Table 2.2 Machine-dependent software for the HP300 in the 4.4BSD kernel.

Category	Lines of code	Percentage of kernel
machine dependent headers	1,562	0.8
device driver headers	3,495	1.7
device driver source	17,506	8.7
virtual memory	3,087	1.5
other machine dependent	6,287	3.1
routines in assembly language	3,014	1.5
HP/UX compatibility	4,683	2.3
total machine dependent	39,634	19.6

on a typical machine. Also, the startup code does not appear in one place in the kernel—it is scattered throughout, and it usually appears in places logically associated with what is being initialized.

2.3   Kernel Services

The boundary between the kernel- and user-level code is enforced by hardware-protection facilities provided by the underlying hardware. The kernel operates in a separate address space that is inaccessible to user processes. Privileged operations—such as starting I/O and halting the central processing unit (CPU)—are available to only the kernel. Applications request services from the kernel with *system calls*. System calls are used to cause the kernel to execute complicated operations, such as writing data to secondary storage, and simple operations, such as returning the current time of day. All system calls appear *synchronous* to applications: The application does not run while the kernel does the actions associated with a system call. The kernel may finish some operations associated with a system call after it has returned. For example, a *write* system call will copy the data to be written from the user process to a kernel buffer while the process waits, but will usually return from the system call before the kernel buffer is written to the disk.

A system call usually is implemented as a hardware trap that changes the CPU's execution mode and the current address-space mapping. Parameters supplied by users in system calls are validated by the kernel before being used. Such checking ensures the integrity of the system. All parameters passed into the kernel are copied into the kernel's address space, to ensure that validated parameters are not changed as a side effect of the system call. System-call results are returned by the kernel, either in hardware registers or by their values being copied to user-specified memory addresses. Like parameters passed into the kernel, addresses used for the return of results must be validated to ensure that they are part of an application's address space. If the kernel encounters an error while processing a system call, it returns an error code to the user. For the C programming language, this error code is stored in the global variable *errno*, and the function that executed the system call returns the value −1.

User applications and the kernel operate independently of each other. 4.4BSD does not store I/O control blocks or other operating-system–related data structures in the application's address space. Each user-level application is provided an independent address space in which it executes. The kernel makes most state changes, such as suspending a process while another is running, invisible to the processes involved.

2.4   Process Management

4.4BSD supports a multitasking environment. Each task or thread of execution is termed a *process*. The *context* of a 4.4BSD process consists of user-level state, including the contents of its address space and the run-time environment, and kernel-level state, which includes scheduling parameters, resource controls, and identification information. The context includes everything used by the kernel in providing services for the process. Users can create processes, control the processes' execution, and receive notification when the processes' execution status changes. Every process is assigned a unique value, termed a *process identifier* (PID). This value is used by the kernel to identify a process when reporting status changes to a user, and by a user when referencing a process in a system call.

The kernel creates a process by duplicating the context of another process. The new process is termed a *child process* of the original *parent process*. The context duplicated in process creation includes both the user-level execution state of the process and the process's system state managed by the kernel. Important components of the kernel state are described in Chapter 4.

The process lifecycle is depicted in Fig. 2.1. A process may create a new process that is a copy of the original by using the *fork* system call. The *fork* call returns twice: once in the parent process, where the return value is the process

Figure 2.1 Process-management system calls.

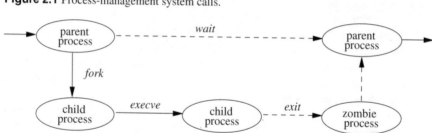

identifier of the child, and once in the child process, where the return value is 0. The parent–child relationship induces a hierarchical structure on the set of processes in the system. The new process shares all its parent's resources, such as file descriptors, signal-handling status, and memory layout.

Although there are occasions when the new process is intended to be a copy of the parent, the loading and execution of a different program is a more useful and typical action. A process can overlay itself with the memory image of another program, passing to the newly created image a set of parameters, using the system call *execve*. One parameter is the name of a file whose contents are in a format recognized by the system—either a binary-executable file or a file that causes the execution of a specified interpreter program to process its contents.

A process may terminate by executing an *exit* system call, sending 8 bits of exit status to its parent. If a process wants to communicate more than a single byte of information with its parent, it must either set up an interprocess-communication channel using pipes or sockets, or use an intermediate file. Interprocess communication is discussed extensively in Chapter 11.

A process can suspend execution until any of its child processes terminate using the *wait* system call, which returns the PID and exit status of the terminated child process. A parent process can arrange to be notified by a signal when a child process exits or terminates abnormally. Using the *wait4* system call, the parent can retrieve information about the event that caused termination of the child process and about resources consumed by the process during its lifetime. If a process is orphaned because its parent exits before it is finished, then the kernel arranges for the child's exit status to be passed back to a special system process (**init**: see Sections 3.1 and 14.6).

The details of how the kernel creates and destroys processes are given in Chapter 5.

Processes are scheduled for execution according to a *process-priority* parameter. This priority is managed by a kernel-based scheduling algorithm. Users can influence the scheduling of a process by specifying a parameter (*nice*) that weights the overall scheduling priority, but are still obligated to share the underlying CPU resources according to the kernel's scheduling policy.

Signals

The system defines a set of *signals* that may be delivered to a process. Signals in 4.4BSD are modeled after hardware interrupts. A process may specify a user-level subroutine to be a *handler* to which a signal should be delivered. When a signal is generated, it is blocked from further occurrence while it is being *caught* by the handler. Catching a signal involves saving the current process context and building a new one in which to run the handler. The signal is then delivered to the handler, which can either abort the process or return to the executing process (perhaps after setting a global variable). If the handler returns, the signal is unblocked and can be generated (and caught) again.

Alternatively, a process may specify that a signal is to be *ignored*, or that a default action, as determined by the kernel, is to be taken. The default action of certain signals is to terminate the process. This termination may be accompanied by creation of a *core file* that contains the current memory image of the process for use in postmortem debugging.

Some signals cannot be caught or ignored. These signals include SIGKILL, which kills runaway processes, and the job-control signal SIGSTOP.

A process may choose to have signals delivered on a special stack so that sophisticated software stack manipulations are possible. For example, a language supporting coroutines needs to provide a stack for each coroutine. The language run-time system can allocate these stacks by dividing up the single stack provided by 4.4BSD. If the kernel does not support a separate signal stack, the space allocated for each coroutine must be expanded by the amount of space required to catch a signal.

All signals have the same *priority*. If multiple signals are pending simultaneously, the order in which signals are delivered to a process is implementation specific. Signal handlers execute with the signal that caused their invocation to be blocked, but other signals may yet occur. Mechanisms are provided so that processes can protect critical sections of code against the occurrence of specified signals.

The detailed design and implementation of signals is described in Section 4.7.

Process Groups and Sessions

Processes are organized into *process groups*. Process groups are used to control access to terminals and to provide a means of distributing signals to collections of related processes. A process inherits its process group from its parent process. Mechanisms are provided by the kernel to allow a process to alter its process group or the process group of its descendents. Creating a new process group is easy; the value of a new process group is ordinarily the process identifier of the creating process.

The group of processes in a process group is sometimes referred to as a *job* and is manipulated by high-level system software, such as the shell. A common kind of job created by a shell is a *pipeline* of several processes connected by pipes, such that the output of the first process is the input of the second, the output of the second is the input of the third, and so forth. The shell creates such a job by forking a process for each stage of the pipeline, then putting all those processes into a separate process group.

A user process can send a signal to each process in a process group, as well as to a single process. A process in a specific process group may receive software interrupts affecting the group, causing the group to suspend or resume execution, or to be interrupted or terminated.

A terminal has a process-group identifier assigned to it. This identifier is normally set to the identifier of a process group associated with the terminal. A job-control shell may create a number of process groups associated with the same terminal; the terminal is the *controlling terminal* for each process in these groups. A process may read from a descriptor for its controlling terminal only if the terminal's process-group identifier matches that of the process. If the identifiers do not match, the process will be blocked if it attempts to read from the terminal. By changing the process-group identifier of the terminal, a shell can arbitrate a terminal among several different jobs. This arbitration is called *job control* and is described, with process groups, in Section 4.8.

Just as a set of related processes can be collected into a process group, a set of process groups can be collected into a *session*. The main uses for sessions are to create an isolated environment for a daemon process and its children, and to collect together a user's login shell and the jobs that that shell spawns.

2.5   Memory Management

Each process has its own private address space. The address space is initially divided into three logical segments: *text*, *data*, and *stack*. The text segment is read-only and contains the machine instructions of a program. The data and stack segments are both readable and writable. The data segment contains the initialized and uninitialized data portions of a program, whereas the stack segment holds the application's run-time stack. On most machines, the stack segment is extended automatically by the kernel as the process executes. A process can expand or contract its data segment by making a system call, whereas a process can change the size of its text segment only when the segment's contents are overlaid with data from the filesystem, or when debugging takes place. The initial contents of the segments of a child process are duplicates of the segments of a parent process.

The entire contents of a process address space do not need to be resident for a process to execute. If a process references a part of its address space that is not resident in main memory, the system *pages* the necessary information into memory. When system resources are scarce, the system uses a two-level approach to maintain available resources. If a modest amount of memory is available, the system will take memory resources away from processes if these resources have not been used recently. Should there be a severe resource shortage, the system will resort to *swapping* the entire context of a process to secondary storage. The *demand paging* and *swapping* done by the system are effectively transparent to processes. A process may, however, advise the system about expected future memory utilization as a performance aid.

BSD Memory-Management Design Decisions

The support of large sparse address spaces, mapped files, and shared memory was a requirement for 4.2BSD. An interface was specified, called *mmap()*, that allowed unrelated processes to request a shared mapping of a file into their address spaces. If multiple processes mapped the same file into their address spaces, changes to the file's portion of an address space by one process would be reflected in the area mapped by the other processes, as well as in the file itself. Ultimately, 4.2BSD was shipped without the *mmap()* interface, because of pressure to make other features, such as networking, available.

Further development of the *mmap*() interface continued during the work on 4.3BSD. Over 40 companies and research groups participated in the discussions leading to the revised architecture that was described in the Berkeley Software Architecture Manual [McKusick, Karels et al, 1994]. Several of the companies have implemented the revised interface [Gingell et al, 1987].

Once again, time pressure prevented 4.3BSD from providing an implementation of the interface. Although the latter could have been built into the existing 4.3BSD virtual-memory system, the developers decided not to put it in because that implementation was nearly 10 years old. Furthermore, the original virtual-memory design was based on the assumption that computer memories were small and expensive, whereas disks were locally connected, fast, large, and inexpensive. Thus, the virtual-memory system was designed to be frugal with its use of memory at the expense of generating extra disk traffic. In addition, the 4.3BSD implementation was riddled with VAX memory-management hardware dependencies that impeded its portability to other computer architectures. Finally, the virtual-memory system was not designed to support the tightly coupled multiprocessors that are becoming increasingly common and important today.

Attempts to improve the old implementation incrementally seemed doomed to failure. A completely new design, on the other hand, could take advantage of large memories, conserve disk transfers, and have the potential to run on multiprocessors. Consequently, the virtual-memory system was completely replaced in 4.4BSD. The 4.4BSD virtual-memory system is based on the Mach 2.0 VM system [Tevanian, 1987], with updates from Mach 2.5 and Mach 3.0. It features efficient support for sharing, a clean separation of machine-independent and machine-dependent features, as well as (currently unused) multiprocessor support. Processes can map files anywhere in their address space. They can share parts of their address space by doing a shared mapping of the same file. Changes made by one process are visible in the address space of the other process, and also are written back to the file itself. Processes can also request private mappings of a file, which prevents any changes that they make from being visible to other processes mapping the file or being written back to the file itself.

Another issue with the virtual-memory system is the way that information is passed into the kernel when a system call is made. 4.4BSD always copies data from the process address space into a buffer in the kernel. For read or write operations that are transferring large quantities of data, doing the copy can be time consuming. An alternative to doing the copying is to remap the process memory into the kernel. The 4.4BSD kernel always copies the data for several reasons:

• Often, the user data are not page aligned and are not a multiple of the hardware page length.

• If the page is taken away from the process, it will no longer be able to reference that page. Some programs depend on the data remaining in the buffer even after those data have been written.

• If the process is allowed to keep a copy of the page (as it is in current 4.4BSD semantics), the page must be made *copy-on-write*. A copy-on-write page is one that is protected against being written by being made read-only. If the process attempts to modify the page, the kernel gets a write fault. The kernel then makes a copy of the page that the process can modify. Unfortunately, the typical process will immediately try to write new data to its output buffer, forcing the data to be copied anyway.

• When pages are remapped to new virtual-memory addresses, most memory-management hardware requires that the hardware address-translation cache be purged selectively. The cache purges are often slow. The net effect is that remapping is slower than copying for blocks of data less than 4 to 8 Kbyte.

The biggest incentives for memory mapping are the needs for accessing big files and for passing large quantities of data between processes. The *mmap()* interface provides a way for both of these tasks to be done without copying.

Memory Management Inside the Kernel

The kernel often does allocations of memory that are needed for only the duration of a single system call. In a user process, such short-term memory would be allocated on the run-time stack. Because the kernel has a limited run-time stack, it is not feasible to allocate even moderate-sized blocks of memory on it. Consequently, such memory must be allocated through a more dynamic mechanism. For example, when the system must translate a pathname, it must allocate a 1-Kbyte buffer to hold the name. Other blocks of memory must be more persistent than a single system call, and thus could not be allocated on the stack even if there was space. An example is protocol-control blocks that remain throughout the duration of a network connection.

Demands for dynamic memory allocation in the kernel have increased as more services have been added. A generalized memory allocator reduces the complexity of writing code inside the kernel. Thus, the 4.4BSD kernel has a single memory allocator that can be used by any part of the system. It has an interface similar to the C library routines *malloc()* and *free()* that provide memory allocation to application programs [McKusick & Karels, 1988]. Like the C library interface, the allocation routine takes a parameter specifying the size of memory that is needed. The range of sizes for memory requests is not constrained; however, physical memory is allocated and is not paged. The free routine takes a pointer to the storage being freed, but does not require the size of the piece of memory being freed.

2.6   I/O System

The basic model of the UNIX I/O system is a sequence of bytes that can be accessed either randomly or sequentially. There are no *access methods* and no *control blocks* in a typical UNIX user process.

Different programs expect various levels of structure, but the kernel does not impose structure on I/O. For instance, the convention for text files is lines of ASCII characters separated by a single newline character (the ASCII line-feed character), but the kernel knows nothing about this convention. For the purposes of most programs, the model is further simplified to being a stream of data bytes, or an *I/O stream*. It is this single common data form that makes the characteristic UNIX tool-based approach work [Kernighan & Pike, 1984]. An I/O stream from one program can be fed as input to almost any other program. (This kind of traditional UNIX I/O stream should not be confused with the Eighth Edition stream I/O system or with the System V, Release 3 STREAMS, both of which can be accessed as traditional I/O streams.)

Descriptors and I/O

UNIX processes use *descriptors* to reference I/O streams. Descriptors are small unsigned integers obtained from the *open* and *socket* system calls. The *open* system call takes as arguments the name of a file and a permission mode to specify whether the file should be open for reading or for writing, or for both. This system call also can be used to create a new, empty file. A *read* or *write* system call can be applied to a descriptor to transfer data. The *close* system call can be used to deallocate any descriptor.

Descriptors represent underlying objects supported by the kernel, and are created by system calls specific to the type of object. In 4.4BSD, three kinds of objects can be represented by descriptors: files, pipes, and sockets.

- A *file* is a linear array of bytes with at least one name. A file exists until all its names are deleted explicitly and no process holds a descriptor for it. A process acquires a descriptor for a file by opening that file's name with the *open* system call. I/O devices are accessed as files.

- A *pipe* is a linear array of bytes, as is a file, but it is used solely as an I/O stream, and it is unidirectional. It also has no name, and thus cannot be opened with *open*. Instead, it is created by the *pipe* system call, which returns two descriptors, one of which accepts input that is sent to the other descriptor reliably, without duplication, and in order. The system also supports a named pipe or FIFO. A FIFO has properties identical to a pipe, except that it appears in the filesystem; thus, it can be opened using the *open* system call. Two processes that wish to communicate each open the FIFO: One opens it for reading, the other for writing.

- A *socket* is a transient object that is used for interprocess communication; it exists only as long as some process holds a descriptor referring to it. A socket is created by the *socket* system call, which returns a descriptor for it. There are different kinds of sockets that support various communication semantics, such as reliable delivery of data, preservation of message ordering, and preservation of message boundaries.

In systems before 4.2BSD, pipes were implemented using the filesystem; when sockets were introduced in 4.2BSD, pipes were reimplemented as sockets.

The kernel keeps for each process a *descriptor table*, which is a table that the kernel uses to translate the external representation of a descriptor into an internal representation. (The descriptor is merely an index into this table.) The descriptor table of a process is inherited from that process's parent, and thus access to the objects to which the descriptors refer also is inherited. The main ways that a process can obtain a descriptor are by opening or creation of an object, and by inheritance from the parent process. In addition, socket IPC allows passing of descriptors in messages between unrelated processes on the same machine.

Every valid descriptor has an associated *file offset* in bytes from the beginning of the object. Read and write operations start at this offset, which is updated after each data transfer. For objects that permit random access, the file offset also may be set with the *lseek* system call. Ordinary files permit random access, and some devices do, as well. Pipes and sockets do not.

When a process terminates, the kernel reclaims all the descriptors that were in use by that process. If the process was holding the final reference to an object, the object's manager is notified so that it can do any necessary cleanup actions, such as final deletion of a file or deallocation of a socket.

Descriptor Management

Most processes expect three descriptors to be open already when they start running. These descriptors are 0, 1, 2, more commonly known as *standard input*, *standard output*, and *standard error*, respectively. Usually, all three are associated with the user's terminal by the login process (see Section 14.6) and are inherited through *fork* and *exec* by processes run by the user. Thus, a program can read what the user types by reading standard input, and the program can send output to the user's screen by writing to standard output. The standard error descriptor also is open for writing and is used for error output, whereas standard output is used for ordinary output.

These (and other) descriptors can be mapped to objects other than the terminal; such mapping is called *I/O redirection*, and all the standard shells permit users to do it. The shell can direct the output of a program to a file by closing descriptor 1 (standard output) and opening the desired output file to produce a new descriptor 1. It can similarly redirect standard input to come from a file by closing descriptor 0 and opening the file.

Pipes allow the output of one program to be input to another program without rewriting or even relinking of either program. Instead of descriptor 1 (standard output) of the source program being set up to write to the terminal, it is set up to be the input descriptor of a pipe. Similarly, descriptor 0 (standard input) of the sink program is set up to reference the output of the pipe, instead of the terminal keyboard. The resulting set of two processes and the connecting pipe is known as a *pipeline*. Pipelines can be arbitrarily long series of processes connected by pipes.

The *open*, *pipe*, and *socket* system calls produce new descriptors with the lowest unused number usable for a descriptor. For pipelines to work, some mechanism must be provided to map such descriptors into 0 and 1. The *dup* system call creates a copy of a descriptor that points to the same file-table entry. The new descriptor is also the lowest unused one, but if the desired descriptor is closed first, *dup* can be used to do the desired mapping. Care is required, however: If descriptor 1 is desired, and descriptor 0 happens also to have been closed, descriptor 0 will be the result. To avoid this problem, the system provides the *dup2* system call; it is like *dup*, but it takes an additional argument specifying the number of the desired descriptor (if the desired descriptor was already open, *dup2* closes it before reusing it).

Devices

Hardware devices have filenames, and may be accessed by the user via the same system calls used for regular files. The kernel can distinguish a *device special file* or *special file*, and can determine to what device it refers, but most processes do not need to make this determination. Terminals, printers, and tape drives are all accessed as though they were streams of bytes, like 4.4BSD disk files. Thus, device dependencies and peculiarities are kept in the kernel as much as possible, and even in the kernel most of them are segregated in the device drivers.

Hardware devices can be categorized as either *structured* or *unstructured*; they are known as *block* or *character* devices, respectively. Processes typically access devices through *special files* in the filesystem. I/O operations to these files are handled by kernel-resident software modules termed *device drivers*. Most network-communication hardware devices are accessible through only the interprocess-communication facilities, and do not have special files in the filesystem name space, because the *raw-socket* interface provides a more natural interface than does a special file.

Structured or block devices are typified by disks and magnetic tapes, and include most random-access devices. The kernel supports read-modify-write–type buffering actions on block-oriented structured devices to allow the latter to be read and written in a totally random byte-addressed fashion, like regular files. Filesystems are created on block devices.

Unstructured devices are those devices that do not support a block structure. Familiar unstructured devices are communication lines, raster plotters, and unbuffered magnetic tapes and disks. Unstructured devices typically support large block I/O transfers.

Unstructured files are called *character devices* because the first of these to be implemented were terminal device drivers. The kernel interface to the driver for these devices proved convenient for other devices that were not block structured.

Device special files are created by the *mknod* system call. There is an additional system call, *ioctl*, for manipulating the underlying device parameters of special files. The operations that can be done differ for each device. This system call allows the special characteristics of devices to be accessed, rather than overloading the semantics of other system calls. For example, there is an *ioctl* on a tape drive to write an end-of-tape mark, instead of there being a special or modified version of *write*.

Socket IPC

The 4.2BSD kernel introduced an IPC mechanism more flexible than pipes, based on *sockets*. A socket is an endpoint of communication referred to by a descriptor, just like a file or a pipe. Two processes can each create a socket, and then connect those two endpoints to produce a reliable byte stream. Once connected, the descriptors for the sockets can be read or written by processes, just as the latter would do with a pipe. The transparency of sockets allows the kernel to redirect the output of one process to the input of another process residing on another machine. A major difference between pipes and sockets is that pipes require a common parent process to set up the communications channel. A connection between sockets can be set up by two unrelated processes, possibly residing on different machines.

System V provides local interprocess communication through FIFOs (also known as *named pipes*). FIFOs appear as an object in the filesystem that unrelated processes can open and send data through in the same way as they would communicate through a pipe. Thus, FIFOs do not require a common parent to set them up; they can be connected after a pair of processes are up and running. Unlike sockets, FIFOs can be used on only a local machine; they cannot be used to communicate between processes on different machines. FIFOs are implemented in 4.4BSD only because they are required by the standard. Their functionality is a subset of the socket interface.

The socket mechanism requires extensions to the traditional UNIX I/O system calls to provide the associated naming and connection semantics. Rather than overloading the existing interface, the developers used the existing interfaces to the extent that the latter worked without being changed, and designed new interfaces to handle the added semantics. The *read* and *write* system calls were used for byte-stream type connections, but six new system calls were added to allow sending and receiving addressed messages such as network datagrams. The system calls for writing messages include *send*, *sendto*, and *sendmsg*. The system calls for reading messages include *recv*, *recvfrom*, and *recvmsg*. In retrospect, the first two in each class are special cases of the others; *recvfrom* and *sendto* probably should have been added as library interfaces to *recvmsg* and *sendmsg*, respectively.

Scatter/Gather I/O

In addition to the traditional *read* and *write* system calls, 4.2BSD introduced the ability to do scatter/gather I/O. Scatter input uses the *readv* system call to allow a single read to be placed in several different buffers. Conversely, the *writev* system call allows several different buffers to be written in a single atomic write. Instead of passing a single buffer and length parameter, as is done with *read* and *write*, the process passes in a pointer to an array of buffers and lengths, along with a count describing the size of the array.

This facility allows buffers in different parts of a process address space to be written atomically, without the need to copy them to a single contiguous buffer. Atomic writes are necessary in the case where the underlying abstraction is record based, such as tape drives that output a tape block on each write request. It is also convenient to be able to read a single request into several different buffers (such as a record header into one place and the data into another). Although an application can simulate the ability to scatter data by reading the data into a large buffer and then copying the pieces to their intended destinations, the cost of memory-to-memory copying in such cases often would more than double the running time of the affected application.

Just as *send* and *recv* could have been implemented as library interfaces to *sendto* and *recvfrom*, it also would have been possible to simulate *read* with *readv* and *write* with *writev*. However, *read* and *write* are used so much more frequently that the added cost of simulating them would not have been worthwhile.

Multiple Filesystem Support

With the expansion of network computing, it became desirable to support both local and remote filesystems. To simplify the support of multiple filesystems, the developers added a new virtual node or *vnode* interface to the kernel. The set of operations exported from the vnode interface appear much like the filesystem operations previously supported by the local filesystem. However, they may be supported by a wide range of filesystem types:

• Local disk-based filesystems

• Files imported using a variety of remote filesystem protocols

• Read-only CD-ROM filesystems

• Filesystems providing special-purpose interfaces—for example, the **/proc** filesystem

A few variants of 4.4BSD, such as FreeBSD, allow filesystems to be loaded dynamically when the filesystems are first referenced by the *mount* system call. The vnode interface is described in Section 6.5; its ancillary support routines are described in Section 6.6; several of the special-purpose filesystems are described in Section 6.7.

2.7   Filesystems

A regular file is a linear array of bytes, and can be read and written starting at any byte in the file. The kernel distinguishes no record boundaries in regular files, although many programs recognize line-feed characters as distinguishing the ends of lines, and other programs may impose other structure. No system-related information about a file is kept in the file itself, but the filesystem stores a small amount of ownership, protection, and usage information with each file.

A *filename* component is a string of up to 255 characters. These filenames are stored in a type of file called a *directory*. The information in a directory about a file is called a *directory entry* and includes, in addition to the filename, a pointer to the file itself. Directory entries may refer to other directories, as well as to plain files. A hierarchy of directories and files is thus formed, and is called a *filesystem*; a small one is shown in Fig. 2.2. Directories may contain subdirectories, and there is no inherent limitation to the depth with which directory nesting may occur. To protect the consistency of the filesystem, the kernel does not permit processes to write directly into directories. A filesystem may include not only plain files and directories, but also references to other objects, such as devices and sockets.

The filesystem forms a tree, the beginning of which is the *root directory*, sometimes referred to by the name **slash**, spelled with a single solidus character (/). The root directory contains files; in our example in Fig. 2.2, it contains **vmunix**, a copy of the kernel-executable object file. It also contains directories; in this example, it contains the **usr** directory. Within the **usr** directory is the **bin** directory, which mostly contains executable object code of programs, such as the files **ls** and **vi**.

A process identifies a file by specifying that file's *pathname*, which is a string composed of zero or more filenames separated by slash (/) characters. The kernel associates two directories with each process for use in interpreting pathnames. A process's *root directory* is the topmost point in the filesystem that the process can access; it is ordinarily set to the root directory of the entire filesystem. A pathname beginning with a slash is called an *absolute pathname*, and is interpreted by the kernel starting with the process's root directory.

Figure 2.2 A small filesystem tree.

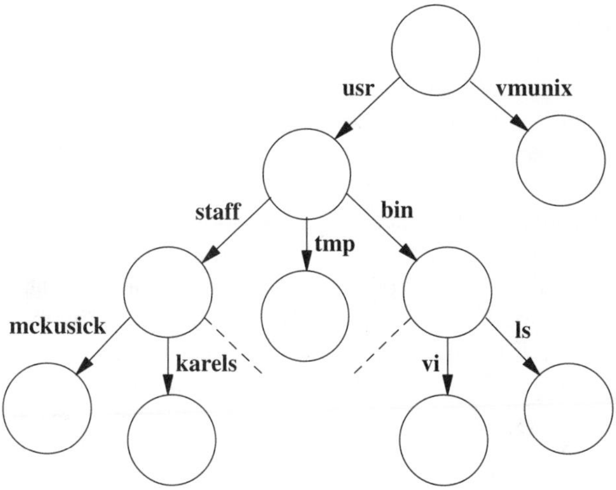

A pathname that does not begin with a slash is called a *relative pathname*, and is interpreted relative to the *current working directory* of the process. (This directory also is known by the shorter names *current directory* or *working directory*.) The current directory itself may be referred to directly by the name *dot*, spelled with a single period (.). The filename *dot-dot* (..) refers to a directory's parent directory. The root directory is its own parent.

A process may set its root directory with the *chroot* system call, and its current directory with the *chdir* system call. Any process may do *chdir* at any time, but *chroot* is permitted only a process with superuser privileges. *Chroot* is normally used to set up restricted access to the system.

Using the filesystem shown in Fig. 2.2, if a process has the root of the filesystem as its root directory, and has **/usr** as its current directory, it can refer to the file **vi** either from the root with the absolute pathname **/usr/bin/vi**, or from its current directory with the relative pathname **bin/vi**.

System utilities and databases are kept in certain well-known directories. Part of the well-defined hierarchy includes a directory that contains the *home directory* for each user—for example, **/usr/staff/mckusick** and **/usr/staff/karels** in Fig. 2.2. When users log in, the current working directory of their shell is set to the home directory. Within their home directories, users can create directories as easily as they can regular files. Thus, a user can build arbitrarily complex subhierarchies.

The user usually knows of only one filesystem, but the system may know that this one virtual filesystem is really composed of several physical filesystems, each on a different device. A physical filesystem may not span multiple hardware devices. Since most physical disk devices are divided into several logical devices, there may be more than one filesystem per physical device, but there will be no more than one per logical device. One filesystem—the filesystem that anchors all absolute pathnames—is called the *root filesystem*, and is always available. Others may be mounted; that is, they may be integrated into the directory hierarchy of the root filesystem. References to a directory that has a filesystem mounted on it are converted transparently by the kernel into references to the root directory of the mounted filesystem.

The *link* system call takes the name of an existing file and another name to create for that file. After a successful *link*, the file can be accessed by either filename. A filename can be removed with the *unlink* system call. When the final name for a file is removed (and the final process that has the file open closes it), the file is deleted.

Files are organized hierarchically in *directories*. A directory is a type of file, but, in contrast to regular files, a directory has a structure imposed on it by the system. A process can read a directory as it would an ordinary file, but only the kernel is permitted to modify a directory. Directories are created by the *mkdir* system call and are removed by the *rmdir* system call. Before 4.2BSD, the *mkdir* and *rmdir* system calls were implemented by a series of *link* and *unlink* system calls being done. There were three reasons for adding systems calls explicitly to create and delete directories:

1. The operation could be made atomic. If the system crashed, the directory would not be left half-constructed, as could happen when a series of link operations were used.

2. When a networked filesystem is being run, the creation and deletion of files and directories need to be specified atomically so that they can be serialized.

3. When supporting non-UNIX filesystems, such as an MS-DOS filesystem, on another partition of the disk, the other filesystem may not support link operations. Although other filesystems might support the concept of directories, they probably would not create and delete the directories with links, as the UNIX filesystem does. Consequently, they could create and delete directories only if explicit directory create and delete requests were presented.

The *chown* system call sets the owner and group of a file, and *chmod* changes protection attributes. *Stat* applied to a filename can be used to read back such properties of a file. The *fchown*, *fchmod*, and *fstat* system calls are applied to a descriptor, instead of to a filename, to do the same set of operations. The *rename* system call can be used to give a file a new name in the filesystem, replacing one of the file's old names. Like the directory-creation and directory-deletion operations, the *rename* system call was added to 4.2BSD to provide atomicity to name changes in the local filesystem. Later, it proved useful explicitly to export renaming operations to foreign filesystems and over the network.

The *truncate* system call was added to 4.2BSD to allow files to be shortened to an arbitrary offset. The call was added primarily in support of the Fortran runtime library, which has the semantics such that the end of a random-access file is set to be wherever the program most recently accessed that file. Without the *truncate* system call, the only way to shorten a file was to copy the part that was desired to a new file, to delete the old file, then to rename the copy to the original name. As well as this algorithm being slow, the library could potentially fail on a full filesystem.

Once the filesystem had the ability to shorten files, the kernel took advantage of that ability to shorten large empty directories. The advantage of shortening empty directories is that it reduces the time spent in the kernel searching them when names are being created or deleted.

Newly created files are assigned the user identifier of the process that created them and the group identifier of the directory in which they were created. A three-level access-control mechanism is provided for the protection of files. These three levels specify the accessibility of a file to

1. The user who owns the file

2. The group that owns the file

3. Everyone else

Each level of access has separate indicators for read permission, write permission, and execute permission.

Files are created with zero length, and may grow when they are written. While a file is open, the system maintains a pointer into the file indicating the current location in the file associated with the descriptor. This pointer can be moved about in the file in a random-access fashion. Processes sharing a file descriptor through a *fork* or *dup* system call share the current location pointer. Descriptors created by separate *open* system calls have separate current location pointers. Files may have *holes* in them. Holes are void areas in the linear extent of the file where data have never been written. A process can create these holes by positioning the pointer past the current end-of-file and writing. When read, holes are treated by the system as zero-valued bytes.

Earlier UNIX systems had a limit of 14 characters per filename component. This limitation was often a problem. For example, in addition to the natural desire of users to give files long descriptive names, a common way of forming filenames is as **basename.extension**, where the extension (indicating the kind of file, such as **.c** for C source or **.o** for intermediate binary object) is one to three characters, leaving 10 to 12 characters for the basename. Source-code–control systems and editors usually take up another two characters, either as a prefix or a suffix, for their purposes, leaving eight to 10 characters. It is easy to use 10 or 12 characters in a single English word as a basename (e.g., "multiplexer").

It is possible to keep within these limits, but it is inconvenient or even dangerous, because other UNIX systems accept strings longer than the limit when creating files, but then *truncate* to the limit. A C language source file named **multiplexer.c** (already 13 characters) might have a source-code–control file with **s.** prepended, producing a filename **s.multiplexer** that is indistinguishable from the source-code–control file for **multiplexer.ms**, a file containing **troff** source for documentation for the C program. The contents of the two original files could easily get confused with no warning from the source-code–control system. Careful coding can detect this problem, but the long filenames first introduced in 4.2BSD practically eliminate it.

2.8   Filestores

The operations defined for local filesystems are divided into two parts. Common to all local filesystems are hierarchical naming, locking, quotas, attribute management, and protection. These features are independent of how the data will be stored. 4.4BSD has a single implementation to provide these semantics.

The other part of the local filesystem is the organization and management of the data on the storage media. Laying out the contents of files on the storage media is the responsibility of the filestore. 4.4BSD supports three different filestore layouts:

• The traditional Berkeley Fast Filesystem

• The log-structured filesystem, based on the Sprite operating-system design [Rosenblum & Ousterhout, 1992]

• A memory-based filesystem

Although the organizations of these filestores are completely different, these differences are indistinguishable to the processes using the filestores.

The Fast Filesystem organizes data into cylinder groups. Files that are likely to be accessed together, based on their locations in the filesystem hierarchy, are stored in the same cylinder group. Files that are not expected to accessed together are moved into different cylinder groups. Thus, files written at the same time may be placed far apart on the disk.

The log-structured filesystem organizes data as a log. All data being written at any point in time are gathered together, and are written at the same disk location. Data are never overwritten; instead, a new copy of the file is written that replaces the old one. The old files are reclaimed by a garbage-collection process that runs when the filesystem becomes full and additional free space is needed.

The memory-based filesystem is designed to store data in virtual memory. It is used for filesystems that need to support fast but temporary data, such as **/tmp**. The goal of the memory-based filesystem is to keep the storage packed as compactly as possible to minimize the usage of virtual-memory resources.

2.9   Network Filesystem

Initially, networking was used to transfer data from one machine to another. Later, it evolved to allowing users to log in remotely to another machine. The next logical step was to bring the data to the user, instead of having the user go to the data—and network filesystems were born. Users working locally do not experience the network delays on each keystroke, so they have a more responsive environment.

Bringing the filesystem to a local machine was among the first of the major client–server applications. The *server* is the remote machine that exports one or more of its filesystems. The *client* is the local machine that imports those filesystems. From the local client's point of view, a remotely mounted filesystem appears in the file-tree name space just like any other locally mounted filesystem. Local clients can change into directories on the remote filesystem, and can read, write, and execute binaries within that remote filesystem identically to the way that they can do these operations on a local filesystem.

When the local client does an operation on a remote filesystem, the request is packaged and is sent to the server. The server does the requested operation and returns either the requested information or an error indicating why the request was denied. To get reasonable performance, the client must cache frequently accessed data. The complexity of remote filesystems lies in maintaining cache consistency between the server and its many clients.

Although many remote-filesystem protocols have been developed over the years, the most pervasive one in use among UNIX systems is the Network Filesystem (NFS), whose protocol and most widely used implementation were done by Sun Microsystems. The 4.4BSD kernel supports the NFS protocol, although the implementation was done independently from the protocol specification [Macklem, 1994]. The NFS protocol is described in Chapter 9.

2.10   Terminals

Terminals support the standard system I/O operations, as well as a collection of terminal-specific operations to control input-character editing and output delays. At the lowest level are the terminal device drivers that control the hardware terminal ports. Terminal input is handled according to the underlying communication characteristics, such as baud rate, and according to a set of software-controllable parameters, such as parity checking.

Layered above the terminal device drivers are line disciplines that provide various degrees of character processing. The default line discipline is selected when a port is being used for an interactive login. The line discipline is run in *canonical mode*; input is processed to provide standard line-oriented editing functions, and input is presented to a process on a line-by-line basis.

Screen editors and programs that communicate with other computers generally run in *noncanonical mode* (also commonly referred to as *raw mode* or *character-at-a-time mode*). In this mode, input is passed through to the reading process immediately and without interpretation. All special-character input processing is disabled, no erase or other line editing processing is done, and all characters are passed to the program that is reading from the terminal.

It is possible to configure the terminal in thousands of combinations between these two extremes. For example, a screen editor that wanted to receive user interrupts asynchronously might enable the special characters that generate signals and enable output flow control, but otherwise run in noncanonical mode; all other characters would be passed through to the process uninterpreted.

On output, the terminal handler provides simple formatting services, including

• Converting the line-feed character to the two-character carriage-return–line-feed sequence

• Inserting delays after certain standard control characters

• Expanding tabs

• Displaying echoed nongraphic ASCII characters as a two-character sequence of the form "ˆC" (i.e., the ASCII caret character followed by the ASCII character that is the character's value offset from the ASCII "@" character).

Each of these formatting services can be disabled individually by a process through control requests.

2.11   Interprocess Communication

Interprocess communication in 4.4BSD is organized in *communication domains.* Domains currently supported include the *local domain,* for communication between processes executing on the same machine; the *internet domain,* for communication between processes using the TCP/IP protocol suite (perhaps within the Internet); the ISO/OSI protocol family for communication between sites required to run them; and the *XNS domain,* for communication between processes using the XEROX Network Systems (XNS) protocols.

Within a domain, communication takes place between communication end-points known as *sockets.* As mentioned in Section 2.6, the *socket* system call creates a socket and returns a descriptor; other IPC system calls are described in Chapter 11. Each socket has a type that defines its communications semantics; these semantics include properties such as reliability, ordering, and prevention of duplication of messages.

Each socket has associated with it a *communication protocol.* This protocol provides the semantics required by the socket according to the latter's type. Applications may request a specific protocol when creating a socket, or may allow the system to select a protocol that is appropriate for the type of socket being created.

Sockets may have addresses bound to them. The form and meaning of socket addresses are dependent on the communication domain in which the socket is created. Binding a name to a socket in the local domain causes a file to be created in the filesystem.

Normal data transmitted and received through sockets are untyped. Data-representation issues are the responsibility of libraries built on top of the interprocess-communication facilities. In addition to transporting normal data, communication domains may support the transmission and reception of specially typed data, termed *access rights.* The local domain, for example, uses this facility to pass descriptors between processes.

Networking implementations on UNIX before 4.2BSD usually worked by overloading the character-device interfaces. One goal of the socket interface was for naive programs to be able to work without change on stream-style connections. Such programs can work only if the *read* and *write* systems calls are unchanged. Consequently, the original interfaces were left intact, and were made to work on stream-type sockets. A new interface was added for more complicated sockets, such as those used to send datagrams, with which a destination address must be presented with each *send* call.

Another benefit is that the new interface is highly portable. Shortly after a test release was available from Berkeley, the socket interface had been ported to System III by a UNIX vendor (although AT&T did not support the socket interface until the release of System V Release 4, deciding instead to use the Eighth Edition stream mechanism). The socket interface was also ported to run in many Ethernet boards by vendors, such as Excelan and Interlan, that were selling into the PC market, where the machines were too small to run networking in the main processor. More recently, the socket interface was used as the basis for Microsoft's Winsock networking interface for Windows.

2.12 Network Communication

Some of the communication domains supported by the *socket* IPC mechanism provide access to network protocols. These protocols are implemented as a separate software layer logically below the socket software in the kernel. The kernel provides many ancillary services, such as buffer management, message routing, standardized interfaces to the protocols, and interfaces to the network interface drivers for the use of the various network protocols.

At the time that 4.2BSD was being implemented, there were many networking protocols in use or under development, each with its own strengths and weaknesses. There was no clearly superior protocol or protocol suite. By supporting multiple protocols, 4.2BSD could provide interoperability and resource sharing among the diverse set of machines that was available in the Berkeley environment. Multiple-protocol support also provides for future changes. Today's protocols designed for 10- to 100-Mbit-per-second Ethernets are likely to be inadequate for tomorrow's 1- to 10-Gbit-per-second fiber-optic networks. Consequently, the network-communication layer is designed to support multiple protocols. New protocols are added to the kernel without the support for older protocols being affected. Older applications can continue to operate using the old protocol over the same physical network as is used by newer applications running with a newer network protocol.

2.13 Network Implementation

The first protocol suite implemented in 4.2BSD was DARPA's Transmission Control Protocol/Internet Protocol (TCP/IP). The CSRG chose TCP/IP as the first network to incorporate into the socket IPC framework, because a 4.1BSD-based implementation was publicly available from a DARPA-sponsored project at Bolt, Beranek, and Newman (BBN). That was an influential choice: The 4.2BSD implementation is the main reason for the extremely widespread use of this protocol suite. Later performance and capability improvements to the TCP/IP implementation have also been widely adopted. The TCP/IP implementation is described in detail in Chapter 13.

The release of 4.3BSD added the Xerox Network Systems (XNS) protocol suite, partly building on work done at the University of Maryland and at Cornell University. This suite was needed to connect isolated machines that could not communicate using TCP/IP.

The release of 4.4BSD added the ISO protocol suite because of the latter's increasing visibility both within and outside the United States. Because of the somewhat different semantics defined for the ISO protocols, some minor changes were required in the socket interface to accommodate these semantics. The changes were made such that they were invisible to clients of other existing protocols. The ISO protocols also required extensive addition to the two-level routing tables provided by the kernel in 4.3BSD. The greatly expanded routing capabilities of 4.4BSD include arbitrary levels of routing with variable-length addresses and network masks.

2.14   System Operation

Bootstrapping mechanisms are used to start the system running. First, the 4.4BSD kernel must be loaded into the main memory of the processor. Once loaded, it must go through an initialization phase to set the hardware into a known state. Next, the kernel must do autoconfiguration, a process that finds and configures the peripherals that are attached to the processor. The system begins running in single-user mode while a start-up script does disk checks and starts the accounting and quota checking. Finally, the start-up script starts the general system services and brings up the system to full multiuser operation.

During multiuser operation, processes wait for login requests on the terminal lines and network ports that have been configured for user access. When a login request is detected, a login process is spawned and user validation is done. When the login validation is successful, a login shell is created from which the user can run additional processes.

Exercises

2.1   How does a user process request a service from the kernel?

2.2   How are data transferred between a process and the kernel? What alternatives are available?

2.3   How does a process access an I/O stream? List three types of I/O streams.

2.4   What are the four steps in the lifecycle of a process?

2.5   Why are process groups provided in 4.3BSD?

2.6   Describe four machine-dependent functions of the kernel?

2.7   Describe the difference between an absolute and a relative pathname.

2.8   Give three reasons why the *mkdir* system call was added to 4.2BSD.

2.9   Define *scatter-gather I/O*. Why is it useful?

2.10   What is the difference between a block and a character device?

2.11   List five functions provided by a terminal driver.

2.12   What is the difference between a pipe and a socket?

2.13   Describe how to create a group of processes in a pipeline.

*2.14 List the three system calls that were required to create a new directory **foo** in the current directory before the addition of the *mkdir* system call.

*2.15 Explain the difference between interprocess communication and networking.

References

Accetta et al, 1986.
M. Accetta, R. Baron, W. Bolosky, D. Golub, R. Rashid, A. Tevanian, & M. Young, "Mach: A New Kernel Foundation for UNIX Development," *USENIX Association Conference Proceedings*, pp. 93–113, June 1986.

Cheriton, 1988.
D. R. Cheriton, "The V Distributed System," *Comm ACM*, vol. 31, no. 3, pp. 314–333, March 1988.

Ewens et al, 1985.
P. Ewens, D. R. Blythe, M. Funkenhauser, & R. C. Holt, "Tunis: A Distributed Multiprocessor Operating System," *USENIX Association Conference Proceedings*, pp. 247–254, June 1985.

Gingell et al, 1987.
R. Gingell, J. Moran, & W. Shannon, "Virtual Memory Architecture in SunOS," *USENIX Association Conference Proceedings*, pp. 81–94, June 1987.

Kernighan & Pike, 1984.
B. W. Kernighan & R. Pike, *The UNIX Programming Environment,* Prentice-Hall, Englewood Cliffs, NJ, 1984.

Macklem, 1994.
R. Macklem, "The 4.4BSD NFS Implementation," in *4.4BSD System Manager's Manual*, pp. 6:1–14, O'Reilly & Associates, Inc., Sebastopol, CA, 1994.

McKusick & Karels, 1988.
M. K. McKusick & M. J. Karels, "Design of a General Purpose Memory

Allocator for the 4.3BSD UNIX Kernel," *USENIX Association Conference Proceedings*, pp. 295–304, June 1988.

McKusick, Karels et al, 1994.

M. K. McKusick, M. J. Karels, S. J. Leffler, W. N. Joy, & R. S. Fabry, "Berkeley Software Architecture Manual, 4.4BSD Edition," in *4.4BSD Programmer's Supplementary Documents*, pp. 5:1–42, O'Reilly & Associates, Inc., Sebastopol, CA, 1994.

Ritchie, 1988.

D. M. Ritchie, "Early Kernel Design," private communication, March 1988.

Rosenblum & Ousterhout, 1992.

M. Rosenblum & J. Ousterhout, "The Design and Implementation of a Log-Structured File System," *ACM Transactions on Computer Systems*, vol. 10, no. 1, pp. 26–52, Association for Computing Machinery, February 1992.

Rozier et al, 1988.

M. Rozier, V. Abrossimov, F. Armand, I. Boule, M. Gien, M. Guillemont, F. Herrmann, C. Kaiser, S. Langlois, P. Leonard, & W. Neuhauser, "Chorus Distributed Operating Systems," *USENIX Computing Systems*, vol. 1, no. 4, pp. 305–370, Fall 1988.

Tevanian, 1987.

A. Tevanian, "Architecture-Independent Virtual Memory Management for Parallel and Distributed Environments: The Mach Approach," Technical Report CMU-CS-88-106, Department of Computer Science, Carnegie-Mellon University, Pittsburgh, PA, December 1987.

CHAPTER 3

Kernel Services

3.1 Kernel Organization

The 4.4BSD kernel can be viewed as a service provider to user processes. Processes usually access these services through system calls. Some services, such as process scheduling and memory management, are implemented as processes that execute in kernel mode or as routines that execute periodically within the kernel. In this chapter, we describe how kernel services are provided to user processes, and what some of the ancillary processing performed by the kernel is. Then, we describe the basic kernel services provided by 4.4BSD, and provide details of their implementation.

System Processes

All 4.4BSD processes originate from a single process that is crafted by the kernel at startup. Three processes are created immediately and exist always. Two of them are *kernel processes*, and function wholly within the kernel. (Kernel processes execute code that is compiled into the kernel's load image and operate with the kernel's privileged execution mode.) The third is the first process to execute a program in user mode; it serves as the parent process for all subsequent processes.

The two kernel processes are the *swapper* and the *pagedaemon*. The *swapper*—historically, process 0—is responsible for scheduling the transfer of whole processes between main memory and secondary storage when system resources are low. The *pagedaemon*—historically, process 2—is responsible for writing parts of the address space of a process to secondary storage in support of the paging facilities of the virtual-memory system. The third process is the **init** process—historically, process 1. This process performs administrative tasks, such as spawning getty processes for each terminal on a machine and handling the orderly shutdown of a system from multiuser to single-user operation. The **init** process is a user-mode process, running outside the kernel (see Section 14.6).

System Entry

Entrances into the kernel can be categorized according to the event or action that initiates it;

• Hardware interrupt

• Hardware trap

• Software-initiated trap

Hardware interrupts arise from external events, such as an I/O device needing attention or a clock reporting the passage of time. (For example, the kernel depends on the presence of a real-time clock or interval timer to maintain the current time of day, to drive process scheduling, and to initiate the execution of system timeout functions.) Hardware interrupts occur *asynchronously* and may not relate to the context of the currently executing process.

Hardware traps may be either synchronous or asynchronous, but *are* related to the current executing process. Examples of hardware traps are those generated as a result of an illegal arithmetic operation, such as divide by zero.

Software-initiated traps are used by the system to force the scheduling of an event such as process rescheduling or network processing, as soon as is possible. For most uses of software-initiated traps, it is an implementation detail whether they are implemented as a hardware-generated interrupt, or as a flag that is checked whenever the priority level drops (e.g., on every exit from the kernel). An example of hardware support for software-initiated traps is the *asynchronous system trap (AST)* provided by the VAX architecture. An AST is posted by the kernel. Then, when a return-from-interrupt instruction drops the interrupt-priority level below a threshold, an AST interrupt will be delivered. Most architectures today do not have hardware support for ASTs, so they must implement ASTs in software.

System calls are a special case of a software-initiated trap—the machine instruction used to initiate a system call typically causes a hardware trap that is handled specially by the kernel.

Run-Time Organization

The kernel can be logically divided into a *top half* and a *bottom half*, as shown in Fig. 3.1. The top half of the kernel provides services to processes in response to system calls or traps. This software can be thought of as a library of routines shared by all processes. The top half of the kernel executes in a privileged execution mode, in which it has access both to kernel data structures and to the context of user-level processes. The context of each process is contained in two areas of memory reserved for process-specific information. The first of these areas is the *process structure*, which has historically contained the information that is necessary even if the process has been swapped out. In 4.4BSD, this information includes the identifiers associated with the process, the process's rights and privileges, its descriptors, its memory map, pending external events and associated

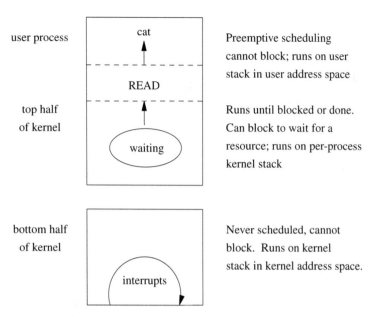

Figure 3.1 Run-time structure of the kernel.

actions, maximum and current resource utilization, and many other things. The second is the *user structure*, which has historically contained the information that is not necessary when the process is swapped out. In 4.4BSD, the user-structure information of each process includes the hardware process control block (PCB), process accounting and statistics, and minor additional information for debugging and creating a core dump. Deciding what was to be stored in the *process structure* and the *user structure* was far more important in previous systems than it was in 4.4BSD. As memory became a less limited resource, most of the user structure was merged into the process structure for convenience; see Section 4.2.

The bottom half of the kernel comprises routines that are invoked to handle hardware interrupts. The kernel requires that hardware facilities be available to block the delivery of interrupts. Improved performance is available if the hardware facilities allow interrupts to be defined in order of priority. Whereas the HP300 provides distinct hardware priority levels for different kinds of interrupts, UNIX also runs on architectures such as the Perkin Elmer, where interrupts are all at the same priority, or the ELXSI, where there are no interrupts in the traditional sense.

Activities in the bottom half of the kernel are *asynchronous*, with respect to the top half, and the software cannot depend on having a specific (or any) process running when an interrupt occurs. Thus, the state information for the process that initiated the activity is not available. (Activities in the bottom half of the kernel are synchronous with respect to the interrupt source.) The top and bottom halves of the kernel communicate through data structures, generally organized around work queues.

The 4.4BSD kernel is never preempted to run another process while executing in the top half of the kernel—for example, while executing a system call—although it will explicitly give up the processor if it must wait for an event or for a shared resource. Its execution may be interrupted, however, by interrupts for the bottom half of the kernel. The bottom half always begins running at a specific *priority level*. Therefore, the top half can block these interrupts by setting the *processor priority level* to an appropriate value. The value is chosen based on the priority level of the device that shares the data structures that the top half is about to modify. This mechanism ensures the consistency of the work queues and other data structures shared between the top and bottom halves.

Processes cooperate in the sharing of system resources, such as the CPU. The top and bottom halves of the kernel also work together in implementing certain system operations, such as I/O. Typically, the top half will start an I/O operation, then relinquish the processor; then the requesting process will sleep, awaiting notification from the bottom half that the I/O request has completed.

Entry to the Kernel

When a process enters the kernel through a trap or an interrupt, the kernel must save the current machine state before it begins to service the event. For the HP300, the machine state that must be saved includes the program counter, the user stack pointer, the general-purpose registers and the processor status longword. The HP300 trap instruction saves the program counter and the processor status longword as part of the exception stack frame; the user stack pointer and registers must be saved by the software trap handler. If the machine state were not fully saved, the kernel could change values in the currently executing program in improper ways. Since interrupts may occur between any two user-level instructions (and, on some architectures, between parts of a single instruction), and because they may be completely unrelated to the currently executing process, an incompletely saved state could cause correct programs to fail in mysterious and not easily reproduceable ways.

The exact sequence of events required to save the process state is completely machine dependent, although the HP300 provides a good example of the general procedure. A trap or system call will trigger the following events:

• The hardware switches into kernel (supervisor) mode, so that memory-access checks are made with kernel privileges, references to the stack pointer use the kernel's stack pointer, and privileged instructions can be executed.

• The hardware pushes onto the per-process kernel stack the program counter, processor status longword, and information describing the type of trap. (On architectures other than the HP300, this information can include the system-call number and general-purpose registers as well.)

• An assembly-language routine saves all state information not saved by the hardware. On the HP300, this information includes the general-purpose registers and the user stack pointer, also saved onto the per-process kernel stack.

After this preliminary state saving, the kernel calls a C routine that can freely use the general-purpose registers as any other C routine would, without concern about changing the unsuspecting process's state.

There are three major kinds of handlers, corresponding to particular kernel entries:

1. *Syscall*( ) for a system call

2. *Trap*( ) for hardware traps and for software-initiated traps other than system calls

3. The appropriate device-driver interrupt handler for a hardware interrupt

Each type of handler takes its own specific set of parameters. For a system call, they are the system-call number and an exception frame. For a trap, they are the type of trap, the relevant floating-point and virtual-address information related to the trap, and an exception frame. (The exception-frame arguments for the trap and system call are not the same. The HP300 hardware saves different information based on different types of traps.) For a hardware interrupt, the only parameter is a unit (or board) number.

Return from the Kernel

When the handling of the system entry is completed, the user-process state is restored, and the kernel returns to the user process. Returning to the user process reverses the process of entering the kernel.

• An assembly-language routine restores the general-purpose registers and user-stack pointer previously pushed onto the stack.

• The hardware restores the program counter and program status longword, and switches to user mode, so that future references to the stack pointer use the user's stack pointer, privileged instructions cannot be executed, and memory-access checks are done with user-level privileges.

Execution then resumes at the next instruction in the user's process.

3.2   System Calls

The most frequent trap into the kernel (after clock processing) is a request to do a system call. System performance requires that the kernel minimize the overhead in fielding and dispatching a system call. The system-call handler must do the following work:

• Verify that the parameters to the system call are located at a valid user address, and copy them from the user's address space into the kernel

• Call a kernel routine that implements the system call

Result Handling

Eventually, the system call returns to the calling process, either successfully or unsuccessfully. On the HP300 architecture, success or failure is returned as the carry bit in the user process's program status longword: If it is zero, the return was successful; otherwise, it was unsuccessful. On the HP300 and many other machines, return values of C functions are passed back through a general-purpose register (for the HP300, data register 0). The routines in the kernel that implement system calls return the values that are normally associated with the global variable *errno*. After a system call, the kernel system-call handler leaves this value in the register. If the system call failed, a C library routine moves that value into *errno*, and sets the return register to −1. The calling process is expected to notice the value of the return register, and then to examine *errno*. The mechanism involving the carry bit and the global variable *errno* exists for historical reasons derived from the PDP-11.

There are two kinds of unsuccessful returns from a system call: those where kernel routines discover an error, and those where a system call is interrupted. The most common case is a system call that is interrupted when it has relinquished the processor to wait for an event that may not occur for a long time (such as terminal input), and a signal arrives in the interim. When signal handlers are initialized by a process, they specify whether system calls that they interrupt should be restarted, or whether the system call should return with an *interrupted system call* (EINTR) error.

When a system call is interrupted, the signal is delivered to the process. If the process has requested that the signal abort the system call, the handler then returns an error, as described previously. If the system call is to be restarted, however, the handler resets the process's program counter to the machine instruction that caused the system-call trap into the kernel. (This calculation is necessary because the program-counter value that was saved when the system-call trap was done is for the instruction after the trap-causing instruction.) The handler replaces the saved program-counter value with this address. When the process returns from the signal handler, it resumes at the program-counter value that the handler provided, and reexecutes the same system call.

Restarting a system call by resetting the program counter has certain implications. First, the kernel must not modify any of the input parameters in the process address space (it can modify the kernel copy of the parameters that it makes). Second, it must ensure that the system call has not performed any actions that cannot be repeated. For example, in the current system, if any characters have been read from the terminal, the read must return with a short count. Otherwise, if the call were to be restarted, the already-read bytes would be lost.

Returning from a System Call

While the system call is running, a signal may be posted to the process, or another process may attain a higher scheduling priority. After the system call completes, the handler checks to see whether either event has occurred.

The handler first checks for a posted signal. Such signals include signals that interrupted the system call, as well as signals that arrived while a system call was in progress, but were held pending until the system call completed. Signals that are ignored, by default or by explicit programmatic request, are never posted to the process. Signals with a default action have that action taken before the process runs again (i.e., the process may be stopped or terminated as appropriate). If a signal is to be caught (and is not currently blocked), the handler arranges to have the appropriate signal handler called, rather than to have the process return directly from the system call. After the handler returns, the process will resume execution at system-call return (or system-call execution, if the system call is being restarted).

After checking for posted signals, the handler checks to see whether any process has a priority higher than that of the currently running one. If such a process exists, the handler calls the context-switch routine to cause the higher-priority process to run. At a later time, the current process will again have the highest priority, and will resume execution by returning from the system call to the user process.

If a process has requested that the system do profiling, the handler also calculates the amount of time that has been spent in the system call, i.e., the system time accounted to the process between the latter's entry into and exit from the handler. This time is charged to the routine in the user's process that made the system call.

3.3   Traps and Interrupts

Traps

Traps, like system calls, occur synchronously for a process. Traps normally occur because of unintentional errors, such as division by zero or indirection through an invalid pointer. The process becomes aware of the problem either by catching a signal or by being terminated. Traps can also occur because of a page fault, in which case the system makes the page available and restarts the process without the process being aware that the fault occurred.

The trap handler is invoked like the system-call handler. First, the process state is saved. Next, the trap handler determines the trap type, then arranges to post a signal or to cause a pagein as appropriate. Finally, it checks for pending signals and higher-priority processes, and exits identically to the system-call handler.

I/O Device Interrupts

Interrupts from I/O and other devices are handled by interrupt routines that are loaded as part of the kernel's address space. These routines handle the console terminal interface, one or more clocks, and several software-initiated interrupts used by the system for low-priority clock processing and for networking facilities.

Unlike traps and system calls, device interrupts occur asynchronously. The process that requested the service is unlikely to be the currently running process, and may no longer exist! The process that started the operation will be notified that the operation has finished when that process runs again. As occurs with traps and system calls, the entire machine state must be saved, since any changes could cause errors in the currently running process.

Device-interrupt handlers run only on demand, and are never scheduled by the kernel. Unlike system calls, interrupt handlers do not have a per-process context. Interrupt handlers cannot use any of the context of the currently running process (e.g., the process's user structure). The stack normally used by the kernel is part of a process context. On some systems (e.g., the HP300), the interrupts are caught on the per-process kernel stack of whichever process happens to be running. This approach requires that all the per-process kernel stacks be large enough to handle the deepest possible nesting caused by a system call and one or more interrupts, and that a per-process kernel stack always be available, even when a process is not running. Other architectures (e.g., the VAX), provide a systemwide interrupt stack that is used solely for device interrupts. This architecture allows the per-process kernel stacks to be sized based on only the requirements for handling a synchronous trap or system call. Regardless of the implementation, when an interrupt occurs, the system must switch to the correct stack (either explicitly, or as part of the hardware exception handling) before it begins to handle the interrupt.

The interrupt handler can never use the stack to save state between invocations. An interrupt handler must get all the information that it needs from the data structures that it shares with the top half of the kernel—generally, its global work queue. Similarly, all information provided to the top half of the kernel by the interrupt handler must be communicated the same way. In addition, because 4.4BSD requires a per-process context for a thread of control to sleep, an interrupt handler cannot relinquish the processor to wait for resources, but rather must always run to completion.

Software Interrupts

Many events in the kernel are driven by hardware interrupts. For high-speed devices such as network controllers, these interrupts occur at a high priority. A network controller must quickly acknowledge receipt of a packet and reenable the controller to accept more packets to avoid losing closely spaced packets. However, the further processing of passing the packet to the receiving process, although time consuming, does not need to be done quickly. Thus, a lower priority is possible for the further processing, so critical operations will not be blocked from executing longer than necessary.

The mechanism for doing lower-priority processing is called a *software interrupt*. Typically, a high-priority interrupt creates a queue of work to be done at a lower-priority level. After queueing of the work request, the high-priority interrupt arranges for the processing of the request to be run at a lower-priority level. When the machine priority drops below that lower priority, an interrupt is generated that calls the requested function. If a higher-priority interrupt comes in during request processing, that processing will be preempted like any other low-priority task. On some architectures, the interrupts are true hardware traps caused by software instructions. Other architectures implement the same functionality by monitoring flags set by the interrupt handler at appropriate times and calling the request-processing functions directly.

The delivery of network packets to destination processes is handled by a packet-processing function that runs at low priority. As packets come in, they are put onto a work queue, and the controller is immediately reenabled. Between packet arrivals, the packet-processing function works to deliver the packets. Thus, the controller can accept new packets without having to wait for the previous packet to be delivered. In addition to network processing, software interrupts are used to handle time-related events and process rescheduling.

3.4   Clock Interrupts

The system is driven by a clock that interrupts at regular intervals. Each interrupt is referred to as a *tick*. On the HP300, the clock ticks 100 times per second. At each tick, the system updates the current time of day as well as user-process and system timers.

Interrupts for clock ticks are posted at a high hardware-interrupt priority. After the process state has been saved, the *hardclock*() routine is called. It is important that the *hardclock*() routine finish its job quickly:

- If *hardclock*() runs for more than one tick, it will miss the next clock interrupt. Since *hardclock*() maintains the time of day for the system, a missed interrupt will cause the system to lose time.

- Because of *hardclock*()s high interrupt priority, nearly all other activity in the system is blocked while *hardclock*() is running. This blocking can cause network controllers to miss packets, or a disk controller to miss the transfer of a sector coming under a disk drive's head.

So that the time spent in *hardclock*() is minimized, less critical time-related processing is handled by a lower-priority software-interrupt handler called *softclock*(). In addition, if multiple clocks are available, some time-related processing can be handled by other routines supported by alternate clocks.

The work done by *hardclock*() is as follows:

- Increment the current time of day.

- If the currently running process has a virtual or profiling interval timer (see Section 3.6), decrement the timer and deliver a signal if the timer has expired.

- If the system does not have a separate clock for statistics gathering, the *hardclock*() routine does the operations normally done by *statclock*(), as described in the next section.

• If *softclock*() needs to be called, and the current interrupt-priority level is low, call *softclock*() directly.

Statistics and Process Scheduling

On historic 4BSD systems, the *hardclock*() routine collected resource-utilization statistics about what was happening when the clock interrupted. These statistics were used to do accounting, to monitor what the system was doing, and to determine future scheduling priorities. In addition, *hardclock*() forced context switches so that all processes would get a share of the CPU.

This approach has weaknesses because the clock supporting *hardclock*() interrupts on a regular basis. Processes can become synchronized with the system clock, resulting in inaccurate measurements of resource utilization (especially CPU) and inaccurate profiling [McCanne & Torek, 1993]. It is also possible to write programs that deliberately synchronize with the system clock to outwit the scheduler.

On architectures with multiple high-precision, programmable clocks, such as the HP300, randomizing the interrupt period of a clock can improve the system resource-usage measurements significantly. One clock is set to interrupt at a fixed rate; the other interrupts at a random interval chosen from times distributed uniformly over a bounded range.

To allow the collection of more accurate profiling information, 4.4BSD supports profiling clocks. When a profiling clock is available, it is set to run at a tick rate that is relatively prime to the main system clock (five times as often as the system clock, on the HP300).

The *statclock*() routine is supported by a separate clock if one is available, and is responsible for accumulating resource usage to processes. The work done by *statclock*() includes

• Charge the currently running process with a tick; if the process has accumulated four ticks, recalculate its priority. If the new priority is less than the current priority, arrange for the process to be rescheduled.

• Collect statistics on what the system was doing at the time of the tick (sitting idle, executing in user mode, or executing in system mode). Include basic information on system I/O, such as which disk drives are currently active.

Timeouts

The remaining time-related processing involves processing timeout requests and periodically reprioritizing processes that are ready to run. These functions are handled by the *softclock*() routine.

When *hardclock*() completes, if there were any *softclock*() functions to be done, *hardclock*() schedules a softclock interrupt, or sets a flag that will cause *softclock*() to be called. As an optimization, if the state of the processor is such that the *softclock*() execution will occur as soon as the hardclock interrupt returns, *hardclock*() simply lowers the processor priority and calls *softclock*() directly, avoiding the cost of returning from one interrupt only to reenter another. The savings can be substantial over time, because interrupts are expensive and these interrupts occur so frequently.

The primary task of the *softclock()* routine is to arrange for the execution of periodic events, such as

• Process real-time timer (see Section 3.6)

• Retransmission of dropped network packets

• Watchdog timers on peripherals that require monitoring

• System process-rescheduling events

An important event is the scheduling that periodically raises and lowers the CPU priority for each process in the system based on that process's recent CPU usage (see Section 4.4). The rescheduling calculation is done once per second. The scheduler is started at boot time, and each time that it runs, it requests that it be invoked again 1 second in the future.

On a heavily loaded system with many processes, the scheduler may take a long time to complete its job. Posting its next invocation 1 second after each completion may cause scheduling to occur less frequently than once per second. However, as the scheduler is not responsible for any time-critical functions, such as maintaining the time of day, scheduling less frequently than once a second is normally not a problem.

The data structure that describes waiting events is called the *callout queue*. Figure 3.2 shows an example of the callout queue. When a process schedules an event, it specifies a function to be called, a pointer to be passed as an argument to the function, and the number of clock ticks until the event should occur.

The queue is sorted in time order, with the events that are to occur soonest at the front, and the most distant events at the end. The time for each event is kept as a difference from the time of the previous event on the queue. Thus, the *hardclock()* routine needs only to check the time to expire of the first element to determine whether *softclock()* needs to run. In addition, decrementing the time to expire of the first element decrements the time for all events. The *softclock()* routine executes events from the front of the queue whose time has decremented to zero until it finds an event with a still-future (positive) time. New events are added to the queue much less frequently than the queue is checked to see whether

Figure 3.2 Timer events in the callout queue.

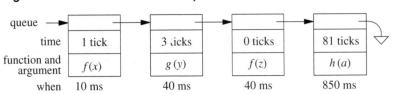

queue →				
time	1 tick	3 ticks	0 ticks	81 ticks
function and argument	$f(x)$	$g(y)$	$f(z)$	$h(a)$
when	10 ms	40 ms	40 ms	850 ms

any events are to occur. So, it is more efficient to identify the proper location to place an event when that event is added to the queue than to scan the entire queue to determine which events should occur at any single time.

The single argument is provided for the callout-queue function that is called, so that one function can be used by multiple processes. For example, there is a single real-time timer function that sends a signal to a process when a timer expires. Every process that has a real-time timer running posts a timeout request for this function; the argument that is passed to the function is a pointer to the process structure for the process. This argument enables the timeout function to deliver the signal to the correct process.

Timeout processing is more efficient when the timeouts are specified in ticks. Time updates require only an integer decrement, and checks for timer expiration require only a comparison against zero. If the timers contained time values, decrementing and comparisons would be more complex. If the number of events to be managed were large, the cost of the linear search to insert new events correctly could dominate the simple linear queue used in 4.4BSD. Other possible approaches include maintaining a heap with the next-occurring event at the top [Barkley & Lee, 1988], or maintaining separate queues of short-, medium- and long-term events [Varghese & Lauck, 1987].

3.5   Memory-Management Services

The memory organization and layout associated with a 4.4BSD process is shown in Fig. 3.3. Each process begins execution with three memory segments, called text, data, and stack. The data segment is divided into initialized data and uninitialized data (also known as bss). The text is read-only and is normally shared by all processes executing the file, whereas the data and stack areas can be written by, and are private to, each process. The text and initialized data for the process are read from the executable file.

An *executable file* is distinguished by its being a plain file (rather than a directory, special file, or symbolic link) and by its having 1 or more of its execute bits set. In the traditional *a.out* executable format, the first few bytes of the file contain a *magic number* that specifies what type of executable file that file is. Executable files fall into two major classes:

1. Files that must be read by an *interpreter*

2. Files that are directly executable

In the first class, the first 2 bytes of the file are the two-character sequence #! followed by the pathname of the interpreter to be used. (This pathname is currently limited by a compile-time constant to 30 characters.) For example, **#!/bin/sh** refers to the Bourne shell. The kernel executes the named interpreter, passing the name of the file that is to be interpreted as an argument. To prevent loops, 4.4BSD allows only one level of interpretation, and a file's interpreter may not itself be interpreted.

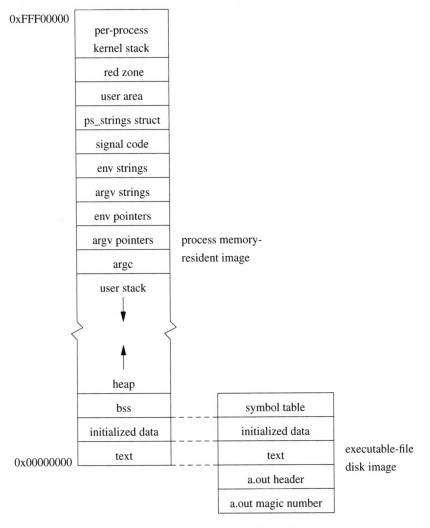

Figure 3.3 Layout of a UNIX process in memory and on disk.

For performance reasons, most files are directly executable. Each directly executable file has a magic number that specifies whether that file can be paged and whether the text part of the file can be shared among multiple processes. Following the magic number is an *exec* header that specifies the sizes of text, initialized data, uninitialized data, and additional information for debugging. (The debugging information is not used by the kernel or by the executing program.) Following the header is an image of the text, followed by an image of the initialized data. Uninitialized data are not contained in the executable file because they can be created on demand using zero-filled memory.

To begin execution, the kernel arranges to have the text portion of the file mapped into the low part of the process address space. The initialized data portion of the file is mapped into the address space following the text. An area equal to the uninitialized data region is created with zero-filled memory after the initialized data region. The stack is also created from zero-filled memory. Although the stack should not need to be zero filled, early UNIX systems made it so. In an attempt to save some startup time, the developers modified the kernel to not zero fill the stack, leaving the random previous contents of the page instead. Numerous programs stopped working because they depended on the local variables in their *main* procedure being initialized to zero. Consequently, the zero filling of the stack was restored.

Copying into memory the entire text and initialized data portion of a large program causes a long startup latency. 4.4BSD avoids this startup time by *demand paging* the program into memory, rather than preloading the program. In demand paging, the program is loaded in small pieces (pages) as it is needed, rather than all at once before it begins execution. The system does demand paging by dividing up the address space into equal-sized areas called pages. For each page, the kernel records the offset into the executable file of the corresponding data. The first access to an address on each page causes a page-fault trap in the kernel. The page-fault handler reads the correct page of the executable file into the process memory. Thus, the kernel loads only those parts of the executable file that are needed. Chapter 5 explains paging details.

The uninitialized data area can be extended with zero-filled pages using the system call *sbrk*, although most user processes use the library routine *malloc()*, a more programmer-friendly interface to *sbrk*. This allocated memory, which grows from the top of the original data segment, is called the *heap*. On the HP300, the stack grows down from the top of memory, whereas the heap grows up from the bottom of memory.

Above the user stack are areas of memory that are created by the system when the process is started. Directly above the user stack is the number of arguments (*argc*), the argument vector (*argv*), and the process environment vector (*envp*) set up when the program was executed. Above them are the argument and environment strings themselves. Above them is the signal code, used when the system delivers signals to the process; above that is the *struct ps_strings* structure, used by *ps* to locate the *argv* of the process. At the top of user memory is the user area (**u.**), the *red zone,* and the per-process kernel stack. The red zone may or may not be present in a port to an architecture. If present, it is implemented as a page of read-only memory immediately below the per-process kernel stack. Any attempt to allocate below the fixed-size kernel stack will result in a memory fault, protecting the user area from being overwritten. On some architectures, it is not possible to mark these pages as read-only, or having the kernel stack attempt to write a write protected page would result in unrecoverable system failure. In these cases, other approaches can be taken—for example, checking during each clock interrupt to see whether the current kernel stack has grown too large.

   In addition to the information maintained in the user area, a process usually requires the use of some global system resources. The kernel maintains a linked list of processes, called the *process table*, which has an entry for each process in the system. Among other data, the process entries record information on scheduling and on virtual-memory allocation. Because the entire process address space, including the user area, may be swapped out of main memory, the process entry must record enough information to be able to locate the process and to bring that process back into memory. In addition, information needed while the process is swapped out (e.g., scheduling information) must be maintained in the process entry, rather than in the user area, to avoid the kernel swapping in the process only to decide that it is not at a high-enough priority to be run.

   Other global resources associated with a process include space to record information about descriptors and page tables that record information about physical-memory utilization.

3.6   Timing Services

The kernel provides several different timing services to processes. These services include timers that run in real time and timers that run only while a process is executing.

Real Time

The system's time offset since January 1, 1970, Universal Coordinated Time (UTC), also known as the Epoch, is returned by the system call *gettimeofday*. Most modern processors (including the HP300 processors) maintain a battery-backup time-of-day register. This clock continues to run even if the processor is turned off. When the system boots, it consults the processor's time-of-day register to find out the current time. The system's time is then maintained by the clock interrupts. At each interrupt, the system increments its global time variable by an amount equal to the number of microseconds per tick. For the HP300, running at 100 ticks per second, each tick represents 10,000 microseconds.

Adjustment of the Time

Often, it is desirable to maintain the same time on all the machines on a network. It is also possible to keep more accurate time than that available from the basic processor clock. For example, hardware is readily available that listens to the set of radio stations that broadcast UTC synchronization signals in the United States. When processes on different machines agree on a common time, they will wish to change the clock on their host processor to agree with the networkwide time value. One possibility is to change the system time to the network time using the *settimeofday* system call. Unfortunately, the *settimeofday* system call will result in time running backward on machines whose clocks were fast. Time running backward can confuse user programs (such as **make**) that expect time to invariably increase. To avoid this problem, the system provides the *adjtime* system call [Gusella et al, 1994]. The *adjtime* system call takes a time delta (either positive or negative) and changes the rate at which time advances by 10 percent, faster or slower, until the time has been corrected. The operating system does the speedup by incrementing the global time by 11,000 microseconds for each tick, and does the slowdown by incrementing the global time by 9,000 microseconds for each tick. Regardless, time increases monotonically, and user processes depending on the ordering of file-modification times are not affected. However, time changes that take tens of seconds to adjust will affect programs that are measuring time intervals by using repeated calls to *gettimeofday*.

External Representation

Time is always exported from the system as microseconds, rather than as clock ticks, to provide a resolution-independent format. Internally, the kernel is free to select whatever tick rate best trades off clock-interrupt–handling overhead with timer resolution. As the tick rate per second increases, the resolution of the system timers improves, but the time spent dealing with hardclock interrupts increases. As processors become faster, the tick rate can be increased to provide finer resolution without adversely affecting user applications.

All filesystem (and other) timestamps are maintained in UTC offsets from the Epoch. Conversion to local time, including adjustment for daylight-savings time, is handled externally to the system in the C library.

Interval Time

The system provides each process with three interval timers. The *real* timer decrements in real time. An example of use for this timer is a library routine maintaining a wakeup-service queue. A SIGALRM signal is delivered to the process when this timer expires. The real-time timer is run from the timeout queue maintained by the *softclock()* routine (see Section 3.4).

The *profiling* timer decrements both in process virtual time (when running in user mode) and when the system is running on behalf of the process. It is designed to be used by processes to profile their execution statistically. A SIG-PROF signal is delivered to the process when this timer expires. The profiling timer is implemented by the *hardclock()* routine. Each time that *hardclock()* runs, it checks to see whether the currently running process has requested a profiling timer; if it has, *hardclock()* decrements the timer, and sends the process a signal when zero is reached.

The *virtual* timer decrements in process virtual time. It runs only when the process is executing in user mode. A SIGVTALRM signal is delivered to the process when this timer expires. The virtual timer is also implemented in *hardclock()* as the profiling timer is, except that it decrements the timer for the current process only if it is executing in user mode, and not if it is running in the kernel.

3.7   User, Group, and Other Identifiers

One important responsibility of an operating system is to implement access-control mechanisms. Most of these access-control mechanisms are based on the notions of individual users and of groups of users. Users are named by a 32-bit number called a *user identifier* (UID). UIDs are not assigned by the kernel—they are assigned by an outside administrative authority. UIDs are the basis for accounting, for restricting access to privileged kernel operations, (such as the request used to reboot a running system), for deciding to what processes a signal may be sent, and as a basis for filesystem access and disk-space allocation. A single user, termed the *superuser* (also known by the user name *root*), is trusted by the system and is permitted to do any supported kernel operation. The superuser is identified not by any specific name, such as *root*, but instead by a UID of zero.

Users are organized into *groups*. Groups are named by a 32-bit number called a *group identifier* (GID). GIDs, like UIDs, are used in the filesystem access-control facilities and in disk-space allocation.

The state of every 4.4BSD process includes a UID and a set of GIDs. A process's filesystem-access privileges are defined by the UID and GIDs of the process (for the filesystem hierarchy beginning at the process's root directory). Normally, these identifiers are inherited automatically from the parent process when a new process is created. Only the superuser is permitted to alter the UID or GID of a process. This scheme enforces a strict compartmentalization of privileges, and ensures that no user other than the superuser can *gain* privileges.

Each file has three sets of permission bits, for read, write, or execute permission for each of owner, group, and other. These permission bits are checked in the following order:

1. If the UID of the file is the same as the UID of the process, only the owner permissions apply; the group and other permissions are not checked.

2. If the UIDs do not match, but the GID of the file matches one of the GIDs of the process, only the group permissions apply; the owner and other permissions are not checked.

3. Only if the UID and GIDs of the process fail to match those of the file are the permissions for all others checked. If these permissions do not allow the requested operation, it will fail.

The UID and GIDs for a process are inherited from its parent. When a user logs in, the login program (see Section 14.6) sets the UID and GIDs before doing the *exec* system call to run the user's login shell; thus, all subsequent processes will inherit the appropriate identifiers.

Often, it is desirable to grant a user limited additional privileges. For example, a user who wants to send mail must be able to append the mail to another user's mailbox. Making the target mailbox writable by all users would permit a user other than its owner to modify messages in it (whether maliciously or unintentionally). To solve this problem, the kernel allows the creation of programs that are granted additional privileges while they are running. Programs that run with a different UID are called *set-user-identifier* (setuid) programs; programs that run with an additional group privilege are called *set-group-identifier* (setgid) programs [Ritchie, 1979]. When a setuid program is executed, the permissions of the process are augmented to include those of the UID associated with the program. The UID of the program is termed the *effective UID* of the process, whereas the original UID of the process is termed the *real UID*. Similarly, executing a setgid program augments a process's permissions with those of the program's GID, and the *effective GID* and *real GID* are defined accordingly.

Systems can use setuid and setgid programs to provide controlled access to files or services. For example, the program that adds mail to the users' mailbox runs with the privileges of the superuser, which allow it to write to any file in the system. Thus, users do not need permission to write other users' mailboxes, but can still do so by running this program. Naturally, such programs must be written carefully to have only a limited set of functionality!

The UID and GIDs are maintained in the per-process area. Historically, GIDs were implemented as one distinguished GID (the effective GID) and a supplementary array of GIDs, which was logically treated as one set of GIDs. In 4.4BSD, the distinguished GID has been made the first entry in the array of GIDs. The supplementary array is of a fixed size (16 in 4.4BSD), but may be changed by recompiling the kernel.

4.4BSD implements the setgid capability by setting the zeroth element of the supplementary groups array of the process that executed the setgid program to the group of the file. Permissions can then be checked as it is for a normal process. Because of the additional group, the setgid program may be able to access more files than can a user process that runs a program without the special privilege. The login program duplicates the zeroth array element into the first array element when initializing the user's supplementary group array, so that, when a setgid program is run and modifies the zeroth element, the user does not lose any privileges.

The setuid capability is implemented by the effective UID of the process being changed from that of the user to that of the program being executed. As it will with setgid, the protection mechanism will now permit access without any change or special knowledge that the program is running setuid. Since a process can have only a single UID at a time, it is possible to lose some privileges while running setuid. The previous real UID is still maintained as the real UID when the new effective UID is installed. The real UID, however, is not used for any validation checking.

A setuid process may wish to revoke its special privilege temporarily while it is running. For example, it may need its special privilege to access a restricted file at only the start and end of its execution. During the rest of its execution, it should have only the real user's privileges. In 4.3BSD, revocation of privilege was done by switching of the real and effective UIDs. Since only the effective UID is used for access control, this approach provided the desired semantics and provided a place to hide the special privilege. The drawback to this approach was that the real and effective UIDs could easily become confused.

In 4.4BSD, an additional identifier, the *saved UID*, was introduced to record the identity of setuid programs. When a program is *exec*'ed, its effective UID is copied to its saved UID. The first line of Table 3.1 shows an unprivileged program for which the real, effective, and saved UIDs are all those of the real user. The second line of Table 3.1 show a setuid program being run that causes the effective UID to be set to its associated special-privilege UID. The special-privilege UID has also been copied to the saved UID.

Also added to 4.4BSD was the new *seteuid* system call that sets only the effective UID; it does not affect the real or saved UIDs. The *seteuid* system call is permitted to set the effective UID to the value of either the real or the saved UID. Lines 3 and 4 of Table 3.1 show how a setuid program can give up and then reclaim its special privilege while continuously retaining its correct real UID. Lines 5 and 6 show how a setuid program can run a subprocess without granting the latter the special privilege. First, it sets its effective UID to the real UID. Then, when it *exec*'s the subprocess, the effective UID is copied to the saved UID, and all access to the special-privilege UID is lost.

A similar saved GID mechanism permits processes to switch between the real GID and the initial effective GID.

Host Identifiers

An additional identifier is defined by the kernel for use on machines operating in a networked environment. A string (of up to 256 characters) specifying the host's name is maintained by the kernel. This value is intended to be defined uniquely for each machine in a network. In addition, in the Internet domain-name system, each machine is given a unique 32-bit number. Use of these identifiers permits applications to use networkwide unique identifiers for objects such as processes, files, and users, which is useful in the construction of distributed applications [Gifford, 1981]. The host identifiers for a machine are administered outside the kernel.

Table 3.1 Actions affecting the real, effective, and saved UIDs. R—real user identifier; S—special-privilege user identifier.

Action	Real	Effective	Saved
1. exec-normal	R	R	R
2. exec-setuid	R	S	S
3. *seteuid*(R)	R	R	S
4. *seteuid*(S)	R	S	S
5. *seteuid*(R)	R	R	S
6. exec-normal	R	R	R

The 32-bit host identifier found in 4.3BSD has been deprecated in 4.4BSD, and is supported only if the system is compiled for 4.3BSD compatibility.

Process Groups and Sessions

Each process in the system is associated with a *process group*. The group of processes in a process group is sometimes referred to as a *job*, and manipulated as a single entity by processes such as the shell. Some signals (e.g., SIGINT) are delivered to all members of a process group, causing the group as a whole to suspend or resume execution, or to be interrupted or terminated.

Sessions were designed by the IEEE POSIX.1003.1 Working Group with the intent of fixing a long-standing security problem in UNIX—namely, that processes could modify the state of terminals that were trusted by another user's processes. A *session* is a collection of process groups, and all members of a process group are members of the same session. In 4.4BSD, when a user first logs onto the system, they are entered into a new session. Each session has a *controlling process*, which is normally the user's login shell. All subsequent processes created by the user are part of process groups within this session, unless they explicitly create a new session. Each session also has an associated *login name*, which is usually the user's login name. This name can be changed by only the superuser.

Each session is associated with a terminal, known as its *controlling terminal*. Each controlling terminal has a process group associated with it. Normally, only processes that are in the terminal's current process group read from or write to the terminal, allowing arbitration of a terminal between several different jobs. When the controlling process exits, access to the terminal is taken away from any remaining processes within the session.

Newly created processes are assigned process IDs distinct from all already-existing processes and process groups, and are placed in the same process group and session as their parent. Any process may set its process group equal to its process ID (thus creating a new process group) or to the value of any process group within its session. In addition, any process may create a new session, as long as it is not already a process-group leader. Sessions, process groups, and associated topics are discussed further in Section 4.8 and in Section 10.5.

3.8   Resource Services

All systems have limits imposed by their hardware architecture and configuration to ensure reasonable operation and to keep users from accidentally (or maliciously) creating resource shortages. At a minimum, the hardware limits must be imposed on processes that run on the system. It is usually desirable to limit processes further, below these hardware-imposed limits. The system measures resource utilization, and allows limits to be imposed on consumption either at or below the hardware-imposed limits.

Process Priorities

The 4.4BSD system gives CPU scheduling priority to processes that have not used CPU time recently. This priority scheme tends to favor processes that execute for only short periods of time—for example, interactive processes. The priority selected for each process is maintained internally by the kernel. The calculation of the priority is affected by the per-process *nice* variable. Positive *nice* values mean that the process is willing to receive less than its share of the processor. Negative values of *nice* mean that the process wants more than its share of the processor. Most processes run with the default *nice* value of zero, asking neither higher nor lower access to the processor. It is possible to determine or change the *nice* currently assigned to a process, to a process group, or to the processes of a specified user. Many factors other than *nice* affect scheduling, including the amount of CPU time that the process has used recently, the amount of memory that the process has used recently, and the current load on the system. The exact algorithms that are used are described in Section 4.4.

Resource Utilization

As a process executes, it uses system resources, such as the CPU and memory. The kernel tracks the resources used by each process and compiles statistics describing this usage. The statistics managed by the kernel are available to a process while the latter is executing. When a process terminates, the statistics are made available to its parent via the *wait* family of system calls.

The resources used by a process are returned by the system call *getrusage*. The resources used by the current process, or by all the terminated children of the current process, may be requested. This information includes

- The amount of user and system time used by the process

- The memory utilization of the process

- The paging and disk I/O activity of the process

- The number of voluntary and involuntary context switches taken by the process

- The amount of interprocess communication done by the process

The resource-usage information is collected at locations throughout the kernel. The CPU time is collected by the *statclock*() function, which is called either by the system clock in *hardclock*(), or, if an alternate clock is available, by the alternate-clock interrupt routine. The kernel scheduler calculates memory utilization by sampling the amount of memory that an active process is using at the same time that it is recomputing process priorities. The *vm_fault*() routine recalculates the paging activity each time that it starts a disk transfer to fulfill a paging request (see Section 5.11). The I/O activity statistics are collected each time that the process has to start a transfer to fulfill a file or device I/O request, as well as when the general system statistics are calculated. The IPC communication activity is updated each time that information is sent or received.

Resource Limits

The kernel also supports limiting of certain per-process resources. These resources include

• The maximum amount of CPU time that can be accumulated

• The maximum bytes that a process can request be locked into memory

• The maximum size of a file that can be created by a process

• The maximum size of a process's data segment

• The maximum size of a process's stack segment

• The maximum size of a core file that can be created by a process

• The maximum number of simultaneous processes allowed to a user

• The maximum number of simultaneous open files for a process

• The maximum amount of physical memory that a process may use at any given moment

For each resource controlled by the kernel, two limits are maintained: a *soft limit* and a *hard limit*. All users can alter the soft limit within the range of 0 to the corresponding hard limit. All users can (irreversibly) lower the hard limit, but only the superuser can raise the hard limit. If a process exceeds certain soft limits, a signal is delivered to the process to notify it that a resource limit has been exceeded. Normally, this signal causes the process to terminate, but the process may either catch or ignore the signal. If the process ignores the signal and fails to release resources that it already holds, further attempts to obtain more resources will result in errors.

Resource limits are generally enforced at or near the locations that the resource statistics are collected. The CPU time limit is enforced in the process context-switching function. The stack and data-segment limits are enforced by a return of allocation failure once those limits have been reached. The file-size limit is enforced by the filesystem.

Filesystem Quotas

In addition to limits on the size of individual files, the kernel optionally enforces limits on the total amount of space that a user or group can use on a filesystem. Our discussion of the implementation of these limits is deferred to Section 7.4.

3.9   System-Operation Services

There are several operational functions having to do with system startup and shut-down. The bootstrapping operations are described in Section 14.2. System shut-down is described in Section 14.7.

Accounting

The system supports a simple form of resource accounting. As each process ter-minates, an accounting record describing the resources used by that process is written to a systemwide accounting file. The information supplied by the system comprises

• The name of the command that ran

• The amount of user and system CPU time that was used

• The elapsed time the command ran

• The average amount of memory used

• The number of disk I/O operations done

• The UID and GID of the process

• The terminal from which the process was started

The information in the accounting record is drawn from the run-time statistics that were described in Section 3.8. The granularity of the time fields is in sixty-fourths of a second. To conserve space in the accounting file, the times are stored in a 16-bit word as a *floating-point* number using 3 bits as a base-8 exponent, and the other 13 bits as the fractional part. For historic reasons, the same floating-point–conversion routine processes the count of disk operations, so the number of disk operations must be multiplied by 64 before it is converted to the floating-point representation.

There are also flags that describe how the process terminated, whether it ever had superuser privileges, and whether it did an *exec* after a *fork*.

The superuser requests accounting by passing the name of the file to be used for accounting to the kernel. As part of a process exiting, the kernel appends an accounting record to the accounting file. The kernel makes no use of the account-ing records; the records' summaries and use are entirely the domain of user-level accounting programs. As a guard against a filesystem running out of space because of unchecked growth of the accounting file, the system suspends account-ing when the filesystem is reduced to only 2 percent remaining free space. Accounting resumes when the filesystem has at least 4 percent free space.

The accounting information has certain limitations. The information on run time and memory usage is only approximate because it is gathered statistically. Accounting information is written only when a process exits, so processes that are still running when a system is shut down unexpectedly do not show up in the accounting file. (Obviously, long-lived system daemons are among such processes.) Finally, the accounting records fail to include much information needed to do accurate billing, including usage of other resources, such as tape drives and printers.

Exercises

3.1   Describe three types of system activity.

3.2   When can a routine executing in the top half of the kernel be preempted? When can it be interrupted?

3.3   Why are routines executing in the bottom half of the kernel precluded from using information located in the user area?

3.4   Why does the system defer as much work as possible from high-priority interrupts to lower-priority software-interrupt processes?

3.5   What determines the shortest (nonzero) time period that a user process can request when setting a timer?

3.6   How does the kernel determine the system call for which it has been invoked?

3.7   How are initialized data represented in an executable file? How are uninitialized data represented in an executable file? Why are the representations different?

3.8   Describe how the "#!" mechanism can be used to make programs that require emulation appear as though they were normal executables.

3.9   Is it possible for a file to have permissions set such that its owner cannot read it, even though a group can? Is this situation possible if the owner is a member of the group that can read the file? Explain your answers.

*3.10   Describe the security implications of not zero filling the stack region at program startup.

*3.11   Why is the conversion from UTC to local time done by user processes, rather than in the kernel?

*3.12   What is the advantage of having the kernel, rather than an application, restart an interrupted system call?

*3.13 Describe a scenario in which the sorted-difference algorithm used for the callout queue does not work well. Suggest an alternative data structure that runs more quickly than does the sorted-difference algorithm for your scenario.

*3.14 The SIGPROF profiling timer was originally intended to replace the *profil* system call to collect a statistical sampling of a program's program counter. Give two reasons why the *profil* facility had to be retained.

**3.15 What weakness in the process-accounting mechanism makes the latter unsuitable for use in a commercial environment?

References

Barkley & Lee, 1988.
R. E. Barkley & T. P. Lee, "A Heap-Based Callout Implementation to Meet Real-Time Needs," *USENIX Association Conference Proceedings*, pp. 213–222, June 1988.

Gifford, 1981.
D. Gifford, "Information Storage in a Decentralized Computer System," PhD Thesis, Electrical Engineering Department, Stanford University, Stanford, CA, 1981.

Gusella et al, 1994.
R. Gusella, S. Zatti, & J. M. Bloom, "The Berkeley UNIX Time Synchronization Protocol," in *4.4BSD System Manager's Manual*, pp. 12:1–10, O'Reilly & Associates, Inc., Sebastopol, CA, 1994.

McCanne & Torek, 1993.
S. McCanne & C. Torek, "A Randomized Sampling Clock for CPU Utilization Estimation and Code Profiling," *USENIX Association Conference Proceedings*, pp. 387–394, January 1993.

Ritchie, 1979.
D. M. Ritchie, "Protection of Data File Contents," *United States Patent*, no. 4,135,240, United States Patent Office, Washington, D.C., January 16, 1979. Assignee: Bell Telephone Laboratories, Inc., Murray Hill, NJ, Appl. No.: 377,591, Filed: Jul. 9, 1973.

Varghese & Lauck, 1987.
G. Varghese & T. Lauck, "Hashed and Hierarchical Timing Wheels: Data Structures for the Efficient Implementation of a Timer Facility," *Proceedings of the Eleventh Symposium on Operating Systems Principles*, pp. 25–38, November 1987.

PART 2

Processes

CHAPTER 4

Process Management

4.1 Introduction to Process Management

A *process* is a program in execution. A process must have system resources, such as memory and the underlying CPU. The kernel supports the illusion of concurrent execution of multiple processes by scheduling system resources among the set of processes that are ready to execute. This chapter describes the composition of a process, the method that the system uses to switch between processes, and the scheduling policy that it uses to promote sharing of the CPU. Later chapters study process creation and termination, signal facilities, and process-debugging facilities.

Two months after the developers began the first implementation of the UNIX operating system, there were two processes: one for each of the terminals of the PDP-7. At age 10 months, and still on the PDP-7, UNIX had many processes, the *fork* operation, and something like the *wait* system call. A process executed a new program by reading in a new program on top of itself. The first PDP-11 system (First Edition UNIX) saw the introduction of *exec*. All these systems allowed only one process in memory at a time. When a PDP-11 with memory management (a KS-11) was obtained, the system was changed to permit several processes to remain in memory simultaneously, to reduce swapping. But this change did not apply to multiprogramming because disk I/O was synchronous. This state of affairs persisted into 1972 and the first PDP-11/45 system. True multiprogramming was finally introduced when the system was rewritten in C. Disk I/O for one process could then proceed while another process ran. The basic structure of process management in UNIX has not changed since that time [Ritchie, 1988].

A process operates in either *user mode* or *kernel mode*. In user mode, a process executes application code with the machine in a nonprivileged protection mode. When a process requests services from the operating system with a system call, it switches into the machine's privileged protection mode via a protected mechanism, and then operates in kernel mode.

The resources used by a process are similarly split into two parts. The resources needed for execution in user mode are defined by the CPU architecture and typically include the CPU's general-purpose registers, the program counter, the processor-status register, and the stack-related registers, as well as the contents of the memory segments that constitute the 4.4BSD notion of a program (the text, data, and stack segments).

Kernel-mode resources include those required by the underlying hardware—such as registers, program counter, and stack pointer—and also by the state required for the 4.4BSD kernel to provide system services for a process. This *kernel state* includes parameters to the current system call, the current process's user identity, scheduling information, and so on. As described in Section 3.1, the kernel state for each process is divided into several separate data structures, with two primary structures: the *process structure* and the *user structure*.

The process structure contains information that must always remain resident in main memory, along with references to a number of other structures that remain resident; whereas the user structure contains information that needs to be resident only when the process is executing (although user structures of other processes also may be resident). User structures are allocated dynamically through the memory-management facilities. Historically, more than one-half of the process state was stored in the user structure. In 4.4BSD, the user structure is used for only the per-process kernel stack and a couple of structures that are referenced from the process structure. Process structures are allocated dynamically as part of process creation, and are freed as part of process exit.

Multiprogramming

The 4.4BSD system supports transparent multiprogramming: the illusion of concurrent execution of multiple processes or programs. It does so by *context switching*—that is, by switching between the execution context of processes. A mechanism is also provided for *scheduling* the execution of processes—that is, for deciding which one to execute next. Facilities are provided for ensuring consistent access to data structures that are shared among processes.

Context switching is a hardware-dependent operation whose implementation is influenced by the underlying hardware facilities. Some architectures provide machine instructions that save and restore the hardware-execution context of the process, including the virtual-address space. On the others, the software must collect the hardware state from various registers and save it, then load those registers with the new hardware state. All architectures must save and restore the software state used by the kernel.

Context switching is done frequently, so increasing the speed of a context switch noticeably decreases time spent in the kernel and provides more time for execution of user applications. Since most of the work of a context switch is expended in saving and restoring the operating context of a process, reducing the amount of the information required for that context is an effective way to produce faster context switches.

Scheduling

Fair scheduling of processes is an involved task that is dependent on the types of executable programs and on the goals of the scheduling policy. Programs are characterized according to the amount of computation and the amount of I/O that they do. Scheduling policies typically attempt to balance resource utilization against the time that it takes for a program to complete. A process's priority is periodically recalculated based on various parameters, such as the amount of CPU time it has used, the amount of memory resources it holds or requires for execution, and so on. An exception to this rule is real-time scheduling, which must ensure that processes finish by a specified deadline or in a particular order; the 4.4BSD kernel does not implement real-time scheduling.

4.4BSD uses a priority-based scheduling policy that is biased to favor *interactive programs*, such as text editors, over long-running batch-type jobs. Interactive programs tend to exhibit short bursts of computation followed by periods of inactivity or I/O. The scheduling policy initially assigns to each process a high execution priority and allows that process to execute for a fixed *time slice*. Processes that execute for the duration of their slice have their priority lowered, whereas processes that give up the CPU (usually because they do I/O) are allowed to remain at their priority. Processes that are inactive have their priority raised. Thus, jobs that use large amounts of CPU time sink rapidly to a low priority, whereas interactive jobs that are mostly inactive remain at a high priority so that, when they are ready to run, they will preempt the long-running lower-priority jobs. An interactive job, such as a text editor searching for a string, may become compute bound briefly, and thus get a lower priority, but it will return to a high priority when it is inactive again while the user thinks about the result.

The system also needs a scheduling policy to deal with problems that arise from not having enough main memory to hold the execution contexts of all processes that want to execute. The major goal of this scheduling policy is to minimize *thrashing*—a phenomenon that occurs when memory is in such short supply that more time is spent in the system handling page faults and scheduling processes than in user mode executing application code.

The system must both detect and eliminate thrashing. It detects thrashing by observing the amount of free memory. When the system has few free memory pages and a high rate of new memory requests, it considers itself to be thrashing. The system reduces thrashing by marking the least-recently run process as not being allowed to run. This marking allows the pageout daemon to push all the pages associated with the process to backing store. On most architectures, the kernel also can push to backing store the user area of the marked process. The effect of these actions is to cause the process to be swapped out (see Section 5.12). The memory freed by blocking the process can then be distributed to the remaining processes, which usually can then proceed. If the thrashing continues, additional processes are selected for being blocked from running until enough memory becomes available for the remaining processes to run effectively. Eventually, enough processes complete and free their memory that blocked processes can resume execution. However, even if there is not enough memory, the blocked processes are allowed to resume execution after about 20 seconds. Usually, the thrashing condition will return, requiring that some other process be selected for being blocked (or that an administrative action be taken to reduce the load).

The orientation of the scheduling policy toward an interactive job mix reflects the original design of 4.4BSD for use in a time-sharing environment. Numerous papers have been written about alternative scheduling policies, such as those used in batch-processing environments or real-time systems. Usually, these policies require changes to the system in addition to alteration of the scheduling policy [Khanna et al, 1992].

4.2   Process State

The layout of process state was completely reorganized in 4.4BSD. The goal was to support multiple *thread*s that share an address space and other resources. Threads have also been called *lightweight processes* in other systems. A thread is the unit of execution of a process; it requires an address space and other resources, but it can share many of those resources with other threads. Threads sharing an address space and other resources are scheduled independently, and can all do system calls simultaneously. The reorganization of process state in 4.4BSD was designed to support threads that can select the set of resources to be shared, known as *variable-weight processes* [Aral et al, 1989]. Unlike some other implementations of threads, the BSD model associates a process ID with each thread, rather than with a collection of threads sharing an address space.

Figure 4.1 Process state.

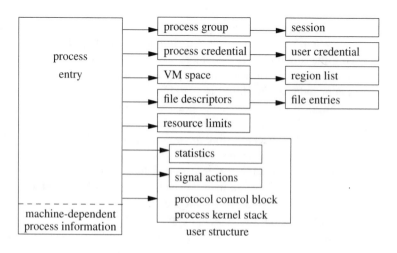

The developers did the reorganization by moving many components of process state from the process and user structures into separate substructures for each type of state information, as shown in Fig. 4.1. The process structure references all the substructures directly or indirectly. The use of global variables in the user structure was completely eliminated. Variables moved out of the user structure include the open file descriptors that may need to be shared among different threads, as well as system-call parameters and error returns. The process structure itself was also shrunk to about one-quarter of its former size. The idea is to minimize the amount of storage that must be allocated to support a thread. The 4.4BSD distribution did not have kernel-thread support enabled, primarily because the C library had not been rewritten to be able to handle multiple threads.

All the information in the substructures shown in Fig. 4.1 can be shared among threads running within the same address space, except the per-thread statistics, the signal actions, and the per-thread kernel stack. These unshared structures need to be accessible only when the thread may be scheduled, so they are allocated in the user structure so that they can be moved to secondary storage when memory resources are low. The following sections describe the portions of these structures that are relevant to process management. The VM space and its related structures are described more fully in Chapter 5.

The Process Structure

In addition to the references to the substructures, the process entry shown in Fig. 4.1 contains the following categories of information:

- **Process identification**. The process identifier and the parent-process identifier

- **Scheduling**. The process priority, user-mode scheduling priority, recent CPU utilization, and amount of time spent sleeping

- **Process state**. The run state of a process (runnable, sleeping, stopped); additional status flags; if the process is sleeping, the *wait channel*, the identity of the event for which the process is waiting (see Section 4.3), and a pointer to a string describing the event

- **Signal state**. Signals pending delivery, signal mask, and summary of signal actions

- **Tracing**. Process tracing information

- **Machine state**. The machine-dependent process information

- **Timers**. Real-time timer and CPU-utilization counters

The process substructures shown in Fig. 4.1 have the following categories of information:

- **Process-group identification**. The process group and the session to which the process belongs

- **User credentials**. The real, effective, and saved user and group identifiers

- **Memory management**. The structure that describes the allocation of virtual address space used by the process

- **File descriptors**. An array of pointers to file entries indexed by the process open file descriptors; also, the open file flags and current directory

- **Resource accounting**. The *rusage* structure that describes the utilization of the many resources provided by the system (see Section 3.8)

- **Statistics**. Statistics collected while the process is running that are reported when it exits and are written to the accounting file; also, includes process timers and profiling information if the latter is being collected

- **Signal actions**. The action to take when a signal is posted to a process

- **User structure**. The contents of the user structure (described later in this section)

A process's state has a value, as shown in Table 4.1. When a process is first created with a *fork* system call, it is initially marked as SIDL. The state is changed to SRUN when enough resources are allocated to the process for the latter to begin execution. From that point onward, a process's state will fluctuate among SRUN (runnable—e.g., ready to execute), SSLEEP (waiting for an event), and SSTOP (stopped by a signal or the parent process), until the process terminates. A deceased process is marked as SZOMB until its termination status is communicated to its parent process.

The system organizes process structures into two lists. Process entries are on the *zombproc* list if the process is in the SZOMB state; otherwise, they are on the *allproc* list. The two queues share the same linkage pointers in the process structure, since the lists are mutually exclusive. Segregating the dead processes from the live ones reduces the time spent both by the *wait* system call, which must scan the zombies for potential candidates to return, and by the scheduler and other functions that must scan all the potentially runnable processes.

Table 4.1 Process states.

State	Description
SIDL	intermediate state in process creation
SRUN	runnable
SSLEEP	awaiting an event
SSTOP	process stopped or being traced
SZOMB	intermediate state in process termination

Most processes, except the currently executing process, are also in one of two queues: a *run queue* or a *sleep queue*. Processes that are in a runnable state are placed on a run queue, whereas processes that are blocked awaiting an event are located on a sleep queue. Stopped processes not also awaiting an event are on neither type of queue. The two queues share the same linkage pointers in the process structure, since the lists are mutually exclusive. The run queues are organized according to process-scheduling priority, and are described in Section 4.4. The sleep queues are organized in a hashed data structure that optimizes finding of a sleeping process by the event number (wait channel) for which the process is waiting. The sleep queues are described in Section 4.3.

Every process in the system is assigned a unique identifier termed the *process identifier*, (*PID*). PIDs are the common mechanism used by applications and by the kernel to reference processes. PIDs are used by applications when the latter are sending a signal to a process and when receiving the exit status from a deceased process. Two PIDs are of special importance to each process: the PID of the process itself and the PID of the process's parent process.

The *p_pglist* list and related lists (*p_pptr*, *p_children*, and *p_siblings*) are used in locating related processes, as shown in Fig. 4.2. When a process spawns a child process, the child process is added to its parent's *p_children* list. The child process also keeps a backward link to its parent in its *p_pptr* field. If a process has more than one child process active at a time, the children are linked together through their *p_sibling* list entries. In Fig. 4.2, process B is a direct descendent of process A, whereas processes C, D, and E are descendents of process B and are siblings of one another. Process B typically would be a shell that started a pipeline (see Sections 2.4 and 2.6) including processes C, D, and E. Process A probably would be the system-initialization process **init** (see Section 3.1 and Section 14.6).

CPU time is made available to processes according to their *scheduling priority*. A process has two scheduling priorities, one for scheduling user-mode execution and one for scheduling kernel-mode execution. The *p_usrpri* field in the process structure contains the user-mode scheduling priority, whereas the *p_priority* field holds the current kernel-mode scheduling priority. The current priority may be

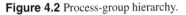

Figure 4.2 Process-group hierarchy.

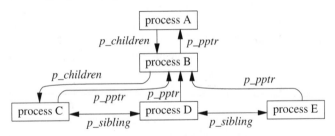

Table 4.2 Process-scheduling priorities.

Priority	Value	Description
PSWP	0	priority while swapping process
PVM	4	priority while waiting for memory
PINOD	8	priority while waiting for file control information
PRIBIO	16	priority while waiting on disk I/O completion
PVFS	20	priority while waiting for a kernel-level filesystem lock
PZERO	22	baseline priority
PSOCK	24	priority while waiting on a socket
PWAIT	32	priority while waiting for a child to exit
PLOCK	36	priority while waiting for user-level filesystem lock
PPAUSE	40	priority while waiting for a signal to arrive
PUSER	50	base priority for user-mode execution

different from the user-mode priority when the process is executing in kernel mode. Priorities range between 0 and 127, with a lower value interpreted as a higher priority (see Table 4.2). User-mode priorities range from PUSER (50) to 127; priorities less than PUSER are used only when a process is *asleep*—that is, awaiting an event in the kernel—and immediately after such a process is awakened. Processes in the kernel are given a higher priority because they typically hold shared kernel resources when they awaken. The system wants to run them as quickly as possible once they get a resource, so that they can use the resource and return it before another process requests it and gets blocked waiting for it.

Historically, a kernel process that is asleep with a priority in the range PZERO to PUSER would be awakened by a signal; that is, it might be awakened and marked runnable if a signal is posted to it. A process asleep at a priority below PZERO would never be awakened by a signal. In 4.4BSD, a kernel process will be awakened by a signal only if it sets the PCATCH flag when it sleeps. The PCATCH flag was added so that a change to a sleep priority does not inadvertently cause a change to the process's interruptibility.

For efficiency, the sleep interface has been divided into two separate entry points: *sleep()* for brief, noninterruptible sleep requests, and *tsleep()* for longer, possibly interrupted sleep requests. The *sleep()* interface is short and fast, to handle the common case of a short sleep. The *tsleep()* interface handles all the special cases including interruptible sleeps, sleeps limited to a maximum time duration, and the processing of restartable system calls. The *tsleep()* interface also includes a reference to a string describing the event that the process awaits; this string is externally visible. The decision of whether to use an interruptible sleep is dependent on how long the process may be blocked. Because it is complex to be prepared to handle signals in the midst of doing some other operation, many sleep requests are not interruptible; that is, a process will not be scheduled to run until the event for which it is waiting occurs. For example, a process waiting for disk I/O will sleep at an uninterruptible priority.

For quickly occurring events, delaying to handle a signal until after they complete is imperceptible. However, requests that may cause a process to sleep for a long period, such as while a process is waiting for terminal or network input, must be prepared to have their sleep interrupted so that the posting of signals is not delayed indefinitely. Processes that sleep at interruptible priorities may abort their system call because of a signal arriving before the event for which they are waiting has occurred. To avoid holding a kernel resource permanently, these processes must check why they have been awakened. If they were awakened because of a signal, they must release any resources that they hold. They must then return the error passed back to them by *tsleep*(), which will be EINTR if the system call is to be aborted after the signal, or ERESTART if it is to be restarted. Occasionally, an event that is supposed to occur quickly, such as a tape I/O, will get held up because of a hardware failure. Because the process is sleeping in the kernel at an uninterruptible priority, it will be impervious to any attempts to send it a signal, even a signal that should cause it to exit unconditionally. The only solution to this problem is to change *sleep*()s on hardware events that may hang to be interruptible. In the remainder of this book, we shall always use *sleep*() when referencing the routine that puts a process to sleep, even when the *tsleep*() interface may be the one that is being used.

The User Structure

The *user structure* contains the process state that may be swapped to secondary storage. The structure was an important part of the early UNIX kernels; it stored much of the state for each process. As the system has evolved, this state has migrated to the process entry or one of its substructures, so that it can be shared. In 4.4BSD, nearly all references to the user structure have been removed. The only place that user-structure references still exist are in the *fork* system call, where the new process entry has pointers set up to reference the two remaining structures that are still allocated in the user structure. Other parts of the kernel that reference these structures are unaware that the latter are located in the user structure; the structures are always referenced from the pointers in the process table. Changing them to dynamically allocated structures would require code changes in only *fork* to allocate them, and *exit* to free them. The user-structure state includes

• The user- and kernel-mode execution states

• The accounting information

• The signal-disposition and signal-handling state

• Selected process information needed by the debuggers and in core dumps

• The per-process execution stack for the kernel

The current execution state of a process is encapsulated in a *process control block* (*PCB*). This structure is allocated in the user structure and is defined by the machine architecture; it includes the general-purpose registers, stack pointers, program counter, processor-status longword, and memory-management registers.

Historically, the user structure was mapped to a fixed location in the virtual address space. There were three reasons for using a fixed mapping:

1. On many architectures, the user structure could be mapped into the top of the user-process address space. Because the user structure was part of the user address space, its context would be saved as part of saving of the user-process state, with no additional effort.

2. The data structures contained in the user structure (also called the *u-dot* (**u.**) *structure,* because all references in C were of the form *u.*) could always be addressed at a fixed address.

3. When a parent forks, its run-time stack is copied for its child. Because the kernel stack is part of the *u.* area, the child's kernel stack is mapped to the same addresses as its parent kernel stack. Thus, all its internal references, such as frame pointers and stack-variable references, work as expected.

On modern architectures with virtual address caches, mapping the user structure to a fixed address is slow and inconvenient. Thus, reason 1 no longer holds. Since the user structure is never referenced by most of the kernel code, reason 2 no longer holds. Only reason 3 remains as a requirement for use of a fixed mapping. Some architectures in 4.4BSD remove this final constraint, so that they no longer need to provide a fixed mapping. They do so by copying the parent stack to the child-stack location. The machine-dependent code then traverses the stack, relocating the embedded stack and frame pointers. On return to the machine-independent fork code, no further references are made to local variables; everything just returns all the way back out of the kernel.

The location of the kernel stack in the user structure simplifies context switching by localizing all a process's kernel-mode state in a single structure. The kernel stack grows down from the top of the user structure toward the data structures allocated at the other end. This design restricts the stack to a fixed size. Because the stack traps page faults, it must be allocated and memory resident before the process can run. Thus, it is not only a fixed size, but also small; usually it is allocated only one or two pages of physical memory. Implementors must be careful when writing code that executes in the kernel to avoid using large local variables and deeply nested subroutine calls, to avoid overflowing the run-time stack. As a safety precaution, some architectures leave an invalid page between the area for the run-time stack and the page holding the other user-structure contents. Thus, overflowing the kernel stack will cause a kernel-access fault, instead of disastrously overwriting the fixed-sized portion of the user structure. On some architectures, interrupt processing takes place on a separate *interrupt stack*, and the size of the kernel stack in the user structure restricts only that code executed as a result of traps and system calls.

4.3   Context Switching

The kernel switches among processes in an effort to share the CPU effectively; this activity is called *context switching*. When a process executes for the duration of its time slice or when it blocks because it requires a resource that is currently unavailable, the kernel finds another process to run and context switches to it. The system can also interrupt the currently executing process to service an asynchronous event, such as a device interrupt. Although both scenarios involve switching the execution context of the CPU, switching between processes occurs *synchronously* with respect to the currently executing process, whereas servicing interrupts occurs *asynchronously* with respect to the current process. In addition, interprocess context switches are classified as *voluntary* or *involuntary*. A voluntary context switch occurs when a process blocks because it requires a resource that is unavailable. An involuntary context switch takes place when a process executes for the duration of its time slice or when the system identifies a higher-priority process to run.

Each type of context switching is done through a different interface. Voluntary context switching is initiated with a call to the *sleep()* routine, whereas an involuntary context switch is forced by direct invocation of the low-level context-switching mechanism embodied in the *mi_switch()* and *setrunnable()* routines. Asynchronous event handling is managed by the underlying hardware and is effectively transparent to the system. Our discussion will focus on how asynchronous event handling relates to synchronizing access to kernel data structures.

Process State

Context switching between processes requires that both the kernel- and user-mode context be changed; to simplify this change, the system ensures that all a process's user-mode state is located in one data structure: the user structure (most kernel state is kept elsewhere). The following conventions apply to this localization:

- **Kernel-mode hardware-execution state**. Context switching can take place in only kernel mode. Thus, the kernel's hardware-execution state is defined by the contents of the PCB that is located at the beginning of the user structure.

- **User-mode hardware-execution state**. When execution is in kernel mode, the user-mode state of a process (such as copies of the program counter, stack pointer, and general registers) always resides on the kernel's execution stack that is located in the user structure. The kernel ensures this location of user-mode state by requiring that the system-call and trap handlers save the contents of the user-mode execution context each time that the kernel is entered (see Section 3.1).

- **The process structure**. The process structure always remains resident in memory.

- **Memory resources**. Memory resources of a process are effectively described by the contents of the memory-management registers located in the PCB and by the values present in the process structure. As long as the process remains in memory, these values will remain valid, and context switches can be done without the associated page tables being saved and restored. However, these values need to be recalculated when the process returns to main memory after being swapped to secondary storage.

Low-Level Context Switching

The localization of the context of a process in the latter's user structure permits the kernel to do context switching simply by changing the notion of the current user structure and process structure, and restoring the context described by the PCB within the user structure (including the mapping of the virtual address space). Whenever a context switch is required, a call to the *mi_switch()* routine causes the highest-priority process to run. The *mi_switch()* routine first selects the appropriate process from the scheduling queues, then resumes the selected process by loading that process's context from its PCB. Once *mi_switch()* has loaded the execution state of the new process, it must also check the state of the new process for a nonlocal return request (such as when a process first starts execution after a *fork*; see Section 4.5).

Voluntary Context Switching

A *voluntary* context switch occurs whenever a process must await the availability of a resource or the arrival of an event. Voluntary context switches happen frequently in normal system operation. For example, a process typically blocks each time that it requests data from an input device, such as a terminal or a disk. In 4.4BSD, voluntary context switches are initiated through the *sleep()* or *tsleep()* routines. When a process no longer needs the CPU, it invokes *sleep()* with a scheduling priority and a *wait channel*. The priority specified in a *sleep()* call is the priority that should be assigned to the process when that process is awakened. This priority does not affect the user-level scheduling priority.

   The wait channel is typically the address of some data structure that identifies the resource or event for which the process is waiting. For example, the address of a disk buffer is used while the process is waiting for the buffer to be filled. When the buffer is filled, processes sleeping on that wait channel will be awakened. In addition to the resource addresses that are used as wait channels, there are some addresses that are used for special purposes:

• The global variable *lbolt* is awakened by the scheduler once per second. Processes that want to wait for up to 1 second can sleep on this global variable. For example, the terminal-output routines sleep on *lbolt* while waiting for output-queue space to become available. Because queue space rarely runs out, it is easier simply to check for queue space once per second during the brief periods of shortages than it is to set up a notification mechanism such as that used for managing disk buffers. Programmers can also use the *lbolt* wait channel as a crude watchdog timer when doing debugging.

- When a parent process does a *wait* system call to collect the termination status of its children, it must wait for one of those children to exit. Since it cannot know which of its children will exit first, and since it can sleep on only a single wait channel, there is a quandary as to how to wait for the next of multiple events. The solution is to have the parent sleep on its own process structure. When a child exits, it awakens its parents process-structure address, rather than its own. Thus, the parent doing the *wait* will awaken independent of which child process is the first to exit.

- When a process does a *sigpause* system call, it does not want to run until it receives a signal. Thus, it needs to do an interruptible sleep on a wait channel that will never be awakened. By convention, the address of the user structure is given as the wait channel.

Sleeping processes are organized in an array of queues (see Fig. 4.3). The *sleep()* and *wakeup()* routines hash wait channels to calculate an index into the sleep queues. The *sleep()* routine takes the following steps in its operation:

1. Prevent interrupts that might cause process-state transitions by raising the hardware-processor priority level to *splhigh* (hardware-processor priority levels are explained in the next section).

2. Record the wait channel in the process structure, and hash the wait-channel value to locate a sleep queue for the process.

3. Set the process's priority to the priority that the process will have when the process is awakened, and set the SSLEEP flag.

Figure 4.3 Queueing structure for sleeping processes.

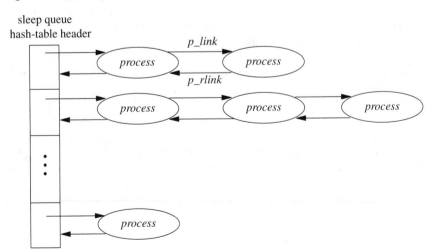

4. Place the process at the *end* of the sleep queue selected in step 2.

5. Call *mi_switch*() to request that a new process be scheduled; the hardware priority level is implicitly reset as part of switching to the other process.

A sleeping process is not selected to execute until it is removed from a sleep queue and is marked runnable. This operation is done by the *wakeup*() routine, which is called to signal that an event has occurred or that a resource is available. *Wakeup*() is invoked with a wait channel, and it awakens *all* processes sleeping on that wait channel. All processes waiting for the resource are awakened to ensure that none are inadvertently left sleeping. If only one process were awakened, it might not request the resource on which it was sleeping, and so any other processes waiting for that resource would be left sleeping forever. A process that needs an empty disk buffer in which to write data is an example of a process that may not request the resource on which it was sleeping. Such a process can use any available buffer. If none is available, it will try to create one by requesting that a dirty buffer be written to disk and then waiting for the I/O to complete. When the I/O finishes, the process will awaken and will check for an empty buffer. If several are available, it may not use the one that it cleaned, leaving any other processes waiting for the buffer that it cleaned sleeping forever.

To avoid having excessive numbers of processes awakened, kernel programmers try to use wait channels with fine enough granularity that unrelated uses will not collide on the same resource. Thus, they put locks on each buffer in the buffer cache, rather than putting a single lock on the buffer cache as a whole. The problem of many processes awakening for a single resource is further mitigated on a uniprocessor by the latter's inherently single-threaded operation. Although many processes will be put into the run queue at once, only one at a time can execute. Since the kernel is nonpreemptive, each process will run its system call to completion before the next one will get a chance to execute. Unless the previous user of the resource blocked in the kernel while trying to use the resource, each process waiting for the resource will be able get and use the resource when it is next run.

A *wakeup*() operation processes entries on a sleep queue from *front* to *back*. For each process that needs to be awakened, *wakeup*()

1. Removes the process from the sleep queue

2. Recomputes the user-mode scheduling priority if the process has been sleeping longer than 1 second

3. Makes the process runnable if it is in a SSLEEP state, and places the process on the run queue if it is not swapped out of main memory; if the process has been swapped out, the *swapin* process will be awakened to load it back into memory (see Section 5.12); if the process is in a SSTOP state, it is left on the queue until it is explicitly restarted by a user-level process, either by a *ptrace* system call or by a *continue* signal (see Section 4.7)

If *wakeup*() moved any processes to the run queue and one of them had a scheduling priority higher than that of the currently executing process, it will also request that the CPU be rescheduled as soon as possible.

The most common use of *sleep*() and *wakeup*() is in scheduling access to shared data structures; this use is described in the next section on *synchronization*.

Synchronization

Interprocess synchronization to a resource typically is implemented by the association with the resource of two flags; a *locked* flag and a *wanted* flag. When a process wants to access a resource, it first checks the locked flag. If the resource is not currently in use by another process, this flag should not be set, and the process can simply set the locked flag and use the resource. If the resource is in use, however, the process should set the wanted flag and call *sleep*() with a wait channel associated with the resource (typically the address of the data structure used to describe the resource). When a process no longer needs the resource, it clears the locked flag and, if the wanted flag is set, invokes *wakeup*() to awaken all the processes that called *sleep*() to await access to the resource.

Routines that run in the bottom half of the kernel do not have a context and consequently cannot wait for a resource to become available by calling *sleep*(). When the top half of the kernel accesses resources that are shared with the bottom half of the kernel, it cannot use the locked flag to ensure exclusive use. Instead, it must prevent the bottom half from running while it is using the resource. Synchronizing access with routines that execute in the bottom half of the kernel requires knowledge of when these routines may run. Although interrupt priorities are machine dependent, most implementations of 4.4BSD order them according to Table 4.3. To block interrupt routines at and below a certain priority level, a critical section must make an appropriate *set-priority-level* call. All the set-priority-

---

Table 4.3 Interrupt-priority assignments, ordered from lowest to highest.

Name	Blocks
spl0()	nothing (normal operating mode)
splsoftclock()	low-priority clock processing
splnet()	network protocol processing
spltty()	terminal multiplexers and low-priority devices
splbio()	disk and tape controllers and high-priority devices
splimp()	network device controllers
splclock()	high-priority clock processing
splhigh()	all interrupt activity

level calls return the previous priority level. When the critical section is done, the priority is returned to its previous level using *splx()*. For example, when a process needs to manipulate a terminal's data queue, the code that accesses the queue is written in the following style:

```
s = spltty();      /* raise priority to block tty processing */
    ...            /* manipulate tty */
splx(s);           /* reset priority level to previous value */
```

Processes must take care to avoid deadlocks when locking multiple resources. Suppose that two processes, A and B, require exclusive access to two resources, R_1 and R_2, to do some operation. If process A acquires R_1 and process B acquires R_2, then a deadlock occurs when process A tries to acquire R_2 and process B tries to acquire R_1. Since a 4.4BSD process executing in kernel mode is never preempted by another process, locking of multiple resources is simple, although it must be done carefully. If a process knows that multiple resources are required to do an operation, then it can safely lock one or more of those resources in any order, as long as it never relinquishes control of the CPU. If, however, a process cannot acquire all the resources that it needs, then it must release any resources that it holds before calling *sleep()* to wait for the currently inaccessible resource to become available.

Alternatively, if resources can be partially ordered, it is necessary only that they be allocated in an increasing order. For example, as the *namei()* routine traverses the filesystem name space, it must lock the next component of a pathname before it relinquishes the current component. A partial ordering of pathname components exists from the root of the name space to the leaves. Thus, translations down the name tree can request a lock on the next component without concern for deadlock. However, when it is traversing up the name tree (i.e., following a pathname component of dot-dot (..)), the kernel must take care to avoid sleeping while holding any locks.

Raising the processor priority level to guard against interrupt activity works for a uniprocessor architecture, but not for a shared-memory multiprocessor machine. Similarly, much of the 4.4BSD kernel implicitly assumes that kernel processing will never be done concurrently. Numerous vendors—such as Sequent, OSF/1, AT&T, and Sun Microsystems—have redesigned the synchronization schemes and have eliminated the uniprocessor assumptions implicit in the standard UNIX kernel, so that UNIX will run on tightly coupled multiprocessor architectures [Schimmel, 1994].

4.4   Process Scheduling

4.4BSD uses a process-scheduling algorithm based on *multilevel feedback queues*. All processes that are runnable are assigned a scheduling priority that determines in which *run queue* they are placed. In selecting a new process to run, the system scans the run queues from highest to lowest priority and chooses the first process on the first nonempty queue. If multiple processes reside on a queue, the system runs them *round robin*; that is, it runs them in the order that they are found on the queue, with equal amounts of time allowed. If a process blocks, it is not put back onto any run queue. If a process uses up the *time quantum* (or *time slice*) allowed it, it is placed at the end of the queue from which it came, and the process at the front of the queue is selected to run.

The shorter the time quantum, the better the interactive response. However, longer time quanta provide higher system throughput, because the system will have less overhead from doing context switches, and processor caches will be flushed less often. The time quantum used by 4.4BSD is 0.1 second. This value was empirically found to be the longest quantum that could be used without loss of the desired response for interactive jobs such as editors. Perhaps surprisingly, the time quantum has remained unchanged over the past 15 years. Although the time quantum was originally selected on centralized timesharing systems with many users, it is still correct for decentralized workstations today. Although workstation users expect a response time faster than that anticipated by the time-sharing users of 10 years ago, the shorter run queues on the typical workstation makes a shorter quantum unnecessary.

The system adjusts the priority of a process dynamically to reflect resource requirements (e.g., being blocked awaiting an event) and the amount of resources consumed by the process (e.g., CPU time). Processes are moved between run queues based on changes in their scheduling priority (hence the word *feedback* in the name *multilevel feedback queue*). When a process other than the currently running process attains a higher priority (by having that priority either assigned or given when it is awakened), the system switches to that process immediately if the current process is in user mode. Otherwise, the system switches to the higher-priority process as soon as the current process exits the kernel. The system tailors this *short-term scheduling algorithm* to favor interactive jobs by raising the scheduling priority of processes that are blocked waiting for I/O for 1 or more seconds, and by lowering the priority of processes that accumulate significant amounts of CPU time.

Short-term process scheduling is broken up into two parts. The next section describes when and how a process's scheduling priority is altered; the section after describes the management of the run queues and the interaction between process scheduling and context switching.

Calculations of Process Priority

A process's scheduling priority is determined directly by two values contained in the process structure: *p_estcpu* and *p_nice*. The value of *p_estcpu* provides an estimate of the recent CPU utilization of the process. The value of *p_nice* is a user-settable weighting factor that ranges numerically between −20 and 20. The normal value for *p_nice* is 0. Negative values increase a process's priority, whereas positive values decrease its priority.

A process's user-mode scheduling priority is calculated every four clock ticks (typically 40 milliseconds) by this equation:

$$p\_usrpri = PUSER + \left[\frac{p\_estcpu}{4} \right] + 2 \times p\_nice. \qquad \text{(Eq. 4.1)}$$

Values less than PUSER are set to PUSER (see Table 4.2); values greater than 127 are set to 127. This calculation causes the priority to decrease linearly based on recent CPU utilization. The user-controllable p_nice parameter acts as a limited weighting factor. Negative values retard the effect of heavy CPU utilization by offsetting the additive term containing p_estcpu. Otherwise, if we ignore the second term, p_nice simply shifts the priority by a constant factor.

The CPU utilization, p_estcpu, is incremented each time that the system clock ticks and the process is found to be executing. In addition, p_estcpu is adjusted once per second via a digital decay filter. The decay causes about 90 percent of the CPU usage accumulated in a 1-second interval to be forgotten over a period of time that is dependent on the system *load average*. To be exact, p_estcpu is adjusted according to

$$p\_estcpu = \frac{(2 \times load)}{(2 \times load + 1)} p\_estcpu + p\_nice, \qquad \text{(Eq. 4.2)}$$

where the *load* is a sampled average of the sum of the lengths of the run queue and do the short-term sleep queue over the previous 1-minute interval of system operation.

To understand the effect of the decay filter, we can consider the case where a single compute-bound process monopolizes the CPU. The process's CPU utilization will accumulate clock ticks at a rate dependent on the clock frequency. The load average will be effectively 1, resulting in a decay of

$$p\_estcpu = 0.66 \times p\_estcpu + p\_nice.$$

If we assume that the process accumulates T_i clock ticks over time interval i, and that p_nice is zero, then the CPU utilization for each time interval will count into the current value of p_estcpu according to

$$p\_estcpu = 0.66 \times T_0$$
$$p\_estcpu = 0.66 \times (T_1 + 0.66 \times T_0) = 0.66 \times T_1 + 0.44 \times T_0$$
$$p\_estcpu = 0.66 \times T_2 + 0.44 \times T_1 + 0.30 \times T_0$$
$$p\_estcpu = 0.66 \times T_3 + \cdots + 0.20 \times T_0$$
$$p\_estcpu = 0.66 \times T_4 + \cdots + 0.13 \times T_0.$$

Thus, after five decay calculations, only 13 percent of T_0 remains present in the current CPU utilization value for the process. Since the decay filter is applied once per second, we can also say that about 90 percent of the CPU utilization is forgotten after 5 seconds.

Processes that are runnable have their priority adjusted periodically as just described. However, the system ignores processes blocked awaiting an event: These processes cannot accumulate CPU usage, so an estimate of their filtered CPU usage can be calculated in one step. This optimization can significantly reduce a system's scheduling overhead when many blocked processes are present. The system recomputes a process's priority when that process is awakened and has been sleeping for longer than 1 second. The system maintains a value, *p_slptime*, that is an estimate of the time a process has spent blocked waiting for an event. The value of *p_slptime* is set to 0 when a process calls *sleep*(), and is incremented once per second while the process remains in an SSLEEP or SSTOP state. When the process is awakened, the system computes the value of *p_estcpu* according to

$$p\_estcpu = \left[\frac{(2 \times load)}{(2 \times load + 1)} \right]^{p\_slptime} \times p\_estcpu, \qquad \text{(Eq. 4.3)}$$

and then recalculates the scheduling priority using Eq. 4.1. This analysis ignores the influence of *p_nice*; also, the *load* used is the current load average, rather than the load average at the time that the process blocked.

Process-Priority Routines

The priority calculations used in the short-term scheduling algorithm are spread out in several areas of the system. Two routines, *schedcpu*() and *roundrobin*(), run periodically. *Schedcpu*() recomputes process priorities once per second, using Eq. 4.2, and updates the value of *p_slptime* for processes blocked by a call to *sleep*(). The *roundrobin*() routine runs 10 times per second and causes the system to reschedule the processes in the highest-priority (nonempty) queue in a round-robin fashion, which allows each process a 100-millisecond time quantum.

  The CPU usage estimates are updated in the system clock-processing module, *hardclock*(), which executes 100 times per second. Each time that a process accumulates four ticks in its CPU usage estimate, *p_estcpu*, the system recalculates the priority of the process. This recalculation uses Eq. 4.1 and is done by the *setpriority*() routine. The decision to recalculate after four ticks is related to the management of the run queues described in the next section. In addition to issuing the call from *hardclock*(), each time *setrunnable*() places a process on a run queue, it also calls *setpriority*() to recompute the process's scheduling priority. This call from *wakeup*() to *setrunnable*() operates on a process other than the currently running process. So, *wakeup*() invokes *updatepri*() to recalculate the CPU usage estimate according to Eq. 4.3 before calling *setpriority*(). The relationship of these functions is shown in Fig. 4.4.

Figure 4.4 Procedural interface to priority calculation.

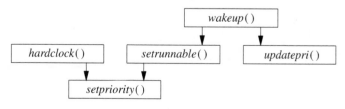

Process Run Queues and Context Switching

The scheduling-priority calculations are used to order the set of runnable processes. The scheduling priority ranges between 0 and 127, with 0 to 49 reserved for processes executing in kernel mode, and 50 to 127 reserved for processes executing in user mode. The number of queues used to hold the collection of runnable processes affects the cost of managing the queues. If only a single (ordered) queue is maintained, then selecting the next runnable process becomes simple, but other operations become expensive. Using 128 different queues can significantly increase the cost of identifying the next process to run. The system uses 32 run queues, selecting a run queue for a process by dividing the process's priority by 4. The processes on each queue are not further sorted by their priorities. The selection of 32 different queues was originally a compromise based mainly on the availability of certain VAX machine instructions that permitted the system to implement the lowest-level scheduling algorithm efficiently, using a 32-bit mask of the queues containing runnable processes. The compromise works well enough today that 32 queues are still used.

The run queues contain all the runnable processes in main memory except the currently running process. Figure 4.5 shows how each queue is organized as a doubly linked list of process structures. The head of each run queue is kept in an array; associated with this array is a bit vector, *whichqs*, that is used in identifying the nonempty run queues. Two routines, *setrunqueue()* and *remrq()*, are used to place a process at the tail of a run queue, and to take a process off the head of a run queue. The heart of the scheduling algorithm is the *cpu_switch()* routine. The *cpu_switch()* routine is responsible for selecting a new process to run; it operates as follows:

Figure 4.5 Queueing structure for runnable processes.

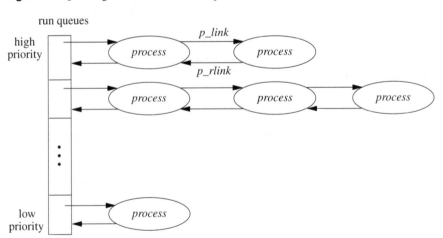

1. Block interrupts, then look for a nonempty run queue. Locate a nonempty queue by finding the location of the first nonzero bit in the *whichqs* bit vector. If *whichqs* is zero, there are no processes to run, so unblock interrupts and loop; this loop is the *idle loop*.

2. Given a nonempty run queue, remove the first process on the queue.

3. If this run queue is now empty as a result of removing the process, reset the appropriate bit in *whichqs*.

4. Clear the *curproc* pointer and the *want_resched* flag. The *curproc* pointer references the currently running process. Clear it to show that *no process is currently running*. The *want_resched* flag shows that a context switch should take place; it is described later in this section.

5. Set the new process running and unblock interrupts.

The context-switch code is broken into two parts. The machine-independent code resides in *mi_switch*(); the machine-dependent part resides in *cpu_switch*(). On most architectures, *cpu_switch*() is coded in assembly language for efficiency.

Given the *mi_switch*() routine and the process-priority calculations, the only missing piece in the scheduling facility is how the system forces an involuntary context switch. Remember that voluntary context switches occur when a process calls the *sleep*() routine. *Sleep*() can be invoked by only a runnable process, so *sleep*() needs only to place the process on a sleep queue and to invoke *mi_switch*() to schedule the next process to run. The *mi_switch*() routine, however, cannot be called from code that executes at interrupt level, because it must be called within the context of the running process.

An alternative mechanism must exist. This mechanism is handled by the machine-dependent *need_resched*() routine, which generally sets a global *reschedule request* flag, named *want_resched*, and then posts an *asynchronous system trap* (*AST*) for the current process. An AST is a trap that is delivered to a process the next time that that process returns to user mode. Some architectures support ASTs directly in hardware; other systems emulate ASTs by checking the *want_resched* flag at the end of every system call, trap, and interrupt of user-mode execution. When the hardware AST trap occurs or the *want_resched* flag is set, the *mi_switch*() routine is called, instead of the current process resuming execution. Rescheduling requests are made by the *wakeup*(), *setpriority*(), *roundrobin*(), *schedcpu*(), and *setrunnable*() routines.

Because 4.4BSD does not preempt processes executing in kernel mode, the worst-case real-time response to events is defined by the longest path through the top half of the kernel. Since the system guarantees no upper bounds on the duration of a system call, 4.4BSD is decidedly not a real-time system. Attempts to retrofit BSD with real-time process scheduling have addressed this problem in different ways [Ferrin & Langridge, 1980; Sanderson et al, 1986].

4.5   Process Creation

In 4.4BSD, new processes are created with the *fork* system call. There is also a
vfork system call that differs from *fork* in how the virtual-memory resources are
treated; *vfork* also ensures that the parent will not run until the child does either an
exec or *exit* system call. The *vfork* system call is described in Section 5.6.

The process created by a *fork* is termed a *child process* of the original *parent
process*. From a user's point of view, the child process is an exact duplicate of the
parent process, except for two values: the child PID, and the parent PID. A call to
fork returns the child PID to the parent and zero to the child process. Thus, a program can identify whether it is the parent or child process after a fork by checking
this return value.

A *fork* involves three main steps:

1. Allocating and initializing a new process structure for the child process

2. Duplicating the context of the parent (including the user structure and virtual-
   memory resources) for the child process

3. Scheduling the child process to run

The second step is intimately related to the operation of the memory-management
facilities described in Chapter 5. Consequently, only those actions related to process management will be described here.

The kernel begins by allocating memory for the new process entry (see
Fig. 4.1). The process entry is initialized in three steps: part is copied from the
parent's process structure, part is zeroed, and the rest is explicitly initialized. The
zeroed fields include recent CPU utilization, wait channel, swap and sleep time,
timers, tracing, and pending-signal information. The copied portions include all
the privileges and limitations inherited from the parent, including

• The process group and session

• The signal state (ignored, caught and blocked signal masks)

• The *p_nice* scheduling parameter

• A reference to the parent's credential

• A reference to the parent's set of open files

• A reference to the parent's limits

The explicitly set information includes

• Entry onto the list of all processes

- Entry onto the child list of the parent and the back pointer to the parent

- Entry onto the parent's process-group list

- Entry onto the hash structure that allows the process to be looked up by its PID

- A pointer to the process's statistics structure, allocated in its user structure

- A pointer to the process's signal-actions structure, allocated in its user structure

- A new PID for the process

The new PID must be unique among all processes. Early versions of BSD verified the uniqueness of a PID by performing a linear search of the process table. This search became infeasible on large systems with many processes. 4.4BSD maintains a range of unallocated PIDs between *nextpid* and *pidchecked*. It allocates a new PID by using the value of *nextpid*, and *nextpid* is then incremented. When *nextpid* reaches *pidchecked*, the system calculates a new range of unused PIDs by making a single scan of all existing processes (not just the active ones are scanned—zombie and swapped processes also are checked).

The final step is to copy the parent's address space. To duplicate a process's image, the kernel invokes the memory-management facilities through a call to *vm_fork*(). The *vm_fork*() routine is passed a pointer to the initialized process structure for the child process and is expected to allocate all the resources that the child will need to execute. The call to *vm_fork*() returns a value of 1 in the child process and of 0 in the parent process.

Now that the child process is fully built, it is made known to the scheduler by being placed on the run queue. The return value from *vm_fork*() is passed back to indicate whether the process is returning in the parent or child process, and determines the return value of the *fork* system call.

4.6   Process Termination

Processes terminate either voluntarily through an *exit* system call, or involuntarily as the result of a signal. In either case, process termination causes a status code to be returned to the parent of the terminating process (if the parent still exists). This termination status is returned through the *wait4* system call. The *wait4* call permits an application to request the status of both stopped and terminated processes. The *wait4* request can wait for any direct child of the parent, or it can wait selectively for a single child process, or for only its children in a particular process group. *Wait4* can also request statistics describing the resource utilization of a terminated child process. Finally, the *wait4* interface allows a process to request status codes without blocking.

Within the kernel, a process terminates by calling the *exit*() routine. *Exit*() first cleans up the process's kernel-mode execution state by

• Canceling any pending timers

• Releasing virtual-memory resources

• Closing open descriptors

• Handling stopped or traced child processes

With the kernel-mode state reset, the process is then removed from the list of active processes—the *allproc* list—and is placed on the list of *zombie processes* pointed to by *zombproc*. The process state is changed, and the global flag *curproc* is marked to show that no process is currently running. The *exit*() routine then

• Records the termination status in the *p_xstat* field of the process structure

• Bundles up a copy of the process's accumulated resource usage (for accounting purposes) and hangs this structure from the *p_ru* field of the process structure

• Notifies the deceased process's parent

Finally, after the parent has been notified, the *cpu_exit*() routine frees any machine-dependent process resources, and arranges for a final context switch from the process.

The *wait4* call works by searching a process's descendant processes for processes that have terminated. If a process in SZOMB state is found that matches the wait criterion, the system will copy the termination status from the deceased process. The process entry then is taken off the zombie list and is freed. Note that resources used by children of a process are accumulated only as a result of a *wait4* system call. When users are trying to analyze the behavior of a long-running program, they would find it useful to be able to obtain this resource usage information before the termination of a process. Although the information is available inside the kernel and within the context of that program, there is no interface to request it outside of that context until process termination.

4.7   Signals

UNIX defines a set of *signals* for software and hardware conditions that may arise during the normal execution of a program; these signals are listed in Table 4.4. Signals may be delivered to a process through application-specified *signal handlers*, or may result in *default* actions, such as process termination, carried out by the system. 4.4BSD signals are designed to be software equivalents of hardware interrupts or traps.

Table 4.4 Signals defined in 4.4BSD.

Name	Default action	Description
SIGHUP	terminate process	terminal line hangup
SIGINT	terminate process	interrupt program
SIGQUIT	create core image	quit program
SIGILL	create core image	illegal instruction
SIGTRAP	create core image	trace trap
SIGIOT	create core image	I/O trap instruction executed
SIGEMT	create core image	emulate instruction executed
SIGFPE	create core image	floating-point exception
SIGKILL	terminate process	kill program
SIGBUS	create core image	bus error
SIGSEGV	create core image	segmentation violation
SIGSYS	create core image	bad argument to system call
SIGPIPE	terminate process	write on a pipe with no one to read it
SIGALRM	terminate process	real-time timer expired
SIGTERM	terminate process	software termination signal
SIGURG	discard signal	urgent condition on I/O channel
SIGSTOP	stop process	stop signal not from terminal
SIGTSTP	stop process	stop signal from terminal
SIGCONT	discard signal	a stopped process is being continued
SIGCHLD	discard signal	notification to parent on child stop or exit
SIGTTIN	stop process	read on terminal by background process
SIGTTOU	stop process	write to terminal by background process
SIGIO	discard signal	I/O possible on a descriptor
SIGXCPU	terminate process	CPU time limit exceeded
SIGXFSZ	terminate process	file-size limit exceeded
SIGVTALRM	terminate process	virtual timer expired
SIGPROF	terminate process	profiling timer expired
SIGWINCH	discard signal	window size changed
SIGINFO	discard signal	information request
SIGUSR1	terminate process	user-defined signal 1
SIGUSR2	terminate process	user-defined signal 2

Each signal has an associated *action* that defines how it should be handled when it is delivered to a process. If a process has not specified an action for a signal, it is given a *default* action that may be any one of

- Ignoring the signal

- Terminating the process

- Terminating the process after generating a *core file* that contains the process's execution state at the time the signal was delivered

- Stopping the process

- Resuming the execution of the process

An application program can use the *sigaction* system call to specify an action for a signal, including

- Taking the default action

- Ignoring the signal

- Catching the signal with a *handler*

A *signal handler* is a user-mode routine that the system will invoke when the signal is received by the process. The handler is said to *catch* the signal. The two signals SIGSTOP and SIGKILL cannot be ignored or caught; this restriction ensures that a software mechanism exists for stopping and killing runaway processes. It is not possible for a user process to decide which signals would cause the creation of a core file by default, but it is possible for a process to prevent the creation of such a file by ignoring, blocking, or catching the signal.

Signals are *posted* to a process by the system when it detects a hardware event, such as an illegal instruction, or a software event, such as a stop request from the terminal. A signal may also be posted by another process through the *kill* system call. A sending process may post signals to only those receiving processes that have the same effective user identifier (unless the sender is the superuser). A single exception to this rule is the *continue signal*, SIGCONT, which always can be sent to any descendent of the sending process. The reason for this exception is to allow users to restart a setuid program that they have stopped from their keyboard.

Like hardware interrupts, the delivery of signals may be *masked* by a process. The execution state of each process contains a set of signals currently masked from delivery. If a signal posted to a process is being masked, the signal is recorded in the process's set of pending signals, but no action is taken until the signal is unmasked. The *sigprocmask* system call modifies a set of masked signals for a process. It can *add* to the set of masked signals, *delete* from the set of masked signals, or *replace* the set of masked signals.

The system does not allow the SIGKILL or SIGSTOP signals to be masked. Although the delivery of the SIGCONT to the signal handler of a process may be masked, the action of resuming that stopped process is not masked.

Two other signal-related system calls are *sigsuspend* and *sigaltstack*. The *sigsuspend* call permits a process to relinquish the processor until that process receives a signal. This facility is similar to the system's *sleep()* routine. The *sigaltstack* call allows a process to specify a run-time stack to use in signal delivery. By default, the system will deliver signals to a process on the latter's normal run-time stack. In some applications, however, this default is unacceptable. For example, if an application is running on a stack that the system does not expand automatically, and the stack overflows, then the signal handler must execute on an alternate stack. This facility is similar to the *interrupt-stack* mechanism used by the kernel.

The final signal-related facility is the *sigreturn* system call. *Sigreturn* is the equivalent of a user-level load-processor-context operation. A pointer to a (machine-dependent) context block that describes the user-level execution state of a process is passed to the kernel. The *sigreturn* system call is used to restore state and to resume execution after a normal return from a user's signal handler.

Comparison with POSIX Signals

Signals were originally designed to model exceptional events, such as an attempt by a user to kill a runaway program. They were not intended to be used as a general interprocess-communication mechanism, and thus no attempt was made to make them reliable. In earlier systems, whenever a signal was caught, its action was reset to the default action. The introduction of job control brought much more frequent use of signals, and made more visible a problem that faster processors also exacerbated: If two signals were sent rapidly, the second could cause the process to die, even though a signal handler had been set up to catch the first signal. Thus, reliability became desirable, so the developers designed a new framework that contained the old capabilities as a subset while accommodating new mechanisms.

The signal facilities found in 4.4BSD are designed around a *virtual-machine* model, in which system calls are considered to be the parallel of machine's hardware instruction set. Signals are the software equivalent of traps or interrupts, and signal-handling routines perform the equivalent function of interrupt or trap service routines. Just as machines provide a mechanism for blocking hardware interrupts so that consistent access to data structures can be ensured, the signal facilities allow software signals to be masked. Finally, because complex run-time stack environments may be required, signals, like interrupts, may be handled on an alternate run-time stack. These machine models are summarized in Table 4.5 (on page 104).

The 4.4BSD signal model was adopted by POSIX, although several significant changes were made.

• In POSIX, system calls interrupted by a signal cause the call to be terminated prematurely and an "interrupted system call" error to be returned. In 4.4BSD, the *sigaction* system call can be passed a flag that requests that system calls interrupted by a signal be restarted automatically whenever possible and reasonable. Automatic restarting of system calls permits programs to service signals without having to check the return code from each system call to determine whether the call should be restarted. If this flag is not given, the POSIX semantics apply. Most applications use the C-library routine *signal*( ) to set up their signal

Table 4.5 Comparison of hardware-machine operations and the corresponding software virtual-machine operations.

Hardware machine	Software virtual machine
instruction set	set of system calls
restartable instructions	restartable system calls
interrupts/traps	signals
interrupt/trap handlers	signal handlers
blocking interrupts	masking signals
interrupt stack	signal stack

handlers. In 4.4BSD, the *signal()* routine calls *sigaction* with the flag that requests that system calls be restarted. Thus, applications running on 4.4BSD and setting up signal handlers with *signal()* continue to work as expected, even though the *sigaction* interface conforms to the POSIX specification.

• In POSIX, signals are always delivered on the normal run-time stack of a process. In 4.4BSD, an alternate stack may be specified for delivering signals with the *sigaltstack* system call. Signal stacks permit programs that manage fixed-sized run-time stacks to handle signals reliably.

• POSIX added a new system call *sigpending*; this routine determines what signals have been posted but have not yet been delivered. Although it appears in 4.4BSD, it had no equivalent in earlier BSD systems because there were no applications that wanted to make use of pending-signal information.

Posting of a Signal

The implementation of signals is broken up into two parts: posting a signal to a process, and recognizing the signal and delivering it to the target process. Signals may be posted by any process or by code that executes at interrupt level. Signal delivery normally takes place within the context of the receiving process. But when a signal forces a process to be stopped, the action can be carried out when the signal is posted.

A signal is posted to a single process with the *psignal()* routine or to a group of processes with the *gsignal()* routine. The *gsignal()* routine invokes *psignal()* for each process in the specified process group. The actions associated with posting a signal are straightforward, but the details are messy. In theory, posting a signal to a process simply causes the appropriate signal to be added to the set of pending signals for the process, and the process is then set to run (or is awakened if it was sleeping at an interruptible priority level). The CURSIG macro calculates the next signal, if any, that should be delivered to a process. It determines the next signal by inspecting the *p_siglist* field that contains the set of signals pending delivery to a process. Each time that a process returns from a call to *sleep()* (with the PCATCH flag set) or prepares to exit the system after processing a system call or trap, it checks to see whether a signal is pending delivery. If a signal is pending and must be delivered in the process's context, it is removed from the pending set, and the process invokes the *postsig*() routine to take the appropriate action.

The work of *psignal*() is a patchwork of special cases required by the process-debugging and job-control facilities, and by intrinsic properties associated with signals. The steps involved in posting a signal are as follows:

1. Determine the action that the receiving process will take when the signal is delivered. This information is kept in the *p_sigignore*, *p_sigmask*, and *p_sigcatch* fields of the process's process structure. If a process is not ignoring, masking, or catching a signal, the default action is presumed to apply. If a process is being traced by its parent—that is, by a debugger—the parent process is always permitted to intercede before the signal is delivered. If the process is ignoring the signal, *psignal*()'s work is done and the routine can return.

2. Given an action, *psignal*() adds the signal to the set of pending signals, *p_siglist*, and then does any implicit actions specific to that signal. For example, if the signal is a *continue signal*, SIGCONT, any pending signals that would normally cause the process to stop, such as SIGTTOU, are removed.

3. Next, *psignal*() checks whether the signal is being masked. If the process is currently masking delivery of the signal, *psignal*()'s work is complete and it may return.

4. If, however, the signal is not being masked, *psignal*() must either do the action directly, or arrange for the process to execute so that the process will take the action associated with the signal. To get the process running, *psignal*() must interrogate the state of the process, which is one of the following:

SSLEEP   The process is blocked awaiting an event. If the process is sleeping at a negative priority, then nothing further can be done. Otherwise, the kernel can apply the action—either directly, or indirectly by waking up the process. There are two actions that can be applied directly. For signals that cause a process to stop, the process is placed in an SSTOP state, and the parent process is notified of the state change by a SIGCHLD signal being posted to it. For signals that are ignored by default, the signal is removed from *p_siglist* and the work is complete. Otherwise, the action associated with the signal must be done in the context of the receiving process, and the process is placed onto the run queue with a call to *setrunnable*().

SSTOP   The process is stopped by a signal or because it is being debugged. If the process is being debugged, then there is nothing to do until the controlling process permits it to run again. If the process is stopped by a signal and the posted signal would cause the process to stop again, then there is nothing to do, and the posted signal is discarded. Otherwise, the signal is either a *continue signal* or a signal that would normally cause the process to terminate (unless the signal is caught). If the signal is SIGCONT, then the process is set running again, unless it is blocked waiting on an event; if the process is blocked, it is returned to the SSLEEP state. If the signal is SIGKILL, then the process is set running again no matter what, so that it can terminate the next time that it is scheduled to run. Otherwise, the signal causes the process to be made *runnable*, but the process is not placed on the run queue because it must wait for a continue signal.

SRUN, SIDL, SZOMB

If the process is not the currently executing process, *need_resched*() is called, so that the signal will be noticed by the receiving process as soon as possible.

The implementation of *psignal*() is complicated, mostly because *psignal*() controls the process-state transitions that are part of the job-control facilities and because it interacts strongly with process-debugging facilities.

Delivering a Signal

Most actions associated with delivering a signal to a process are carried out within the context of that process. A process checks its process structure for pending signals at least once each time that it enters the system, by calling the CURSIG macro.

If CURSIG determines that there are any unmasked signals in *p_siglist*, it calls *issignal*() to find the first unmasked signal in the list. If delivering the signal causes a signal handler to be invoked or a core dump to be made, the caller is notified that a signal is pending, and actual delivery is done by a call to *postsig*(). That is,

```
if (sig = CURSIG(p))
        postsig(sig);
```

Otherwise, the action associated with the signal is done within *issignal*() (these actions mimic the actions carried out by *psignal*()).

The *postsig*() routine has two cases to handle:

1. Producing a core dump

2. Invoking a signal handler

The former task is done by the *coredump*() routine and is always followed by a call to *exit*() to force process termination. To invoke a signal handler, *postsig*() first calculates a set of masked signals and installs that set in *p_sigmask*. This set normally includes the signal being delivered, so that the signal handler will not be invoked recursively by the same signal. Any signals specified in the *sigaction*

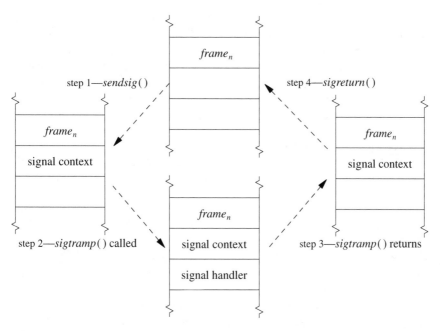

Figure 4.6 Delivery of a signal to a process.

system call at the time the handler was installed also will be included. *Postsig()* then calls the *sendsig()* routine to arrange for the signal handler to execute immediately after the process returns to user mode. Finally, the signal in *p_cursig* is cleared and *postsig()* returns, presumably to be followed by a return to user mode.

The implementation of the *sendsig()* routine is machine dependent. Figure 4.6 shows the flow of control associated with signal delivery. If an alternate stack has been requested, the user's stack pointer is switched to point at that stack. An argument list and the process's current user-mode execution context are stored on the (possibly new) stack. The state of the process is manipulated so that, on return to user mode, a call will be made immediately to a body of code termed the *signal-trampoline code*. This code invokes the signal handler with the appropriate argument list, and, if the handler returns, makes a *sigreturn* system call to reset the process's signal state to the state that existed before the signal.

4.8   Process Groups and Sessions

A *process group* is a collection of related processes, such as a shell pipeline, all of which have been assigned the same *process-group identifier*. The process-group identifier is the same as the PID of the process group's initial member; thus process-group identifiers share the name space of process identifiers. When a new process group is created, the kernel allocates a process-group structure to be associated with it. This process-group structure is entered into a process-group hash table so that it can be found quickly.

A process is always a member of a single process group. When it is created, each process is placed into the process group of its parent process. Programs such as shells create new process groups, usually placing related child processes into a group. A process can change its own process group or that of a child process by creating a new process group or by moving a process into an existing process group using the *setpgid* system call. For example, when a shell wants to set up a new pipeline, it wants to put the processes in the pipeline into a process group different from its own, so that the pipeline can be controlled independently of the shell. The shell starts by creating the first process in the pipeline, which initially has the same process-group identifier as the shell. Before executing the target program, the first process does a *setpgid* to set its process-group identifier to the same value as its PID. This system call creates a new process group, with the child process as the *process-group leader* of the process group. As the shell starts each additional process for the pipeline, each child process uses *setpgid* to join the existing process group.

In our example of a shell creating a new pipeline, there is a race. As the additional processes in the pipeline are spawned by the shell, each is placed in the process group created by the first process in the pipeline. These conventions are enforced by the *setpgid* system call. It restricts the set of process-group identifiers to which a process may be set to either a value equal its own PID or a value of another process-group identifier in its session. Unfortunately, if a pipeline process other than the process-group leader is created before the process-group leader has completed its *setpgid* call, the *setpgid* call to join the process group will fail. As the *setpgid* call permits parents to set the process group of their children (within some limits imposed by security concerns), the shell can avoid this race by making the *setpgid* call to change the child's process group both in the newly created child and in the parent shell. This algorithm guarantees that, no matter which process runs first, the process group will exist with the correct process-group leader. The shell can also avoid the race by using the *vfork* variant of the *fork* system call that forces the parent process to wait until the child process either has done an *exec* system call or has exited. In addition, if the initial members of the process group exit before all the pipeline members have joined the group—for example if the process-group leader exits before the second process joins the group, the *setpgid* call could fail. The shell can avoid this race by ensuring that all child processes are placed into the process group without calling the *wait* system call, usually by blocking the SIGCHLD signal so that the shell will not be notified yet if a child exits. As long as a process-group member exists, even as a zombie process, additional processes can join the process group.

There are additional restrictions on the *setpgid* system call. A process may join process groups only within its current session (discussed in the next section), and it cannot have done an *exec* system call. The latter restriction is intended to avoid unexpected behavior if a process is moved into a different process group after it has begun execution. Therefore, when a shell calls *setpgid* in both parent and child processes after a *fork*, the call made by the parent will fail if the child has already made an *exec* call. However, the child will already have joined the process group successfully, and the failure is innocuous.

Sessions

Just as a set of related processes are collected into a process group, a set of process groups are collected into a *session*. A session is a set of one or more process groups and may be associated with a terminal device. The main uses for sessions are to collect together a user's login shell and the jobs that it spawns, and to create an isolated environment for a daemon process and its children. Any process that is not already a process-group leader may create a session using the *setsid* system call, becoming the *session leader* and the only member of the session. Creating a session also creates a new process group, where the process-group ID is the PID of the process creating the session, and the process is the process-group leader. By definition, all members of a process group are members of the same session.

A session may have an associated *controlling terminal* that is used by default for communicating with the user. Only the session leader may allocate a controlling terminal for the session, becoming a *controlling process* when it does so. A device can be the controlling terminal for only one session at a time. The terminal I/O system (described in Chapter 10) synchronizes access to a terminal by permitting only a single process group to be the *foreground* process group for a controlling terminal at any time. Some terminal operations are allowed by only members of the session. A session can have at most one controlling terminal. When a session is created, the session leader is dissociated from its controlling terminal if it had one.

A login session is created by a program that prepares a terminal for a user to log into the system. That process normally executes a shell for the user, and thus the shell is created as the controlling process. An example of a typical login session is shown in Fig. 4.7 (on page 110).

The data structures used to support sessions and process groups in 4.4BSD are shown in Fig. 4.8. This figure parallels the process layout shown in Fig. 4.7. The *pg_members* field of a process-group structure heads the list of member processes; these processes are linked together through the *p_pglist* list entry in the process structure. In addition, each process has a reference to its process-group structure in the *p_pgrp* field of the process structure. Each process-group structure has a pointer to its enclosing session. The session structure tracks per-login information, including the process that created and controls the session, the controlling terminal for the session, and the login name associated with the session. Two processes wanting to determine whether they are in the same session can traverse their *p_pgrp* pointers to find their process-group structures, and then compare the *pg_session* pointers to see whether the latter are the same.

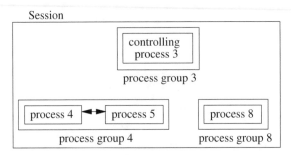

Figure 4.7 A session and its processes. In this example, process 3 is the initial member of the session—the session leader—and is referred to as the controlling process if it has a controlling terminal. It is contained in its own process group, 3. Process 3 has spawned two jobs: one is a pipeline composed of processes 4 and 5, grouped together in process group 4, and the other one is process 8, which is in its own process group, 8. No process-group leader can create a new session; thus, processes 3, 4, or 8 could not start their own session, but process 5 would be allowed to do so.

Job Control

Job control is a facility first provided by the C shell [Joy, 1994], and today provided by most shells. It permits a user to control the operation of groups of processes termed *jobs*. The most important facilities provided by job control are the abilities to suspend and restart jobs and to do the multiplexing of access to the user's terminal. Only one job at a time is given control of the terminal and is able to read from and write to the terminal. This facility provides some of the advantages of window systems, although job control is sufficiently different that it is often used in combination with window systems on those systems that have the latter. Job control is implemented on top of the process group, session, and signal facilities.

Each job is a process group. Outside the kernel, a shell manipulates a job by sending signals to the job's process group with the *killpg* system call, which delivers a signal to all the processes in a process group. Within the system, the two main users of process groups are the terminal handler (Chapter 10) and the inter-process-communication facilities (Chapter 11). Both facilities record process-group identifiers in private data structures and use them in delivering signals. The terminal handler, in addition, uses process groups to multiplex access to the controlling terminal.

For example, special characters typed at the keyboard of the terminal (e.g., control-C or control-\) result in a signal being sent to all processes in one job in the session; that job is in the *foreground*, whereas all other jobs in the session are in the *background*. A shell may change the foreground job by using the *tcsetpgrp*() function, implemented by the TIOCSPGRP *ioctl* on the controlling terminal. Background jobs will be sent the SIGTTIN signal if they attempt to read from the terminal, normally stopping the job. The SIGTTOU signal is sent to background jobs that attempt an *ioctl* system call that would alter the state of the

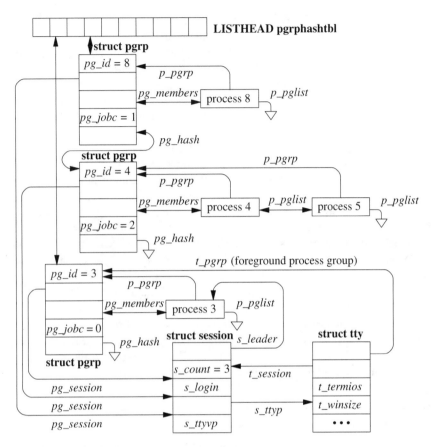

Figure 4.8 Process-group organization.

terminal, and, if the TOSTOP option is set for the terminal, if they attempt to write to the terminal.

The foreground process group for a session is stored in the *t_pgrp* field of the session's controlling terminal tty structure (see Chapter 10). All other process groups within the session are in the background. In Fig. 4.8, the session leader has set the foreground process group for its controlling terminal to be its own process group. Thus, its two jobs are in background, and the terminal input and output will be controlled by the session-leader shell. Job control is limited to processes contained within the same session and to the terminal associated with the session. Only the members of the session are permitted to reassign the controlling terminal among the process groups within the session.

If a controlling process exits, the system revokes further access to the controlling terminal and sends a SIGHUP signal to the foreground process group. If a process such as a job-control shell exits, each process group that it created will become an *orphaned process group*: a process group in which no member has a parent that is a member of the same session but of a different process group. Such a parent would normally be a job-control shell capable of resuming stopped child processes. The *pg_jobc* field in Fig. 4.8 counts the number of processes within the process group that have the controlling process as a parent; when that count goes to zero, the process group is orphaned. If no action were taken by the system, any orphaned process groups that were stopped at the time that they became orphaned would be unlikely ever to resume. Historically, the system dealt harshly with such stopped processes: They were killed. In POSIX and 4.4BSD, an orphaned process group is sent a hangup and a continue signal if any of its members are stopped when it becomes orphaned by the exit of a parent process. If processes choose to catch or ignore the hangup signal, they can continue running after becoming orphaned. The system keeps a count of processes in each process group that have a parent process in another process group of the same session. When a process exits, this count is adjusted for the process groups of all child processes. If the count reaches zero, the process group has become orphaned. Note that a process can be a member of an orphaned process group even if its original parent process is still alive. For example, if a shell starts a job as a single process A, that process then forks to create process B, and the parent shell exits, then process B is a member of an orphaned process group but is not an orphaned process.

To avoid stopping members of orphaned process groups if they try to read or write to their controlling terminal, the kernel does not send them SIGTTIN and SIGTTOU signals, and prevents them from stopping in response to those signals. Instead, attempts to read or write to the terminal produce an error.

4.9   Process Debugging

4.4BSD provides a simplistic facility for controlling and debugging the execution of a process. This facility, accessed through the *ptrace* system call, permits a parent process to control a child process's execution by manipulating user- and kernel-mode execution state. In particular, with *ptrace*, a parent process can do the following operations on a child process:

• Read and write address space and registers

• Intercept signals posted to the process

• Single step and continue the execution of the process

• Terminate the execution of the process

The *ptrace* call is used almost exclusively by program debuggers, such as **gdb**.

When a process is being traced, any signals posted to that process cause it to enter the SSTOP state. The parent process is notified with a SIGCHLD signal and may interrogate the status of the child with the *wait4* system call. On most machines, *trace traps*, generated when a process is single stepped, and *breakpoint faults*, caused by a process executing a breakpoint instruction, are translated by

4.4BSD into SIGTRAP signals. Because signals posted to a traced process cause it to stop and result in the parent being notified, a program's execution can be controlled easily.

To start a program that is to be debugged, the debugger first creates a child process with a *fork* system call. After the fork, the child process uses a *ptrace* call that causes the process to be flagged as *traced* by setting the P_TRACED bit in the *p_flag* field of the process structure. The child process then sets the *trace trap* bit in the process's processor status word and calls *execve* to load the image of the program that is to be debugged. Setting this bit ensures that the first instruction executed by the child process after the new image is loaded will result in a hardware trace trap, which is translated by the system into a SIGTRAP signal. Because the parent process is notified about all signals to the child, it can intercept the signal and gain control over the program before it executes a single instruction.

All the operations provided by *ptrace* are carried out in the context of the process being traced. When a parent process wants to do an operation, it places the parameters associated with the operation into a data structure named *ipc* and sleeps on the address of *ipc*. The next time that the child process encounters a signal (immediately if it is currently stopped by a signal), it retrieves the parameters from the *ipc* structure and does the requested operation. The child process then places a return result in the *ipc* structure and does a *wakeup*() call with the address of *ipc* as the wait channel. This approach minimizes the amount of extra code needed in the kernel to support debugging. Because the child makes the changes to its own address space, any pages that it tries to access that are not resident in memory are brought into memory by the existing page-fault mechanisms. If the parent tried to manipulate the child's address space, it would need special code to find and load any pages that it wanted to access that were not resident in memory.

The *ptrace* facility is inefficient for three reasons. First, *ptrace* uses a single global data structure for passing information back and forth between all the parent and child processes in the system. Because there is only one structure, it must be interlocked to ensure that only one parent–child process pair will use it at a time. Second, because the data structure has a small, fixed size, the parent process is limited to reading or writing 32 bits at a time. Finally, since each request by a parent process must be done in the context of the child process, two context switches need to be done for each request—one from the parent to the child to send the request, and one from the child to the parent to return the result of the operation.

To address these problems, 4.4BSD added a **/proc** filesystem, similar to the one found in UNIX Eighth Edition [Killian, 1984]. In the **/proc** system, the address space of another process can be accessed with *read* and *write* system calls, which allows a debugger to access a process being debugged with much greater efficiency. The page (or pages) of interest in the child process is mapped into the kernel address space. The requested data can then be copied directly from the kernel to the parent address space. This technique avoids the need to have a data structure to pass messages back and forth between processes, and avoids the context switches between the parent and child processes. Because the *ipc* mechanism was derived from the original UNIX code, it was not included in the freely redistributable 4.4BSD-Lite release. Most reimplementations simply converted the *ptrace* requests into calls on **/proc**, or map the process pages directly into the kernel memory. The result is a much simpler and faster implementation of *ptrace*.

Exercises

4.1   What are three implications of not having the user structure mapped at a fixed virtual address in the kernel's address space?

4.2   Why is the performance of the context-switching mechanism critical to the performance of a highly multiprogrammed system?

4.3   What effect would increasing the time quantum have on the system's interactive response and total throughput?

4.4   What effect would reducing the number of run queues from 32 to 16 have on the scheduling overhead and on system performance?

4.5   Give three reasons for the system to select a new process to run.

4.6   What type of scheduling policy does 4.4BSD use? What type of jobs does the policy favor? Propose an algorithm for identifying these favored jobs.

4.7   Is job control still a useful facility, now that window systems are widely available? Explain your answer.

4.8   When and how does process scheduling interact with the memory-management facilities?

4.9   After a process has exited, it may enter the state of being a zombie, SZOMB, before disappearing from the system entirely. What is the purpose of the SZOMB state? What event causes a process to exit from SZOMB?

4.10   Suppose that the data structures shown in Fig. 4.2 do not exist. Instead assume that each process entry has only its own PID and the PID of its parent. Compare the costs in space and time to support each of the following operations:

a.   Creation of a new process

b.   Lookup of the process's parent

c.   Lookup of all a process's siblings

d.   Lookup of all a process's descendents

e.   Destruction of a process

4.11   The system raises the hardware priority to *splhigh* in the *sleep*() routine before altering the contents of a process's process structure. Why does it do so?

4.12 A process blocked with a priority less than PZERO may never be awakened by a signal. Describe two problems a noninterruptible sleep may cause if a disk becomes unavailable while the system is running.

4.13 For each state listed in Table 4.1, list the system queues on which a process in that state might be found.

*4.14 Define three properties of a real-time system. Give two reasons why 4.4BSD is not a real-time system.

*4.15 In 4.4BSD, the signal SIGTSTP is delivered to a process when a user types a "suspend character." Why would a process want to catch this signal before it is stopped?

*4.16 Before the 4.4BSD signal mechanism was added, signal handlers to catch the SIGTSTP signal were written as

```
catchstop()
{
    prepare to stop;
    signal(SIGTSTP, SIG_DFL);
    kill(getpid(), SIGTSTP);
    signal(SIGTSTP, catchstop);
}
```

This code causes an infinite loop in 4.4BSD. Why does it do so? How should the code be rewritten?

*4.17 The process-priority calculations and accounting statistics are all based on sampled data. Describe hardware support that would permit more accurate statistics and priority calculations.

*4.18 What are the implications of adding a fixed-priority scheduling algorithm to 4.4BSD?

*4.19 Why are signals a poor interprocess-communication facility?

**4.20 A *kernel-stack-invalid* trap occurs when an invalid value for the kernel-mode stack pointer is detected by the hardware. Assume that this trap is received on an interrupt stack in kernel mode. How might the system terminate gracefully a process that receives such a trap while executing on the kernel's run-time stack contained in the user structure?

**4.21 Describe a synchronization scheme that would work in a tightly coupled multiprocessor hardware environment. Assume that the hardware supports a *test-and-set* instruction.

**4.22 Describe alternatives to the *test-and-set* instruction that would allow you to build a synchronization mechanism for a multiprocessor 4.4BSD system.

**4.23   A *lightweight process* is a thread of execution that operates within the context of a normal 4.4BSD process. Multiple lightweight processes may exist in a single 4.4BSD process and share memory, but each is able to do blocking operations, such as system calls. Describe how lightweight processes might be implemented entirely in user mode.

References

Aral et al, 1989.
> Z. Aral, J. Bloom, T. Doeppner, I. Gertner, A. Langerman, & G. Schaffer, "Variable Weight Processes with Flexible Shared Resources," *USENIX Association Conference Proceedings*, pp. 405–412, January 1989.

Ferrin & Langridge, 1980.
> T. E. Ferrin & R. Langridge, "Interactive Computer Graphics with the UNIX Time-Sharing System," *Computer Graphics*, vol. 13, pp. 320–331, 1980.

Joy, 1994.
> W. N. Joy, "An Introduction to the C Shell," in *4.4BSD User's Supplementary Documents*, pp. 4:1–46, O'Reilly & Associates, Inc., Sebastopol, CA, 1994.

Khanna et al, 1992.
> S. Khanna, M. Sebree, & J. Zolnowsky, "Realtime Scheduling in SunOS 5.0," *USENIX Association Conference Proceedings*, pp. 375–390, January 1992.

Killian, 1984.
> T. J. Killian, "Processes as Files," *USENIX Association Conference Proceedings*, pp. 203–207, June 1984.

Ritchie, 1988.
> D. M. Ritchie, "Multi-Processor UNIX," private communication, April 25, 1988.

Sanderson et al, 1986.
> T. Sanderson, S. Ho, N. Heijden, E. Jabs, & J. L. Green, "Near-Realtime Data Transmission During the ICE-Comet Giacobini-Zinner Encounter," *ESA Bulletin*, vol. 45, no. 21, 1986.

Schimmel, 1994.
> C. Schimmel, *UNIX Systems for Modern Architectures, Symmetric Multiprocessing, and Caching for Kernel Programmers,* Addison-Wesley, Reading, MA, 1994.

CHAPTER 5

Memory Management

5.1 Terminology

A central component of any operating system is the *memory-management system.*
As the name implies, memory-management facilities are responsible for the management of memory resources available on a machine. These resources are typically layered in a hierarchical fashion, with memory-access times inversely related
to their proximity to the CPU (see Fig. 5.1). The primary memory system is *main
memory*; the next level of storage is *secondary storage* or *backing storage.* Main-
memory systems usually are constructed from random-access memories, whereas
secondary stores are placed on moving-head disk drives. In certain workstation
environments, the common two-level hierarchy is becoming a three-level

Figure 5.1 Hierarchical layering of memory.

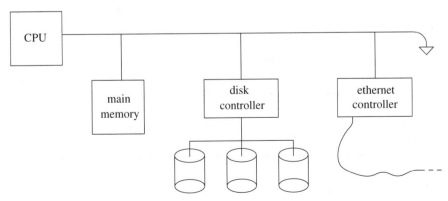

hierarchy, with the addition of file-server machines connected to a workstation via a local-area network [Gingell, Moran, & Shannon, 1987].

In a multiprogrammed environment, it is critical for the operating system to share available memory resources effectively among the processes. The operation of any memory-management policy is directly related to the memory required for a process to execute. That is, if a process must reside entirely in main memory for it to execute, then a memory-management system must be oriented toward allocating large units of memory. On the other hand, if a process can execute when it is only partially resident in main memory, then memory-management policies are likely to be substantially different. Memory-management facilities usually try to optimize the number of runnable processes that are resident in main memory. This goal must be considered with the goals of the process scheduler (Chapter 4), so that conflicts that can adversely affect overall system performance are avoided.

Although the availability of secondary storage permits more processes to exist than can be resident in main memory, it also requires additional algorithms that can be complicated. Space management typically requires algorithms and policies different from those used for main memory, and a policy must be devised for deciding when to move processes between main memory and secondary storage.

Processes and Memory

Each process operates on a *virtual machine* that is defined by the architecture of the underlying hardware on which it executes. We are interested in only those machines that include the notion of a *virtual address space*. A virtual address space is a range of memory locations that a process references independently of the physical memory present in the system. In other words, the virtual address space of a process is independent of the physical address space of the CPU. For a machine to support virtual memory, we also require that the whole of a process's virtual address space does not need to be resident in main memory for that process to execute.

References to the virtual address space—*virtual addresses*—are translated by hardware into references to physical memory. This operation, termed *address translation*, permits programs to be loaded into memory at any location without requiring position-dependent addresses in the program to be changed. Address translation and virtual addressing are also important in efficient sharing of a CPU, because position independence usually permits context switching to be done quickly.

Most machines provide a contiguous virtual address space for processes. Some machines, however, choose to partition visibly a process's virtual address space into regions termed *segments* [Intel, 1984]; such segments usually must be physically contiguous in main memory and must begin at fixed addresses. We shall be concerned with only those systems that do not visibly segment their virtual address space. This use of the word *segment* is not the same as its earlier use in Section 3.5, when we were describing 4.4BSD process segments, such as text and data segments.

When multiple processes are coresident in main memory, we must protect the physical memory associated with each process's virtual address space to ensure that one process cannot alter the contents of another process's virtual address space. This protection is implemented in hardware and is usually tightly coupled with the implementation of address translation. Consequently, the two operations usually are defined and implemented together as hardware termed the *memory-management unit*.

Virtual memory can be implemented in many ways, some of which are software based, such as *overlays*. Most effective virtual-memory schemes are, however, hardware based. In these schemes, the virtual address space is divided into fixed-sized units, termed *pages*, as shown in Fig. 5.2. Virtual-memory references are resolved by the address-translation unit to a page in main memory and an offset within that page. Hardware protection is applied by the memory-management unit on a page-by-page basis.

Some systems provide a two-tiered virtual-memory system in which pages are grouped into segments [Organick, 1975]. In these systems, protection is usually at the segment level. In the remainder of this chapter, we shall be concerned with only those virtual-memory systems that are page based.

Paging

Address translation provides the implementation of virtual memory by decoupling the virtual address space of a process from the physical address space of the CPU. Each page of virtual memory is marked as *resident* or *nonresident* in main memory. If a process references a location in virtual memory that is not resident, a hardware trap termed a *page fault* is generated. The servicing of page faults, or *paging*, permits processes to execute even if they are only partially resident in main memory.

Figure 5.2 Paged virtual-memory scheme. Key: MMU—memory-management unit.

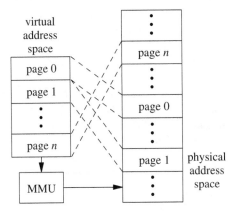

Coffman and Denning [1973] characterize paging systems by three important policies:

1. When the system loads pages into memory—the *fetch policy*

2. Where the system places pages in memory—the *placement policy*

3. How the system selects pages to be removed from main memory when pages are unavailable for a placement request—the *replacement policy*

In normal circumstances, all pages of main memory are equally good, and the placement policy has no effect on the performance of a paging system. Thus, a paging system's behavior is dependent on only the fetch policy and the replacement policy. Under a *pure demand-paging* system, a demand-fetch policy is used, in which only the missing page is fetched, and replacements occur only when main memory is full. Consequently, the performance of a pure demand-paging system depends on only the system's replacement policy. In practice, paging systems do not implement a pure demand-paging algorithm. Instead, the fetch policy often is altered to do *prepaging*—fetching pages of memory other than the one that caused the page fault—and the replacement policy is invoked before main memory is full.

Replacement Algorithms

The replacement policy is the most critical aspect of any paging system. There is a wide range of algorithms from which we can select in designing a replacement strategy for a paging system. Much research has been carried out in evaluating the performance of different page-replacement algorithms [Belady, 1966; King, 1971; Marshall, 1979].

A process's paging behavior for a given input is described in terms of the pages referenced over the time of the process's execution. This sequence of pages, termed a *reference string*, represents the behavior of the process at discrete times during the process's lifetime. Corresponding to the sampled references that constitute a process's reference string are real-time values that reflect whether or not the associated references resulted in a page fault. A useful measure of a process's behavior is the *fault rate*, which is the number of page faults encountered during processing of a reference string, normalized by the length of the reference string.

Page-replacement algorithms typically are evaluated in terms of their effectiveness on reference strings that have been collected from execution of real programs. Formal analysis can also be used, although it is difficult to perform unless many restrictions are applied to the execution environment. The most common metric used in measuring the effectiveness of a page-replacement algorithm is the fault rate.

Page-replacement algorithms are defined in terms of the criteria that they use for selecting pages to be reclaimed. For example, the *optimal replacement policy*

[Denning, 1970] states that the "best" choice of a page to replace is the one with the longest expected time until its next reference. Clearly, this policy is not applicable to dynamic systems, as it requires a priori knowledge of the paging characteristics of a process. The policy is useful for evaluation purposes, however, as it provides a yardstick for comparing the performance of other page-replacement algorithms.

Practical page-replacement algorithms require a certain amount of state information that the system uses in selecting replacement pages. This state typically includes the reference pattern of a process, sampled at discrete time intervals. On some systems, this information can be expensive to collect [Babaoğlu & Joy, 1981]. As a result, the "best" page-replacement algorithm may not be the most efficient.

Working-Set Model

The working-set model assumes that processes exhibit a slowly changing locality of reference. For a period of time, a process operates in a set of subroutines or loops, causing all its memory references to refer to a fixed subset of its address space, termed the *working set*. The process periodically changes its working set, abandoning certain areas of memory and beginning to access new ones. After a period of transition, the process defines a new set of pages as its working set. In general, if the system can provide the process with enough pages to hold that process's working set, the process will experience a low page-fault rate. If the system cannot provide the process with enough pages for the working set, the process will run slowly and will have a high page-fault rate.

Precise calculation of the working set of a process is impossible without a priori knowledge of that process's memory-reference pattern. However, the working set can be approximated by various means. One method of approximation is to track the number of pages held by a process and that process's page-fault rate. If the page-fault rate increases above a high watermark, the working set is assumed to have increased, and the number of pages held by the process is allowed to grow. Conversely, if the page-fault rate drops below a low watermark, the working set is assumed to have decreased, and the number of pages held by the process is reduced.

Swapping

Swapping is the term used to describe a memory-management policy in which entire processes are moved to and from secondary storage when main memory is in short supply. Swap-based memory-management systems usually are less complicated than are demand-paged systems, since there is less bookkeeping to do. However, pure swapping systems are typically less effective than are paging systems, since the degree of multiprogramming is lowered by the requirement that processes be fully resident to execute. Swapping is sometimes combined with paging in a two-tiered scheme, whereby paging satisfies memory demands until a severe memory shortfall requires drastic action, in which case swapping is used.

In this chapter, a portion of secondary storage that is used for paging or swapping is termed a *swap area* or *swap space*. The hardware devices on which these areas reside are termed *swap devices*.

Advantages of Virtual Memory

There are several advantages to the use of virtual memory on computers capable of supporting this facility properly. Virtual memory allows large programs to be run on machines with main-memory configurations that are smaller than the program size. On machines with a moderate amount of memory, it allows more programs to be resident in main memory to compete for CPU time, as the programs do not need to be completely resident. When programs use sections of their program or data space for some time, leaving other sections unused, the unused sections do not need to be present. Also, the use of virtual memory allows programs to start up faster, as they generally require only a small section to be loaded before they begin processing arguments and determining what actions to take. Other parts of a program may not be needed at all during individual runs. As a program runs, additional sections of its program and data spaces are paged in on demand (*demand paging*). Finally, there are many algorithms that are more easily programmed by sparse use of a large address space than by careful packing of data structures into a small area. Such techniques are too expensive for use without virtual memory, but may run much faster when that facility is available, without using an inordinate amount of physical memory.

On the other hand, the use of virtual memory can degrade performance. It is more efficient to load a program all at one time than to load it entirely in small sections on demand. There is a finite cost for each operation, including saving and restoring state and determining which page must be loaded. So, some systems use demand paging for only those programs that are larger than some minimum size.

Hardware Requirements for Virtual Memory

Nearly all versions of UNIX have required some form of memory-management hardware to support transparent multiprogramming. To protect processes from modification by other processes, the memory-management hardware must prevent programs from changing their own address mapping. The 4.4BSD kernel runs in a privileged mode (*kernel mode* or *system mode*) in which memory mapping can be controlled, whereas processes run in an unprivileged mode (*user mode*). There are several additional architectural requirements for support of virtual memory. The CPU must distinguish between resident and nonresident portions of the address space, must suspend programs when they refer to nonresident addresses, and must resume programs' operation once the operating system has placed the required section in memory. Because the CPU may discover missing data at various times during the execution of an instruction, it must provide a mechanism to save the machine state, so that the instruction can be continued or restarted later. The CPU may implement restarting by saving enough state when an instruction begins that the state can be restored when a fault is discovered. Alternatively, instructions could delay any modifications or side effects until after any faults would be discovered, so that the instruction execution does not need to back up before restarting. On some computers, instruction backup requires the assistance of the operating system.

Most machines designed to support demand-paged virtual memory include hardware support for the collection of information on program references to memory. When the system selects a page for replacement, it must save the contents of that page if they have been modified since the page was brought into memory. The hardware usually maintains a per-page flag showing whether the page has been modified. Many machines also include a flag recording any access to a page for use by the replacement algorithm.

5.2   Overview of the 4.4BSD Virtual-Memory System

The 4.4BSD virtual-memory system differs completely from the system that was used in 4.3BSD and predecessors. The implementation is based on the Mach 2.0 virtual-memory system [Tevanian, 1987], with updates from Mach 2.5 and Mach 3.0. The Mach virtual-memory system was adopted because it features efficient support for sharing and a clean separation of machine-independent and machine-dependent features, as well as (currently unused) multiprocessor support. None of the original Mach system-call interface remains. It has been replaced with the interface first proposed for 4.2BSD that has been widely adopted by the UNIX industry; the 4.4BSD interface is described in Section 5.5.

The virtual-memory system implements protected address spaces into which can be mapped data sources (objects) such as files or private, anonymous pieces of swap space. Physical memory is used as a cache of recently used pages from these objects, and is managed by a global page-replacement algorithm much like that of 4.3BSD.

The virtual address space of most architectures is divided into two parts. Typically, the top 30 to 100 Mbyte of the address space is reserved for use by the kernel. The remaining address space is a available for use by processes. A traditional UNIX layout is shown in Fig. 5.3 (on page 124). Here, the kernel and its associated data structures reside at the top of the address space. The initial text and data areas start at or near the beginning of memory. Typically, the first 4 or 8 Kbyte of memory are kept off limits to the process. The reason for this restriction is to ease program debugging; indirecting through a null pointer will cause an invalid address fault, instead of reading or writing the program text. Memory allocations made by the running process using the *malloc*() library routine (or the *sbrk* system call) are done on the heap that starts immediately following the data area and grows to higher addresses. The argument vector and environment vectors are at the top of the user portion of the address space. The user's stack starts just below these vectors and grows to lower addresscs. Subject to only administrative limits, the stack and heap can each grow until they meet. At that point, a process running on a 32-bit machine will be using nearly 4 Gbyte of address space.

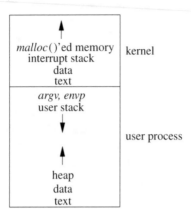

Figure 5.3 Layout of virtual address space.

In 4.4BSD and other modern UNIX systems that support the *mmap* system call, address-space usage is less structured. Shared library implementations may place text or data arbitrarily, rendering the notion of predefined regions obsolete. For compatibility, 4.4BSD still supports the *sbrk* call that *malloc*( ) uses to provide a contiguous heap region, and the kernel has a designated stack region where adjacent allocations are performed automatically.

At any time, the currently executing process is mapped into the virtual address space. When the system decides to context switch to another process, it must save the information about the current-process address mapping, then load the address mapping for the new process to be run. The details of this address-map switching are architecture dependent. Some architectures need to change only a few memory-mapping registers that point to the base, and to give the length of memory-resident page tables. Other architectures store the page-table descriptors in special high-speed static RAM. Switching these maps may require dumping and reloading hundreds of map entries.

Both the kernel and user processes use the same basic data structures for the management of their virtual memory. The data structures used to manage virtual memory are as follows:

vmspace	Structure that encompasses both the machine-dependent and machine-independent structures describing a process's address space
vm_map	Highest-level data structure that describes the machine-independent virtual address space
vm_map_entry	Structure that describes a virtually contiguous range of address space that shares protection and inheritance attributes
object	Structure that describes a source of data for a range of addresses

shadow object   Special object that represents modified copy of original data

vm_page   The lowest-level data structure that represents the physical mem-
                   ory being used by the virtual-memory system

In the remainder of this section, we shall describe briefly how all these data structures fit together. The remainder of this chapter will describe what the details of
the structures are and how the structures are used.

Figure 5.4 shows a typical process address space and associated data structures. The *vmspace* structure encapsulates the virtual-memory state of a particular
process, including the machine-dependent and machine-independent data structures, as well as statistics. The machine-dependent *vm_pmap* structure is opaque
to all but the lowest level of the system, and contains all information necessary to
manage the memory-management hardware. This *pmap layer* is the subject of
Section 5.13 and is ignored for the remainder of the current discussion. The
machine-independent data structures include the address space that is represented
by a *vm_map* structure. The *vm_map* contains a linked list of *vm_map_entry*
structures, hints for speeding up lookups during memory allocation and page-fault
handling, and a pointer to the associated machine-dependent *vm_pmap* structure
contained in the *vmspace*. A *vm_map_entry* structure describes a virtually contiguous range of address space that has the same protection and inheritance
attributes. Every *vm_map_entry* points to a chain of *vm_object* structures that
describes sources of data (objects) that are mapped at the indicated address range.
At the tail of the chain is the original mapped data object, usually representing a
persistent data source, such as a file. Interposed between that object and the map
entry are one or more transient *shadow* objects that represent modified copies of
the original data. These shadow objects are discussed in detail in Section 5.5.

Figure 5.4 Data structures that describe a process address space.

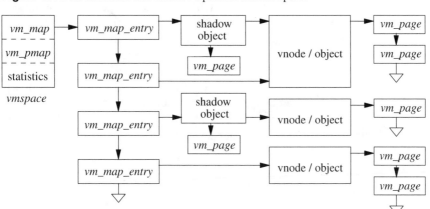

Each *vm_object* structure contains a linked list of *vm_page* structures representing the physical-memory cache of the object, as well as a pointer to the *pager_struct* structure that contains information on how to page in or page out data from its backing store. There is a *vm_page* structure allocated for every page of physical memory managed by the virtual-memory system, where a page here may be a collection of multiple, contiguous hardware pages that will be treated by the machine-dependent layer as though they were a single unit. The structure also contains the status of the page (e.g., modified or referenced) and links for various paging queues.

All structures contain the necessary interlocks for multithreading in a multiprocessor environment. The locking is fine grained, with at least one lock per instance of a data structure. Many of the structures contain multiple locks to protect individual fields.

5.3   Kernel Memory Management

There are two ways in which the kernel's memory can be organized. The most common is for the kernel to be permanently mapped into the high part of every process address space. In this model, switching from one process to another does not affect the kernel portion of the address space. The alternative organization is to switch between having the kernel occupy the whole address space and mapping the currently running process into the address space. Having the kernel permanently mapped does reduce the amount of address space available to a large process (and the kernel), but it also reduces the cost of data copying. Many system calls require data to be transferred between the currently running user process and the kernel. With the kernel permanently mapped, the data can be copied via the efficient block-copy instructions. If the kernel is alternately mapped with the process, data copying requires the use of special instructions that copy to and from the previously mapped address space. These instructions are usually a factor of 2 slower than the standard block-copy instructions. Since up to one-third of the kernel time is spent in copying between the kernel and user processes, slowing this operation by a factor of 2 significantly slows system throughput.

Although the kernel is able freely to read and write the address space of the user process, the converse is not true. The kernel's range of virtual address space is marked inaccessible to all user processes. The reason for restricting writing is so that user processes cannot tamper with the kernel's data structures. The reason for restricting reading is so that user processes cannot watch sensitive kernel data structures, such as the terminal input queues, that include such things as users typing their passwords.

Usually, the hardware dictates which organization can be used. All the architectures supported by 4.4BSD map the kernel into the top of the address space.

Kernel Maps and Submaps

When the system boots, the first task that the kernel must do is to set up data structures to describe and manage its address space. Like any process, the kernel has a *vm_map* with a corresponding set of *vm_map_entry* structures that describe the use of a range of addresses. Submaps are a special kernel-only construct used to isolate and constrain address-space allocation for kernel subsystems. One use is in subsystems that require contiguous pieces of the kernel address space. So that intermixing of unrelated allocations within an address range is avoided, that range is covered by a submap, and only the appropriate subsystem can allocate from that map. For example, several network buffer (*mbuf*) manipulation macros use address arithmetic to generate unique indices, thus requiring the network buffer region to be contiguous. Parts of the kernel may also require addresses with particular alignments or even specific addresses. Both can be ensured by use of submaps. Finally, submaps can be used to limit statically the amount of address space and hence the physical memory consumed by a subsystem.

A typical layout of the kernel map is shown in Fig. 5.5. The kernel's address space is described by the *vm_map* structure shown in the upper-left corner of the

Figure 5.5 Kernel address-space maps.

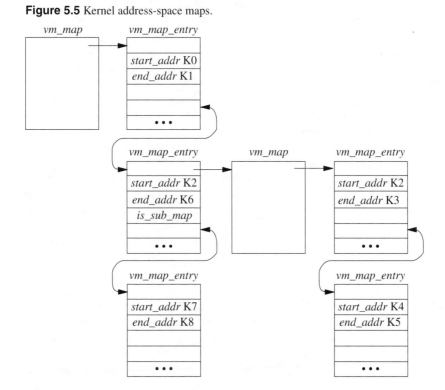

figure. Pieces of the address space are described by the *vm_map_entry* structures that are linked in ascending address order from K0 to K8 on the *vm_map* structure. Here, the kernel text, initialized data, uninitialized data, and initially allocated data structures reside in the range K0 to K1 and are represented by the first *vm_map_entry*. The next *vm_map_entry* is associated with the address range from K2 to K6; this piece of the kernel address space is being managed via a submap headed by the referenced *vm_map* structure. This submap currently has two parts of its address space used: the address range K2 to K3, and the address range K4 to K5. These two submaps represent the kernel malloc arena and the network buffer arena, respectively. The final part of the kernel address space is being managed in the kernel's main map; the address range K7 to K8 representing the kernel I/O staging area.

Kernel Address-Space Allocation

The virtual-memory system implements a set of primitive functions for allocating and freeing the page-aligned, page-rounded virtual-memory ranges that the kernel uses. These ranges may be allocated either from the main kernel-address map or from a submap. The allocation routines take a map and size as parameters, but do not take an address. Thus, specific addresses within a map cannot be selected. There are different allocation routines for obtaining nonpageable and pageable memory ranges.

A nonpageable, or *wired*, range has physical memory assigned at the time of the call, and this memory is not subject to replacement by the pageout daemon. Wired pages must never cause a page fault that might result in a blocking operation. Wired memory is allocated with *kmem_alloc*() and *kmem_malloc*(). *Kmem_alloc*() returns zero-filled memory and may block if insufficient physical memory is available to honor the request. It will return a failure only if no address space is available in the indicated map. *Kmem_malloc*() is a variant of *kmem_alloc*() used by only the general allocator, *malloc*(), described in the next subsection. This routine has a nonblocking option that protects callers against inadvertently blocking on kernel data structures; it will fail if insufficient physical memory is available to fill the requested range. This nonblocking option allocates memory at interrupt time and during other critical sections of code. In general, wired memory should be allocated via the general-purpose kernel allocator. *Kmem_alloc*() should be used only to allocate memory from specific kernel submaps.

Pageable kernel virtual memory can be allocated with *kmem_alloc_pageable*() and *kmem_alloc_wait*(). A pageable range has physical memory allocated on demand, and this memory can be written out to backing store by the pageout daemon as part of the latter's normal replacement policy. *Kmem_alloc_pageable*() will return an error if insufficient address space is available for the desired allocation; *kmem_alloc_wait*() will block until space is available. Currently, pageable kernel memory is used only for temporary storage of *exec* arguments and for the kernel stacks of processes that have been swapped out.

Kmem_free() deallocates kernel wired memory and pageable memory allocated with *kmem_alloc_pageable*(). *Kmem_free_wakeup*() should be used with *kmem_alloc_wait*() because it wakes up any processes waiting for address space in the specified map.

Kernel Malloc

The kernel also provides a generalized nonpageable memory-allocation and freeing mechanism that can handle requests with arbitrary alignment or size, as well as allocate memory at interrupt time. Hence, it is the preferred way to allocate kernel memory. This mechanism has an interface similar to that of the well-known memory allocator provided for applications programmers through the C library routines *malloc*() and *free*(). Like the C library interface, the allocation routine takes a parameter specifying the size of memory that is needed. The range of sizes for memory requests are not constrained. The free routine takes a pointer to the storage being freed, but does not require the size of the piece of memory being freed.

Often, the kernel needs a memory allocation for the duration of a single system call. In a user process, such short-term memory would be allocated on the run-time stack. Because the kernel has a limited run-time stack, it is not feasible to allocate even moderate blocks of memory on it. Consequently, such memory must be allocated dynamically. For example, when the system must translate a pathname, it must allocate a 1-Kbyte buffer to hold the name. Other blocks of memory must be more persistent than a single system call, and have to be allocated from dynamic memory. Examples include protocol control blocks that remain throughout the duration of a network connection.

The design specification for a kernel memory allocator is similar to, but not identical to, the design criteria for a user-level memory allocator. One criterion for a memory allocator is that the latter make good use of the physical memory. Use of memory is measured by the amount of memory needed to hold a set of allocations at any point in time. Percentage utilization is expressed as

$$utilization = \frac{requested}{required}.$$

Here, *requested* is the sum of the memory that has been requested and not yet freed; *required* is the amount of memory that has been allocated for the pool from which the requests are filled. An allocator requires more memory than requested because of fragmentation and a need to have a ready supply of free memory for future requests. A perfect memory allocator would have a utilization of 100 percent. In practice, a 50-percent utilization is considered good [Korn & Vo, 1985].

Good memory utilization in the kernel is more important than in user processes. Because user processes run in virtual memory, unused parts of their address space can be paged out. Thus, pages in the process address space that are part of the required pool that are not being requested do not need to tie up physical memory. Since the kernel malloc arena is not paged, all pages in the required pool are held by the kernel and cannot be used for other purposes. To keep the kernel-utilization percentage as high as possible, the kernel should release unused memory in the required pool, rather than hold it, as is typically done with user processes. Because the kernel can manipulate its own page maps directly, freeing unused memory is fast; a user process must do a system call to free memory.

The most important criterion for a kernel memory allocator is that the latter be fast. A slow memory allocator will degrade the system performance because memory allocation is done frequently. Speed of allocation is more critical when executing in the kernel than it is in user code because the kernel must allocate many data structures that user processes can allocate cheaply on their run-time stack. In addition, the kernel represents the platform on which all user processes run, and, if it is slow, it will degrade the performance of every process that is running.

Another problem with a slow memory allocator is that programmers of frequently used kernel interfaces will think that they cannot afford to use the memory allocator as their primary one. Instead, they will build their own memory allocator on top of the original by maintaining their own pool of memory blocks. Multiple allocators reduce the efficiency with which memory is used. The kernel ends up with many different free lists of memory, instead of a single free list from which all allocations can be drawn. For example, consider the case of two subsystems that need memory. If they have their own free lists, the amount of memory tied up in the two lists will be the sum of the greatest amount of memory that each of the two subsystems has ever used. If they share a free list, the amount of memory tied up in the free list may be as low as the greatest amount of memory that either subsystem used. As the number of subsystems grows, the savings from having a single free list grow.

The kernel memory allocator uses a hybrid strategy. Small allocations are done using a power-of-2 list strategy; the typical allocation requires only a computation of the list to use and the removal of an element if that element is available, so it is fast. Only if the request cannot be fulfilled from a list is a call made to the allocator itself. To ensure that the allocator is always called for large requests, the lists corresponding to large allocations are always empty.

Freeing a small block also is fast. The kernel computes the list on which to place the request, and puts the request there. The free routine is called only if the block of memory is considered to be a large allocation.

Because of the inefficiency of power-of-2 allocation strategies for large allocations, the allocation method for large blocks is based on allocating pieces of memory in multiples of pages. The algorithm switches to the slower but more memory-efficient strategy for allocation sizes larger than $2 \times pagesize$. This value is chosen because the power-of-2 algorithm yields sizes of 1, 2, 4, 8, ..., n pages, whereas the large block algorithm that allocates in multiples of pages yields sizes of 1, 2, 3, 4, ..., n pages. Thus, for allocations of sizes between one and two pages, both algorithms use two pages; a difference emerges beginning with allocations of sizes between two and three pages, where the power-of-2 algorithm will use four pages, whereas the large block algorithm will use three pages. Thus, the threshold between the large and small allocators is set to two pages.

Large allocations are first rounded up to be a multiple of the page size. The allocator then uses a "first-fit" algorithm to find space in the kernel address arena set aside for dynamic allocations. On a machine with a 4-Kbyte page size, a request for a 20-Kbyte piece of memory will use exactly five pages of memory, rather than the eight pages used with the power-of-2 allocation strategy. When a large piece of memory is freed, the memory pages are returned to the free-memory pool and the *vm_map_entry* structure is deleted from the submap, effectively coalescing the freed piece with any adjacent free space.

Another technique to improve both the efficiency of memory utilization and the speed of allocation is to cluster same-sized small allocations on a page. When a list for a power-of-2 allocation is empty, a new page is allocated and is divided into pieces of the needed size. This strategy speeds future allocations because several pieces of memory become available as a result of the call into the allocator.

Because the size is not specified when a block of memory is freed, the allocator must keep track of the sizes of the pieces that it has handed out. Many allocators increase the allocation request by a few bytes to create space to store the size of the block in a header just before the allocation. However, this strategy doubles the memory requirement for allocations that request a power-of-2–sized block. Therefore, instead of storing the size of each piece of memory with the piece itself, the kernel associates the size information with the memory page. Figure 5.6 shows how the kernel determines the size of a piece of memory that is being freed, by calculating the page in which it resides and looking up the size associated with that page. Locating the allocation size outside of the allocated block improved utilization far more than expected. The reason is that many allocations in the kernel are for blocks of memory whose size is exactly a power of 2. These requests would be nearly doubled in size if the more typical strategy were used. Now they can be accommodated with no wasted memory.

The allocator can be called both from the top half of the kernel that is willing to wait for memory to become available, and from the interrupt routines in the bottom half of the kernel that cannot wait for memory to become available. Clients show their willingness (and ability) to wait with a flag to the allocation routine. For clients that are willing to wait, the allocator guarantees that their request will

---

Figure 5.6 Calculation of allocation size. Key: free—unused page; cont—continuation of previous page.

```
char *kmembase
kmemsizes[ ] = {  4096, 1024,  2048,  12288, cont,   cont,   512,   free,  cont,   cont,


usage: memsize(char *addr)
       {
            return(kmemsizes[(addr - kmembase) / PAGESIZE]);
       }
```

succeed. Thus, these clients do not need to check the return value from the allocator. If memory is unavailable and the client cannot wait, the allocator returns a null pointer. These clients must be prepared to cope with this (hopefully infrequent) condition (usually by giving up and hoping to succeed later). The details of the kernel memory allocator are further described in [McKusick & Karels, 1988].

5.4   Per-Process Resources

As we have already seen, a process requires a process entry and a kernel stack. The next major resource that must be allocated is its virtual memory. The initial virtual-memory requirements are defined by the header in the process's executable. These requirements include the space needed for the program text, the initialized data, the uninitialized data, and the run-time stack. During the initial startup of the program, the kernel will build the data structures necessary to describe these four areas. Most programs need to allocate additional memory. The kernel typically provides this additional memory by expanding the uninitialized data area.

Most 4.4BSD systems also provide shared libraries. The header for the executable will describe the libraries that it needs (usually the C library, and possibly others). The kernel is not responsible for locating and mapping these libraries during the initial execution of the program. Finding, mapping, and creating the dynamic linkages to these libraries is handled by the user-level startup code prepended to the file being executed. This startup code usually runs before control is passed to the main entry point of the program [Gingell et al, 1987].

4.4BSD Process Virtual-Address Space

The initial layout of the address space for a process is shown in Fig. 5.7. As discussed in Section 5.2, the address space for a process is described by that process's *vmspace* structure. The contents of the address space are defined by a list of *vm_map_entry* structures, each structure describing a *region* of virtual address space that resides between a *start* and an *end* address. A region describes a range of memory that is being treated in the same way. For example, the text of a program is a region that is read-only and is demand paged from the file on disk that contains it. Thus, the *vm_map_entry* also contains the protection mode to be applied to the region that it describes. Each *vm_map_entry* structure also has a pointer to the object that provides the initial data for the region. It also stores the modified contents either transiently when memory is being reclaimed or more permanently when the region is no longer needed. Finally, each *vm_map_entry* structure has an offset that describes where within the object the mapping begins.

The example shown in Fig. 5.7 represents a process just after it has started execution. The first two map entries both point to the same object; here, that object is the executable. The executable consists of two parts: the text of the program that resides at the beginning of the file and the initialized data area that

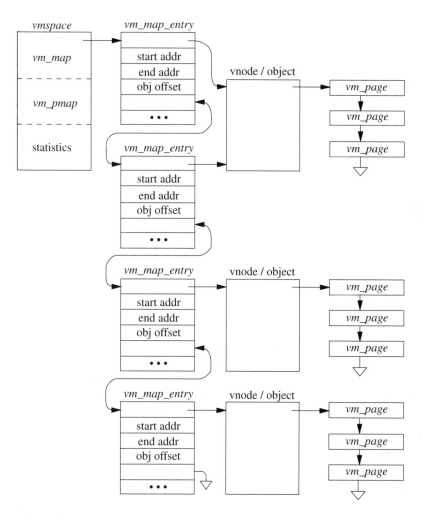

Figure 5.7 Layout of an address space.

follows at the end of the text. Thus, the first *vm_map_entry* describes a read-only region that maps the text of the program. The second *vm_map_entry* describes the copy-on-write region that maps the initialized data of the program that follows the program text in the file (copy-on-write is described in Section 5.6). The offset field in the entry reflects this different starting location. The third and fourth *vm_map_entry* structures describe the uninitialized data and stack areas, respectively. Both of these areas are represented by *anonymous objects*. An anonymous object provides a zero-filled page on first use, and arranges to store modified pages in the swap area if memory becomes tight. Anonymous objects are described in more detail later in this section.

Page-Fault Dispatch

When a process attempts to access a piece of its address space that is not currently resident, a page fault occurs. The page-fault handler in the kernel is presented with the virtual address that caused the fault. The fault is handled with the following four steps:

1. Find the *vmspace* structure for the faulting process; from that structure, find the head of the *vm_map_entry* list.

2. Traverse the *vm_map_entry* list starting at the entry indicated by the map hint; for each entry, check whether the faulting address falls within its start and end address range. If the kernel reaches the end of the list without finding any valid region, the faulting address is not within any valid part of the address space for the process, so send the process a segment fault signal.

3. Having found a *vm_map_entry* that contains the faulting address, convert that address to an offset within the underlying object. Calculate the offset within the object as

$$
\begin{aligned}
\text{object\_offset} = {} & \text{fault\_address} \\
& - \text{vm\_map\_entry} \rightarrow \text{start\_address} \\
& + \text{vm\_map\_entry} \rightarrow \text{object\_offset}
\end{aligned}
$$

   Subtract off the start address to give the offset into the region mapped by the *vm_map_entry*. Add in the object offset to give the absolute offset of the page within the object.

4. Present the absolute object offset to the underlying object, which allocates a *vm_page* structure and uses its pager to fill the page. The object then returns a pointer to the *vm_page* structure, which is mapped into the faulting location in the process address space.

Once the appropriate page has been mapped into the faulting location, the page-fault handler returns and reexecutes the faulting instruction.

Mapping to Objects

Objects are used to hold information about either a file or about an area of anonymous memory. Whether a file is mapped by a single process in the system or by many processes in the system, it will always be represented by a single object. Thus, the object is responsible for maintaining all the state about those pages of a file that are resident. All references to that file will be described by *vm_map_entry* structures that reference the same object. An object never stores the same page of a file in more than one memory page, so that all mappings will get a consistent view of the file.

An object stores the following information:

- A list of the pages for that object that are currently resident in main memory; a page may be mapped into multiple address spaces, but it is always claimed by exactly one object

- A count of the number of *vm_map_entry* structures or other objects that reference the object

- The size of the file or anonymous area described by the object

- The number of memory-resident pages held by the object

- Pointers to copy or shadow objects (described in Section 5.5)

- A pointer to the *pager* for the object; the pager is responsible for providing the data to fill a page, and for providing a place to store the page when it has been modified (pagers are covered in Section 5.10)

There are four types of objects in the system:

- *Named* objects represent files; they may also represent hardware devices that are able to provide mapped memory such as frame buffers.

- *Anonymous* objects represent areas of memory that are zero filled on first use; they are abandoned when they are no longer needed.

- *Shadow* objects hold private copies of pages that have been modified; they are abandoned when they are no longer referenced.

- *Copy* objects hold old pages from files that have been modified after they were privately mapped; they are abandoned when the private mapping is abandoned.

These objects are often referred to as "internal" objects in the source code. The type of an object is defined by the pager that that object uses to fulfill page-fault requests.

A named object uses either (an instance of) the device pager, if it maps a hardware device, or the vnode pager, if it is backed by a file in the filesystem. A pager services a page fault by returning the appropriate address for the device being mapped. Since the device memory is separate from the main memory on the machine, it will never be selected by the pageout daemon. Thus, the device pager never has to handle a pageout request.

The vnode pager provides an interface to objects that represent files in the filesystem. A vnode-pager instance keeps a reference to a vnode that represents the file being mapped by the object. A vnode pager services a pagein request by doing a read on the vnode; it services a pageout request by doing a write to the vnode. Thus, the file itself stores the modified pages. In cases where it is not appropriate to modify the file directly, such as an executable that does not want to modify its initialized data pages, the kernel must interpose an anonymous shadow object between the *vm_map_entry* and the object representing the file.

Anonymous objects use the swap pager. An anonymous object services pagein requests by getting a page of memory from the free list, and zeroing that page. When a pageout request is made for a page for the first time, the swap pager is responsible for finding an unused page in the swap area, writing the contents of the page to that space, and recording where that page is stored. If a pagein request comes for a page that had been previously paged out, the swap pager is responsible for finding where it stored that page and reading back the contents into a free page in memory. A later pageout request for that page will cause the page to be written out to the previously allocated location.

Shadow objects and copy objects also use the swap pager. They work just like anonymous objects, except that the swap pager provides their initial pages by copying existing pages in response to copy-on-write faults, instead of by zero-filling pages.

Further details on the pagers are given in Section 5.10.

Objects

Each virtual-memory object has a pager associated with it; objects that map files have a vnode pager associated with them. Each instance of a vnode pager is associated with a particular vnode. Objects are stored on a hash chain and are identified by their associated pager. When a fault occurs for a file that is mapped into memory, the kernel checks its vnode pager cache to see whether a pager already exists for that file. If a pager exists, the kernel then looks to see whether there is an object still associated with that pager. If the object exists, it can be checked to see whether the faulted page is resident. If the page is resident, it can be used. If the page is not resident, a new page is allocated, and the pager is requested to fill the new page.

Caching in the virtual-memory system is identified by an object that is associated with a file or region that it represents. Each object contains pages that are the cached contents of its associated file or region. Objects that represent anonymous memory are reclaimed as soon as the reference count drops to zero. However, objects that refer to files are persistent. When their reference count drops to zero, the object is stored on a least-recently used (LRU) list known as the *object cache*. The object remains on its hash chain, so that future uses of the associated file will cause the existing object to be found. The pages associated with the object are moved to the *inactive list*, which is described in Section 5.12. However, their identity is retained, so that, if the object is reactivated and a page fault occurs before the associated page is freed, that page can be reattached, rather than being reread from disk.

This cache is similar to the text cache found in earlier versions of BSD in that it provides performance improvements for short-running but frequently executed programs. Frequently executed programs include those to list the contents of directories, to show system status, or to do the intermediate steps involved in compiling a program. For example, consider a typical application that is made up of multiple source files. Each of several compiler steps must be run on each file in turn. The first time that the compiler is run, the objects associated with its various components are read in from the disk. For each file compiled thereafter, the previously created objects are found, alleviating the need to reload them from disk each time.

Objects to Pages

When the system is first booted, the kernel looks through the physical memory on the machine to find out how many pages are available. After the physical memory that will be dedicated to the kernel itself has been deducted, all the remaining pages of physical memory are described by *vm_page* structures. These *vm_page* structures are all initially placed on the memory free list. As the system starts running and processes begin to execute, they generate page faults. Each page fault is matched to the object that covers the faulting piece of address space. The first time that a piece of an object is faulted, it must allocate a page from the free list, and must initialize that page either by zero filling it or by reading its contents from the filesystem. That page then becomes associated with the object. Thus, each object has its current set of *vm_page* structures linked to it. A page can be associated with at most one object at a time. Although a file may be mapped into several processes at once, all those mappings reference the same object. Having a single object for each file ensures that all processes will reference the same physical pages. One anomaly is that the object offset in a *vm_map_entry* structure may not be page aligned (the result of an *mmap* call with a non–page-aligned offset parameter). Consequently, a *vm_page* may be filled and associated with the object with a non–page-aligned tag that will not match another access to the same object at the page-aligned boundary. Hence, if two processes map the same object with offsets of 0 and 32, two *vm_pages* will be filled with largely the same data, and that can lead to inconsistent views of the file.

If memory becomes scarce, the paging daemon will search for pages that have not been used recently. Before these pages can be used by a new object, they must be removed from all the processes that currently have them mapped, and any modified contents must be saved by the object that owns them. Once cleaned, the pages can be removed from the object that owns them and can be placed on the free list for reuse. The details of the paging system are described in Section 5.12.

5.5   Shared Memory

In Section 5.4, we explained how the address space of a process is organized. This section shows the additional data structures needed to support shared address space between processes. Traditionally, the address space of each process was completely isolated from the address space of all other processes running on the system. The only exception was read-only sharing of program text. All interprocess communication was done through well-defined channels that passed through the kernel: pipes, sockets, files, and special devices. The benefit of this isolated approach is that, no matter how badly a process destroys its own address space, it cannot affect the address space of any other process running on the system. Each process can precisely control when data are sent or received; it can also precisely identify the locations within its address space that are read or written. The drawback of this approach is that all interprocess communication requires at least two system calls: one from the sending process and one from the receiving process. For high volumes of interprocess communication, especially when small packets of data are being exchanged, the overhead of the system calls dominates the communications cost.

Shared memory provides a way to reduce interprocess-communication costs dramatically. Two or more processes that wish to communicate map the same piece of read–write memory into their address space. Once all the processes have mapped the memory into their address space, any changes to that piece of memory are visible to all the other processes, without any intervention by the kernel. Thus, interprocess communication can be achieved without any system-call overhead, other than the cost of the initial mapping. The drawback to this approach is that, if a process that has the memory mapped corrupts the data structures in that memory, all the other processes mapping that memory also are corrupted. In addition, there is the complexity faced by the application developer who must develop data structures to control access to the shared memory, and must cope with the race conditions inherent in manipulating and controlling such data structures that are being accessed concurrently.

Some variants of UNIX have a kernel-based semaphore mechanism to provide the needed serialization of access to the shared memory. However, both getting and setting such semaphores require system calls. The overhead of using such semaphores is comparable to that of using the traditional interprocess-communication methods. Unfortunately, these semaphores have all the complexity of shared memory, yet confer little of its speed advantage. The primary reason to introduce the complexity of shared memory is for the commensurate speed gain. If this gain is to be obtained, most of the data-structure locking needs to be done in the shared memory segment itself. The kernel-based semaphores should be used for only those rare cases where there is contention for a lock and one process must wait. Consequently, modern interfaces, such as POSIX Pthreads, are designed such that the semaphores can be located in the shared memory region. The common case of setting or clearing an uncontested semaphore can be done by the user process, without calling the kernel. There are two cases where a process must do a system call. If a process tries to set an already-locked semaphore, it must call the kernel to block until the semaphore is available. This system call has little effect on performance because the lock is contested, so it is impossible to proceed and the kernel has to be invoked to do a context switch anyway. If a process clears a semaphore that is wanted by another process, it must call the kernel to awaken that process. Since most locks are uncontested, the applications can run at full speed without kernel intervention.

Mmap Model

When two processes wish to create an area of shared memory, they must have some way to name the piece of memory that they wish to share, and they must be able to describe its size and initial contents. The system interface describing an area of shared memory accomplishes all these goals by using files as the basis for describing a shared memory segment. A process creates a shared memory segment by using

```
caddr_t addr = mmap(
     caddr_t addr,    /* base address */
     size_t len,      /* length of region */
     int prot,        /* protection of region */
     int flags,       /* mapping flags */
     int fd,          /* file to map */
     off_t offset);   /* offset to begin mapping */
```

to map the file referenced by descriptor *fd* starting at file offset *offset* into its address space starting at *addr* and continuing for *len* bytes with access permission *prot*. The *flags* parameter allows a process to specify whether it wants to make a *shared* or *private* mapping. Changes made to a shared mapping are written back to the file and are visible to other processes. Changes made to a private mapping are not written back to the file and are not visible to other processes. Two processes that wish to share a piece of memory request a shared mapping of the same file into their address space. Thus, the existing and well-understood filesystem name space is used to identify shared objects. The contents of the file are used as the initial value of the memory segment. All changes made to the mapping are reflected back into the contents of the file, so long-term state can be maintained in the shared memory region, even across invocations of the sharing processes.

   Some applications want to use shared memory purely as a short-term inter-process-communication mechanism. They need an area of memory that is initially zeroed and whose contents are abandoned when they are done using it. Such processes neither want to pay the relatively high start-up cost associated with paging in the contents of a file to initialize a shared memory segment, nor to pay the shut-down costs of writing modified pages back to the file when they are done with the memory. Although an alternative naming scheme was considered to provide a rendezvous mechanism for such short-term shared memory, the designers ulti-mately decided that all naming of memory objects should use the filesystem name space. To provide an efficient mechanism for short-term shared memory, they cre-ated a virtual-memory–resident filesystem for transient objects. The details of the virtual-memory–resident filesystem are described in Section 8.4. Unless memory is in high demand, files created in the virtual-memory–resident filesystem reside entirely in memory. Thus, both the initial paging and later write-back costs are eliminated. Typically, a virtual-memory–resident filesystem is mounted on **/tmp**. Two processes wishing to create a transient area of shared memory create a file in **/tmp** that they can then both map into their address space.

When a mapping is no longer needed, it can be removed using

```
munmap(caddr_t addr, size_t len);
```

The *munmap* system call removes any mappings that exist in the address space, starting at *addr* and continuing for *len* bytes. There are no constraints between previous mappings and a later *munmap*. The specified range may be a subset of a previous *mmap* or it may encompass an area that contains many *mmap*'ed files. When a process exits, the system does an implied *munmap* over its entire address space.

During its initial mapping, a process can set the protections on a page to allow reading, writing, and/or execution. The process can change these protections later by using

```
mprotect(caddr_t addr, int len, int prot);
```

This feature can be used by debuggers when they are trying to track down a memory-corruption bug. By disabling writing on the page containing the data structure that is being corrupted, the debugger can trap all writes to the page and verify that they are correct before allowing them to occur.

Traditionally, programming for real-time systems has been done with specially written operating systems. In the interests of reducing the costs of real-time applications and of using the skills of the large body of UNIX programmers, companies developing real-time applications have expressed increased interest in using UNIX-based systems for writing these applications. Two fundamental requirements of a real-time system are maximum guaranteed latencies and predictable execution times. Predictable execution time is difficult to provide in a virtual-memory–based system, since a page fault may occur at any point in the execution of a program, resulting in a potentially large delay while the faulting page is retrieved from the disk or network. To avoid paging delays, the system allows a process to force its pages to be resident, and not paged out, by using

```
mlock(caddr_t addr, size_t len);
```

As long as the process limits its accesses to the locked area of its address space, it can be sure that it will not be delayed by page faults. To prevent a single process from acquiring all the physical memory on the machine to the detriment of all other processes, the system imposes a resource limit to control the amount of memory that may be locked. Typically, this limit is set to no more than one-third of the physical memory, and it may be set to zero by a system administrator that does not want random processes to be able to monopolize system resources.

When a process has finished with its time-critical use of an *mlock*'ed region, it can release the pages using

```
munlock(caddr_t addr, size_t len);
```

After the *munlock* call, the pages in the specified address range are still accessible, but they may be paged out if memory is needed and they are not accessed.

The architecture of some multiprocessing machines does not provide consistency between a high-speed cache local to a CPU and the machine's main memory. For these machines, it may be necessary to flush the cache to main memory before the changes made in that memory are visible to processes running on other CPUs. A process does this synchronization using

```
msync(caddr_t addr, int len);
```

For a region containing a mapped file, *msync* also writes back any modified pages to the filesystem.

Shared Mapping

When multiple processes map the same file into their address space, the system must ensure that all the processes view the same set of memory pages. As shown in Section 5.4, each file that is being used actively by a client of the virtual-memory system is represented by an object. Each mapping that a process has to a piece of a file is described by a *vm_map_entry* structure. An example of two processes mapping the same file into their address space is shown in Fig. 5.8. When a page fault occurs in one of these processes, the process's *vm_map_entry* references the object to find the appropriate page. Since all mappings reference the same object, the processes will all get references to the same set of physical memory, thus ensuring that changes made by one process will be visible in the address spaces of the other processes as well.

A second organization arises when a process with a shared mapping does a *fork*. Here, the kernel interposes a *sharing map* between the two processes and the shared object, so that both processes' map entries reference this map, instead of the object. A sharing map is identical in structure to an address map: It is a linked

---

Figure 5.8 Multiple mappings to a file.

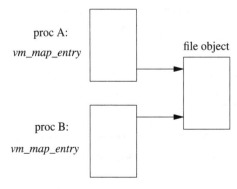

list of map entries. The intent is that a sharing map, referenced by all processes inheriting a shared memory region, will be the focus of map-related operations that should affect all the processes. Sharing maps are useful in the creation of shadow objects for copy-on-write operations because they affect part or all of the shared region. Here, all sharing processes should use the same shadow object, so that all will see modifications made to the region. Sharing maps are an artifact of the virtual-memory code's early Mach origin; they do not work well in the 4.4BSD environment because they work for only that memory shared by inheritance. Shared mappings established with *mmap* do not use them. Hence, even if a sharing map exists for a shared region, it does not necessarily reflect all processes involved. The only effect that sharing maps have in 4.4BSD is to extend across forks the delayed creation of shadow and copy objects. This delay does not offer a significant advantage, and the small advantage is outweighed by the added amount and complexity of code necessary to handle sharing maps. For this reason, sharing maps probably will be eliminated from systems derived from 4.4BSD, as they were from later versions of Mach.

Private Mapping

A process may request a *private mapping* of a file. A private mapping has two main effects:

1. Changes made to the memory mapping the file are not reflected back into the mapped file.

2. Changes made to the memory mapping the file are not visible to other processes mapping the file.

An example of the use of a private mapping would be during program debugging. The debugger will request a private mapping of the program text so that, when it sets a breakpoint, the modification is not written back into the executable stored on the disk and is not visible to the other (presumably nondebugging) processes executing the program.

The kernel uses shadow objects to prevent changes made by a process from being reflected back to the underlying object. The use of a shadow object is shown in Fig. 5.9. When the initial private mapping is requested, the file object is mapped into the requesting-process address space, with copy-on-write semantics. If the process attempts to write a page of the object, a page fault occurs and traps into the kernel. The kernel makes a copy of the page to be modified and hangs it from the shadow object. In this example, process A has modified page 0 of the file object. The kernel has copied page 0 to the shadow object that is being used to provide the private mapping for process A.

If free memory is limited, it would be better simply to move the modified page from the file object to the shadow object. The move would reduce the immediate demand on the free memory, because a new page would not have to be allocated. The drawback to this optimization is that, if there is a later access to the file object by some other process, the kernel will have to allocate a new page. The

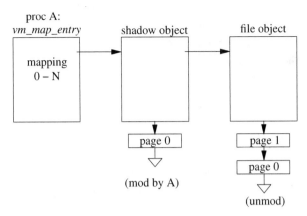

Figure 5.9 Use of a shadow object for a private mapping.

kernel will also have to pay the cost of doing an I/O operation to reload the page contents. In 4.4BSD, the virtual-memory system never moves the page rather than copying it.

When a page fault for the private mapping occurs, the kernel traverses the list of objects headed by the *vm_map_entry*, looking for the faulted page. The first object in the chain that has the desired page is the one that is used. If the search gets to the final object on the chain without finding the desired page, then the page is requested from that final object. Thus, pages on a shadow object will be used in preference to the same pages in the file object itself. The details of page-fault handling are given in Section 5.11.

When a process removes a mapping from its address space (either explicitly from an *munmap* request or implicitly when the address space is freed on process exit), pages held by its shadow object are not written back to the file object. The shadow-object pages are simply placed back on the memory free list for immediate reuse.

When a process forks, it does not want changes to its private mappings to be visible in its child; similarly, the child does not want its changes to be visible in its parent. The result is that each process needs to create a shadow object if it continues to make changes in a private mapping. When process A in Fig. 5.9 forks, a set of shadow object chains is created, as shown in Fig. 5.10 (on page 144). In this example, process A modified page 0 before it forked, then later modified page 1. Its modified version of page 1 hangs off its new shadow object, so that those modifications will not be visible to its child. Similarly, its child has modified page 0. If the child were to modify page 0 in the original shadow object, that change would be visible in its parent. Thus, the child process must make a new copy of page 0 in its own shadow object.

If the system runs short of memory, the kernel may need to reclaim inactive memory held in a shadow object. The kernel assigns to the swap pager the task of backing the shadow object. The swap pager creates a swap map that is large enough to describe the entire contents of the shadow object. It then allocates

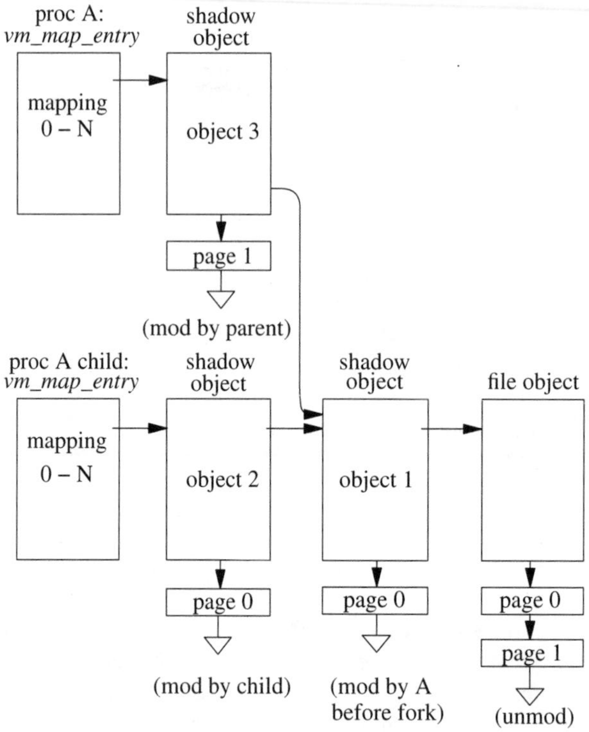

Figure 5.10 Shadow-object chains.

enough swap space to hold the requested shadow pages and writes them to that area. These pages can then be freed for other uses. If a later page fault requests a swapped-out page, then a new page of memory is allocated and its contents are reloaded with an I/O from the swap area.

Collapsing of Shadow Chains

When a process with a private mapping removes that mapping either explicitly with an *munmap* system call or implicitly by exiting, its parent or child process may be left with a chain of shadow objects. Usually, these chains of shadow objects can be collapsed into a single shadow object, often freeing up memory as part of the collapse. Consider what happens when process A exits in Fig. 5.10. First, shadow object 3 can be freed, along with its associated page of memory. This deallocation leaves shadow objects 1 and 2 in a chain with no intervening references. Thus, these two objects can be collapsed into a single shadow object. Since they both contain a copy of page 0, and since only the page 0 in shadow object 2 can be accessed by the remaining child process, the page 0 in shadow object 1 can be freed, along with shadow object 1 itself.

If the child of process A were to exit, then shadow object 2 and the associated page of memory could be freed. Shadow objects 1 and 3 would then be in a chain that would be eligible for collapse. Here, there are no common pages, so the remaining collapsed shadow object would contain page 0 from shadow object 1, as well as page 1 from shadow object 3. A limitation of the implementation is that it cannot collapse two objects if either of them has allocated a pager. This limitation is serious, since pagers are allocated when the system begins running short of memory—precisely the time when reclaiming of memory from collapsed objects is most necessary.

Private Snapshots

When a process makes read accesses to a private mapping of an object, it continues to see changes made to that object by other processes that are writing to the object through the filesystem or that have a shared mapping to the object. When a process makes a write access to a private mapping of an object, a snapshot of the corresponding page of the object is made and is stored in the shadow object, and the modification is made to that snapshot. Thus, further changes to that page made by other processes that are writing to the page through the filesystem or that have a shared mapping to the object are no longer visible for that page. However, changes to unmodified pages of the object continue to be visible. This mix of changing and unchanging parts of the file can be confusing.

To provide a more consistent view of a file, a process may want to take a snapshot of the file at the time that it is initially privately mapped. A process takes such a snapshot by using a copy object, as shown in Fig. 5.11 (on page 146). In this example, process B has a shared mapping to the file object, whereas process A has a private mapping. Modifications made by process B will be reflected in the file, and hence will be visible to any other process (such as process A) that is mapping that file. To avoid seeing the modifications made by process B after process B has done its mapping, process A interposes a copy object between itself and the file object. At the same time, it changes the protections on the file object to be copy-on-write. Thereafter, when process B tries to modify the file object, it will generate a page fault. The page-fault handler will save a copy of the unmodified page in the copy object, then will allow process B to write the original page. If process A later tries to access one of the pages that process B has modified, it will get the page that was saved in the copy object, instead of getting the version that process B changed.

In 4.4BSD, private snapshots work correctly only if all processes modifying the file do so through the virtual-memory interface. For example, in Fig. 5.11, assume that a third process C writes page 2 of the file using *write* before A or B reference page 2. Now, even though A has made a snapshot of the file, it will see the modified version of page 2, since the virtual-memory system has no knowledge that page 2 was written. This behavior is an unwelcome side effect of the separate virtual memory and filesystem caches; it would be eliminated if the two caches were integrated.

Most non-BSD systems that provide the *mmap* interface do not provide copy-object semantics. Thus, 4.4BSD does not provide copy semantics by default; such semantics are provided only when they are requested explicitly. It is debatable

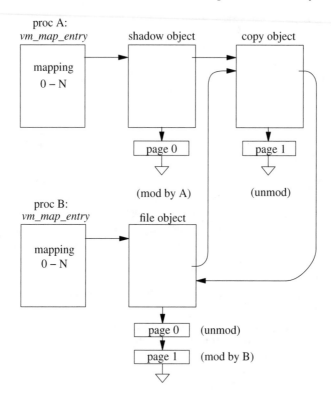

Figure 5.11 Use of a copy object.

whether the copy semantics are worth providing at all, because a process can obtain them trivially by reading the file in a single request into a buffer in the process address space. The added complexity and overhead of copy objects may well exceed the value of providing copy semantics in the *mmap* interface.

5.6   Creation of a New Process

Processes are created with a *fork* system call. The *fork* is usually followed shortly thereafter by an *exec* system call that overlays the virtual address space of the child process with the contents of an executable image that resides in the filesystem. The process then executes until it terminates by exiting, either voluntarily or involuntarily, by receiving a signal. In Sections 5.6 to 5.9, we trace the management of the memory resources used at each step in this cycle.

A *fork* system call duplicates the address space of an existing process, creating an identical child process. *Fork* is the only way that new processes are created in 4.4BSD (except for its variant, *vfork*, which is described in the last subsection of this section). *Fork* duplicates all the resources of the original process, and copies that process's address space.

The virtual-memory resources of the process that must be allocated for the child include the process structure and its associated substructures, and the user area that includes both the user structure and the kernel stack. In addition, the kernel must reserve storage (either memory, filesystem space, or swap space) used to back the process. The general outline of the implementation of a *fork* is as follows:

• Reserve virtual address space for the child process.

• Allocate a process entry for the child process, and fill it in.

• Copy to the child the parent's process group, credentials, file descriptors, limits, and signal actions.

• Allocate a new user area, copying the current one to initialize it.

• Allocate a *vmspace* structure.

• Duplicate the address space, by creating copies of the parent *vm_map_entry* structures marked copy-on-write.

• Arrange for the child process to return 0, to distinguish its return value from the new PID that is returned by the parent process.

The allocation and initialization of the process structure, and the arrangement of the return value, were covered in Chapter 4. The remainder of this section discusses the other steps involved in duplicating a process.

Reserving Kernel Resources

The first resource to be reserved when an address space is duplicated is the required virtual address space. To avoid running out of memory resources, the kernel must ensure that it does not promise to provide more virtual memory than it is able to deliver. The total virtual memory that can be provided by the system is limited to the amount of physical memory available for paging plus the amount of swap space that is provided. A few pages are held in reserve to stage I/O between the swap area and main memory.

The reason for this restriction is to ensure that processes get synchronous notification of memory limitations. Specifically, a process should get an error back from a system call (such as *sbrk*, *fork*, or *mmap*) if there are insufficient resources to allocate the needed virtual memory. If the kernel promises more virtual memory than it can support, it can deadlock trying to service a page fault. Trouble arises when it has no free pages to service the fault and no available swap space to save an active page. Here, the kernel has no choice but to send a segmentation-fault signal to the process unfortunate enough to be page faulting. Such asynchronous notification of insufficient memory resources is unacceptable.

Excluded from this limit are those parts of the address space that are mapped read-only, such as the program text. Any pages that are being used for a read-only part of the address space can be reclaimed for another use without being saved because their contents can be refilled from the original source. Also excluded from this limit are parts of the address space that map shared files. The kernel can reclaim any pages that are being used for a shared mapping after writing their contents back to the filesystem from which they are mapped. Here, the filesystem is being used as an extension of the swap area. Finally, any piece of memory that is used by more than one process (such as an area of anonymous memory being shared by several processes) needs to be counted only once toward the virtual-memory limit.

The limit on the amount of virtual address space that can be allocated causes problems for applications that want to allocate a large piece of address space, but want to use the piece only sparsely. For example, a process may wish to make a private mapping of a large database from which it will access only a small part. Because the kernel has no way to guarantee that the access will be sparse, it takes the pessimistic view that the entire file will be modified and denies the request. One extension that many BSD derived systems have made to the *mmap* system call is to add a flag that tells the kernel that the process is prepared to accept asynchronous faults in the mapping. Such a mapping would be permitted to use up to the amount of virtual memory that had not been promised to other processes. If the process then modifies more of the file than this available memory, or if the limit is reduced by other processes allocating promised memory, the kernel can then send a segmentation-fault signal to the process. On receiving the signal, the process must *munmap* an unneeded part of the file to release resources back to the system. The process must ensure that the code, stack, and data structures needed to handle the segment-fault signal do not reside in the part of the address space that is subject to such faults.

Tracking the outstanding virtual memory accurately is a complex task. The 4.4BSD system makes no effort to calculate the outstanding-memory load and can be made to promise more than it can deliver. When memory resources run out, it either picks a process to kill or simply hangs. An important future enhancement is to track the amount of virtual memory being used by the processes in the system.

Duplication of the User Address Space

The next step in *fork* is to allocate and initialize a new process structure. This operation must be done before the address space of the current process is duplicated because it records state in the process structure. From the time that the process structure is allocated until all the needed resources are allocated, the parent process is locked against swapping to avoid deadlock. The child is in an inconsistent state and cannot yet run or be swapped, so the parent is needed to complete the copy of its address space. To ensure that the child process is ignored by the scheduler, the kernel sets the process's state to SIDL during the entire fork procedure.

Historically, the *fork* system call operated by copying the entire address space of the parent process. When large processes fork, copying the entire user address space is expensive. All the pages that are on secondary storage must be read back into memory to be copied. If there is not enough free memory for both complete copies of the process, this memory shortage will cause the system to begin paging to create enough memory to do the copy (see Section 5.12). The copy operation may result in parts of the parent and child processes being paged out, as well as the paging out of parts of unrelated processes.

The technique used by 4.4BSD to create processes without this overhead is called *copy-on-write*. Rather than copy each page of a parent process, both the child and parent processes resulting from a fork are given references to the same physical pages. The page tables are changed to prevent either process from modifying a shared page. Instead, when a process attempts to modify a page, the kernel is entered with a protection fault. On discovering that the fault was caused by an attempt to modify a shared page, the kernel simply copies the page and changes the protection field for the page to allow modification once again. Only pages modified by one of the processes need to be copied. Because processes that fork typically overlay the child process with a new image with *exec* shortly thereafter, this technique significantly improves the performance of *fork*.

The next step in *fork* is to traverse the list of *vm_map_entry* structures in the parent and to create a corresponding entry in the child. Each entry must be analyzed and the appropriate action taken:

• If the entry maps a read-only region, the child can take a reference to it.

• If the entry maps a privately mapped region (such as the data area or stack), the child must create a copy-on-write mapping of the region. The parent must be converted to a copy-on-write mapping of the region. If either process later tries to write the region, it will create a shadow map to hold the modified pages.

• If the entry maps a shared region, a sharing map is created referencing the shared object, and both map entries are set to reference this map.

Map entries for a process are never merged (simplified). Only entries for the kernel map itself can be merged. The kernel-map entries need to be simplified so that excess growth is avoided. It might be worthwhile to do such a merge of the map entries for a process when it forks, especially for large or long-running processes.

With the virtual-memory resources allocated, the system sets up the kernel- and user-mode state of the new process, including the hardware memory-management registers and the user area. It then clears the SIDL flag and places the process on the run queue; the new process can then begin execution.

Creation of a New Process Without Copying

When a process (such as a shell) wishes to start another program, it will generally *fork*, do a few simple operations such as redirecting I/O descriptors and changing signal actions, and then start the new program with an *exec*. In the meantime, the parent shell suspends itself with *wait* until the new program completes. For such operations, it is not necessary for both parent and child to run simultaneously, and therefore only one copy of the address space is required. This frequently occurring set of system calls led to the implementation of the *vfork* system call. In

4.4BSD, the *vfork* system call still exists, but it is implemented using the same copy-on-write algorithm described in this section. Its only difference is that it ensures that the parent does not run until the child has done either an *exec* or an *exit*.

The historic implementation of *vfork* will always be more efficient than the copy-on-write implementation because the kernel avoids copying the address space for the child. Instead, the kernel simply *passes* the parent's address space to the child and suspends the parent. The child process needs to allocate only new process and user structures, receiving everything else from the parent. The child process returns from the *vfork* system call with the parent still suspended. The child does the usual activities in preparation for starting a new program, then calls *exec*. Now the address space is passed back to the parent process, rather than being abandoned, as in a normal *exec*. Alternatively, if the child process encounters an error and is unable to execute the new program, it will *exit*. Again, the address space is passed back to the parent, instead of being abandoned.

With *vfork*, the entries describing the address space do not need to be copied, and the page-table entries do not need to be marked and then cleared of copy-on-write. *Vfork* is likely to remain more efficient than copy-on-write or other schemes that must duplicate the process's virtual address space. The architectural quirk of the *vfork* call is that the child process may modify the contents and even the size of the parent's address space while the child has control. Modification of the parent's address space is bad programming practice. Some programs that took advantage of this quirk broke when they were ported to 4.4BSD, which implemented *vfork* using copy-on-write.

5.7   Execution of a File

The *exec* system call was described in Sections 2.4 and 3.1; it replaces the address space of a process with the contents of a new program obtained from an executable file. During an *exec*, the target executable image is validated, then the arguments and environment are copied from the current process image into a temporary area of pageable kernel virtual memory.

To do an *exec*, the system must allocate resources to hold the new contents of the virtual address space, set up the mapping for this address space to reference the new image, and release the resources being used for the existing virtual memory.

The first step is to reserve memory resources for the new executable image. The algorithm for the calculation of the amount of virtual address space that must be reserved was described in Section 5.6. For an executable that is not being debugged (and hence will not have its text space modified), a space reservation needs to be made for only the data and stack space of the new executable. *Exec* does this reservation without first releasing the currently assigned space, because the system must be able to continue running the old executable until it is sure that it will be able to run the new one. If the system released the current space and the memory reservation failed, the *exec* would be unable to return to the original process. Once the reservation is made, the address space and virtual-memory resources of the current process are then freed as though the process were exiting; this mechanism is described in Section 5.9.

Now, the process has only a user structure and kernel stack. The kernel now allocates a new *vmspace* structure and creates the list of four *vm_map_entry* structures:

1. A copy-on-write, fill-from-file entry maps the text segment. A copy-on-write mapping is used, rather than a read-only one, to allow active text segments to have debugging breakpoints set without affecting other users of the binary. In 4.4BSD, some legacy code in the kernel debugging interface disallows the setting of break points in binaries being used by more than one process. This legacy code prevents the use of the copy-on-write feature.

2. A private (copy-on-write), fill-from-file entry maps the initialized data segment.

3. An anonymous zero-fill-on-demand entry maps the uninitialized data segment.

4. An anonymous zero-fill-on-demand entry maps the stack segment.

No further operations are needed to create a new address space during an *exec* system call; the remainder of the work comprises copying the arguments and environment out to the top of the new stack. Initial values are set for the registers: The program counter is set to the entry point, and the stack pointer is set to point to the argument vector. The new process image is then ready to run.

5.8   Process Manipulation of Its Address Space

Once a process begins execution, it has several ways to manipulate its address space. The system has always allowed processes to expand their uninitialized data area (usually done with the *malloc*() library routine). The stack is grown on an as-needed basis. The 4.4BSD system also allows a process to map files and devices into arbitrary parts of its address space, and to change the protection of various parts of its address space, as described in Section 5.5. This section describes how these address-space manipulations are done.

Change of Process Size

A process can change its size during execution by explicitly requesting more data space with the *sbrk* system call. Also, the stack segment will be expanded automatically if a protection fault is encountered because of an attempt to grow the stack below the end of the stack region. In either case, the size of the process address space must be changed. The size of the request is always rounded up to a multiple of page size. New pages are marked fill-with-zeros, as there are no contents initially associated with new sections of the address space.

The first step of enlarging a process's size is to check whether the new size would violate the size limit for the process segment involved. If the new size is in range, the following steps are taken to enlarge the data area:

1. Verify that the virtual-memory resources are available.

2. Verify that the address space of the requested size immediately following the current end of the data area is not already mapped.

3. If the existing *vm_map_entry* is not constrained to be a fixed size because of the allocation of swap space, increment its ending address by the requested size. If the entry has had one or more of its pages written to swap space, then the current implementation of the swap pager will not permit it to grow. Consequently, a new *vm_map_entry* must be created with a starting address immediately following the end of the previous fixed-sized entry. Its ending address is calculated to give it the size of the request. Until a pageout forces the allocation of a fixed-sized swap partition of this new entry, the latter will be able to continue growing.

If the change is to reduce the size of the data segment, the operation is easy: Any memory allocated to the pages that will no longer be part of the address space is freed. The ending address of the *vm_map_entry* is reduced by the size. If the requested size reduction is bigger than the range defined by the *vm_map_entry*, the entire entry is freed, and the remaining reduction is applied to the *vm_map_entry* that precedes it. This algorithm is applied until the entire reduction has been made. Future references to these addresses will result in protection faults, as access is disallowed when the address range has been deallocated.

The allocation of the stack segment is considerably different. At *exec* time, the stack is allocated at its maximum possible size. Due to the *lazy* allocation of virtual-memory resources, this operation involves allocating only sufficient address space. Physical memory and swap space are allocated on demand as the stack grows. Hence, only step 3 of the data-growth algorithm applies to stack-growth–related page faults. An additional step is required to check that the desired growth does not exceed the dynamically changeable stack-size limit.

File Mapping

The *mmap* system call requests that a file be mapped into an address space. The system call may request either that the mapping be done at a particular address or that the kernel to pick an unused area. If the request is for a particular address range, the kernel first checks to see whether that part of the address space is already in use. If it is in use, the kernel first does an *munmap* of the existing mapping, then proceeds with the new mapping.

The kernel implements the *munmap* system call by traversing the list of *vm_map_entry* structures for the process. The various overlap conditions to consider are shown in Fig. 5.12. The five cases are as follows:

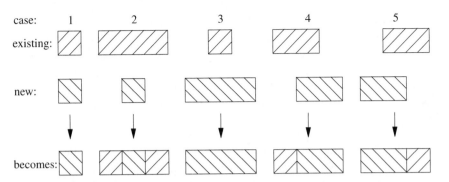

Figure 5.12 Five types of overlap that the kernel must consider when adding a new address mapping.

1. The new mapping exactly overlaps an existing mapping. The old mapping is deallocated as described in Section 5.9. The new mapping is created in its place as described in the paragraph following this list.

2. The new mapping is a subset of the existing mapping. The existing mapping is split into three pieces (two pieces if the new mapping begins at the beginning or ends at the end of the existing mapping). The existing *vm_map_entry* structure is augmented with one or two additional *vm_map_entry* structures: one mapping the remaining part of the existing mapping before the new mapping, and one mapping the remaining part of the existing mapping following the new mapping. Its overlapped piece is replaced by the new mapping, as described in the paragraph following this list.

3. The new mapping is a superset of an existing mapping. The old mapping is deallocated as described in Section 5.9, and a new mapping is created as described in the paragraph following this list.

4. The new mapping starts part way into and extends past the end of an existing mapping. The existing mapping has its length reduced by the size of the unmapped area. Its overlapped piece is replaced by the new mapping, as described in the paragraph following this list.

5. The new mapping extends into the beginning of an existing mapping. The existing mapping has its starting address incremented and its length reduced by the size of the covered area. Its overlapped piece is replaced by the new mapping, as described in the paragraph following this list.

In addition to the five basic types of overlap listed, a new mapping request may span several existing mappings. Specifically, a new request may be composed of zero or one of type 4, zero to many of type 3, and zero or one of type 5. When a mapping is shortened, any shadow or copy pages associated with it are released, as they are no longer needed.

Once the address space is zero filled, the kernel creates a new *vm_map_entry* to describe the new address range. If the object being mapped is already being mapped by another process, the new entry gets a reference to the existing object. This reference is obtained in the same way, as described in Section 5.6, when a new process is being created and needs to map each of the regions in its parent. If this request is the first mapping of an object, then the kernel checks the object cache to see whether a previous instance of the object still exists. If one does, then that object is activated and referenced by the new *vm_map_entry*.

If the object is not found, then a new object must be created. First, a new object is allocated. Next, the kernel must determine what is being mapped, so that it can associate the correct pager with the object (pagers are described in Section 5.10). Once the object and its pager have been set up, the new *vm_map_entry* can be set to reference the object.

Change of Protection

A process may change the protections associated with a region of its virtual memory by using the *mprotect* system call. The size of the region to be protected may be as small as a single page. Because the kernel depends on the hardware to enforce the access permissions, the granularity of the protection is limited by the underlying hardware. A region may be set for any combination of read, write, and execute permissions. Many architectures do not distinguish between read and execute permissions; on such architectures, the execute permission is treated as read permission.

The kernel implements the *mprotect* system call by finding the existing *vm_map_entry* structure or structures that cover the region specified by the call. If the existing permissions are the same as the request, then no further action is required. Otherwise, the new permissions are compared to the maximum protection value associated with the *vm_map_entry*. The maximum value is set at *mmap* time and reflects the maximum value allowed by the underlying file. If the new permissions are valid, one or more new *vm_map_entry* structures have to be set up to describe the new protections. The set of overlap conditions that must be handled is similar to that described in the previous subsection. Instead of replacing the object underlying the new *vm_map_entry* structures, these *vm_map_entry* structures still reference the same object; the difference is that they grant different access permissions to it.

5.9   Termination of a Process

The final change in process state that relates to the operation of the virtual-memory system is *exit*; this system call terminates a process, as described in Chapter 4. The part of *exit* that is discussed here is the release of the virtual-memory resources of the process. The release is done in two steps:

1. The user portions of the address space are freed, both in memory and on swap space.

2. The user area is freed.

These two operations are complicated because the kernel stack in the user area must be used until the process relinquishes the processor for the final time.

The first step—freeing the user address space—is identical to the one that occurs during *exec* to free the old address space. The free operation proceeds entry by entry through the list of *vm_map_entry* structures associated with the address space. The first step in freeing an entry is to traverse the latter's list of shadow and copy objects. If the entry is the last reference to a shadow or copy object, then any memory or swap space that is associated with the object can be freed. In addition, the machine-dependent routines are called to unmap and free up any page table or data structures that are associated with the object. If the shadow or copy object is still referenced by other *vm_map_entry* structures, its resources cannot be freed, but the kernel still needs to call the machine-dependent routines to unmap and free the resources associated with the current process mapping. Finally, if the underlying object referenced by the *vm_map_entry* is losing its last reference, then that object is a candidate for deallocation. If it is an object that will never have any chance of a future reuse (such as an anonymous object associated with a stack or uninitialized data area), then its resources are freed as though it were a shadow or copy object. However, if the object maps a file (such as an executable) that might be used again soon, the object is saved in the object cache, where it can be found by newly executing processes or by processes mapping in a file. The number of unreferenced cached objects is limited to a threshold set by the system (typically 100). If adding this new object would cause the cache to grow beyond its limit, the least recently used object in the cache is removed and deallocated.

Next, the memory used by the user area must be freed. This operation begins the problematic time when the process must free resources that it has not yet finished using. It would be disastrous if a page from the user structure or kernel stack were reallocated and reused before the process had finished the *exit*(). Memory is allocated either synchronously by the page-fault handler or asynchronously from interrupt handlers that use *malloc*(), such as the network when packets arrive (see Chapter 12). To block any allocation of memory, it is necessary to delay interrupts by raising the processor interrupt-priority level. The process may then free the pages of its user area, safe from having them reused until it has relinquished the processor. The next context switch will lower the priority so that interrupts may resume.

With all its resources free, the exiting process finishes detaching itself from its process group, and notifies its parent that it is done. The process has now become a zombie process—one with no resources, not even a kernel stack. Its parent will collect its exit status with a *wait* call, and will free its process structure.

There is nothing for the virtual-memory system to do when *wait* is called: All virtual-memory resources of a process are removed when *exit* is done. On *wait*, the system just returns the process status to the caller, and deallocates the process-table entry and the small amount of space in which the resource-usage information was kept.

5.10 The Pager Interface

The *pager interface* provides the mechanism by which data are moved between backing store and physical memory. The 4.4BSD pager interface is a modification of the interface present in Mach 2.0. The interface is page based, with all data requests made in multiples of the software page size. *Vm_page* structures are passed around as descriptors providing the backing-store offset and physical cache-page address of the desired data. This interface should not be confused with the current Mach 3.0 *external* paging interface [Young, 1989], where pagers are typically user applications outside the kernel and are invoked via asynchronous remote procedure calls using the Mach interprocess-communication mechanism. The 4.4BSD interface is *internal* in the sense that the pagers are compiled into the kernel and pager routines are invoked via simple function calls.

Associated with each object is a *pager_struct* structure representing an instance of the pager type responsible for supplying the contents of pages within the object. This structure contains pointers to type-specific routines for reading and writing data, as well as a pointer to instance-specific storage. Conceptually, the *pager_struct* structure describes a logically contiguous piece of backing store, such as a chunk of swap space or a disk file. A *pager_struct* and any associated instance-specific data are collectively known as a *pager instance* in the following discussion.

A pager instance is typically created at the same time as the object when a file, device, or piece of anonymous memory is mapped into a process address space. The pager instance continues to exist until the object is deallocated. When a page fault occurs for a virtual address mapping a particular object, the fault-handling code allocates a *vm_page* structure and converts the faulting address to an offset within the object. This offset is recorded in the *vm_page* structure, and the page is added to the list of pages cached by the object. The page frame and the object's pager instance are then passed to the underlying pager routine. The pager routine is responsible for filling the *vm_page* structure with the appropriate initial value for that offset of the object that it represents.

The pager instance is also responsible for saving the contents of a dirty page if the system decides to push out the latter to backing store. When the pageout daemon decides that a particular page is no longer needed, it requests the object that owns the page to free the page. The object first passes the page with the associated logical offset to the underlying pager instance, to be saved for future use. The pager instance is responsible for finding an appropriate place to save the page, doing any I/O necessary for the save, and then notifying the object that the page can be freed. When it is done, the pager instance notifies the pageout daemon to move the *vm_page* structure from the object to the free list for future use.

There are seven routines associated with each pager type. The *pgo_init* routine is called at boot time to do any one-time type-specific initializations, such as allocating a pool of private pager structures. The *pgo_alloc* and *pgo_dealloc* routines are called when an instance of a pager should be created or destroyed. The allocation routine is called whenever the corresponding object is mapped into an address space via *mmap*. Hence, only the first call should create the structure; successive calls just increment the reference count for the associated object and return a pointer to the existing pager instance. The deallocation routine is called only when the object reference count drops to zero.

Pgo_getpages is called to return one or more pages of data from a pager instance either synchronously or asynchronously. Currently, this routine is called from only the page-fault handler to synchronously fill single pages. *Pgo_putpages* writes back one or more pages of data. This routine is called by the pageout daemon to write back one or more pages asynchronously, and by *msync* to write back single pages synchronously or asynchronously. Both the get and put routines are called with an array of *vm_page* structures indicating the affected pages.

Pgo_cluster takes an offset and returns an enclosing offset range representing an optimal I/O transfer unit for the backing store. This range can be used with *pgo_getpages* and *pgo_putpages* to help do informed prefetching or clustered cleaning. Currently, it is used by only the pageout daemon for the latter task. The *pgo_haspage* routine queries a pager instance to see whether that instance has data at a particular backing-store offset. This routine is used in only the page-fault handler, to determine whether an internal copy object already has received a copy of a particular page.

The three types of pagers supported by the system are described in the next three subsections.

Vnode Pager

The *vnode pager* handles objects that map files in a filesystem. Whenever a file is mapped either explicitly by *mmap* or implicitly by *exec*, the vnode-pager allocation routine is called. If the call represents the first mapping of the vnode, the necessary vnode-pager–specific structure is created, and an object of the appropriate size is allocated and is associated with the pager instance. The vnode-pager structure contains a pointer to the vnode and a copy of the latter's current size. The vnode reference count is incremented to reflect the pager reference. If this initialization call is not the first for a vnode, the existing pager structure is located. In either case, the associated object's reference count is incremented, and a pointer to the pager instance is returned.

When a pagein request is received by the vnode-pager read routine, the provided physical page is mapped into the kernel address space long enough for the pager instance to call the filesystem VOP_READ vnode operation to load the page with the file contents. Once the page is filled, the kernel mapping can be dropped, and the page can be returned.

When the vnode pager is asked to save a page to be freed, it simply arranges to write back the page to the part of the file from which the page came. The page is mapped into the kernel address space long enough for the pager routine to call the filesystem VOP_WRITE vnode operation to store the page back into the file. Once the page is stored, the kernel mapping can be dropped, and the object can be notified that the page can be freed.

If a file is being privately mapped, then modified pages cannot be written back to the filesystem. Such private mapping must use a shadow object with a swap pager for all pages that are modified. Thus, a privately mapped object will never be asked to save any dirty pages to the underlying file.

When the last address-space mapping of a vnode is removed by *munmap* or *exit*, the vnode-pager deallocation routine is called. This routine releases the vnode reference and frees the vnode-pager structure.

The vnode-pager I/O routines use the VOP_READ and VOP_WRITE vnode operations that pass data through any caches maintained by filesystems (e.g., the buffer cache used by UFS and NFS). The problem with this approach is that the virtual-memory system maintains a cache of file pages that is independent of the filesystem caches, resulting in potential double caching of file data. This condition leads to inefficient cache use, and worse, to the potential for inconsistencies between the two caches. Modifications to files that are mapped into memory are not seen by processes that read those files until the mapped file is written back to the filesystem and reread into the filesystem cache. Similarly, changes to files written to the filesystem are not visible to processes that map those files until the file is written back to disk and then page faulted into the process. The writeback and rereading may take seconds to hours, depending on the level of memory activity.

In 4.4BSD, this problem is addressed in an ad hoc and incomplete fashion. Two vnode-pager–specific routines are called from various points in the VFS code. *Vnode_pager_setsize*( ) is invoked when a file changes size. If the file has shrunk, any excess cached pages are removed from the object. This page removal guarantees that future mapped references to those pages will cause page faults, and in turn, will generate a signal to the mapping process. *Vnode_pager_uncache*( ) removes the object representing a vnode from the object cache. Recall that the object cache contains only objects that are not currently referenced; thus, this routine will not help to maintain consistency for an object that is currently mapped.

A more consistent interface can be obtained by using a common cache for both the virtual-memory system and the filesystem. Three approaches to merging the two caches are being undertaken. One approach is to have the filesystem use objects in the virtual-memory system as its cache; a second approach is to have the virtual-memory objects that map files use the existing filesystem cache; the third approach is to create a new cache that is a merger of the two existing caches, and to convert both the virtual memory and the filesystems to use this new cache. Each of these approaches has its merits and drawbacks; it is not yet clear which approach will work best.

Device Pager

The device pager handles objects representing memory-mapped hardware devices. Memory-mapped devices provide an interface that looks like a piece of memory. An example of a memory-mapped device is a frame buffer, which presents a range of memory addresses with one word per pixel on the screen. The kernel provides access to memory-mapped devices by mapping the device memory into a process's address space. The process can then access that memory without further operating-system intervention. Writing to a word of the frame-buffer memory causes the corresponding pixel to take on the appropriate color and brightness.

The device pager is fundamentally different from the other two pagers in that it does not fill provided physical-memory pages with data. Instead, it creates and manages its own *vm_page* structures, each of which describes a page of the device space. This approach makes device memory look like wired physical memory. Thus, no special code should be needed in the remainder of the virtual-memory system to handle device memory.

When a device is first mapped, the device-pager allocation routine will validate the desired range by calling the device *d_mmap*() routine. If the device allows the requested access for all pages in the range, the device pager creates a device-pager structure and associated object. It does not create *vm_page* structures at this time—they are created individually by the page-get routine as they are referenced. The reason for this late allocation is that some devices export a large memory range in which either not all pages are valid or the pages may not be accessed for common operations. Complete allocation of *vm_page* structures for these sparsely accessed devices would be wasteful.

The first access to a device page will cause a page fault and will invoke the device-pager page-get routine. The pager instance creates a *vm_page* structure, initializes the latter with the appropriate object offset and a physical address returned by the device *d_mmap*() routine, and flags the page as fictitious. This *vm_page* structure is added to the list of all such allocated pages in the device-pager structure. Since the fault code has no special knowledge of the device pager, it has preallocated a physical-memory page to fill and has associated that *vm_page* structure with the object. The device-pager routine removes that *vm_page* structure from the object, returns the structure to the free list, and inserts its own *vm_page* structure in the same place.

The device-pager page-put routine expects never to be called and will panic if it is. This behavior is based on the assumption that device-pager pages are never entered into any of the paging queues and hence will never be seen by the pageout daemon. However, it is possible to *msync* a range of device memory. This operation brings up an exception to the higher-level virtual-memory system's ignorance of device memory: The object page-cleaning routine will skip pages that are flagged as fictitious.

Finally, when a device is unmapped, the device-pager deallocation routine is invoked. This routine deallocates the *vm_page* structures that it allocated, as well as the device-pager structure itself.

Swap Pager

The term *swap pager* refers to two functionally different pagers. In the most common use, *swap pager* refers to the pager that is used by objects that map anonymous memory. This pager has sometimes been referred to as the *default pager* because it is the pager that is used if no other pager has been requested. It provides what is commonly known as *swap space*: nonpersistent backing store that is zero filled on first reference. The zero filling is really done by the fault-handling code, without ever invoking the swap pager. Because of the zero-filling optimization and the transient nature of the backing store, allocation of swap-pager resources for a particular object may be delayed until the first pageout operation. Until that time, the pager-structure pointer in the object is NULL. While the object is in this state, page faults (getpage) are handled by zero filling, and page queries (haspage) are not necessary. The expectation is that free memory will be plentiful enough that it will not be necessary to swap out any pages. The object will simply create zero-filled pages during the process lifetime that can all be returned to the free list when the process exits.

The role of the swap pager is swap-space management: figuring out where to store dirty pages and how to find dirty pages when they are needed again. Shadow objects require that these operations be efficient. A typical shadow object is sparsely populated: It may cover a large range of pages, but only those pages that have been modified will be in the shadow object's backing store. In addition, long chains of shadow objects may require numerous pager queries to locate the correct copy of an object page to satisfy a page fault. Hence, determining whether a pager instance contains a particular page needs to be fast, preferably requiring no I/O operations. A final requirement of the swap pager is that it can do asynchronous writeback of dirty pages. This requirement is necessitated by the pageout daemon, which is a single-threaded process. If the pageout daemon blocked waiting for a page-clean operation to complete before starting the next operation, it is unlikely that it could keep enough memory free in times of heavy memory demand.

In theory, any pager that meets these criteria can be used as the swap pager. In Mach 2.0, the vnode pager was used as the swap pager. Special paging files could be created in any filesystem and registered with the kernel. The swap pager would then suballocate pieces of the files to back particular anonymous objects. Asynchronous writes were a side effect of the filesystem's use of the buffer cache. One obvious advantage of using the vnode pager is that swap space can be expanded by the addition of more swap files or the extension of existing ones dynamically (i.e., without rebooting or reconfiguring of the kernel). The main disadvantage is that, in the past, the filesystem has not been able to deliver a respectable fraction of the disk bandwidth.

The desire to provide the highest possible disk bandwidth led to the creation of a special *raw-partition pager* to use as the swap pager for 4.4BSD. Previous versions of BSD also used dedicated disk partitions, commonly known as *swap partitions*; hence, this partition pager became the *swap pager*. The remainder of this section describes how the partition pager is implemented, and how it provides the necessary capabilities for backing anonymous objects.

As mentioned, a swap-pager instance will not be created until the first time that a page from the object is replaced in memory. At that time, a structure is allocated to describe the swap space that can hold the object. This swap space is described by an array of fixed-sized swap blocks. The size of each swap block is selected based on the size of the object that the swap pager is managing. For a small object, a minimal-sized (32-Kbyte) swap block will be used; for a large object, each swap block may be as large as $32 \times pagesize$. For a machine such as the HP300 with a pagesize of 4 Kbyte, the maximum swap-block size will be 128 Kbyte. A swap block is always an integral number of virtual-memory pages, because those are the units used in the pager interface.

The two structures created by the swap pager are shown in Fig. 5.13. The *swpager* structure describes the swap area being managed by the pager. It records the total size of the object (object size), the size of each swap block being managed (block size), and the number of swap blocks that make up the swap area for the object (block count). It also has a pointer to an array of block-count *swblock* structures, each containing a device block number and a bit mask. The block number gives the address of the first device block in a contiguous chunk of block-size DEV_BSIZE–sized blocks that form the swap block, or is zero if a swap block has never been allocated. A mask of 1 bit per page-sized piece within this swap block records which pages in the block contain valid data. A bit is set when the corresponding page is first written to the swap area. Together, the *swblock* array and associated bit masks provide a two-level page table describing the backing store of an object. This structure provides efficient swap-space allocation for sparsely populated objects, since a given swap block does not need to be allocated until the first time that a page in its block-size range is written back. The structure also allows efficient page lookup: at most an array-indexing operation and a bit-mask operation.

The size of the object is frozen at the time of allocation. Thus, if the anonymous area continues to grow (such as the stack or heap of a process), a new object must be created to describe the expanded area. On a system that is short of memory, the result is that a large process may acquire many anonymous objects. Changing the swap pager to handle growing objects would cut down on this object proliferation dramatically.

Figure 5.13 Structures used to manage swap space.

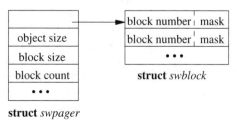

struct *swpager*   struct *swblock*

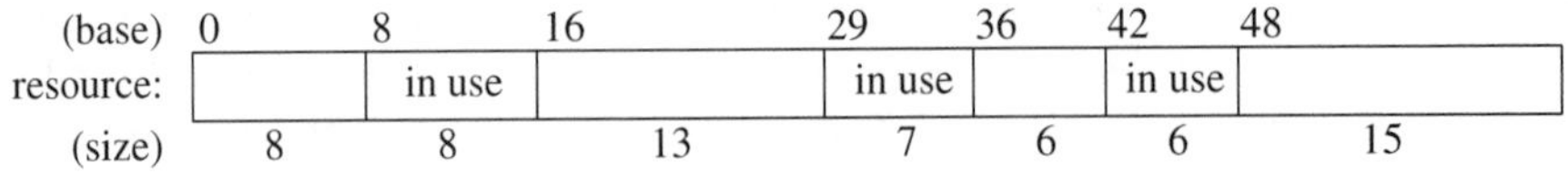

(base)	0		8		16		29		36	42		48	
resource:			in use				in use			in use			
(size)		8		8		13		7		6		6		15

resource map: <0,8>, <16,13>, <36,6>, <48,15>

Figure 5.14 A kernel resource map.

Allocation of swap blocks from the system's pool of swap space is managed with a *resource map* called *swapmap*. Resource maps are ordered arrays of <base, size> pairs describing the free segments of a resource (see Fig. 5.14). A segment of a given size is allocated from a resource map by *rmalloc()*, using a first-fit algorithm, and is subsequently freed with *rmfree()*. The swapmap is initialized at boot time to contain all the available swap space. An index into the swapmap at which space has been allocated is used as the index of the disk address within the swap area.

The swap pager is complicated considerably by the requirement that it handle asynchronous writes from the pageout daemon. The protocol for managing these writes is described in Section 5.12.

5.11 Paging

When the memory-management hardware detects an invalid virtual address, it generates a trap to the system. This page-fault trap can occur for several reasons. Most BSD programs are created in a format that permits the executable image to be paged into main memory directly from the filesystem. When a program in a demand-paged format is first run, the kernel marks as invalid the pages for the text and initialized data regions of the executing process. The text and initialized data regions share an object that provides fill-on-demand from the filesystem. As each page of the text or initialized data region is first referenced, a page fault occurs.

Page faults can also occur when a process first references a page in the uninitialized data region of a program. Here, the anonymous object managing the region automatically allocates memory to the process and initializes the newly assigned page to zero. Other types of page faults arise when previously resident pages have been reclaimed by the system in response to a memory shortage.

The handling of page faults is done with the *vm_fault()* routine; this routine services all page faults. Each time *vm_fault()* is invoked, it is provided the virtual address that caused the fault. The first action of *vm_fault()* is to traverse the *vm_map_entry* list of the faulting process to find the entry associated with the fault. The routine then computes the logical page within the underlying object and traverses the list of objects to find or create the needed page. Once the page has been found, *vm_fault()* must call the machine-dependent layer to validate the faulted page, and return to restart the process.

The details of calculating the address within the object were described in Section 5.4. Having computed the offset within the object and determined the object's protection and object list from the *vm_map_entry*, the kernel is ready to find or create the associated page. The page-fault–handling algorithm is shown in Fig 5.15 (on pages 164 and 165). In the following overview, the lettered points are references to the tags down the left side of the code.

A. The loop traverses the list of shadow, copy, anonymous, and file objects until it either finds an object that holds the sought-after page, or reaches the final object in the list. If no page is found, the final object will be requested to produce it.

B. An object with the desired page has been found. If the page is busy, another process may be in the middle of faulting it in, so this process is blocked until the page is no longer busy. Since many things could have happened to the affected object while the process was blocked, it must restart the entire fault-handling algorithm. If the page was not busy, the algorithm exits the loop with the page.

C. Anonymous objects (such as those used to represent shadow and copy objects) do not allocate a pager until the first time that they need to push a page to backing store. Thus, if an object has a pager, then there is a chance that the page previously existed but was paged out. If the object does have a pager, then the kernel needs to allocate a page to give to the pager to be filled (see D). The special case for the object being the first object is to avoid a race condition with two processes trying to get the same page. The first process through will create the sought after page in the first object, but keep it marked as busy. When the second process tries to fault the same page it will find the page created by the first process and block on it (see B). When the first process completes the pagein processing, it will unlock the first page, causing the second process to awaken, retry the fault, and find the page created by the first process.

D. If the page is present in the file or swap area, the pager will bring it back into the newly allocated page. If the pagein succeeds, then the sought after page has been found. If the page never existed, then the pagein request will fail. Unless this object is the first, the page is freed and the search continues. If this object is the first, the page is not freed, so that it will act as a block to further searches by other processes (as described in C).

E. If the kernel created a page in the first object but did not use that page, it will have to remember that page so that it can free the page when the pagein is done (see M).

F. If the search has reached the end of the object list and has not found the page, then the fault is on an anonymous object chain, and the first object in the list will handle the page fault using the page allocated in C. The first_page entry is set to NULL to show that it does not need to be freed, the page is zero filled, and the loop is exited.

```
/* Handle a page fault occurring at the given address,
 * requiring the given permissions, in the map specified.
 * If successful, insert the page into the associated
 * physical map. */
vm_fault(map, addr, type)
{
RetryFault:
    lookup address in map returning object/offset/prot;
    first_object = object;
[A] for (;;) {
        page = lookup page at object/offset;
[B]     if (page found) {
            if (page busy)
                block and goto RetryFault;
            remove from paging queues;
            mark page as busy;
            break;
        }
[C]     if (object has pager or object == first_object) {
            page = allocate a page for object/offset;
            if (no pages available)
                block and goto RetryFault;
        }
[D]     if (object has pager) {
            call pager to fill page;
            if (IO error)
                return an error;
            if (pager has page)
                break;
            if (object != first_object)
                free page;
        }
        /* no pager, or pager does not have page */
[E]     if (object == first_object)
            first_page = page;
        next_object = next object;
[F]     if (no next object) {
            if (object != first_object) {
                object = first_object;
                page = first_page;
            }
            first_page = NULL;
            zero fill page;
            break;
        }
        object = next_object;
    }
[G] /* appropriate page has been found or allocated */
    orig_page = page;
```

Figure 5.15 Page-fault handling.

```
[H] if (object != first_object) {
        if (fault type == WRITE) {
            copy page to first_page;
            deactivate page;
            page = first_page;
            object = first_object;
        } else {
            prot &= ~WRITE;
            mark page copy-on-write;
            first_page = NULL;
        }
    }
    if (first_object has copy object) {
[I]     if (fault type != WRITE) {
            prot &= ~WRITE;
            mark page copy-on-write;
        } else {
            copy_object = first_object copy object;
            lookup page in copy_object;
[J]         if (page exists) {
                if (page busy)
                    block and goto RetryFault;
            } else {
[K]             allocate a blank page;
                if (no pages available)
                    block and goto RetryFault;
                if (copy_object has pager) {
                    call pager to see if page exists;
                    if (page exists)
                        free blank page;
                }
                if (page doesn't exist) {
                    copy page to copy_object page;
                    remove orig_page from pmaps;
                    activate copy page;
                }
            }
            mark page not copy-on-write;
        }
    }
[L] if (prot & WRITE)
        mark page not copy-on-write;
    enter mapping for page;
[M] activate and unbusy page;
    if (first_page != NULL)
        unbusy and free first_page;
}
```

Figure 5.15 Page-fault handling (continued).

G. The search exits the loop with `page` as the page that has been found or allocated and initialized, and `object` as the owner of that page. The page has been filled with the correct data at this point.

H. If the object providing the page is not the first object, then this mapping must be private, with the first object being a shadow object of the object providing the page. If pagein is handling a write fault, then the contents of the page that it has found have to be copied to the page that it allocated for the first object. Having made the copy, it can release the object and page from which the copy came, as the first object and first page will be used to finish the page-fault service. If pagein is handling a read fault, it can use the page that it found, but it has to mark the page copy-on-write to avoid the page being modified in the future.

I. Pagein is handling a read fault. It can use the page that it found, but has to mark the page copy-on-write to avoid the page being modified before pagein has had a chance to copy the page for the copy object.

J. If the copy object already has a copy of the page in memory, then pagein does not have to worry about saving the one that it just created.

K. If there is no page in memory, the copy object may still have a copy in its backing store. If the copy object has a pager, the *vm_pager_has_page*() routine is called to find out if the copy object still has a copy of the page in its backing store. This routine does not return any data; the blank page is allocated to avoid a race with other faults. Otherwise, the page does not exist, so pagein must copy the page that it found to the page owned by the copy object. After doing this copying, pagein has to remove all existing mappings for the page from which it copied, so that future attempts to access that page will fault and find the page that pagein left in the copy object.

L. If pagein is handling a write fault, then it has made any copies that were necessary, so it can safely make the page writable.

M. As the page and possibly the first_page are released, any processes waiting for that page of the object will get a chance to run to get their own references.

Note that the page and object locking has been elided in Fig. 5.15 to simplify the explanation. In 4.4BSD, no clustering is done on pagein; only the requested page is brought in from the backing store.

5.12 Page Replacement

The service of page faults and other demands for memory may be satisfied from the free list for some time, but eventually memory must be reclaimed for reuse. Some pages are reclaimed when processes exit. On systems with a large amount of memory and low memory demand, exiting processes may provide enough free memory to fill demand. This case arises when there is enough memory for the kernel and for all pages that have ever been used by any current process. Obviously, many computers do not have enough main memory to retain all pages in memory. Thus, it eventually becomes necessary to move some pages to secondary storage—to the swap space. Bringing in a page is demand driven. For paging it out, however, there is no immediate indication when a page is no longer needed by a process. The kernel must implement some strategy for deciding which pages to move out of memory so that it can replace these pages with the ones that are currently needed in memory. Ideally, the strategy will choose pages for replacement that will not be needed soon. An approximation to this strategy is to find pages that have not been used recently.

The system implements demand paging with a page-replacement algorithm that approximates global least-recently used [Corbato, 1968; Easton & Franaszek, 1979]. It is an example of a *global replacement algorithm*: one in which the choice of a page for replacement is made according to system wide criteria. A *local replacement algorithm* would choose a process for which to replace a page, and then chose a page based on per-process criteria. Although the algorithm in 4.4BSD is similar in nature to that in 4.3BSD, its implementation is considerably different.

The kernel scans physical memory on a regular basis, considering pages for replacement. The use of a systemwide list of pages forces all processes to compete for memory on an equal basis. Note that it is also consistent with the way that 4.4BSD treats other resources provided by the system. A common alternative to allowing all processes to compete equally for memory is to partition memory into multiple independent areas, each localized to a collection of processes that compete with one another for memory. This scheme is used, for example, by the VMS operating system [Kenah & Bate, 1984]. With this scheme, system administrators can guarantee that a process, or collection of processes, will always have a minimal percentage of memory. Unfortunately, this scheme can be difficult to administer. Allocating too small a number of pages to a partition can result in underutilization of memory and excessive I/O activity to secondary-storage devices, whereas setting the number too high can result in excessive swapping [Lazowska & Kelsey, 1978].

The kernel divides the main memory into four lists:

1. *Wired*: Wired pages are locked in memory and cannot be paged out. Typically, these pages are being used by the kernel or have been locked down with *mlock*. In addition, all the pages being used to hold the user areas of loaded (i.e., not swapped-out) processes are also wired. Wired pages cannot be paged out.

2. *Active*: Active pages are being used by one or more regions of virtual memory. Although the kernel can page them out, doing so is likely to cause an active process to fault them back again.

3. *Inactive*: Inactive pages have contents that are still known, but they are not usually part of any active region. If the system becomes short of memory, the

pageout daemon may try to move active pages to the inactive list in the hopes of finding pages that are not really in use. The selection criteria that are used by the pageout daemon to select pages to move from the active list to the inactive list are described later in this section. When the free-memory list drops too low, the pageout daemon traverses the inactive list to create more free pages.

4. *Free*: Free pages have no useful contents, and will be used to fulfill new page-fault requests.

The pages of main memory that can be used by user processes are those on the active, inactive, and free lists.

Ideally, the kernel would maintain a working set for each process in the system. It would then know how much memory to provide to each process to minimize the latter's page-fault behavior. The 4.4BSD virtual-memory system does not use the working-set model because it lacks accurate information about the reference pattern of a process. It does track the number of pages held by a process via the *resident-set size*, but it does not know which of the resident pages constitute the working set. In 4.3BSD, the count of resident pages was used in making decisions on whether there was enough memory for a process to be swapped in when that process wanted to run. This feature was not carried over to the 4.4BSD virtual-memory system. Because it worked well during periods of high memory demand, this feature should be incorporated in future 4.4BSD systems.

Paging Parameters

The memory-allocation needs of processes compete constantly, through the page-fault handler, with the overall system goal of maintaining a minimum threshold of pages in the free list. As the system operates, it monitors main-memory utilization, and attempts to run the pageout daemon frequently enough to keep the amount of free memory at or above the minimum threshold. When the page-allocation routine, *vm_page_alloc*(), determines that more memory is needed, it awakens the pageout daemon.

The work of the pageout daemon is controlled by several parameters that are calculated during system startup. These parameters are fine tuned by the pageout daemon as it runs based on the memory available for processes to use. In general, the goal of this policy is to maintain free memory at, or above, a minimum threshold. The pageout daemon implements this policy by reclaiming pages for the free list. The number of pages to be reclaimed by the pageout daemon is a function of the memory needs of the system. As more memory is needed by the system, more pages are scanned. This scanning causes the number of pages freed to increase.

The pageout daemon determines the memory needed by comparing the number of free memory pages against several parameters. The first parameter, *free_target*, specifies a threshold (in pages) for stopping the pageout daemon. When available memory is above this threshold, no pages will be paged out by the pageout daemon. *Free_target* is normally 7 percent of user memory. The other interesting limit specifies the minimum free memory considered tolerable, *free_min*; this limit is normally 5 percent of user memory. If the amount of free memory goes below *free_min*, the pageout daemon is started. The desired size of the list of inactive pages is kept in *inactive_target*; this limit is normally 33 percent of available user memory. The size of this threshold changes over time as more or less of the system memory is wired down by the kernel. If the number of inactive pages goes below *inactive_target*, the pageout daemon begins scanning the active pages to find candidates to move to the inactive list.

The desired values for the paging parameters are communicated to the pageout daemon through global variables. Likewise, the pageout daemon records its progress in a global variable. Progress is measured by the number of pages scanned over each interval that it runs.

The Pageout Daemon

Page replacement is done by the *pageout daemon*. When the pageout daemon reclaims pages that have been modified, it is responsible for writing them to the swap area. Thus, the pageout daemon must be able to use normal kernel-synchronization mechanisms, such as *sleep*( ). It therefore runs as a separate process, with its own process structure, user structure, and kernel stack. Like **init**, the pageout daemon is created by an internal *fork* operation during system startup (see Section 14.5); unlike **init**, however, it remains in kernel mode after the fork. The pageout daemon simply enters *vm_pageout*( ) and never returns. Unlike other users of the disk I/O routines, the pageout process needs to do its disk operations asynchronously so that it can continue scanning in parallel with disk writes.

The goal of the pageout daemon is to keep at least 5 percent of the memory on the free list. Whenever an operation that uses pages causes the amount of free memory to fall below this threshold, the pageout daemon is awakened. It starts by checking to see whether any processes are eligible to be swapped out (see the next subsection). If the pageout daemon finds and swaps out enough eligible processes to meet the free-page target, then the pageout daemon goes to sleep to await another memory shortage.

If there is still not enough free memory, the pageout daemon scans the queue of inactive pages, starting with the oldest page and working toward the youngest. It frees those pages that it can until the free-page target is met or it reaches the end of the inactive list. The following list enumerates the possible actions that can be taken with each page:

• If the page is clean and unreferenced, move it to the free list and increment the free-list count.

• If the page has been referenced by an active process, move it from the inactive list back to the active list.

• If the page is dirty and is being written to the swap area or the filesystem, skip it for now. The expectation is that the I/O will have completed by the next time that the pageout daemon runs, so the page will be clean and can be freed.

• If the page is dirty but is not actively being written to the swap space or the filesystem, then start an I/O operation to get it written. As long as a pageout is needed to save the current page, adjacent pages of the region that are resident, inactive, and dirty are clustered together so that the whole group can be written to the swap area or filesystem in a single I/O operation. If they are freed before they are next modified, the free operation will not require the page to be written.

When the scan of the inactive list completes, the pageout daemon checks the size of the inactive list. Its target is to keep one-third of the available (nonwired) pages on the inactive list. If the inactive queue has gotten too small, the pageout daemon moves pages from the active list over to the inactive list until it reaches its target. Like the inactive list, the active list is sorted into a least recently activated order: The pages selected to be moved to the inactive list are those that were activated least recently. *Vm_pageout*( ) then goes to sleep until free memory drops below the target.

The procedure for writing the pages of a process to the swap device, a *page push*, is somewhat complicated. The mechanism used by the pageout daemon to write pages to the swap area differs from normal I/O in two important ways:

1. The dirty pages are mapped into the virtual address space of the kernel, rather than being part of the virtual address space of the process.

2. The write operation is done asynchronously.

Both these operations are done by the *swap_pager_putpage*( ) routine. Because the pageout daemon does not synchronously wait while the I/O is done, it does not regain control after the I/O operation completes. Therefore, *swap_pager_putpage*( ) marks the buffer with a callback flag and sets the routine for the callback to be *swap_pager_iodone*( ). When the push completes, *swap_pager_iodone*( ) is called; it places the buffer on the list of completed page-outs. If the pageout daemon has finished initiating paging I/O and has gone to sleep, *swap_pager_iodone*( ) awakens it so that it can process the completed page-out list. If the pageout daemon is still running, it will find the buffer the next time that it processes the completed pageout list.

Doing the write asynchronously allows the pageout daemon to continue examining pages, possibly starting additional pushes. Because the number of swap buffers is constant, the kernel must take care to ensure that a buffer is available before a commitment to a new page push is made. If the pageout daemon has used all the swap buffers, *swap_pager_putpage*( ) waits for at least one write operation to complete before it continues. When pageout operations complete, the buffers are added to the list of completed pageouts and, if a *swap_pager_putpage*( ) was blocked awaiting a buffer, *swap_pager_putpage*( ) is awakened.

The list of completed pageouts is processed by *swap_pager_clean*( ) each time a swap-pager instance is deallocated, before a new swap operation is started, and before the pageout daemon sleeps. For each pageout operation on the list, each page (including each in a page cluster) is marked as clean, has its busy bit cleared, and has any processes waiting for it awakened. The page is not moved from its active or inactive list to the free list. If a page remains on the inactive list, it will eventually be moved to the free list during a future pass of the pageout daemon. A count of *pageouts in progress* is kept for the pager associated with each object; this count is decremented when the pageout completes, and, if the count goes to zero, a *wakeup*( ) is issued. This operation is done so that an object that is deallocating a swap pager can wait for the completion of all pageout operations before freeing the pager's references to the associated swap space.

Swapping

Although swapping is generally avoided, there are several times when it is used in 4.4BSD to address a serious resource shortage. Swapping is done in 4.4BSD when any of the following occurs:

• The system becomes so short of memory that the paging process cannot free memory fast enough to satisfy the demand. For example, a memory shortfall may happen when multiple large processes are run on a machine lacking enough memory for the minimum working sets of the processes.

• Processes are completely inactive for more than 20 seconds. Otherwise, such processes would retain a few pages of memory associated with the user structure and kernel stack.

Swap operations completely remove a process from main memory, including the process page tables, the pages of the data and the stack segments that are not already in swap space, and the user area.

Process swapping is invoked only when paging is unable to keep up with memory needs or when short-term resource needs warrant swapping a process. In general, the swap-scheduling mechanism does not do well under heavy load; system performance is much better when memory scheduling can be done by the page-replacement algorithm than when the swap algorithm is used.

Swapout is driven by the pageout daemon. If the pageout daemon can find any processes that have been sleeping for more than 20 seconds (*maxslp*, the cutoff for considering the time sleeping to be "a long time"), it will swap out the one sleeping for the longest time. Such processes have the least likelihood of making good use of the memory that they occupy; thus, they are swapped out even if they are small. If none of these processes are available, the pageout daemon will swap out a process that has been sleeping for a shorter time. If memory is still desperately low, it will select to swap out the runnable process that has been resident the longest. These criteria attempt to avoid swapping entirely until the pageout daemon is clearly unable to keep enough memory free. Once swapping of runnable processes has begun, the processes eligible for swapping should take turns in memory so that no process is frozen out entirely.

The mechanics of doing a swap out are simple. The swapped-in process flag P_INMEM is cleared to show that the process is not resident in memory, and, if necessary, the process is removed from the runnable process queue. Its user area is then marked as pageable, which allows the user area pages, along with any other remaining pages for the process, to be paged out via the standard pageout mechanism. The swapped-out process cannot be run until after it is swapped back into memory.

The Swap-In Process

Swap-in operations are done by the swapping process, process 0. This process is the first one created by the system when the latter is started. The swap-in policy of the *swapper* is embodied in the *scheduler()* routine. This routine swaps processes back in when memory is available and they are ready to run. At any time, the swapper is in one of three states:

1. **Idle**: No swapped-out processes are ready to be run. Idle is the normal state.

2. **Swapping in**: At least one runnable process is swapped out, and *scheduler()* attempts to find memory for it.

3. **Swapping out**: The system is short of memory or there is not enough memory to swap in a process. Under these circumstances, *scheduler()* awakens the pageout daemon to free pages and to swap out other processes until the memory shortage abates.

If more than one swapped-out process is runnable, the first task of the *swapper* is to decide which process to swap in. This decision may affect the decision whether to swap out another process. Each swapped-out process is assigned a priority based on

• The length of time it has been swapped out

• Its *nice* value

• The amount of time it was asleep since it last ran

In general, the process that has been swapped out longest or was swapped out because it was not runnable will be brought in first. Once a process is selected, the *swapper* checks to see whether there is enough memory free to swap in the process. Historically, the 4.3BSD system required as much memory to be available as was occupied by the process before that process was swapped. Under 4.4BSD, this requirement was reduced to a requirement that only enough memory be available to hold the swapped-process user structure and kernel stack. If there is enough memory available, the process is brought back into memory. The user area is swapped in immediately, but the process loads the rest of its working set by demand paging from the swap device. Thus, not all the memory that is committed to the process is used immediately.

The procedure for swapin of a process is the reverse of that for swapout:

1. Memory is allocated for the user structure and kernel stack, and they are read back from swap space.

2. The process is marked as resident and is returned to the run queue if it is runnable (i.e., is not stopped or sleeping).

After the swapin completes, the process is ready to run like any other, except that it has no resident pages. It will bring in the pages that it needs by faulting them.

5.13 Portability

Everything discussed in this chapter up to this section has been part of the machine-independent data structures and algorithms. These parts of the virtual-memory system require little change when 4.4BSD is ported to a new architecture. This section will describe the machine-dependent parts of the virtual-memory system; the parts of the virtual-memory system that must be written as part of a port of 4.4BSD to a new architecture. The machine-dependent parts of the virtual-memory system control the hardware *memory-management unit* (*MMU*). The MMU implements address translation and access control when virtual memory is mapped onto physical memory.

One common MMU design uses memory-resident *forward-mapped page tables*. These page tables are large contiguous arrays indexed by the virtual address. There is one element, or *page-table entry*, in the array for each virtual page in the address space. This element contains the physical page to which the virtual page is mapped, as well as access permissions, status bits telling whether the page has been referenced or modified, and a bit indicating whether the entry contains valid information. For a 4-Gbyte address space with 4-Kbyte virtual pages and a 32-bit page-table entry, 1 million entries, or 4 Mbyte, would be needed to describe an entire address space. Since most processes use little of their address space, most of the entries would be invalid, and allocating 4 Mbyte of physical memory per process would be wasteful. Thus, most page-table structures are hierarchical, using two or more levels of mapping. With a hierarchical structure, different portions of the virtual address are used to index the various levels of the page tables. The intermediate levels of the table contain the addresses of the next lower level of the page table. The kernel can mark as unused large contiguous regions of an address space by inserting invalid entries at the higher levels of the page table, eliminating the need for invalid page descriptors for each individual unused virtual page.

This hierarchical page-table structure requires the hardware to make frequent memory references to translate a virtual address. To speed the translation process, most page-table–based MMUs also have a small, fast, fully associative hardware cache of recent address translations, a structure known commonly as a *translation lookaside buffer* (*TLB*). When a memory reference is translated, the TLB is first consulted and, only if a valid entry is not found there, the page-table structure for the current process is traversed. Because most programs exhibit spatial locality in their memory-access patterns, the TLB does not need to be large; many are as small as 64 entries.

As address spaces grew beyond 32 to 48 and, more recently, 64 bits, simple indexed data structures become unwieldy, with three or more levels of tables required to handle address translation. A response to this page-table growth is the *inverted page table*, also known as the *reverse-mapped page table*. In an inverted page table, the hardware still maintains a memory-resident table, but that table contains one entry per physical page and is indexed by physical address, instead of by virtual address. An entry contains the virtual address to which the physical page is currently mapped, as well as protection and status attributes. The hardware does virtual-to-physical address translation by computing a hash function on the virtual address to select an entry in the table. The system handles collisions by linking together table entries and making a linear search of this chain until it finds the matching virtual address.

The advantages of an inverted page table are that the size of the table is proportional to the amount of physical memory and that only one global table is needed, rather than one table per process. A disadvantage to this approach is that there can be only one virtual address mapped to any given physical page at any one time. This limitation makes *virtual-address aliasing*—having multiple virtual addresses for the same physical page—difficult to handle. As it is with the forward-mapped page table, a hardware TLB is typically used to speed the translation process.

A final common MMU organization consists of just a TLB. This architecture is the simplest hardware design. It gives the software maximum flexibility by allowing the latter to manage translation information in whatever structure it desires.

The machine-dependent part of the virtual-memory system also may need to interact with the memory cache. Because the speed of CPUs has increased far more rapidly than the speed of main memory, most machines today require the use of a memory cache to allow the CPU to operate near its full potential. There are several cache-design choices that require cooperation with the virtual-memory system.

The design option with the biggest effect is whether the cache uses virtual or physical addressing. A physically addressed cache takes the address from the CPU, runs it through the MMU to get the address of the physical page, then uses this physical address to find out whether the requested memory location is available in the cache. Although the TLB significantly reduces the average latency of the translation, there is still a delay in going through the MMU. A virtually addressed cache uses the virtual address as that address comes from the CPU to find out whether the requested memory location is available in the cache. The virtual-address cache is faster than the physical-address cache because it avoids the time to run the address through the MMU. However, the virtual-address cache must be flushed completely after each context switch, because virtual addresses from one process are indistinguishable from the virtual addresses of another process. By contrast, a physical-address cache needs to flush only a few individual entries when their associated physical page is reassigned. In a system with many short-running processes, a virtual-address cache gets flushed so frequently that it is seldom useful.

A further refinement to the virtual-address cache is to add a process tag to each cache entry. At each context switch, the kernel loads a hardware context register with the tag assigned to the process. Each time an entry is recorded in the cache, both the virtual address and the process tag that faulted it are recorded. The cache looks up the virtual address as before, but, when it finds an entry, it compares the tag associated with that entry to the hardware context register. If they match, the cached value is returned. If they do not match, the correct value and current process tag replace the old cached value. When this technique is used, the cache does not need to be flushed completely at each context switch, since multiple processes can have entries in the cache. The drawback is that the kernel must manage the process tags. Usually, there are fewer tags (eight to 16) than there are processes. The kernel must assign the tags to the active set of processes. When an old process drops out of the active set to allow a new one to enter, the kernel must flush the cache entries associated with the tag that it is about to reuse.

A final consideration is a write-through versus a write-back cache. A write-through cache writes the data back to main memory at the same time as it is writing to the cache, forcing the CPU to wait for the memory access to conclude. A write-back cache writes the data to only the cache, delaying the memory write until an explicit request or until the cache entry is reused. The write-back cache allows the CPU to resume execution more quickly and permits multiple writes to the same cache block to be consolidated into a single memory write.

Often, a port to another architecture with a similar memory-management organization can be used as a starting point for a new port. Most models of the HP300 line of workstations, built around the Motorola 68000 family of processors, use the typical two-level page-table organization shown in Fig. 5.16 (on page 176). An address space is broken into 4-Kbyte virtual pages, with each page identified by a 32-bit entry in the *page table*. Each page-table entry contains the physical page number assigned to the virtual page, the access permissions allowed, modify and reference information, and a bit indicating that the entry contains valid information. The 4 Mbyte of page-table entries are likewise divided into 4-Kbyte *page-table pages*, each of which is described by a single 32-bit entry in the *segment table*. Segment-table entries are nearly identical to page-table entries: They contain access bits, modify and reference bits, a valid bit, and the physical page number of the page-table page described. One 4-Kbyte page—1024 segment-table entries—covers the maximum-sized 4-Gbyte address space. A hardware register contains the physical address of the segment-table for the currently active process.

In Fig. 5.16, translation of a virtual address to a physical address during a CPU access proceeds as follows:

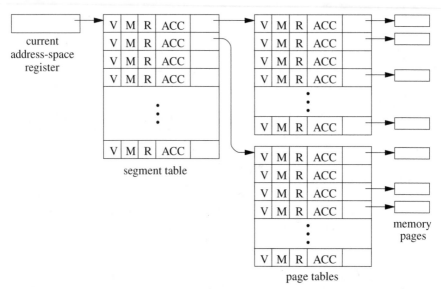

Figure 5.16 Two-level page-table organization. Key: V—page-valid bit; M—page-modified bit; R—page-referenced bit; ACC—page-access permissions.

- The 10 most significant bits of the virtual address are used to index into the active segment table.

- If the selected segment-table entry is valid and the access permissions grant the access being made, the next 10 bits of the virtual address are used to index into the page-table page referenced by the segment-table entry.

- If the selected page-table entry is valid and the access permissions match, the final 12 bits of the virtual address are combined with the physical page referenced by the page-table entry to form the physical address of the access.

The Role of the *pmap* Module

The machine-dependent code describes how the *physical mapping* is done between the user-processes and kernel virtual addresses and the physical addresses of the main memory. This mapping function includes management of access rights in addition to address translation. In 4.4BSD, the *physical mapping (pmap) module* manages machine-dependent translation and access tables that are used either directly or indirectly by the memory-management hardware. For example, on the HP300, the *pmap* maintains the memory-resident segment and page tables for each process, as well as for the kernel. The machine-dependent state required to describe the translation and access rights of a single page is often referred to as a *mapping* or *mapping structure*.

The 4.4BSD *pmap* interface is nearly identical to that in Mach 3.0: it shares many design characteristics. The *pmap* module is intended to be logically independent of the higher levels of the virtual-memory system. The interface deals strictly in machine-independent page-aligned virtual and physical addresses and in machine-independent protections. The machine-independent page size may be a multiple of the architecture-supported page size. Thus, *pmap* operations must be able to affect more than one physical page per logical page. The machine-independent protection is a simple encoding of read, write, and execute permission bits. The *pmap* must map all possible combinations into valid architecture-specific values.

A process's *pmap* is considered to be a cache of mapping information kept in a machine-dependent format. As such, it does not need to contain complete state for all valid mappings. Mapping state is the responsibility of the machine-independent layer. With one exception, the *pmap* module may throw away mapping state at its discretion to reclaim resources. The exception is wired mappings, which should never cause a fault that reaches the machine-independent *vm_fault()* routine. Thus, state for wired mappings must be retained in the *pmap* until it is removed explicitly.

In theory, the *pmap* module may also delay most interface operations, such as removing mappings or changing their protection attributes. It can then do many of them batched together, before doing expensive operations such as flushing the TLB. In practice, however, this delayed operation has never been used, and it is unclear whether it works completely. This feature was dropped from later releases of the Mach 3.0 *pmap* interface.

In general, *pmap* routines may act either on a set of mappings defined by a virtual address range or on all mappings for a particular physical address. Being able to act on individual or all virtual mappings for a physical page requires that the mapping information maintained by the *pmap* module be indexed by both virtual and physical address. For architectures such as the HP300 that support memory-resident page tables, the virtual-to-physical, or forward, lookup may be a simple emulation of the hardware page-table traversal. Physical-to-virtual, or reverse, lookup requires an *inverted page table*: an array with one entry per physical page indexed by the physical page number. Entries in this table may be either a single mapping structure, if only one virtual translation is allowed per physical page, or a pointer to a list of mapping structures, if *virtual-address aliasing* is allowed. The kernel typically handles forward lookups in a system without page tables by using a hash table to map virtual addresses into mapping structures in the inverted page table.

There are two strategies that can be used for management of *pmap* memory resources, such as user-segment or page-table memory. The traditional and easiest approach is for the *pmap* module to manage its own memory. Under this strategy, the *pmap* module can grab a fixed amount of wired physical memory at system boot time, map that memory into the kernel's address space, and allocate pieces of the memory as needed for its own data structures. The primary benefit is that this approach isolates the *pmap* module's memory needs from those of the rest of the system and limits the *pmap* module's dependencies on other parts of the system. This design is consistent with a layered model of the virtual-memory system in which the *pmap* is the lowest, and hence self-sufficient, layer.

The disadvantage is that this approach requires the duplication of many of the memory-management functions. The *pmap* module has its own memory allocator and deallocator for its private heap—a heap that is statically sized and cannot be adjusted for varying systemwide memory demands. For an architecture with memory-resident page tables, it must keep track of noncontiguous chunks of processes' page tables, because a process may populate its address space sparsely. Handling this requirement entails duplicating much of the standard list-management code, such as that used by the *vm_map* code.

An alternative approach, used by the HP300, is to use the higher-level virtual-memory code recursively to manage some *pmap* resources. Here, the page table for a user process appears as a virtually contiguous 4-Mbyte array of page-table entries in the kernel's address space. Using higher-level allocation routines, such as *kmem_alloc_wait*( ), ensures that physical memory is allocated only when needed and from the systemwide free-memory pool. Page tables and other *pmap* resources also can be allocated from pageable kernel memory. This approach easily and efficiently supports large sparse address spaces, including the kernel's own address space.

The primary drawback is that this approach violates the independent nature of the interface. In particular, the recursive structure leads to deadlock problems with global multiprocessor spin locks that can be held while the kernel is calling a *pmap* routine. Another problem for page-table allocation is that page tables are typically hierarchically arranged; they are not flat, as this technique represents them. With a two-level organization present on some HP300 machines, the *pmap* module must be aware that a new page has been allocated within the 4-Mbyte range, so that the page's physical address can be inserted into the segment table. Thus, the advantage of transparent allocation of physical memory is partially lost. Although the problem is not severe in the two-level case, the technique becomes unwieldy for three or more levels.

The *pmap* data structures are contained in the machine-dependent include directory in the file **pmap.h**. Most of the code for these routines is in the machine-dependent source directory **pmap.c**. The main tasks of the *pmap* module are these:

- System initialization and startup (*pmap_bootstrap_alloc*( ), *pmap_bootstrap*( ), *pmap_init*( ))

- Allocation and deallocation of mappings of physical to virtual pages (*pmap_enter*( ), *pmap_remove*( ))

- Change of access protections and other attributes of mappings (*pmap_change_wiring*( ), *pmap_page_protect*( ), *pmap_protect*( ))

- Maintenance of physical page-usage information (*pmap_clear_modify*( ), *pmap_clear_reference*( ), *pmap_is_modified*( ), *pmap_is_referenced*( ))

- Initialization of physical pages (*pmap_copy_page*( ), *pmap_zero_page*( ))

• Management of internal data structures (*pmap_create*(), *pmap_reference*(),
  pmap_destroy(), *pmap_pinit*(), *pmap_release*(), *pmap_copy*(),
  pmap_pageable(), *pmap_collect*(), *pmap_update*())

Each of these tasks will be described in the following subsections.

Initialization and Startup

The first step in starting up the system is for the loader to bring the kernel image
from a disk or the network into the physical memory of the machine. The kernel
load image looks much like that of any other process; it contains a text segment,
an initialized data segment, and an uninitialized data segment. The loader places
the kernel contiguously into the beginning of physical memory. Unlike a user process that is demand paged into memory, the text and data for the kernel are read
into memory in their entirety. Following these two segments, the loader zeros an
area of memory equal to the size of the kernel's uninitialized memory segment.
After loading the kernel, the loader passes control to the starting address given in
the kernel executable image. When the kernel begins executing, it is executing
with the MMU turned off. Consequently, all addressing is done using the direct
physical addresses.

    The first task undertaken by the kernel is to set up the kernel *pmap*, and any
other data structures that are necessary to describe the kernel's virtual address
space and to make it possible to enable the MMU. This task is done in
pmap_bootstrap(). On the HP300, bootstrap tasks include allocating and initializing the segment and page tables that map the statically loaded kernel image and
memory-mapped I/O address space, allocating a fixed amount of memory for kernel page-table pages, allocating and initializing the user structure and kernel stack
for the initial process, allocating the empty segment table initially shared by all
processes, reserving special areas of the kernel's address space, and initializing
assorted critical *pmap*-internal data structures. After this call, the MMU is
enabled, and the kernel begins running in the context of process zero.

    Once the kernel is running in its virtual address space, it proceeds to initialize
the rest of the system. This initialization starts with a call to set up the machine-
independent portion of the virtual-memory system and concludes with a
call to *pmap_init*(). Any subsystem that requires dynamic memory allocation
between enabling of the MMU and the call to *pmap_init*() must use
pmap_bootstrap_alloc(). Memory allocated by this routine will not be managed
by the virtual-memory system and is effectively wired down. *Pmap_init*() allocates all resources necessary to manage multiple user address spaces and synchronizes the higher level kernel virtual-memory data structures with the kernel *pmap*.

    On the HP300, it first marks as in use the areas of the kernel's *vm_map* that
were allocated during the bootstrap. These marks prevent future high-level allocations from trying to use those areas. Next, it allocates a range of kernel virtual
address space, via a kernel submap, to use for user-process page tables. Pieces of
this address range are allocated when processes are created and are deallocated

when the processes exit. These areas are not populated with memory on allocation. Page-table pages are allocated on demand when a process first accesses memory that is mapped by an entry in that page of the page table. This allocation is discussed later, in the mapping-allocation subsection. Page tables are allocated from their own submap to limit the amount of kernel virtual address space that they consume. At 4 Mbyte per process page table, 1024 active processes would occupy the entire kernel address space. The available page-table address-space limit is approximately one-half of the entire address space.

Pmap_init allocates a fixed amount of wired memory to use for kernel page-table pages. In theory, these pages could be allocated on demand from the general free-memory pool, as user page-table pages are; in practice, however, this approach leads to deadlocks, so a fixed pool of memory is used.

After determining the number of pages of physical memory remaining, the startup code allocates the inverted page table, *pv_table*. This table is an array of *pv_entry* structures. Each *pv_entry* describes a single address translation and includes the virtual address, a pointer to the associated *pmap* structure for that virtual address, a link for chaining together multiple entries mapping this physical address, and additional information specific to entries mapping page-table pages. Figure 5.17 shows the *pv_entry* references for a set of pages that have a single mapping. The *pv_table* contains actual instances of *pv_entry* structures, rather than pointers; this strategy optimizes the common case where physical pages have only one mapping. The purpose of the *pv_entry* structures is to identify the address space that has the page mapped. Rather than having a pointer from the *vm_page* structure to its corresponding *pv_entry*, the relationship is based on the array index of the two entries. In Fig. 5.17, the object is using pages 5, 18, and 79; thus, the corresponding *pv_entry* structures 5, 18, and 79 point to the physical map for the address space that has page tables referencing those pages.

Each *pv_entry* can reference only one physical map. When an object becomes shared between two or more processes, each physical page of memory becomes mapped into two or more sets of page tables. To track these multiple references, the *pmap* module must create chains of *pv_entry* structures, as shown in

---

Figure 5.17 Physical pages with a single mapping.

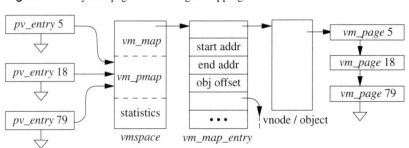

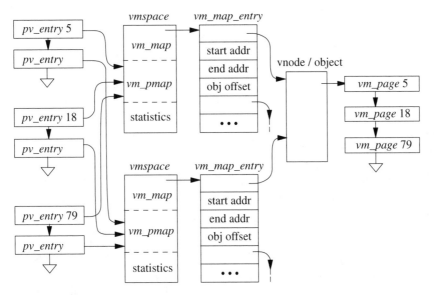

Figure 5.18 Physical pages with multiple mappings.

Fig. 5.18. These additional structures are allocated dynamically and are linked from a list headed by the *pv_entry* that was allocated in the initial table. For example, implementation of copy-on-write requires that the page tables be set to read-only in all the processes sharing the object. The *pmap* module can implement this request by walking the list of pages associated with the object to be made copy-on-write. For each page, it finds that pages' corresponding *pv_entry* structure. It then makes the appropriate change to the page table associated with that *pv_entry* structure. If that *pv_entry* structure has any additional *pv_entry* structures linked off it, the *pmap* module traverses them, making the same modification to their referenced page-table entry.

Finally, a *page-attribute* array is allocated with 1 byte per physical page. This array contains reference and dirty information and is described later in the subsection on the management of page usage information. The first and last physical addresses of the area covered by both the *pv_entry* and attribute arrays are recorded, and are used by other routines for bounds checking. This area is referred to as the *pmap-managed memory*.

Mapping Allocation and Deallocation

The primary responsibility of the *pmap* module is validating (allocating) and invalidating (deallocating) mappings of physical pages to virtual addresses. The physical pages represent cached portions of an object that is providing data from a file or an anonymous memory region. A physical page is bound to a virtual address because that object is being mapped into a process's address space either explicitly by *mmap* or implicitly by *fork* or *exec*. Physical-to-virtual address mappings are not created at the time that the object is mapped; rather, their creation is delayed until the first reference to a particular page is made. At that point, an access fault will occur, and *pmap_enter()* will be called. *Pmap_enter* is responsible for any required side effects associated with creation of a new mapping. Such side effects are largely the result of entering a second translation for an already mapped physical page—for example, as the result of a copy-on-write operation. Typically, this operation requires flushing uniprocessor or multiprocessor TLB or cache entries to maintain consistency.

In addition to its use to create new mappings, *pmap_enter()* may also be called to modify the wiring or protection attributes of an existing mapping or to rebind an existing mapping for a virtual address to a new physical address. The kernel can handle changing attributes by calling the appropriate interface routine, described in the next subsection. Changing the target physical address of a mapping is simply a matter of first removing the old mapping and then handling it like any other new mapping request.

Pmap_enter() is the only routine that cannot lose state or delay its action. When called, it must create a mapping as requested, and it must validate that mapping before returning to the caller. On the HP300, *pmap_enter()* takes the following actions:

1. If no page-table exists for the process, a 4-Mbyte range is allocated in the kernel's address space to map the process's address space.

2. If the process has no segment table of its own (i.e., it still references the initial shared segment table), a private one is allocated.

3. If a physical page has not yet been allocated to the process page-table at the location required for the new mapping, that is done now. Kernel page-table pages are acquired from the reserved pool allocated at bootstrap time. For user processes, the kernel does the allocation by simulating a fault on the appropriate location in the 4-Mbyte page-table range. This fault forces allocation of a zero-filled page and makes a recursive call to *pmap_enter()* to enter the mapping of that page in the kernel's *pmap*. For either kernel or user page-table pages, the kernel mapping for the new page is flagged as being a page-table page, and the physical address of the page is recorded in the segment table. Recording this address is more complicated on the 68040 that has the top two levels of the page-table hierarchy squeezed into the single segment-table page.

After ensuring that all page-table resources exist for the mapping being entered, *pmap_enter()* validates or modifies the requested mapping as follows:

1. Check to see whether a mapping structure already exists for this virtual-to-physical address translation. If one does, the call must be one to change the protection or wiring attributes of the mapping; it is handled as described in the next subsection.

2. Otherwise, if a mapping exists for this virtual address but it references a differ-
    ent physical address, that mapping is removed.

3. If the indicated mapping is for a user process, the kernel page-table page con-
    taining that page-table entry is marked as nonpageable. Making this marking
    is an obscure way of keeping page-table pages wired as long as they contain
    any valid mappings. The *vm_map_pageable*() routine keeps a *wired count* for
    every virtual page, wiring the page when the count is incremented from zero
    and unwiring the page when the count is decremented to zero. The wiring and
    unwiring calls trigger a call to *pmap_pageable*(), whose function is described
    in the last subsection on the management of internal data structures. Wiring a
    page-table page avoids having it involuntarily paged out, effectively invalidat-
    ing all pages that it currently maps. A beneficial side effect is that, when a
    page-table page is finally unwired, it contains no useful information and does
    not need to be paged out. Hence, no backing store is required for page-table
    pages.

4. If the physical address is outside the range managed by the *pmap* module (e.g.,
    a frame-buffer page), no *pv_table* entry is allocated; only a page-table entry is
    created. Otherwise, for the common case of a new mapping for a managed
    physical page, a *pv_table* entry is created.

5. For HP300 machines with a virtually-indexed cache, a check is made to see
    whether this physical page already has other mappings. If it does, all map-
    pings may need to be marked cache inhibited, to avoid cache inconsistencies.

6. A page-table entry is created and validated, with cache and TLB entries flushed
    as necessary.

When an object is unmapped from an address space, either explicitly by
munmap() or implicitly on process exit, the *pmap* module is invoked to invalidate
and remove the mappings for all physical pages caching data for the object.
Unlike *pmap_enter*(), *pmap_remove*() can be called with a virtual-address range
encompassing more than one mapping. Hence, the kernel does the unmapping by
looping over all virtual pages in the range, ignoring those for which there is no
mapping and removing those for which there is one. Also unlike *pmap_enter*(),
the implied action can be delayed until *pmap_update*(), described in the next subsection, is called. This delay may enable the *pmap* to optimize the invalidation
process by aggregating individual operations.

Pmap_remove() on the HP300 is simple. It loops over the specified address
range, invalidating individual page mappings. Since *pmap_remove*() can be
called with large sparsely allocated regions, such as an entire process virtual
address range, it needs to skip efficiently invalid entries within the range. It skips
invalid entries by first checking the segment-table entry for a particular address
and, if an entry is invalid, skipping to the next 4-Mbyte boundary. This check also
prevents unnecessary allocation of a page-table page for the empty area. When all
page mappings have been invalidated, any necessary global cache flushing is done.

To invalidate a single mapping, the kernel locates and marks as invalid the appropriate page-table entry. The reference and modify bits for the page are saved in the separate attribute array for future retrieval. If this mapping was a user mapping, *vm_map_pageable*() is called to decrement the wired count on the page-table page. When the count reaches zero, the page-table page can be reclaimed because it contains no more valid mappings. If the physical address from the mapping is outside the managed range, nothing more is done. Otherwise, the *pv_table* entry is found and is deallocated. When a user page-table page is removed from the kernel's address space (i.e., as a result of removal of the final valid user mapping from that page), the process's segment table must be updated. The kernel does this update by invalidating the appropriate segment-table entry.

Change of Access and Wiring Attributes for Mappings

An important role of the *pmap* module is to manipulate the hardware access protections for pages. These manipulations may be applied to all mappings covered by a virtual-address range within a *pmap* via *pmap_protect*(), or they may be applied to all mappings of a particular physical page across *pmap*s via *pmap_page_protect*(). There are two features common to both calls. First, either form may be called with a protection value of VM_PROT_NONE to remove a range of virtual addresses or to remove all mappings for a particular physical page. Second, these routines should never add write permission to the affected mappings; thus, calls including VM_PROT_WRITE should make no changes. This restriction is necessary for the copy-on-write mechanism to function properly. Write permission is added only via calls to *pmap_enter*().

Pmap_protect() is used primarily by the *mprotect* system call to change the protection for a region of process address space. The strategy is similar to that of *pmap_remove*(): Loop over all virtual pages in the range and apply the change to all valid mappings that are found. Invalid mappings are left alone. As occurs with *pmap_remove*(), the action may be delayed until *pmap_update*() is called.

For the HP300, *pmap_protect*() first checks for the special cases. If the requested permission is VM_PROT_NONE, it calls *pmap_remove*() to handle the revocation of all access permission. If VM_PROT_WRITE is included, it just returns immediately. For a normal protection value, *pmap_remove*() loops over the given address range, skipping invalid mappings. For valid mappings, the page-table entry is looked up and, if the new protection value differs from the current value, the entry is modified and any TLB and cache flushing done. As occurs with *pmap_remove*(), any global cache actions are delayed until the entire range has been modified.

Pmap_page_protect() is used internally by the virtual-memory system for two purposes. It is called to set read-only permission when a copy-on-write operation is set up (e.g., during *fork*). It also removes all access permissions before doing page replacement to force all references to a page to block pending the completion of its operation. In Mach, this routine used to be two separate routines—*pmap_copy_on_write*() and *pmap_remove_all*()—and many *pmap* modules implement *pmap_page_protect*() as a call to one or the other of these functions, depending on the protection argument.

In the HP300 implementation of *pmap_page_protect*(), a check is made to ensure that this page is a managed physical page and that VM_PROT_WRITE was not specified. If either of these conditions is not met, *pmap_page_protect*() returns without doing anything. Otherwise, it locates the *pv_table* entry for the specified physical page. If the request requires the removal of mappings, *pmap_page_protect*() loops over all *pv_entry* structures that are chained together for this page, invalidating the individual mappings as described in the previous subsection. Note that TLB and cache flushing differ from those for *pmap_remove*(), since they must invalidate entries from multiple process contexts, rather than invalidating multiple entries from a single process context.

If *pmap_page_protect*() is called to make mappings read-only, then it loops over all *pv_entry* structures for the physical address, modifying the appropriate page-table entry for each. As occurs with *pmap_protect*(), the entry is checked to ensure that it is changing before expensive TLB and cache flushes are done.

Pmap_change_wiring() is called to wire or unwire a single machine-independent virtual page within a *pmap*. As described in the previous subsection, wiring informs the *pmap* module that a mapping should not cause a hardware fault that reaches the machine-independent *vm_fault*() code. Wiring is typically a software attribute that has no affect on the hardware MMU state: It simply tells the *pmap* not to throw away state about the mapping. As such, if a *pmap* module never discards state, then it is not strictly necessary for the module even to track the wired status of pages. The only side effect of not tracking wiring information in the *pmap* is that the *mlock* system call cannot be completely implemented without a wired page-count statistic.

The HP300 *pmap* implementation maintains wiring information. An unused bit in the page-table–entry structure records a page's wired status. *Pmap_change_wiring*() sets or clears this bit when it is invoked with a valid virtual address. Since the wired bit is ignored by the hardware, there is no need to modify the TLB or cache when the bit is changed.

Management of Page-Usage Information

The machine-independent page-management code needs to be able to get basic information about the usage and modification of pages from the underlying hardware. The *pmap* module facilitates the collection of this information without requiring the machine-independent code to understand the details of the mapping tables by providing a set of interfaces to query and clear the reference and modify bits. The pageout daemon can call *pmap_is_modified*() to determine whether a page is dirty. If the page is dirty, the pageout daemon can write it to backing store, then call *pmap_clear_modify*() to clear the modify bit. Similarly, when the pageout daemon pages out or inactivates a page, it uses *pmap_clear_reference*() to clear the reference bit for the page. Later, when it considers moving the page from the inactive list, it uses *pmap_is_referenced*() to check whether the page has been used since the page was inactivated. If the page has been used, it is moved back to the active list; otherwise, it is moved to the free list.

One important feature of the query routines is that they should return valid information even if there are currently no mappings for the page in question.

Thus, referenced and modified information cannot just be gathered from the hardware-maintained bits of the various page-table or TLB entries; rather, there must be an auxiliary array where the information is retained when a mapping is removed.

The HP300 implementation of these routines is simple. As mentioned in the subsection on initialization and startup, a page-attribute array with one entry per managed physical page is allocated at boot time. Initially zeroed, the entries are updated whenever a mapping for a page is removed. The query routines return FALSE if they are not passed a managed physical page. Otherwise, they test the referenced or modified bit of the appropriate attribute-array entry and, if the bit is set, return TRUE immediately. Since this attribute array contains only past information, they still need to check status bits in the page-table entries for currently valid mappings of the page. Thus, they loop over all *pv_entry* structures associated with the physical page and examine the appropriate page-table entry for each. They can return TRUE as soon as they encounter a set bit or FALSE if the bit is not set in any page-table entry.

The clear routines also return immediately if they are not passed a managed physical page. Otherwise, the referenced or modified bit is cleared in the attribute array, and they loop over all *pv_entry* structures associated with the physical page, clearing the hardware-maintained page-table–entry bits. This final step may involve TLB or cache flushes along the way or afterward.

Initialization of Physical Pages

Two interfaces are provided to allow the higher-level virtual-memory routines to initialize physical memory. *Pmap_zero_page*() takes a physical address and fills the page with zeros. *Pmap_copy_page*() takes two physical addresses and copies the contents of the first page to the second page. Since both take physical addresses, the *pmap* module will most likely have first to map those pages into the kernel's address space before it can access them. Since mapping and unmapping single pages dynamically may be expensive, an alternative is to have all physical memory permanently mapped into the kernel's address space at boot time. With this technique, addition of an offset to the physical address is all that is needed to create a usable kernel virtual address.

The HP300 implementation has a pair of global kernel virtual addresses reserved for zeroing and copying pages, and thus is not as efficient as it could be. *Pmap_zero_page*() calls *pmap_enter*() with the reserved virtual address and the specified physical address, calls *bzero*() to clear the page, and then removes the temporary mapping with the single translation-invalidation primitive used by *pmap_remove*(). Similarly, *pmap_copy_page*() creates mappings for both physical addresses, uses *bcopy*() to make the copy, and then removes both mappings.

Management of Internal Data Structures

The remaining *pmap* interface routines are used for management and synchronization of internal data structures. *Pmap_create*() creates an instance of the machine-dependent *pmap* structure. The value returned is the handle used for all other *pmap* routines. *Pmap_reference*() increments the reference count for a particular *pmap*. In theory this reference count allows a *pmap* to be shared by multiple processes; in practice, only the kernel submaps that use the kernel's *pmap* share references. Since kernel submaps as well as the kernel map are permanent, there is currently no real need to maintain a reference count. *Pmap_destroy*() decrements the reference count of the given *pmap* and deallocates the *pmap*'s resources when the count drops to zero.

Because of an incomplete transition in the virtual-memory code, there is also another set of routines to create and destroy *pmap*s effectively. *Pmap_pinit*() initializes an already-existing *pmap* structure, and *pmap_release*() frees any resources associated with a *pmap* without freeing the *pmap* structure itself. These routines were added in support of the *vm_space* structure that encapsulates all storage associated with a process's virtual-memory state.

On the HP300, the create and destroy routines use the kernel *malloc*() and *free*() routines to manage space for the *pmap* structure, and then use *pmap_pinit*() and *pmap_release*() to initialize and release the *pmap*. *Pmap_pinit*() sets the process segment-table pointer to the common empty segment table. As noted earlier in the subsection on mapping allocation and deallocation, page-table allocation is delayed until the first access to the process's address space. *Pmap_release*() simply frees the process segment and page tables.

Pmap_copy() and *pmap_pageable*() are optional interface routines that are used to provide hints to the *pmap* module about the use of virtual-memory regions. *Pmap_copy*() is called when a copy-on-write operation has been done. Its parameters include the source and destination *pmap*, and the virtual address and the length of the region copied. On the HP300, this routine does nothing. *Pmap_pageable*() indicates that the specified address range has been either wired or unwired. The HP300 *pmap* module uses this interface to detect when a page-table page is empty and can be released. The current implementation does not free the page-table page; it just clears the modified state of the page and allows the page to be reclaimed by the pageout daemon as needed. Clearing the modify bit is necessary to prevent the empty page from being wastefully written out to backing store.

Pmap_update() is called to notify the *pmap* module that all delayed actions for all *pmap*s should be done now. On the HP300, this routine does nothing. *Pmap_collect*() is called to inform the *pmap* module that the given *pmap* is not expected to be used for some time, allowing the *pmap* module to reclaim resources that could be used more effectively elsewhere. Currently, it is called whenever a process is about to be swapped out. The HP300 *pmap* module does not use this information for user processes, but it does use the information to attempt to reclaim unused kernel page-table pages when none are available on the free list.

Exercises

5.1   What does it mean for a machine to support virtual memory? What four hardware facilities are typically required for a machine to support virtual memory?

5.2   What is the relationship between paging and swapping on a demand-paged virtual-memory system? Explain whether it is desirable to provide both mechanisms in the same system. Can you suggest an alternative to providing both mechanisms?

5.3   What three policies characterize paging systems? Which of these policies usually has no effect on the performance of a paging system?

5.4   Describe a disadvantage of the scheme used for the management of swap space that holds the dynamic per-process segments. *Hint*: Consider what happens when a process on a heavily paging system expands in many small increments.

5.5   What is *copy-on-write*? In most UNIX applications, the *fork* system call is followed almost immediately by an *exec* system call. Why does this behavior make it particularly attractive to use copy-on-write in implementing *fork*?

5.6   Explain why the *vfork* system call will always be more efficient than a clever implementation of the *fork* system call.

5.7   When a process exits, all its pages may not be placed immediately on the memory free list. Explain this behavior.

5.8   What is clustering? Where is it used in the virtual-memory system?

5.9   What purpose does the pageout-daemon process serve in the virtual-memory system? What facility is used by the pageout daemon that is not available to a normal user process?

5.10   Why is the *sticky bit* no longer useful in 4.4BSD?

5.11   Give two reasons for swapping to be initiated.

*5.12   The 4.3BSD virtual-memory system had a text cache that retained the identity of text pages from one execution of a program to the next. How does the object cache in 4.4BSD improve on the performance of the 4.3BSD text cache?

*5.13   Postulate a scenario under which the HP300 kernel would deadlock if it were to allocate kernel page-table pages dynamically.

References

Babaoğlu & Joy, 1981.
      O. Babaoğlu & W. N. Joy, "Converting a Swap-Based System to Do Paging in an Architecture Lacking Page-Referenced Bits," *Proceedings of the Eighth Symposium on Operating Systems Principles*, pp. 78–86, December 1981.

Belady, 1966.
L. A. Belady, "A Study of Replacement Algorithms for Virtual Storage Systems," *IBM Systems Journal*, vol. 5, no. 2, pp. 78–101, 1966.

Coffman & Denning, 1973.
E. G. Coffman, Jr. & P. J. Denning, *Operating Systems Theory*, p. 243, Prentice-Hall, Englewood Cliffs, NJ, 1973.

Corbato, 1968.
F. J. Corbato, "A Paging Experiment with the Multics System," Project MAC Memo MAC-M-384, Massachusetts Institute of Technology, Boston, MA, July 1968.

Denning, 1970.
P. J. Denning, "Virtual Memory," *Computer Surveys*, vol. 2, no. 3, pp. 153–190, September 1970.

Easton & Franaszek, 1979.
M. C. Easton & P. A. Franaszek, "Use Bit Scanning in Replacement Decisions," *IEEE Transactions on Computing*, vol. 28, no. 2, pp. 133–141, February 1979.

Gingell et al, 1987.
R. Gingell, M. Lee, X. Dang, & M. Weeks, "Shared Libraries in SunOS," *USENIX Association Conference Proceedings*, pp. 131–146, June 1987.

Gingell, Moran, & Shannon, 1987.
R. Gingell, J. Moran, & W. Shannon, "Virtual Memory Architecture in SunOS," *USENIX Association Conference Proceedings*, pp. 81–94, June 1987.

Intel, 1984.
Intel, "Introduction to the iAPX 286," Order Number 210308, Intel Corporation, Santa Clara, CA, 1984.

Kenah & Bate, 1984.
L. J. Kenah & S. F. Bate, *VAX/VMS Internals and Data Structures*, Digital Press, Bedford, MA, 1984.

King, 1971.
W. F. King, "Analysis of Demand Paging Algorithms," *IFIP*, pp. 485–490, North Holland, Amsterdam, 1971.

Korn & Vo, 1985.
D. Korn & K. Vo, "In Search of a Better Malloc," *USENIX Association Conference Proceedings*, pp. 489–506, June 1985.

Lazowska & Kelsey, 1978.
E. D. Lazowska & J. M. Kelsey, "Notes on Tuning VAX/VMS.," Technical Report 78-12-01, Department of Computer Science, University of Washington, Seattle, WA, December 1978.

Marshall, 1979.
W. T. Marshall, "A Unified Approach to the Evaluation of a Class of 'Working Set Like' Replacement Algorithms," PhD Thesis, Department of Computer Engineering, Case Western Reserve University, Cleveland, OH, May 1979.

McKusick & Karels, 1988.
> M. K. McKusick & M. J. Karels, "Design of a General Purpose Memory Allocator for the 4.3BSD UNIX Kernel," *USENIX Association Conference Proceedings*, pp. 295–304, June 1988.

Organick, 1975.
> E. I. Organick, *The Multics System: An Examination of Its Structure,* MIT Press, Cambridge, MA, 1975.

Tevanian, 1987.
> A. Tevanian, "Architecture-Independent Virtual Memory Management for Parallel and Distributed Environments: The Mach Approach," Technical Report CMU-CS-88-106, Department of Computer Science, Carnegie-Mellon University, Pittsburgh, PA, December 1987.

Young, 1989.
> M. W. Young, *Exporting a User Interface to Memory Management from a Communication-Oriented Operating System,* CMU-CS-89-202, Department of Computer Science, Carnegie-Mellon University, November 1989.

PART 3

I/O System

CHAPTER 6

I/O System Overview

6.1 I/O Mapping from User to Device

Computers store and retrieve data through supporting peripheral I/O devices. These devices typically include mass-storage devices, such as moving-head disk drives, magnetic-tape drives, and network interfaces. Storage devices such as disks and tapes are accessed through I/O controllers that manage the operation of their *slave* devices according to I/O requests from the CPU.

Many hardware device peculiarities are hidden from the user by high-level kernel facilities, such as the filesystem and socket interfaces. Other such peculiarities are hidden from the bulk of the kernel itself by the I/O system. The I/O system consists of buffer-caching systems, general device-driver code, and drivers for specific hardware devices that must finally address peculiarities of the specific devices. The various I/O systems are summarized in Fig. 6.1 (on page 194).

There are four main kinds of I/O in 4.4BSD: the *filesystem*, the *character-device* interface, the *block-device* interface, and the *socket* interface with its related network devices. The character and block interfaces appear in the filesystem name space. The character interface provides *unstructured* access to the underlying hardware, whereas the block device provides *structured* access to the underlying hardware. The network devices do not appear in the filesystem; they are accessible through only the socket interface. Block and character devices are described in Sections 6.2 and 6.3 respectively. The filesystem is described in Chapters 7 and 8. Sockets are described in Chapter 11.

A block-device interface, as the name indicates, supports only block-oriented I/O operations. The block-device interface uses the buffer cache to minimize the number of I/O requests that require an I/O operation, and to synchronize with filesystem operations on the same device. All I/O is done to or from I/O buffers that reside in the kernel's address space. This approach requires at least one memory-to-memory copy operation to satisfy a user request, but also allows 4.4BSD to support I/O requests of nearly arbitrary size and alignment.

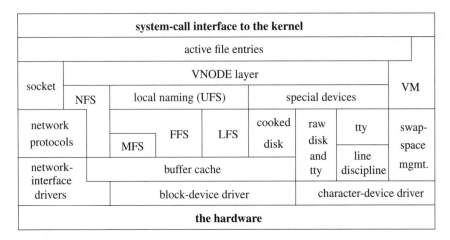

Figure 6.1 Kernel I/O structure.

A character-device interface comes in two styles that depend on the character-istics of the underlying hardware device. For some character-oriented hardware devices, such as terminal multiplexers, the interface is truly character oriented, although higher-level software, such as the terminal driver, may provide a line-oriented interface to applications. However, for block-oriented devices such as disks and tapes, a character-device interface is an *unstructured* or *raw* interface. For this interface, I/O operations do not go through the buffer cache; instead, they are made directly between the device and buffers in the application's virtual address space. Consequently, the size of the operations must be a multiple of the underlying *block size* required by the device, and, on some machines, the application's I/O buffer must be aligned on a suitable boundary.

Internal to the system, I/O devices are accessed through a fixed set of entry points provided by each device's *device driver*. The set of entry points varies according to whether the I/O device supports a block- or character-device interface. For a block-device interface, a device driver is described by a *bdevsw* structure, whereas for character-device interface, it accesses a *cdevsw* structure. All the *bdevsw* structures are collected in the *block-device table*, whereas *cdevsw* structures are similarly organized in a *character-device table*.

Devices are identified by a *device number* that is constructed from a *major* and a *minor* device number. The *major device number* uniquely identifies the type of device (really of the device driver) and is the index of the device's entry in the block- or character-device table. Devices that support both block- and character-device interfaces have two major device numbers, one for each table. The *minor device* number is interpreted solely by the device driver and is used by the driver to identify to which, of potentially many, hardware devices an I/O request refers. For magnetic tapes, for example, minor device numbers identify a specific controller and tape transport. The minor device number may also specify a section of a device—for example, a channel of a multiplexed device, or optional handling parameters.

Device Drivers

A device driver is divided into three main sections:

1. Autoconfiguration and initialization routines

2. Routines for servicing I/O requests (the top half)

3. Interrupt service routines (the bottom half)

The autoconfiguration portion of a driver is responsible for *probing* for a hardware device to see whether the latter is present and to initialize the device and any associated software state that is required by the device driver. This portion of the driver is typically called only once, when the system is initialized. Autoconfiguration is described in Section 14.4.

The section of a driver that services I/O requests by the system is invoked because of system calls or for the virtual-memory system. This portion of the device driver executes synchronously in the top half of the kernel and is permitted to block by calling the *sleep()* routine. We commonly refer to this body of code as the *top half* of a device driver.

Interrupt service routines are invoked when the system fields an interrupt from a device. Consequently, these routines cannot depend on any per-process state and cannot block. We commonly refer to a device driver's interrupt service routines as the *bottom half* of a device driver.

In addition to these three sections of a device driver, an optional *crash-dump* routine may be provided. This routine, if present, is invoked when the system recognizes an unrecoverable error and wishes to record the contents of physical memory for use in postmortem analysis. Most device drivers for disk controllers, and some for tape controllers, provide a crash-dump routine. The use of the crash-dump routine is described in Section 14.7.

I/O Queueing

Device drivers typically manage one or more queues of I/O requests in their normal operation. When an input or output request is received by the top half of the driver, it is recorded in a data structure that is placed on a per-device queue for processing. When an input or output operation completes, the device driver receives an interrupt from the controller. The interrupt service routine removes the appropriate request from the device's queue, notifies the requester that the command has completed, and then starts the next request from the queue. The I/O queues are the primary means of communication between the top and bottom halves of a device driver.

Because I/O queues are shared among asynchronous routines, access to the queues must be synchronized. Routines that make up the top half of a device driver must raise the processor priority level (using *splbio()*, *spltty()*, etc.) to prevent the bottom half from being entered as a result of an interrupt while a top-half routine is manipulating an I/O queue. Synchronization among multiple processes starting I/O requests also must be done. This synchronization is done using the mechanisms described in Section 4.3.

Interrupt Handling

Interrupts are generated by devices to signal that an operation has completed or that a change in status has occurred. On receiving a device interrupt, the system invokes the appropriate device-driver interrupt service routine with one or more parameters that identify uniquely the device that requires service. These parameters are needed because device drivers typically support multiple devices of the same type. If the interrupting device's identity were not supplied with each interrupt, the driver would be forced to poll all the potential devices to identify the device that interrupted.

The system arranges for the unit-number parameter to be passed to the interrupt service routine for each device by installing the address of an auxiliary glue routine in the interrupt-vector table. This glue routine, rather than the actual interrupt service routine, is invoked to service the interrupt; it takes the following actions:

1. Save all volatile registers.

2. Update statistics on device interrupts.

3. Call the interrupt service routine with the appropriate unit number parameter.

4. Restore the volatile registers saved in step 1.

5. Return from the interrupt.

Because a glue routine is interposed between the interrupt-vector table and the interrupt service routine, device drivers do not need to be concerned with saving and restoring machine state. In addition, special-purpose instructions that cannot be generated from C, which are needed by the hardware to support interrupts, can be kept out of the device driver; this interposition of a glue routine permits device drivers to be written without assembly language.

6.2   Block Devices

Block devices include disks and tapes. The task of the block-device interface is to convert from the user abstraction of a disk as an array of bytes to the structure imposed by the underlying physical medium. Although the user may wish to write a single byte to a disk, the hardware can read and write only in multiples of sectors. Hence, the system must arrange to read in the sector containing the byte to be modified, to replace the affected byte, and to write back the sector to the disk. This operation of converting random access to an array of bytes to reads and writes of disk sectors is known as *block I/O*. Block devices are accessible directly through appropriate device special files, but are more commonly accessed indirectly through the filesystem (see Section 8.2).

Processes may read data in sizes smaller than a disk block. The first time that a small read is required from a particular disk block, the block will be transferred from the disk into a kernel buffer. Later reads of parts of the same block then require only copying from the kernel buffer to the memory of the user process. Multiple small writes are treated similarly. A buffer is allocated from the cache when the first write to a disk block is made, and later writes to part of the same block are then likely to require only copying into the kernel buffer, and no disk I/O.

In addition to providing the abstraction of arbitrary alignment of reads and writes, the block buffer cache reduces the number of disk I/O transfers required by filesystem accesses. Because system-parameter files, commands, and directories are read repeatedly, their data blocks are usually in the buffer cache when they are needed. Thus, the kernel does not need to read them from the disk every time that they are requested.

If the system crashes while data for a particular block are in the cache but have not yet been written to disk, the filesystem on the disk will be incorrect and those data will be lost. (Critical system data, such as the contents of directories, however, are written synchronously to disk, to ensure filesystem consistency; operations requiring synchronous I/O are described in the last subsection of Section 8.2.) So that lost data are minimized, writes are forced periodically for dirty buffer blocks. These forced writes are done (usually every 30 seconds) by a user process, **update**, which uses the *sync* system call. There is also a system call, *fsync*, that a process can use to force all dirty blocks of a single file to be written to disk immediately; this synchronization is useful for ensuring database consistency or before removing an editor backup file.

Most magnetic-tape accesses are done through the appropriate raw tape device, bypassing the block buffer cache. When the cache is used, tape blocks must still be written in order, so the tape driver forces synchronous writes for them.

Entry Points for Block-Device Drivers

Device drivers for block devices are described by an entry in the *bdevsw* table. Each *bdevsw* structure contains the following entry points:

open   Open the device in preparation for I/O operations. A device's open entry point will be called for each *open* system call on a block special device file, or, internally, when a device is prepared for mounting a filesystem with the *mount* system call. The *open*( ) routine will commonly verify the integrity of the associated medium. For example, it will verify that the device was identified during the autoconfiguration phase and, for tape and disk drives, that a medium is present and online.

strategy Start a read or write operation, and return immediately. I/O requests to or from filesystems located on a device are translated by the system into calls to the block I/O routines *bread*( ) and *bwrite*( ). These block I/O routines in turn call the device's strategy routine to read or write data not in the cache. Each call to the strategy routine specifies a pointer to a *buf* structure containing the parameters for an I/O request.

If the request is synchronous, the caller must sleep (on the address of the *buf* structure) until I/O completes.

close   Close a device. The *close()* routine is called after the final client interested in using the device terminates. These semantics are defined by the higher-level I/O facilities. Disk devices have nothing to do when a device is closed, and thus use a null *close()* routine. Devices that support access to only a single client must mark the device as available once again. Closing a tape drive that was open for writing typically causes end-of-file marks to be written on the tape and the tape to be rewound.

dump   Write all physical memory to the device. The dump entry point saves the contents of memory on secondary storage. The system automatically takes a dump when it detects an unrecoverable error and is about to *crash*. The dump is used in a postmortem analysis of the problem that caused the system to crash. The dump routine is invoked with the processor priority at its highest level; thus, the device driver must poll for device status, rather than wait for interrupts. All disk devices are expected to support this entry point; some tape devices do as well.

psize   Return the size of a disk-drive partition. The driver is supplied a logical unit and is expected to return the size of that unit, typically a disk-drive partition, in DEV_BSIZE blocks. This entry point is used during the bootstrap procedure to calculate the location at which a crash dump should be placed and to determine the sizes of the swap devices.

Sorting of Disk I/O Requests

The kernel provides a generic *disksort()* routine that can be used by all the disk device drivers to sort I/O requests into a drive's request queue using an *elevator sorting algorithm*. This algorithm sorts requests in a cyclic, ascending, cylinder order, so that requests can be serviced with a minimal number of one-way scans over the drive. This ordering was originally designed to support the normal read-ahead requested by the filesystem as well as to counteract the filesystem's random placement of data on a drive. With the improved placement algorithms in the current filesystem, the effect of the *disksort()* routine is less noticeable; *disksort()* produces the largest effect when there are multiple simultaneous users of a drive.

The *disksort()* algorithm is shown in Fig. 6.2. A drive's request queue is made up of one or two lists of requests ordered by cylinder number. The request at the front of the first list indicates the current position of the drive. If a second list is present, it is made up of requests that lie before the current position. Each new request is sorted into either the first or the second list, according to the request's location. When the heads reach the end of the first list, the drive begins servicing the other list.

Disk sorting can also be important on machines that have a fast processor, but that do not sort requests within the device driver. In this situation, if a write of

```
disksort(dq, bp)
    drive queue *dq;
    buffer *bp;
{
    if (drive queue is empty) {
        place the buffer at the front of the drive queue;
        return;
    }
    if (request lies before the first active request) {
        locate the beginning of the second request list;
        sort bp into the second request list;
    } else
        sort bp into the current request list;
}
```

Figure 6.2 Algorithm for *disksort*().

---

several Kbyte is honored in order of queueing, it can block other processes from accessing the disk while it completes. Sorting requests provides some scheduling, which more fairly distributes accesses to the disk controller.

Disk Labels

Many disk controllers require the device driver to identify the location of disk sectors that are to be transferred by their cylinder, track, and rotational offset. For maximum throughput efficiency, this information is also needed by the filesystem when deciding how to lay out files. Finally, a disk may be broken up into several partitions, each of which may be used for a separate filesystem or swap area.

Historically, the information about the geometry of the disk and about the layout of the partitions was compiled into the kernel device drivers. This approach had several flaws. First, it was cumbersome to have all the possible disk types and partitions compiled into the kernel. Any time that a disk with a new geometry was added, the driver tables had to be updated and the kernel recompiled. It was also restrictive in that there was only one choice of partition table for each drive type. Choosing a different set of tables required modifying the disk driver and rebuilding the kernel. Installing new tables also required dumping all the disks of that type on the system, then booting the new kernel and restoring them onto the new partitions. Disks with different partition layouts could not be moved from one system to another. An additional problem arose when nonstandard partition tables were used; new releases from the vendor had to have the partition tables modified before they could be used on an existing system.

For all these reasons, 4.4BSD and most commercial UNIX vendors added *disk labels*. A disk label contains detailed geometry information, including cylinder, track, and sector layout, along with any other driver-specific information. It also contains information about the partition layout and usage, the latter describing partition usage: type of filesystem, swap partition, or unused. For the fast filesystem, the partition usage contains enough additional information to enable the filesystem check program (**fsck**) to locate the alternate superblocks for the filesystem.

Having labels on each disk means that partition information can be different for each disk, and that it carries over when the disk is moved from one system to another. It also means that, when previously unknown types of disks are connected to the system, the system administrator can use them without changing the disk driver, recompiling, and rebooting the system.

The label is located near the beginning of each drive—usually, in block zero. It must be located in the first track, because the device driver does not know the geometry of the disk until the driver has read the label. Thus, it must assume that the label is in cylinder zero, track zero, at some valid offset within that track. Most architectures have hardware (or first-level) bootstrap code stored in read-only memory (ROM). When the machine is powered up or the reset button is pressed, the CPU executes the hardware bootstrap code from the ROM. The hardware bootstrap code typically reads the first few sectors on the disk into the main memory, then branches to the address of the first location that it read. The program stored in these first few sectors is the second-level bootstrap. Having the disk label stored in the part of the disk read as part of the hardware bootstrap allows the second-level bootstrap to have the disk-label information. This information gives it the ability to find the root filesystem and hence the files, such as the kernel, needed to bring up 4.4BSD. The size and location of the second-level bootstrap are dependent on the requirements of the hardware bootstrap code. Since there is no standard for disk-label formats and the hardware bootstrap code usually understands only the vendor label, it is often necessary to support both the vendor and the 4.4BSD disk labels. Here, the vendor label must be placed where the hardware bootstrap ROM code expects it; the 4.4BSD label must be placed out of the way of the vendor label but within the area that is read in by the hardware bootstrap code, so that it will be available to the second-level bootstrap.

6.3   Character Devices

Almost all peripherals on the system, except network interfaces, have a character-device interface. A character device usually maps the hardware interface into a byte stream, similar to that of the filesystem. Character devices of this type include terminals (e.g., **/dev/tty00**), line printers (e.g, **/dev/lp0**), an interface to physical main memory (**/dev/mem**), and a bottomless sink for data and an endless source of end-of-file markers (**/dev/null**). Some of these character devices, such as terminal devices, may display special behavior on line boundaries, but in general are still treated as byte streams.

Devices emulating terminals use buffers that are smaller than those used for disks and tapes. This buffering system involves small (usually 64-byte) blocks of characters kept in linked lists. Although all free character buffers are kept in a single free list, most device drivers that use them limit the number of characters that can be queued at one time for a single terminal port.

Devices such as high-speed graphics interfaces may have their own buffers or may always do I/O directly into the address space of the user; they too are classed as character devices. Some of these drivers may recognize special types of records, and thus be further from the plain byte-stream model.

The character interface for disks and tapes is also called the *raw device interface*; it provides an unstructured interface to the device. Its primary task is to arrange for direct I/O to and from the device. The disk driver isolates the details of tracks, cylinders, and the like from the rest of the kernel. It also handles the asynchronous nature of I/O by maintaining and ordering an active queue of pending transfers. Each entry in the queue specifies whether it is for reading or writing, the main-memory address for the transfer, the device address for the transfer (usually a disk sector number), and the transfer size (in bytes).

All other restrictions of the underlying hardware are passed through the character interface to its clients, making character-device interfaces the furthest from the byte-stream model. Thus, the user process must abide by the sectoring restrictions imposed by the underlying hardware. For magnetic disks, the file offset and transfer size must be a multiple of the sector size. The character interface does not copy the user data into a kernel buffer before putting them on an I/O queue. Rather, it arranges to have the I/O done directly to or from the address space of the process. The size and alignment of the transfer is limited by the physical device. However, the transfer size is not restricted by the maximum size of the internal buffers of the system, because these buffers are not used.

The character interface is typically used by only those system utility programs that have an intimate knowledge of the data structures on the disk or tape. The character interface also allows user-level prototyping; for example, the 4.2BSD filesystem implementation was written and largely tested as a user process that used a raw disk interface, before the code was moved into the kernel.

Character devices are described by entries in the *cdevsw* table. The entry points in this table (see Table 6.1 on page 202) are used to support raw access to block-oriented devices, as well as normal access to character-oriented devices through the terminal driver. Because of the diverse requirements of these two types of devices, the set of entry points is the union of two disjoint sets. Raw devices support a subset of the entry points that correspond to those entry points found in a block-device driver, whereas character devices support the full set of entry points. Each is described in the following sections.

Raw Devices and Physical I/O

Most raw devices differ from block devices only in the way that they do I/O. Whereas block devices read and write data to and from the system buffer cache, raw devices transfer data to and from user data buffers. Bypassing the buffer cache eliminates the memory-to-memory copy that must be done by block devices, but also denies applications the benefits of data caching. In addition, for devices that support both raw- and block-device access, applications must take

Table 6.1 Entry points for character and raw device drivers.

Entry point	Function
open()	open the device
close()	close the device
ioctl()	do an I/O control operation
mmap()	map device offset to memory location
read()	do an input operation
reset()	reinitialize device after a bus reset
select()	poll device for I/O readiness
stop()	stop output on the device
write()	do an output operation

care to preserve consistency between data in the buffer cache and data written directly to the device; the raw device should be used only when the block device is idle. Raw-device access is used by many filesystem utilities, such as the filesystem check program, **fsck**, and by programs that read and write magnetic tapes— for example, **tar**, **dump**, and **restore**.

Because raw devices bypass the buffer cache, they are responsible for managing their own buffer structures. Most devices borrow swap buffers to describe their I/O. The read and write routines use the *physio*() routine to start a raw I/O operation (see Fig. 6.3). The *strategy* parameter identifies a block-device strategy routine that starts I/O operations on the device. The buffer indicated by *bp* is used by *physio*() in constructing the request(s) made to the strategy routine. The device, read–write flag, and *uio* parameters completely specify the I/O operation that should be done. The *minphys*() routine is called by *physio*() to adjust the size of each I/O transfer before the latter is passed to the strategy routine; this call to *minphys*() allows the transfer to be done in sections, according to the maximum transfer size supported by the device.

Raw-device I/O operations request the hardware device to transfer data directly to or from the data buffer in the user program's address space described by the *uio* parameter. Thus, unlike I/O operations that do direct memory access (DMA) from buffers in the kernel address space, raw I/O operations must check that the user's buffer is accessible by the device, and must lock it into memory for the duration of the transfer.

Character-Oriented Devices

Character-oriented I/O devices are typified by terminal multiplexers, although they also include printers and other character- or line-oriented devices. These devices are usually accessed through the terminal driver, described in Chapter 10. The

```
physio(strategy, bp, dev, flags, minphys, uio)
    int strategy();
    buffer *bp;
    device dev;
    int flags;
    int minphys();
    struct uio *uio;
{
    if no buffer passed in, allocate a swap buffer;
    while (uio is not exhausted) {
        check user read/write access at uio location;
        if buffer passed in, wait until not busy;
        mark the buffer busy for physical I/O;
        set up the buffer for a maximum sized transfer;
        call minphys to bound the transfer size;
        lock the part of the user address space
            involved in the transfer;
        map the user pages into the buffer;
        call strategy to start the transfer;
        raise the priority level to splbio;
        wait for the transfer to complete;
        unmap the user pages from the buffer;
        unlock the part of the address space previously
            locked;
        wake up anybody waiting on the buffer;
        lower the priority level;
        deduct the transfer size from the total number
            of data to transfer;
    }
    if using swap buffer, free it;
}
```

Figure 6.3 Algorithm for physical I/O.

---

close tie to the terminal driver has heavily influenced the structure of character-device drivers. For example, several entry points in the *cdevsw* structure exist for communication between the generic terminal handler and the terminal multiplexer hardware drivers.

Entry Points for Character-Device Drivers

A device driver for a character device is defined by an entry in the *cdevsw* table. This structure contains many of the same entry points found in an entry in the *bdevsw* table.

open   Open or close a character device. The *open*() and *close*() entry points
          provide functions similar to those of a block device driver. For character
close   devices that simply provide raw access to a block device, these entry
          points are usually the same. But some block devices do not have these
          entry points, whereas most character devices do have them.

read   Read data from a device. For raw devices, this entry point normally just
          calls the *physio*() routine with device-specific parameters. For terminal-
          oriented devices, a read request is passed immediately to the terminal
          driver. For other devices, a read request requires that the specified data be
          copied into the kernel's address space, typically with the *uiomove*() rou-
          tine, and then be passed to the device.

write   Write data to a device. This entry point is a direct parallel of the read
          entry point: Raw devices use *physio*(), terminal-oriented devices call the
          terminal driver to do this operation, and other devices handle the request
          internally.

ioctl   Do an operation other than a read or write. This entry point originally
          provided a mechanism to get and set device parameters for terminal
          devices; its use has expanded to other types of devices as well. Histori-
          cally, *ioctl*() operations have varied widely from device to device.
          4.4BSD, however, defines a set of operations that is supported by all tape
          devices. These operations position tapes, return unit status, write end-of-
          file marks, and place a tape drive off-line.

select Check the device to see whether data are available for reading, or space is
          available for writing, data. The select entry point is used by the *select* sys-
          tem call in checking file descriptors associated with device special files.
          For raw devices, a select operation is meaningless, since data are not
          buffered. Here, the entry point is set to *seltrue*(), a routine that returns
          true for any select request. For devices used with the terminal driver, this
          entry point is set to *ttselect*(), a routine described in Chapter 10.

stop   Stop output on a device. The stop routine is defined for only those
          devices used with the terminal driver. For these devices, the stop routine
          halts transmission on a line when the terminal driver receives a *stop char-
          acter*—for example, "^S"—or when it prepares to flush its output queues.

mmap   Map a device offset into a memory address. This entry point is called by
          the virtual-memory system to convert a logical mapping to a physical
          address. For example, it converts an offset in **/dev/mem** to a kernel
          address.

reset   Reset device state after a bus reset. The reset routine is called from the
          bus-adapter support routines after a bus reset is made. The device driver
          is expected to reinitialize the hardware to set into a known state—typi-
          cally the state it has when the system is initially booted.

6.4   Descriptor Management and Services

For user processes, all I/O is done through descriptors. The user interface to descriptors was described in Section 2.6. This section describes how the kernel manages descriptors, and how it provides descriptor services, such as locking and selecting.

System calls that refer to open files take a file descriptor as an argument to specify the file. The file descriptor is used by the kernel to index into the *descriptor table* for the current process (kept in the *filedesc* structure, a substructure of the process structure for the process) to locate a *file entry*, or *file structure*. The relations of these data structures are shown in Fig. 6.4.

The file entry provides a file type and a pointer to an underlying object for the descriptor. For data files, the file entry points to a *vnode* structure that references a substructure containing the filesystem-specific information described in Chapters 7, 8, and 9. The vnode layer is described in Section 6.5. Special files do not have data blocks allocated on the disk; they are handled by the *special-device* filesystem that calls appropriate drivers to handle I/O for them. The 4.4BSD file entry may also reference a *socket*, instead of a file. Sockets have a different file type, and the file entry points to a system block that is used in doing interprocess communication. The virtual-memory system supports the mapping of files into a process's address space. Here, the file descriptor must reference a vnode that will be partially or completely mapped into the user's address space.

Open File Entries

The set of file entries is the focus of activity for file descriptors. They contain the information necessary to access the underlying objects and to maintain common information.

The file entry is an object-oriented data structure. Each entry contains a type and an array of function pointers that translate the generic operations on file descriptors into the specific actions associated with their type. In 4.4BSD, there are two descriptor types: files and sockets. The operations that must be implemented for each type are as follows:

Figure 6.4 File-descriptor reference to a file entry.

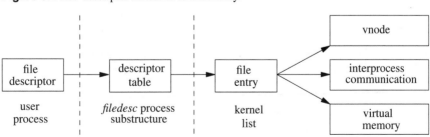

• Read from the descriptor

• Write to the descriptor

• Select on the descriptor

• Do *ioctl* operations on the descriptor

• Close and possibly deallocate the object associated with the descriptor

Note that there is no *open* routine defined in the object table. 4.4BSD treats descriptors in an object-oriented fashion only after they are created. This approach was taken because sockets and files have different characteristics. Generalizing the interface to handle both types of descriptors at open time would have complicated an otherwise simple interface.

Each file entry has a pointer to a data structure that contains information specific to the instance of the underlying object. The data structure is opaque to the routines that manipulate the file entry. A reference to the data structure is passed on each call to a function that implements a file operation. All state associated with an instance of an object must be stored in that instance's data structure; the underlying objects are not permitted to manipulate the file entry themselves.

The *read* and *write* system calls do not take an offset in the file as an argument. Instead, each read or write updates the current *file offset* in the file according to the number of bytes transferred. The offset determines the position in the file for the next read or write. The offset can be set directly by the *lseek* system call. Since more than one process may open the same file, and each such process needs its own offset for the file, the offset cannot be stored in the per-object data structure. Thus, each *open* system call allocates a new file entry, and the open file entry contains the offset.

Some semantics associated with all file descriptors are enforced at the descriptor level, before the underlying system call is invoked. These semantics are maintained in a set of flags associated with the descriptor. For example, the flags record whether the descriptor is open for reading, writing, or both reading and writing. If a descriptor is marked as open for reading only, an attempt to write it will be caught by the descriptor code. Thus, the functions defined for doing reading and writing do not need to check the validity of the request; we can implement them knowing that they will never receive an invalid request.

Other information maintained in the flags includes

• The *no-delay* (*NDELAY*) flag: If a read or a write would cause the process to block, the system call returns an error (EWOULDBLOCK) instead.

• The *asynchronous* (*ASYNC*) flag: The kernel watches for a change in the status of the descriptor, and arranges to send a signal (SIGIO) when a read or write becomes possible.

Other information that is specific to regular files also is maintained in the flags field:

- Information on whether the descriptor holds a shared or exclusive lock on the underlying file: The locking primitives could be extended to work on sockets, as well as on files. However, the descriptors for a socket rarely refer to the same file entry. The only way for two processes to share the same socket descriptor is for a parent to share the descriptor with its child by forking, or for one process to pass the descriptor to another in a message.

- The *append* flag: Each time that a write is made to the file, the offset pointer is first set to the end of the file. This feature is useful when, for example, multiple processes are writing to the same log file.

Each file entry has a *reference count*. A single process may have multiple references to the entry because of calls to the *dup* or *fcntl* system calls. Also, file structures are inherited by the child process after a *fork*, so several different processes may reference the same file entry. Thus, a read or write by either process on the twin descriptors will advance the file offset. This semantic allows two processes to read the same file or to interleave output to the same file. Another process that has independently opened the file will refer to that file through a different file structure with a different file offset. This functionality was the original reason for the existence of the file structure; the file structure provides a place for the file offset intermediate between the descriptor and the underlying object.

   Each time that a new reference is created, the reference count is incremented. When a descriptor is closed (any one of (1) explicitly with a *close*, (2) implicitly after an *exec* because the descriptor has been marked as close-on-exec, or (3) on process exit), the reference count is decremented. When the reference count drops to zero, the file entry is freed.

   The AF_LOCAL domain interprocess-communication facility allows descriptors to be sent between processes. While a descriptor is in transit between processes, it may not have any explicit references. It must not be deallocated, as it will be needed when the message is received by the destination process. However, the message might never be received; thus, the file entry also holds a *message count* for each entry. The message count is incremented for each descriptor that is in transit, and is decremented when the descriptor is received. The file entry might need to be reclaimed when all the remaining references are in messages. For more details on message passing in the AF_LOCAL domain, see Section 11.6.

   The close-on-exec flag is kept in the descriptor table, rather than in the file entry. This flag is not shared among all the references to the file entry because it is an attribute of the file descriptor itself. The close-on-exec flag is the only piece of information that is kept in the descriptor table, rather than being shared in the file entry.

Management of Descriptors

The *fcntl* system call manipulates the file structure. It can be used to make the following changes to a descriptor:

• Duplicate a descriptor as though by a *dup* system call.

• Get or set the close-on-exec flag. When a process *forks*, all the parent's descriptors are duplicated in the child. The child process then *execs* a new process. Any of the child's descriptors that were marked close-on-exec are closed. The remaining descriptors are available to the newly executed process.

• Set the descriptor into nonblocking mode. If any data are available for a read operation, or if any space is available for a write operation, an immediate partial read or write is done. If no data are available for a read operation, or if a write operation would block, the system call returns an error showing that the operation would block, instead of putting the process to sleep. This facility was not implemented for regular files in 4.4BSD, because filesystem I/O is always expected to complete within a few milliseconds.

• Force all writes to append data to the end of the file, instead of at the descriptor's current location in the file.

• Send a signal to the process when it is possible to do I/O.

• Send a signal to a process when an exception condition arises, such as when urgent data arrive on an interprocess-communication channel.

• Set or get the process identifier or process-group identifier to which the two I/O–related signals in the previous steps should be sent.

• Test or change the status of a lock on a range of bytes within an underlying file. Locking operations are described in the next subsection.

The implementation of the *dup* system call is easy. If the process has reached its limit on open files, the kernel returns an error. Otherwise, the kernel scans the current process's descriptor table, starting at descriptor zero, until it finds an unused entry. The kernel allocates the entry to point to the same file entry as does the descriptor being duplicated. The kernel then increments the reference count on the file entry, and returns the index of the allocated descriptor-table entry. The *fcntl* system call provides a similar function, except that it specifies a descriptor from which to start the scan.

Sometimes, a process wants to allocate a specific descriptor-table entry. Such a request is made with the *dup2* system call. The process specifies the descriptor-table index into which the duplicated reference should be placed. The kernel implementation is the same as for *dup*, except that the scan to find a free entry is changed to close the requested entry if that entry is open, and then to allocate the entry as before. No action is taken if the new and old descriptors are the same.

The system implements getting or setting the close-on-exec flag via the *fcntl* system call by making the appropriate change to the flags field of the associated descriptor-table entry. Other attributes that *fcntl* can get or set manipulate the flags in the file entry. However, the implementation of the various flags cannot be handled by the generic code that manages the file entry. Instead, the file flags must be passed through the object interface to the type-specific routines to do the appropriate operation on the underlying object. For example, manipulation of the nonblocking flag for a socket must be done by the socket layer, since only that layer knows whether an operation can block.

The implementation of the *ioctl* system call is broken into two major levels. The upper level handles the system call itself. The *ioctl* call includes a descriptor, a command, and pointer to a data area. The command argument encodes what the size is of the data area for the parameters, and whether the parameters are input, output, or both input and output. The upper level is responsible for decoding the command argument, allocating a buffer, and copying in any input data. If a return value is to be generated and there is no input, the buffer is zeroed. Finally, the *ioctl* is dispatched through the file-entry *ioctl* function, along with the I/O buffer, to the lower-level routine that implements the requested operation.

The lower level does the requested operation. Along with the command argument, it receives a pointer to the I/O buffer. The upper level has already checked for valid memory references, but the lower level may do more precise argument validation because it knows more about the expected nature of the arguments. However, it does not need to copy the arguments in or out of the user process. If the command is successful and produces output, the lower level places the results in the buffer provided by the top level. When the lower level returns, the upper level copies the results to the process.

File-Descriptor Locking

Early UNIX systems had no provision for locking files. Processes that needed to synchronize access to a file had to use a separate *lock file*. A process would try to create a lock file. If the creation succeeded, then the process could proceed with its update; if the creation failed, the process would wait, and then try again. This mechanism had three drawbacks:

1. Processes consumed CPU time by looping over attempts to create locks.

2. Locks left lying around because of system crashes had to be removed (normally in a system-startup command script).

3. Processes running as the special system-administrator user, the *superuser*, are always permitted to create files, and so were forced to use a different mechanism.

Although it is possible to work around all these problems, the solutions are not straightforward, so a mechanism for locking files was added in 4.2BSD.

The most general locking schemes allow multiple processes to update a file concurrently. Several of these techniques are discussed in [Peterson, 1983]. A simpler technique is to serialize access to a file with locks. For standard system applications, a mechanism that locks at the granularity of a file is sufficient. So, 4.2BSD and 4.3BSD provided only a fast whole-file locking mechanism. The semantics of these locks include allowing locks to be inherited by child processes and releasing locks only on the last close of a file.

Certain applications require the ability to lock pieces of a file. Locking facilities that support a byte-level granularity are well understood [Bass, 1981]. Unfortunately, they are not powerful enough to be used by database systems that require nested hierarchical locks, but are complex enough to require a large and cumbersome implementation compared to the simpler whole-file locks. Because byte-range locks are mandated by the POSIX standard, the developers added them to 4.4BSD reluctantly. The semantics of byte-range locks come from the lock's initial implementation in System V, which included releasing all locks held by a process on a file every time a *close* system call was done on a descriptor referencing that file. The 4.2BSD whole-file locks are removed only on the last close. A problem with the POSIX semantics is that an application can lock a file, then call a library routine that opens, reads, and closes the locked file. Calling the library routine will have the unexpected effect of releasing the locks held by the application. Another problem is that a file must be open for writing to be allowed to get an exclusive lock. A process that does not have permission to open a file for writing cannot get an exclusive lock on that file. To avoid these problems, yet remain POSIX compliant, 4.4BSD provides separate interfaces for byte-range locks and whole-file locks. The byte-range locks follow the POSIX semantics; the whole-file locks follow the traditional 4.2BSD semantics. The two types of locks can be used concurrently; they will serialize against each other properly.

Both whole-file locks and byte-range locks use the same implementation; the whole-file locks are implemented as a range lock over an entire file. The kernel handles the other differing semantics between the two implementations by having the byte-range locks be applied to processes whereas the whole-file locks are applied to descriptors. Because descriptors are shared with child processes, the whole-file locks are inherited. Because the child process gets its own process structure, the byte-range locks are not inherited. The last-close versus every-close semantics are a small bit of special-case code in the close routine that checks whether the underlying object is a process or a descriptor. It releases locks on every call if the lock is associated with a process, and only when the reference count drops to zero if the lock is associated with a descriptor.

Locking schemes can be classified according to the extent that they are enforced. A scheme in which locks are enforced for every process without choice is said to use *mandatory locks*, whereas a scheme in which locks are enforced for only those processes that request them is said to use *advisory locks*. Clearly, advisory locks are effective only when all programs accessing a file use the locking scheme. With mandatory locks, there must be some override policy implemented in the kernel. With advisory locks, the policy is left to the user programs. In the 4.4BSD system, programs with superuser privilege are allowed to override any protection scheme. Because many of the programs that need to use locks must also run as the superuser, 4.2BSD implemented advisory locks, rather than creating an additional protection scheme that was inconsistent with the UNIX philosophy or that could not be used by privileged programs. The use of advisory locks carried over to the POSIX specification of byte-range locks and is retained in 4.4BSD.

The 4.4BSD file-locking facilities allow cooperating programs to apply advisory *shared* or *exclusive* locks on ranges of bytes within a file. Only one process may have an exclusive lock on a byte range, whereas multiple shared locks may be present. Both shared and exclusive locks cannot be present on a byte range at the same time. If any lock is requested when another process holds an exclusive lock, or an exclusive lock is requested when another process holds any lock, the lock request will block until the lock can be obtained. Because shared and exclusive locks are only advisory, even if a process has obtained a lock on a file, another process may access the file if it ignores the locking mechanism.

So that there are no races between creating and locking a file, a lock can be requested as part of opening a file. Once a process has opened a file, it can manipulate locks without needing to close and reopen the file. This feature is useful, for example, when a process wishes to apply a shared lock, to read information, to determine whether an update is required, then to apply an exclusive lock and to update the file.

A request for a lock will cause a process to block if the lock cannot be obtained immediately. In certain instances, this blocking is unsatisfactory. For example, a process that wants only to check whether a lock is present would require a separate mechanism to find out this information. Consequently, a process can specify that its locking request should return with an error if a lock cannot be obtained immediately. Being able to request a lock conditionally is useful to *daemon* processes that wish to service a spooling area. If the first instance of the daemon locks the directory where spooling takes place, later daemon processes can easily check to see whether an active daemon exists. Since locks exist only while the locking processes exist, locks can never be left active after the processes exit or if the system crashes.

The implementation of locks is done on a per-filesystem basis. The implementation for the local filesystems is described in Section 7.5. A network-based filesystem has to coordinate locks with a central lock manager that is usually located on the server exporting the filesystem. Client lock requests must be sent to the lock manager. The lock manager arbitrates among lock requests from processes running on its server and from the various clients to which it is exporting the filesystem. The most complex operation for the lock manager is recovering lock state when a client or server is rebooted or becomes partitioned from the rest of the network. The 4.4BSD system does not have a network-based lock manager.

Multiplexing I/O on Descriptors

A process sometimes wants to handle I/O on more than one descriptor. For example, consider a remote login program that wants to read data from the keyboard and to send them through a socket to a remote machine. This program also wants to read data from the socket connected to the remote end and to write them to the screen. If a process makes a read request when there are no data available, it is normally blocked in the kernel until the data become available. In our example, blocking is unacceptable. If the process reads from the keyboard and blocks, it will be unable to read data from the remote end that are destined for the screen. The user does not know what to type until more data arrive from the remote end; hence, the session deadlocks. Conversely, if the process reads from the remote end when there are no data for the screen, it will block and will be unable to read from the terminal. Again, deadlock would occur if the remote end were waiting for output before sending any data. There is an analogous set of problems to blocking on the writes to the screen or to the remote end. If a user has stopped output to their screen by typing the stop character, the write will block until they type the start character. In the meantime, the process cannot read from the keyboard to find out that the user wants to flush the output.

Historic UNIX systems have handled the multiplexing problem by using multiple processes that communicate through pipes or some other interprocess-communication facility, such as shared memory. This approach, however, can result in significant overhead as a result of context switching among the processes if the cost of processing input is small compared to the cost of a context switch. Furthermore, it is often more straightforward to implement applications of this sort in a single process. For these reasons, 4.4BSD provides three mechanisms that permit multiplexing I/O on descriptors: *polling I/O*, *nonblocking I/O*, and *signal-driven I/O*. Polling is done with the *select* system call, described in the next subsection. Operations on nonblocking descriptors complete immediately, partially complete an input or output operation and return a partial count, or return an error that shows that the operation could not be completed at all. Descriptors that have signaling enabled cause the associated process or process group to be notified when the I/O state of the descriptor changes.

There are four possible alternatives that avoid the blocking problem:

1. Set all the descriptors into nonblocking mode. The process can then try operations on each descriptor in turn, to find out which descriptors are ready to do I/O. The problem with this approach is that the process must run continuously to discover whether there is any I/O to be done.

2. Enable all descriptors of interest to signal when I/O can be done. The process can then wait for a signal to discover when it is possible to do I/O. The drawback to this approach is that signals are expensive to catch. Hence, signal-driven I/O is impractical for applications that do moderate to large amounts of I/O.

3. Have the system provide a method for asking which descriptors are capable of doing I/O. If none of the requested descriptors are ready, the system can put the process to sleep until a descriptor becomes ready. This approach avoids the problem of deadlock, because the process will be awakened whenever it is possible to do I/O, and will be told which descriptor is ready. The drawback is that the process must do two system calls per operation: one to poll for the descriptor that is ready to do I/O and another to do the operation itself.

4. Have the process notify the system of all the descriptors that it is interested in reading, then do a blocking read on that set of descriptors. When the read returns, the process is notified on which descriptor the read completed. The benefit of this approach is that the process does a single system call to specify the set of descriptors, then loops doing only reads [Accetta et al, 1986].

The first approach is available in 4.4BSD as nonblocking I/O. It typically is used for output descriptors, because the operation typically will not block. Rather than doing a *select*, which nearly always succeeds, followed immediately by a *write*, it is more efficient to try the *write* and revert to using *select* only during periods when the *write* returns a blocking error. The second approach is available in 4.4BSD as signal-driven I/O. It typically is used for rare events, such as for the arrival of out-of-band data on a socket. For such rare events, the cost of handling an occasional signal is lower than that of checking constantly with *select* to find out whether there are any pending data.

The third approach is available in 4.4BSD via the *select* system call. Although less efficient than the fourth approach, it is a more general interface. In addition to handling reading from multiple descriptors, it handles writes to multiple descriptors, notification of exceptional conditions, and timeout when no I/O is possible.

The *select* interface takes three masks of descriptors to be monitored, corresponding to interest in reading, writing, and exceptional conditions. In addition, it takes a timeout value for returning from *select* if none of the requested descriptors becomes ready before a specified amount of time has elapsed. The *select* call returns the same three masks of descriptors after modifying them to show that the descriptors that are able to do reading, to do writing, or to provide an exceptional condition. If none of the descriptors has become ready in the timeout interval, *select* returns showing that no descriptors are ready for I/O.

Implementation of *Select*

The implementation of *select*, like that of much other kernel functionality, is divided into a generic top layer and many device- or socket-specific bottom pieces.

At the top level, *select* decodes the user's request and then calls the appropriate lower-level select functions. The top level takes the following steps:

1. Copy and validate the descriptor masks for read, write, and exceptional conditions. Doing validation requires checking that each requested descriptor is currently open by the process.

2. Set the *selecting* flag for the process.

3. For each descriptor in each mask, poll the device by calling its select routine. If the descriptor is not able to do the requested I/O operation, the device select routine is responsible for recording that the process wants to do I/O. When I/O becomes possible for the descriptor—usually as a result of an interrupt

from the underlying device—a notification must be issued for the selecting process.

4. Because the selection process may take a long time, the kernel does not want to block out I/O during the time it takes to poll all the requested descriptors. Instead, the kernel arranges to detect the occurrence of I/O that may affect the status of the descriptors being polled. When such I/O occurs, the select-notification routine, *selwakeup*(), clears the *selecting* flag. If the top-level select code finds that the *selecting* flag for the process has been cleared while it has been doing the polling, and it has not found any descriptors that are ready to do an operation, then the top level knows that the polling results are incomplete and must be repeated starting at step 2. The other condition that requires the polling to be repeated is a *collision*. Collisions arise when multiple processes attempt to select on the same descriptor at the same time. Because the select routines have only enough space to record a single process identifier, they cannot track multiple processes that need to be awakened when I/O is possible. In such rare instances, all processes that are selecting must be awakened.

5. If no descriptors are ready and the *select* specified a timeout, the kernel posts a timeout for the requested amount of time. The process goes to sleep, giving the address of the kernel global variable *selwait*. Normally, a descriptor will become ready and the process will be notified by *selwakeup*(). When the process is awakened, it repeats the polling process and returns the available descriptors. If none of the descriptors become ready before the timer expires, the process returns with a timed-out error and an empty list of available descriptors.

Each of the low-level polling routines in the terminal drivers and the network protocols follows roughly the same set of steps. A piece of the select routine for a terminal driver is shown in Fig. 6.5. The steps involved in a device select routine are as follows:

1. The socket or device select entry is called with flag of FREAD, FWRITE, or 0 (exceptional condition). The example in Fig. 6.5 shows the FREAD case; the others cases are similar.

2. The poll returns success if the requested operation is possible. In Fig. 6.5, it is possible to read a character if the number of unread characters is greater than zero. In addition, if the carrier has dropped, it is possible to get a read error. A return from *select* does not necessarily mean that there are data to read; rather, it means that a read will not block.

3. If the requested operation is not possible, the process identifier is recorded with the socket or device for later notification. In Fig. 6.5, the recording is done by the *selrecord*() routine. That routine first checks to see whether the current process was the one that was recorded previously for this record; if it

```
struct selinfo {
    pid_t   si_pid;     /* process to be notified */
    short   si_flags;   /* SI_COLL - collision occurred */
};
struct tty *tp;

case FREAD:
    if (nread > 0 || (tp->t_state & TS_CARR_ON) == 0)
        return (1);
    selrecord(curproc, &tp->t_rsel);
    return (0);

selrecord(selector, sip)
    struct proc *selector;
    struct selinfo *sip;
{
    struct proc *p;
    pid_t mypid;

    mypid = selector->p_pid;
    if (sip->si_pid == mypid)
        return;
    if (sip->si_pid && (p = pfind(sip->si_pid)) &&
        p->p_wchan == (caddr_t)&selwait)
        sip->si_flags |= SI_COLL;
    else
        sip->si_pid = mypid;
}
```

Figure 6.5 *Select* code to check for data to read in a terminal driver.

was, then no further action is needed. The second **if** statement checks for a collision. The first part of the conjunction checks to see whether any process identifier is recorded already. If there is none, then there is no collision. If there is a process identifier recorded, it may remain from an earlier call on *select* by a process that is no longer selecting because one of its other descriptors became ready. If that process is still selecting, it will be sleeping on *selwait* (when it is sleeping, the address of the sleep event is stored in *p_wchan*). If it is sleeping on some other event, its *p_wchan* will have a value different from that of *selwait*. If it is running, its *p_wchan* will be zero. If it is not sleeping on *selwait*, there is no collision, and the process identifier is saved in *si_pid*.

4. If multiple processes are selecting on the same socket or device, a collision is recorded for the socket or device, because the structure has only enough space

for a single process identifier. In Fig. 6.5, a collision occurs when the second **if** statement in the *selrecord*() function is true. There is a *tty* structure for each terminal line (or pseudoterminal) on the machine. Normally, only one process at a time is selecting to read from the terminal, so collisions are rare.

Selecting processes must be notified when I/O becomes possible. The steps involved in a status change awakening a process are as follows:

1. The device or socket detects a change in status. Status changes normally occur because of an interrupt (e.g., a character coming in from a keyboard or a packet arriving from the network).

2. *Selwakeup*() is called with a pointer to the *selinfo* structure used by *selrecord*() to record the process identifier, and with a flag showing whether a collision occurred.

3. If the process is sleeping on *selwait*, it is made runnable (or is marked ready, if it is stopped). If the process is sleeping on some event other than *selwait*, it is not made runnable. A spurious call to *selwakeup*() can occur when the process returns from *select* to begin processing one descriptor and then another descriptor on which it had been selecting also becomes ready.

4. If the process has its *selecting* flag set, the flag is cleared so that the kernel will know that its polling results are invalid and must be recomputed.

5. If a collision has occurred, all sleepers on *selwait* are awakened to rescan to see whether one of their descriptors became ready. Awakening all selecting processes is necessary because the *selrecord*() routine could not record all the processes that needed to be awakened. Hence, it has to wake up all processes that could possibly have been interested. Empirically, collisions occur infrequently. If they were a frequent occurrence, it would be worthwhile to store multiple process identifiers in the *selinfo* structure.

Movement of Data Inside the Kernel

Within the kernel, I/O data are described by an array of vectors. Each *I/O vector* or *iovec* has a base address and a length. The I/O vectors are identical to the I/O vectors used by the *readv* and *writev* system calls.

The kernel maintains another structure, called a *uio* structure, that holds additional information about the I/O operation. A sample *uio* structure is shown in Fig. 6.6; it contains

• A pointer to the *iovec* array

• The number of elements in the *iovec* array

• The file offset at which the operation should start

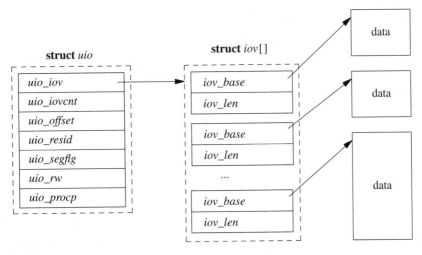

Figure 6.6 A *uio* structure.

- The sum of the lengths of the I/O vectors

- A flag showing whether the source and destination are both within the kernel, or whether the source and destination are split between the user and the kernel

- A flag showing whether the data are being copied from the *uio* structure to the kernel (UIO_WRITE) or from the kernel to the *uio* structure (UIO_READ)

- A pointer to the process whose data area is described by the *uio* structure (the pointer is NULL if the *uio* structure describes an area within the kernel)

All I/O within the kernel is described with *iovec* and *uio* structures. System calls such as *read* and *write* that are not passed an *iovec* create a *uio* to describe their arguments; this *uio* structure is passed to the lower levels of the kernel to specify the parameters of an I/O operation. Eventually, the *uio* structure reaches the part of the kernel responsible for moving the data to or from the process address space: the filesystem, the network, or a device driver. In general, these parts of the kernel do not interpret *uio* structures directly. Instead, they arrange a kernel buffer to hold the data, then use *uiomove()* to copy the data to or from the buffer or buffers described by the *uio* structure. The *uiomove()* routine is called with a pointer to a kernel data area, a data count, and a *uio* structure. As it moves data, it updates the counters and pointers of the *iovec* and *uio* structures by a corresponding amount. If the kernel buffer is not as large as the areas described by the *uio* structure, the *uio* structure will point to the part of the process address space just beyond the location completed most recently. Thus, while servicing a request, the kernel may call *uiomove()* multiple times, each time giving a pointer to a new kernel buffer for the next block of data.

Character device drivers that do not copy data from the process generally do not interpret the *uio* structure. Instead, there is one low-level kernel routine that arranges a direct transfer to or from the address space of the process. Here, a separate I/O operation is done for each *iovec* element, calling back to the driver with one piece at a time.

Historic UNIX systems used global variables in the user area to describe I/O. This approach has several problems. The lower levels of the kernel are not reentrant, because there is exactly one context to describe an I/O operation. The system cannot do scatter-gather I/O, since there is only a single base and size variable per process. Finally, the bottom half of the kernel cannot do I/O, because it does not have a user area.

The one part of the 4.4BSD kernel that does not use *uio* structures is the block-device drivers. The decision not to change these interfaces to use *uio* structures was largely pragmatic. The developers would have had to change many drivers. The existing buffer interface was already decoupled from the user structure; hence, the interface was already reentrant and could be used by the bottom half of the kernel. The only gain was to allow scatter-gather I/O. The kernel does not need scatter-gather operations on block devices, however, and user operations on block devices are done through the buffer cache.

6.5   The Virtual-Filesystem Interface

In 4.3BSD, the file entries directly referenced the local filesystem *inode*. An inode is a data structure that describes the contents of a file; it is more fully described in Section 7.2. This approach worked fine when there was a single filesystem implementation. However, with the advent of multiple filesystem types, the architecture had to be generalized. The new architecture had to support importing of filesystems from other machines including other machines that were running different operating systems.

One alternative would have been to connect the multiple filesystems into the system as different file types. However, this approach would have required massive restructuring of the internal workings of the system, because current directories, references to executables, and several other interfaces used inodes instead of file entries as their point of reference. Thus, it was easier and more logical to add a new object-oriented layer to the system below the file entry and above the inode. This new layer was first implemented by Sun Microsystems, which called it the virtual-node, or *vnode*, layer. Interfaces in the system that had referred previously to inodes were changed to reference generic vnodes. A vnode used by a local filesystem would refer to an inode. A vnode used by a remote filesystem would refer to a protocol control block that described the location and naming information necessary to access the remote file.

Contents of a Vnode

The vnode is an extensible object-oriented interface. It contains information that is generically useful independent of the underlying filesystem object that it represents. The information stored in a vnode includes the following:

- Flags are used for locking the vnode and identifying generic attributes. An example generic attribute is a flag to show that a vnode represents an object that is the root of a filesystem.

- The various reference counts include the number of file entries that are open for reading and/or writing that reference the vnode, the number of file entries that are open for writing that reference the vnode, and the number of pages and buffers that are associated with the vnode.

- A pointer to the mount structure describes the filesystem that contains the object represented by the vnode.

- Various information is used to do file read-ahead.

- A reference to an NFS lease is included; see Section 9.3.

- A reference to state about special devices, sockets, and FIFOs is included.

- There is a pointer to the set of vnode operations defined for the object. These operations are described in the next subsection.

- A pointer to private information needed for the underlying object is included. For the local filesystem, this pointer will reference an inode; for NFS, it will reference an nfsnode.

- The type of the underlying object (e.g., regular file, directory, character device, etc.) is given. The type information is not strictly necessary, since a vnode client could always call a vnode operation to get the type of the underlying object. However, because the type often is needed, the type of underlying objects does not change, and it takes time to call through the vnode interface, the object type is cached in the vnode.

- There are clean and dirty buffers associated with the vnode. Each valid buffer in the system is identified by its associated vnode and the starting offset of its data within the object that the vnode represents. All the buffers that have been modified, but have not yet been written back, are stored on their vnode dirty-buffer list. All buffers that have not been modified, or have been written back since they were last modified, are stored on their vnode clean list. Having all the dirty buffers for a vnode grouped onto a single list makes the cost of doing an *fsync* system call to flush all the dirty blocks associated with a file proportional to the amount of dirty data. In 4.3BSD, the cost was proportional to the smaller of the size of the file or the size of the buffer pool. The list of clean buffers is used to free buffers when a file is deleted. Since the file will never be read again, the kernel can immediately cancel any pending I/O on its dirty buffers, and reclaim all its clean and dirty buffers and place them at the head of the buffer free list, ready for immediate reuse.

• A count is kept of the number of buffer write operations in progress. To speed the flushing of dirty data, the kernel does this operation by doing asynchronous writes on all the dirty buffers at once. For local filesystems, this simultaneous push causes all the buffers to be put into the disk queue, so that they can be sorted into an optimal order to minimize seeking. For remote filesystems, this simultaneous push causes all the data to be presented to the network at once, so that it can maximize their throughput. System calls that cannot return until the data are on stable store (such as *fsync*) can sleep on the count of pending output operations, waiting for the count to reach zero.

The position of vnodes within the system was shown in Fig. 6.1. The vnode itself is connected into several other structures within the kernel, as shown in Fig. 6.7. Each mounted filesystem within the kernel is represented by a generic mount structure that includes a pointer to a filesystem-specific control block. All the vnodes associated with a specific mount point are linked together on a list headed by this generic mount structure. Thus, when it is doing a *sync* system call for a filesystem, the kernel can traverse this list to visit all the files active within that filesystem. Also shown in the figure are the lists of clean and dirty buffers associated with each vnode. Finally, there is a free list that links together all the vnodes in the system that are not being used actively. The free list is used when a filesystem needs to allocate a new vnode, so that the latter can open a new file; see Section 6.4.

Vnode Operations

Vnodes are designed as an object-oriented interface. Thus, the kernel manipulates them by passing requests to the underlying object through a set of defined operations. Because of the many varied filesystems that are supported in 4.4BSD, the set of operations defined for vnodes is both large and extensible. Unlike the original Sun Microsystems vnode implementation, that in 4.4BSD allows dynamic addition of vnode operations at system boot time. As part of the booting process, each filesystem registers the set of vnode operations that it is able to support. The kernel then builds a table that lists the union of all operations supported by any filesystem. From that table, it builds an operations vector for each filesystem. Supported operations are filled in with the entry point registered by the filesystem. Filesystems may opt to have unsupported operations filled in with either a default routine (typically a routine to bypass the operation to the next lower layer; see Section 6.7), or a routine that returns the characteristic error "operation not supported" [Heidemann & Popek, 1994].

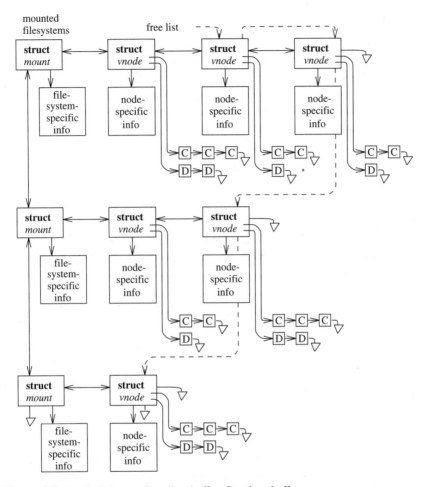

Figure 6.7 Vnode linkages. D—dirty buffer; C—clean buffer.

In 4.3BSD, the local filesystem code provided both the semantics of the hierarchical filesystem naming and the details of the on-disk storage management. These functions are only loosely related. To enable experimentation with other disk-storage techniques without having to reproduce the entire naming semantics, 4.4BSD splits the naming and storage code into separate modules. This split is evident at the vnode layer, where there are a set of operations defined for hierarchical filesystem operations and a separate set of operations defined for storage of variable-sized objects using a flat name space. About 60 percent of the traditional filesystem code became the name-space management, and the remaining 40 percent became the code implementing the on-disk file storage. The naming scheme and its vnode operations are described in Chapter 7. The disk-storage scheme and its vnode operations are explained in Chapter 8.

Pathname Translation

The translation of a pathname requires a series of interactions between the vnode interface and the underlying filesystems. The pathname-translation process proceeds as follows:

1. The pathname to be translated is copied in from the user process or, for a remote filesystem request, is extracted from the network buffer.

2. The starting point of the pathname is determined as either the root directory or the current directory (see Section 2.7). The vnode for the appropriate directory becomes the *lookup directory* used in the next step.

3. The vnode layer calls the filesystem-specific *lookup()* operation, and passes to that operation the remaining components of the pathname and the current *lookup directory*. Typically, the underlying filesystem will search the *lookup directory* for the next component of the pathname and will return the resulting vnode (or an error if the name does not exist).

4. If an error is returned, the top level returns the error. If the pathname has been exhausted, the pathname lookup is done, and the returned vnode is the result of the lookup. If the pathname has not been exhausted, and the returned vnode is not a directory, then the vnode layer returns the "not a directory" error. If there are no errors, the top layer checks to see whether the returned directory is a mount point for another filesystem. If it is, then the *lookup directory* becomes the mounted filesystem; otherwise, the *lookup directory* becomes the vnode returned by the lower layer. The lookup then iterates with step 3.

Although it may seem inefficient to call through the vnode interface for each pathname component, doing so usually is necessary. The reason is that the underlying filesystem does not know which directories are being used as mount points. Since a mount point will redirect the lookup to a new filesystem, it is important that the current filesystem not proceed past a mounted directory. Although it might be possible for a local filesystem to be knowledgeable about which directories are mount points, it is nearly impossible for a server to know which of the directories within its exported filesystems are being used as mount points by its clients. Consequently, the conservative approach of traversing only a single pathname component per *lookup()* call is used. There are a few instances where a filesystem will know that there are no further mount points in the remaining path, and will traverse the rest of the pathname. An example is crossing into a *portal*, described in Section 6.7.

Exported Filesystem Services

The vnode interface has a set of services that the kernel exports from all the filesystems supported under the interface. The first of these is the ability to support the update of generic mount options. These options include the following:

noexec   Do not execute any files on the filesystem. This option is often used
when a server exports binaries for a different architecture that cannot be
executed on the server itself. The kernel will even refuse to execute
shell scripts; if a shell script is to be run, its interpreter must be invoked
explicitly.

nosuid   Do not honor the set-user-id or set-group-id flags for any executables on
the filesystem. This option is useful when a filesystem of unknown origin is mounted.

nodev   Do not allow any special devices on the filesystem to be opened. This
option is often used when a server exports device directories for a different architecture. The values of the major and minor numbers are non-
sensical on the server.

Together, these options allow reasonably secure mounting of untrusted or foreign filesystems. It is not necessary to unmount and remount the filesystem to
change these flags; they may be changed while a filesystem is mounted. In addition, a filesystem that is mounted read-only can be upgraded to allow writing.
Conversely, a filesystem that allows writing may be downgraded to read-only provided that no files are open for modification. The system administrator can
forcibly downgrade the filesystem to read-only by requesting that any files open
for writing have their access revoked.

Another service exported from the vnode interface is the ability to get information about a mounted filesystem. The *statfs* system call returns a buffer that
gives the numbers of used and free disk blocks and inodes, along with the filesystem mount point, and the device, location, or program from which the filesystem
is mounted. The *getfsstat* system call returns information about all the mounted
filesystems. This interface avoids the need to track the set of mounted filesystems
outside the kernel, as is done in many other UNIX variants.

6.6   Filesystem-Independent Services

The vnode interface not only supplies an object-oriented interface to the underlying filesystems, but also provides a set of management routines that can be used
by the client filesystems. These facilities are described in this section.

When the final file-entry reference to a file is closed, the usage count on the
vnode drops to zero and the vnode interface calls the *inactive*() vnode operation.
The *inactive*() call notifies the underlying filesystem that the file is no longer
being used. The filesystem will often use this call to write dirty data back to the
file, but will not typically reclaim the buffers. The filesystem is permitted to cache
the file so that the latter can be reactivated quickly (i.e., without disk or network
I/O) if the file is reopened.

In addition to the *inactive*() vnode operation being called when the reference
count drops to zero, the vnode is placed on a systemwide free list. Unlike most

vendor's vnode implementations, which have a fixed number of vnodes allocated to each filesystem type, the 4.4BSD kernel keeps a single systemwide collection of vnodes. When an application opens a file that does not currently have an in-memory vnode, the client filesystem calls the *getnewvnode*() routine to allocate a new vnode. The *getnewvnode*() routine removes the least recently used vnode from the front of the free list and calls the *reclaim*() operation to notify the filesystem currently using the vnode that that vnode is about to be reused. The *reclaim*() operation writes back any dirty data associated with the underlying object, removes the underlying object from any lists that it is on (such as hash lists used to find it), and frees up any auxiliary storage that was being used by the object. The vnode is then returned for use by the new client filesystem.

The benefit of having a single global vnode table is that the kernel memory dedicated to vnodes is used more efficiently than when several filesystem-specific collections of vnodes are used. Consider a system that is willing to dedicate memory for 1000 vnodes. If the system supports 10 filesystem types, then each filesystem type will get 100 vnodes. If most of the activity moves to a single filesystem (e.g., during the compilation of a kernel located in a local filesystem), all the active files will have to be kept in the 100 vnodes dedicated to that filesystem while the other 900 vnodes sit idle. In a 4.4BSD system, all 1000 vnodes could be used for the active filesystem, allowing a much larger set of files to be cached in memory. If the center of activity moved to another filesystem (e.g., compiling a program on an NFS mounted filesystem), the vnodes would migrate from the previously active local filesystem over to the NFS filesystem. Here, too, there would be a much larger set of cached files than if only 100 vnodes were available using a partitioned set of vnodes.

The *reclaim*() operation is a disassociation of the underlying filesystem object from the vnode itself. This ability, combined with the ability to associate new objects with the vnode, provides functionality with usefulness that goes far beyond simply allowing vnodes to be moved from one filesystem to another. By replacing an existing object with an object from the *dead* filesystem—a filesystem in which all operations except *close* fail—the kernel revokes the object. Internally, this revocation of an object is provided by the *vgone*() routine.

This revocation service is used for session management, where all references to the controlling terminal are revoked when the session leader exits. Revocation works as follows. All open terminal descriptors within the session reference the vnode for the special device representing the session terminal. When *vgone*() is called on this vnode, the underlying special device is detached from the vnode and is replaced with the dead filesystem. Any further operations on the vnode will result in errors, because the open descriptors no longer reference the terminal. Eventually, all the processes will exit and will close their descriptors, causing the reference count to drop to zero. The *inactive*() routine for the dead filesystem returns the vnode to the front of the free list for immediate reuse, because it will never be possible to get a reference to the vnode again.

The revocation service is used to support forcible unmounting of filesystems. If it finds an active vnode when unmounting a filesystem, the kernel simply calls the *vgone*() routine to disassociate the active vnode from the filesystem object. Processes with open files or current directories within the filesystem find that they have simply vanished, as though they had been removed. It is also possible to downgrade a mounted filesystem from read-write to read-only. Instead of access being revoked on every active file within the filesystem, only those files with a nonzero number of references for writing have their access revoked.

Finally, the ability to revoke objects is exported to processes through the *revoke* system call. This system call can be used to ensure controlled access to a device such as a pseudo-terminal port. First, the ownership of the device is changed to the desired user and the mode is set to owner-access only. Then, the device name is revoked to eliminate any interlopers that already had it open. Thereafter, only the new owner is able to open the device.

The Name Cache

Name-cache management is another service that is provided by the vnode management routines. The interface provides a facility to add a name and its corresponding vnode, to look up a name to get the corresponding vnode, and to delete a specific name from the cache. In addition to providing a facility for deleting specific names, the interface also provides an efficient way to invalidate all names that reference a specific vnode. Directory vnodes can have many names that reference them—notably, the .. entries in all their immediate descendents. The kernel could revoke all names for a vnode by scanning the entire name table, looking for references to the vnode in question. This approach would be slow, however, given that the name table may store thousands of names. Instead, each vnode is given a *capability*—a 32-bit number guaranteed to be unique. When all the numbers have been exhausted, all outstanding capabilities are purged, and numbering restarts from scratch. Purging is possible, because all capabilities are easily found in kernel memory; it needs to be done only if the machine remains running for nearly 1 year. When an entry is made in the name table, the current value of the vnode's capability is copied to the associated name entry. A vnode's capability is invalidated each time it is reused by *getnewvnode*() or, when specifically requested by a client (e.g., when a file is being renamed), by assignment of a new capability to the vnode. When a name is found during a cached lookup, the capability assigned to the name is compared with that of the vnode. If they match, the lookup is successful; if they do not match, the cache entry is freed and failure is returned.

The cache-management routines also allow for negative caching. If a name is looked up in a directory and is not found, that name can be entered in the cache, along with a null pointer for its corresponding vnode. If the name is later looked up, it will be found in the name table, and thus the kernel can avoid scanning the entire directory to determine that the name is not there. If a directory is modified, then potentially one or more of the negative entries may be wrong. So, when the directory is modified, the kernel must invalidate all the negative names for that directory vnode by assigning the directory a new capability. Negative caching provides a significant performance improvement because of path searching in command shells. When executing a command, many shells will look at each path in turn, looking for the executable. Commonly run executables will be searched for repeatedly in directories in which they do not exist. Negative caching speeds these searches.

An obscure but tricky issue has to do with detecting and properly handling special device aliases. Special devices and FIFOs are hybrid objects. Their naming and attributes (such as owner, timestamps, and permissions) are maintained by the filesystem in which they reside. However, their operations (such as read and write) are maintained by the kernel on which they are being used. Since a special device is identified solely by its major and minor number, it is possible for two or more instances of the same device to appear within the filesystem name space, possibly in different filesystems. Each of these different names has its own vnode and underlying object, yet all these vnodes must be treated as one from the perspective of identifying blocks in the buffer cache and in other places where the vnode and logical block number are used as a key. To ensure that the set of vnodes is treated as a single vnode, the vnode layer provides a routine *checkalias*( ) that is called each time that a new special device vnode comes into existence. This routine looks for other instances of the device, and if it finds them, links them together so that they can act as one.

Buffer Management

Another important service provided by the filesystem-independent layer is the management of the kernel's buffer space. The task of the *buffer cache* is two-fold. One task is to manage the memory that buffers data being transferred to and from the disk or network. The second, and more important, task is to act as a cache of recently used blocks. The semantics of the filesystem imply much I/O. If every implied transfer had to be done, the CPU would spend most of its time waiting for I/O to complete. On a typical 4.4BSD system, over 85 percent of the implied disk or network transfers can be skipped, because the requested block already resides in the buffer cache. Depending on available memory, a system is configured with from 100 to 1000 buffers. The larger the number of buffers is, the longer a given block can be retained in memory, and the greater the chance that actual I/O can be avoided.

Figure 6.8 shows the format of a buffer. The buffer is composed of two parts. The first part is the buffer header, which contains information used to find the buffer and to describe the buffer's contents. The content information includes the vnode (i.e., a pointer to the vnode whose data the buffer holds), the starting offset within the file, and the number of bytes contained in the buffer. The flags entry tracks status information about the buffer, such as whether the buffer contains useful data, whether the buffer is in use, and whether the data must be written back to the file before the buffer can be reused.

The second part is the actual buffer contents. Rather than the header being prepended to the data area of the buffer, as is done with mbufs (see Section 11.3), the data areas are maintained separately. Thus, there is a pointer to the buffer contents and a field that shows the size of the data-buffer contents. The buffer size is always at least as big as the size of the data block that the buffer contains. Data

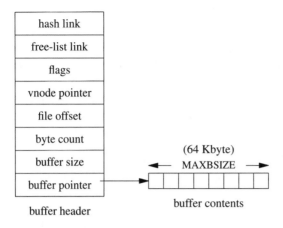

Figure 6.8 Format of a buffer.

are maintained separately from the header to allow easy manipulation of buffer sizes via the page-mapping hardware. If the headers were prepended, either each header would have to be on a page by itself or the kernel would have to avoid remapping buffer pages that contained headers.

The sizes of buffer requests from a filesystem range from 512 bytes up to 65,536 bytes. If many small files are being accessed, then many small buffers are needed. Alternatively, if several large files are being accessed, then fewer large buffers are needed. To allow the system to adapt efficiently to these changing needs, the kernel allocates to each buffer MAXBSIZE bytes of virtual memory, but the address space is not fully populated with physical memory. Initially, each buffer is assigned 4096 bytes of physical memory. As smaller buffers are allocated, they give up their unused physical memory to buffers that need to hold more than 4096 bytes. The algorithms for managing the physical memory are described in the next subsection.

In earlier versions of BSD and in most other versions of UNIX, buffers were identified by their physical disk block number. 4.4BSD changes this convention to identify buffers by their logical block number within the file. For filesystems such as NFS, the local client has no way to compute the physical block address of a logical file block on the server, so only a logical block number can be used. Using the logical block number also speeds lookup, because it is no longer necessary to compute the physical block number before checking for the block in the cache. For a local filesystem where the computation may require traversing up to three indirect blocks, the savings are considerable. The drawback to using a logical-address cache is that it is difficult to detect aliases for a block belonging to a local file and the same block accessed through the block device disk whose logical-block address is the same as the physical-block address. The kernel handles these aliases by administratively preventing them from occurring. The kernel does not allow the block device for a partition to be opened while that partition is mounted.

Conversely, the kernel will not allow a partition on a block device disk to be mounted if the latter is already open.

The internal kernel interface to the buffer pool is simple. The filesystem allocates and fills buffers by calling the *bread*() routine. *Bread*() takes a vnode, a logical block number, and a size, and returns a pointer to a locked buffer. Any other process that tries to obtain the buffer will be put to sleep until the buffer is released. A buffer can be released in one of four ways. If the buffer has not been modified, it can simply be released through use of *brelse*(), which returns it to the free list and awakens any process that are waiting for it.

If the buffer has been modified, it is called *dirty*. Dirty buffers must eventually be written back to their filesystem. Three routines are available based on the urgency with which the data must be written. In the typical case, *bdwrite*() is used; since the buffer may be modified again soon, it should be marked as dirty, but should not be written immediately. After the buffer is marked as dirty, it is returned to the free list and any processes waiting for it are awakened. The heuristic is that, if the buffer will be modified again soon, the I/O would be wasted. Because the buffer is held for an average of 15 seconds before it is written, a process doing many small writes will not repeatedly access the disk or network.

If a buffer has been filled completely, then it is unlikely to be written again soon, so it should be released with *bawrite*(). *Bawrite*() schedules an I/O on the buffer, but allows the caller to continue running while the output completes.

The final case is *bwrite*(), which ensures that the write is complete before proceeding. Because *bwrite*() can introduce a long latency to the writer, it is used only when a process explicitly requests the behavior (such as the *fsync* system call), when the operation is critical to ensure the consistency of the filesystem after a system crash, or when a stateless remote filesystem protocol such as NFS is being served. Buffers that are written using *bawrite*() or *bwrite*() are placed on the appropriate output queue. When the output completes, the *brelse*() routine is called to return them to the free list and to awaken any processes that are waiting for them.

Figure 6.9 shows a snapshot of the buffer pool. A buffer with valid contents is contained on exactly one *bufhash* hash chain. The kernel uses the hash chains to determine quickly whether a block is in the buffer pool, and if it is, to locate it. A buffer is removed only when its contents become invalid or it is reused for different data. Thus, even if the buffer is in use by one process, it can still be found by another process, although the *busy* flag will be set so that it will not be used until its contents are consistent.

In addition to appearing on the hash list, each unlocked buffer appears on exactly one free list. The first free list is the *LOCKED* list. Buffers on this list cannot be flushed from the cache. This list was originally intended to hold superblock data; in 4.4BSD, it is used by only the log-structured filesystem.

The second list is the *LRU* list. When a buffer is found—typically on the LRU list—it is removed and used. The buffer is then returned to the end of the LRU list. When new buffers are needed, they are taken from the front of the LRU list. Thus, buffers used repeatedly will continue to migrate to the end of the LRU list and are

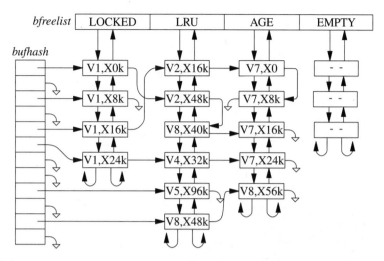

Figure 6.9 Snapshot of the buffer pool. V—vnode; X—file offset

not likely to be reused for new blocks. As its name suggests, this list implements a least recently used (LRU) algorithm.

The third free list is the *AGE* list. This list holds blocks that have not proved their usefulness, but are expected to be used soon, or have already been used and are not likely to be reused. Buffers can be pushed onto either end of this list: Buffers containing no useful data are pushed on the front (where they will be reclaimed quickly), and other buffers are pushed on the end (where they might remain long enough to be used again). When a file is unlinked, its buffers are placed at the front of the AGE list. In Fig. 6.9, the file associated with vnode 7 has just been deleted. The AGE list is also used to hold read-ahead blocks. In Fig. 6.9, vnode 8 has just finished using the buffer starting with offset 48 Kbyte (which, being a full-sized block, contains logical blocks 48 through 55), and will probably use its read-ahead, contained in the buffer starting with offset 56 Kbyte at end of the AGE list. If a requested block is found on the AGE list, it is returned to the end of the LRU list, because it has proved its usefulness. When a new buffer is needed, the AGE list is searched first; only when that list is empty is the LRU list used.

The final list is the list of empty buffers, the *EMPTY* list. The empty buffers have had all their physical memory stripped away by other buffers. They are held on this list waiting for another buffer to be reused for a smaller block and thus to give up its extra physical memory.

Implementation of Buffer Management

Having looked at the function and algorithms used to manage the buffer pool, we shall now turn our attention to the implementation requirements for ensuring the consistency of the data in the buffer pool. Figure 6.10 (on page 230) shows the

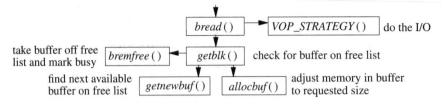

Figure 6.10 Procedural interface to the buffer-allocation system.

support routines that implement the interface for getting buffers. The primary interface to getting a buffer is through *bread()*, which is called with a request for a data block of a specified size for a specified vnode. There is also a related interface, *breadn()*, that both gets a requested block and starts read-ahead for additional blocks. *Bread()* first calls *getblk()* to find out whether the data block is available in a buffer that is already in memory. If the block is available in a buffer, *getblk()* calls *bremfree()* to take the buffer off whichever free list it is on and to mark it busy; *bread()* can then return the buffer to the caller.

If the block is not already in memory, *getblk()* calls *getnewbuf()* to allocate a new buffer. The new buffer is then passed to *allocbuf()*, which ensures that the buffer has the right amount of physical memory. *Getblk()* then returns the buffer to *bread()* marked busy and unfilled. Noticing that the buffer is unfilled, *bread()* passes the buffer to the *strategy()* routine for the underlying filesystem to have the data read in. When the read completes, the buffer is returned.

The task of *allocbuf()* is to ensure that the buffer has enough physical memory allocated to it. Figure 6.11 shows the virtual memory for the data part of a buffer. The data area for each buffer is allocated MAXBSIZE bytes of virtual address space. The *bufsize* field in the buffer header shows how much of the virtual address space is backed by physical memory. *Allocbuf()* compares the size of the intended data block with the amount of physical memory already allocated to the buffer. If there is excess physical memory and there is a buffer available on the EMPTY list, a buffer is taken off the EMPTY list, the excess memory is put into the empty buffer, and that buffer is then inserted onto the front of the AGE list. If

Figure 6.11 Allocation of buffer memory.

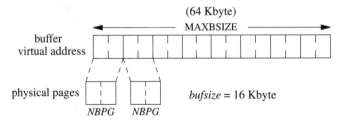

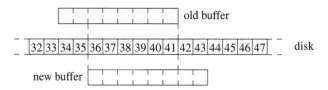

Figure 6.12 Potentially overlapping allocation of buffers.

there are no buffers on the EMPTY list, the excess physical memory is retained in the original buffer.

If the buffer has insufficient memory, *allocbuf*() takes memory from other buffers. *Allocbuf*() does the allocation by calling *getnewbuf*() to a second buffer and then transferring the physical memory in the second buffer to the new buffer under construction. If there is memory remaining in the second buffer, the second buffer is released to the front of the AGE list; otherwise, the second buffer is released to the EMPTY list. If the new buffer still does not have enough physical memory, the process is repeated. *Allocbuf*() ensures that each physical-memory page is mapped into exactly one buffer at all times.

To maintain the consistency of the filesystem, the kernel must ensure that a disk block is mapped into at most one buffer. If the same disk block were present in two buffers, and both buffers were marked dirty, the system would be unable to determine which buffer had the most current information. Figure 6.12 shows a sample allocation. In the middle of the figure are the blocks on the disk. Above the disk is shown an old buffer containing a 4096-byte fragment for a file that presumably has been removed or shortened. The new buffer is going to be used to hold a 3072-byte fragment for a file that is presumably being created and that will reuse part of the space previously held by the old file. The kernel maintains the consistency by purging old buffers when files are shortened or removed. Whenever a file is removed, the kernel traverses its list of dirty buffers. For each buffer, the kernel cancels its write request and marks the buffer invalid, so that the buffer cannot be found in the buffer pool again. Each invalid buffer is put at the front of the AGE list, so that it will be used before any buffers with potentially useful data. For a file being partially truncated, only the buffers following the truncation point are invalidated. The system can then allocate the new buffer knowing that the buffer maps the corresponding disk blocks uniquely.

6.7   Stackable Filesystems

The early vnode interface was simply an object-oriented interface to an underlying filesystem. As the demand grew for new filesystem features, it became desirable to find ways of providing them without having to modify the existing and stable filesystem code. One approach is to provide a mechanism for stacking several filesystems on top of one another other [Rosenthal, 1990]. The stacking ideas were refined and implemented in the 4.4BSD system [Heidemann & Popek, 1994]. The bottom of a vnode stack tends to be a disk-based filesystem, whereas the layers used above it typically transform their arguments and pass on those arguments to a lower layer.

In all UNIX systems, the *mount* command takes a special device as a source and maps that device onto a directory mount point in an existing filesystem. When a filesystem is mounted on a directory, the previous contents of the directory are hidden; only the contents of the root of the newly mounted filesystem are visible. To most users, the effect of the series of mount commands done at system startup is the creation of a single seamless filesystem tree.

Stacking also uses the *mount* command to create new layers. The *mount* command pushes a new layer onto a vnode stack; an *unmount* command removes a layer. Like the mounting of a filesystem, a vnode stack is visible to all processes running on the system. The *mount* command identifies the underlying layer in the stack, creates the new layer, and attaches that layer into the filesystem name space. The new layer can be attached to the same place as the old layer (covering the old layer) or to a different place in the tree (allowing both layers to be visible). An example is shown in the next subsection.

If layers are attached to different places in the name space then the same file will be visible in multiple places. Access to the file under the name of the new layer's name space will go to the new layer, whereas that under the old layer's name space will go to only the old layer.

When a file access (e.g., an *open*, *read*, *stat*, or *close*) occurs to a vnode in the stack, that vnode has several options:

• Do the requested operations and return a result.

• Pass the operation without change to the next-lower vnode on the stack. When the operation returns from the lower vnode, it may modify the results, or simply return them.

• Modify the operands provided with the request, then pass it to the next-lower vnode. When the operation returns from the lower vnode, it may modify the results, or simply return them.

If an operation is passed to the bottom of the stack without any layer taking action on it, then the interface will return the error "operation not supported."

Vnode interfaces released before 4.4BSD implemented vnode operations as indirect function calls. The requirements that intermediate stack layers bypass operations to lower layers and that new operations can be added into the system at boot time mean that this approach is no longer adequate. Filesystems must be able to bypass operations that may not have been defined at the time that the filesystem was implemented. In addition to passing through the function, the filesystem layer must also pass through the function parameters, which are of unknown type and number.

```
{
    ...
    /*
     * Check for read permission on file ''vp''.
     */
    if (error = VOP_ACCESS(vp, VREAD, cred, p))
        return (error);
    ...
}

/*
 * Check access permission for a file.
 */
int
ufs_access(ap)
    struct vop_access_args {
        struct vnodeop_desc *a_desc;  /* operation descrip. */
        struct vnode *a_vp;           /* file to be checked */
        int a_mode;                   /* access mode sought */
        struct ucred *a_cred;         /* user seeking access */
        struct proc *a_p;             /* associated process */
    } *ap;
{

    if (permission granted)
        return (1);
    return (0);
}
```

Figure 6.13 Call to and function header for *access* vnode operation.

To resolve these two problems in a clean and portable way, the kernel places the vnode operation name and its arguments into an argument structure. This argument structure is then passed as a single parameter to the vnode operation. Thus, all calls on a vnode operation will always have exactly one parameter, which is the pointer to the argument structure. If the vnode operation is one that is supported by the filesystem, then it will know what the arguments are and how to interpret them. If it is an unknown vnode operation, then the generic bypass routine can call the same operation in the next-lower layer, passing to the operation the same argument structure that it received. In addition, the first argument of every operation is a pointer to the vnode operation description. This description provides to a bypass routine the information about the operation, including the operation's name and the location of the operation's parameters. An example access-check call and its implementation for the UFS filesystem are shown in Fig. 6.13. Note that the *vop_access_args* structure is normally declared in a header file, but here is declared at the function site to simplify the example.

Simple Filesystem Layers

The simplist filesystem layer is *nullfs*. It makes no transformations on its arguments, simply passing through all requests that it receives and returning all results that it gets back. Although it provides no useful functionality if it is simply stacked on top of an existing vnode, *nullfs* can provide a loopback filesystem by mounting the filesystem rooted at its source vnode at some other location in the filesystem tree. The code for *nullfs* is also an excellent starting point for designers who want to build their own filesystem layers. Examples that could be built include a compression layer or an encryption layer.

A sample vnode stack is shown in Fig. 6.14. The figure shows a local filesystem on the bottom of the stack that is being exported from **/local** via an NFS layer. Clients within the administrative domain of the server can import the **/local** filesystem directly, because they are all presumed to use a common mapping of UIDs to user names.

The *umapfs* filesystem works much like the *nullfs* filesystem in that it provides a view of the file tree rooted at the **/local** filesystem on the **/export** mount point. In addition to providing a copy of the **/local** filesystem at the **/export** mount point, it transforms the credentials of each system call made to files within the **/export** filesystem. The kernel does the transformation using a mapping that was provided as part of the *mount* system call that created the *umapfs* layer.

The **/export** filesystem can be exported to clients from an outside administrative domain that uses different UIDs and GIDs. When an NFS request comes in for the **/export** filesystem, the *umapfs* layer modifies the credential from the foreign client by mapping the UIDs used on the foreign client to the corresponding UIDs used on the local system. The requested operation with the modified credential is passed down to the lower layer corresponding to the **/local** filesystem, where it is processed identically to a local request. When the result is returned to the mapping layer, any returned credentials are mapped inversely so that they are converted from the local UIDs to the outside UIDs, and this result is sent back as the NFS response.

Figure 6.14 Stackable vnodes.

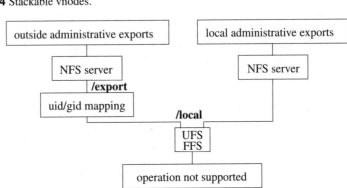

There are three benefits to this approach:

1. There is no cost of mapping imposed on the local clients.

2. There are no changes required to the local filesystem code or the NFS code to support mapping.

3. Each outside domain can have its own mapping. Domains with simple mappings consume small amounts of memory and run quickly; domains with large and complex mappings can be supported without detracting from the performance of simpler environments.

Vnode stacking is an effective approach for adding extensions, such as the *umapfs* service.

The Union Mount Filesystem

The *union* filesystem is another example of a middle filesystem layer. Like the *nullfs*, it does not store data; it just provides a name-space transformation. It is loosely modeled on the work on the 3-D filesystem [Korn & Krell, 1989], on the Translucent filesystem [Hendricks, 1990], and on the Automounter [Pendry & Williams, 1994]. The *union* filesystem takes an existing filesystem and transparently overlays the latter on another filesystem. Unlike most other filesystems, a union mount does not cover up the directory on which the filesystem is mounted. Instead, it shows the logical merger of both directories and allows both directory trees to be accessible simultaneously [Pendry & McKusick, 1995].

A small example of a union-mount stack is shown in Fig. 6.15. Here, the bottom layer of the stack is the **src** filesystem that includes the source for the **shell** program. Being a simple program, it contains only one source and one header file. The upper layer that has been union mounted on top of **src** initially contains just the **src** directory. When the user changes directory into **shell**, a directory of the same name is created in the top layer. Directories in the top layer corresponding to directories in the lower layer are created only as they are encountered while the top layer is traversed. If the user were to run a recursive traversal of the tree rooted at the top of the union-mount location, the result would be a complete tree of directories matching the underlying filesystem. In our example, the user now types *make* in the **shell** directory. The **sh** executable is created in the upper layer

Figure 6.15 A union-mounted filesystem.

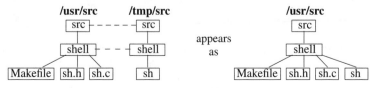

of the union stack. To the user, a directory listing shows the sources and executable all apparently together, as shown on the right in Fig. 6.15.

All filesystem layers, except the top one, are treated as though they were read-only. If a file residing in a lower layer is opened for reading, a descriptor is returned for that file. If a file residing in a lower layer is opened for writing, the kernel first copies the file to the top layer, then returns a descriptor referencing the copy of the file. The result is that there are two copies of the file: the original unmodified file in the lower layer and the modified copy of the file in the upper layer. When the user does a directory listing, any duplicate names in the lower layer are suppressed. When a file is opened, a descriptor for the file in the upper-most layer in which the name appears is returned. Thus, once a file has been copied to the top layer, instances of the file in lower layers become inaccessible.

The tricky part of the *union* filesystem is handling the removal of files that reside in a lower layer. Since the lower layers cannot be modified, the only way to remove a file is to hide it by creating a *whiteout* directory entry in the top layer. A whiteout is an entry in a directory that has no corresponding file; it is distinguished by having an inode number of 1. If the kernel finds a whiteout entry while searching for a name, the lookup is stopped and the "no such file or directory" error is returned. Thus, the file with the same name in a lower layer appears to have been removed. If a file is removed from the top layer, it is necessary to create a whiteout entry for it only if there is a file with the same name in the lower level that would reappear.

When a process creates a file with the same name as a whiteout entry, the whiteout entry is replaced with a regular name that references the new file. Because the new file is being created in the top layer, it will mask out any files with the same name in a lower layer. When a user does a directory listing, white-out entries and the files that they mask usually are not shown. However, there is an option that causes them to appear.

One feature that has long been missing in UNIX systems is the ability to recover files after they have been deleted. For the union filesystem, the kernel can implement file recovery trivially simply by removing the whiteout entry to expose the underlying file. The LFS filesystem also has the (currently unimplemented) ability to recover deleted files, because it never overwrites previously written data. Deleted versions of files may not be reclaimed until the filesystem becomes nearly full and the LFS garbage collector runs. For filesystems that provide file recovery, users can recover files by using a special option to the remove command; processes can recover files by using the *undelete* system call.

When a directory whose name appears in a lower layer is removed, a whiteout entry is created just as it would be for a file. However, if the user later attempts to create a directory with the same name as the previously deleted directory, the union filesystem must treat the new directory specially to avoid having the previous contents from the lower-layer directory reappear. When a directory that replaces a whiteout entry is created, the union filesystem sets a flag in the directory metadata to show that this directory should be treated specially. When a directory scan is done, the kernel returns information about only the top-level directory; it suppresses the list of files from the directories of the same name in the lower layers.

The *union* filesystem can be used for many purposes:

- It allows several different architectures to build from a common source base. The source pool is NFS mounted onto each of several machines. On each host machine, a local filesystem is union mounted on top of the imported source tree. As the build proceeds, the objects and binaries appear in the local filesystem that is layered above the source tree. This approach not only avoids contaminating the source pool with binaries, but also speeds the compilation, because most of the filesystem traffic is on the local filesystem.

- It allows compilation of sources on read-only media such as CD-ROMs. A local filesystem is union mounted above the CD-ROM sources. It is then possible to change into directories on the CD-ROM and to give the appearance of being able to edit and compile in that directory.

- It allows creation of a private source directory. The user creates a source directory in her own work area, then union mounts the system sources underneath that directory. This feature is possible because the restrictions on the *mount* command have been relaxed. Any user can do a mount if she owns the directory on which the mount is being done and she has appropriate access permissions on the device or directory being mounted (read permission is required for a read-only mount, read–write permission is required for a read–write mount). Only the user who did the mount or the superuser can unmount a filesystem.

Other Filesystems

There are several other filesystems included as part of 4.4BSD. The *portal* filesystem mounts a process onto a directory in the file tree. When a pathname that traverses the location of the portal is used, the remainder of the path is passed to the process mounted at that point. The process interprets the path in whatever way it sees fit, then returns a descriptor to the calling process. This descriptor may be for a socket connected to the portal process. If it is, further operations on the descriptor will be passed to the portal process for the latter to interpret. Alternatively, the descriptor may be for a file elsewhere in the filesystem.

Consider a portal process mounted on **/dialout** used to manage a bank of dialout modems. When a process wanted to connect to an outside number, it would open **/dialout/15105551212/9600** to specify that it wanted to dial 1-510-555-1212 at 9600 baud. The portal process would get the final two pathname components. Using the final component, it would determine that it should find an unused 9600-baud modem. It would use the other component as the number to which to place the call. It would then write an accounting record for future billing, and would return the descriptor for the modem to the process.

One of the more interesting uses of the portal filesystem is to provide an Internet service directory. For example, with an Internet portal process mounted on **/net**, an open of **/net/tcp/McKusick.COM/smtp** returns a TCP socket descriptor to the calling process that is connected to the SMTP server on **McKusick.COM**. Because access is provided through the normal filesystem, the calling process does not need to be aware of the special functions necessary to create a TCP socket and to establish a TCP connection [Stevens & Pendry, 1995].

There are several filesystems that are designed to provide a convenient interface to kernel information. The *procfs* filesystem is normally mounted at **/proc** and provides a view of the running processes in the system. Its primary use is for debugging, but it also provides a convenient interface for collecting information about the processes in the system. A directory listing of **/proc** produces a numeric list of all the processes in the system. Each process entry is itself a directory that contains the following:

ctl   A file to control the process, allowing the process to be stopped, continued, and signaled

file   The executable for the process

mem   The virtual memory of the process

regs   The registers for the process

status   A text file containing information about the process.

The *fdesc* filesystem is normally mounted on **/dev/fd**, and provides a list of all the active file descriptors for the currently running process. An example where this is useful is specifying to an application that it should read input from its standard input. Here, you can use the pathname **/dev/fd/0**, instead of having to come up with a special convention, such as using the name – to tell the application to read from its standard input.

The *kernfs* filesystem is normally mounted on **/kern**, and contains files that have various information about the system. It includes information such as the host name, time of day, and version of the system.

Finally there is the *cd9660* filesystem. It allows ISO-9660–compliant filesystems, with or without Rock Ridge extensions, to be mounted. The ISO-9660 filesystem format is most commonly used on CD-ROMs.

Exercises

6.1   Where are the read and write attributes of an open file descriptor stored?

6.2   Why is the close-on-exec bit located in the per-process descriptor table, instead of in the system file table?

6.3   Why are the file-table entries reference counted?

6.4   What three shortcomings of lock files are addressed by the 4.4BSD descriptor-locking facilities?

6.5   What two problems are raised by mandatory locks?

6.6   Why is the implementation of *select* split between the descriptor-manage-ment code and the lower-level routines?

6.7   Describe how the *process selecting flag* is used in the implementation of *select*.

6.8   The *update* program is usually started shortly after the system is booted. Once every 30 seconds, it does a *sync* system call. What problem could arise if this program were not run?

6.9   The special device **/dev/kmem** provides access to the kernel's virtual address space. Would you expect it to be a character or a block device? Explain your answer.

6.10   Many tape drives provide a block-device interface. Is it possible to support a filesystem on a such a tape drive?

6.11   When is a vnode placed on the free list?

6.12   Why must the lookup routine call through the vnode interface once for each component in a pathname?

6.13   Give three reasons for revoking access to a vnode.

6.14   Why are the buffer headers allocated separately from the memory that holds the contents of the buffer?

6.15   How does the maximum filesystem block size affect the buffer cache?

*6.16   Why are there both an AGE list and an LRU list, instead of all buffers being managed on the LRU list?

*6.17   Filenames can be up to 255 characters long. How could you implement the systemwide name cache to avoid allocating 255 bytes for each entry?

*6.18   If a process reads a large file, the blocks of the file will fill the buffer cache completely, flushing out all other contents. All other processes in the sys-tem then will have to go to disk for all their filesystem accesses. Write an algorithm to control the purging of the buffer cache.

*6.19   Discuss the tradeoff between dedicating memory to the buffer cache and making the memory available to the virtual-memory system for use in ful-filling paging requests. Give a policy for moving memory between the buffer pool and the virtual-memory system.

*6.20   Vnode operation parameters are passed between layers in structures. What alternatives are there to this approach? Explain why your approach is more or less efficient, compared to the current approach, when there are less than five layers in the stack. Also compare the efficiency of your solution when there are more than five layers in the stack.

*6.21 True asynchronous I/O is not supported in 4.4BSD. What problems arise with providing asynchronous I/O in the existing read–write interface?

References

Accetta et al, 1986.
>   M. Accetta, R. Baron, W. Bolosky, D. Golub, R. Rashid, A. Tevanian, & M. Young, "Mach: A New Kernel Foundation for UNIX Development," *USENIX Association Conference Proceedings*, pp. 93–113, June 1986.

Bass, 1981.
>   J. Bass, *Implementation Description for File Locking,* Onyx Systems Inc., 73 E. Trimble Road, San Jose, CA, January 1981.

Heidemann & Popek, 1994.
>   J. S. Heidemann & G. J. Popek, "File-System Development with Stackable Layers," *ACM Transactions on Computer Systems*, vol. 12, no. 1, pp. 58–89, February 1994.

Hendricks, 1990.
>   D. Hendricks, "A Filesystem for Software Development," *USENIX Association Conference Proceedings*, pp. 333–340, June 1990.

Korn & Krell, 1989.
>   D. Korn & E. Krell, "The 3-D File System," *USENIX Association Conference Proceedings*, pp. 147–156, June 1989.

Pendry & McKusick, 1995.
>   J. Pendry & M. McKusick, "Union Mounts in 4.4BSD-Lite," *USENIX Association Conference Proceedings*, pp. 25–33, January 1995.

Pendry & Williams, 1994.
>   J. Pendry & N. Williams, "AMD: The 4.4BSD Automounter Reference Manual," in *4.4BSD System Manager's Manual*, pp. 13:1–57, O'Reilly & Associates, Inc., Sebastopol, CA, 1994.

Peterson, 1983.
>   G. Peterson, "Concurrent Reading While Writing," *ACM Transactions on Programming Languages and Systems*, vol. 5, no. 1, pp. 46–55, January 1983.

Rosenthal, 1990.
>   D. Rosenthal, "Evolving the Vnode Interface," *USENIX Association Conference Proceedings*, pp. 107–118, June 1990.

Stevens & Pendry, 1995.
>   R. Stevens & J. Pendry, "Portals in 4.4BSD," *USENIX Association Conference Proceedings*, pp. 1–10, January 1995.

CHAPTER 7

Local Filesystems

7.1 Hierarchical Filesystem Management

The operations defined for local filesystems are divided into two parts. Common to all local filesystems are hierarchical naming, locking, quotas, attribute management, and protection. These features, which are independent of how data are stored, are provided by the UFS code described in this chapter. The other part of the local filesystem is concerned with the organization and management of the data on the storage media. Storage is managed by the datastore filesystem operations described in Chapter 8.

The vnode operations defined for doing hierarchical filesystem operations are shown in Table 7.1. The most complex of these operations is that for doing a lookup. The filesystem-independent part of the lookup was described in Section 6.5. The algorithm used to look up a pathname component in a directory is described in Section 7.3.

Table 7.1 Hierarchical filesystem operations.

Operation done	Operator names
pathname searching	lookup
name creation	create, mknod, link, symlink, mkdir
name change/deletion	rename, remove, rmdir
attribute manipulation	access, getattr, setattr
object interpretation	open, readdir, readlink, mmap, close
process control	advlock, ioctl, select
object management	lock, unlock, inactive, reclaim, abortop

There are five operators for creating names. The operator used depends on the type of object being created. The *create* operator creates regular files and also is used by the networking code to create AF_LOCAL domain sockets. The *link* operator creates additional names for existing objects. The *symlink* operator creates a symbolic link (see Section 7.3 for a discussion of symbolic links). The *mknod* operator creates block and character special devices; it is also used to create FIFOs. The *mkdir* operator creates directories.

There are three operators for changing or deleting existing names. The *rename* operator deletes a name for an object in one location and creates a new name for the object in another location. The implementation of this operator is complex when the kernel is dealing with the movement of a directory from one part of the filesystem tree to another. The *remove* operator removes a name. If the removed name is the final reference to the object, the space associated with the underlying object is reclaimed. The *remove* operator operates on all object types except directories; they are removed using the *rmdir* operator.

Three operators are supplied for object attributes. The kernel retrieves attributes from an object using the *getattr* operator; it stores them using the *setattr* operator. Access checks for a given user are provided by the *access* operator.

Five operators are provided for interpreting objects. The *open* and *close* operators have only peripheral use for regular files, but, when used on special devices, are used to notify the appropriate device driver of device activation or shutdown. The *readdir* operator converts the filesystem-specific format of a directory to the standard list of directory entries expected by an application. Note that the interpretation of the contents of a directory is provided by the hierarchical filesystem-management layer; the filestore code considers a directory as just another object holding data. The *readlink* operator returns the contents of a symbolic link. As it does directories, the filestore code considers a symbolic link as just another object holding data. The *mmap* operator prepares an object to be mapped into the address space of a process.

Three operators are provided to allow process control over objects. The *select* operator allows a process to find out whether an object is ready to be read or written. The *ioctl* operator passes control requests to a special device. The *advlock* operator allows a process to acquire or release an advisory lock on an object. None of these operators modifies the object in the filestore. They are simply using the object for naming or directing the desired operation.

There are five operations for management of the objects. The *inactive* and *reclaim* operators were described in Section 6.6. The *lock* and *unlock* operators allow the callers of the vnode interface to provide hints to the code that implement operations on the underlying objects. Stateless filesystem such as NFS ignore these hints. Stateful filesystems, however, can use hints to avoid doing extra work. For example, an *open* system call requesting that a new file be created requires two steps. First, a *lookup* call is done to see if the file already exists. Before the lookup, is started a *lock* request is made on the directory being searched. While scanning through the directory checking for the name, the lookup code also identifies a location within the directory that contains enough space to hold the new name. If the lookup returns successfully (meaning that the name does not already exist), the *open* code verifies that the user has permission to create the file. If the user is not eligible to create the new file, then the *abortop* operator is called to release any resources held in reserve. Otherwise, the *create* operation is called. If the filesystem is stateful and has been able to lock the directory, then it can simply create the name in the previously identified space, because it knows that no other processes will have had access to the directory. Once the name is created, an *unlock* request is made on the directory. If the filesystem is stateless, then it cannot lock the directory, so the *create* operator must rescan the directory to find space and to verify that the name has not been created since the lookup.

7.2   Structure of an Inode

To allow files to be allocated concurrently and random access within files, 4.4BSD uses the concept of an *index node*, or *inode*. The inode contains information about the contents of the file, as shown in Fig. 7.1. This information includes

Figure 7.1 The structure of an inode.

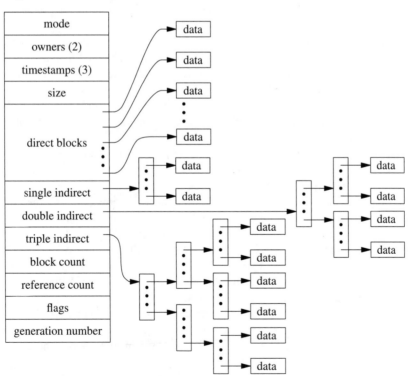

- The type and access mode for the file

- The file's owner

- The group-access identifier

- The time that the file was most recently read and written

- The time that the inode was most recently updated by the system

- The size of the file in bytes

- The number of physical blocks used by the file (including blocks used to hold indirect pointers)

- The number of references to the file

- The flags that describe characteristics of the file

- The generation number of the file (a unique number selected to be the approximate creation time of the file and assigned to the inode each time that the latter is allocated to a new file; the generation number is used by NFS to detect references to deleted files)

Notably missing in the inode is the filename. Filenames are maintained in directories, rather than in inodes, because a file may have many names, or links, and the name of a file may be large (up to 255 bytes in length). Directories are described in Section 7.3.

To create a new name for a file, the system increments the count of the number of names referring to that inode. Then, the new name is entered in a directory, along with the number of the inode. Conversely, when a name is deleted, the entry is deleted from a directory, and the name count for the inode is then decremented. When the name count reaches zero, the system deallocates the inode by putting all the inode's blocks back on a list of free blocks and by putting the inode back on a list of unused inodes.

The inode also contains an array of pointers to the blocks in the file. The system can convert from a logical block number to a physical sector number by indexing into the array using the logical block number. A null array entry shows that no block has been allocated and will cause a block of zeros to be returned on a read. On a write of such an entry, a new block is allocated, the array entry is updated with the new block number, and the data are written to the disk.

Inodes are statically allocated and most files are small, so the array of pointers must be small for efficient use of space. The first 12 array entries are allocated in the inode itself. For typical filesystems, this allows the first 48 or 96 Kbyte of data to be located directly via a simple indexed lookup.

For somewhat larger files, Fig. 7.1 shows that the inode contains a *single indirect pointer* that points to a *single indirect block* of pointers to data blocks. To find the one-hundredth logical block of a file, the system first fetches the block identified by the indirect pointer, then indexes into the eighty-eighth block (100 minus 12 direct pointers), and fetches that data block.

For files that are bigger than a few Mbyte, the single indirect block is eventually exhausted; these files must resort to using a *double indirect block*, which is a pointer to a block of pointers to pointers to data blocks. For files of multiple Gbyte, the system uses a *triple indirect block*, which contains three levels of pointer before reaching the data block.

Although indirect blocks appear to increase the number of disk accesses required to get a block of data, the overhead of the transfer is typically much lower. In Section 6.6, we discussed the management of the filesystem cache that holds recently used disk blocks. The first time that a block of indirect pointers is needed, it is brought into the filesystem cache. Further accesses to the indirect pointers find the block already resident in memory; thus, they require only a single disk access to get the data.

Inode Management

Most of the activity in the local filesystem revolves around inodes. As described in Section 6.6, the kernel keeps a list of active and recently accessed vnodes. The decisions regarding how many and which files should be cached are made by the vnode layer based on information about activity across all filesystems. Each local filesystem will have a subset of the system vnodes to manage. Each uses an inode supplemented with some additional information to identify and locate the set of files for which it is responsible. Figure 7.2 shows the location of the inodes within the system.

Reviewing the material in Section 6.4, each process has a *process open-file table* that has slots for up to a system-imposed limit of file descriptors; this table is maintained as part of the process state. When a user process opens a file (or socket), an unused slot is located in the process's open-file table; the small integer file descriptor that is returned on a successful *open* is an index value into this table.

The per-process file-table entry points to a *system open-file entry*, which contains information about the underlying file or socket represented by the descriptor. For files, the file table points to the vnode representing the open file. For the local filesystem, the vnode references an inode. It is the inode that identifies the file itself.

Figure 7.2 Layout of kernel tables.

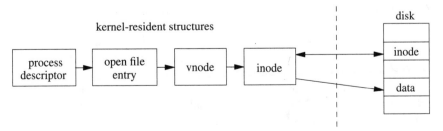

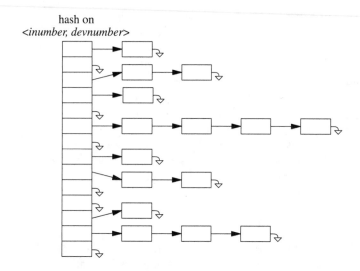

hash on
<inumber, devnumber>

Figure 7.3 Structure of the inode table.

The first step in opening a file is to find the file's associated vnode. The lookup request is given to the filesystem associated with the directory currently being searched. When the local filesystem finds the name in the directory, it gets the inode number of the associated file. First, the filesystem searches its collection of inodes to see whether the requested inode is already in memory. To avoid doing a linear scan of all its entries, the system keeps a set of hash chains keyed on inode number and filesystem identifier, as shown in Fig. 7.3. If the inode is not in the table, such as the first time a file is opened, the filesystem must request a new vnode. When a new vnode is allocated to the local filesystem, a new structure to hold the inode is allocated.

The next step is to locate the disk block containing the inode and to read that block into a buffer in system memory. When the disk I/O completes, the inode is copied from the disk buffer into the newly allocated inode entry. In addition to the information contained in the disk portion of the inode, the inode table itself maintains supplemental information while the inode is in memory. This information includes the hash chains described previously, as well as flags showing the inode's status, reference counts on its use, and information to manage locks. The information also contains pointers to other kernel data structures of frequent interest, such as the superblock for the filesystem containing the inode.

When the last reference to a file is closed, the local filesystem is notified that the file has become inactive. When it is inactivated, the inode times will be updated, and the inode may be written to disk. However, it remains on the hash list so that it can be found if it is reopened. After being inactive for a period determined by the vnode layer based on demand for vnodes in all the filesystems, the vnode will be reclaimed. When a vnode for a local file is reclaimed, the inode is removed from the previous filesystem's hash chain and, if the inode is dirty, its contents are written back to disk. The space for the inode is then deallocated, so that the vnode will be ready for use by a new filesystem client.

7.3   Naming

Filesystems contain files, most of which contain ordinary data. Certain files are distinguished as directories and contain pointers to files that may themselves be directories. This hierarchy of directories and files is organized into a tree structure; Fig. 7.4 shows a small filesystem tree. Each of the circles in the figure represents an inode with its corresponding inode number inside. Each of the arrows represents a name in a directory. For example, inode 4 is the **/usr** directory with entry **.**, which points to itself, and entry **..**, which points to its parent, inode 2, the root of the filesystem. It also contains the name **bin**, which references directory inode 7, and the name **foo**, which references file inode 6.

Directories

Directories are allocated in units called *chunks*; Fig. 7.5 (on page 248) shows a typical directory chunk. The size of a chunk is chosen such that each allocation can be transferred to disk in a single operation; the ability to change a directory in a single operation makes directory updates atomic. Chunks are broken up into variable-length directory entries to allow filenames to be of nearly arbitrary length. No directory entry can span multiple chunks. The first four fields of a directory entry are of fixed length and contain

1. An index into a table of on-disk inode structures; the selected entry describes the file (inodes were described in Section 7.2)

Figure 7.4 A small filesystem tree.

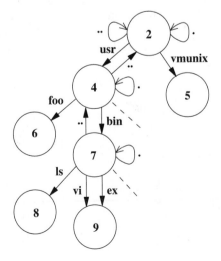

a directory block with three entries

an empty directory block

Figure 7.5 Format of directory chunks.

2. The size of the entry in bytes

3. The type of the entry

4. The length of the filename contained in the entry in bytes

The remainder of an entry is of variable length and contains a null-terminated filename, padded to a 4-byte boundary. The maximum length of a filename in a
directory is 255 characters.

The filesystem records free space in a directory by having entries accumulate
the free space in their size fields. Thus, some directory entries are larger than
required to hold the entry name plus fixed-length fields. Space allocated to a
directory should always be accounted for completely by the total of the sizes of
the directory's entries. When an entry is deleted from a directory, the system coa-
lesces the entry's space into the previous entry in the same directory chunk by
increasing the size of the previous entry by the size of the deleted entry. If the first
entry of a directory chunk is free, then the pointer to the entry's inode is set to zero
to show that the entry is unallocated.

Applications obtain chunks of directories from the kernel by using the *getdirentries* system call. For the local filesystem, the on-disk format of directories is
identical to that expected by the application, so the chunks are returned uninterpreted. When directories are read over the network or from non-BSD filesystems
such as MS-DOS, the *getdirentries* system call has to convert the on-disk representation of the directory to that described.

Normally, programs want to read directories one entry at a time. This interface is provided by the directory-access routines. The *opendir*() function returns a
structure pointer that is used by *readdir*() to get chunks of directories using *getdirentries*; *readdir*() returns the next entry from the chunk on each call. The
closedir() function deallocates space allocated by *opendir*() and closes the directory. In addition, there is the *rewinddir*() function to reset the read position to the
beginning, the *telldir*() function that returns a structure describing the current
directory position, and the *seekdir*() function that returns to a position previously
obtained with *telldir*().

Finding of Names in Directories

A common request to the filesystem is to look up a specific name in a directory. The kernel usually does the lookup by starting at the beginning of the directory and going through, comparing each entry in turn. First, the length of the sought-after name is compared with the length of the name being checked. If the lengths are identical, a string comparison of the name being sought and the directory entry is made. If they match, the search is complete; if they fail, either in the length or in the string comparison, the search continues with the next entry. Whenever a name is found, its name and containing directory are entered into the systemwide name cache described in Section 6.6. Whenever a search is unsuccessful, an entry is made in the cache showing that the name does not exist in the particular directory. Before starting a directory scan, the kernel looks for the name in the cache. If either a positive or negative entry is found, the directory scan can be avoided.

Another common operation is to look up all the entries in a directory. For example, many programs do a *stat* system call on each name in a directory in the order that the names appear in the directory. To improve performance for these programs, the kernel maintains the directory offset of the last successful lookup for each directory. Each time that a lookup is done in that directory, the search is started from the offset at which the previous name was found (instead of from the beginning of the directory). For programs that step sequentially through a directory with *n* files, search time decreases from $Order(n^2)$ to $Order(n)$.

One quick benchmark that demonstrates the maximum effectiveness of the cache is running the *ls −l* command on a directory containing 600 files. On a system that retains the most recent directory offset, the amount of system time for this test is reduced by 85 percent on a directory containing 600 files. Unfortunately, the maximum effectiveness is much greater than the average effectiveness. Although the cache is 90-percent effective when hit, it is applicable to only about 25 percent of the names being looked up. Despite the amount of time spent in the lookup routine itself decreasing substantially, the improvement is diminished because more time is spent in the routines that that routine calls. Each cache miss causes a directory to be accessed twice—once to search from the middle to the end, and once to search from the beginning to the middle.

Pathname Translation

We are now ready to describe how the filesystem looks up a pathname. The small filesystem introduced in Fig. 7.4 is expanded to show its internal structure in Fig. 7.6 (on page 250). Each of the files in Fig. 7.4 is shown expanded into its constituent inode and data blocks. As an example of how these data structures work, consider how the system finds the file **/usr/bin/vi**. It must first search the root directory of the filesystem to find the directory **usr**. It first finds the inode that describes the root directory. By convention, inode 2 is always reserved for the root directory of a filesystem; therefore, the system finds and brings inode 2 into memory. This inode shows where the data blocks are for the root directory; these data blocks must also be brought into memory so that they can be searched for the entry **usr**. Having found the entry for **usr**, the system knows that the

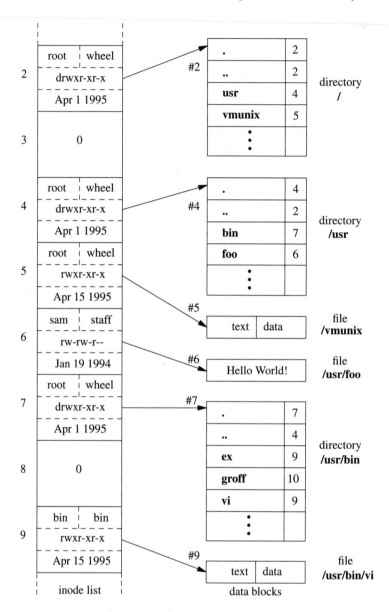

Figure 7.6 Internal structure of a small filesystem.

contents of **usr** are described by inode 4. Returning once again to the disk, the system fetches inode 4 to find where the data blocks for **usr** are located. Searching these blocks, it finds the entry for **bin**. The **bin** entry points to inode 7. Next, the system brings in inode 7 and its associated data blocks from the disk, to search for the entry for **vi**. Having found that **vi** is described by inode 9, the system can fetch this inode and the blocks that contain the **vi** binary.

Links

Each file has a single inode, but multiple directory entries in the same filesystem may reference that inode (i.e., the inode may have multiple names). Each directory entry creates a *hard link* of a filename to the inode that describes the file's contents. The link concept is fundamental; inodes do not reside in directories, but rather exist separately and are referenced by links. When all the links to an inode are removed, the inode is deallocated. If one link to a file is removed and the filename is recreated with new contents, the other links will continue to point to the old inode. Figure 7.7 shows two different directory entries, **foo** and **bar**, that reference the same file; thus, the inode for the file shows a reference count of 2.

The system also supports a *symbolic link*, or *soft link*. A symbolic link is implemented as a file that contains a pathname. When the system encounters a symbolic link while looking up a component of a pathname, the contents of the symbolic link are prepended to the rest of the pathname; the lookup continues with the resulting pathname. If a symbolic link contains an absolute pathname, that absolute pathname is used; otherwise, the contents of the symbolic link are evaluated relative to the location of the link in the file hierarchy (not relative to the current working directory of the calling process).

An example symbolic link is shown in Fig. 7.8 (on page 252). Here, there is a hard link, **foo**, that points to the file. The other reference, **bar**, points to a different inode whose contents are a pathname of the referenced file. When a process opens **bar**, the system interprets the contents of the symbolic link as a pathname to find the file the link references. Symbolic links are treated like data files by the system, rather than as part of the filesystem structure; thus, they can point at directories or files on other filesystems. If a filename is removed and replaced, any symbolic links that point to it will access the new file. Finally, if the filename is not replaced, the symbolic link will point at nothing, and any attempt to access it will be an error.

Figure 7.7 Hard links to a file.

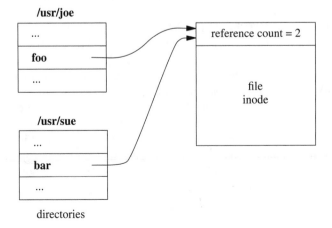

directories

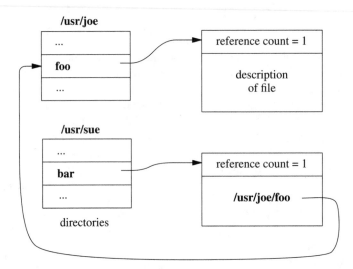

Figure 7.8 Symbolic link to a file.

When *open* is applied to a symbolic link, it returns a file descriptor for the file pointed to, not for the link itself. Otherwise, it would be necessary to use indirection to access the file pointed to—and that file, rather than the link, is what is usually wanted. For the same reason, most other system calls that take pathname arguments also follow symbolic links. Sometimes, it is useful to be able to detect a symbolic link when traversing a filesystem or when making an archive tape. So, the *lstat* system call is available to get the status of a symbolic link, instead of the object at which that link points.

A symbolic link has several advantages over a hard link. Since a symbolic link is maintained as a pathname, it can refer to a directory or to a file on a different filesystem. So that loops in the filesystem hierarchy are prevented, unprivileged users are not permitted to create hard links (other than **.** and **..**) that refer to a directory. The implementation of hard links prevents hard links from referring to files on a different filesystem.

There are several interesting implications of symbolic links. Consider a process that has current working directory **/usr/keith** and does *cd* **src**, where **src** is a symbolic link to directory **/usr/src**. If the process then does a *cd* **..**, then the current working directory for the process will be in **/usr** instead of in **/usr/keith**, as it would have been if **src** was a normal directory instead of a symbolic link. The kernel could be changed to keep track of the symbolic links that a process has traversed, and to interpret **..** differently if the directory has been reached through a symbolic link. There are two problems with this implementation. First, the kernel would have to maintain a potentially unbounded amount of information. Second, no program could depend on being able to use **..**, since it could not be sure how the name would be interpreted.

Many shells keep track of symbolic-link traversals. When the user changes directory through .. from a directory that was entered through a symbolic link, the shell returns the user to the directory from which they came. Although the shell might have to maintain an unbounded amount of information, the worst that will happen is that the shell will run out of memory. Having the shell fail will affect only the user silly enough to traverse endlessly through symbolic links. Tracking of symbolic links affects only change-directory commands in the shell; programs can continue to depend on .. referencing its true parent. Thus, tracking symbolic links outside of the kernel in a shell is reasonable.

Since symbolic links may cause loops in the filesystem, the kernel prevents looping by allowing at most eight symbolic link traversals in a single pathname translation. If the limit is reached, the kernel produces an error (ELOOP).

7.4   Quotas

Resource sharing always has been a design goal for the BSD system. By default, any single user can allocate all the available space in the filesystem. In certain environments, uncontrolled use of disk space is unacceptable. Consequently, 4.4BSD includes a quota mechanism to restrict the amount of filesystem resources that a user or members of a group can obtain. The quota mechanism sets limits on both the number of files and the number of disk blocks that a user or members of a group may allocate. Quotas can be set separately for each user and group on each filesystem.

Quotas support both hard and soft limits. When a process exceeds its soft limit, a warning is printed on the user's terminal; the offending process is not prevented from allocating space unless it exceeds its hard limit. The idea is that users should stay below their soft limit between login sessions, but may use more resources while they are active. If a user fails to correct the problem for longer than a grace period, the soft limit starts to be enforced as the hard limit. The grace period is set by the system administrator and is 7 days by default. These quotas are derived from a larger resource-limit package that was developed at the University of Melbourne in Australia by Robert Elz [Elz, 1984].

Quotas connect into the system primarily as an adjunct to the allocation routines. When a new block is requested from the allocation routines, the request is first validated by the quota system with the following steps:

1. If there is a user quota associated with the file, the quota system consults the quota associated with the owner of the file. If the owner has reached or exceeded their limit, the request is denied.

2. If there is a group quota associated with the file, the quota system consults the quota associated with the group of the file. If the group has reached or exceeded its limit, the request is denied.

3. If the quota tests pass, the request is permitted and is added to the usage statistics for the file.

When either a user or group quota would be exceeded, the allocator returns a failure as though the filesystem were full. The kernel propagates this error up to the process doing the *write* system call.

Quotas are assigned to a filesystem after it has been mounted. A system call associates a file containing the quotas with the mounted filesystem. By convention, the file with user quotas is named **quota.user**, and the file with group quotas is named **quota.group**. These files typically reside either in the root of the mounted filesystem or in the **/var/quotas** directory. For each quota to be imposed, the system opens the appropriate quota file and holds a reference to it in the mount-table entry associated with the mounted filesystem. Figure 7.9 shows the mount-table reference. Here, the root filesystem has a quota on users, but has none on groups. The **/usr** filesystem has quotas imposed on both users and groups. As quotas for different users or groups are needed, they are taken from the appropriate quota file.

Quota files are maintained as an array of quota records indexed by user or group identifiers; Fig. 7.10 shows a typical record in a user quota file. To find the quota for user identifier i, the system seeks to location $i \times$ **sizeof**(quota structure) in the quota file and reads the quota structure at that location. Each quota structure contains the limits imposed on the user for the associated filesystem. These limits include the hard and soft limits on the number of blocks and inodes that the user may have, the number of blocks and inodes that the user currently has allocated, and the amount of time that the user has remaining before the soft limit is enforced as the hard limit. The group quota file works in the same way, except that it is indexed by group identifier.

Figure 7.9 References to quota files.

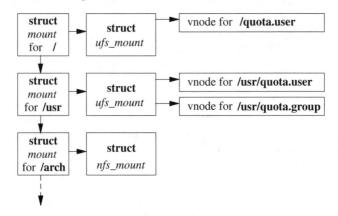

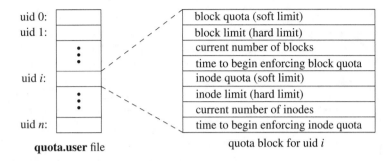

Figure 7.10 Contents of a quota record.

Active quotas are held in system memory in a data structure known as a *dquot entry*; Fig. 7.11 shows two typical entries. In addition to the quota limits and usage extracted from the quota file, the dquot entry maintains information about the quota while the quota is in use. This information includes fields to allow fast access and identification. Quotas are checked by the *chkdq*() routine. Since quotas may have to be updated on every write to a file, *chkdq*() must be able to find and manipulate them quickly. Thus, the task of finding the dquot structure associated with a file is done when the file is first opened for writing. When an access

Figure 7.11 Dquot entries.

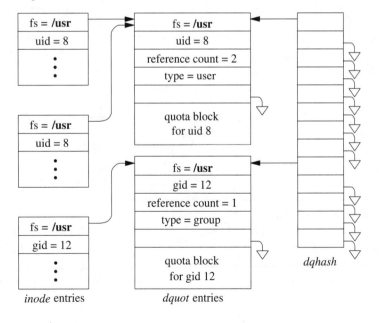

check is done to check for writing, the system checks to see whether there is either a user or a group quota associated with the file. If one or more quotas exist, the inode is set up to hold a reference to the appropriate dquot structures for as long as the inode is resident. The *chkdq*( ) routine can determine that a file has a quota simply by checking whether the dquot pointer is nonnull; if it is, all the necessary information can be accessed directly. If a user or a group has multiple files open on the same filesystem, all inodes describing those files point to the same dquot entry. Thus, the number of blocks allocated to a particular user or a group can always be known easily and consistently.

The number of dquot entries in the system can grow large. To avoid doing a linear scan of all the dquot entries, the system keeps a set of hash chains keyed on the filesystem and on the user or group identifier. Even with hundreds of dquot entries, the kernel needs to inspect only about five entries to determine whether a requested dquot entry is memory resident. If the dquot entry is not resident, such as the first time a file is opened for writing, the system must reallocate a dquot entry and read in the quota from disk. The dquot entry is reallocated from the least recently used dquot entry. So that it can find the oldest dquot entry quickly, the system keeps unused dquot entries linked together in an LRU chain. When the reference count on a dquot structure drops to zero, the system puts that dquot onto the end of the LRU chain. The dquot structure is not removed from its hash chain, so if the structure is needed again soon, it can still be located. Only when a dquot structure is recycled with a new quota record is it removed and relinked into the hash chain. The dquot entry on the front of the LRU chain yields the least recently used dquot entry. Frequently used dquot entries are reclaimed from the middle of the LRU chain and are relinked at the end after use.

The hashing structure allows dquot structures to be found quickly. However, it does not solve the problem of how to discover that a user has no quota on a particular filesystem. If a user has no quota, a lookup for the quota will fail. The cost of going to disk and reading the quota file to discover that the user has no quota imposed would be prohibitive. To avoid doing this work each time that a new file is accessed for writing, the system maintains nonquota dquot entries. When an inode owned by a user or group that does not already have a dquot entry is first accessed, a dummy dquot entry is created that has infinite values filled in for the quota limits. When the *chkdq*( ) routine encounters such an entry, it will update the usage fields, but will not impose any limits. When the user later writes other files, the same dquot entry will be found, thus avoiding additional access to the on-disk quota file. Ensuring that a file will always have a dquot entry improves the performance of the writing data, since *chkdq*( ) can assume that the dquot pointer is always valid, rather than having to check the pointer before every use.

Quotas are written back to the disk when they fall out of the cache, whenever the filesystem does a sync, or when the filesystem is unmounted. If the system crashes, leaving the quotas in an inconsistent state, the system administrator must run the **quotacheck** program to rebuild the usage information in the quota files.

7.5   File Locking

Locks may be placed on any arbitrary range of bytes within a file. These semantics are supported in 4.4BSD by a list of locks, each of which describes a lock of a specified byte range. An example of a file containing several range locks is shown in Fig. 7.12. The list of currently held or active locks appears across the top of the figure, headed by the *i_lockf* field in the inode, and linked together through the *lf_next* field of the lock structures. Each lock structure identifies the type of the lock (exclusive or shared), the byte range over which the lock applies, and the identity of the lock holder. A lock may be identified either by a pointer to a process entry or by a pointer to a file entry. A process pointer is used for POSIX-style range locks; a file-entry pointer is used for BSD-style whole file locks. The examples in this section show the identity as a pointer to a process entry. In this example, there are three active locks: an exclusive lock held by process 1 on bytes 1 to 3, a shared lock held by process 2 on bytes 7 to 12, and a shared lock held by process 3 on bytes 7 to 14.

In addition to the active locks, there are other processes that are sleeping waiting to get a lock applied. Pending locks are headed by the *lf_block* field of the

Figure 7.12 A set of range locks on a file.

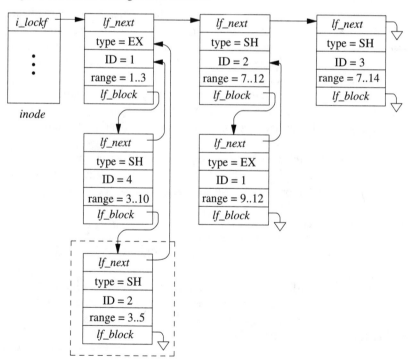

active lock that prevents them from being applied. If there are multiple pending locks, they are linked through their *lf_block* fields. New lock requests are placed at the end of the list; thus, processes tend to be granted locks in the order that they requested the locks. Each pending lock uses its *lf_next* field to identify the active lock that currently blocks it. In the example in Fig. 7.12, the first active lock has two other locks pending. There is also a pending request for the range 9 to 12 that is currently linked onto the second active entry. It could equally well have been linked onto the third active entry, since the third entry also blocks it. When an active lock is released, all pending entries for that lock are awakened, so that they can retry their request. If the second active lock were released, the result would be that its currently pending request would move over to the blocked list for the last active entry.

A problem that must be handled by the locking implementation is the detection of potential deadlocks. To see how deadlock is detected, consider the addition of the lock request by process 2 outlined in the dashed box in Fig. 7.12. Since the request is blocked by an active lock, process 2 must sleep waiting for the active lock on range 1 to 3 to clear. We follow the *lf_next* pointer from the requesting lock (the one in the dashed box), to identify the active lock for the 1-to-3 range as being held by process 1. The wait channel for process 1 shows that that process too is sleeping, waiting for a lock to clear, and identifies the pending lock structure as the pending lock (range 9 to 12) hanging off the *lf_block* field of the second active lock (range 7 to 12). We follow the *lf_next* field of this pending lock structure (range 9 to 12) to the second active lock (range 7 to 12) that is held by the lock requester, process 2. Thus, the lock request is denied, as it would lead to a deadlock between processes 1 and 2. This algorithm works on cycles of locks and processes of arbitrary size.

As we note, the pending request for the range 9 to 12 could equally well have been hung off the third active lock for the range 7 to 14. Had it been, the request for adding the lock in the dashed box would have succeeded, since the third active lock is held by process 3, rather than by process 2. If the next lock request on this file were to release the third active lock, then deadlock detection would occur when process 1's pending lock got shifted to the second active lock (range 7 to 12). The difference is that process 1, instead of process 2, would get the deadlock error.

When a new lock request is made, it must first be checked to see whether it is blocked by existing locks held by other processes. If it is not blocked by other processes, it must then be checked to see whether it overlaps any existing locks already held by the process making the request. There are five possible overlap cases that must be considered; these possibilities are shown in Fig. 7.13. The assumption in the figure is that the new request is of a type different from that of the existing lock (i.e., an exclusive request against a shared lock, or vice versa); if the existing lock and the request are of the same type, the analysis is a bit simpler. The five cases are as follows:

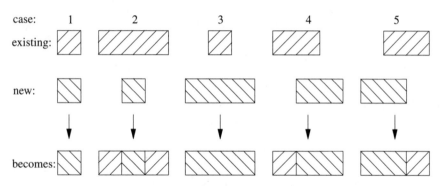

Figure 7.13 Five types of overlap considered by the kernel when a range lock is added.

1. The new request exactly overlaps the existing lock. The new request replaces the existing lock. If the new request downgrades from exclusive to shared, all requests pending on the old lock are awakened.

2. The new request is a subset of the existing lock. The existing lock is broken into three pieces (two if the new lock begins at the beginning or ends at the end of the existing lock). If the type of the new request differs from that of the existing lock, all requests pending on the old lock are awakened, so that they can be reassigned to the correct new piece, blocked on a lock held by some other process, or granted.

3. The new request is a superset of an existing lock. The new request replaces the existing lock. If the new request downgrades from exclusive to shared, all requests pending on the old lock are awakened.

4. The new request extends past the end of an existing lock. The existing lock is shortened, and its overlapped piece is replaced by the new request. All requests pending on the existing lock are awakened, so that they can be reassigned to the correct new piece, blocked on a lock held by some other process, or granted.

5. The new request extends into the beginning of an existing lock. The existing lock is shortened, and its overlapped piece is replaced by the new request. All requests pending on the existing lock are awakened, so that they can be reassigned to the correct new piece, blocked on a lock held by some other process, or granted.

In addition to the five basic types of overlap outlined, a request may span several existing locks. Specifically, a new request may be composed of zero or one of type 4, zero or more of type 3, and zero or one of type 5.

To understand how the overlap is handled, we can consider the example shown in Fig. 7.14. This figure shows a file that has all its active range locks held by process 1, plus a pending lock for process 2.

Now consider a request by process 1 for an exclusive lock on the range 3 to 13. This request does not conflict with any active locks (because all the active locks are already held by process 1). The request does overlap all three active locks, so the three active locks represent a type 4, type 3, and type 5 overlap respectively. The result of processing the lock request is shown in Fig. 7.15. The first and third active locks are trimmed back to the edge of the new request, and the second lock is replaced entirely. The request that had been held pending on the first lock is awakened. It is no longer blocked by the first lock, but is blocked by the newly installed lock. So, it now hangs off the blocked list for the second lock. The first and second locks could have been merged, because they are of the same type and are held by the same process. However, the current implementation makes no effort to do such merges, because range locks are normally released over the same range that they were created. If the merger were done, it would probably have to be split again when the release was requested.

Lock-removal requests are simpler than addition requests; they need only to consider existing locks held by the requesting process. Figure 7.16 shows the five possible ways that a removal request can overlap the locks of the requesting process:

1. The unlock request exactly overlaps an existing lock. The existing lock is deleted, and any lock requests that were pending on that lock are awakened.

2. The unlock request is a subset of an existing lock. The existing lock is broken into two pieces (one if the unlock request begins at the beginning or ends at

---

Figure 7.14 Locks before addition of exclusive-lock request by process 1 on range 3..13.

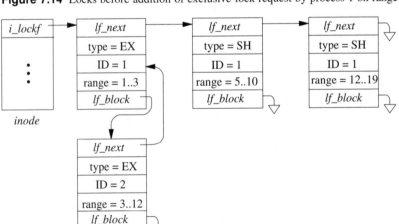

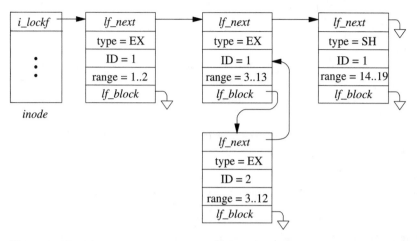

Figure 7.15 Locks after addition of exclusive-lock request by process 1 on range 3..13.

the end of the existing lock). Any locks that were pending on that lock are awakened, so that they can be reassigned to the correct new piece, blocked on a lock held by some other process, or granted.

3. The unlock request is a superset of an existing lock. The existing lock is deleted, and any locks that were pending on that lock are awakened.

4. The unlock request extends past the end of an existing lock. The end of the existing lock is shortened. Any locks that were pending on that lock are awakened, so that they can be reassigned to the shorter lock, blocked on a lock held by some other process, or granted.

5. The unlock request extends into the beginning of an existing lock. The beginning of the existing lock is shortened. Any locks that were pending on that

Figure 7.16 Five types of overlap considered by the kernel when a range lock is deleted.

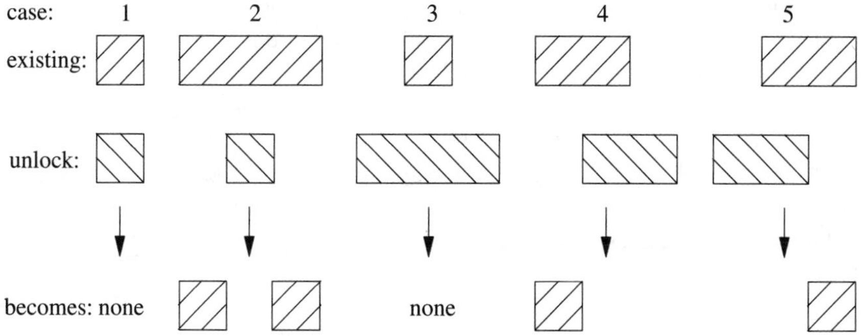

case: 1   2   3   4   5

existing:

unlock:

becomes: none

lock are awakened, so that they can be reassigned to the shorter lock, blocked on a lock held by some other process, or granted.

In addition to the five basic types of overlap outlined, an unlock request may span several existing locks. Specifically, a new request may be composed of zero or one of type 4, zero or more of type 3, and zero or one of type 5.

7.6 Other Filesystem Semantics

Two major new filesystem features were introduced in 4.4BSD. The first of these features was support for much larger file sizes. The second was the introduction of file metadata.

Large File Sizes

Traditionally, UNIX systems supported a maximum file and filesystem size of 2^{31} bytes. When the filesystem was rewritten in 4.2BSD, the inodes were defined to allow a 64-bit file sizes. However, the interface to the filesystem was still limited to 31-bit sizes. With the advent of ever-larger disks, the developers decided to expand the 4.4BSD interface to allow larger files. Export of 64-bit file sizes from the filesystem requires that the defined type *off_t* be a 64-bit integer (referred to as *long long* or *quad* in most compilers).

The number of affected system calls is surprisingly low:

- *lseek* has to be able to specify 64-bit offsets

- *stat*, *fstat*, and *lstat* have to return 64-bit sizes

- *truncate* and *ftruncate* have to set 64-bit sizes

- *mmap* needs to start a mapping at any 64-bit point in the file

- *getrlimit* and *setrlimit* need to get and set 64-bit filesize limits

Changing these interfaces did cause applications to break. No trouble was encountered with the *stat* family of system calls returning larger data values; recompiling with the redefined *stat* structure caused applications to use the new larger values. The other system calls are all changing one of their parameters to be a 64-bit value. Applications that fail to cast the 64-bit argument to *off_t* may get an incorrect parameter list. Except for *lseek*, most applications do not use these system calls, so they are not affected by their change. However, many applications use *lseek* and cast the seek value explicitly to type *long*. So that there is no need to make changes to many applications, a prototype for *lseek* is placed in the commonly included header file **<sys/types.h>**. After this change was made, most applications recompiled and ran without difficulty.

For completeness, the type of *size_t* also should have been changed to be a 64-bit integer. This change was not made because it would have affected too many system calls. Also, on 32-bit address-space machines, an application cannot read more than can be stored in a 32-bit integer. Finally, it is important to minimize the use of 64-bit arithmetic that is slow on 32-bit processors.

File Flags

4.4BSD added two new system calls, *chflags* and *fchflags*, that set a 32-bit flags word in the inode. The flags are included in the *stat* structure so that they can be inspected.

The owner of the file or the superuser can set the low 16 bits. Currently, there are flags defined to mark a file as append-only, immutable, and not needing to be dumped. An *immutable* file may not be changed, moved, or deleted. An *append-only* file is immutable except that data may be appended to it. The user append-only and immutable flags may be changed by the owner of the file or the superuser.

Only the superuser can set the high 16 bits. Currently, there are flags defined to mark a file as append-only and immutable. Once set, the append-only and immutable flags in the top 16 bits cannot be cleared when the system is secure.

The kernel runs with four different levels of security. Any superuser process can raise the security level, but only the **init** process can lower that level (the **init** program is described in Section 14.6). Security levels are defined as follows:

−1. *Permanently insecure mode*: Always run system in level 0 mode (must be compiled into the kernel).

0. *Insecure mode*: Immutable and append-only flags may be turned off. All devices can be read or written, subject to their permissions.

1. *Secure mode*: The superuser-settable immutable and append-only flags cannot be cleared; disks for mounted filesystems and kernel memory (**/dev/mem** and **/dev/kmem**) are read-only.

2. *Highly secure mode*: This mode is the same as secure mode, except that disks are always read-only whether mounted or not. This level precludes even a superuser process from tampering with filesystems by unmounting them, but also inhibits formatting of new filesystems.

Normally, the system runs with level 0 security while in single-user mode, and with level 1 security while in multiuser mode. If level 2 security is desired while the system is running in multiuser mode, it should be set in the **/etc/rc** startup script (the **/etc/rc** script is described in Section 14.6).

Files marked immutable by the superuser cannot be changed, except by someone with physical access to either the machine or the system console. Files marked immutable include those that are frequently the subject of attack by intruders (e.g., **login** and **su**). The append-only flag is typically used for critical system logs. If an intruder breaks in, he will be unable to cover his tracks. Although simple in concept, these two features improve the security of a system dramatically.

Exercises

7.1   What are the seven classes of operations handled by the hierarchical filesystem?

7.2   What is the purpose of the inode data structure?

7.3   How does the system select an inode for replacement when a new inode must be brought in from disk?

7.4   Why are directory entries not allowed to span chunks?

7.5   Describe the steps involved in looking up a pathname component.

7.6   Why are hard links not permitted to span filesystems?

7.7   Describe how the interpretation of a symbolic link containing an absolute pathname is different from that of a symbolic link containing a relative pathname.

7.8   Explain why unprivileged users are not permitted to make hard links to directories, but are permitted to make symbolic links to directories.

7.9   How can hard links be used to gain access to files that could not be accessed if a symbolic link were used instead?

7.10   How does the system recognize loops caused by symbolic links? Suggest an alternative scheme for doing loop detection.

7.11   How do quotas differ from the file-size resource limits described in Section 3.8?

7.12   How does the kernel determine whether a file has an associated quota?

7.13   Draw a picture showing the effect of processing an exclusive-lock request by process 1 on bytes 7 to 10 to the lock list shown in Fig. 7.14. Which of the overlap cases of Fig. 7.13 apply to this example?

*7.14   Give an example where the file-locking implementation is unable to detect a potential deadlock.

**7.15 Design a system that allows the security level of the system to be lowered while the system is still running in multiuser mode.

References

Elz, 1984.
    K. R. Elz, "Resource Controls, Privileges, and Other MUSH," *USENIX Association Conference Proceedings*, pp. 183–191, June 1984.

CHAPTER 8

Local Filestores

This chapter describes the organization and management of data on storage media. 4.4BSD provides three different filestore managers: the traditional Berkeley Fast Filesystem (FFS), the recently added Log-Structured Filesystem (LFS), and the Memory-based Filesystem (MFS) that uses much of the FFS code base. The FFS filestore was designed on the assumption that buffer caches would be small and thus that files would need to be read often. It tries to place files likely to be accessed together in the same general location on the disk. It is described in Section 8.2. The LFS filestore was designed for fast machines with large buffer caches. It assumes that writing data to disk is the bottleneck, and it tries to avoid seeking by writing all data together in the order in which they were created. It assumes that active files will remain in the buffer cache, so is little concerned with the time that it takes to retrieve files from the filestore. It is described in Section 8.3. The MFS filestore was designed as a fast-access repository for transient data. It is used primarily to back the **/tmp** filesystem. It is described in Section 8.4.

8.1 Overview of the Filestore

The vnode operations defined for doing the datastore filesystem operations are shown in Table 8.1 (on page 266). These operators are fewer and semantically simpler than are those used for managing the name space.

There are two operators for allocating and freeing objects. The *valloc* operator creates a new object. The identity of the object is a number returned by the operator. The mapping of this number to a name is the responsibility of the name-space code. An object is freed by the *vfree* operator. The object to be freed is identified by only its number.

The attributes of an object are changed by the *update* operator. This layer does no interpretation of these attributes; they are simply fixed-size auxiliary data

Table 8.1 Datastore filesystem operations.

Operation done	Operator names
object creation and deletion	valloc, vfree
attribute update	update
object read and write	vget, blkatoff, read, write, fsync
change in space allocation	truncate

stored outside the main data area of the object. They are typically file attributes, such as the owner, group, permissions, and so on.

There are five operators for manipulating existing objects. The *vget* operator retrieves an existing object from the filestore. The object is identified by its number and must have been created previously by *valloc*. The *read* operator copies data from an object to a location described by a *uio* structure. The *blkatoff* operator is similar to the *read* operator, except that the *blkatoff* operator simply returns a pointer to a kernel memory buffer with the requested data, instead of copying the data. This operator is designed to increase the efficiency of operations where the name-space code interprets the contents of an object (i.e., directories), instead of just returning the contents to a user process. The *write* operator copies data to an object from a location described by a *uio* structure. The *fsync* operator requests that all data associated with the object be moved to stable storage (usually by their all being written to disk). There is no need for an analog of *blkatoff* for writing, as the kernel can simply modify a buffer that it received from *blkatoff*, mark that buffer as dirty, and then do an *fsync* operation to have the buffer written back.

The final datastore operation is *truncate*. This operation changes the amount of space associated with an object. Historically, it could be used only to decrease the size of an object. In 4.4BSD, it can be used both to increase and to decrease the size of an object.

Each disk drive has one or more subdivisions, or *partitions*. Each such partition can contain only one filestore, and a filestore never spans multiple partitions.

The filestore is responsible for the management of the space within its disk partition. Within that space, its responsibility is the creation, storage, retrieval, and removal of files. It operates in a flat name space. When asked to create a new file, it allocates an inode for that file and returns the assigned number. The naming, access control, locking, and attribute manipulation for the file are all handled by the hierarchical filesystem-management layer above the filestore.

The filestore also handles the allocation of new blocks to files as the latter grow. Simple filesystem implementations, such as those used by early microcomputer systems, allocate files contiguously, one after the next, until the files reach the end of the disk. As files are removed, holes occur. To reuse the freed space, the system must compact the disk to move all the free space to the end. Files can be created only one at a time; for the size of a file other than the final one on the disk to be increased, the file must be copied to the end, then expanded.

As we saw in Section 7.2, each file in a filestore is described by an inode; the locations of its data blocks are given by the block pointers in its inode. Although the filestore may cluster the blocks of a file to improve I/O performance, the inode can reference blocks scattered anywhere throughout the partition. Thus, multiple files can be written simultaneously, and all the disk space can be used without the need for compaction.

The filestore implementation converts from the user abstraction of a file as an array of bytes to the structure imposed by the underlying physical medium. Consider a typical medium of a magnetic disk with fixed-sized sectoring. Although the user may wish to write a single byte to a file, the disk supports reading and writing only in multiples of sectors. Here, the system must read in the sector containing the byte to be modified, replace the affected byte, and write the sector back to the disk. This operation—converting random access to an array of bytes to reads and writes of disk sectors—is called *block I/O*.

First, the system breaks the user's request into a set of operations to be done on *logical block*s of the file. Logical blocks describe block-sized pieces of a file. The system calculates the logical blocks by dividing the array of bytes into file-store-sized pieces. Thus, if a filestore's block size is 8192 bytes, then logical block 0 would contain bytes 0 to 8191, logical block 1 would contain bytes 8192 to 16,383, and so on.

The data in each logical block are stored in a *physical block* on the disk. A physical block is the location on the disk to which the system maps a logical block. A physical disk block is constructed from one or more contiguous sectors. For a disk with 512-byte sectors, an 8192-byte filestore block would be built up from 16 contiguous sectors. Although the contents of a logical block are contiguous on disk, the logical blocks of the file do not need to be laid out contiguously. The data structure used by the system to convert from logical blocks to physical blocks was described in Section 7.2.

Figure 8.1 (on page 268) shows the flow of information and work required to access the file on the disk. The abstraction shown to the user is an array of bytes. These bytes are collectively described by a file descriptor that refers to some location in the array. The user can request a write operation on the file by presenting the system with a pointer to a buffer, with a request for some number of bytes to be written. As shown in Fig. 8.1, the requested data do not need to be aligned with the beginning or end of a logical block. Further, the size of the request is not constrained to a single logical block. In the example shown, the user has requested data to be written to parts of logical blocks 1 and 2. Since the disk can transfer data only in multiples of sectors, the filestore must first arrange to read in the data for any part of the block that is to be left unchanged. The system must arrange an intermediate staging area for the transfer. This staging is done through one or more system buffers, as described in Section 6.6.

In our example, the user wishes to modify data in logical blocks 1 and 2. The operation iterates over five steps:

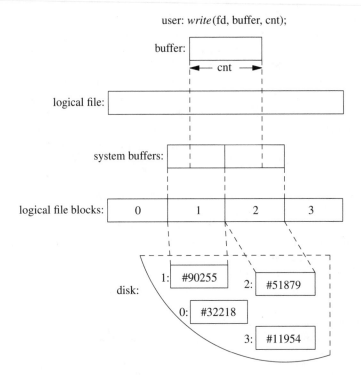

Figure 8.1 The block I/O system.

1. Allocate a buffer.

2. Determine the location of the corresponding physical block on the disk.

3. Request the disk controller to read the contents of the physical block into the system buffer and wait for the transfer to complete.

4. Do a memory-to-memory copy from the beginning of the user's I/O buffer to the appropriate portion of the system buffer.

5. Write the block to the disk and continue without waiting for the transfer to complete.

If the user's request is incomplete, the process is repeated with the next logical block of the file. In our example, the system fetches logical block 2 of the file and is able to complete the user's request. Had an entire block been written, the system could have skipped step 3 and have simply written the data to the disk without first reading in the old contents. This incremental filling of the write request is transparent to the user's process because that process is blocked from running during the entire procedure. The filling is transparent to other processes; because the inode is locked during the process, any attempted access by any other process will be blocked until the write has completed.

8.2   The Berkeley Fast Filesystem

A traditional UNIX filesystem is described by its superblock, which contains the basic parameters of the filesystem. These parameters include the number of data blocks in the filesystem, a count of the maximum number of files, and a pointer to the *free list*, which is a list of all the free blocks in the filesystem.

A 150-Mbyte traditional UNIX filesystem consists of 4 Mbyte of inodes followed by 146 Mbyte of data. That organization segregates the inode information from the data; thus, accessing a file normally incurs a long seek from the file's inode to its data. Files in a single directory typically are not allocated consecutive slots in the 4 Mbyte of inodes, causing many nonconsecutive disk blocks to be read when many inodes in a single directory are accessed.

The allocation of data blocks to files also is suboptimal. The traditional filesystem implementation uses a 512-byte physical block size. But the next sequential data block often is not on the same cylinder, so seeks between 512-byte data transfers are required frequently. This combination of small block size and scattered placement severely limits filesystem throughput.

The first work on the UNIX filesystem at Berkeley attempted to improve both the reliability and the throughput of the filesystem. The developers improved reliability by staging modifications to critical filesystem information so that the modifications could be either completed or repaired cleanly by a program after a crash [McKusick & Kowalski, 1994]. Doubling the block size of the filesystem improved the performance of the 4.0BSD filesystem by a factor of more than 2 when compared with the 3BSD filesystem. This doubling caused each disk transfer to access twice as many data blocks and eliminated the need for indirect blocks for many files. In the remainder of this section, we shall refer to the filesystem with these changes as the *old filesystem*.

The performance improvement in the old filesystem gave a strong indication that increasing the block size was a good method for improving throughput. Although the throughput had doubled, the old filesystem was still using only about 4 percent of the maximum disk throughput. The main problem was that the order of blocks on the free list quickly became scrambled, as files were created and removed. Eventually, the free-list order became entirely random, causing files to have their blocks allocated randomly over the disk. This randomness forced a seek before every block access. Although the old filesystem provided transfer rates of up to 175 Kbyte per second when it was first created, the scrambling of the free list caused this rate to deteriorate to an average of 30 Kbyte per second after a few weeks of moderate use. There was no way of restoring the performance of an old filesystem except to recreate the system.

Organization of the Berkeley Fast Filesystem

The first version of the current BSD filesystem appeared in 4.2BSD [McKusick et al, 1984]. In the 4.4BSD filesystem organization (as in the old filesystem organization), each disk drive contains one or more filesystems. A 4.4BSD filesystem is described by its *superblock*, located at the beginning of the filesystem's disk partition. Because the superblock contains critical data, it is replicated to protect against catastrophic loss. This replication is done when the filesystem is created; since the superblock data do not change, the copies do not need to be referenced unless a disk failure causes the default superblock to be corrupted.

So that files as large as 2^{32} bytes can be created with only two levels of indirection, the minimum size of a filesystem block is 4096 bytes. The block size can be any power of 2 greater than or equal to 4096. The block size is recorded in the filesystem's superblock, so it is possible for filesystems with different block sizes to be accessed simultaneously on the same system. The block size must be selected at the time that the filesystem is created; it cannot be changed subsequently without the filesystem being rebuilt.

The BSD filesystem organization divides a disk partition into one or more areas, each of which is called a *cylinder group*. Figure 8.2 shows a set of cylinder groups, each comprising one or more consecutive cylinders on a disk. Each cylinder group contains bookkeeping information that includes a redundant copy of the superblock, space for inodes, a bitmap describing available blocks in the cylinder group, and summary information describing the usage of data blocks within the cylinder group. The bitmap of available blocks in the cylinder group replaces the traditional filesystem's free list. For each cylinder group, a static number of inodes is allocated at filesystem-creation time. The default policy is to allocate one inode for each 2048 bytes of space in the cylinder group, with the expectation that this amount will be far more than will ever be needed. The default may be changed at the time that the filesystem is created.

Figure 8.2 Layout of cylinder groups.

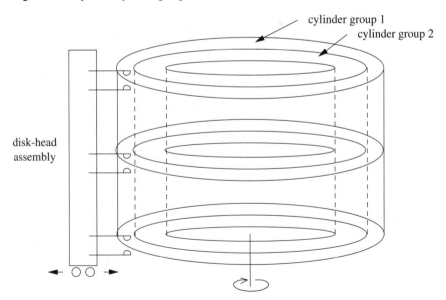

The rationale for using cylinder groups is to create clusters of inodes that are spread over the disk close to the blocks that they reference, instead of them all being located at the beginning of the disk. The filesystem attempts to allocate file blocks close to the inodes that describe them to avoid long seeks between getting the inode and getting its associated data. Also, when the inodes are spread out, there is less chance of losing all of them in a single disk failure.

All the bookkeeping information could be placed at the beginning of each cylinder group. If this approach were used, however, all the redundant information would be on the same platter of a disk. A single hardware failure could then destroy all copies of the superblock. Thus, the bookkeeping information begins at a varying offset from the beginning of the cylinder group. The offset for each successive cylinder group is calculated to be about one track farther from the beginning than is the preceding cylinder group. In this way, the redundant information spirals down into the pack, so that any single track, cylinder, or platter can be lost without all copies of the superblock also being lost. Except for the first cylinder group, which leaves space for a boot block, the space between the beginning of the cylinder group and the beginning of the cylinder-group information is used for data blocks.

Optimization of Storage Utilization

Data are laid out such that large blocks can be transferred in a single disk operation, greatly increasing filesystem throughput. A file in the new filesystem might be composed of 8192-byte data blocks, as compared to the 512-byte blocks of the old filesystem; disk accesses would thus transfer up to 16 times as much information per disk transaction. In large files, several blocks can be allocated consecutively, so that even larger data transfers are possible before a seek is required.

The main problem with larger blocks is that most BSD filesystems contain primarily small files. A uniformly large block size will waste space. Table 8.2

Table 8.2 Amount of space wasted as a function of block size.

Percent total waste	Percent data waste	Percent inode waste	Organization
0.0	0.0	0.0	data only, no separation between files
1.1	1.1	0.0	data only, files start on 512-byte boundary
7.4	1.1	6.3	data + inodes, 512-byte block
8.8	2.5	6.3	data + inodes, 1024-byte block
11.7	5.4	6.3	data + inodes, 2048-byte block
15.4	12.3	3.1	data + inodes, 4096-byte block
29.4	27.8	1.6	data + inodes, 8192-byte block
62.0	61.2	0.8	data + inodes, 16384-byte block

shows the effect of filesystem block size on the amount of wasted space in the filesystem. The measurements used to compute this table were collected from a survey of the Internet conducted in 1993 [Irlam, 1993]. The survey covered 12 million files residing on 1000 filesystems with a total size of 250 Gbyte. The investigators found that the median file size was under 2048 bytes; the average file size was 22 Kbyte. The space wasted is calculated to be the percentage of disk space not containing user data. As the block size increases, the amount of space reserved for inodes decreases, but the amount of unused data space at the end of blocks rises quickly to an intolerable 29.4 percent waste with a minimum allocation of 8192-byte filesystem blocks.

For large blocks to be used without significant waste, small files must be stored more efficiently. To increase space efficiency, the filesystem allows the division of a single filesystem block into one or more *fragments*. The fragment size is specified at the time that the filesystem is created; each filesystem block optionally can be broken into two, four, or eight fragments, each of which is addressable. The lower bound on the fragment size is constrained by the disk-sector size, which is typically 512 bytes. The block map associated with each cylinder group records the space available in a cylinder group in fragments; to determine whether a block is available, the system examines aligned fragments. Figure 8.3 shows a piece of a block map from a filesystem with 4096-byte blocks and 1024-byte fragments, hereinafter referred to as a *4096/1024 filesystem*.

On a 4096/1024 filesystem, a file is represented by zero or more 4096-byte blocks of data, possibly plus a single fragmented block. If the system must fragment a block to obtain space for a small number of data, it makes the remaining fragments of the block available for allocation to other files. As an example, consider an 11000-byte file stored on a 4096/1024 filesystem. This file would use two full-sized blocks and one three-fragment portion of another block. If no block with three aligned fragments were available at the time that the file was created, a full-sized block would be split, yielding the necessary fragments and a single unused fragment. This remaining fragment could be allocated to another file as needed.

Figure 8.3 Example of the layout of blocks and fragments in a 4096/1024 filesystem. Each bit in the map records the status of a fragment; a "-" means that the fragment is in use, whereas a "1" means that the fragment is available for allocation. In this example, fragments 0 through 5, 10, and 11 are in use, whereas fragments 6 through 9 and 12 through 15 are free. Fragments of adjacent blocks cannot be used as a full block, even if they are large enough. In this example, fragments 6 through 9 cannot be allocated as a full block; only fragments 12 through 15 can be coalesced into a full block.

bits in map	----	--11	11--	1111
fragment numbers	0-3	4-7	8-11	12-15
block numbers	0	1	2	3

Reading and Writing to a File

Having opened a file, a process can do reads or writes on it. The procedural path through the kernel is shown in Fig. 8.4. If a read is requested, it is channeled through the *ffs_read*() routine. *Ffs_read*() is responsible for converting the read into one or more reads of logical file blocks. A logical block request is then handed off to *ufs_bmap*(). *Ufs_bmap*() is responsible for converting a logical block number to a physical block number by interpreting the direct and indirect block pointers in an inode. *Ffs_read*() requests the block I/O system to return a buffer filled with the contents of the disk block. If two or more logically sequential blocks are read from a file, the process is assumed to be reading the file sequentially. Here, *ufs_bmap*() returns two values: first, the disk address of the requested block; then, the number of contiguous blocks that follow that block on disk. The requested block and the number of contiguous blocks that follow it are passed to the *cluster*() routine. If the file is being accessed sequentially, the *cluster*() routine will do a single large I/O on the entire range of sequential blocks. If the file is not being accessed sequentially (as determined by a seek to a different part of the file preceding the read), only the requested block or a subset of the cluster will be read. If the file has had a long series of sequential reads, or if the number of contiguous blocks is small, the system will issue one or more requests for read-ahead blocks in anticipation that the process will soon want those blocks. The details of block clustering are described at the end of this section.

Figure 8.4 Procedural interface to reading and writing.

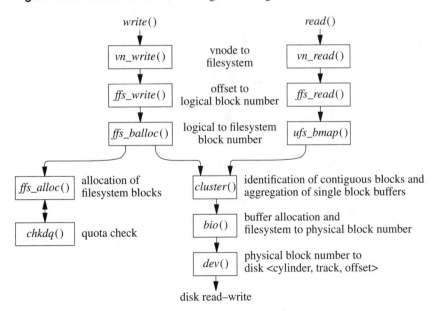

disk read–write

Each time that a process does a *write* system call, the system checks to see whether the size of the file has increased. A process may overwrite data in the middle of an existing file, in which case space would usually have been allocated already (unless the file contains a hole in that location). If the file needs to be extended, the request is rounded up to the next fragment size, and only that much space is allocated (see "Allocation Mechanisms" later in this section for the details of space allocation). The *write* system call is channeled through the *ffs_write*() routine. *Ffs_write*() is responsible for converting the write into one or more writes of logical file blocks. A logical block request is then handed off to *ffs_balloc*(). *Ffs_balloc*() is responsible for interpreting the direct and indirect block pointers in an inode to find the location for the associated physical block pointer. If a disk block does not already exist, the *ffs_alloc*() routine is called to request a new block of the appropriate size. After calling *chkdq*() to ensure that the user has not exceeded their quota, the block is allocated, and the address of the new block is stored in the inode or indirect block. The address of the new or already-existing block is returned. *Ffs_write*() allocates a buffer to hold the contents of the block. The user's data are copied into the returned buffer, and the buffer is marked as dirty. If the buffer has been filled completely, it is passed to the *cluster*() routine. When a maximally sized cluster has been accumulated, a noncontiguous block is allocated, or a seek is done to another part of the file, and the accumulated blocks are grouped together into a single I/O operation that is queued to be written to the disk. If the buffer has not been filled completely, it is not considered immediately for writing. Rather, the buffer is held in the expectation that the process will soon want to add more data to it. It is not released until it is needed for some other block—that is, until it has reached the head of the free list, or until a user process does a *sync* system call. There is normally a user process called *update* that does a *sync* every 30 seconds.

Repeated small write requests may expand the file one fragment at a time. The problem with expanding a file one fragment at a time is that data may be copied many times as a fragmented block expands to a full block. Fragment reallocation can be minimized if the user process writes a full block at a time, except for a partial block at the end of the file. Since filesystems with different block sizes may reside on the same system, the filesystem interface provides application programs with the optimal size for a read or write. This facility is used by the standard I/O library that many application programs use, and by certain system utilities, such as archivers and loaders, that do their own I/O management.

If the layout policies (described at the end of this section) are to be effective, a filesystem cannot be kept completely full. A parameter, termed the *free-space reserve*, gives the minimum percentage of filesystem blocks that should be kept free. If the number of free blocks drops below this level, only the superuser is allowed to allocate blocks. This parameter can be changed any time that the filesystem is unmounted. When the number of free blocks approaches zero, the filesystem throughput tends to be cut in half because the filesystem is unable to localize blocks in a file. If a filesystem's throughput drops because of overfilling, it can be restored by removal of files until the amount of free space once again reaches the minimum acceptable level. Users can restore locality to get faster access rates for files created during periods of little free space by copying the file to a new one and removing the original one when enough space is available.

Filesystem Parameterization

Except for the initial creation of the free list, the old filesystem ignores the parameters of the underlying hardware. It has no information about either the physical characteristics of the mass-storage device or the hardware that interacts with the filesystem. A goal of the new filesystem is to parameterize the processor capabilities and mass-storage characteristics so that blocks can be allocated in an optimum configuration-dependent way. Important parameters include the speed of the processor, the hardware support for mass-storage transfers, and the characteristics of the mass-storage devices. These parameters are summarized in Table 8.3. Disk technology is constantly improving, and a given installation can have several different disk technologies running on a single processor. Each filesystem is parameterized so that it can be adapted to the characteristics of the disk on which it is located.

For mass-storage devices such as disks, the new filesystem tries to allocate a file's new blocks on the same cylinder and rotationally well positioned. The distance between *rotationally optimal* blocks varies greatly; optimal blocks can be consecutive or rotationally delayed, depending on system characteristics. For disks attached to a dedicated I/O processor or accessed by a track-caching controller, two consecutive disk blocks often can be accessed without time lost because of an intervening disk revolution. Otherwise, the main processor must field an interrupt and prepare for a new disk transfer. The expected time to service this interrupt and to schedule a new disk transfer depends on the speed of the main processor.

The physical characteristics of each disk include the number of blocks per track and the rate at which the disk spins. The allocation routines use this information to calculate the number of milliseconds required to skip over a block. The

---

Table 8.3 Important parameters maintained by the filesystem.

Name	Meaning
maxbpg	maximum blocks per file in a cylinder group
maxcontig	maximum contiguous blocks before a *rotdelay* gap
minfree	minimum percentage of free space
nsect	sectors per track
rotdelay	rotational delay between contiguous blocks
rps	revolutions per second
tracks	tracks per cylinder
trackskew	track skew in sectors

characteristics of the processor include the expected time to service an interrupt and to schedule a new disk transfer. Given a block allocated to a file, the allocation routines calculate the number of blocks to skip over such that the next block in the file will come into position under the disk head in the expected amount of time that it takes to start a new disk-transfer operation. For sequential access to large numbers of data, this strategy minimizes the amount of time spent waiting for the disk to position itself.

The parameter that defines the minimum number of milliseconds between the completion of a data transfer and the initiation of another data transfer on the same cylinder can be changed at any time. If a filesystem is parameterized to lay out blocks with a rotational separation of 2 milliseconds, and the disk is then moved to a system that has a processor requiring 4 milliseconds to schedule a disk operation, the throughput will drop precipitously because of lost disk revolutions on nearly every block. If the target machine is known, the filesystem can be parameterized for that machine, even though it is initially created on a different processor. Even if the move is not known in advance, the rotational-layout delay can be reconfigured after the disk is moved, so that all further allocation is done based on the characteristics of the new machine.

Layout Policies

The filesystem layout policies are divided into two distinct parts. At the top level are global policies that use summary information to make decisions regarding the placement of new inodes and data blocks. These routines are responsible for deciding the placement of new directories and files. They also calculate rotationally optimal block layouts and decide when to force a long seek to a new cylinder group because there is insufficient space left in the current cylinder group to do reasonable layouts. Below the global-policy routines are the local-allocation routines. These routines use a locally optimal scheme to lay out data blocks. The original intention was to bring out these decisions to user level so that they could be ignored or replaced by user processes. Thus, they are definitely policies, rather than simple mechanisms.

Two methods for improving filesystem performance are to increase the locality of reference to minimize seek latency [Trivedi, 1980], and to improve the layout of data to make larger transfers possible [Nevalainen & Vesterinen, 1977]. The global layout policies try to improve performance by clustering related information. They cannot attempt to localize all data references, but must instead try to spread unrelated data among different cylinder groups. If too much localization is attempted, the local cylinder group may run out of space, forcing further related data to be scattered to nonlocal cylinder groups. Taken to an extreme, total localization can result in a single huge cluster of data resembling the old filesystem. The global policies try to balance the two conflicting goals of localizing data that are concurrently accessed while spreading out unrelated data.

One allocatable resource is inodes. Inodes of files in the same directory frequently are accessed together. For example, the list-directory command, **ls**, may access the inode for each file in a directory. The inode layout policy tries to place all the inodes of files in a directory in the same cylinder group. To ensure that files are distributed throughout the filesystem, the system uses a different policy to allocate directory inodes. New directories are placed in cylinder groups with a greater-than-average number of free inodes and with the smallest number of directories. The intent of this policy is to allow inode clustering to succeed most of the time. The filesystem allocates inodes within a cylinder group using a next-free strategy. Although this method allocates the inodes randomly within a cylinder group, all the inodes for a particular cylinder group can be accessed with 10 to 20 disk transfers. This allocation strategy puts a small and constant upper bound on the number of disk transfers required to access the inodes for all the files in a directory. In contrast, the old filesystem typically requires one disk transfer to fetch the inode for each file in a directory.

The other major resource is data blocks. Data blocks for a file typically are accessed together. The policy routines try to place data blocks for a file in the same cylinder group, preferably at rotationally optimal positions in the same cylinder. The problem with allocating all the data blocks in the same cylinder group is that large files quickly use up the available space, forcing a spillover to other areas. Further, using all the space causes future allocations for any file in the cylinder group also to spill to other areas. Ideally, none of the cylinder groups should ever become completely full. The heuristic chosen is to redirect block allocation to a different cylinder group after every few Mbyte of allocation. The spillover points are intended to force block allocation to be redirected when any file has used about 25 percent of the data blocks in a cylinder group. In day-to-day use, the heuristics appear to work well in minimizing the number of completely filled cylinder groups. Although this heuristic appears to benefit small files at the expense of the larger files, it really aids both file sizes. The small files are helped because there are nearly always blocks available in the cylinder group for them to use. The large files benefit because they are able to use rotationally well laid out space and then to move on, leaving behind the blocks scattered around the cylinder group. Although these scattered blocks are fine for small files that need only a block or two, they slow down big files that are best stored on a single large group of blocks that can be read in a few disk revolutions.

The newly chosen cylinder group for block allocation is the next cylinder group that has a greater-than-average number of free blocks left. Although big files tend to be spread out over the disk, several Mbyte of data typically are accessible before a seek to a new cylinder group is necessary. Thus, the time to do one long seek is small compared to the time spent in the new cylinder group doing the I/O.

Allocation Mechanisms

The global-policy routines call local-allocation routines with requests for specific blocks. The local-allocation routines will always allocate the requested block if it is free; otherwise, they will allocate a free block of the requested size that is rotationally closest to the requested block. If the global layout policies had complete information, they could always request unused blocks, and the allocation routines would be reduced to simple bookkeeping. However, maintaining complete information is costly; thus, the global layout policy uses heuristics based on the partial information that is available.

If a requested block is not available, the local allocator uses a four-level allocation strategy:

1. Use the next available block rotationally closest to the requested block on the same cylinder. It is assumed that head-switching time is zero. On disk controllers where this assumption is not valid, the time required to switch between disk platters is incorporated into the rotational layout tables when they are constructed.

2. If no blocks are available on the same cylinder, choose a block within the same cylinder group.

3. If the cylinder group is full, quadratically hash the cylinder-group number to choose another cylinder group in which to look for a free block. Quadratic hash is used because of its speed in finding unused slots in nearly full hash tables [Knuth, 1975]. Filesystems that are parameterized to maintain at least 10 percent free space rarely need to use this strategy. Filesystems used without free space typically have so few free blocks available that almost any allocation is random; the most important characteristic of the strategy used under such conditions is that it be fast.

4. Apply an exhaustive search to all cylinder groups. This search is necessary because the quadratic rehash may not check all cylinder groups.

The task of managing block and fragment allocation is done by *ffs_balloc*(). If the file is being written and a block pointer is zero or points to a fragment that is too small to hold the additional data, *ffs_balloc*() calls the allocation routines to obtain a new block. If the file needs to be extended, one of two conditions exists:

1. The file contains no fragmented blocks (and the final block in the file contains insufficient space to hold the new data). If space exists in a block already allocated, the space is filled with new data. If the remainder of the new data consists of more than a full block, a full block is allocated and the first full block of new data is written there. This process is repeated until less than a full block of new data remains. If the remaining new data to be written will fit in less than a full block, a block with the necessary number of fragments is located; otherwise, a full block is located. The remaining new data are written into the located space. However, to avoid excessive copying for slowly growing files, the filesystem allows only direct blocks of files to refer to fragments.

2. The file contains one or more fragments (and the fragments contain insufficient space to hold the new data). If the size of the new data plus the size of the data already in the fragments exceeds the size of a full block, a new block is allocated. The contents of the fragments are copied to the beginning of the block, and the remainder of the block is filled with new data. The process then continues as in step 1. Otherwise, a set of fragments big enough to hold the

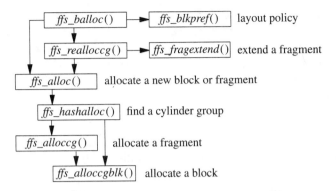

Figure 8.5 Procedural interface to block allocation.

data is located; if enough of the rest of the current block is free, the filesystem can avoid a copy by using that block. The contents of the existing fragments, appended with the new data, are written into the allocated space.

Ffs_balloc() is also responsible for allocating blocks to hold indirect pointers. It must also deal with the special case in which a process seeks past the end of a file and begins writing. Because of the constraint that only the final block of a file may be a fragment, *ffs_balloc()* must first ensure that any previous fragment has been upgraded to a full-sized block.

On completing a successful allocation, the allocation routines return the block or fragment number to be used; *ffs_balloc()* then updates the appropriate block pointer in the inode. Having allocated a block, the system is ready to allocate a buffer to hold the block's contents so that the block can be written to disk.

The procedural description of the allocation process is shown in Fig. 8.5. *Ffs_balloc()* is the routine responsible for determining when a new block must be allocated. It first calls the layout-policy routine *ffs_blkpref()* to select the most desirable block based on the preference from the global-policy routines that were described earlier in this section. If a fragment has already been allocated and needs to be extended, *ffs_balloc()* calls *ffs_realloccg()*. If nothing has been allocated yet, *ffs_balloc()* calls *ffs_alloc()*.

Ffs_realloccg() first tries to extend the current fragment in place. Consider the sample block of an allocation map with two fragments allocated from it, shown in Fig. 8.6. The first fragment can be extended from a size 2 fragment to a size 3 or a size 4 fragment, since the two adjacent fragments are unused. The second

Figure 8.6 Sample block with two allocated fragments.

entry in table	1	-	-	1	1	-	-	-
allocated fragments		size 2				size 3		

fragment cannot be extended, as it occupies the end of the block, and fragments are not allowed to span blocks. If *ffs_realloccg*() is able to expand the current fragment in place, the map is updated appropriately and it returns. If the fragment cannot be extended, *ffs_realloccg*() calls the *ffs_alloc*() routine to get a new fragment. The old fragment is copied to the beginning of the new fragment, and the old fragment is freed.

The bookkeeping tasks of allocation are handled by *ffs_alloc*(). It first verifies that a block is available in the desired cylinder group by checking the filesystem summary information. If the summary information shows that the cylinder group is full, *ffs_alloc*() quadratically rehashes through the summary information looking for a cylinder group with free space. Having found a cylinder group with space, *ffs_alloc*() calls either the fragment-allocation routine or the block-allocation routine to acquire a fragment or block.

The block-allocation routine is given a preferred block. If that block is available, it is returned. If the block is unavailable, the allocation routine tries to find another block on the same cylinder that is rotationally close to the requested block. So that the task of locating rotationally optimal blocks is simplified, the summary information for each cylinder group includes a count of the available blocks at different rotational positions. By default, eight rotational positions are distinguished; that is, the resolution of the summary information is 2 milliseconds for a 3600 revolution-per-minute drive. The superblock contains an array of lists called the *rotational-layout table*. The array is indexed by rotational position. Each entry in the array lists the index into the block map for every data block contained in its rotational position. When searching for a block to allocate, the system first looks through the summary information for a rotational position with a nonzero block count. It then uses the index of the rotational position to find the appropriate list of rotationally optimal blocks. This list enables the system to limit its scan of the free-block map to only those parts that contain free, rotationally well-placed blocks.

The fragment-allocation routine is given a preferred fragment. If that fragment is available, it is returned. If the requested fragment is not available, and the filesystem is configured to optimize for space utilization, the filesystem uses a best-fit strategy for fragment allocation. The fragment-allocation routine checks the cylinder-group summary information, starting with the entry for the desired size, and scanning larger sizes until an available fragment is found. If there are no fragments of the appropriate size or larger, then a full-sized block is allocated and is broken up.

If an appropriate-sized fragment is listed in the fragment summary, then the allocation routine expects to find it in the allocation map. To speed up the process

---

Figure 8.7 Map entry for an 8192/1024 filesystem.

bits in map	decimal value
-111--11	115

of scanning the potentially large allocation map, the filesystem uses a table-driven algorithm. Each byte in the map is treated as an index into a *fragment-descriptor table*. Each entry in the fragment-descriptor table describes the fragments that are free for that corresponding map entry. Thus, by doing a logical AND with the bit corresponding to the desired fragment size, the allocator can determine quickly whether the desired fragment is contained within a given allocation-map entry. As an example, consider the entry from an allocation map for the 8192/1024 filesystem shown in Fig. 8.7. The map entry shown has already been fragmented, with a single fragment allocated at the beginning and a size 2 fragment allocated in the middle. Remaining unused is another size 2 fragment, and a size 3 fragment. Thus, if we look up entry 115 in the fragment table, we find the entry shown in Fig. 8.8. If we were looking for a size 3 fragment, we would inspect the third bit and find that we had been successful; if we were looking for a size 4 fragment, we would inspect the fourth bit and find that we needed to continue. The C code that implements this algorithm is as follows:

```
for (i = 0; i < MAPSIZE; i++)
    if (fragtbl[allocmap[i]] & (1 << (size - 1)))
        break;
```

Using a best-fit policy has the benefit of minimizing disk fragmentation; however, it has the undesirable property that it maximizes the number of fragment-to-fragment copies that must be made when a process writes a file in many small pieces. To avoid this behavior, the system can configure filesystems to optimize for time, rather than for space. The first time that a process does a small write on a filesystem configured for time optimization, it is allocated a best-fit fragment. On the second small write, however, a full-sized block is allocated, with the unused portion being freed. Later small writes are able to extend the fragment in place, rather than requiring additional copy operations. Under certain circumstances, this policy can cause the disk to become heavily fragmented. The system tracks this condition, and automatically reverts to optimizing for space if the percentage of fragmentation reaches one-half of the minimum free-space limit.

Block Clustering

Most machines running 4.4BSD do not have separate I/O processors. The main CPU must take an interrupt after each disk I/O operation; if there is more disk I/O to be done, it must select the next buffer to be transferred and must start the operation on that buffer. Before the advent of track-caching controllers, the filesystem

Figure 8.8 Fragment-table entry for entry 115.

entry in table	0	0	0	0	0	1	1	0
available fragment size	8	7	6	5	4	3	2	1

obtained its highest throughput by leaving a gap after each block to allow time for the next I/O operation to be scheduled. If the blocks were laid out without a gap, the throughput would suffer because the disk would have to rotate nearly an entire revolution to pick up the start of the next block.

Track-caching controllers have a large buffer in the controller that continues to accumulate the data coming in from the disk even after the requested data have been received. If the next request is for the immediately following block, the controller will already have most of the block in its buffer, so it will not have to wait a revolution to pick up the block. Thus, for the purposes of reading, it is possible to nearly double the throughput of the filesystem by laying out the files contiguously, rather than leaving gaps after each block.

Unfortunately, the track cache is less useful for writing. Because the kernel does not provide the next data block until the previous one completes, there is still a delay during which the controller does not have the data to write, and it ends up waiting a revolution to get back to the beginning of the next block. One solution to this problem is to have the controller give its completion interrupt after it has copied the data into its cache, but before it has finished writing them. This early interrupt gives the CPU time to request the next I/O before the previous one completes, thus providing a continuous stream of data to write to the disk.

This approach has one seriously negative side effect. When the I/O completion interrupt is delivered, the kernel expects the data to be on stable store. Filesystem integrity and user applications using the *fsync* system call depend on these semantics. These semantics will be violated if the power fails after the I/O completion interrupt but before the data are written to disk. Some vendors eliminate this problem by using nonvolatile memory for the controller cache and providing microcode restart after power fail to determine which operations need to be completed. Because this option is expensive, few controllers provide this functionality.

The 4.4BSD system uses I/O clustering to avoid this dilemma. Clustering was first done by Santa Cruz Operations [Peacock, 1988] and Sun Microsystems [McVoy & Kleiman, 1991]; the idea was later adapted to 4.4BSD [Seltzer et al, 1993]. As a file is being written, the allocation routines try to allocate up to 64 Kbyte of data in contiguous disk blocks. Instead of the buffers holding these blocks being written as they are filled, their output is delayed. The cluster is completed when the limit of 64 Kbyte of data is reached, the file is closed, or the cluster cannot grow because the next sequential block on the disk is already in use by another file. If the cluster size is limited by a previous allocation to another file, the filesystem is notified and is given the opportunity to find a larger set of contiguous blocks into which the cluster may be placed. If the reallocation is successful, the cluster continues to grow. When the cluster is complete, the buffers making up the cluster of blocks are aggregated and passed to the disk controller as a single I/O request. The data can then be streamed out to the disk in a single uninterrupted transfer.

A similar scheme is used for reading. If the *ffs_read*() discovers that a file is being read sequentially, it inspects the number of contiguous blocks returned by *ufs_bmap*() to look for clusters of contiguously allocated blocks. It then allocates a set of buffers big enough to hold the contiguous set of blocks and passes them to the disk controller as a single I/O request. The I/O can then be done in one operation. Although read clustering is not needed when track-caching controllers are available, it reduces the interrupt load from systems that have them, and it speeds low-cost systems that do not have them.

For clustering to be effective, the filesystem must be able to allocate large clusters of contiguous blocks to files. If the filesystem always tried to begin allocation for a file at the beginning of a large set of contiguous blocks, it would soon use up its contiguous space. Instead, it uses an algorithm similar to that used for the management of fragments. Initially, file blocks are allocated via the standard algorithm described in the previous two subsections. Reallocation is invoked when the standard algorithm does not result in a contiguous allocation. The reallocation code searches a *cluster map* that summarizes the available clusters of blocks in the cylinder group. It allocates the first free cluster that is large enough to hold the file, then moves the file to this contiguous space. This process continues until the current allocation has grown to a size equal to the maximum permissible contiguous set of blocks (typically 16 blocks). At that point, the I/O is done, and the process of allocating space begins again.

Unlike fragment reallocation, block reallocation to different clusters of blocks does not require extra I/O or memory-to-memory copying. The data to be written are held in delayed write buffers. Within that buffer is the disk location to which the data are to be written. When the location of the block cluster is relocated, it takes little time to walk the list of buffers in the cluster and to change the disk addresses to which they are to be written. When the I/O occurs, the final destination has been selected and will not change.

To speed the operation of finding clusters of blocks, the filesystem maintains a cluster map with 1 bit per block (in addition to the map with 1 bit per fragment). It also has summary information showing how many sets of blocks there are for each possible cluster size. The summary information allows it to avoid looking for cluster sizes that do not exist. The cluster map is used because it is faster to scan than is the much larger fragment bitmap. The size of the map is important because the map must be scanned bit by bit. Unlike fragments, clusters of blocks are not constrained to be aligned within the map. Thus, the table-lookup optimization done for fragments cannot be used for look up of clusters.

The filesystem relies on the allocation of contiguous blocks to achieve high levels of performance. The fragmentation of free space may increase with time or with filesystem utilization. This fragmentation can degrade performance as the filesystem ages. The effects of utilization and aging were measured on over 50 filesystems at Harvard University. The measured filesystems ranged in age since initial creation from 1 to 3 years. The fragmentation of free space on most of the measured filesystems caused performance to degrade no more than 10 percent from that of a newly created empty filesystem. The most severe degradation measured was 30 percent on a highly active filesystem that had many small files and was used to spool USENET news [Seltzer et al, 1995].

Synchronous Operations

If the system crashes or stops suddenly because of a power failure, the filesystem may be in an inconsistent state. To ensure that the on-disk state of the filesystem can always be returned deterministically to a consistent state, the system must do three operations synchronously:

1. Write a newly allocated inode to disk before its name is entered into a directory.

2. Remove a directory name before the inode is deallocated.

3. Write a deallocated inode to disk before its blocks are placed into the cylinder-group free list.

These synchronous operations ensure that directory names always reference valid inodes, and that no block is ever claimed by more than one inode. Because the filesystem must do two synchronous operations for each file that it creates, and for each file that it deletes, the filesystem throughput is limited to the disk-write speed when many files are created or deleted simultaneously.

Three techniques have been used to eliminate these synchronous operations:

1. Put stable store (battery–backed-up memory) on the disk-controller board. Filesystem operations can then proceed as soon as the block to be written is copied into the stable store. If the system fails, unfinished disk operations can be completed from the stable store when the system is rebooted [Moran et al, 1990].

2. Keep a log of filesystem updates on a separate disk or in stable store. Filesystem operations can then proceed as soon as the operation to be done is written into the log. If the system fails, unfinished filesystem operations can be completed from the log when the system is rebooted [Chutani et al, 1992].

3. Maintain a partial ordering on filesystem update operations. Before committing a change to disk, ensure that all operations on which it depends have been completed. For example, an operation that would write an inode with a newly allocated block to disk would ensure that a deallocated inode that previously owned the block had been written to disk first. Using a technique of partial rollback to break circular dependencies, this algorithm can eliminate 95 percent of the synchronous writes [Ganger & Patt, 1994].

The first technique ensures that the filesystem is always consistent after a crash and can be used as soon as the system reboots. The second technique ensures that the filesystem is consistent as soon as a log rollback has been done. The third technique still requires that the filesystem-check program be run to restore the consistency of the filesystem; however, it does not require any specialized hardware or additional disk space to do logging. All these techniques have been developed in derivatives of the FFS, although none of them are currently part of the 4.4BSD distribution.

8.3   The Log-Structured Filesystem

The factors that limited the performance of the implementation of the FFS found in historic versions of 4BSD are the FFS's requirement for synchronous I/O during file creation and deletion, and the seek times between I/O requests for different files. The synchronous I/O used during file creation and deletion is necessary for filesystem recoverability after failures. The worst-case example is that it normally takes five separate disk I/O's (two synchronous, three asynchronous), each preceded by a seek, to create a new file in the FFS: The file inode is written twice, the containing directory is written once, the containing directory's inode is written once, and, of course, the file's data are written. This synchronous behavior is rarely an issue. Unimaginative benchmarks to the contrary, few applications create large numbers of files, and fewer still immediately delete those files.

Seek times between I/O requests to a single file are significant only when the file has been allocated poorly on disk. The FFS does an excellent job of laying out files on disk, and, as long as the disk remains empty enough to permit good allocation, it can read and write individual files at roughly 50 percent of the disk bandwidth, skipping one disk block for every one read or written. In 4.4BSD, where clustering has been added, or when using a disk controller that supports track caching, the FFS can transfer at close to the full bandwidth of the disk. For these reasons, the seek times between I/O requests for different files will often dominate performance. (As an example, on a typical disk, an average seek takes only slightly less time than a disk rotation, so many blocks can be written in the time that it takes to seek to a new location on the disk.)

As the main-memory buffer cache has become larger over the past decade, applications have tended to experience this problem only when writing to the disk. Repeated reads of data will go to the disk only the first time, after which the data are cached and no further I/O is required. In addition, doing read-ahead further amends this problem, as sequential reads of a file will wait for only the first data block to transfer from disk. Later reads will find the data block already in the cache, although a separate I/O will still have been done. In summary, the problem to be solved in modern filesystem design is that of writing a large volume of data, from multiple files, to the disk. If the solution to this problem eliminates any synchronous I/O, so much the better.

The LFS, as proposed by Ousterhout and Douglis [Ousterhout & Douglis, 1989], attempted to address both the problem and the issue of synchronous I/O. The fundamental idea of the LFS is to improve filesystem performance by storing all filesystem data in a single, contiguous log. The LFS is optimized for writing, and no seek is required between writes, regardless of the file to which the writes belong. It is also optimized for reading files written in their entirety over a brief period (as is the norm in workstation environments) because the files are placed contiguously on disk.

The FFS provides logical locality, as it attempts to place related files (e.g., files from the same directory) in the same cylinder group. The LFS provides temporal locality, as it places files created at about the same time together on disk, relying on the buffer cache to protect the application from any adverse effects of this decision. It is important to realize that no performance characteristics of the disk or processor are taken into account by the LFS. The assumption that the LFS makes is that reads are cached, and that writes are always contiguous. Therefore, a simpler model of disk activity suffices.

Organization of the Log-Structured Filesystem

The LFS is described by a superblock similar to the one used by the FFS. In addition, to minimize the additional software needed for the LFS, FFS index structures (inodes) and directories are used almost without change, making tools written to analyze the FFS immediately applicable to the LFS (a useful result in itself). Where the LFS differs from the FFS is in the layout of the inode, directory and file data blocks on disk.

The underlying structure of the LFS is that of a sequential, append-only *log*. The disk is statically partitioned into fixed-sized contiguous segments, (which are generally 0.5 to 1 Mbyte), as shown by the disk-layout column of Fig. 8.9. The initial superblock is in the same location as in the FFS, and is replicated throughout the disk in selected segments. All writes to the disk are appended to the logical end of the log. Although the log logically grows forever, portions of the log that have already been written must be made available periodically for reuse because the disk is not infinite in length. This process is called *cleaning*, and the

Figure 8.9 Log-Structured Filesystem layout.

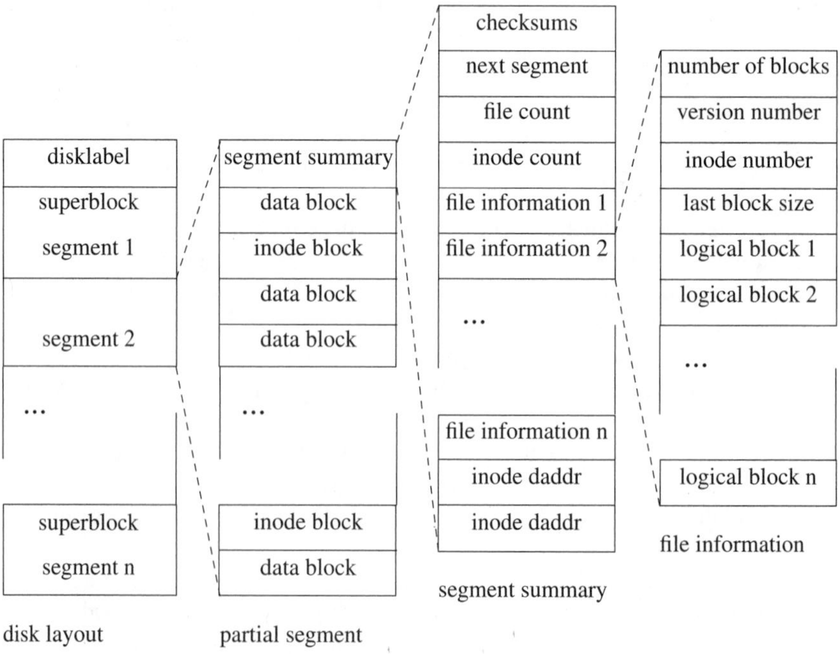

utility that performs this reclamation is called the *cleaner*. The need for cleaning is the reason that the disk is logically divided into segments. Because the disk is divided into reasonably large static areas, it is easy to segregate the portions of the disk that are currently being written from those that are currently being cleaned. The logical order of the log is not fixed, and the log should be viewed as a linked list of segments, with segments being periodically cleaned, detached from their current position in the log, and reattached after the end of the log.

In ideal operation, the LFS accumulates dirty blocks in memory. When enough blocks have been accumulated to fill a segment, they are written to the disk in a single, contiguous I/O operation. Since it makes little sense to write data blocks contiguously and continue to require seeks and synchronous writes to update their inode-modification times, the modified inodes are written into the segment at the same time as the data. As a result of this design goal, inodes are no longer in fixed locations on the disk, and the LFS requires an additional data structure called the *inode map*, which maps inode numbers to the current disk addresses of the blocks containing them. So that fast recovery after crashes is facilitated, the inode map is also stored on disk (the inode map would be time consuming to recreate after system failure).

As the LFS writes dirty data blocks to the logical end of the log (that is, into the next available segment), modified blocks will be written to the disk in locations different from those of the original blocks. This behavior is called a *no-overwrite* policy, and it is the responsibility of the cleaner to reclaim space resulting from deleted or rewritten blocks. Generally, the cleaner reclaims space in the filesystem by reading a segment, discarding *dead* blocks (blocks that belong to deleted files or that have been superseded by rewritten blocks), and rewriting any *live* blocks to the end of the log.

In a workstation environment, the LFS usually will not accumulate many dirty data blocks before having to write at least some portion of the accumulated data. Reasons that writes must happen include the requirement of the Network Filesystem (NFS) that write operations be flushed to the disk before the write call returns, and that UNIX filesystems (and POSIX standards) have historically guaranteed that closing a file descriptor both updates the inode and flushes pending write operations to the disk.

Because the LFS can only rarely write full segments, each segment is further partitioned into one or more *partial segments*. A partial segment can be thought of as the result of a single write operation to disk. Each partial segment is composed of a single *partial-segment summary*, and inode blocks and data blocks, as shown by the partial-segment column of Fig. 8.9. The segment summary describes the inode and data blocks in the partial segment, and is shown by the segment-summary column of Fig. 8.9. The partial-segment summary contains the following information:

• Checksums for the summary information and for the entire partial segment

• The time that the partial segment was written (not shown in Fig. 8.9)

- Directory-operation information (not shown in Fig. 8.9)

- The disk address of the segment to be written immediately after this segment

- The number of file-information structures and the number of inode disk addresses that follow

- A file-information structure for each separate file for which blocks are included in this partial segment (described next)

- A disk address for each block of inodes included in this partial segment

The checksums are necessary for the recovery agent to determine that the partial segment is complete. Because disk controllers do not guarantee that data are written to disk in the order that write operations are issued, it is necessary to be able to determine that the entire partial segment has been written to the disk successfully. Writing a single disk sector's worth of the partial-segment summary after the rest of the partial segment was known to have been written successfully would largely avoid this problem; however, it would have a catastrophic effect on filesystem performance, as there would be a significant rotational latency between the two writes. Instead, a checksum of 4 bytes in each block of the partial segment is created and provides validation of the partial segment, permitting the filesystem to write multiple partial segments without an intervening seek or rotation.

The file-information structures and inode disk addresses describe the rest of the partial segment. The number of file-information structures and blocks of inodes in the partial segment is specified in the segment-summary portion of the partial segment. The inode blocks are identical to the FFS inode blocks. The disk address of each inode block is also specified in the partial-segment summary information, and can be retrieved easily from that structure. Blocks in the partial segment that are not blocks of inodes are file data blocks, in the order listed in the partial-segment summary information.

The file-information structures are as shown by the file-information column of Fig. 8.9. They contain the following information:

- The number of data blocks for this file contained in this partial segment

- A version number for the file, intended for use by the cleaner

- The file's inode number

- The size of the block written most recently to the file in this partial segment

- The logical block number for the data blocks in this partial segment

Index File

The final data structure in the LFS is known as the *index file* (shown in Fig. 8.10), because it contains a mapping from the inode number to the disk address of the block that contains the inode. The index file is maintained as a regular, read-only file visible in the filesystem, named *ifile* by convention.

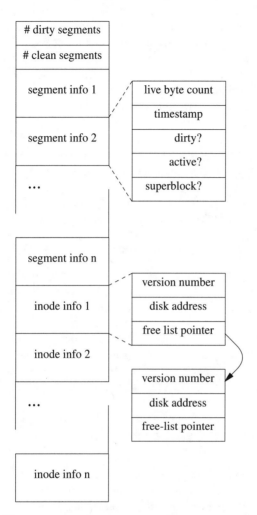

Figure 8.10 Log-Structured Filesystem index-file structure.

There are two reasons for the index file to be implemented as a regular file. First, because the LFS does not allocate a fixed position for each inode when created, there is no reason to limit the number of inodes in the filesystem, as is done in the FFS. This feature permits the LFS to support a larger range of uses because the filesystem can change from being used to store a few, large files (e.g., an X11 binary area) to storing many files (e.g., a home directory or news partition) without the filesystem being recreated. In addition, there is no hard limit to the number of files that can be stored in the filesystem. However, this lack of constraints requires that the inode map be able to grow and shrink based on the filesystem's inode usage. Using an already established mechanism (the kernel file code) minimizes the special-case code in the kernel.

Second, the information found in the index file is used by the cleaner. The LFS cleaner is implemented as a user-space process, so it is necessary to make the index-file information accessible to application processes. Again, because the index file is visible in the filesystem, no additional mechanism is required, minimizing the special-case code in both the kernel and the cleaner.

Because the index file's inode and data blocks are themselves written to new locations each time that they are written, there must be a fixed location on the disk that can be used to find them. This location is the superblock. The first superblock is always in the same position on the disk and contains enough information for the kernel to find the disk address of the block of inodes that contains the index file's inode.

In addition to the inode map, the index file includes the other information that is shared between the kernel and the cleaner. The index file contains information:

- It contains the number of clean and dirty segments.

- It records segment-usage information, one entry per segment (rather than per partial segment) on the disk. The segment-usage information includes the number of live bytes currently found in the segment; the most recent modification time of the segment; and flags that show whether the segment is currently being written, whether the segment was written since the most recent checkpoint (checkpoints are described in the writing to the log subsection), whether the segment has been cleaned, and whether the segment contains a copy of the superblock. Because segment-based statistics are maintained on the amount of useful information that is currently in the segment, it is possible to clean segments that contain a high percentage of useless data, so that the maximum amount of space is made available for reuse with the minimal amount of cleaning.

- It maintains inode information, one entry per current inode in the filesystem. The inode information includes the current version number of the inode, the disk address of the block of inodes that contains the inode, and a pointer if the inode is unused and is on the current list of free inodes.

So that calculations are simplified, segment-summary-information entries and inode-map entries are block aligned and are not permitted to span block boundaries, resulting in a fixed number of each type of entry per block. This alignment makes it possible for the filesystem to calculate easily the logical block of the index file that contains the correct entry.

Reading of the Log

To clarify the relationships among these structures, we shall consider the steps necessary to read a single block of a file if the file's inode number is known and there is no other information available.

1. Read in the superblock. The superblock contains the index file's inode number, and the disk address of the block of inodes that contains the index file's inode.

2. Read in the block of inodes that contains the index file's inode. Search the block and find the index file's inode. Inode blocks are searched linearly. No more complicated search or data structure is used, because, on the average, in an 8-Kbyte–block filesystem, only 32 or so memory locations need to be checked for any given inode in a block to be located.

3. Use the disk addresses in the index file's inode and read in the block of the index file that contains the inode-map entry for the requested file's inode.

4. Take the disk address found in the inode-map entry and use it to read in the block of inodes that contains the inode for the requested file. Search the block to find the file's inode.

5. Use the disk addresses found in the file's inode to read in the blocks of the requested file.

Normally, all this information would be cached in memory, and the only real I/O would be a single I/O operation to bring the file's data block into memory. However, it is important to minimize the information stored in the index file to ensure that the latter does not reserve unacceptable amounts of memory.

Writing to the Log

When a dirty block must be flushed to the disk for whatever reason (e.g., because of a *fsync* or *sync* system call, or because of closing a file descriptor), the LFS gathers all the dirty blocks for the filesystem and writes them sequentially to the disk in one or more partial segments. In addition, if the number of currently dirty buffers approaches roughly one-quarter of the total number of buffers in the system, the LFS will initiate a segment write regardless.

The filesystem does the write by traversing the vnode lists linked to the filesystem mount point and collecting the dirty blocks. The dirty blocks are sorted by file and logical block number (so that files and blocks within files will be written as contiguously as possible), and then are assigned disk addresses. Their associated meta-data blocks (inodes and indirect blocks) are updated to reflect the new disk addresses, and the meta-data blocks are added to the information to be written. This information is formatted into one or more partial segments, partial segment summaries are created, checksums are calculated, and the partial segments are written into the next available segment. This process continues until all dirty blocks in the filesystem have been written.

Periodically, the LFS synchronizes the information on disk, such that all disk data structures are completely consistent. This state is known as a filesystem *checkpoint*. Normally, a checkpoint occurs whenever the *sync* system call is made by the *update* utility, although there is no reason that it cannot happen more or less often. The only effect of changing how often the filesystem checkpoints is that the time needed to recover the filesystem after system failure is inversely proportional to the frequency of the checkpoints. The only requirement is that the filesystem be checkpointed between the time that a segment is last written and the time that the segment is cleaned, to avoid a window where system failure during cleaning of a segment could cause the loss of data that the kernel has already confirmed as being written safely to disk.

For the filesystem to be checkpointed, additional data structures must be written to disk. First, because each file inode is written into a new location each time that it is written, the index file must also be updated and its dirty meta-data blocks written. The flags in the segment usage information that note if each segment was written since the most recent checkpoint must be toggled and written as part of this update. Second, because the index-file inode will have been modified, it too must be written, and the superblock must be updated to reflect its new location. Finally, the superblock must be written to the disk. When these objects have been updated and written successfully, the filesystem is considered checkpointed.

The amount of information needing to be written during a filesystem checkpoint is proportional to the amount of effort the recovery agent is willing to make after system failure. For example, it would be possible for the recovery agent to detect that a file was missing an indirect block, if a data block existed for which there was no appropriate indirect block, in which case, indirect blocks for files would not have to be written during normal writes or checkpoints. Or, the recovery agent could find the current block of inodes that contains the latest copy of the index file inode by searching the segments on the disk for a known inode number, in which case the superblock would not need to be updated during checkpoint. More aggressively, it would be possible to rebuild the index file after system failure by reading the entire disk, so the index file would not have to be written to complete a checkpoint. Like the decision of how often to checkpoint, the determination of the tradeoff between what is done by the system during filesystem checkpoint and what is done by the recovery agent during system recovery is a flexible decision.

Writes to a small fragment of a LFS are shown in Fig. 8.11. Note that the no-overwrite policy of the LFS results in the latter using far more disk space than is used by the FFS, a classic space–time tradeoff: Although more space is used, because the disk I/O is contiguous on disk, it requires no intermediate seeks.

Block Accounting

Block accounting in the LFS is far more complex than in the FFS. In the FFS, blocks are allocated as needed, and, if no blocks are available, the allocation fails. The LFS requires two different types of block accounting.

The first form of block accounting is similar to that done by the FFS. The LFS maintains a count of the number of disk blocks that do not currently contain useful data. The count is decremented whenever a newly dirtied block enters the buffer cache. Many files die in the cache, so this number must be incremented

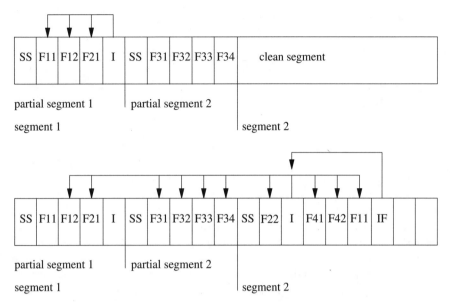

Figure 8.11 Log-Structured Filesystem fragment. In the first snapshot, the first partial segment contains a segment summary (SS), two blocks from file 1 (F11 and F12), a single block from file 2 (F21), and a block of inodes (I). The block of inodes contains the inodes (and therefore the disk addresses) for files F1 and F2. The second partial segment contains a segment summary and four blocks from file 3. In the second snapshot, a block has been appended to file 2 (F22); a new file, file 4, has been written that has two blocks (F41 and F42); and the first block of file 1 (F11) has been modified and therefore rewritten. Because the disk addresses for files 1 and 2 have changed, and the inodes for files 3 and 4 have not yet been written, those files' inodes are written (I). Note that this inode block still references disk addresses in the first and second partial segments, because blocks F12 and F21, and the blocks from file 3, are still live. Since the locations of the files' inodes have changed, if the filesystem is to be consistent on disk, the modified blocks from the index file (IF) must be written as well.

whenever blocks are deleted, even if the blocks were never written to disk. This count provides a system-administration view of how much of the filesystem is currently in use. However, this count cannot be used to authorize the acceptance of a write from an application because the calculation implies that blocks can be written successfully into the cache that will later fail to be written to disk. For example, this failure could be caused by the disk filling up because the additional blocks necessary to write dirty blocks (e.g., meta-data blocks and partial-segment summary blocks) were not considered in this count. Even if the disk were not full, all the available blocks might reside in uncleaned segments, and new data could not written.

The second form of block accounting is a count of the number of disk blocks currently available for writing—that is, that reside in segments that are clean and ready to be written. This count is decremented whenever a newly dirtied block enters the cache, and the count is not incremented until the block is discarded or the segment into which it is written is cleaned. This accounting value is the value that controls cleaning initiation. If an application attempts to write data, but there is no space currently available for writing, the application will block until space is available. Using this pessimistic accounting to authorize writing guarantees that, if the operating system accepts a write request from the user, it will be able to do that write, barring system failure.

The accounting support in the LFS is complex. This complexity arises because allocation of a block must also consider the allocation of any necessary meta-data blocks and any necessary inode and partial-segment summary blocks. Determining the actual disk space required for any block write is difficult because inodes are not collected into inode blocks, and indirect blocks and segment summaries are not created until the partial segments are actually written. Every time an inode is modified in the inode cache, a count of inodes to be written is incremented. When blocks are dirtied, the number of available disk blocks is decremented. To decide whether there is enough disk space to allow another write into the cache, the system computes the number of segment summaries necessary to write the dirty blocks already in the cache, adds the number of inode blocks necessary to write the dirty inodes, and compares that number to the amount of space currently available to be written. If insufficient space is available, either the cleaner must run or dirty blocks in the cache must be deleted.

The Buffer Cache

Before the integration of the LFS into 4BSD, the buffer cache was thought to be filesystem-independent code. However, the buffer cache contained assumptions about how and when blocks are written to disk. The most significant problem was that the buffer cache assumed that any single dirty block could be flushed to disk at any time to reclaim the memory allocated to the block. There are two problems with this assumption:

1. Flushing blocks a single block at a time would destroy any possible performance advantage of the LFS, and, because of the modified meta-data and partial-segment summary blocks, the LFS would use enormous amounts of disk space.

2. Also because of the modified meta-data and partial-segment summary blocks, the LFS requires additional memory to write: If the system were completely out of memory, it would be impossible for the LFS to write anything at all.

For these reasons, the LFS needs to guarantee that it can obtain the additional buffers that it needs when it writes a segment, and that it can prevent the buffer cache from attempting to flush blocks backed by a LFS. To handle these problems, the LFS maintains its dirty buffers on the kernel LOCKED queue, instead of on the traditional LRU queue, so that the buffer cache does not attempt to reclaim them. Unfortunately, maintaining these buffers on the LOCKED queue exempts most of the dirty LFS blocks from traditional buffer-cache behavior, which undoubtedly alters system performance in unexpected ways. To prevent the LFS from locking down all the available buffers and to guarantee that there are always additional buffers available when they are needed for segment writing, the LFS begins segment writing as described previously, when the number of locked-down buffers exceeds a threshold. In addition, the kernel blocks any process attempting to acquire a block from a LFS if the number of currently locked blocks is above a related access threshold. Buffer allocation and management will be much more reasonably handled by systems with better integration of the buffer cache and virtual memory.

Another problem with the historic buffer cache was that it was a logical buffer cache, hashed by vnode and file logical block number. In the FFS, since indirect blocks did not have logical block numbers, they were hashed by the vnode of the raw device (the file that represents the disk partition) and the disk address. Since the LFS does not assign disk addresses until the blocks are written to disk, indirect blocks have no disk addresses on which to hash. So that this problem could be solved, the block name space had to incorporate meta-data block numbering. Block numbers were changed to be signed integers, with negative block numbers referencing indirect blocks and zero and positive numbers referencing data blocks. Singly indirect blocks take on the negative block number of the first data block to which they point. Doubly and triply indirect blocks take the next-lower negative number of the singly or doubly indirect block to which they point. This approach makes it possible for the filesystem to traverse the indirect block chains in either direction, facilitating reading a block or creating indirect blocks. Because it was possible for the FFS also to use this scheme, the current hash chains for both filesystems are done in this fashion.

Directory Operations

Directory operations include those system calls that affect more than one inode (typically a directory and a file). They include *create, link, mkdir, mknod, remove, rename, rmdir,* and *symlink.* These operations pose a special problem for the LFS. Since the basic premise of the LFS is that small I/O operations can be postponed and then coalesced to provide larger I/O operations, retaining the synchronous behavior of directory operations would make little sense. In addition, the UNIX semantics of directory operations are defined to preserve ordering (e.g., if the creation of one file precedes the creation of another, any recovery state of the filesystem that includes the second file must also include the first). This semantic is used in UNIX filesystems to provide mutual exclusion and other locking protocols. Since directory operations affect multiple inodes, we must guarantee that either all inodes and associated changes are written successfully to the disk, or that any partially written information is ignored during recovery.

The basic unit of atomicity in LFS is the partial segment because the checksum information guarantees that either all or none of the partial segment will be considered valid. Although it would be possible to guarantee that the inodes for any single directory operation would fit into a partial segment, that would require each directory operation to be flushed to the disk before any vnode participating in it is allowed to participate in another directory operation, or a potentially extremely complex graph of vnode interdependencies has to be maintained. Instead, a mechanism was introduced to permit directory operations to span multiple partial segments. First, all vnodes participating in any directory operation are flagged. When the partial segment containing the first of the flagged vnodes is written, the segment summary flag SS_DIROP is set. If the directory-operation information spans multiple partial segments, the segment summary flag SS_CONT also is set. So that the number of partial segments participating in a set of directory operations is minimized, vnodes are included in partial segments based on whether they participated in a directory operation. Finally, so that directory operations are prevented from being only partially reflected in a segment, no new directory operations are begun while the segment writer is writing a partial segment containing directory operations, and the segment writer will not write a partial segment containing directory operations while any directory operation is in progress.

During recovery, partial segments with the SS_DIROP or SS_CONT flag set are ignored unless the partial segment completing the directory operation was written successfully to the disk. For example, if the recovery agent finds a segment with both SS_DIROP and SS_CONT set, it ignores all such partial segments until it finds a later partial segment with SS_DIROP set and SS_CONT unset (i.e. the final partial segment including any part of this set of directory operations). If no such partial segment is ever found, then all the segments from the initial directory operation on are discarded.

Creation of a File

Creating a file in the LFS is a simple process. First, a new inode must be allocated from the filesystem. There is a field in the superblock that points to the first free inode in the linked list of free inodes found in the index file. If this pointer references an inode, that inode is allocated in the index file, and the pointer is updated from that inode's free-list pointer. Otherwise, the index file is extended by a block, and the block is divided into index-file inode entries. The first of these entries is then allocated as the new inode.

The inode version number is then incremented by some value. The reason for this increment is that it makes the cleaner's task simpler. Recall that there is an inode version number stored with each file-information structure in the segment. When the cleaner reviews a segment for live data, mismatching version numbers or an unallocated index file inode makes detection of file removal simple.

Conversely, deleting a file from the LFS adds a new entry to the index file's free-inode list. Contrasted to the multiple synchronous operations required by the FFS when a file is created, creating a file in LFS is conceptually simple and blindingly fast. However, the LFS pays a price for avoiding the synchronous behavior: It cannot permit segments to be written at the same time as files are being created, and the maintenance of the allocation information is significantly more complex.

Reading and Writing to a File

Having created a file, a process can do reads or writes on it. The procedural path through the kernel is largely identical to that of the FFS, as shown by Fig. 8.4 with the *ffs_* routines changed to *lfs_*. The code for *ffs_read*() and *lfs_read*(), and that for *ffs_write*() and *lfs_write*(), is the same, with some C preprocessing *#define*s added for minor tailoring. As in the FFS, each time that a process does a *write* system call, the system checks to see whether the size of the file has increased. If the file needs to be extended, the request is rounded up to the next fragment size, and only that much space is allocated. A logical block request is handed off to *lfs_balloc*(), which performs the same functions as *ffs_balloc*(), allocating any necessary indirect blocks and the data block if it has not yet been allocated, and reallocating and rewriting fragments as necessary.

Filesystem Cleaning

Because the disk is not infinite, cleaning must be done periodically to make new segments available for writing. Cleaning is the most challenging aspect of the LFS, in that its effect on performance and its interactions with other parts of the system are still not fully understood.

Although a cleaner was simulated extensively in the original LFS design [Rosenblum & Ousterhout, 1992], the simulated cleaner was never implemented, and none of the implemented cleaners (including the one in 4BSD) have ever been simulated. Cleaning must be done often enough that the filesystem does not fill up; however, the cleaner can have a devastating effect on performance. Recent research [Seltzer et al, 1995] shows that cleaning segments while the LFS is active (i.e., writing other segments) can result in a performance degradation of about 35 to 40 percent for some transaction-processing–oriented applications. This degradation is largely unaffected by how full the filesystem is; it occurs even when the filesystem is half empty. However, even at 40-percent degradation, the LFS performs comparably to the FFS on these applications. Recent research also shows that typical workstation workloads can permit cleaning during disk idle periods [Blackwell et al, 1995], without introducing any user-noticeable latency.

Cleaning in the LFS is implemented by a user utility named *lfs_cleanerd*. This functionality was placed in user space for three major reasons.

First, experimentation with different algorithms, such as migrating rarely accessed data to the same segment or restricting cleaning to disk idle times, probably will prove fruitful, and making this experimentation possible outside the operating system will encourage further research. In addition, a single cleaning algorithm is unlikely to perform equally well for all possible workloads. For example, coalescing randomly updated files during cleaning should dramatically improve later sequential-read performance for some workloads.

Second, the cleaner may potentially require large amounts of memory and processor time, and previous implementations of the cleaner in the kernel have caused noticeable latency problems in user response. When the cleaner is moved to user space, it competes with other processes for processor time and virtual memory, instead of tying down a significant amount of physical memory.

Third, given the negative effect that the cleaner can have on performance, and the many possible algorithms for deciding when and what segments to clean, running the cleaner is largely a policy decision, always best implemented outside the kernel.

The number of live bytes of information in a segment, as determined from the segment-usage information in the index file, is used as a measure of *cleaning importance*. A simple algorithm for cleaning would be always to clean the segment that contains the fewest live bytes, based on the argument that this rule would result in the most free disk space for the least effort. The cleaning algorithm in the current LFS implementation is based on the simulation in Rosenblum and Ousterhout, 1992. This simulation shows that selection of segments to clean is an important design parameter in minimizing cleaning overhead, and that the cost–benefit policy defined there does well for the simulated workloads. Briefly restated, each segment is assigned a *cleaning cost* and *benefit*. The I/O *cost* to clean a segment is equal to

$$1 + utilization,$$

where 1 represents the cost to read the segment to be cleaned, and *utilization* is the fraction of live data in the segment that must be written back into the log. The *benefit* of cleaning a segment is

$$free\ bytes\ generated \times age\ of\ segment,$$

where *free bytes generated* is the fraction of dead blocks in the segment $(1 - utilization)$ and *age of segment* is the number of seconds since the segment was written to disk. The selection of the *age of segment* metric can have dramatic effects on the frequency with which the cleaner runs (and interferes with system performance).

When the filesystem needs to reclaim space, the cleaner selects the segment with the largest *benefit*-to-*cost* ratio:

$$\frac{benefit}{cost} = \frac{(1 - utilization) \times age\ of\ segment}{1 + utilization}$$

Once a segment has been selected for cleaning, by whatever mechanism, cleaning proceeds as follows:

1. Read one (or more) target segments.

2. Determine the blocks that contain useful data. For the cleaner to determine the blocks in a segment that are live, it must be able to identify each block in a segment; so, the summary block of each partial segment identifies the inode and logical block number of every block in the partial segment.

3. Write the live blocks back into the filesystem.

4. Mark the segments as clean.

The cleaner shares information with the kernel via four new system calls and the index file. The new system calls interface to functionality that was used by the kernel (e.g., the translation of file logical block numbers to disk addresses done by *ufs_bmap*()) and to functionality that must be in the kernel to avoid races between the cleaner and other processes.

The four system calls added for the cleaner are as follows:

1. *lfs_bmapv*: Take an array of inode number and logical block number pairs, and return the current disk address, if any, for each block. If the disk address returned to the cleaner is the one in the segment that it is considering, the block is live.

2. *lfs_markv*: Take an array of inode number and logical block number pairs and write their associated data blocks into the filesystem in the current partial segment. Although it would be theoretically possible for the cleaner to accomplish this task itself, the obvious race with other processes writing or deleting the same blocks, and the need to do the write without updating the inode's access or modification times, made it simpler for this functionality to be in the kernel.

3. *lfs_segclean*: Mark a segment clean. After the cleaner has rewritten all the live data in the segment, this system call marks the segment clean for reuse. It is a system call so that the kernel does not have to search the index file for new segments and so that the cleaner does not have to modify the index file.

4. *lfs_segwait*: Make a special-purpose sleep call. The calling process is put to sleep until a specified timeout period has elapsed or, optionally, until a segment has been written. This operation lets the cleaner pause until there may be a requirement for further cleaning.

When a segment is selected and read into memory, the cleaner processes each partial segment in the segment sequentially. The segment summary specifies the blocks that are in the partial segment. Periodically, the cleaner constructs an array of pairs consisting of an inode number and a logical block number, for file blocks found in the segment, and uses the *lfs_bmapv* system call to obtain the current disk address for each block. If the returned disk address is the same as the location of the block in the segment being examined, the block is live. The cleaner uses the *lfs_markv* system call to rewrite each live block into another segment in the filesystem.

Before rewriting these blocks, the kernel must verify that none of the blocks have been superseded or deleted since the cleaner called *lfs_bmapv*. Once the call to *lfs_markv* begins, only blocks specified by the cleaner are written into the log, until the *lfs_markv* call completes, so that, if cleaned blocks die after the *lfs_markv* call verifies that they are alive, the partial segments written after the *lfs_markv* partial segments will update their status properly.

The separation of the *lfs_bmapv* and *lfs_markv* functionality was done deliberately to make it easier for LFS to support new cleaning algorithms. There is no

requirement that the cleaner always call *lfs_markv* after each call to *lfs_bmapv*, or
that it call *lfs_markv* with the same arguments. For example, the cleaner might
use *lfs_markv* to do block coalescing from several segments.

When the cleaner has written the live blocks using *lfs_markv*, the cleaner calls
lfs_segclean to mark the segment clean. When the cleaner has cleaned enough
segments, it calls *lfs_segwait*, sleeping until the specified timeout elapses or a new
segment is written into the filesystem.

Since the cleaner is responsible for producing free space, the blocks that it
writes must get preference over all other dirty blocks to be written, so that the system avoids running out of free space. In addition, there are degenerative cases
where cleaning a segment can consume more space than it reclaims. So that the
cleaner can always run and will eventually generate free space, all writing by any
process other than the cleaner is blocked by the kernel when the number of clean
segments drops below 3.

Filesystem Parameterization

Parameterization in the LFS is minimal. At filesystem-creation time, it is possible
to specify the filesystem block and fragment size, the segment size, and the percentage of space reserved from normal users. Only the last of these parameters
may be altered after filesystem creation without recreation of the filesystem.

Filesystem-Crash Recovery

Historic UNIX systems spend a significant amount of time in filesystem checks
while rebooting. As disks become ever larger, this time will continue to increase.
There are two aspects to filesystem recovery: bringing the filesystem to a physically consistent state and verifying the logical structure of the filesystem. When
the FFS or the LFS adds a block to a file, there are several different pieces of information that may be modified: the block itself, its inode, indirect blocks, and, of
course, the location of the most recent allocation. If the system crashes between
any of the operations, the filesystem is likely be left in a physically inconsistent
state.

There is currently no way for the FFS to determine where on the disk or in the
filesystem hierarchy an inconsistency is likely to occur. As a result, it must
rebuild the entire filesystem state, including cylinder-group bitmaps and all meta-
data after each system failure. At the same time, the FFS verifies the filesystem
hierarchy. Traditionally, **fsck** is the utility that performs both of these functions.
Although the addition of filesystem-already-clean flags and tuning *fsck* has provided a significant decrease in the time that it takes to reboot in 4BSD, it can still
take minutes per filesystem before applications can be run.

Because writes are localized in the LFS, the recovery agent can determine
where any filesystem inconsistencies caused by the system crash are located, and
needs to check only those segments, so bringing a LFS to a consistent state normally requires only a few seconds per filesystem. The minimal time required to
achieve filesystem consistency is a major advantage for the LFS over the FFS.
However, although fast recovery from system failure is desirable, reliable recovery
from media failure is necessary. The high level of robustness that *fsck* provides

for the FFS is not maintained by this consistency checking. For example, *fsck* is capable of recovering from the corruption of data on the disk by hardware, or by errant software overwriting filesystem data structures such as a block of inodes.

Recovery in the LFS has been separated into two parts. The first part involves bringing the filesystem into a consistent state after a system crash. This part of recovery is more similar to standard database recovery than to *fsck*. It consists of three steps:

1. Locate the most recent checkpoint—the last time at which the filesystem was consistent on disk.

2. Initialize all the filesystem structures based on that checkpoint.

3. *Roll forward*, reading each partial segment from the checkpoint to the end of the log, in write order, and incorporating any modifications that occurred, except as noted previously for directory operations.

Support for rolling forward is the purpose of much of the information included in the partial-segment summary. The next-segment pointers are provided so that the recovery agent does not have to search the disk to find the next segment to read. The recovery agent uses the partial-segment checksums to identify valid partial segments (ones that were written completely to the disk). It uses the partial segment time-stamps to distinguish partial segments written after the checkpoint from those that were written before the checkpoint and that were later reclaimed by the cleaner. It uses the file and block numbers in the file-information structures to update the index file (the inode map and segment-usage information) and the file inodes, to make the blocks in the partial segment appear in the file. The latter actions are similar to those taken in cleaning. As happens in database recovery, the filesystem-recovery time is proportional to the interval between filesystem checkpoints.

The second part of recovery in the LFS involves the filesystem-consistency checks performed for the FFS by *fsck*. This check is similar to the functionality of *fsck*, and, like *fsck*, will take a long time to run. (This functionality has not been implemented in 4.4BSD.)

The LFS implementation permits fast recovery, and applications are able to start running as soon as the roll forward has been completed, while basic sanity checking of the filesystem is done in the background. There is the obvious problem of what to do if the sanity check fails. If that happens, the filesystem must be downgraded forcibly to read-only status, and fixed. Then, writes can be enabled once again. The only applications affected by this downgrade are those that were writing to the filesystem. Of course, the root filesystem must always be checked completely after every reboot, to avoid a cycle of reboot followed by crash followed by reboot if the root has become corrupted,

Like the FFS, the LFS replicates the superblock, copying the latter into several segments. However, no cylinder placement is taken into account in this replication, so it is theoretically possible that all copies of the superblock would be on the same disk cylinder or platter.

8.4   The Memory-Based Filesystem

Memory-based filesystems have existed for a long time; they have generally been marketed as random-access–memory disks (RAM-disk) or sometimes as software packages that use the machine's general-purpose memory. A RAM disk is designed to appear like any other disk peripheral connected to a machine. It is normally interfaced to the processor through the I/O bus, and is accessed through a device driver similar or sometimes identical to the device driver used for a normal magnetic disk. The device driver sends requests for blocks of data to the device, and the hardware then transfers the requested data to or from the requested disk sectors. Instead of storing its data on a rotating magnetic disk, the RAM disk stores its data in a large array of RAM or bubble memory. Thus, the latency of accessing the RAM disk is nearly zero, whereas 15 to 50 milliseconds of latency are incurred when rotating magnetic media are accessed. RAM disks also have the benefit of being able to transfer data at the memory bandwidth of the system, whereas magnetic disks are typically limited by the rate at which the data pass under the disk head.

Software packages simulating RAM disks operate by allocating a fixed partition of the system memory. The software then provides a device-driver interface similar to the one used by disk hardware. Because the memory used by the RAM disk is not available for other purposes, software RAM-disk solutions are used primarily for machines with limited addressing capabilities, such as 16-bit computers that do not have an effective way to use the extra memory.

Most software RAM disks lose their contents when the system is powered down or rebooted. The system can save the contents either by using battery–backed-up memory, or by storing critical filesystem data structures in the filesystem and running a consistency-check program after each reboot. These conditions increase the hardware cost and potentially slow down the speed of the disk. Thus, RAM-disk filesystems are not typically designed to survive power failures; because of their volatility, their usefulness is limited to storage of transient or easily recreated information, such as might be found in **/tmp**. Their primary benefit is that they have higher throughput than do disk-based filesystems [Smith, 1981]. This improved throughput is particularly useful for utilities that make heavy use of temporary files, such as compilers. On fast processors, nearly one-half of the elapsed time for a compilation is spent waiting for synchronous operations required for file creation and deletion. The use of the MFS nearly eliminates this waiting time.

Use of dedicated memory to support a RAM disk exclusively is a poor use of resources. The system can improve overall throughput by using the memory for the locations with high access rates. These locations may shift between supporting process virtual address spaces and caching frequently used disk blocks. Memory dedicated to the filesystem is used more effectively in a buffer cache than as a RAM disk. The buffer cache permits faster access to the data because it requires only a single memory-to-memory copy from the kernel to the user process. The use of memory in a RAM-disk configuration may require two memory-to-memory copies: one from the RAM disk to the buffer cache, then another from the buffer cache to the user process.

The 4.4BSD system avoids these problems by building its RAM-disk filesystem in pageable memory, instead of in dedicated memory. The goal is to provide the speed benefits of a RAM disk without paying the performance penalty inherent in dedicating to the RAM disk part of the physical memory on the machine. When the filesystem is built in pageable memory, it competes with other processes for the available memory. When memory runs short, the paging system pushes its least recently used pages to backing store. Being pageable also allows the filesystem to be much larger than would be practical if it were limited by the amount of physical memory that could be dedicated to that purpose. The **/tmp** filesystem can be allocated a virtual address space that is larger than the physical memory on the machine. Such a configuration allows small files to be accessed quickly, while still allowing **/tmp** to be used for big files, although at a speed more typical of normal, disk-based filesystems.

An alternative to building a MFS would be to have a filesystem that never did operations synchronously, and that never flushed its dirty buffers to disk. However, we believe that such a filesystem either would use a disproportionately large percentage of the buffer-cache space, to the detriment of other filesystems, or would require the paging system to flush its dirty pages. Waiting for other filesystems to push dirty pages subjects all filesystems to delays while they are waiting for the pages to be written [Ohta & Tezuka, 1990].

Organization of the Memory-Based Filesystem

The implementation of the MFS in 4.4BSD was done before the FFS had been split into semantic and filestore modules. Thus, to avoid rewriting the semantics of the 4.4BSD filesystem, it instead used the FFS in its entirety. The current design does not take advantage of the memory-resident nature of the filesystem. A future implementation probably will use the existing semantic layer, but will rewrite the filestore layer to reduce its execution expense and to make more efficient use of the memory space.

The user creates a filesystem by invoking a modified version of the *newfs* utility, with an option telling *newfs* to create a MFS. The *newfs* utility allocates a section of virtual address space of the requested size, and builds a filesystem in the memory, instead of on a disk partition. When the filesystem has been built, *newfs* does a *mount* system call specifying a filesystem type of MFS. The auxiliary data parameter to the mount call specifies a pointer to the base of the memory in which it has built the filesystem. The *mount* call does not return until the filesystem is unmounted. Thus, the *newfs* process provides the context to support the MFS.

The *mount* system call allocates and initializes a mount-table entry, and then calls the filesystem-specific mount routine. The filesystem-specific routine is responsible for doing the mount and for initializing the filesystem-specific portion of the mount-table entry. It allocates a block-device vnode to represent the memory disk device. In the private area of this vnode, it stores the base address of the

filesystem and the process identifier of the *newfs* process for later reference when
doing I/O. It also initializes an I/O list that it uses to record outstanding I/O
requests. It can then call the normal FFS *mount* system call, passing the special
block-device vnode that it has created, instead of the usual disk block-device
vnode. The mount proceeds just like any other local mount, except that requests
to read from the block device are vectored through the MFS block-device vnode,
instead of through the usual block-device I/O function. When the mount is completed, *mount* does not return as most other filesystem *mount* system calls do;
instead, it sleeps in the kernel awaiting I/O requests. Each time an I/O request is
posted for the filesystem, a wakeup is issued for the corresponding *newfs* process.
When awakened, the process checks for requests on its I/O list. The filesystem
services a read request by copying to a kernel buffer data from the section of the
newfs address space corresponding to the requested disk block. Similarly, the
filesystem services a write request by copying data to the section of the *newfs*
address space corresponding to the requested disk block from a kernel buffer.
When all the requests have been serviced, the *newfs* process returns to sleep to
await more requests.

Once the MFS is mounted, all operations on files are handled by the FFS code
until they get to the point where the filesystem needs to do I/O on the device.
Here, the filesystem encounters the second piece of the MFS. Instead of calling
the special-device strategy routine, it calls the memory-based strategy routine.
Usually, the filesystem services the request by linking the buffer onto the I/O list
for the MFS vnode, and issuing a wakeup to the *newfs* process. This wakeup
results in a context switch to the *newfs* process, which does a copyin or copyout,
as described previously. The strategy routine must be careful to check whether the
I/O request is coming from the *newfs* process itself, however. Such requests happen during mount and unmount operations, when the kernel is reading and writing
the superblock. Here, the MFS strategy routine must do the I/O itself, to avoid
deadlock.

The final piece of kernel code to support the MFS is the close routine. After
the filesystem has been unmounted successfully, the device close routine is called.
This routine flushes any pending I/O requests, then sets the I/O list head to a special value that is recognized by the I/O servicing loop as an indication that the
filesystem is unmounted. The *mount* system call exits, in turn causing the *newfs*
process to exit, resulting in the filesystem vanishing in a cloud of dirty pages.

The paging of the filesystem does not require any additional code beyond that
already in the kernel to support virtual memory. The *newfs* process competes with
other processes on an equal basis for the machine's available memory. Data pages
of the filesystem that have not yet been used are zero-fill-on-demand pages that do
not occupy memory. As long as memory is plentiful, the entire contents of the
filesystem remain memory resident. When memory runs short, the oldest pages of
newfs are pushed to backing store as part of the normal paging activity. The pages
that are pushed usually hold the contents of files that have been created in the
MFS, but that have not been accessed recently (or have been deleted).

Filesystem Performance

The performance of the current MFS is determined by the memory-to-memory copy speed of the processor. Empirically, the throughput is about 45 percent of this memory-to-memory copy speed. The basic set of steps for each block written is as follows:

1. Memory-to-memory copy from the user process doing the write to a kernel buffer

2. Context switch to the *newfs* process

3. Memory-to-memory copy from the kernel buffer to the *newfs* address space

4. Context switch back to the writing process

Thus, each write requires at least two memory-to-memory copies, accounting for about 90 percent of the CPU time. The remaining 10 percent is consumed in the context switches and in the filesystem-allocation and block-location code. The actual context-switch count is only about one-half of the worst case outlined previously because read-ahead and write-behind allow multiple blocks to be handled with each context switch.

The added speed of the MFS is most evident for processes that create and delete many files. The reason for the speedup is that the filesystem must do two synchronous operations to create a file: first, writing the allocated inode to disk; then, creating the directory entry. Deleting a file similarly requires at least two synchronous operations. Here, the low latency of the MFS is noticeable compared to that of a disk-based filesystem because a synchronous operation can be done with just two context switches, instead of incurring the disk latency.

Future Work

The most obvious shortcoming of the current implementation is that filesystem blocks are copied twice: once between the *newfs* process address space and the kernel buffer cache, and once between the kernel buffer and the requesting process. These copies are done in different process contexts, necessitating two context switches per group of I/O requests. When the MFS was built, the virtual-memory system did not support paging of any part of the kernel address space. Thus, the only way to build a pageable filesystem was to do so in the context of a normal process. The current virtual-memory system allows parts of the kernel address space to be paged. Thus, it is now possible to build a MFS that avoids the double copy and context switch. One potential problem with such a scheme is that many kernels are limited to a small address space (usually a few Mbyte). This restriction limits the size of MFS that such a machine can support. On such a machine, the kernel can describe a MFS that is larger than its address space and can use a window to map the larger filesystem address space into its limited address space. The window maintains a cache of recently accessed pages. The problem with this scheme is that, if the working set of active pages is greater than the size of the window, then much time is spent remapping pages and invalidating translation buffers. Alternatively, a separate address space could be constructed for each MFS, as in the current implementation. The memory-resident pages of each address space could be mapped exactly as other cached pages are accessed.

The current system uses the existing local filesystem structures and code to implement the MFS. The major advantages of this approach are the sharing of code and the simplicity of the approach. There are several disadvantages, however. One is that the size of the filesystem is fixed at mount time. Thus, only a fixed number of files and data blocks can be supported. Currently, this approach requires enough swap space for the entire filesystem and prevents expansion and contraction of the filesystem on demand. The current design also prevents the filesystem from taking advantage of the memory-resident character of the filesystem. For example, the current filesystem structure is optimized for magnetic disks. It includes replicated control structures, cylinder groups with separate allocation maps and control structures, and data structures that optimize rotational layout of files. None of these optimizations are useful in a MFS (at least when the backing store for the filesystem is allocated dynamically and is not contiguous on a single disk type). Alternatively, directories could be implemented using dynamically allocated memory organized as linked lists or trees, rather than as files stored in disk blocks. Allocation and location of pages for file data might use virtual-memory primitives and data structures, rather than direct and indirect blocks.

Exercises

8.1   What are the four classes of operations handled by the datastore filesystem?

8.2   Under what circumstances can a write request avoid reading a block from the disk?

8.3   What is the difference between a logical block and a physical block? Why is this distinction important?

8.4   Give two reasons why increasing the basic block size in the old filesystem from 512 bytes to 1024 bytes more than doubled the system's throughput.

8.5   Why is the per-cylinder group information placed at varying offsets from the beginning of the cylinder group?

8.6   How many blocks and fragments are allocated to a 31,200-byte file on a FFS with 4096-byte blocks and 1024-byte fragments? How many blocks and fragments are allocated to this file on a FFS with 4096-byte blocks and 512-byte fragments? Also answer these two questions assuming that an inode had only six direct block pointers, instead of 12.

8.7   Explain why the FFS maintains a 5 to 10 percent reserve of free space. What problems would arise if the free-space reserve were set to zero?

8.8   What is a quadratic hash? Describe for what it is used in the FFS, and why it is used for that purpose.

8.9   Why are the allocation policies for inodes different from those for data blocks?

8.10   Under what circumstances does block clustering provide benefits that cannot be obtained with a disk-track cache?

8.11   What are the FFS performance bottlenecks that the LFS filesystem attempts to address?

8.12   Why does the LFS provide on-disk checksums for partial segments?

8.13   Why does the LFS segment writer require that no directory operations occur while it runs?

8.14   Which three FFS operations must be done synchronously to ensure that the filesystem can always be recovered deterministically after a crash (barring unrecoverable hardware errors)?

*8.15   What problems would arise if files had to be allocated in a single contiguous piece of the disk? Consider the problems created by multiple processes, random access, and files with holes.

*8.16   Construct an example of an LFS segment where cleaning would lose, rather than gain, free blocks.

**8.17 Inodes could be allocated dynamically as part of a directory entry. Instead, inodes are allocated statically when the filesystem is created. Why is the latter approach used?

**8.18 The no-overwrite policy of the LFS offers the ability to support new features such as *unrm*, which offers the ability to un-remove a file. What changes would have to be made to the system to support this feature?

**8.19 The LFS causes wild swings in the amount of memory used by the buffer cache and the filesystem, as compared to the FFS. What relationship should the LFS have with the virtual-memory subsystem to guarantee that this behavior does not cause deadlock?

References

Blackwell et al, 1995.
    T. Blackwell, J. Harris, & M. Seltzer, "Heuristic Cleaning Algorithms in Log-Structured File Systems," *USENIX Association Conference Proceedings*, pp. 277–288, January 1995.

Chutani et al, 1992.
  S. Chutani, O. Anderson, M. Kazar, W. Mason, & R. Sidebotham, "The Episode File System," *USENIX Association Conference Proceedings*, pp. 43–59, January 1992.

Ganger & Patt, 1994.
  G. Ganger & Y. Patt, "Metadata Update Performance in File Systems," *USENIX Symposium on Operating Systems Design and Implementation*, pp. 49–60, November 1994.

Irlam, 1993.
  G. Irlam, *Unix File Size Survey—1993,* http://www.base.com/gordoni/-/ufs93.html, email:<gordoni@home.base.com>, November 1993.

Knuth, 1975.
  D. Knuth, *The Art of Computer Programming, Volume 3—Sorting and Searching,* pp. 506–549, Addison-Wesley, Reading, MA, 1975.

McKusick et al, 1984.
  M. K. McKusick, W. N. Joy, S. J. Leffler, & R. S. Fabry, "A Fast File System for UNIX," *ACM Transactions on Computer Systems*, vol. 2, no. 3, pp. 181–197, Association for Computing Machinery, August 1984.

McKusick & Kowalski, 1994.
  M. K. McKusick & T. J. Kowalski, "Fsck: The UNIX File System Check Program," in *4.4BSD System Manager's Manual*, pp. 3:1–21, O'Reilly & Associates, Inc., Sebastopol, CA, 1994.

McVoy & Kleiman, 1991.
  L. McVoy & S. Kleiman, "Extent-Like Performance from a Unix File System," *USENIX Association Conference Proceedings*, pp. 33–44, January 1991.

Moran et al, 1990.
  J. Moran, R. Sandberg, D. Coleman, J. Kepecs, & B. Lyon, "Breaking Through the NFS Performance Barrier," *Proceedings of the Spring 1990 European UNIX Users Group Conference*, pp. 199–206, April 1990.

Nevalainen & Vesterinen, 1977.
  O. Nevalainen & M. Vesterinen, "Determining Blocking Factors for Sequential Files by Heuristic Methods," *The Computer Journal*, vol. 20, no. 3, pp. 245–247, August 1977.

Ohta & Tezuka, 1990.
  M. Ohta & H. Tezuka, "A Fast /tmp File System by Async Mount Option," *USENIX Association Conference Proceedings*, pp. 145–150, June 1990.

Ousterhout & Douglis, 1989.
  J. Ousterhout & F. Douglis, "Beating the I/O Bottleneck: A Case for Log-Structured File Systems," *Operating Systems Review*, vol. 23, 1, pp. 11–27, January 1989.

Peacock, 1988.
  J. Peacock, "The Counterpoint Fast File System," *USENIX Association Conference Proceedings*, pp. 243–249, January 1988.

Rosenblum & Ousterhout, 1992.

M. Rosenblum & J. Ousterhout, "The Design and Implementation of a Log-Structured File System," *ACM Transactions on Computer Systems*, vol. 10, no. 1, pp. 26–52, Association for Computing Machinery, February 1992.

Seltzer et al, 1993.

M. Seltzer, K. Bostic, M. K. McKusick, & C. Staelin, "An Implementation of a Log-Structured File System for UNIX," *USENIX Association Conference Proceedings*, pp. 307–326, January 1993.

Seltzer et al, 1995.

M. Seltzer, K. Smith, H. Balakrishnan, J. Chang, S. McMains, & V. Padmanabhan, "File System Logging Versus Clustering: A Performance Comparison," *USENIX Association Conference Proceedings*, pp. 249–264, January 1995.

Smith, 1981.

A. J. Smith, "Bibliography on File and I/O System Optimizations and Related Topics," *Operating Systems Review*, vol. 14, no. 4, pp. 39–54, October 1981.

Trivedi, 1980.

K. Trivedi, "Optimal Selection of CPU Speed, Device Capabilities, and File Assignments," *Journal of the ACM*, vol. 27, no. 3, pp. 457–473, July 1980.

CHAPTER 9

The Network Filesystem

This chapter is divided into three main sections. The first gives a brief history of remote filesystems. The second describes the client and server halves of NFS and the mechanics of how they operate. The final section describes the techniques needed to provide reasonable performance for remote filesystems in general, and NFS in particular.

9.1 History and Overview

When networking first became widely available in 4.2BSD, users who wanted to share files all had to log in across the net to a central machine on which the shared files were located. These central machines quickly became far more loaded than the user's local machine, so demand quickly grew for a convenient way to share files on several machines at once. The most easily understood sharing model is one that allows a server machine to export its filesystems to one or more client machines. The clients can then import these filesystems and present them to the user as though they were just another local filesystem.

Numerous remote-filesystem protocol designs and protocols were proposed and implemented. The implementations were attempted at all levels of the kernel. Remote access at the top of the kernel resulted in semantics that nearly matched the local filesystem, but had terrible performance. Remote access at the bottom of the kernel resulted in awful semantics, but great performance. Modern systems place the remote access in the middle of the kernel at the vnode layer. This level gives reasonable performance and acceptable semantics.

An early remote filesystem, *UNIX United*, was implemented near the top of the kernel at the system-call dispatch level. It checked for file descriptors representing remote files and sent them off to the server. No caching was done on the

311

client machine. The lack of caching resulted in slow performance, but in semantics nearly identical to a local filesystem. Because the current directory and executing files are referenced internally by vnodes rather than by descriptors, UNIX United did not allow users to change directory into a remote filesystem and could not execute files from a remote filesystem without first copying the files to a local filesystem.

At the opposite extreme was Sun Microsystem's *network disk,* implemented near the bottom of the kernel at the device-driver level. Here, the client's entire filesystem and buffering code was used. Just as in the local filesystem, recently read blocks from the disk were stored in the buffer cache. Only when a file access requested a block that was not already in the cache would the client send a request for the needed physical disk block to the server. The performance was excellent because the buffer cache serviced most of the file-access requests just as it does for the local filesystem. Unfortunately, the semantics suffered because of incoherency between the client and server caches. Changes made on the server would not be seen by the client, and vice versa. As a result, the network disk could be used only by a single client or as a read-only filesystem.

The first remote filesystem shipped with System V was *RFS* [Rifkin et al, 1986]. Although it had excellent UNIX semantics, its performance was poor, so it met with little use. Research at Carnegie-Mellon lead to the *Andrew filesystem* [Howard, 1988]. The Andrew filesystem was commercialized by Transarc and eventually became part of the Distributed Computing Environment promulgated by the Open Software Foundation, and was supported by many vendors. It is designed to handle widely distributed servers and clients and also to work well with mobile computers that operate while detached from the network for long periods.

The most commercially successful and widely available remote-filesystem protocol is the *network filesystem* (*NFS*) designed and implemented by Sun Microsystems [Walsh et al, 1985; Sandberg et al, 1985]. There are two important components to the success of NFS. First, Sun placed the protocol specification for NFS in the public domain. Second, Sun sells that implementation to all people who want it, for less than the cost of implementing it themselves. Thus, most vendors chose to buy the Sun implementation. They are willing to buy from Sun because they know that they can always legally write their own implementation if the price of the Sun implementation is raised to an unreasonable level. The 4.4BSD implementation was written from the protocol specification, rather than being incorporated from Sun, because of the developers desire to be able to redistribute it freely in source form.

NFS was designed as a client–server application. Its implementation is divided into a client part that imports filesystems from other machines and a server part that exports local filesystems to other machines. The general model is shown in Fig. 9.1. Many goals went into the NFS design:

• The protocol is designed to be stateless. Because there is no state to maintain or recover, NFS can continue to operate even during periods of client or server failures. Thus, it is much more robust than a system that operates with state.

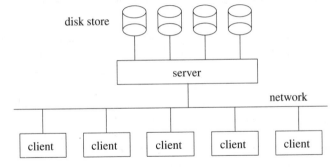

Figure 9.1 The division of NFS between client and server.

- NFS is designed to support UNIX filesystem semantics. However, its design also allows it to support the possibly less rich semantics of other filesystem types, such as MS-DOS.

- The protection and access controls follow the UNIX semantics of having the process present a UID and set of groups that are checked against the file's owner, group, and other access modes. The security check is done by filesystem-dependent code that can do more or fewer checks based on the capabilities of the filesystem that it is supporting. For example, the MS-DOS filesystem cannot implement the full UNIX security validation and makes access decisions solely based on the UID.

- The protocol design is transport independent. Although it was originally built using the UDP datagram protocol, it was easily moved to the TCP stream protocol. It has also been ported to run over numerous other non–IP-based protocols.

Some of the design decisions limit the set of applications for which NFS is appropriate:

- The design envisions clients and servers being connected on a locally fast network. The NFS protocol does not work well over slow links or between clients and servers with intervening gateways. It also works poorly for mobile computing that has extended periods of disconnected operation.

- The caching model assumes that most files will not be shared. Performance suffers when files are heavily shared.

- The stateless protocol requires some loss of traditional UNIX semantics. Filesystem locking (*flock*) has to be implemented by a separate stateful daemon. Deferral of the release of space in an unlinked file until the final process has closed the file is approximated with a heuristic that sometimes fails.

Despite these limitations, NFS proliferated because it makes a reasonable tradeoff between semantics and performance; its low cost of adoption has now made it ubiquitous.

9.2   NFS Structure and Operation

NFS operates as a typical client–server application. The server receives *remote-procedure-call* (*RPC*) requests from its various clients. An RPC operates much like a local procedure call: The client makes a procedure call, then waits for the result while the procedure executes. For a remote procedure call, the parameters must be *marshalled* together into a message. Marshalling includes replacing pointers by the data to which they point and converting binary data to the canonical network byte order. The message is then sent to the server, where it is unmarshalled (separated out into its original pieces) and processed as a local filesystem operation. The result must be similarly marshalled and sent back to the client. The client splits up the result and returns that result to the calling process as though the result were being returned from a local procedure call [Birrell & Nelson, 1984]. The NFS protocol uses the Sun's RPC and external data-representation (XDR) protocols [Reid, 1987]. Although the kernel implementation is done by hand to get maximum performance, the user-level daemons described later in this section use Sun's public-domain RPC and XDR libraries.

The NFS protocol can run over any available stream- or datagram-oriented protocol. Common choices are the TCP stream protocol and the UDP datagram protocol. Each NFS RPC message may need to be broken into multiple packets to be sent across the network. A big performance problem for NFS running under UDP on an Ethernet is that the message may be broken into up to six packets; if any of these packets are lost, the entire message is lost and must be resent. When running under TCP on an Ethernet, the message may also be broken into up to six packets; however, individual lost packets, rather than the entire message, can be retransmitted. Section 9.3 discusses performance issues in greater detail.

The set of RPC requests that a client can send to a server is shown in Table 9.1. After the server handles each request, it responds with the appropriate data, or with an error code explaining why the request could not be done. As noted in the table, most operations are *idempotent*. An idempotent operation is one that can be repeated several times without the final result being changed or an error being caused. For example, writing the same data to the same offset in a file is idempotent because it will yield the same result whether it is done once or many times. However, trying to remove the same file more than once is nonidempotent because the file will no longer exist after the first try. Idempotency is an issue when the server is slow, or when an RPC acknowledgment is lost and the client retransmits the RPC request. The retransmitted RPC will cause the server to try to do the same operation twice. For a nonidempotent request, such as a request to remove a file, the retransmitted RPC, if undetected by the server recent-request cache [Juszczak, 1989], will cause a "no such file" error to be returned, because the file will have been removed already by the first RPC. The user may be confused by the error, because they will have successfully found and removed the file.

Each file on the server can be identified by a unique *file handle*. A file handle is the token by which clients refer to files on a server. Handles are globally unique and are passed in operations, such as read and write, that reference a file. A file

RPC request	Action	Idempotent
GETATTR	get file attributes	yes
SETATTR	set file attributes	yes
LOOKUP	look up file name	yes
READLINK	read from symbolic link	yes
READ	read from file	yes
WRITE	write to file	yes
CREATE	create file	yes
REMOVE	remove file	no
RENAME	rename file	no
LINK	create link to file	no
SYMLINK	create symbolic link	yes
MKDIR	create directory	no
RMDIR	remove directory	no
READDIR	read from directory	yes
STATFS	get filesystem attributes	yes

Table 9.1 NFS, Version 2, RPC requests.

handle is created by the server when a pathname-translation request (lookup) is sent from a client to the server. The server must find the requested file or directory and ensure that the requesting user has access permission. If permission is granted, the server returns a file handle for the requested file to the client. The file handle identifies the file in future access requests by the client. Servers are free to build file handles from whatever information they find convenient. In the 4.4BSD NFS implementation, the file handle is built from a filesystem identifier, an inode number, and a *generation number*. The server creates a unique filesystem identifier for each of its locally mounted filesystems. A generation number is assigned to an inode each time that the latter is allocated to represent a new file. Each generation number is used only once. Most NFS implementations use a random-number generator to select a new generation number; the 4.4BSD implementation selects a generation number that is approximately equal to the creation time of the file. The purpose of the file handle is to provide the server with enough information to find the file in future requests. The filesystem identifier and inode provide a unique identifier for the inode to be accessed. The generation number verifies that the inode still references the same file that it referenced when the file was first accessed. The generation number detects when a file has been deleted, and a new file is later created using the same inode. Although the new file has the same filesystem identifier and inode number, it is a completely different file from the one that the previous file handle referenced. Since the generation number is included in the file handle, the generation number in a file handle for a previous use of the inode will not match the new generation number in the same inode. When an old-generation file handle is presented to the server by a client, the server refuses to accept it, and instead returns the "stale file handle" error message.

The use of the generation number ensures that the file handle is *time stable*. Distributed systems define a time-stable identifier as one that refers uniquely to some entity both while that entity exists and for a long time after it is deleted. A time-stable identifier allows a system to remember an identity across transient failures and allows the system to detect and report errors for attempts to access deleted entities.

The NFS Protocol

The NFS protocol is *stateless*. Being stateless means that the server does not need to maintain any information about which clients it is serving or about the files that they currently have open. Every RPC request that is received by the server is completely self-contained. The server does not need any additional information beyond that contained in the RPC to fulfill the request. For example, a read request will include the credential of the user doing the request, the file handle on which the read is to be done, the offset in the file to begin the read, and the number of bytes to be read. This information allows the server to open the file, verifying that the user has permission to read it, to seek to the appropriate point, to read the desired contents, and to close the file. In practice, the server caches recently accessed file data. However, if there is enough activity to push the file out of the cache, the file handle provides the server with enough information to reopen the file.

In addition to reducing the work needed to service incoming requests, the server cache also detects retries of previously serviced requests. Occasionally, a UDP client will send a request that is processed by the server, but the acknowledgment returned by the server to the client is lost. Receiving no answer, the client will timeout and resend the request. The server will use its cache to recognize that the retransmitted request has already been serviced. Thus, the server will not repeat the operation, but will just resend the acknowledgment. To detect such retransmissions properly, the server cache needs to be large enough to keep track of at least the most recent few seconds of NFS requests.

The benefit of the stateless protocol is that there is no need to do state recovery after a client or server has crashed and rebooted, or after the network has been partitioned and reconnected. Because each RPC is self-contained, the server can simply begin servicing requests as soon as it begins running; it does not need to know which files its clients have open. Indeed, it does not even need to know which clients are currently using it as a server.

There are drawbacks to the stateless protocol. First, the semantics of the local filesystem imply state. When files are unlinked, they continue to be accessible until the last reference to them is closed. Because NFS knows neither which files are open on clients nor when those files are closed, it cannot properly know when to free file space. As a result, it always frees the space at the time of the unlink of the last name to the file. Clients that want to preserve the freeing-on-last-close semantics convert unlink's of open files to renames to obscure names on the server. The names are of the form *.nfsAxxxx4.4*, where the *xxxx* is replaced with the hexadecimal value of the process identifier, and the *A* is successively incremented until an unused name is found. When the last close is done on the client, the client sends an unlink of the obscure filename to the server. This heuristic works for file access on only a single client; if one client has the file open and another client removes the file, the file will still disappear from the first client at the time of the remove. Other stateful semantics include the advisory locking described in Section 7.5. The locking semantics cannot be handled by the NFS protocol. On most systems, they are handled by a separate lock manager; the 4.4BSD version of NFS does not implement them at all.

The second drawback of the stateless protocol is related to performance. For version 2 of the NFS protocol, all operations that modify the filesystem must be committed to stable-storage before the RPC can be acknowledged. Most servers do not have battery-backed memory; the stable store requirement means that all written data must be on the disk before they can reply to the RPC. For a growing file, an update may require up to three synchronous disk writes: one for the inode to update its size, one for the indirect block to add a new data pointer, and one for the new data themselves. Each synchronous write takes several milliseconds; this delay severely restricts the write throughput for any given client file.

Version 3 of the NFS protocol eliminates some of the synchronous writes by adding a new asynchronous write RPC request. When such a request is received by the server, it is permitted to acknowledge the RPC without writing the new data to stable storage. Typically, a client will do a series of asynchronous write requests followed by a commit RPC request when it reaches the end of the file or it runs out of buffer space to store the file. The commit RPC request causes the server to write any unwritten parts of the file to stable store before acknowledging the commit RPC. The server benefits by having to write the inode and indirect blocks for the file only once per batch of asynchronous writes, instead of on every write RPC request. The client benefits from having higher throughput for file writes. The client does have the added overhead of having to save copies of all asynchronously written buffers until a commit RPC is done, because the server may crash before having written one or more of the asynchronous buffers to stable store. When the client sends the commit RPC, the acknowledgment to that RPC tells which of the asynchronous blocks were written to stable store. If any of the asynchronous writes done by the client are missing, the client knows that the server has crashed during the asynchronous-writing period, and resends the unacknowledged blocks. Once all the asynchronously written blocks have been acknowledged, they can be dropped from the client cache.

The NFS protocol does not specify the granularity of the buffering that should be used when files are written. Most implementations of NFS buffer files in 8-Kbyte blocks. Thus, if an application writes 10 bytes in the middle of a block, the client reads the entire block from the server, modifies the requested 10 bytes, and then writes the entire block back to the server. The 4.4BSD implementation also uses 8-Kbyte buffers, but it keeps additional information that describes which bytes in the buffer are modified. If an application writes 10 bytes in the middle of a block, the client reads the entire block from the server, modifies the requested 10 bytes, but then writes back only the 10 modified bytes to the server. The block read is necessary to ensure that, if the application later reads back other unmodified parts of the block, it will get valid data. Writing back only the modified data has two benefits:

1. Fewer data are sent over the network, reducing contention for a scarce resource.

2. Nonoverlapping modifications to a file are not lost. If two different clients simultaneously modify different parts of the same file block, both modifications will show up in the file, since only the modified parts are sent to the server. When clients send back entire blocks to the server, changes made by the first client will be overwritten by data read before the first modification was made, and then will be written back by the second client.

The 4.4BSD NFS Implementation

The NFS implementation that appears in 4.4BSD was written by Rick Macklem at the University of Guelph using the specifications of the Version 2 protocol published by Sun Microsystems [Sun Microsystems, 1989; Macklem, 1991]. This NFS Version 2 implementation had several 4.4BSD-only extensions added to it; the extended version became known as the *Not Quite NFS* (*NQNFS*) protocol [Macklem, 1994a]. This protocol provides

• Sixty-four–bit file offsets and sizes

• An access RPC that provides server permission checking on file open, rather than having the client guess whether the server will allow access

• An append option on the write RPC

• Extended file attributes to support 4.4BSD filesystem functionality more fully

• A variant of short-term *leases* with delayed-write client caching that give distributed cache consistency and improved performance [Gray & Cheriton, 1989]

Many of the NQNFS extensions were incorporated into the revised NFS Version 3 specification [Sun Microsystems, 1993; Pawlowski et al, 1994]. Others, such as leases, are still available only with NQNFS. The NFS implementation distributed in 4.4BSD supports clients and servers running the NFS Version 2, NFS Version 3, or NQNFS protocol [Macklem, 1994b]. The NQNFS protocol is described in Section 9.3.

The 4.4BSD client and server implementations of NFS are kernel resident. NFS interfaces to the network with sockets using the kernel interface available through *sosend*( ) and *soreceive*( ) (see Chapter 11 for a discussion of the socket interface). There are connection-management routines for support of sockets using connection-oriented protocols; there are timeout and retransmit support for datagram sockets on the client side.

The less time-critical operations, such as mounting and unmounting, as well as determination of which filesystems may be exported and to what set of clients they may be exported are managed by user-level system daemons. For the server side to function, the **portmap**, **mountd**, and **nfsd** daemons must be running. The **portmap** daemon acts as a registration service for programs that provide RPC-based services. When an RPC daemon is started, it tells the **portmap** daemon to what port number it is listening and what RPC services it is prepared to serve. When a client wishes to make an RPC call to a given service, it will first contact the **portmap** daemon on the server machine to determine the port number to which RPC messages should be sent.

The interactions between the client and server daemons when a remote filesystem is mounted are shown in Fig. 9.2. The **mountd** daemon handles two important functions:

1. On startup and after a hangup signal, **mountd** reads the **/etc/exports** file and creates a list of hosts and networks to which each local filesystem may be exported. It passes this list into the kernel using the *mount* system call; the

Figure 9.2 Daemon interaction when a remote filesystem is mounted. Step 1: The client's **mount** process sends a message to the well-known port of the server's **portmap** daemon, requesting the port address of the server's **mountd** daemon. Step 2: The server's **portmap** daemon returns the port address of its server's **mountd** daemon. Step 3: The client's **mount** process sends a request to the server's **mountd** daemon with the pathname of the filesystem that it wants to mount. Step 4: The server's **mountd** daemon requests a file handle for the desired mount point from its kernel. If the request is successful, the file handle is returned to the client's **mount** process. Otherwise, the error from the file-handle request is returned. If the request is successful, the client's **mount** process does a *mount* system call, passing in the file handle that it received from the server's **mountd** daemon.

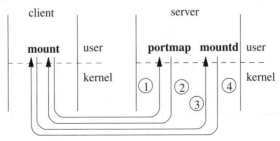

kernel links the list to the associated local filesystem mount structure so that
the list is readily available for consultation when an NFS request is received.

2. Client mount requests are directed to the **mountd** daemon. After verifying
   that the client has permission to mount the requested filesystem, **mountd**
   returns a file handle for the requested mount point. This file handle is used by
   the client for later traversal into the filesystem.

The **nfsd** master daemon forks off children that enter the kernel using the
nfssvc system call. The children normally remain kernel resident, providing a process context for the NFS RPC daemons. Typical systems run four to six **nfsd** daemons. If **nfsd** is providing datagram service, it will create a datagram socket
when it is started. If **nfsd** is providing stream service, connected stream sockets
will be passed in by the master **nfsd** daemon in response to connection-oriented
connection requests from clients, When a request arrives on a datagram or stream
socket, there is an upcall from the socket layer that invokes the *nfsrv_rcv()* routine. The *nfsrv_rcv()* call takes the message from the socket receive queue and
dispatches that message to an available **nfsd** daemon. The **nfsd** daemon verifies
the sender, and then passes the request to the appropriate local filesystem for processing. When the result returns from the filesystem, it is returned to the requesting client. The **nfsd** daemon is then ready to loop back and to service another
request. The maximum degree of concurrency on the server is determined by the
number of **nfsd** daemons that are started.

For connection-oriented transport protocols, such as TCP, there is one connection for each client-to-server mount point. For datagram-oriented protocols, such
as UDP, the server creates a fixed number of incoming RPC sockets when it starts
its **nfsd** daemons; clients create one socket for each imported mount point. The
socket for a mount point is created by the **mount** command on the client, which
then uses it to communicate with the **mountd** daemon on the server. Once the
client-to-server connection is established, the daemon processes on a connection-
oriented protocol may do additional verification, such as Kerberos authentication.
Once the connection is created and verified, the socket is passed into the kernel. If
the connection breaks while the mount point is still active, the client will attempt a
reconnect with a new socket.

The client side can operate without any daemons running, but the system
administrator can improved performance by running several **nfsiod** daemons
(these daemons provide the same service as the Sun **biod** daemons). The purpose
of the **nfsiod** daemons is to do asynchronous read-aheads and write-behinds.
They are typically started when the kernel begins running multiuser. They enter
the kernel using the *nfssvc* system call, and they remain kernel resident, providing
a process context for the NFS RPC client side. In their absence, each read or write
of an NFS file that cannot be serviced from the local client cache must be done in
the context of the requesting process. The process sleeps while the RPC is sent to
the server, the RPC is handled by the server, and a reply sent back. No read-
aheads are done, and write operations proceed at the disk-write speed of the

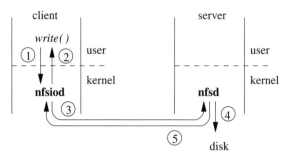

Figure 9.3 Daemon interaction when I/O is done. Step 1: The client's process does a *write* system call. Step 2: The data to be written are copied into a kernel buffer on the client, and the *write* system call returns. Step 3: An **nfsiod** daemon awakens inside the client's kernel, picks up the dirty buffer, and sends the buffer to the server. Step 4: The incoming write request is delivered to the next available **nfsd** daemon running inside the kernel on the server. The server's **nfsd** daemon writes the data to the appropriate local disk, and waits for the disk I/O to complete. Step 5: After the I/O has completed, the server's **nfsd** daemon sends back an acknowledgment of the I/O to the waiting **nfsiod** daemon on the client. On receipt of the acknowledgment, the client's **nfsiod** daemon marks the buffer as clean.

server. When present, the **nfsiod** daemons provide a separate context in which to issue RPC requests to a server. When a file is written, the data are copied into the buffer cache on the client. The buffer is then passed to a waiting **nfsiod** that does the RPC to the server and awaits the reply. When the reply arrives, **nfsiod** updates the local buffer to mark that buffer as written. Meanwhile, the process that did the write can continue running. The Sun Microsystems reference port of the NFS protocol flushes all the blocks of a file to the server when that file is closed. If all the dirty blocks have been written to the server when a process closes a file that it has been writing, it will not have to wait for them to be flushed. The NQNFS protocol does not flush all the blocks of a file to the server when that file is closed.

When reading a file, the client first hands a read-ahead request to the **nfsiod** that does the RPC to the server. It then looks up the buffer that it has been requested to read. If the sought-after buffer is already in the cache because of a previous read-ahead request, then it can proceed without waiting. Otherwise, it must do an RPC to the server and wait for the reply. The interactions between the client and server daemons when I/O is done are shown in Fig. 9.3.

Client–Server Interactions

A local filesystem is unaffected by network service disruptions. It is always available to the users on the machine unless there is a catastrophic event, such as a disk or power failure. Since the entire machine hangs or crashes, the kernel does not need to concern itself with how to handle the processes that were accessing the filesystem. By contrast, the client end of a network filesystem must have ways to handle processes that are accessing remote files when the client is still running, but the server becomes unreachable or crashes. Each NFS mount point is provided with three alternatives for dealing with server unavailability:

1. The default is a *hard mount* that will continue to try to contact the server "forever" to complete the filesystem access. This type of mount is appropriate when processes on the client that access files in the filesystem do not tolerate I/O system calls that return transient errors. A hard mount is used for processes for which access to the filesystem is critical for normal system operation. It is also useful if the client has a long-running program that simply wants to wait for the server to resume operation (e.g., after the server is taken down to run dumps).

2. The other extreme is a *soft mount* that retries an RPC a specified number of times, and then the corresponding system call returns with a transient error. For a connection-oriented protocol, the actual RPC request is not retransmitted; instead, NFS depends on the protocol retransmission to do the retries. If a response is not returned within the specified time, the corresponding system call returns with a transient error. The problem with this type of mount is that most applications do not expect a transient error return from I/O system calls (since they never occur on a local filesystem). Often, they will mistakenly interpret the transient error as a permanent error, and will exit prematurely. An additional problem is deciding how long to set the timeout period. If it is set too low, error returns will start occurring whenever the NFS server is slow because of heavy load. Alternately, a large retry limit can result in a process hung for a long time because of a crashed server or network partitioning.

3. Most system administrators take a middle ground by using an *interruptible mount* that will wait forever like a hard mount, but checks to see whether a termination signal is pending for any process that is waiting for a server response. If a signal (such as an interrupt) is sent to a process waiting for an NFS server, the corresponding I/O system call returns with a transient error. Normally, the process is terminated by the signal. If the process chooses to catch the signal, then it can decide how to handle the transient failure. This mount option allows interactive programs to be aborted when a server fails, while allowing long-running processes to await the server's return.

The original NFS implementation had only the first two options. Since neither of these two options was ideal for interactive use of the filesystem, the third option was developed as a compromise solution.

RPC Transport Issues

The NFS Version 2 protocol runs over UDP/IP transport by sending each request-reply message in a single UDP datagram. Since UDP does not guarantee datagram delivery, a timer is started, and if a timeout occurs before the corresponding RPC reply is received, the RPC request is retransmitted. At best, an extraneous RPC request retransmit increases the load on the server and can result in damaged files on the server or spurious errors being returned to the client when nonidempotent RPCs are redone. A recent-request cache normally is used on the server to minimize the negative effect of redoing a duplicate RPC request [Juszczak, 1989].

The amount of time that the client waits before resending an RPC request is called the *round-trip timeout* (*RTT*). Figuring out an appropriate value for the RTT is difficult. The RTT value is for the entire RPC operation, including transmitting the RPC message to the server, queuing at the server for an **nfsd**, doing any required I/O operations, and sending the RPC reply message back to the client. It can be highly variable for even a moderately loaded NFS server. As a result, the RTT interval must be a conservative (large) estimate to avoid extraneous RPC request retransmits. Adjusting the RTT interval dynamically and applying a congestion window on outstanding requests has been shown to be of some help with the retransmission problem [Nowicki, 1989].

On an Ethernet with the default 8-Kbyte read–write data size, the read–write reply-request will be an 8+-Kbyte UDP datagram that normally must be broken into at least six fragments at the IP layer for transmission. For IP fragments to be reassembled successfully into the IP datagram at the receive end, all fragments must be received at the destination. If even one fragment is lost or damaged in transit, the entire RPC message must be retransmitted, and the entire RPC redone. This problem can be exaggerated if the server is multiple hops away from the client through routers or slow links. It can also be nearly fatal if the network interface on the client or server cannot handle the reception of back-to-back network packets [Kent & Mogul, 1987].

An alternative to all this madness is to run NFS over TCP transport, instead of over UDP. Since TCP provides reliable delivery with congestion control, it avoids the problems associated with UDP. Because the retransmissions are done at the TCP level, instead of at the RPC level, the only time that a duplicate RPC will be sent to the server is when the server crashes or there is an extended network partition that causes the TCP connection to break after an RPC has been received but not acknowledged to the client. Here, the client will resend the RPC after the server reboots, because it does not know that the RPC has been received.

The use of TCP also permits the use of read and write data sizes greater than the 8-Kbyte limit for UDP transport. Using large data sizes allows TCP to use the full duplex bandwidth of the network effectively, before being forced to stop and wait for RPC response from the server. NFS over TCP usually delivers comparable to significantly better performance than NFS over UDP, unless the client or server processor is slow. For processors running at less than 10 million instructions per second (MIPS), the extra CPU overhead of using TCP transport becomes significant.

The main problem with using TCP transport with Version 2 of NFS is that it is supported between only BSD clients and servers. However, the clear superiority demonstrated by the Version 2 BSD TCP implementation of NFS convinced the group at Sun Microsystems implementing NFS Version 3 to make TCP the default transport. Thus, a Version 3 Sun client will first try to connect using TCP; only if the server refuses will it fall back to using UDP.

Security Issues

NFS is not secure because the protocol was not designed with security in mind. Despite several attempts to fix security problems, NFS security is still limited. Encryption is needed to build a secure protocol, but robust encryption cannot be exported from the United States. So, even if building a secure protocol were possible, doing so would be pointless, because all the file data are sent around the net in clear text. Even if someone is unable to get your server to send them a sensitive file, they can just wait until a legitimate user accesses it, and then can pick it up as it goes by on the net.

NFS export control is at the granularity of local filesystems. Associated with each local filesystem mount point is a list of the hosts to which that filesystem may be exported. A local filesystem may be exported to a specific host, to all hosts that match a subnet mask, or to all other hosts (the world). For each host or group of hosts, the filesystem can be exported read-only or read–write. In addition, a server may specify a set of subdirectories within the filesystem that may be mounted. However, this list of mount points is enforced by only the **mountd** daemon. If a malicious client wishes to do so, it can access any part of a filesystem that is exported to it.

The final determination of exportability is made by the list maintained in the kernel. So, even if a rogue client manages to snoop the net and to steal a file handle for the mount point of a valid client, the kernel will refuse to accept the file handle unless the client presenting that handle is on the kernel's export list. When NFS is running with TCP, the check is done once when the connection is established. When NFS is running with UDP, the check must be done for every RPC request.

The NFS server also permits limited remapping of user credentials. Typically, the credential for the superuser is not trusted and is remapped to the low-privilege user "nobody." The credentials of all other users can be accepted as given or also mapped to a default user (typically "nobody"). Use of the client UID and GID list unchanged on the server implies that the UID and GID space are common between the client and server (i.e., UID N on the client must refer to the same user on the server). The system administrator can support more complex UID and GID mappings by using the **umapfs** filesystem described in Section 6.7.

The system administrator can increase security by using Kerberos credentials, instead of accepting arbitrary user credentials sent without encryption by clients of unknown trustworthiness [Steiner et al, 1988]. When a new user on a client wants to begin accessing files in an NFS filesystem that is exported using Kerberos, the client must provide a Kerberos ticket to authenticate the user on the server. If successful, the system looks up the Kerberos principal in the server's password and group databases to get a set of credentials, and passes in to the server **nfsd** a local translation of the client UID to these credentials. The **nfsd** daemons run entirely within the kernel except when a Kerberos ticket is received. To avoid putting all the Kerberos authentication into the kernel, the **nfsd** returns from the kernel temporarily to verify the ticket using the Kerberos libraries, and then returns to the kernel with the results.

The NFS implementation with Kerberos uses encrypted timestamps to avert replay attempts. Each RPC request includes a timestamp that is encrypted by the client and decrypted by the server using a session key that has been exchanged as part of the initial Kerberos authentication. Each timestamp can be used only once, and must be within a few minutes of the current time recorded by the server. This implementation requires that the client and server clocks be kept within a few minutes of synchronization (this requirement is already imposed to run Kerberos). It also requires that the server keep copies of all timestamps that it has received that are within the time range that it will accept, so that it can verify that a timestamp is not being reused. Alternatively, the server can require that timestamps from each of its clients be monotonically increasing. However, this algorithm will cause RPC requests that arrive out of order to be rejected. The mechanism of using Kerberos for authentication of NFS requests is not well defined, and the 4.4BSD implementation has not been tested for interoperability with other vendors. Thus, Kerberos can be used only between 4.4BSD clients and servers.

9.3   Techniques for Improving Performance

Remote filesystems provide a challenging performance problem: Providing both a coherent networkwide view of the data and delivering that data quickly are often conflicting goals. The server can maintain coherency easily by keeping a single repository for the data and sending them out to each client when the clients need them; this approach tends to be slow, because every data access requires the client to wait for an RPC round-trip time. The delay is further aggravated by the huge load that it puts on a server that must service every I/O request from its clients. To increase performance and to reduce server load, remote filesystem protocols attempt to cache frequently used data on the clients themselves. If the cache is designed properly, the client will be able to satisfy many of the client's I/O requests directly from the cache. Doing such accesses is faster than communicating with the server, reducing latency on the client and load on the server and network. The hard part of client caching is keeping the caches coherent—that is, ensuring that each client quickly replaces any cached data that are modified by writes done on other clients. If a first client writes a file that is later read by a second client, the second client wants to see the data written by the first client, rather than the stale data that were in the file previously. There are two main ways that the stale data may be read accidentally:

1. If the second client has stale data sitting in its cache, the client may use those data because it does not know that newer data are available.

2. The first client may have new data sitting in its cache, but may not yet have written those data back to the server. Here, even if the second client asks the server for up-to-date data, the server may return the stale data because it does not know that one of its clients has a newer version of the file in that client's cache.

The second of these problems is related to the way that client writing is done. Synchronous writing requires that all writes be pushed through to the server during the *write* system call. This approach is the most consistent, because the server always has the most recently written data. It also permits any write errors, such as "filesystem out of space," to be propagated back to the client process via the *write* system-call return. With an NFS filesystem using synchronous writing, error returns most closely parallel those from a local filesystem. Unfortunately, this approach restricts the client to only one write per RPC round-trip time.

An alternative to synchronous writing is delayed writing, where the *write* system call returns as soon as the data are cached on the client; the data are written to the server sometime later. This approach permits client writing to occur at the rate of local storage access up to the size of the local cache. Also, for cases where file truncation or deletion occurs shortly after writing, the write to the server may be avoided entirely, because the data have already been deleted. Avoiding the data push saves the client time and reduces load on the server.

There are some drawbacks to delayed writing. To provide full consistency, the server must notify the client when another client wants to read or write the file, so that the delayed writes can be written back to the server. There are also problems with the propagation of errors back to the client process that issued the *write* system call. For example, a semantic change is introduced by delayed-write caching when the file server is full. Here, delayed-write RPC requests can fail with an "out of space" error. If the data are sent back to the server when the file is closed, the error can be detected if the application checks the return value from the *close* system call. For delayed writes, written data may not be sent back to the server until after the process that did the write has exited—long after it can be notified of any errors. The only solution is to modify programs writing an important file to do an *fsync* system call and to check for an error return from that call, instead of depending on getting errors from *write* or *close*. Finally, there is a risk of the loss of recently written data if the client crashes before the data are written back to the server.

A compromise between synchronous writing and delayed writing is asynchronous writing. The write to the server is started during the *write* system call, but the *write* system call returns before the write completes. This approach minimizes the risk of data loss because of a client crash, but negates the possibility of reducing server write load by discarding writes when a file is truncated or deleted.

The simplest mechanism for maintaining full cache consistency is the one used by Sprite that disables all client caching of the file whenever concurrent write sharing might occur [Nelson et al, 1988]. Since NFS has no way of knowing when write sharing might occur, it tries to bound the period of inconsistency by writing the data back when a file is closed. Files that are open for long periods are written back at 30-second intervals when the filesystem is synchronized. Thus, the NFS implementation does a mix of asynchronous and delayed writing, but always pushes all writes to the server on close. Pushing the delayed writes on close negates much of the performance advantage of delayed writing, because the delays that were avoided in the *write* system calls are observed in the *close* system call. With this approach, the server is always aware of all changes made by its clients with a maximum delay of 30 seconds and usually sooner, because most files are open only briefly for writing.

The server maintains read consistency by always having a client verify the contents of its cache before using that cache. When a client reads data, it first checks for the data in its cache. Each cache entry is stamped with an attribute that shows the most recent time that the server says that the data were modified. If the data are found in the cache, the client sends a timestamp RPC request to its server to find out when the data were last modified. If the modification time returned by the server matches that associated with the cache, the client uses the data in its cache; otherwise, it arranges to replace the data in its cache with the new data.

The problem with checking with the server on every cache access is that the client still experiences an RPC round-trip delay for each file access, and the server is still inundated with RPC requests, although they are considerably quicker to handle than are full I/O operations. To reduce this client latency and server load, most NFS implementations track how recently the server has been asked about each cache block. The client then uses a tunable parameter that is typically set at a few seconds to delay asking the server about a cache block. If an I/O request finds a cache block and the server has been asked about the validity of that block within the delay period, the client does not ask the server again, but rather just uses the block. Because certain blocks are used many times in succession, the server will be asked about them only once, rather than on every access. For example, the directory block for the **/usr/include** directory will be accessed once for each **#include** in a source file that is being compiled. The drawback to this approach is that changes made by other clients may not be noticed for up to the delay number of seconds.

A more consistent approach used by some network filesystems is to use a *callback* scheme where the server keeps track of all the files that each of its clients has cached. When a cached file is modified, the server notifies the clients holding that file so that they can purge it from their cache. This algorithm dramatically reduces the number of queries from the client to the server, with the effect of decreasing client I/O latency and server load [Howard et al, 1988]. The drawback is that this approach introduces state into the server because the server must remember the clients that it is serving and the set of files that they have cached. If the server crashes, it must rebuild this state before it can begin running again. Rebuilding the server state is a significant problem when everything is running properly; it gets even more complicated and time consuming when it is aggravated by network partitions that prevent the server from communicating with some of its clients [Mogul, 1993].

The 4.4BSD NFS implementation uses asynchronous writes while a file is open, but synchronously waits for all data to be written when the file is closed. This approach gains the speed benefit of writing asynchronously, yet ensures that any delayed errors will be reported no later than the point at which the file is closed. The implementation will query the server about the attributes of a file at most once every 3 seconds. This 3-second period reduces network traffic for files accessed frequently, yet ensures that any changes to a file are detected with no more than a 3-second delay. Although these heuristics provide tolerable semantics, they are noticeably imperfect. More consistent semantics at lower cost are available with the NQNFS lease protocol described in the next section.

Leases

The NQNFS protocol is designed to maintain full cache consistency between clients in a crash-tolerant manner. It is an adaptation of the NFS protocol such that the server supports both NFS and NQNFS clients while maintaining full consistency between the server and NQNFS clients. The protocol maintains cache consistency by using short-term leases instead of hard-state information about open files [Gray & Cheriton, 1989]. A *lease* is a ticket permitting an activity that is valid until some expiration time. As long as a client holds a valid lease, it knows that the server will give it a callback if the file status changes. Once the lease has expired, the client must contact the server if it wants to use the cached data.

Leases are issued using time intervals rather than absolute times to avoid the requirement of time-of-day clock synchronization. There are three important time constants known to the server. The *maximum_lease_term* sets an upper bound on lease duration—typically, 30 seconds to 1 minute. The *clock_skew* is added to all lease terms on the server to correct for differing clock speeds between the client and server. The *write_slack* is the number of seconds that the server is willing to wait for a client with an expired write-caching lease to push dirty writes.

Contacting the server after the lease has expired is similar to the NFS technique for reducing server load by checking the validity of data only every few seconds. The main difference is that the server tracks its clients' cached files, so there are never periods of time when the client is using stale data. Thus, the time used for leases can be considerably longer than the few seconds that clients are willing to tolerate possibly stale data. The effect of this longer lease time is to reduce the number of server calls almost to the level found in a full callback implementation such as the Andrew Filesystem [Howard et al, 1988]. Unlike the callback mechanism, state recovery with leases is trivial. The server needs only to wait for the lease's expiration time to pass, and then to resume operation. Once all the leases have expired, the clients will always communicate with the server before using any of their cached data. The lease expiration time is usually shorter than the time it takes most servers to reboot, so the server can effectively resume operation as soon as it is running. If the machine does manage to reboot more quickly than the lease expiration time, then it must wait until all leases have expired before resuming operation.

An additional benefit of using leases rather than hard state information is that leases use much less server memory. If each piece of state requires 64 bytes, a large server with hundreds of clients and a peak throughput of 2000 RPC requests per second will typically only use a few hundred Kbyte of memory for leases, with a worst case of about 3 Mbyte. Even if a server has exhausted lease storage, it can simply wait a few seconds for a lease to expire and free up a record. By contrast, a server with hard state must store records for all files currently open by all clients. The memory requirements are 3 to 12 Mbyte of memory per 100 clients served.

Whenever a client wishes to cache data for a file, it must hold a valid lease. There are three types of leases: noncaching, read caching, and write caching. A *noncaching lease* requires that all file operations be done synchronously with the server. A *read-caching lease* allows for client data caching, but no file modifications may be done. A *write-caching lease* allows for client caching of writes for the period of the lease. If a client has cached write data that are not yet written to the server when a write-cache lease has almost expired, it will attempt to extend the lease. If the extension fails, the client is required to push the written data.

If all the clients of a file are reading it, they will all be granted a read-caching lease. A read-caching lease allows one or more clients to cache data, but they may not make any modifications to the data. Figure 9.4 shows a typical read-caching scenario. The vertical solid black lines depict the lease records. Note that the time lines are not drawn to scale, since a client–server interaction will normally take less than 100 milliseconds, whereas the normal lease duration is 30 seconds.

Figure 9.4 Read-caching leases. Solid vertical lines represent valid leases.

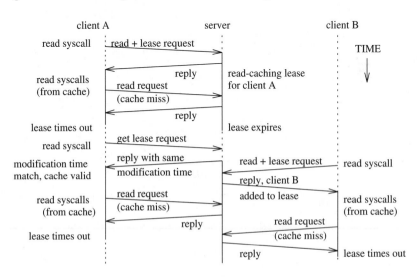

Every lease includes the time that the file was last modified. The client can use this timestamp to ensure that its cached data are still current. Initially, client A gets a read-caching lease for the file. Later, client A renews that lease and uses it to verify that the data in its cache are still valid. Concurrently, client B is able to obtain a read-caching lease for the same file.

If a single client wants to write a file and there are no readers of that file, the client will be issued a write-caching lease. A write-caching lease permits delayed write caching, but requires that all data be pushed to the server when the lease expires or is terminated by an *eviction notice*. When a write-caching lease has almost expired, the client will attempt to extend the lease if the file is still open, but is required to push the delayed writes to the server if renewal fails (see Fig. 9.5). The writes may not arrive at the server until after the write lease has expired on the client. A consistency problem is avoided because the server keeps its write lease valid for *write_slack* seconds longer than the time given in the lease issued to the client. In addition, writes to the file by the lease-holding client cause the lease expiration time to be extended to at least *write_slack* seconds. This *write_slack* period is conservatively estimated as the extra time that the client will need to write back any written data that it has cached. If the value selected for *write_slack* is too short, a write RPC may arrive after the write lease has expired on the server. Although this write RPC will result in another client seeing an inconsistency, that inconsistency is no more problematic than the semantics that NFS normally provides.

Figure 9.5 Write-caching lease. Solid vertical lines represent valid leases.

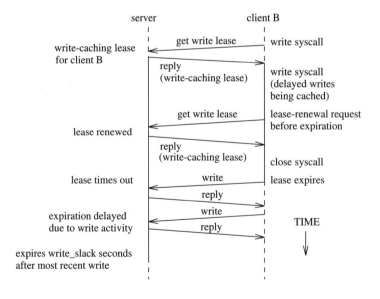

The server is responsible for maintaining consistency among the NQNFS clients by disabling client caching whenever a server file operation would cause inconsistencies. The possibility of inconsistencies occurs whenever a client has a write-caching lease and any other client or a local operation on the server tries to access the file, or when a modify operation is attempted on a file being read cached by clients. If one of these conditions occurs, then all clients will be issued noncaching leases. With a noncaching lease, all reads and writes will be done through the server, so clients will always get the most recent data. Figure 9.6 shows how read and write leases are replaced by a noncaching lease when there is the potential for write sharing. Initially, the file is read by client A. Later, it is written by client B. While client B is still writing, client A issues another read request. Here, the server sends an "eviction notice" message to client B, and then waits for lease termination. Client B writes back its dirty data, then sends a "vacated" message. Finally, the server issues noncaching leases to both clients. In general, lease termination occurs when a "vacated" message has been received from all the clients that have signed the lease or when the lease has expired. The server does not wait for a reply for the message pair "eviction notice" and

Figure 9.6 Write-sharing leases. Solid vertical lines represent valid leases.

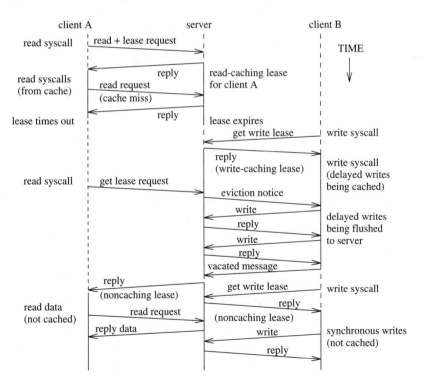

"vacated," as it does for all other RPC messages; they are sent asynchronously to avoid the server waiting indefinitely for a reply from a dead client.

A client gets leases either by doing a specific lease RPC or by including a lease request with another RPC. Most NQNFS RPC requests allow a lease request to be added to them. Combining lease requests with other RPC requests minimizes the amount of extra network traffic. A typical combination can be done when a file is opened. The client must do an RPC to get the handle for the file to be opened. It can combine the lease request, because it knows at the time of the open whether it will need a read or a write lease. All leases are at the granularity of a file, because all NFS RPC requests operate on individual files, and NFS has no intrinsic notion of a file hierarchy. Directories, symbolic links, and file attributes may be read cached but are not write cached. The exception is the file-size attribute that is updated during cached writing on the client to reflect a growing file. Leases have the advantage that they are typically required only at times when other I/O operations occur. Thus, lease requests can almost always be piggy-backed on other RPC requests, avoiding some of the overhead associated with the explicit open and close RPC required by a long-term callback implementation.

The server handles operations from local processes and from remote clients that are not using the NQNFS protocol by issuing short-term leases for the duration of each file operation or RPC. For example, a request to create a new file will get a short-term write lease on the directory in which the file is being created. Before that write lease is issued, the server will vacate the read leases of all the NQNFS clients that have cached data for that directory. Because the server gets leases for all non-NQNFS activity, consistency is maintained between the server and NQNFS clients, even when local or NFS clients are modifying the filesystem. The NFS clients will continue to be no more or less consistent with the server than they were without leases.

Crash Recovery

The server must maintain the state of all the current leases held by its clients. The benefit of using short-term leases is that, *maximum_lease_term* seconds after the server stops issuing leases, it knows that there are no current leases left. As such, server crash recovery does not require any state recovery. After rebooting, the server simply refuses to service any RPC requests except for writes (predominantly from clients that previously held write leases) until *write_slack* seconds after the final lease would have expired. For machines that cannot calculate the time that they crashed, the final-lease expiration time can be estimated safely as

$$boot\_time + maximum\_lease\_term + write\_slack + clock\_skew$$

Here, *boot_time* is the time that the kernel began running after the kernel was booted. With a *maximum_lease_term* 30 to 60 seconds, and *clock_skew* and *write_slack* at most a few seconds, this delay amounts to about 1 minute, which for most systems is taken up with the server rebooting process. When this time has passed, the server will have no outstanding leases. The clients will have had at least *write_slack* seconds to get written data to the server, so the server should be up to date. After this, the server resumes normal operation.

There is another failure condition that can occur when the server is congested. In the worst-case scenario, the client pushes dirty writes to the server, but a large request queue on the server delays these writes for more than *write_slack* seconds. In an effort to minimize the effect of these *recovery storms*, the server replies "try again later" to the RPC requests that it is not yet ready to service [Baker & Ousterhout, 1991]. The server takes two steps to ensure that all clients have been able to write back their written data. First, a write-caching lease is terminated on the server only when there are have been no writes to the file during the previous *write_slack* seconds. Second, the server will not accept any requests other than writes until it has not been overloaded during the previous *write_slack* seconds. A server is considered overloaded when there are pending RPC requests and all its **nfsd** processes are busy.

Another problem that is solved by short-term leases is how to handle a crashed or partitioned client that holds a lease that the server wishes to vacate. The server detects this problem when it needs to vacate a lease so that it can issue a lease to a second client, and the first client holding the lease fails to respond to the vacate request. Here, the server can simply wait for the first client's lease to expire before issuing the new one to the second client. When the first client reboots or gets reconnected to the server, it simply reacquires any leases it now needs. If a client-to-server network connection is severed just before a write-caching lease expires, the client cannot push the dirty writes to the server. Other clients that can contact the server will continue to be able to access the file and will see the old data. Since the write-caching lease has expired on the client, the client will synchronize with the server as soon as the network connection has been re-established. This delay can be avoided with a write-through policy.

A detailed comparison of the effects of leases on performance is given in [Macklem, 1994a]. Briefly, leases are most helpful when a server or network is loaded heavily. Here, leases allow up to 30 to 50 percent more clients to use a network and server before beginning to experience a level of congestion equal to what they would on a network and server that were not using leases. In addition, leases provide better consistency and lower latency for clients, independent of the load. Although leases are new enough that they are not widely used in commercial implementations of NFS today, leases or a similar mechanism will need to be added to commercial versions of NFS if NFS is to be able to compete effectively against other remote filesystems, such as Andrew.

Exercises

9.1   Describe the functions done by an NFS client.

9.2   Describe the functions done by an NFS server.

9.3   Describe three benefits that NFS derives from being stateless.

9.4   Give two reasons why TCP is a better protocol to use than is UDP for handling the NFS RPC protocol.

9.5   Describe the contents of a file handle in 4.4BSD. How is a file handle used?

9.6   When is a new generation number assigned to a file? What purpose does the generation number serve?

9.7   Describe the three ways that an NFS client can handle filesystem-access attempts when its server crashes or otherwise becomes unreachable.

9.8   Give two reasons why leases are given a limited lifetime.

9.9   What is a callback? When is it used?

9.10   A server may issue three types of leases: noncaching, read caching, and write caching. Describe what a client can do with each of these leases.

9.11   Describe how an NQNFS server recovers after a crash.

*9.12   Suppose that there is a client that supports both versions 2 and 3 of the NFS protocol running on both the TCP and UDP protocols, but a server that supports only version 2 of NFS running on UDP. Show the protocol negotiation between the client and server, assuming that the client prefers to run using version 3 of NFS using TCP.

**9.13   Assume that leases have an unlimited lifetime. Design a system for recovering the lease state after a client or server crash.

References

Baker & Ousterhout, 1991.
     M. Baker & J. Ousterhout, "Availability in the Sprite Distributed File System," *ACM Operating System Review*, vol. 25, no. 2, pp. 95–98, April 1991.
Birrell & Nelson, 1984.
     A. D. Birrell & B. J. Nelson, "Implementing Remote Procedure Calls," *ACM Transactions on Computer Systems*, vol. 2, no. 1, pp. 39–59, Association for Computing Machinery, February 1984.
Gray & Cheriton, 1989.
     C. Gray & D. Cheriton, "Leases: An Efficient Fault-Tolerant Mechanism for Distributed File Cache Consistency," *Proceedings of the Twelfth Symposium on Operating Systems Principles*, pp. 202–210, December 1989.
Howard, 1988.
     J. Howard, "An Overview of the Andrew File System," *USENIX Association Conference Proceedings*, pp. 23–26, January 1988.
Howard et al, 1988.
     J. Howard, M. Kazar, S. Menees, D. Nichols, M. Satyanarayanan, R.

Sidebotham, & M. West, "Scale and Performance in a Distributed File System," *ACM Transactions on Computer Systems*, vol. 6, no. 1, pp. 51–81, Association for Computing Machinery, February 1988.

Juszczak, 1989.
C. Juszczak, "Improving the Performance and Correctness of an NFS Server," *USENIX Association Conference Proceedings*, pp. 53–63, January 1989.

Kent & Mogul, 1987.
C. Kent & J. Mogul, "Fragmentation Considered Harmful," Research Report 87/3, Digital Equipment Corporation Western Research Laboratory, Palo Alto, CA, December 1987.

Macklem, 1991.
R. Macklem, "Lessons Learned Tuning the 4.3BSD-Reno Implementation of the NFS Protocol," *USENIX Association Conference Proceedings*, pp. 53–64, January 1991.

Macklem, 1994a.
R. Macklem, "Not Quite NFS, Soft Cache Consistency for NFS," *USENIX Association Conference Proceedings*, pp. 261–278, January 1994.

Macklem, 1994b.
R. Macklem, "The 4.4BSD NFS Implementation," in *4.4BSD System Manager's Manual*, pp. 6:1–14, O'Reilly & Associates, Inc., Sebastopol, CA, 1994.

Mogul, 1993.
J. Mogul, "Recovery in Spritely NFS," Research Report 93/2, Digital Equipment Corporation Western Research Laboratory, Palo Alto, CA, June 1993.

Nelson et al, 1988.
M. Nelson, B. Welch, & J. Ousterhout, "Caching in the Sprite Network File System," *ACM Transactions on Computer Systems*, vol. 6, no. 1, pp. 134–154, Association for Computing Machinery, February 1988.

Nowicki, 1989.
B. Nowicki, "Transport Issues in the Network File System," *Computer Communications Review*, vol. 19, no. 2, pp. 16–20, April 1989.

Pawlowski et al, 1994.
B. Pawlowski, C. Juszczak, P. Staubach, C. Smith, D. Lebel, & D. Hitz, "NFS Version 3: Design and Implementation," *USENIX Association Conference Proceedings*, pp. 137–151, June 1994.

Reid, 1987.
Irving Reid, "RPCC: A Stub Compiler for Sun RPC," *USENIX Association Conference Proceedings*, pp. 357–366, June 1987.

Rifkin et al, 1986.
A. Rifkin, M. Forbes, R. Hamilton, M. Sabrio, S. Shah, & K. Yueh, "RFS Architectural Overview," *USENIX Association Conference Proceedings*, pp. 248–259, June 1986.

Sandberg et al, 1985.

> R. Sandberg, D. Goldberg, S. Kleiman, D. Walsh, & B. Lyon, "Design and Implementation of the Sun Network Filesystem," *USENIX Association Conference Proceedings*, pp. 119–130, June 1985.

Steiner et al, 1988.

> J. Steiner, C. Neuman, & J. Schiller, "Kerberos: An Authentication Service for Open Network Systems," *USENIX Association Conference Proceedings*, pp. 191–202, February 1988.

Sun Microsystems, 1989.

> Sun Microsystems, "NFS: Network File System Protocol Specification," RFC 1094, available by anonymous FTP from ds.internic.net, March 1989.

Sun Microsystems, 1993.

> Sun Microsystems, *NFS: Network File System Version 3 Protocol Specification,* Sun Microsystems, Mountain View, CA, June 1993.

Walsh et al, 1985.

> D. Walsh, B. Lyon, G. Sager, J. Chang, D. Goldberg, S. Kleiman, T. Lyon, R. Sandberg, & P. Weiss, "Overview of the Sun Network File System," *USENIX Association Conference Proceedings*, pp. 117–124, January 1985.

CHAPTER 10

███████

Terminal Handling

A common type of peripheral device found on 4.4BSD systems is a hardware interface supporting one or more terminals. The most common type of interface is a *terminal multiplexer*, a device that connects multiple, asynchronous RS-232 serial lines, which may be used to connect terminals, modems, printers, and similar devices. Unlike the block storage devices described in Section 6.2 and the network devices to be considered in Chapter 11, terminal devices commonly process data one character at a time. Like other character devices described in Section 6.3, terminal multiplexers are supported by device drivers specific to the actual hardware.

Terminal interfaces interrupt the processor asynchronously to present input, which is independent of process requests to read user input. Data are processed when they are received, and then are stored until a process requests them, thus allowing *type-ahead*. Many terminal ports attach local or remote terminals on which users may log in to the system. When used in this way, terminal input represents the keystrokes of users, and terminal output is printed on the users' screens or printers. We shall deal mostly with this type of terminal line usage in this chapter. Asynchronous serial lines also connect modems for computer-to-computer communications or serial-interface printers. When serial interfaces are used for these purposes, they generally use a subset of the system's terminal-handling capability. Sometimes, they use special processing modules for higher efficiency. We shall discuss alternate terminal modules at the end of this chapter.

The most common type of user session in 4.4BSD uses a pseudo-terminal, or *pty*. The pseudo-terminal driver provides support for a device-pair, termed the *master* and *slave* devices. The slave device provides a process an interface identical to the one described for terminals in this chapter. However, whereas all other devices that provide this interface are supported by a hardware device of some sort, the slave device has, instead, another process manipulating it through the master half of the pseudo-terminal. That is, anything written on the master device is provided to the slave device as input, and anything written on the slave device is presented to the master device as input. The driver for the master device emulates all specific hardware support details described in the rest of this chapter.

10.1   Terminal-Processing Modes

4.4BSD supports several modes of terminal processing. Much of the time, terminals are in *canonical mode* (also commonly referred to as *cooked mode* or *line mode*), in which input characters are echoed by the operating system as they are typed by the user, but are buffered internally until a newline character is received. Only after the receipt of a newline character is the entire line made available to the shell or other process reading from the terminal. If the process attempts to read from the terminal line before a complete line is ready, the process will sleep until a newline character is received, regardless of a partial line already having been received. (The common case where a carriage return behaves like a newline character and causes the line to be made available to the waiting process is implemented by the operating system, and is configurable by the user or process.) In canonical mode, the user may correct typing errors, deleting the most recently typed character with the *erase character*, deleting the most recent word with the *word-erase character*, or deleting the entire current line with the *kill character*. Other special characters generate signals sent to processes associated with the terminal; these signals may abort processing or may suspend it. Additional characters start and stop output, flush output, or prevent special interpretation of the succeeding character. The user can type several lines of input, up to an implementation-defined limit, without waiting for input to be read and then removed from the input queue. The user can specify the special processing characters or can selectively disable them.

Screen editors and programs that communicate with other computers generally run in *noncanonical mode* (also commonly referred to as *raw mode* or *character-at-a-time mode*). In this mode, the system makes each typed character available to be read as input as soon as that character is received. All special-character input processing is disabled, no erase or other line-editing processing is done, and all characters are passed to the program reading from the terminal.

It is possible to configure the terminal in thousands of combinations between these two extremes. For example, a screen editor that wanted to receive user interrupts asynchronously might enable the special characters that generate signals, but otherwise run in noncanonical mode.

In addition to processing input characters, terminal interface drivers must do certain processing on output. Most of the time, this processing is simple: Newline characters are converted to a carriage return plus a line feed, and the interface hardware is programmed to generate appropriate parity bits on output characters. In addition to doing character processing, the terminal output routines must manage flow control, both with the user (using stop and start characters) and with the process. Because terminal devices are slow in comparison with other computer peripherals, a program writing to the terminal may produce output much faster than that output can be sent to the terminal. When a process has filled the terminal output queue, it will be put to sleep; it will be restarted when enough output has drained.

10.2   Line Disciplines

Most of the character processing done for terminal interfaces is independent of the type of hardware device used to connect the terminals to the computer. Therefore, most of this processing is done by common routines in the *tty driver* or terminal handler. Each hardware interface type is supported by a specific device driver. The hardware driver is a device driver like those described in Chapter 6; it is responsible for programming the hardware multiplexer. It is responsible for receiving and transmitting characters, and for handling some of the synchronization with the process doing output. The hardware driver is called by the tty driver to do output; in turn, it calls the tty driver with input characters as they are received. Because serial lines may be used for more than just connection of terminals, a modular interface between the hardware driver and the tty driver allows either part to be replaced with alternate versions. The tty driver interfaces with the rest of the system as a *line discipline*. A line discipline is a processing module used to provide semantics on an asynchronous serial interface (or, as we shall see, on a software emulation of such an interface). It is described by a procedural interface, the *linesw* (line-switch) structure.

The *linesw* structure specifies the entry points of a line discipline, much as the character-device switch *cdevsw* lists the entry points of a character-device driver. The entry points of a line discipline are listed in Table 10.1. Like all device drivers, a terminal driver is divided into the top half, which runs synchronously

Table 10.1 Entry points of a line discipline.

Routine	Called from	Usage
l_open	above	initial entry to discipline
l_close	above	exit from discipline
l_read	above	read from line
l_write	above	write to line
l_ioctl	above	control operations
l_rint	below	received character
l_start	below	completion of transmission
l_modem	below	modem carrier transition

when called to process a system call, and the bottom half, which runs
asynchronously when device interrupts occur. The line discipline provides routines that do common terminal processing for both the top and bottom halves of a
terminal driver.

Device drivers for serial terminal interfaces support the normal set of character-device–driver entry points specified by the character-device switch. Several
of the standard driver entry points (*read*, *write*, and *ioctl*) immediately transfer
control to the line discipline when called. (The standard tty select routine
ttselect() usually is used as the device driver *select* entry in the character-device
switch.) The *open* and *close* routines are similar; the line-discipline open entry is
called when a line first enters a discipline, either at initial open of the line or when
the discipline is changed. Similarly, the discipline close routine is called to exit
from a discipline. All these routines are called from above, in response to a corresponding system call. The remaining line-discipline entries are called by the bottom half of the device driver to report input or status changes detected at interrupt
time. The *l_rint* (receiver interrupt) entry is called with each character received on
a line. The corresponding entry for transmit-complete interrupts is the *l_start* routine, which is called when output operations complete. This entry gives the line
discipline a chance to start additional output operations. For the normal terminal
line discipline, this routine simply calls the driver's output routine to start the next
block of output. Transitions in modem-control lines (see Section 10.7) may be
detected by the hardware driver, in which case the *l_modem* routine is called with
an indication of the new state.

The system includes several different types of line disciplines. Most lines use
the terminal-oriented discipline described in Section 10.3. Other disciplines in the
system support graphics tablets on serial lines and asynchronous serial network
interfaces.

10.3   User Interface

The terminal line discipline used by default on most terminal lines is derived from
a discipline that was present in System V, as modified by the POSIX standard, and
then was modified further to provide reasonable compatibility with previous
Berkeley line disciplines. The base structure used to describe terminal state in
System V was the *termio structure*. The base structure used by POSIX and by
4.4BSD is the *termios structure*.

The standard programmatic interface for control of the terminal line discipline
is the *ioctl* system call. This call changes disciplines, sets and gets values for special processing characters and modes, sets and gets hardware serial line parameters, and performs other control operations. Most *ioctl* operations require one
argument in addition to a file descriptor and the command; the argument is the
address of an integer or structure from which the system gets parameters, or into
which information is placed. Because the POSIX Working Group thought that the
ioctl system call was difficult and undesirable to specify—because of its use of

arguments that varied in size, in type, and in whether they were being read or written—the group members chose to introduce new interfaces for each of the *ioctl* calls that they believed were necessary for application portability. Each of these calls is named with a *tc* prefix. In the 4.4BSD system, each of these calls is translated (possibly after preprocessing) into an *ioctl* call.

The following set of *ioctl* commands apply specifically to the standard terminal line discipline, although all line disciplines must support at least the first two. Other disciplines generally support other *ioctl* commands. This list is not exhaustive, although it presents all the commands that are used commonly.

TIOCGETD TIOCSETD	Get (set) the line discipline for this line.
TIOCGETA TIOCSETA	Get (set) the termios parameters for this line, including line speed, behavioral parameters, and special characters (e.g., erase and kill characters).
TIOCSETAW	Set the termios parameters for this line after waiting for the output buffer to drain (but without discarding any characters from the input buffer).
TIOCSETAF	Set the termios parameters for this line after waiting for the output buffer to drain and discarding any characters from the input buffer.
TIOCFLUSH	Discard all characters from the input and output buffers.
TIOCDRAIN	Wait for the output buffer to drain.
TIOCEXCL TIOCNXCL	Get (release) exclusive use of the line.
TIOCCBRK TIOCSBRK	Clear (set) the terminal hardware BREAK condition for the line.
TIOCCDTR TIOCSDTR	Clear (set) data terminal ready on the line.
TIOCGPGRP TIOCSPGRP	Get (set) the process group associated with this terminal (see Section 10.5).
TIOCOUTQ	Return the number of characters in the terminal's output buffer.
TIOCSTI	Enter characters into the terminal's input buffer as though they were typed by the user.
TIOCNOTTY	Disassociate the current controlling terminal from the process (see Section 10.5).
TIOCSCTTY	Make the terminal the controlling terminal for the process (see Section 10.5).

| TIOCSTART | Start (stop) output on the terminal. |
| TIOCSTOP | |

| TIOCGWINSZ | Get (set) the terminal or window size for the terminal line; the |
| TIOCSWINSZ | window size includes width and height in characters and (optionally, on graphical displays) in pixels. |

10.4 The *tty* Structure

Each terminal hardware driver has a data structure to contain the state of each line that it supports. This structure, the *tty structure* (see Table 10.2), contains state information, the input and output queues, the modes and options set by the *ioctl* operations listed in Section 10.3, and the line-discipline number. The *tty* structure is shared by the hardware driver and the line discipline. The calls to the line discipline all require a *tty* structure as a parameter; the driver locates the correct *tty* according to the minor device number. This structure also contains information about the device driver needed by the line discipline.

The sections of the *tty* structure include:

• State information about the hardware terminal line. The *t_state* field includes line state (open, carrier present, or waiting for carrier) and major file options (e.g., signal-driven I/O). Transient state for flow control and synchronization is also stored here.

Table 10.2 The *tty* structure.

Type	Description
character queues	raw input queue
	canonical input queue
	device output queue
	high/low watermarks
hardware parameters	device number
	start/stop output functions
	set hardware state function
selecting	process selecting for reading
	process selecting for writing
state	termios state
	process group
	session
	terminal column number
	number of rows and columns

- Input and output queues. The hardware driver transmits characters placed in the output queue, *t_outq*. Line disciplines generally use the *t_rawq* and *t_canq* (noncanonical and canonical queues) for input; in line mode, the canonical queue contains full lines, and the noncanonical queue contains any current partial line. In addition, *t_hiwat* and *t_lowat* provide boundaries where processes attempting to write to the terminal will be put to sleep, waiting for the output queue to drain.

- Hardware and software modes and parameters, and special characters. The *t_termios* structure contains the information set by TIOCSETA, TIOCSETAF and TIOCSETAW. Specifically, line speed appears in the *c_ispeed* and *c_ospeed* fields of the *t_termios* structure, control information in the *c_iflag*, *c_oflag*, *c_cflag* and *c_lflag* fields, and special characters (end-of-file, end-of-line, alternate end-of-line, erase, word-erase, kill, reprint, interrupt, quit, suspend, start, stop, escape-next-character, status-interrupt, flush-output and VMIN and VTIME information) in the *c_cc* field.

- Hardware driver information. This information includes *t_oproc* and *t_stop*, the driver procedures that start (stop) transmissions after data are placed in the output queue; *t_param*, the driver procedure that sets the hardware state; and *t_dev*, the device number of the terminal line.

- Terminal line-discipline software state. This state includes the terminal column number and counts for tab and erase processing (*t_column*, *t_rocount* and *t_rocol*), the process group of the terminal (*t_pgrp*), the session associated with the terminal (*t_session*), and information about any processes selecting for input or output (*t_rsel* and *t_wsel*).

- Terminal or window size (*t_winsize*). This information is not used by the kernel, but it is stored here to present consistent and correct information to applications. In addition, 4.4BSD supplies the SIGWINCH signal (derived from Sun Microsystems' SunOS) that can be sent when the size of a window changes. This signal is useful for windowing packages such as X Window System [Scheifler & Gettys, 1986] that allow users to resize windows dynamically; programs such as text editors running in such a window need to be informed that something has changed and that they should recheck the window size.

The *tty* structure is initialized by the hardware terminal driver's open routine and by the line-discipline open routine.

10.5   Process Groups, Sessions, and Terminal Control

The process-control (job-control) facilities described in Section 4.8 depend on the terminal I/O system to control access to the terminal. Each job (a process group that is manipulated as a single entity) is known by a process-group ID.

Each terminal structure contains a pointer to an associated session. When a process creates a new session, that session has no associated terminal. To acquire an associated terminal, the session leader must make an *ioctl* system call using a file descriptor associated with the terminal and specifying the TIOCSCTTY flag. When the *ioctl* succeeds, the session leader is known as the *controlling process*. In addition, each terminal structure contains the process group ID of the foreground process group. When a session leader acquires an associated terminal, the terminal process group is set to the process group of the session leader. The terminal process group may be changed by making an *ioctl* system call using a file descriptor associated with the terminal and specifying the TIOCSPGRP flag. Any process group in the session is permitted to become the foreground process group for the terminal.

Signals that are generated by characters typed at the terminal are sent to all the processes in the terminal's foreground process group. By default, some of those signals cause the process group to stop. The shell creates jobs as process groups, setting the process group ID to be the PID of the first process in the process group. Each time it places a new job in the foreground, the shell sets the terminal process group to the new process group. Thus, the terminal process group is the identifier for the process group that is currently in control of the terminal— that is, for the process group running in the *foreground*. Other process groups may run in the *background*. If a background process attempts to read from the terminal, its process group is sent another signal, which stops the process group. Optionally, background processes that attempt terminal output may be stopped as well. These rules for control of input and output operations apply to only those operations on the controlling terminal.

When carrier is lost for the terminal—for example, at modem disconnect—the session leader of the session associated with the terminal is sent a SIGHUP signal. If the session leader exits, the controlling terminal is revoked, and that invalidates any open file descriptors in the system for the terminal. This revocation ensures that processes holding file descriptors for a terminal cannot still access the terminal after the terminal is acquired by another user. The revocation operates at the vnode layer. It is possible for a process to have a read or write sleeping for some reason—for example, it was in a background process group. Since such a process would have already resolved the file descriptor through the vnode layer, a single read or write by the sleeping process could complete after the *revoke* system call. To avoid this security problem, the system checks a tty generation number when a process wakes up from sleeping on a terminal, and, if the number has changed, restarts the read or write system call.

10.6 C-lists

The terminal I/O system deals with data in blocks of widely varying sizes. Most input and output operations deal with single characters (typed input characters and their output echoes). Input characters are usually aggregated with previous input to form lines of varying sizes. Some output operations involve larger numbers of data, such as screen updates or other command output. The data structures

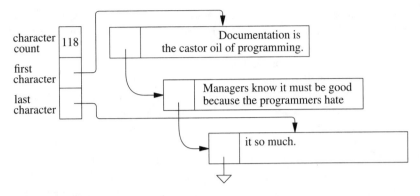

Figure 10.1 A C-list structure.

originally designed for terminal drivers, the character block, *C-block*, and
character list, *C-list*, are still in use in 4.4BSD. Each C-block is a fixed-size buffer
that contains a linkage pointer and space for buffered characters and quoting information. Its size is a power of 2, and it is aligned such that the system can compute
boundaries between blocks by masking off the low-order bits of a pointer. 4.4BSD
uses 64-byte C-blocks, storing 52 characters and an array of quoting flags (1-bit
per character). A queue of input or output characters is described by a C-list,
which contains pointers to the first and final characters, and a count of the number
of characters in the queue (see Fig. 10.1). Both of the pointers point to characters
stored in C-blocks. When a character is removed from a C-list queue, the count is
decremented, and the pointer to the first character is incremented. If the pointer
has advanced beyond the end of the first C-block on the queue, the pointer to the
next C-block is obtained from the forward pointer at the start of the current C-
block. After the forward pointer is updated, the empty C-block is placed on a free
chain. A similar process adds a character to a queue. If there is no room in the
current buffer, another buffer is allocated from the free list, the linkage pointer of
the last buffer is set to point at the new buffer, and the tail pointer is set to the first
storage location of the new buffer. The character is stored where indicated by the
tail pointer, the tail pointer is incremented, and the character count is incremented.
A set of utility routines manipulates C-lists: *getc*() removes the next character
from a C-list and returns that character; *putc*() adds a character to the end of a C-
list. The *getc*() routine takes an integer as an argument, and the *putc*() routine
returns an integer. The lower 8 bits of this value are the actual character. The
upper bits are used to provide quoting and other information. Groups of characters may be added to or removed from C-lists with *b_to_q*() and *q_to_b*(), respectively, in which case no additional information (e.g., quoting information) can be
specified or returned. The terminal driver also requires the ability to remove a
character from the end of a queue with *unputc*(), to examine characters in the
queue with *nextc*(), and to concatenate queues with *catq*().

When UNIX was developed on computers with small address spaces, the design of buffers for the use of terminal drivers was a challenge. The C-list and C-block provided an elegant solution to the problem of storing arbitrary-length queues of data for terminal input and output queues when the latter were designed for machines with small memories. On modern machines that have far larger address spaces, it would be better to use a data structure that uses less CPU time per character at a cost of reduced space efficiency. 4.4BSD still uses the original C-list data structure because of the high labor cost of converting to a new data structure; a change to the queue structure would require changes to all the line disciplines and to all the terminal device drivers, which would be a substantial amount of work. The developers could just change the implementations of the interface routines, but the routines would still be called once per character unless the actual interface was changed, and changing the interface would require changing the drivers.

10.7   RS-232 and Modem Control

Most terminals and modems are connected via asynchronous RS-232 serial ports. This type of connection supports several lines, in addition to those that transmit and receive data. The system typically supports only a few of these lines. The most commonly used lines are those showing that the equipment on each end is ready for data transfer. The RS-232 electrical specification is asymmetrical: Each line is driven by one of the two devices connected and is sampled by the other device. Thus, one end in any normal connection must be wired as data-terminal equipment (DTE), such as a terminal, and the other as data-communications equipment (DCE), such as a modem. Note that *terminal* in DTE means *endpoint*: A terminal on which people type is a DTE, and a computer also is a DTE. The data-terminal ready (DTR) line is the output of the DTE end that serves as a *ready* indicator. In the other direction, the data-carrier detect (DCD) line indicates that the DCE device is ready for data transfer. Historically, VAX terminal interfaces were all wired as DTE (they may be connected directly to modems, or connected to local terminals with null modem cables). The terminology used in the 4.4BSD terminal drivers and commands reflects this orientation, even though many computers incorrectly use the opposite convention.

When terminal devices are opened, the DTR output is asserted so that the connected modem or other equipment may begin operation. If *modem control* is supported on a line, the open does not complete unless the O_NONBLOCK option was specified or the CLOCAL control flag is set for the line, and no data are transferred until the DCD input *carrier* is detected or the CLOCAL flag is set. Thus, an open on a line connected to a modem will block until a connection is made; the connection commonly occurs when a call is received from a remote modem. Data then can be transferred for as long as carrier remains on. If the modem loses the connection, the DCD line is turned off, and subsequent reads and writes fail.

Ports that are used with local terminals or other DTE equipment are connected with a *null-modem* cable that connects DTR on each end to DCD on the other end. Alternatively, the DTR output on the host port can be *looped back* to the DCD input. If the cable or device does not support modem control, the system will ignore the state of the modem control signals when the CLOCAL control flag is set for the line, Finally, some drivers may be configured to ignore modem-control inputs.

10.8 Terminal Operations

Now that we have examined the overall structure of the terminal I/O system and have described that system's data structures, as well as the hardware that the system controls, we continue with a description of the terminal I/O system operation. We shall examine the operation of a generalized terminal hardware device driver and the usual terminal line discipline. We shall not cover the autoconfiguration routines present in each driver; they function in the same way as do those described in Section 14.4.

Open

Each time that the special file for a terminal-character device is opened, the hardware driver's open routine is called. The open routine checks that the requested device was configured into the system and was located during autoconfiguration, then initializes the *tty* structure. If the device was not yet open, the default modes and line speed are set. The *tty* state is set to TS_WOPEN, waiting for open. Then, if the device supports modem-control lines, the open routine enables the DTR output line. If the CLOCAL control flag is not set for the terminal and the *open* call did not specify the O_NONBLOCK flag, the open routine blocks awaiting assertion of the DCD input line. Some drivers support *device flags* to override modem control; these flags are set in the system-configuration file and are stored in the driver data structures. If the bit corresponding to a terminal line number is set in a device's flags, modem-control lines are ignored on input. When a carrier signal is detected on the line, the TS_CARR_ON bit is set in the terminal state. The driver then passes control to the initial (or current) line discipline through its open entry.

The default line discipline when a device is first opened is the *termios* terminal-driver discipline. If the line was not already open, the terminal-size information for the line is set to zero, indicating an unknown size. The line is then marked as open (state bit TS_OPEN).

Output Line Discipline

After a line has been opened, a write on the resulting file descriptor produces output to be transmitted on the terminal line. Writes to character devices result in calls to the device write entry, *d_write*, with a device number, a *uio* structure describing the data to be written, and a flag specifying whether the I/O is nonblocking. Terminal hardware drivers use the device number to locate the correct *tty* structure, then call the line discipline *l_write* entry with the *tty* structure and *uio* structure as parameters.

The line-discipline write routine does most of the work of output translation and flow control. It is responsible for copying data into the kernel from the user process calling the routine and for placing the translated data onto the terminal's output queue for the hardware driver. The terminal-driver write routine, *ttwrite*(), first checks that the terminal line still has carrier asserted (or that modem control is being ignored). If carrier is significant and not asserted, the process will be put to sleep awaiting carrier if the terminal has not yet been opened, or an error will be returned. If carrier is being ignored or is asserted, *ttwrite*() then checks whether the current process is allowed to write to the terminal at this time. The user may set a *tty* option to allow only the foreground process (see Section 10.5) to do output. If this option is set, and if the terminal line is the controlling terminal for the process, then the process should do output immediately only if it is in the foreground process group (i.e., if the process groups of the process and of the terminal are the same). If the process is not in the foreground process group, and a SIGTTOU signal would cause the process to be suspended, a SIGTTOU signal is sent to the process group of the process. In this case, the write will be attempted again when the user moves the process group to the foreground. If the process is in the foreground process group, or a SIGTTOU signal would not suspend the process, the write proceeds as usual.

When *ttwrite*() has confirmed that the write is permitted, it enters a loop that copies the data to be written into the kernel, checks for any output translation that is required, and places the data on the output queue for the terminal. It prevents the queue from becoming overfull by blocking if the queue fills before all characters have been processed. The limit on the queue size, the *high watermark*, is dependent on the output line speed; the difference between the *low watermark* and *high watermark* is approximately 1 second's worth of output. When forced to wait for output to drain before proceeding, *ttwrite*() sets a flag in the *tty* structure

---

Figure 10.2 Pseudocode for checking the output queue in a line discipline.

```
        struct tty *tp;

        ttstart(tp);
        s = spltty();
        if (tp->t_outq.c_cc > high-water-mark) {
            tp->t_state |= TS_ASLEEP;
            ttysleep(&tp->t_outq);
        }
        splx(s);
```

state, TS_ASLEEP, so that the transmit-complete interrupt handler will awaken it when the queue is reduced to the *low watermark*. The check of the queue size and subsequent sleep must be ordered such that any interrupt is guaranteed to occur after the sleep. See Fig. 10.2 for an example, presuming a uniprocessor machine.

Once errors, permissions, and flow control have been checked, *ttwrite*() copies the user's data into a local buffer in chunks of at most 100 characters using *uiomove*(). (A value of 100 is used because the buffer is stored on the stack, and so cannot be large.) When the terminal driver is configured in noncanonical mode, no per-character translations are done, and the entire buffer is processed at once. In canonical mode, the terminal driver locates groups of characters requiring no translation by scanning through the output string, looking up each character in turn in a table that marks characters that might need translation (e.g., newline), or characters that need expansion (e.g., tabs). Each group of characters that requires no special processing is placed into the output queue using *b_to_q*(). Trailing special characters are output with *ttyoutput*(). In either case, *ttwrite*() must check that enough C-list blocks are available; if they are not, it waits for a short time (by sleeping on *lbolt* for up to 1 second), then retries.

The routine that does output with translation is *ttyoutput*(), which accepts a single character, processes that character as necessary, and places the result on the output queue. The following translations may be done, depending on the terminal mode:

- Tabs may be expanded to spaces.

- Newlines may be replaced with a carriage return plus a line feed.

As soon as data are placed on the output queue of a *tty*, *ttstart*() is called to initiate output. Unless output is already in progress or has been suspended by receipt of a *stop* character, *ttstart*() calls the hardware-driver start routine specified in the *tty*'s *t_oproc* field. Once all the data have been processed and have been placed into the output queue, *ttwrite*() returns an indication that the *write* completed successfully, and the actual serial character transmission is managed asynchronously by the device driver.

Output Top Half

The device driver handles the hardware-specific operation of character transmission, as well as synchronization and flow control for output. The structure of the *start*() routine varies little from one driver to another. There are two general classes of output mechanisms, depending on the type of hardware device. The first class operates on devices that are capable of direct-memory-access (DMA) output, which can fetch the data directly from the *C-list* block. For this class of device, the device fetches the data from main memory, transmits each of the characters in turn, and interrupts the CPU when the transmission is complete. Because the hardware fetches data directly from main memory, there may be additional requirements on where the *C-lists* can be located in physical memory.

The other extreme for terminal interfaces are those that do *programmed I/O*, potentially on a character-by-character basis. One or more characters are loaded into the device's output-character register for transmission. The CPU must then wait for the transmit-complete interrupt before sending more characters. Because of the many interrupts generated in this mode of operation, several variants have been developed to minimize the overhead of terminal I/O.

One approach is to compute in advance as much as possible of the information needed at interrupt time. (Generally, the information needed is a pointer to the next character to be transmitted, the number of characters to be transmitted, and the address of the hardware device register that will receive the next character.) This strategy is known as *pseudo-DMA*; the precomputed information is stored in a *pdma* structure. A small assembly-language routine receives each hardware transmit-complete interrupt, transmits the next character, and returns. When there are no characters left to transmit, it calls a C-language interrupt routine with an indication of the line that completed transmission. The normal driver thus has the illusion of DMA output, because it is not called until the entire block of characters has been transmitted.

Another approach is found on hardware that supports periodic polling interrupts instead of per-character interrupts. Usually, the period is settable based on the line speed. A final variation is found in hardware that can buffer several characters at a time in a *silo* and that will interrupt only when the silo has been emptied completely. In addition, some hardware devices are capable of both DMA and a variant of character-at-a-time I/O, and can be programmed by the operating system to operate in either mode.

After an output operation is started, the terminal state is marked with TS_BUSY so that new transmissions will not be attempted until the current one completes.

Output Bottom Half

When transmission of a block of characters has been completed, the hardware multiplexer interrupts the CPU; the transmit interrupt routine is then called with the unit number of the device. Usually, the device has a register that the driver can read to determine which of the device's lines have completed transmit operations. For each line that has finished output, the interrupt routine clears the TS_BUSY flag. The characters that have been transmitted were removed from the *C-list* when copied to a local buffer by the device driver using *getc*( ) or *q_to_b*( ); or if they were not, the driver removes them from the output queue using *ndflush*( ). These steps complete one section of output.

The line-discipline start routine is called to start the next operation; as noted, this routine generally does nothing but call the driver start routine specified in the terminal *t_oproc* field. The start routine now checks to see whether the output queue has been reduced to the low watermark, and, if it has been, whether the top half is waiting for space in the output queue. If the TS_ASLEEP flag is set, the output process is awakened. In addition, *selwakeup*( ) is called, and, if a process is recorded in *t_wsel* as selecting for output, that process is notified. Then, if the output queue is not empty, the next operation is started as before.

Input Bottom Half

Unlike output, terminal input is not initiated by a system call, but rather arrives asynchronously when the terminal line receives characters from the keyboard or other input device. Thus, the input processing in the terminal system occurs mostly at interrupt time. Most hardware multiplexers interrupt each time that a character is received on any line. They usually provide a silo that stores received characters, along with the line number on which the characters were received and any associated status information, until the device handler retrieves the characters. Use of the silo prevents characters from being lost if the CPU has not processed a received-character interrupt by the time that the next character arrives. On many devices, the system can avoid per-character interrupts by programming the device to interrupt only after the silo is partially or completely full. However, the driver must then check the device periodically so that characters do not stagnate in the silo if additional input does not trigger an interrupt. If the device can also be programmed to interrupt a short time after the first character enters the silo, regardless of additional characters arriving, these periodic checks of the device by the driver can be avoided. Characters cannot be allowed to stagnate because input flow-control characters must be processed without much delay, and users will notice any significant delay in character echo as well. The drivers in 4.4BSD for devices with such timers always use the silo interrupts. Other terminal drivers use per-character interrupts until the input rate is high enough to warrant the use of the silo alarm and a periodic scan of the silo.

When a device receiver interrupt occurs, or when a timer routine detects input, the receiver-interrupt routine reads each character from the input silo, along with the latter's line number and status information. Normal characters are passed as input to the terminal line discipline for the receiving *tty* through the latter's *l_rint* entry:

```
(*linesw[tp->t_line].l_rint)(input-character, tp);
```

The input character is passed to the *l_rint* routine as an integer. The bottom 8 bits of the integer are the actual character. Characters received with hardware-detected parity errors, break characters, or framing errors have flags set in the upper bits of the integer to indicate these conditions.

The receiver-interrupt (*l_rint*) routine for the normal terminal line discipline is *ttyinput()*. When a *break* condition is detected (a longer-than-normal character with only 0 bits), it is ignored, or an interrupt character or a null is passed to the process, depending on the terminal mode. The interpretation of terminal input described in Section 10.1 is done here. Input characters are echoed if desired. In noncanonical mode, characters are placed into the raw input queue without interpretation. Otherwise, most of the work done by *ttyinput()* is to check for characters with special meanings and to take the requested actions. Other characters are placed into the raw queue. In canonical mode, if the received character is a carriage return or another character that causes the current line to be made available to the program reading the terminal, the contents of the raw queue are added to the canonicalized queue and *ttwakeup()* is called to notify any process waiting for input. In noncanonical mode, *ttwakeup*() is called when each character is processed. It will awaken any process sleeping on the raw queue awaiting input for a *read* and will notify processes selecting for input. If the terminal has been set for signal-driven I/O using *fcntl* and the FASYNC flag, a SIGIO signal is sent to the process group controlling the terminal.

Ttyinput() must also check that the input queue does not become too large, exhausting the supply of C-list blocks; input characters are discarded when the limit (1024 characters) is reached. If the IXOFF termios flag is set, end-to-end flow control is invoked when the queue reaches half full by output of a stop character (normally XOFF or control-S).

Up to this point, all processing is asynchronous, and occurs independent of whether a *read* call is pending on the terminal device. In this way, type-ahead is allowed to the limit of the input queues.

Input Top Half

Eventually, a *read* call is made on the file descriptor for the terminal device. Like all calls to read from a character-special device, this one results in a call to the device driver's *d_read* entry with a device number, a *uio* structure describing the data to be read, and a flag specifying whether the I/O is nonblocking. Terminal device drivers use the device number to locate the *tty* structure for the device, then call the line discipline *l_read* entry to process the system call.

The *l_read* entry for the terminal driver is *ttread*(). Like *ttwrite*(), *ttread*() first checks that the terminal line still has carrier (and that carrier is significant); if not, it goes to sleep or returns an error. It then checks to see whether the process is part of the session and the process group currently associated with the terminal. If the process is not a member of the session currently associated with the terminal, if any, or is a member of the current process group, the read proceeds. Otherwise, if a SIGTTIN would suspend the process, a SIGTTIN is sent to that process group. In this case, the read will be attempted again when the user moves the process group to the foreground. Otherwise, an error is returned. Finally, *ttread*() checks for data in the appropriate queue (the canonical queue in canonical mode, the raw queue in noncanonical mode). If no data are present, *ttread*() returns the error EWOULDBLOCK if the terminal is using nonblocking I/O; otherwise, it sleeps on the address of the raw queue. When *ttread*() is awakened, it restarts processing from the beginning because the terminal state or process group might have changed while it was asleep.

When characters are present in the queue for which *ttread*() is waiting, they are removed from the queue one at a time with *getc*() and are copied out to the user's buffer with *ureadc*(). In canonical mode, certain characters receive special processing as they are removed from the queue: The delayed-suspension character causes the current process group to be stopped with signal SIGTSTP, and the end-of-file character terminates the read without being passed back to the user program. If there was no previous character, the end-of-file character results in the read returning zero characters, and that is interpreted by user programs as indicating end-of-file. However, most special processing of input characters is done when the character is entered into the queue. For example, translating carriage returns to newlines based on the ICRNL flag must be done when the character is first received because the newline character wakes up waiting processes in canonical mode. In noncanonical mode, the characters are not examined as they are processed.

Characters are processed and returned to the user until the character count in the *uio* structure reaches zero, the queue is exhausted, or, if in canonical mode, a line terminator is reached. When the *read*() call returns, the returned character count will be the amount by which the requested count was decremented as characters were processed.

After the read completes, if terminal output was blocked by a stop character being sent because the queue was filling up, and the queue is now less than 20-percent full, a start character (normally XON, control-Q) is sent.

The *stop* Routine

Character output on terminal devices is done in blocks as large as possible, for efficiency. However, there are two events that should cause a pending output operation to be stopped. The first event is the receipt of a stop character, which should stop output as quickly as possible; sometimes, the device receiving output is a printer or other output device with a limited buffer size. The other event that stops output is the receipt of a special character that causes output to be discarded, possibly because of a signal. In either case, the terminal line discipline calls the character device driver's *d_stop* entry to stop any current output operation. Two parameters are provided: a *tty* structure and a flag that indicates whether output is to be flushed or suspended. Theoretically, if output is flushed, the terminal discipline removes all the data in the output queue after calling the device stop routine. More practically, the flag is ignored by most current device drivers.

The implementation of the *d_stop* routine is hardware dependent. Different drivers stop output by disabling the transmitter, thus suspending output, or by changing the current character count to zero. Drivers using pseudo-DMA may change the limit on the current block of characters so that the pseudo-DMA routine will call the transmit-complete interrupt routine after the current character is transmitted. Most drivers set a flag in the *tty* state, TS_FLUSH, when a stop is to flush data, and the aborted output operation will cause an interrupt. When the transmit-complete interrupt routine runs, it checks the TS_FLUSH flag, and avoids updating the output-queue character count (the queue has probably already been flushed by the time the interrupt occurs). If output is to be stopped but not flushed, the TS_TTSTOP flag is set in the *tty* state; the driver must stop output such that it may be resumed from the current position.

The *ioctl* Routine

Section 10.3 described the user interface to terminal drivers and line disciplines, most of which is accessed via the *ioctl* system call. Most of these calls manipulate software options in the terminal line discipline; some of them also affect the

```
error = (*linesw[tp->t_line].l_ioctl)(tp, cmd, data, flag);
if (error >= 0)
    return (error);
error = ttioctl(tp, cmd, data, flag);
if (error >= 0)
    return (error);
switch (cmd) {
case TIOCSBRK:          /* hardware specific commands */
    ...
    return (0);
case TIOCCBRK:
    ...
    return (0);
default:
    return (ENOTTY);
}
```

Figure 10.3 Handling of an error return from a line discipline.

operation of the asynchronous serial port hardware. In particular, the hardware line speed, word size, and parity are derived from these settings. So, *ioctl* calls are processed both by the current line discipline and by the hardware driver.

The device driver *d_ioctl* routine is called with a device number, an *ioctl* command, and a pointer to a data buffer when an *ioctl* is done on a character-special file, among other arguments. Like the read and write routines, most terminal-driver *ioctl* routines locate the *tty* structure for the device, then pass control to the line discipline. The line-discipline *ioctl* routine does discipline-specific actions, including change of line discipline. If the line-discipline routine fails, the driver will immediately return an error, as shown in Fig. 10.3. Otherwise, the driver will then call the *ttioctl*() routine that does most common terminal processing, including changing terminal parameters. If *ttioctl*() fails, the driver will immediately return an error. Otherwise, some drivers implement additional *ioctl* commands that do hardware specific processing—for example, manipulating modem-control outputs. These commands are not recognized by the line discipline, or by common terminal processing, and thus must be handled by the driver. The *ioctl* routine returns an error number if an error is detected, or returns zero if the command has been processed successfully. The *errno* variable is set to ENOTTY if the command is not recognized.

Modem Transitions

The way in which the system uses modem-control lines on terminal lines was introduced in Section 10.7. Most terminal multiplexers support at least the set of modem-control lines used by 4.4BSD; those that do not act instead as though carrier were always asserted. When a device is opened, the DTR output is enabled, and then the state of the carrier input is checked. If the state of the carrier input changes later, this change must be detected and processed by the driver. Some devices have a separate interrupt that reports changes in modem-control status; others report such changes along with other status information with received characters. Some devices do not interrupt when modem-control lines change, and the driver must check their status periodically. When a change is detected, the line discipline is notified by a call to its *l_modem* routine with the new state of the carrier input.

The normal terminal-driver modem routine, *ttymodem*( ), maintains the state of the TS_CARR_ON flag in the *tty* structure and processes corresponding state changes. When carrier establishment is detected, a wakeup is issued for any process waiting for an open to complete. When carrier drops on an open line, the leader of the session associated with the terminal (if any) is sent a hangup signal, SIGHUP, and the terminal queues are flushed. The return value of *ttymodem*( ) indicates whether the driver should maintain its DTR output. If the value is zero, DTR should be turned off. *Ttymodem*( ) also implements an obscure terminal option to use the carrier line for flow-control handshaking, stopping output when carrier drops and resuming when it returns.

Closing of Terminal Devices

When the final reference to a terminal device is closed, or the *revoke* system call is made on the device, the device-driver close routine is called. Both the line discipline and the hardware driver may need to close down gracefully. The device-driver routine first calls the line-discipline close routine. The standard line-discipline close entry, *ttylclose*( ), waits for any pending output to drain (if the terminal was not opened with the O_NONBLOCK flag set and the carrier is still on), then flushes the input and output queues. (Note that the close may be interrupted by a signal while waiting for output to complete.) The hardware driver may clear any pending operations, such as transmission of a break. If the state bit TS_HUPCLS has been set with the TIOCHPCL *ioctl*, DTR is disabled to hang up the line. Finally, the device-driver routine calls *ttyclose*( ), which flushes all the queues, increments the generation number so that pending reads and writes can detect reuse of the terminal, and clears the terminal state.

10.9   Other Line Disciplines

We have examined the operation of the terminal I/O system using the standard terminal-oriented line-discipline routines. For completeness, we now describe two other line disciplines in the system. Note that the preceding discussion of the operation of the terminal multiplexer drivers applies when these disciplines are used, as well as when the terminal-oriented disciplines are used.

Serial Line IP Discipline

The *serial line IP* (*SLIP*) line discipline is used by networking software to encapsulate and transfer Internet Protocol (IP) datagrams over asynchronous serial lines [Romkey, 1988]. (See Chapter 13 for information about IP.) The **slattach** program opens a serial line, sets the line's speed, and enters the SLIP line discipline. The SLIP line discipline's open routine associates the terminal line with a preconfigured network interface and prepares to send and receive network packets. Once the interface's network address is set with the **ifconfig** program, the network will route packets through the SLIP line to the system to which it connects. Packets are framed with a simple scheme; a framing character (0300 octal) separates packets. Framing characters that occur within packets are quoted with an escape character (0333 octal) and are transposed (to 0334 octal). Escape characters within the packet are escaped and transposed (to 0335 octal).

The output path is started every time a packet is output to the SLIP interface. Packets are enqueued on one of two queues: one for interactive traffic and one for other traffic. Interactive traffic takes precedence over other traffic. The SLIP discipline places the framing character and the data of the next packet onto the output queue of the *tty*, escaping the framing and the escape characters as needed, and in some cases compressing packet headers. It then starts transmission by calling *ttstart*( ), which in turn calls the device's start routine referenced in the *tty t_oproc* field. It may place multiple packets onto the output queue before returning, as long as the system is not running short of C-list blocks. However, it stops moving packets into the *tty* output queue when the character count has reached a fairly low limit (60 bytes), so that future interactive traffic is not blocked by noninteractive traffic already in the output queue. When transmission completes, the device driver calls the SLIP start routine, which continues to place data onto the output queue until all packets have been sent or the queue hits the limit again.

When characters are received on a line that is using the SLIP discipline, the escaped characters are translated and data characters are placed into a network buffer. When a framing character ends the packet, the packet header is uncompressed if necessary, the packet is presented to the network protocol, and the buffer is reinitialized.

The SLIP discipline allows moderate-speed network connections to machines without specialized high-speed network hardware. It has a simple design, but has several limitations. A newer protocol, the *point-to-point protocol* (or *PPP*), addresses some of the limitations [Simpson, 1994]. However, PPP is not included in 4.4BSD.

Graphics Tablet Discipline

The *tablet line discipline* connects graphic devices, such as digitizing tablets, to the system using a serial line. Once the discipline is entered, it receives graphics data from the device continuously, and allows the application program to poll for the most recent information by reading from the line. The format of the information returned is dependent on that provided by the device; several different formats are supported.

Exercises

10.1   What are the two general modes of terminal input? Which mode is most commonly in use when users converse with an interactive screen editor?

10.2   Explain why there are two character queues for dealing with terminal input. Describe the use of each.

10.3   What do we mean when we say that modem control is supported on a terminal line? How are terminal lines of this sort typically used?

10.4   What signal is sent to what process associated with a terminal if a user disconnects the modem line in the middle of a session?

10.5   How is the high watermark on a terminal's output queue determined?

10.6   Describe two methods to reduce the overhead of a hardware device that transmits a single character at a time. List the hardware requirements of each.

*10.7   Consider a facility that allowed a tutor on one terminal to monitor and assist students working on other terminals. Everything the students typed would be transmitted both to the system as input and to the tutor's terminal as output. Everything the tutor typed would be directed to the students' terminals as input. Describe how this facility might be implemented with a special-purpose line discipline. Describe further useful generalizations of this facility.

*10.8   The terminal line discipline supports logical erasure of input text when characters, words, and lines are erased. Remembering that other system activities continue while a user types an input line, explain what complications must be considered in the implementation of this feature. Name three exceptional cases, and describe their effects on the implementation.

**10.9   What are the advantages of the use of line disciplines by device drivers for terminal multiplexers? What are the limitations? Propose an alternative approach to the current structure of the terminal I/O system.

**10.10 Propose another buffering scheme to replace C-lists.

References

Romkey, 1988.
    J. Romkey, "A Nonstandard for Transmission of IP Datagrams Over Serial Lines: SLIP," RFC 1055, available by anonymous FTP from ds.internic.net, June 1988.
Scheifler & Gettys, 1986.
    R. W. Scheifler & J. Gettys, "The X Window System," *ACM Transactions on Graphics*, vol. 5, no. 2, pp. 79–109, April 1986.
Simpson, 1994.
    W. Simpson, "The Point-to-Point Protocol (PPP)," RFC 1661, available by anonymous FTP from ds.internic.net, July 1994.

PART 4

Interprocess Communication

CHAPTER 11

Interprocess Communication

Historically, UNIX systems were weak in the area of *interprocess communication.* Before the release of 4.2BSD, the only standard interprocess-communication facility found in UNIX was the *pipe*—a reliable, flow-controlled, byte stream that could be established only between two related processes on the same machine. The limiting nature of pipes inspired many experimental facilities, such as the Rand Corporation UNIX system's *ports* [Sunshine, 1977], *multiplexed files* that were an experimental part of Version 7 UNIX [UPMV7, 1983], and the Accent IPC facility developed at Carnegie-Mellon University [Rashid, 1980]. Some communication facilities were developed for use in application-specific versions of UNIX—for example, the shared memory, semaphores, and message queues that were part of the *Columbus UNIX System.* The requirements of the DARPA research community, which drove much of the design and development of 4.2BSD, resulted in a significant effort to address the lack of a comprehensive set of interprocess-communication facilities in UNIX. The facilities designed and implemented in 4.2BSD were refined following that version's release. As a result, 4.4BSD provides a rich set of interprocess-communication facilities intended to support the construction of *distributed programs* built on top of communications primitives.

The interprocess-communication facilities are described in this chapter. The layer of software that implements these facilities is strongly intertwined with the network subsystem. The architecture of the network system is described in Chapter 12, and the networking protocols themselves are examined in Chapter 13. You will find it easiest to understand the material in these three chapters if you first read Chapter 11, and then Chapters 12 and 13. At the end of Chapter 13 is a section devoted to tying everything together.

11.1   Interprocess-Communication Model

There were several goals in the design of the interprocess-communication enhancements to UNIX. The most immediate need was to provide access to communication networks such as the DARPA Internet [Cerf, 1978]. Previous work in providing network access had focused on the implementation of the network protocols, exporting the transport facilities to applications via special-purpose—and often awkward—character-device interfaces [D. Cohen, 1977; Gurwitz, 1981]. As a result, each new network implementation resulted in a different application interface, requiring most existing programs to be altered significantly or rewritten completely. The 4.2BSD interprocess-communication facilities were intended to provide a sufficiently general interface to allow network-based applications to be constructed independently of the underlying communication facilities.

The second goal was to allow multiprocess programs, such as distributed databases, to be implemented. The UNIX *pipe* requires all communicating processes to be derived from a common parent process. The use of pipes forced systems such as the Ingres database system to be designed with a somewhat contorted structure [Kalash et al, 1986]. New communication facilities were needed to support communication between unrelated processes residing locally on a single host computer and residing remotely on multiple host machines.

Finally, the emerging networking and workstation technology required that the new communication facilities allow construction of local-area network services, such as file servers. The intent was to provide facilities that could be used easily in supporting resource sharing in a distributed environment; the intention was not to build a distributed UNIX system.

The interprocess-communication facilities were designed to support the following:

- **Transparency**: Communication between processes should not depend on whether the processes are on the same machine.

- **Efficiency**: The applicability of any interprocess-communication facility is limited by the performance of the facility. In 4.2BSD, interprocess communication was layered on top of network communication for performance reasons. The alternative is to provide network communication as a service accessed via the interprocess-communication facilities. Although this design is more modular, it would have required that network-communication facilities be accessed through one or more server processes. At the time that 4.2BSD was designed, the prevalent hardware on which the system ran had such a slow process context-switch time that the performance of the communication facilities in a distributed environment would have been seriously constrained. Thus, the most efficient implementation of interprocess-communication facilities layers interprocess communication on top of network-communication facilities. Although current hardware is much faster than was the hardware used at the time of the initial design, the desire for maximal network performance is no less.

• **Compatibility**: Existing naive processes should be usable in a distributed environment without change. A *naive process* is characterized as a process that performs its work by reading from the standard input file and writing to the standard output file. A *sophisticated process* is one that manages other processes or uses knowledge about specific devices, such as a terminal. A major reason why UNIX has been successful is the operating system's support for modularity by naive processes that act as byte-stream filters. Although sophisticated applications such as shells and screen editors exist, they are far outnumbered by the collection of naive application programs.

While designing the interprocess-communication facilities, the developers identified the following requirements to support these goals, and they developed a unifying concept for each:

• The system must support communication networks that use different sets of protocols, different naming conventions, different hardware, and so on. The notion of a *communication domain* was defined for these reasons. A communication domain embodies the standard semantics of communication and naming. Different networks almost always have different standards for specifying the name of a communication endpoint. Names may also vary in their properties. In one network, a name may be a fixed address for a communication endpoint, whereas in another it may be used to locate a process that can move between locations. The semantics of communication can include the cost associated with the reliable transport of data, the support for multicast transmissions, the ability to pass access rights or capabilities, and so on. By distinguishing communication properties, applications can select a domain appropriate to their needs.

• A unified abstraction for an endpoint of communication is needed that can be manipulated with a file descriptor. The *socket* is the abstract object from which messages are sent and received. Sockets are created within a communication domain, just as files are created within a filesystem. Unlike files, however, sockets exist only as long as they are referenced.

• The semantic aspects of communication must be made available to applications in a controlled and uniform way. That is, applications must be able to request styles of communication, such as virtual circuits or datagrams, but these styles must be provided consistently across all communication domains. All sockets are *typed* according to their communication semantics. Types are defined by the subset of semantic properties that a socket supports. These properties are

1. In-order delivery of data

2. Unduplicated delivery of data

3. Reliable delivery of data

4. Preservation of message boundaries

5. Support for out-of-band messages

6. Connection-oriented communication

Pipes have the first three properties, but not the fourth. An out-of-band message is one that is delivered to the receiver outside the normal stream of incoming,
in-band data. It usually is associated with an urgent or exceptional condition. A
connection is a mechanism that protocols use to avoid having to transmit the identity of the sending socket with each packet of data. Instead, the identity of each
endpoint of communication is exchanged before transmission of any data, and is
maintained at each end so that it can be presented at any time. On the other hand,
connectionless communications require a source and destination address associated with each transmission. A *datagram socket* models potentially unreliable,
connectionless packet communication; a *stream socket* models a reliable connection-based byte stream that may support out-of-band data transmission; and a
sequenced packet socket models sequenced, reliable, unduplicated connection-
based communication that preserves message boundaries. In the latter case, a
message is also known as a *record*. Other types of sockets are desirable and can
be added.

• Processes must be able to locate endpoints of communication so that they can
  rendezvous without being related; hence, sockets can be *named*. A socket's
  name is meaningfully interpreted only within the context of the communication
  domain in which the socket is created. The names used by most applications are
  human-readable strings. However, the name for a socket that is used within a
  communication domain is usually a low-level *address*. Rather than placing
  name-to-address translation functions in the kernel, 4.4BSD provides functions
  for application programs to use in translating names to addresses. In the remainder of this chapter, we refer to the name of a socket as an *address*.

Use of Sockets

Use of sockets is reasonably straightforward. First, a socket must be created with
the *socket* system call:

```
s = socket(domain, type, protocol);
int s, domain, type, protocol;
```

The type of socket is selected according to the characteristic properties required by
the application. For example, if reliable communication is required, a stream
socket might be selected. The *type* parameter is a socket type defined in a system
header file. The *domain* parameter specifies the communication domain (or *protocol family*, see Section 11.4) in which the socket should be created; this domain is
dependent on the environment in which the application is working. The most common domain for intermachine communication is the Internet communication
domain because of the many hosts that support the Internet communication
protocols. The final parameter, the *protocol*, can be used to indicate a specific

communication protocol for use in supporting the socket's operation. Protocols are indicated by well-known (standard) constants specific to each communication domain. If the protocol is specified as zero, the system picks an appropriate protocol. The *socket* system call returns a file descriptor (a small integer number; see Section 6.4) that is then used in later socket operations. The *socket* call is similar to *open*, except that it creates a new instance of an object of the specified type, whereas *open* creates a new reference to an existing object, such as a file or device.

After a socket has been created, the next step depends on the type of socket being used. The most commonly used type of socket requires a *connection* before it can be used. Creation of a connection between two sockets usually requires that each socket have an address bound to it. Applications may explicitly specify a socket's address or may permit the system to assign one. A socket's address is normally immutable, although some protocols refine an under-specified address as needed. Socket addresses may be reused if the communication domain permits, although domains normally ensure that a socket address is unique on each host, so that the association between two sockets is unique within the communication domain. The address to be bound to a socket must be formulated in a *socket address structure*. Applications find addresses of well-known services by looking up their names in a database. The format of addresses can vary among domains; to permit a wide variety of different formats, the system treats addresses as variable-length byte arrays, which are prefixed with a length and a tag that identifies their format. The call to bind an address to a socket is

```
error = bind(s, addr, addrlen);
int error, s;
struct sockaddr *addr;
int addrlen;
```

where *s* is the descriptor returned from a previous *socket* system call.

For several reasons, binding a name to a socket was separated from creating a socket. First, sockets are potentially useful without names. If all sockets had to be named, users would be forced to devise meaningless names without reason. Second, in some communication domains, it may be necessary to supply additional, nonstandard information to the system before binding a name to a socket— for example, the "type of service" required when a socket is used. If a socket's name had to be specified at the time that the socket was created, supplying this information would not be possible without further complicating the interface.

In connection-based communication, the process that initiates a connection normally is termed a *client process*, whereas the process that receives, or responds to, a connection is termed a *server process*. In the *client process*, a connection is initiated with a *connect* system call:

```
error = connect(s, serveraddr, serveraddrlen);
int error, s;
struct sockaddr *serveraddr;
int serveraddrlen;
```

In the *server process*, the socket is first marked to specify that incoming connections are to be accepted on it:

```
error = listen(s, backlog);
int error, s, backlog;
```

Connections are then received, one at a time, with

```
snew = accept(s, clientaddr, clientaddrlen);
int snew, s;
struct sockaddr *clientaddr;
int *clientaddrlen;
```

The *backlog* parameter in the *listen* call specifies an upper bound on the number of
pending connections that should be queued for acceptance. Processes can obtain a
new connected socket with the *accept* call, and can also obtain the address of the
client by specifying the *clientaddr* and *clientaddrlen* parameters. Note that *accept*
returns a file descriptor associated with a *new* socket. This new socket is the
socket through which client–server communication can take place. The original
socket *s* is used solely for managing the queue of connection requests in the
server.

Sockets that are not connection based may also use the *connect* system call to
fix a peer's address, although this step is not required. The system calls available
for sending and receiving data (described later in this subsection) permit connectionless sockets to be used without a fixed peer address via specification of the
destination with each transmitted message. Likewise, connectionless sockets do
not need to bind an address to a socket before using the socket to transmit data.
However, in some communication domains, addresses are assigned to sockets
when the latter are first used, if no specific address was bound.

A variety of calls is available for sending and receiving data. The usual *read*
(*readv*) and *write* (*writev*) system calls, as well as the newer *send* and *recv* calls,
can be used with sockets that are in a connected state. *Send* and *recv* differ from
the more common interface in that they both support an additional *flags* parameter.
The *flags* can be used to *peek* at incoming data on reception (MSG_PEEK), to send
or receive out-of-band data (MSG_OOB), and to send data without network routing
(MSG_DONTROUTE). The *sendto* and *recvfrom* system calls have all the capabilities of *send* and *recv* and, in addition, permit callers to specify or receive the
address of the peer with whom they are communicating; these calls are most useful for connectionless sockets, where the peer may vary on each message transmitted or received. (The *send* and *recv* calls were originally system calls; they are
now implemented as library routines using *sendto* and *recvfrom* with null
addresses.) Finally, the *sendmsg* and *recvmsg* system calls support the full interface to the interprocess-communication facilities. Besides scatter-gather operations being possible, an address may be specified or received, the optional flags
described previously are available, and specially interpreted *ancillary data* or

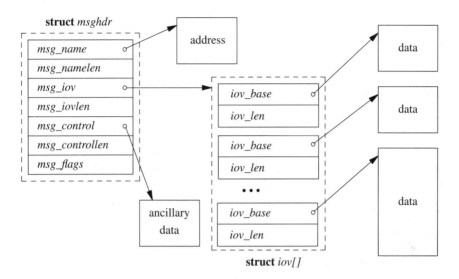

Figure 11.1 Data structures for the *sendmsg* and *recvmsg* system calls.

control information may be passed (see Fig. 11.1). Ancillary data may include protocol-specific data, such as addressing or options, and also specially interpreted data, called *access rights*.

In addition to these system calls, several other calls are provided to access miscellaneous services. The *socketpair* call provides a mechanism by which two connected sockets can be created without binding addresses. This facility is almost identical to a pipe, except for the potential for bidirectional flow of data; pipes are implemented internally as a pair of sockets. The *getsockname* call returns the locally bound address of a socket, whereas the *getpeername* call returns the address of the socket at the remote end of a connection. The *shutdown* call terminates data transmission or reception at a socket, and two *ioctl*-style calls—*setsockopt* and *getsockopt*—can be used to set and retrieve various parameters that control the operation of a socket or of the underlying network protocols. These options include the ability to transmit broadcast messages, to set the size of a socket's send and receive data buffers, and to await the transmission of queued data when a socket is destroyed. Sockets are discarded with the normal *close* system call.

The interface to the interprocess-communication facilities was purposely designed to be orthogonal to the existing standard system interfaces—that is, to the *open*, *read*, and *write* system calls. This decision was made to avoid overloading the familiar interface with undue complexity. In addition, the developers thought that using an interface that was completely independent of the filesystem would improve the portability of software, because, for example, pathnames would not be involved. Backward compatibility, for the sake of naive processes,

was still deemed important; thus, the familiar read–write interface was augmented
to permit access to the new communication facilities wherever that made sense
(e.g., when connected stream sockets were used).

11.2 Implementation Structure and Overview

The interprocess-communication facilities are layered on top of the networking
facilities, as shown in Fig. 11.2. Data flows from the application through the
socket layer to the networking support, and vice versa. State required by the
socket level is fully encapsulated in the socket layer, whereas any protocol-related
state is maintained in auxiliary data structures that are specific to the supporting
protocols. Responsibility for storage associated with transmitted data is passed
from the socket level to the network level. Consistent adherence to this rule
assists in simplifying details of storage management. Within the socket layer, the
socket data structure is the focus of all activity. The system-call interface routines
manage the actions related to a system call, collecting the system-call parameters
(see Section 3.2) and converting user data into the format expected by the second-
level routines. Most of the socket abstraction is implemented within the second-
level routines. All second-level routines have names with a *so* prefix, and directly
manipulate socket data structures and manage the synchronization between asynchronous activities; these routines are listed in Table 11.1.

The remainder of this chapter focuses on the implementation of the socket
layer. Section 11.3 discusses how memory is managed at the socket level and
below in the networking subsystem; Section 11.4 covers the socket and related
data structures; Section 11.5 presents the algorithms for connection setup; Section
11.6 discusses data transfer; and Section 11.7 describes connection shutdown.
Throughout this chapter, references to the supporting facilities provided by the
network-communication protocols are made with little elaboration; a complete
description of the interaction between the network protocols and the socket layer
appears in Chapter 12, and the internals of the network protocols are presented in
Chapter 13.

Figure 11.2 Interprocess-communication implementation layering. The boxes on the left
name the standard layers; the boxes on the right name specific examples of the layers that
might be used by an individual socket.

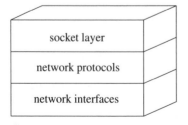
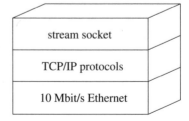

socket layer	stream socket
network protocols	TCP/IP protocols
network interfaces	10 Mbit/s Ethernet

Table 11.1 Socket-layer support routines.

Routine	Function
socreate( )	create a new socket
sobind( )	bind a name to a socket
solisten( )	mark a socket as listening for connection requests
soclose( )	close a socket
soabort( )	abort connection on a socket
soaccept( )	accept a pending connection on a socket
soconnect( )	initiate a connection to another socket
soconnect2( )	create a connection between two sockets
sodisconnect( )	initiate a disconnect on a connected socket
sosend( )	send data
soreceive( )	receive data
soshutdown( )	shut down data transmission or reception
sosetopt( )	set the value of a socket option
sogetopt( )	get the value of a socket option

11.3 Memory Management

The requirements placed on a memory-management scheme by interprocess-communication and network protocols tend to be substantially different from those of other parts of the operating system. Although all require the efficient allocation and reclamation of memory, communication protocols in particular need memory in widely varying sizes. Memory is needed for variable-sized structures such as communication protocol packets. Protocol implementations must frequently prepend headers or remove headers from packetized data. As packets are sent and received, buffered data may need to be divided into packets, and received packets may be combined into a single *record*. In addition, packets and other data objects must be queued when awaiting transmission or reception. A special-purpose memory-management facility was created for use by the interprocess-communication and networking systems to address these needs.

Mbufs

The memory-management facilities revolve around a data structure called an *mbuf* (see Fig. 11.3 on page 370). Mbufs, or memory buffers, are 128 bytes long, with 100 or 108 bytes of this space reserved for data storage. For large messages, the system can associate larger sections of data with an mbuf by referencing an external *mbuf cluster* from a private virtual memory area. The size of an mbuf cluster may vary by architecture, and is specified by the macro MCLBYTES (traditionally 1 Kbyte).

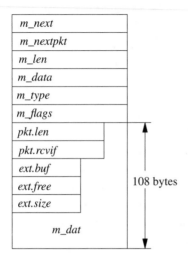

Figure 11.3 Memory-buffer (mbuf) data structure.

There are three sets of header fields that might be present in an mbuf. The first set is always present and resides at the beginning of the mbuf structure. The second set of header fields is optional. The third set of header fields is used when an external mbuf cluster is associated with an mbuf.

Data are stored either in the internal data area or in the external cluster, but never in both. Data in either location are accessed via a data pointer within the mbuf, and thus may begin at a location other than the beginning of the buffer area. In addition to the data-pointer field used to reference the data associated with an mbuf, a length field also is maintained. The length field shows the number of bytes of valid data to be found at the data-pointer location. The data and length fields allow routines to trim data efficiently at the start or end of an mbuf. In deletion of data at the start of an mbuf, the pointer is incremented and the length is decremented. In deletion of data at the end of an mbuf, only the length is decremented. When space is available within an mbuf, data can be added at either end. This flexibility to add and delete space without copying is particularly useful in communication-protocol implementation. Protocols routinely strip protocol information off the front or back of a message before the message's contents are handed to a higher-level processing module, or add protocol information as a message is passed to lower levels.

The ability to refer to mbuf clusters from an mbuf permits data to be copied without a memory-to-memory copy operation. When multiple copies of a block of data are required, the same mbuf cluster can be referenced from multiple mbufs to avoid physical copies. An array of reference counts is maintained for a virtual array of mbuf clusters to support this style of sharing (see the next subsection).

Multiple mbufs can be linked to hold an arbitrary quantity of data. This linkage is done with the *m_next* field of the mbuf. By convention, a chain of mbufs linked in this way is treated as a single object. For example, the communication protocols build packets from chains of mbufs. A second field, *m_nextpkt*, links objects built from chains of mbufs into lists of objects. (This field was previously known as *m_act*.) Throughout our discussions, a collection of mbufs linked together with the *m_next* field will be called a *chain*; chains of mbufs linked together with the *m_nextpkt* field will be called a *queue*.

The mbuf structure also contains a type field. Each mbuf is typed according to its use. The mbuf type serves two purposes. The only operational use of the type is to distinguish optional components of a message in an mbuf chain that is queued for reception on a socket data queue. Otherwise, the type information is used in maintaining statistics about storage use and, if there are problems, as an aid in tracking mbufs.

The final header component of the standard mbuf structure is the flags field. The flags are logically divided into two sets: flags that describe the usage of an individual mbuf and those that describe an object stored in an mbuf chain. The flags describing an mbuf specify whether the mbuf references external storage (M_EXT), whether the second set of header fields is present (M_PKTHDR), and whether the mbuf completes a *record* (M_EOR). A packet normally would be stored in an mbuf chain (of one or more mbufs) with the M_PKTHDR flag set on the first mbuf of the chain. The mbuf flags describing the packet would be set in the first mbuf and could include either the broadcast flag (M_BCAST) or the multi-cast flag (M_MCAST). The latter flags specify that a transmitted packet should be sent as a broadcast or multicast, respectively, or that a received packet was sent in that manner.

If the M_PKTHDR flag is set on an mbuf, the mbuf has a second set of header fields immediately following the standard header. This addition causes the mbuf data area to shrink from 108 bytes to 100 bytes. The second header is used on only the first mbuf of a chain. It includes two fields: the total length of the object in the mbuf chain, and, for received packets, a field that identifies the network interface on which the packet was received.

An mbuf that uses external storage is marked with the M_EXT flag. Here, a third header area overlays the internal data area of an mbuf. The fields in this header describe the external storage, including the start of the buffer and its size. A third field is designated to point to a routine to free the buffer, in theory allow-ing various types of buffers to be mapped by mbufs. In the current implementa-tion, however, the free function is not used, and the external storage is assumed to be a standard mbuf cluster.

Mbufs have fixed-sized, rather than variable-sized, data areas for several rea-sons. First, the fixed size minimizes memory fragmentation. This consideration was important at the time the networking software was designed originally, as a targeted machine was the BBN C70, which had a 20-bit physical address space. Second, communication protocols are frequently required to prepend or append headers to existing data areas, to split data areas, or to trim data from the begin-ning or end of a data area. The mbuf facilities are designed to handle such changes without reallocation or copying whenever possible. Finally, the *dtom*()

function, described in the subsection on mbuf utility routines later in this section, would be much more expensive if mbufs were not fixed in size. (Note, however, that the *dtom*() function is now deprecated.)

The mbuf structure has changed substantially since its initial design. The flags field and the two optional sets of header fields were added since 4.3BSD. In addition, the data pointer replaces a field used as an offset in the initial version of the mbuf. The use of an offset was not portable when the data referenced could be in an mbuf cluster. The addition of a flags field allowed the use of a flag indicating external storage; earlier versions tested the magnitude of the offset to see whether the data were in the internal mbuf data area. The addition of the broadcast flag allowed network-level protocols to know whether packets were received as link-level broadcasts, as was required for standards conformance.

The two new headers were designed to avoid redundant calculations of the size of an object, to make it easier to identify the incoming network interface of a received packet, and to generalize the use of external storage by an mbuf. The design has not been completely successful. The packet header contains only two fields (8 bytes), although we anticipated that a timestamp or other fields would be added. It is probably not worth the complexity of having a variable-sized header on an mbuf for the packet header; instead, those fields probably should have been included in all mbufs, even if they were not used. Also, as we noted, the header describing the external storage includes a pointer to a free function. The header file includes an unused sample macro to use that function, in theory allowing other types of external storage. However, the example is incorrect. The problem is that the code continues to use the array of mbuf-cluster reference counts, which is one for one with mbuf clusters. If an mbuf mapped some other external buffer, indexing into this array of reference counts would be incorrect. Rather than providing a function to free the buffer, the mbuf header should have a function to adjust the reference count, freeing the buffer when the final reference is removed.

Storage-Management Algorithms

The system allocates mbuf structures with the standard memory allocator, the *malloc*() function. Mbuf clusters are managed differently, via three central resources: a pool of pages allocated from the system memory allocator, a fixed-sized area of kernel virtual memory for mapping pages used for mbuf clusters, and an array of counters used in maintaining reference counts on mbuf clusters. A free list is maintained for mbuf clusters. When additional mbuf clusters are required, the system allocates a page of memory, maps the page into the reserved area of kernel virtual memory, and divides the page into one or more mbuf clusters, depending on the page size. The array of reference counts is large enough for every mbuf cluster that could be allocated within this area of virtual memory, and is one for one with the virtual array of clusters. When the system is booted, the mbuf-allocation routines initialize the free list by allocating 4 Kbyte of physical memory for mbuf clusters. Further memory may be allocated as the system operates, up to a compile-time configurable limit (256 Kbyte by default, or 512 Kbyte if the GATEWAY configuration option is enabled). Once memory is allocated for mbuf clusters, it is never freed.

Mbuf-allocation requests indicate either that they must be fulfilled immediately or that they can wait for available resources. If a request is marked as "can wait" and the requested resources are unavailable, the process is put to sleep to await available resources. The nonblocking allocation request is necessary for code that executes at interrupt level. If mbuf allocation has reached its limit or kernel memory is unavailable, the mbuf-allocation routines ask the network-protocol modules to give back any available resources that they can spare. A nonblocking request will fail if no resources are available.

An mbuf-allocation request is made through a call to *m_get*(), *m_gethdr*(), or through an equivalent macro used for efficiency purposes. Space for the mbuf is allocated by the *malloc*() function and is then initialized. For *m_gethdr*(), the mbuf is initialized with the optional packet header. The MCLGET macro adds an mbuf cluster to an mbuf.

Release of mbuf resources is straightforward; *m_free*() frees a single mbuf, and *m_freem*() frees a chain of mbufs. When an mbuf that references an mbuf cluster is freed, the reference count for the cluster is decremented. Mbuf clusters are placed onto the free list when their reference counts reach zero.

Mbuf Utility Routines

Many useful utility routines exist for manipulating mbufs within the kernel networking subsystem. Those routines that will be used in Chapter 12 are described briefly here.

The *m_copym*() routine makes a copy of an mbuf chain starting at a logical offset, in bytes, from the start of the data. This routine may be used to copy all or only part of a chain of mbufs. If an mbuf is associated with an mbuf cluster, the copy will reference the same data by incrementing the reference count on the cluster; otherwise, the data portion is copied as well. The *m_copydata*() function is similar, but copies data from an mbuf chain into a caller-provided buffer.

The *m_adj*() routine adjusts the data in an mbuf chain by a specified number of bytes, shaving data off either the front or back. No data are ever copied; *m_adj*() operates purely by manipulating the offset and length fields in the mbuf structures.

The *mtod*() macro takes a pointer to an mbuf header and a data type and returns a pointer to the data in the buffer, cast to the given type. The *dtom*() function is the inverse: It takes a pointer to an arbitrary address in the data of an mbuf, and returns a pointer to the mbuf header (rather than to the head of the mbuf chain). This operation is done through simple truncation of the data address to an mbuf-sized boundary. This function works only when data reside within the mbuf. In part because this restriction may force extra data copies, this function has been deprecated; it is no longer used in the main code paths of the network.

The *m_pullup*() routine rearranges an mbuf chain such that a specified number of bytes of data resides in a contiguous data area within the mbuf (not in

external storage). This operation is used so that objects such as protocol headers
are contiguous and can be treated as normal data structures, and so that *dtom()*
will work when the object is freed. (If the *dtom()* macro is eventually removed,
m_pullup() will no longer be forced to move data from mbuf clusters.) If there is
room, *m_pullup()* will increase the size of the contiguous region up to the maximum size of a protocol header in an attempt to avoid being called in the future.

The *M_PREPEND()* macro adjusts an mbuf chain to prepend a specified number of bytes of data. If possible, space is made in place, but an additional mbuf
may have to be allocated at the beginning of the chain. It is not currently possible
to prepend data within an mbuf cluster because different mbufs might refer to data
in different portions of the cluster.

11.4 Data Structures

Sockets are the basic objects used by communicating processes. A socket's type
defines the basic set of communication semantics, whereas the communication
domain defines auxiliary properties important to the use of the socket, and may
refine the set of available communication semantics. Table 11.2 shows the four
types of sockets currently supported by the system. To create a new socket, applications must specify the socket type and communication domain in which the
socket is to be created. The request may also indicate a specific network protocol
to be used by the socket. If no protocol is specified, the system selects an appropriate protocol from the set of protocols supported by the communication domain.
If the communication domain is unable to support the type of socket requested
(i.e., no suitable protocol is available), the request will fail.

Sockets are described by a *socket* data structure that is dynamically created at
the time of a *socket* system call. Communication domains are described by a

Table 11.2 Socket types supported by the system.

Name	Type	Properties
SOCK_STREAM	stream	reliable, sequenced, data transfer; may support out-of-band data
SOCK_DGRAM	datagram	unreliable, unsequenced, data transfer, with message boundaries preserved
SOCK_SEQPACKET	sequenced packet	reliable, sequenced, data transfer, with message boundaries preserved
SOCK_RAW	raw	direct access to the underlying communication protocols

domain data structure that is statically defined within the system based on the system's configuration (see Section 14.5). Communication protocols within a domain are described by a *protosw* structure that is also statically defined within the system for each protocol implementation configured. When a request is made to create a socket, the system uses the value of the communication domain to search linearly the list of configured domains. If the domain is found, the domain's table of supported protocols is consulted for a protocol appropriate for the type of socket being created or for a specific protocol requested. (A wildcard entry may exist for a raw socket.) Should multiple protocol entries satisfy the request, the first is selected. We shall begin discussion of the data structures by examining the *domain* structure. The *protosw* structure is discussed in Section 12.1.

Communication Domains

The *domain* structure is shown in Fig. 11.4. The *dom_name* field is the ASCII name of the communication domain. (In the original design, communication domains were to be specified with ASCII strings; they are now specified with manifest constants.) The *dom_family* field identifies the *protocol family* used by the domain; possible values are shown in Table 11.3 (on page 376). *Protocol families* refer to the suite of communication protocols of a domain used to support the communication semantics of a socket. A protocol family generally has an associated *address family* defining an addressing structure, although it can use other addressing formats. The *dom_protosw* field points to the table of protocols supported by the communication domain, and the *dom_NPROTOSW* pointer marks the end of the table. The remaining entries contain pointers to domain-specific routines used in the management and transfer of access rights (described in Section 11.6) and fields relating to routing initialization for the domain.

Figure 11.4 Communication-domain data structure.

dom_family	PF_UNIX
dom_name	"unix"
dom_init	...
dom_externalize	*unp_externalize( )*
dom_dispose	*unp_dispose( )*
dom_protosw	*unixsw*
dom_protoswNPROTOSW	*&unixsw[3]*
dom_rtattach	
dom_rtoffset	
dom_maxrtkey	
dom_next	

Table 11.3 Protocol families.

Name	Description
PF_LOCAL	(PF_UNIX) local communication
PF_INET	DARPA Internet (TCP/IP)
PF_IMPLINK	old 1822 Interface Message Processor link layer
PF_PUP	old Xerox network
PF_CHAOS	MIT Chaos network
PF_NS	Xerox Network System (XNS) architecture
PF_ISO	OSI network protocols
PF_ECMA	European Computer Manufacturers network
PF_DATAKIT	AT&T Datakit network
PF_CCITT	CCITT protocols, e.g., X.25
PF_SNA	IBM System Network Architecture (SNA)
PF_DECnet	DEC network
PF_DLI	direct link interface
PF_LAT	local-area–network terminal interface
PF_HYLINK	Network Systems Corporation Hyperchannel (raw)
PF_APPLETALK	AppleTalk network
PF_ROUTE	communication with kernel routing layer
PF_LINK	raw link-layer access
PF_XTP	eXpress Transfer Protocol
PF_COIP	Connection-oriented IP (ST II)
PF_CNT	Computer Network Technology
PF_IPX	Novell Internet protocol

Sockets

The *socket* data structure is shown in Fig. 11.5. Storage for the *socket* structure is allocated dynamically via the *malloc()* routine. Sockets contain information about their type, the supporting protocol in use, and their state (Table 11.4). Data being transmitted or received are queued at the socket as a list of mbuf chains. Various fields are present for managing queues of sockets created during connection establishment. Each socket structure also holds a process-group identifier. The process-group identifier is used in delivering the SIGURG and SIGIO signals; SIGURG is sent when an urgent condition exists for a socket, and SIGIO is used by the asynchronous I/O facility (see Section 6.4). The socket contains an error field, which is needed for storing asynchronous errors to be reported to the owner of the socket.

Sockets are located through a process's file descriptor via the file table. When a socket is created, the *f_data* field of the file structure is set to point at the socket

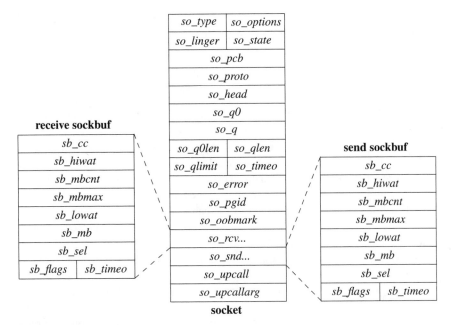

Figure 11.5 Socket data structure.

structure, and the *f_ops* field to point to the set of routines defining socket-specific file operations. In this sense, the socket structure is a direct parallel of the *vnode* structure used by the filesystems.

The socket structure acts as a queueing point for data being transmitted and received. As data enter the system as a result of system calls, such as *write* or *send*, the socket layer passes the data to the networking subsystem as a chain of mbufs for immediate transmission. If the supporting protocol module decides to

Table 11.4 Socket states.

State	Description
SS_NOFDREF	no file-table reference
SS_ISCONNECTED	connected to a peer
SS_ISCONNECTING	in process of connecting to peer
SS_ISDISCONNECTING	in process of disconnecting from peer
SS_CANTSENDMORE	cannot send more data to peer
SS_CANTRCVMORE	cannot receive more data from peer
SS_RCVATMARK	at out-of-band mark on input
SS_ISCONFIRMING	peer awaiting connection confirmation

postpone transmission of the data, or if a copy of the data is to be maintained until an acknowledgment is received, the data are queued in the socket's transmit buffer. When the network has consumed the data, it discards them from the outgoing queue. On reception, the network passes data up to the socket layer, also in mbuf chains, where they are then queued until the application makes a system call to request them. The socket layer can also make an *upcall* to an internal kernel client of the network when data arrive, allowing the data to be processed without a context switch. Upcalls are used by the NFS server (see Chapter 9).

To avoid resource exhaustion, sockets impose upper bounds on the number of bytes of data that can be queued in a socket data buffer, and also on the amount of storage space that can be used for data. This *high watermark* is initially set by the protocol, although an application can change the value up to a system maximum, normally 256 Kbyte. The network protocols can examine the high watermark and use the value in flow-control policies. A *low watermark* also is present in each socket data buffer. The low watermark allows applications to control data flow by specifying a minimum number of bytes required to satisfy a reception request, with a default of 1 byte and a maximum of the high watermark. For output, the low watermark sets the minimum amount of space available before transmission can be attempted; the default is the size of an mbuf cluster. These values also control the operation of the *select* system call when it is used to test for ability to read or write the socket.

When connection indications are received at the communication-protocol level, the connection may require further processing to complete. Depending on the protocol, that processing may be done before the connection is returned to the listening process, or the listening process may be allowed to confirm or reject the connection request. Sockets used to accept incoming connection requests maintain two queues of sockets associated with connection requests. The list of sockets headed by the *so_q0* field represents a queue of connections that must be completed at the protocol level before being returned. The *so_q* field heads a list of sockets that are ready to be returned to the listening process. Like the data queues, the queues of connections also have an application-controllable limit. The limit applies to both queues. Because the limit may include sockets that cannot yet be accepted, the system enforces a limit 50-percent larger than the nominal limit.

Note that, although a connection may be established by the network protocol, the application may choose not to accept the established connection, or may close down the connection immediately after discovering the identity of the client. It is also possible for a network protocol to delay completion of a connection until after the application has obtained control with the *accept* system call. The application might then accept or reject the connection explicitly with a protocol-specific mechanism. Otherwise, if the application does a data transfer, the connection is confirmed; if the application closes the socket immediately, the connection is rejected.

Socket Addresses

Sockets may be labeled so that peers can connect to them. The socket layer treats an address as an opaque object. Applications supply and receive addresses as tagged, variable-length byte strings. Addresses are placed in mbufs within the

sa_len	sa_family	sa_data
◄— 1 byte —►◄— 1 byte —►◄————————— variable ————————————►

Figure 11.6 Socket-address template structure.

socket layer. A structure called a *sockaddr*, shown in Fig. 11.6, may be used as a template for referring to the identifying tag and length of each address. Most protocol layers support a single address type as identified by the tag, known as the *address family*. In general, the address-family values are one-for-one with protocol family values.

It is common for addresses passed in by an application to reside in mbufs only long enough for the socket layer to pass them to the supporting protocol for transfer into a fixed-sized address structure, for example, when a protocol records an address in a protocol state block. The *sockaddr* structure is the common means by which the socket layer and network-support facilities exchange addresses. The size of the generic data array was chosen to be large enough to hold many addresses directly, although generic code cannot depend on having sufficient space in a *sockaddr* structure for an arbitrary address. The local communication domain (formerly known as the UNIX domain), for example, stores filesystem pathnames in mbufs and allows socket names as large as 104 bytes, as shown in Fig. 11.7. The Internet communication domain, on the other hand, uses a fixed-size structure that combines a DARPA Internet address and a port number. The Internet protocols reserve space for addresses in an Internet control-block data structure, and free up mbufs that contain addresses after copying the addresses. The ISO (OSI) domain uses a variable-sized structure with a fixed-size initial component. The initial portion has space for a network-level address plus a local transport selector.

Figure 11.7 Network system, Internet, and local-domain address structures.

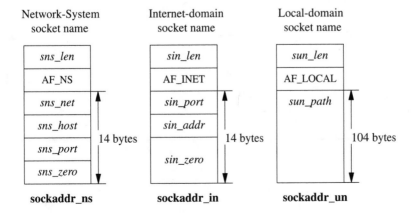

A larger space may be needed for larger transport selectors or for higher-level selectors. Another example of a variable-length structure is the link-layer address format, which includes an optional network interface name as a string, an optional interface index, and an optional link-layer address.

11.5   Connection Setup

For two processes to pass information between them, an *association* must be established. The steps involved in creating an association (*socket, connect, listen, accept,* etc.) were described in Section 11.1. In this section, we shall study the operation of the socket layer in establishing associations. As the state associated with a connectionless transfer of data is fully encapsulated in each message that is sent, our discussion will focus on connection-based associations established with the *connect, listen,* and *accept* system calls.

Connection establishment in the client–server model is asymmetric. A client process actively initiates a connection to obtain service, whereas a server process passively accepts connections to provide service. Fig. 11.8 shows the state-transition diagram for a socket used to initiate or accept connections. State transitions are initiated either by user actions (i.e., system calls) or by protocol actions that result from receiving network messages or servicing timers that expire.

Sockets are normally used to send and receive data. When they are used in establishing a connection, they are treated somewhat differently. If a socket is to be used to accept a connection, a *listen* system call must be used. The *listen* call

Figure 11.8 Socket state transitions during process rendezvous.

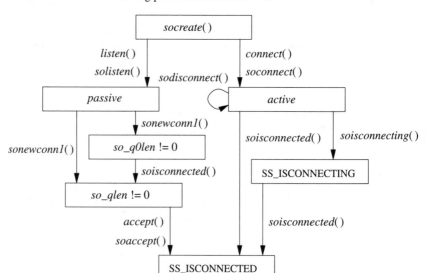

invokes *solisten*(), which notifies the supporting protocol that the socket will be receiving connections, establishes an empty list of pending connections at the socket (through the *so_q* field), and then marks the socket as *accepting connections*, SO_ACCEPTCON. At the time a *listen* is done, a backlog parameter is specified by the application. This parameter sets a limit on the number of incoming connections that the system will queue awaiting acceptance by the application. (The system enforces a maximum on this limit.) Once a socket is set up to receive connections, the remainder of the work in creating connections is managed by the protocol layers. For each connection established at the server side, a new socket is created with the *sonewconn1*() routine. These new sockets may be placed on the socket's queue of partially established connections while the connections are being completed, or they may be placed directly into the queue of connections ready to be passed to the application via the *accept* call. The new sockets might be ready to be passed to the application either because no further protocol action is necessary to establish the connection, or because the protocol allows the listening process to confirm or reject the connection request. In the latter case, the socket is marked as *confirming* (state bit SS_CONFIRMING), so that the pending connection request will be confirmed or rejected as needed. Once sockets on the queue of partly established connections are ready, they are moved to the queue of connections completed and pending acceptance by an application (see Fig. 11.9). When an *accept* system call is made to obtain a connection, the system verifies that a connection is present on the socket's queue of ready connections. If no connection is ready to be returned, the system puts the process to sleep until one arrives (unless nonblocking I/O is being used with the socket, in which case an error is returned). When a connection is available, the associated socket is removed from the queue, a new file descriptor is allocated to reference the socket, and the result is returned to the caller. If the *accept* call indicates that the peer's identity is to be returned, the peer's address is obtained from the protocol layer and is copied into the supplied buffer.

Figure 11.9 Connections queued at a socket awaiting an *accept*() call.

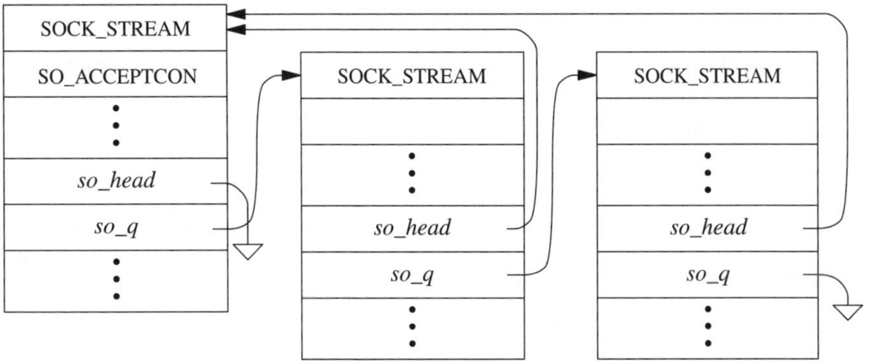

On the client side, an application requests a connection with the *connect* system call, supplying the address of the peer socket to which to connect. The system verifies that a connection attempt is not already in progress for that socket, then invokes *soconnect( )* to initiate the connection. The *soconnect( )* routine first checks the socket to see whether the latter is already connected. If the socket is already connected, the existing connection is first terminated (this disconnection is done with datagram sockets only). With the socket in an unconnected state, *soconnect( )* then marks the state as connecting, and makes a request to the protocol layer to initiate the new connection. Once the connection request has been passed to the protocol layer, if the connection request is incomplete, the system puts the process to sleep to await notification by the protocol layer that a completed connection exists. A nonblocking connect may return at this point, but a process awaiting a completed connection will awaken only when the connection request has been completed—either successfully or with an error condition.

A socket's state during connection establishment is managed jointly by the socket layer and the supporting protocol layer. The socket's state value is never altered directly by a protocol; to promote modularity, all modifications are performed by surrogate socket-layer routines, such as *soisconnected( )*. These routines modify the socket state as indicated and notify any waiting processes. The supporting protocol layers never use process synchronization or signaling facilities directly. Errors that are detected asynchronously are communicated to a socket in its *so_error* field. For example, if a connection request fails because the protocol layer detects that the requested service is unavailable, the *so_error* field usually is set to ECONNREFUSED before the requesting process is awakened. The socket layer always inspects the value of *so_error* on return from a call to *tsleep( )*; this field is used to report errors detected asynchronously by the protocol layers.

11.6 Data Transfer

Most of the work done by the socket layer lies in sending and receiving data. Note that the socket layer itself explicitly refrains from imposing any structure on data transmitted or received via sockets other than optional record boundaries. This policy is in contrast to that of other interprocess-communication facilities [Fitzgerald & Rashid, 1986]. Within the overall interprocess-communication model, any data interpretation or structuring is logically isolated in the implementation of the communication domain. An example of this logical isolation is the ability to pass file descriptors between processes using local-domain sockets.

Sending and receiving of data can be done with any one of several system calls. The system calls vary according to the amount of information to be transmitted and received, and according to the state of the socket doing the operation. For example, the *write* system call may be used with a socket that is in a connected state, as the destination of the data is implicitly specified by the connection; but the *sendto* or *sendmsg* system calls allow the process to specify the destination for a message explicitly. Likewise, when data are received, the *read* system call allows a process to receive data on a connected socket without receiving the sender's address; the *recvfrom* and *recvmsg* system calls allow the process to retrieve the incoming message and the sender's address. The *recvmsg* and *sendmsg* system calls allow scatter-gather I/O with multiple user-provided buffers. In addition, *recvmsg* reports additional information about a received message, such as whether it was expedited (out of band), whether it completes a record, or whether it was truncated because a buffer was too small. The decision to provide many different system calls, rather than to provide only a single general interface, is debatable. It would have been possible to implement a single system-call interface and to provide simplified interfaces to applications via user-level library routines. However, the single system call would have to be the most general call, which has somewhat higher overhead. Internally, all transmission and reception requests are converted to a uniform format and are passed to the socket-layer *sendit()* and *recvit()* routines, respectively.

Transmitting Data

The *sendit()* routine is responsible for gathering all system-call parameters that the application has specified into the kernel's address space (except the actual data), and then for invoking the *sosend()* routine to do the transmission. The parameters may include the following components, illustrated in Fig. 11.1:

- An address to which data will be sent, if the socket has not been connected

- Optional *ancillary data* (control data) associated with the message; ancillary data can include protocol-specific data associated with a message, protocol option information, or access rights

- Normal data, specified as an array of buffers (see Section 6.4)

- Optional flags, including out-of-band and end-of-record flags

The *sosend()* routine handles most of the socket-level data-transmission options, including requests for transmission of out-of-band data and of transmission without network routing. This routine is also responsible for checking socket state— for example, seeing whether a required connection has been made, whether transmission is still possible on the socket, and whether a pending error should be reported rather than transmission attempted. In addition, *sosend()* is responsible for putting processes to sleep when their data transmissions exceed the buffering available in the socket's send buffer. The actual transmission of data is done by the supporting communication protocol; *sosend()* copies data from the user's address space into mbufs in the kernel's address space, and then makes calls to the protocol to transfer the data.

Most of the work done by *sosend()* lies in checking the socket state, handling flow control, checking for termination conditions, and breaking up an application's transmission request into one or more protocol transmission requests. The request must be broken up only when the size of the user's request plus the number of data queued in the socket's send data buffer exceeds the socket's high watermark. It is not permissible to break up a request if the protocol is *atomic*, because each request made by the socket layer to the protocol modules implicitly indicates a boundary in the data stream. Most datagram protocols are of this type. Honoring each socket's high watermark ensures that a protocol will always have space in the socket's send buffer to enqueue unacknowledged data. It also ensures that no process, or group of processes, can monopolize system resources.

For sockets that guarantee reliable data delivery, a protocol will normally maintain a copy of all transmitted data in the socket's send queue until receipt is acknowledged by the receiver. Protocols that provide no assurance of delivery normally accept data from *sosend()* and directly transmit the data to the destination without keeping a copy. But *sosend()* itself does not distinguish between reliable and unreliable delivery.

Sosend() always ensures that a socket's send buffer has enough space available to store the next section of data to be transmitted. If a socket has insufficient space in its send buffer to hold all the data to be transmitted, *sosend()* uses the following strategy. If the protocol is atomic, *sosend()* verifies that the message is no larger than the send buffer size; if the message is larger, it returns an EMSGSIZE error. If the available space in the send queue is less then the send low watermark, the transmission is deferred; if the process is not using nonblocking I/O, the process is put to sleep until more space is available in the send buffer; otherwise, an error is returned. When space is available, a protocol transmit request is formulated according to the available space in the send buffer. *Sosend()* copies data from the user's address space into mbuf clusters whenever the data would fill more than two mbufs, on the theory that two allocations are required for an mbuf plus a cluster. If a transmission request for a nonatomic protocol is large, each protocol transmit request will normally contain a full mbuf cluster. Although additional data could be appended to the mbuf chain before delivery to the protocol, it is preferable to pass the data to lower levels immediately. This strategy allows better pipelining, as data reach the bottom of the protocol stack earlier, and can begin physical transmission sooner. This procedure is repeated until insufficient space remains; it resumes each time that additional space becomes available.

This strategy tends to preserve the application-specified message size and helps to avoid fragmentation at the network level. The latter benefit is important, because system performance is significantly improved when data-transmission units are large, e.g. the mbuf cluster size.

The *sosend()* routine, in manipulating a socket's send data buffer, takes care to ensure that access to the buffer is synchronized among multiple sending processes. It does so by bracketing accesses to the data structure with calls to *sblock()* and *sbunlock()*. Interlocking against asynchronous network activity is also a concern here, as the network-protocol modules that operate at network-interrupt level cannot wait for access to a data structure such as a socket data buffer. Thus, they do not honor the locking protocol used between processes. To block network-protocol modules, *sosend()* must raise the processor priority level to *splnet* to ensure that no protocol processing takes place that might alter the state of a socket being manipulated while it is testing that state.

Receiving Data

The *soreceive*() routine receives data queued at a socket. As the counterpart to *sosend*(), *soreceive*() appears at the same level in the internal software structure and does similar tasks. Three types of data may be queued for reception at a socket: in-band data, out-of-band data, and ancillary data such as access rights. In-band data may also be tagged with the sender's address. Handling of out-of-band data varies by protocol. They may be placed at the beginning of the receive buffer, may be placed at the end of the buffer to appear in order with other data, or may be managed in the protocol layer separate from the socket's receive buffer. In the first two cases, they are returned by normal receive operations. In the final case, they are retrieved through a special interface when requested by the user. These options allow varying styles of urgent data transmission.

Soreceive() checks the socket's state, including the received data buffer, for incoming data, errors, or state transitions, and processes queued data according to their type and the actions specified by the caller. A system-call request may specify that only out-of-band data should be retrieved (MSG_OOB), or that data should be returned but not removed from the data buffer (by specifying the MSG_PEEK flag). Receive calls normally return as soon as the low watermark is reached; thus, by default, the call returns when any data are present. The MSG_WAITALL flag specifies that the call should block until it can return all the requested data if possible. On the other hand, the MSG_DONTWAIT flag causes the call to act as though the socket was in nonblocking mode, returning EWOULDBLOCK rather than blocking.

Data present in the receive data buffer are organized in one of several ways, depending on whether message boundaries are preserved. There are three common cases, for stream, datagram, and sequenced-packet sockets. In the general case, the receive data buffer is organized as a list of messages (see Fig. 11.10 on page 386). Each message can include a sender's address (for datagram protocols), ancillary data, and normal data. Depending on the protocol, it is also possible for expedited or out-of-band data to be placed into the normal receive buffer. Each mbuf chain on a list represents a single message or, for the final chain, a possibly incomplete record. Protocols that supply the sender's address with each message place a single mbuf containing the address at the front of message. Immediately following any address is an optional mbuf containing any ancillary data. Regular data mbufs follow the ancillary data. Names and ancillary data are distinguished by the type field in an mbuf; addresses are marked as MT_SONAME, whereas ancillary data are tagged as MT_CONTROL. Each message other than the final one is considered to be terminated. The final message is terminated implicitly when an atomic protocol is used, such as most datagram protocols. Sequenced packet protocols could treat each message as an atomic record, or they could support records that could be arbitrarily long (as is done in OSI). In the latter case, the final record in the buffer might or might not be complete, and a flag on the final mbuf, M_EOR, marks the termination of a record. Record boundaries (if any) are generally ignored by a stream protocol. However, transition from out-of-band data to normal data in the buffer, or presence of ancillary data, causes logical boundaries. A single receive operation never returns data that cross a logical boundary. Note that the storage

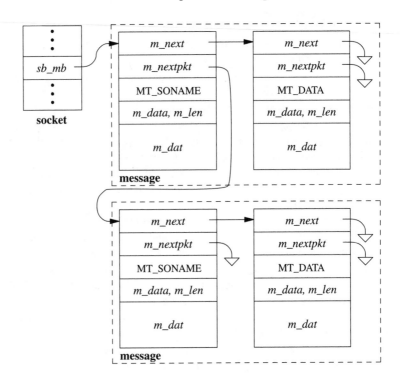

Figure 11.10 Data queueing for datagram socket.

scheme used by sockets allows them to compact data of the same type into the minimal number of mbufs required to hold those data.

On entry to *soreceive*(), a check is made to see whether out-of-band data are being requested. If they are, the protocol layer is queried to see whether any such data are available; if the data are available, they are returned to the caller. As regular data cannot be retrieved simultaneously with out-of-band data, *soreceive*() then returns. Otherwise, data from the normal queue have been requested. The *soreceive*() function first checks whether the socket is in *confirming* state, with the peer awaiting confirmation of a connection request. If it is, no data can arrive until the connection is confirmed, and the protocol layer is notified that the connection should be completed. *Soreceive*() then checks the receive-data-buffer character count to see whether data are available. If they are, the call returns with at least the data currently available. If no data are present, *soreceive*() consults the socket's state to find out whether data might be forthcoming. Data may no longer be received because the socket is disconnected (and a connection is required to receive data), or because the reception of data has been terminated with a *shutdown* by the socket's peer. In addition, if an error from a previous operation was detected asynchronously, the error needs to be returned to the user;

soreceive( ) checks the *so_error* field after checking for data. If no data or error exists, data might still arrive, and if the socket is not marked for nonblocking I/O, *soreceive*( ) puts the process to sleep to await the arrival of new data.

When data arrive for a socket, the supporting protocol notifies the socket layer by calling *sorwakeup*( ). *Soreceive*( ) can then process the contents of the receive buffer, observing the data-structuring rules described previously. *Soreceive*( ) first removes any address that must be present, then optional ancillary data, and finally normal data. If the application has provided a buffer for the receipt of ancillary data, they are passed to the application in that buffer; otherwise, they are discarded. The removal of data is slightly complicated by the interaction between in-band and out-of-band data managed by the protocol. The location of the next out-of-band datum can be marked in the in-band data stream and used as a record boundary during in-band data processing. That is, when an indication of out-of-band data is received by a protocol that holds out-of-band data separately from the normal buffer, the corresponding point in the in-band data stream is marked. Then, when a request is made to receive in-band data, only data up to the mark will be returned. This mark allows applications to synchronize the in-band and out-of-band data streams, so that, for example, received data can be flushed up to the point at which out-of-band data are received. Each socket has a field, *so_oobmark*, that contains the character offset from the front of the receive data buffer to the point in the data stream at which the last out-of-band message was received. When in-band data are removed from the receive buffer, the offset is updated, so that data past the mark will not be mixed with data preceding the mark. The SS_RCVATMARK bit in a socket's state field is set when *so_oobmark* reaches zero to show that the out-of-band data mark is at the beginning of the socket receive buffer. An application can test the state of this bit with the SIOCATMARK *ioctl* call to find out whether all in-band data have been read up to the point of the mark.

Once data have been removed from a socket's receive buffer, *soreceive*( ) updates the state of the socket and notifies the protocol layer that data have been received by the user. The protocol layer can use this information to release internal resources, to trigger end-to-end acknowledgment of data reception, to update flow-control information, or to start a new data transfer. Finally, if any access rights were received as ancillary data, *soreceive*( ) passes them to a communication-domain–specific routine to convert them from their internal representation to the external representation.

The *soreceive*( ) function returns a set of flags that are supplied to the caller of the *recvmsg* system call via the *msg_flags* field of the *msghdr* structure (see Fig. 11.1). The possible flags include MSG_EOR to specify that the received data complete a record for a nonatomic sequenced packet protocol, MSG_OOB to specify that expedited (out-of-band) data were received from the normal socket receive buffer, MSG_TRUNC to specify that an atomic record was truncated because the supplied buffer was too small, and MSG_CTRUNC to specify that ancillary data were truncated because the control buffer was too small.

Passing Access Rights

In addition to the transmission and reception of uninterpreted data, the system also supports the passage of typed ancillary data that have special meaning, either to a protocol layer or to an application. Access rights are one such type of ancillary data. These data normally represent the right to do operations on associated objects. The data used to represent access rights, or capabilities, normally are meaningful only within the context of the process that created or obtained the right; thus, their transmission requires system support to make them meaningful in a receiving process's context. For example, in 4.4BSD, access rights to files in the filesystem or sockets are encapsulated as file descriptors. A file descriptor is a small integer number that is meaningful only in the context of the process that opened or created the associated file. To pass a file descriptor from one process to another, the system must create a reference to the associated file-table structure in the receiving process's user structure.

Access rights, or capabilities, are categorized as *internalized* or *externalized*. Internalized capabilities require the support of trusted agents to be useful. Keys associated with these capabilities are created by a trusted agent, and, when presented for accessing a protected object, are deemed valid according to their interpretation in the context of the presenter.

Externalized capabilities, on the other hand, use keys that require no specific trusted agent for their use. That is, the validation of the right to access an object is based solely on the possession and presentation of the requisite key. Systems that use externalized capabilities frequently use a public-key encryption algorithm. Keys for externalized capabilities normally have the properties that they are long lived and that they may be stored in locations such as a filesystem without losing their usefulness.

No specific system support is required to support externalized capabilities. To support internalized capabilities, however, the operating system, acting as a trusted agent, must verify and translate keys when transmitting them as messages between processes. The interprocess-communication system provides facilities, on a per-communication domain basis, to process all access rights transmitted and received in messages, and to dispose of rights that are not received.

Sending and receiving of access rights requires the internalization and externalization of these rights. Internalization converts a key held by a sending process into an internal form that can be passed as data in a message. Externalization reverses this process, converting the internal form into an external form that is meaningful in the context of the receiving process. Internalization of access rights is done at the protocol layer when the *sosend*() routine requests transmission of data containing access rights. The access rights to be transmitted are passed as an mbuf chain separate from the regular data. When *soreceive*() encounters access rights on the receive data queue, it invokes the communication domain's *dom_externalize* routine to externalize the rights. The socket layer implicitly presumes that access rights stored in socket data queues will be valid as long as the system remains up. That is, there are no mechanisms to expedite the delivery of access rights, or to time out or invalidate rights stored on a socket data queue.

Passing Access Rights in the Local Domain

In the local domain, the internalization of file descriptors results in their conversion to system file-table pointers, whereas externalization requires allocation of new file descriptors for the receiving process. File descriptors passed in messages are really duplicates of the ones held by the sending process (as though they had been created by *dup*). The sending process must explicitly close a file descriptor after that descriptor has been sent to give the descriptor away.

A *garbage-collection* facility is provided to reclaim resources associated with access rights that are not delivered properly. Access rights may not be delivered for several reasons: because the receiving socket has insufficient space, because the user does not request them with the proper system call when receiving data from the socket, or because the socket is closed while access rights are still present in the receive buffer. In addition, it is possible for access rights in a socket receive buffer to become inaccessible because the socket itself is not accessible. For example, if a socket pair is created, each socket of the pair is sent as access rights on one of the sockets, and then both sockets are closed; then all the remaining references to the two sockets will be in access rights that can never be received. Garbage collection is used because of this problem, and because normal message processing does not permit a protocol to access a message after the protocol has passed on that message for delivery. This inability to access a message after it has been transmitted means that, if access rights in a message are not delivered, these rights will be discarded without being reclaimed. In the local domain, reclamation of access rights ensures that files associated with these rights are closed, so that system resources, such as file-table entries, are not depleted.

For garbage collection to be implemented, each file-table entry must contain a count of references held by file descriptors present in socket receive queues, *f_msgcount*. Another variable, *unp_rights*, tracks the number of file descriptors held in all the local-domain sockets in use. When a file descriptor is internalized to a file-table pointer for transmission, the *f_msgcount* for the file is incremented. On reception, when the file descriptor is externalized, *f_msgcount* is decremented. When a local-domain socket is reclaimed and *unp_rights* is nonzero, the garbage-collection routine, *unp_gc()*, is invoked to scan the file table and all local-domain sockets to reclaim unaccounted-for file-table references.

Unp_gc() uses a *mark-and-sweep algorithm* in doing its duties [J. Cohen, 1981]. The basic strategy is to locate all references to files that are accessible and to *mark* them. Files in a process's open file array have a reference not in a message, and are thus accessible. If the file is a socket that is accessible, access rights held in its receive buffer can be accessed once received, and thus the files to which they refer are *marked* as well.† This search is repeated while there are newly marked files whose buffers have not been scanned, accounting for sockets that are reachable only via receipt of access rights, which in turn contain other access rights. The garbage collector can then reclaim lost references by searching the file

---

†If a listening socket is accessible, then any queued connections that it holds are also accessible; the garbage collector in 4.4BSD fails to take this fact into account.

table for un*marked* entries for which all references are indicated as being in socket
receive queues.

Note that the garbage collector is invoked only when a local-domain socket is
closed and file descriptors are known to be queued awaiting reception; thus, the
overhead associated with the garbage collector is limited. Also, the garbage collector reclaims only those file-table entries that were lost while being passed in
messages; references that might be lost in other parts of the system are not
reclaimed.

11.7   Socket Shutdown

Although closing a socket and reclaiming its resources at first glance appears to be
a straightforward operation, it can be complicated. The complexity arises because
of the implicit semantics of the *close* system call. In certain situations (e.g., when
a process exits), a *close* call is never expected to fail. However, when a socket
promising reliable delivery of data is closed with data still queued for transmission
or awaiting acknowledgment of reception, the socket must attempt to transmit the
data, perhaps indefinitely, for the *close* call to maintain the socket's advertised
semantics. If the socket discards the queued data to allow the *close* to complete
successfully, it violates its promise to deliver data reliably. Discarding data can
cause naive processes, which depend on the implicit semantics of *close*, to work
unreliably in a network environment. However, if sockets block until all data have
been transmitted successfully, then, in some communication domains, a *close* may
never complete!

The socket layer compromises in an effort to address this problem yet to
maintain the semantics of the *close* system call. Figure 11.11 shows the possible
state transitions for a socket from a connected to a closed state. In normal

Figure 11.11 Socket-state transitions during shutdown.

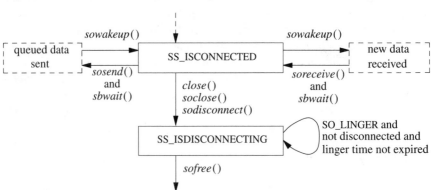

operation, closing a socket causes any queued but unaccepted connections to be discarded. If the socket is in a connected state, a disconnect is initiated. The socket is marked to indicate that a file descriptor is no longer referencing it, and the close operation returns successfully. When the disconnect request completes, the network support notifies the socket layer and the socket resources are reclaimed. The network layer may attempt to transmit any data queued in the socket's send buffer, although there is no guarantee that it will. However, commonly used connection-oriented protocols generally attempt to transmit any queued data asynchronously after the *close* call returns, preserving the normal semantics of *close* on a file.

Alternatively, a socket may be marked explicitly to force the application process to *linger* when closing until pending data have drained and the connection has shut down. This option is marked in the *socket* data structure using the *setsockopt* system call with the SO_LINGER option. When an application indicates that a socket is to linger, it also specifies a duration for the lingering period. The application can then block for as long as the specified duration while waiting for pending data to drain. If the lingering period expires before the disconnect is completed, the socket layer then notifies the network that it is closing, possibly discarding any data still pending. Some protocols handle the linger option differently; in particular, if the linger option is set with a duration of zero, the protocol may discard pending data, rather than attempt to deliver them asynchronously.

Exercises

11.1 What limitation in the use of pipes inspired the developers to design alternative interprocess-communication facilities?

11.2 Why are the 4.4BSD interprocess-communication facilities designed to be independent of the filesystem for naming sockets?

11.3 Why is interprocess communication layered on top of networking in 4.4BSD, rather than the other way around?

11.4 Would a screen editor be considered a naive or a sophisticated program, according to the definitions given in this chapter? Explain your answer.

11.5 What are out-of-band data? What types of socket support the communication of out-of-band data? Describe one use for out-of-band data.

11.6 Give two requirements that interprocess communication places on a memory-management facility.

11.7 How many mbufs and mbuf clusters would be needed to hold a 3024-byte message? Draw a picture of the necessary mbuf chain and any associated mbuf clusters.

11.8   Why does an mbuf have two link pointers? For what is each pointer used?

11.9   Each socket's send and receive data buffers have high and low watermarks. For what are these watermarks used?

11.10   Consider a socket with a network connection that is queued at the socket awaiting an *accept* system call. Is this socket on the queue headed by the *so_q* or by the *so_q0* field in the socket structure? What is the use of the queue that does *not* contain the socket?

11.11   Describe two types of protocols that would immediately place incoming connection requests into the queue headed by the *so_q* field in the socket structure.

11.12   How does the protocol layer communicate an asynchronous error to the socket layer?

11.13   Sockets explicitly refrain from interpreting the data that they send and receive. Do you believe that this approach is correct? Explain your answer.

11.14   Why does the *sosend*() routine ensure there is enough space in a socket's send buffer before making a call to the protocol layer to transmit data?

11.15   How is the type information in each mbuf used in the queueing of data at a datagram socket? How is this information used in the queueing of data at a stream socket?

11.16   Why does the *soreceive*() routine optionally notify the protocol layer when data are removed from a socket's receive buffer?

11.17   Describe an application where the ability to pass file descriptors is useful. Is there another way to simulate this facility in 4.4BSD?

11.18   What is the difference between an internalized capability and an externalized capability? Would file descriptors be considered externalized or internalized capabilities, according to the definitions given in this chapter?

11.19   What might cause a connection to linger forever when closing?

*11.20 What effect might storage compaction have on the performance of network-communication protocols?

**11.21 Why is releasing mbuf-cluster storage back to the system complicated? Explain why it might be desirable.

**11.22 In the original design of the interprocess-communication facilities, a reference to a communication domain was obtained with a *domain* system call,

```
int d; d = domain("inet");
```

(where *d* is a descriptor, much like a file descriptor), and sockets then were created with

```
s = socket(type, d, protocol);
int s, type, protocol;
```

What advantages and disadvantages does this scheme have compared to the one that is used in 4.4BSD? What effect does the introduction of a domain descriptor type have on the management and use of descriptors within the kernel?

References

Cerf, 1978.
V. Cerf, "The Catenet Model for Internetworking," Technical Report IEN 48, SRI Network Information Center, Menlo Park, CA, July 1978.

D. Cohen, 1977.
D. Cohen, "Network Control Protocol (NCP) Software," University of Illinois Software Distribution, University of Illinois, Champaign-Urbana, IL, 1977.

J. Cohen, 1981.
J. Cohen, "Garbage Collection of Linked Data Structures," *Computing Surveys*, vol. 13, no. 3, pp. 341–367, September 1981.

Fitzgerald & Rashid, 1986.
R. Fitzgerald & R. F. Rashid, "The Integration of Virtual Memory Management and Interprocess Communication in Accent," *ACM Transactions on Computer Systems*, vol. 4, no. 2, pp. 147–177, May 1986.

Gurwitz, 1981.
R. F. Gurwitz, "VAX-UNIX Networking Support Project—Implementation Description," Technical Report IEN 168, SRI Network Information Center, Menlo Park, CA, January 1981.

Kalash et al, 1986.
J. Kalash, L. Rodgin, Z. Fong, & J. Anton, "Ingres Version 8 Reference Manual," in *UNIX Programmer's Supplementary Documents, Volume 2, 4.3 Berkeley Software Distribution, Virtual VAX-11 Version*, pp. 10:1–88, USENIX Association, Berkeley, CA, 1986.

Rashid, 1980.
R. F. Rashid, "An Inter-Process Communication Facility for UNIX," Technical Report, Carnegie-Mellon University, Pittsburgh, PA, August 14, 1980.

Sunshine, 1977.
C. Sunshine, "Interprocess Communication Extensions for the UNIX Operating System: Design Considerations," Technical Report R-2064/1-AF, Rand Corporation, Santa Monica, CA, June 1977.

UPMV7, 1983.
UPMV7, *UNIX Programmer's Manual,* Seventh ed, Volumes 1 and 2, Holt, Rinehart & Winston, New York, NY, 1983.

CHAPTER 12

Network Communication

In this chapter, we shall study the internal structure of the network subsystem provided in 4.4BSD. The networking facilities provide a framework within which many *network architectures* may coexist. A network architecture comprises a set of network-communication protocols, the *protocol family*; conventions for naming communication endpoints, the *address family* or *address format*; and any additional facilities that may fall outside the realm of connection management and data transfer. Networking facilities are accessed through the *socket* abstraction described in Chapter 11. The network subsystem provides a general-purpose framework within which network services are implemented. These facilities include

- A structured interface to the socket level that allows the development of network-independent application software

- A consistent interface to the hardware devices used to transmit and receive data

- Network-independent support for message routing

- Memory management

We describe the internal structure of the network subsystem in Section 12.1. Then, we discuss the interface between the socket layer and the network facilities, and examine the interfaces between the layers of software that make up the network subsystem. In Section 12.5, we discuss the routing services used by the network protocols; in Section 12.6, we describe the mechanisms provided to manage buffering and to control congestion. We present the *raw-socket* interface that provides direct access to lower-level network protocols in Section 12.7. Finally, in Section 12.8, we discuss an assortment of issues and facilities, including out-of-band data, subnetwork addressing, and the Address Resolution Protocol.

After we have discussed the framework in which the network protocols fit, we shall examine the implementations of several existing network protocols in Chapter 13. A detailed description of the internal data structures and functions of the network layers and protocols can be found in [Wright & Stevens, 1995].

12.1 Internal Structure

The network subsystem is logically divided into three layers. These three layers manage the following tasks:

1. Interprocess data transport

2. Internetwork addressing and message routing

3. Transmission-media support

The first two layers are made up of modules that implement communication protocols. The software in the third layer generally includes a protocol sublayer, as well as a sublayer that is structurally much like a device driver (see Section 6.3).

The topmost layer in the network subsystem is termed the *transport layer*. The transport layer must provide an addressing structure that permits communication between sockets and any protocol mechanisms necessary for socket semantics, such as reliable data delivery. The second layer, the *network layer*, is responsible for the delivery of data destined for remote transport or for network-layer protocols. In providing internetwork delivery, the network layer must manage a private routing database or use the systemwide facility for routing messages to their destination host. The bottom layer, the *network-interface layer*, or *link layer*, is responsible for transporting messages between hosts connected to a common transmission medium. The network-interface layer is mainly concerned with driving the transmission media involved and doing any necessary link-level protocol *encapsulation* and *decapsulation*.

The transport, network, and network-interface layers of the network subsystem most closely resemble the bottom three levels (2 through 0) of the Xerox Network System (XNS) architecture. These layers correspond to the *transport*, *network*, and *link* layers of the ISO Open Systems Interconnection Reference Model [ISO, 1984], respectively. The internal structure of the networking software is not directly visible to users. Instead, all networking facilities are accessed through the socket layer described in Chapter 11. Each communication protocol that permits access to its facilities exports a user request routine to the socket layer. This routine is used by the socket layer in providing access to network services.

The layering described here is a *logical layering*. The software that implements network services may use more or fewer communication protocols according to the design of the network architecture being supported. For example, raw sockets often use a null implementation at one or more layers. At the opposite extreme, *tunneling* of one protocol through another uses one network protocol to encapsulate and deliver packets for another protocol, and involves multiple instances of some layers.

Data Flow

Data flow down to the network subsystem from the socket layer through calls to the transport-layer modules that support the socket abstraction. Data received at a network interface flow upward through communication protocols until they are placed in the receive queue of the destination socket. The downward flow of data typically is started by system calls. Data flowing upward are received asynchronously, and are passed from the network-interface layer to the appropriate communication protocol through per-protocol input message queues, as shown in Fig. 12.1. The system schedules network protocol processing from the network-interface layer by marking a bit assigned to the protocol in the system's network-interrupt status word, and posting a *software interrupt* reserved for triggering

Figure 12.1 Example of upward flow of a data packet in the network subsystem. ETHER—Ethernet header; IP—Internet Protocol header; TCP—Transmission Control Protocol header.

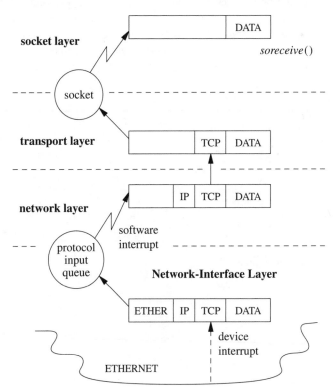

network activity. Software interrupts are used to schedule asynchronous network activity, rather than protocols being run as independent processes, to avoid context-switching overhead. If a message received by a communication protocol is destined for a higher-level protocol, this protocol is invoked directly at software-interrupt level to process the message. Alternatively, if the message is destined for another host and the system is configured as a *router*, the message may be returned to the network-interface layer for retransmission.

Communication Protocols

A network protocol is defined by a set of conventions, including packet formats, states, and state transitions. A communication-protocol module implements a protocol, and is made up of a collection of procedures and private data structures. Protocol modules are described by a *protocol-switch* structure that contains the set of externally visible entry points and certain attributes, shown in Fig. 12.2. The socket layer interacts with a communication protocol solely through the latter's protocol-switch structure, recording the structure's address in a socket's *so_proto* field. This isolation of the socket layer from the networking subsystem is important in ensuring that the socket layer provides users with a consistent interface to all the protocols supported by a system. When a socket is created, the socket layer looks up the *domain* for the protocol family to find the array of protocol-switch structures for the family (see Section 11.4). A protocol is selected from the array based on the type of socket supported (the *pr_type* field) and optionally a specific protocol number (the *pr_protocol* field). The protocol switch has a back pointer to the domain (*pr_domain*). Within a protocol family, every protocol capable of supporting a socket directly (for example, most transport protocols) must provide a

Figure 12.2 Protocol-switch structure.

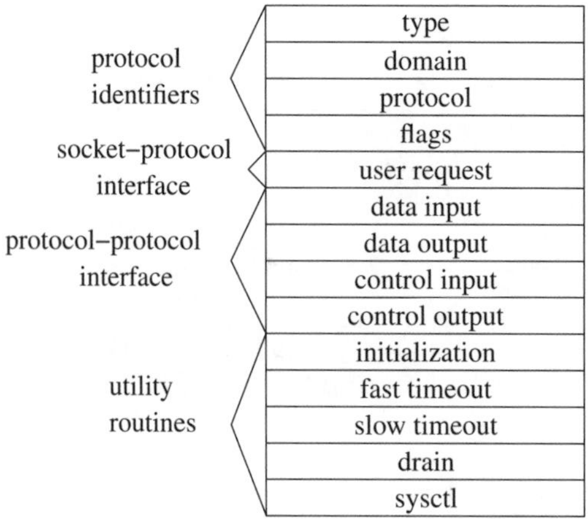

protocol-switch structure describing the protocol. Lower-level protocols such as network-layer protocols may also have protocol-switch entries, although whether they do can depend on conventions within the family.

Before a protocol is first used, the protocol's initialization routine is invoked. Thereafter, the protocol will be invoked for timer-based actions every 200 milliseconds if the *pr_fasttimo()* entry is present, and every 500 milliseconds if the *pr_slowtimo()* entry point is present. In general, protocols use the slower timer for most timer processing; the major use of the fast timeout is for delayed-acknowledgment processing. The *pr_drain()* entry is provided so that the system can notify the protocol if the system is low on space and would like any noncritical data to be discarded. Finally, the *pr_sysctl()* entry implements *sysctl* configuration operations specific to the protocol.

Protocols may pass data among themselves in chains of mbufs (see Section 11.3) using the *pr_input()* and *pr_output()* routines. The *pr_input()* routine passes data *up* toward the user, whereas the *pr_output()* routine passes data *down* toward the network. Similarly, control information passes up and down via the *pr_ctlinput()* and *pr_ctloutput()* routines. The *user request routine, pr_usrreq()*, is the interface between a protocol and the socket level; it is described in detail in Section 12.2.

In general, a protocol is responsible for storage space occupied by any of the arguments passed downward via these procedures and must either pass the space onward or dispose of it. On output, the lowest level reached must free space passed as arguments; on input, the highest level is responsible for freeing space passed up to it. Auxiliary storage needed by protocols is allocated from the mbuf store. This space is used temporarily to formulate messages or to hold variable-sized socket addresses. (Some protocols also use mbufs for data structures such as state control blocks, although many such uses have been converted to use *malloc()* directly.) Mbufs allocated by a protocol for private use must be freed by that protocol when they are no longer in use.

The *pr_flags* field in a protocol's protocol-switch structure describes the protocol's capabilities and certain aspects of its operation that are pertinent to the operation of the socket level; the flags are listed in Table 12.1. Protocols that are

Table 12.1 Protocol flags.

Flag	Description
PR_ATOMIC	messages sent separately, each in a single packet
PR_ADDR	protocol presents address with each message
PR_CONNREQUIRED	connection required for data transfer
PR_WANTRCVD	protocol notified on user receipt of data
PR_RIGHTS	protocol supports passing access rights

connection based specify the PR_CONNREQUIRED flag, so that socket routines will never attempt to send data before a connection has been established. If the PR_WANTRCVD flag is set, the socket routines will notify the protocol when the user has removed data from a socket's receive queue. This notification allows a protocol to implement acknowledgment on user receipt, and also to update flow-control information based on the amount of space available in the receive queue. The PR_ADDR field indicates that any data placed in a socket's receive queue by the protocol will be preceded by the address of the sender. The PR_ATOMIC flag specifies that each *user* request to send data must be done in a single *protocol* send request; it is the protocol's responsibility to maintain record boundaries on data to be sent. This flag also implies that messages must be received and delivered to processes atomically. The PR_RIGHTS flag indicates that the protocol supports the transfer of access rights; this flag is currently used by only those protocols in the local communication domain (see Section 11.6).

Network Interfaces

Each network interface configured in a system defines a link-layer path through which messages can be sent and received. A *link-layer path* is a path that allows a message to be sent via a single transmission to its destination, without network-level forwarding. Normally, a hardware device is associated with this interface, although there is no requirement that one be (e.g., all systems have a software *loopback* interface used for most network traffic sent to local sockets). In addition to manipulating the hardware device, a network-interface module is responsible for encapsulation and decapsulation of any link-layer protocol header required to deliver a message to its destination. For common interface types, the link-layer protocol is implemented in a separate sublayer that is shared by various hardware drivers. The selection of the interface to use in delivering a packet is a routing decision carried out at the network-protocol layer. An interface may have addresses in one or more address families. Each address is set at boot time using an *ioctl* system call on a socket in the appropriate domain; this operation is implemented by the protocol family after the network interface verifies the operation with an *ioctl* entry point provided by the network interface. The network-interface abstraction provides protocols with a consistent interface to all hardware devices that may be present on a machine.

An interface and its addresses are defined by the structures shown in Fig. 12.3. As interfaces are found at startup time, the *ifnet* structures are initialized and are placed on a linked list. The network-interface module generally maintains the *ifnet* interface data structure as part of a larger structure that also contains information used in driving the underlying hardware device. Similarly, the *ifaddr* interface address structure is often part of a larger structure containing additional protocol information about the interface or its address. Because network socket addresses are variable in size, the protocol is responsible for allocating the space referenced by the address, mask, and broadcast or destination address pointers in the *ifaddr* structure.

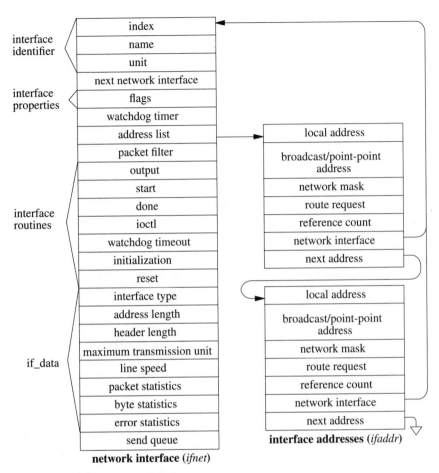

Figure 12.3 Network-interface data structures.

Each network interface contains identification of the interface in two forms: a character string identifying the driver plus a unit number for the driver (e.g. *en0*) and a binary systemwide index number. The index is used as a shorthand identifier—for example, when a route that refers to the interface is established. As each interface is found during system startup, the system creates an array of pointers to the *ifnet* structures for the interfaces. It can thus locate an interface quickly given an index number, whereas the lookup using a string name is less efficient. Some operations, such as interface address assignment, name the interface with a string for convenience because performance is not critical. Other operations, such as route establishment, pass a newer style of identifier that can use either a string or an index. The new identifier uses a *sockaddr* structure in a new address family, AF_LINK, indicating a link-layer address. The family-specific version of the

sdl_len	20
sdl_family	AF_LINK
sdl_index	1
sdl_type	IFT_ETHER
sdl_nlen	3
sdl_alen	6
sdl_slen	0
adl_data	'e' 'n' '0' 00:00:c0:c2:59:0b
struct *sockaddr_dl*	example **struct** *sockaddr_dl*

Figure 12.4 Link-layer address structure. The box on the left names the elements of the *sockaddr_dl* structure. The box on the right shows sample values for these elements for an Ethernet interface. The *sdl_data* array may contain a name (if *sdl_nlen* is nonzero, a link-layer address (if *sdl_alen* is nonzero), and an address selector (if *sdl_slen* is nonzero). For an Ethernet, *sdl_data* contains a three-character name, *en0*, followed by a 6-byte Ethernet address.

---

structure is a *sockaddr_dl* structure, shown in Fig. 12.4, which may contain up to three identifiers. It includes an interface name as a string plus a length, with a length of zero denoting the absence of a name. It also includes an interface index as an integer, with a value of zero indicating that the index is not set. Finally, it may include a binary link-level address, such as an Ethernet address, and the length of the address. An address of this form is created for each network interface as the interface is configured by the system, and is returned in the list of local addresses for the system along with network protocol addresses (see later in this subsection). Figure 12.4 shows a structure describing an Ethernet interface that is the second interface on the system; the structure contains the interface name, the index, and the link-layer (Ethernet) address.

The interface data structure includes an *if_data* structure, which contains the externally visible description of the interface. It includes the link-layer type of the interface, the maximum network-protocol packet size that is supported, and the sizes of the link-layer header and address. It also contains numerous statistics, such as packets and bytes sent and received, input and output errors, and other data required by network-management protocols.

The state of an interface and certain externally visible characteristics are stored in the *if_flags* field described in Table 12.2. The first set of flags characterizes an interface. If an interface is connected to a network that supports transmission of *broadcast* messages, the IFF_BROADCAST flag will be set, and the interface's address list will contain a broadcast address to be used in sending and receiving such messages. If an interface is associated with a point-to-point hardware link (e.g., a serial interface to a telephone circuit), the IFF_POINTOPOINT flag will be set, and the interface's address list will contain the address of the host on the other side of the connection. (Note that the broadcast and point-to-point attributes are

Table 12.2 Network interface flags.

Flag	Description
IFF_UP	interface is available for use
IFF_BROADCAST	broadcast is supported
IFF_DEBUG	enable debugging in the interface software
IFF_LOOPBACK	this is a software loopback interface
IFF_POINTOPOINT	interface is for a point-to-point link
IFF_RUNNING	interface resources have been allocated
IFF_PROMISC	interface receives packets for all destinations
IFF_ALLMULTI	interface receives all multicast packets
IFF_OACTIVE	interface is busy doing output
IFF_SIMPLEX	interface cannot receive its own transmissions
IFF_LINK0	link-layer specific
IFF_LINK1	link-layer specific
IFF_LINK2	link-layer specific
IFF_MULTICAST	multicast is supported

mutually exclusive, and that the two addresses share storage in the interface address structure.) These addresses and the local address of an interface are used by network-layer protocols in filtering incoming packets. The IFF_MULTICAST flag is set by interfaces that support multicast packets in addition to IFF_BROADCAST. Multicast packets are sent to one of several *group* addresses, and are intended for all members of the group.

Additional interface flags describe the operational state of an interface. An interface sets the IFF_RUNNING flag after it has allocated system resources and has posted an initial read on the device that it manages. This state bit avoids multiple allocation requests when an interface's address is changed. The IFF_UP flag is set when the interface is configured and is ready to transmit messages. The IFF_OACTIVE flag is used to coordinate between the *if_output* and *if_start* routines, described later in this subsection; it is set when no additional output may be attempted. The IFF_PROMISC flag is set by network-monitoring programs to enable *promiscuous* reception: when they wish to receive packets for all destinations, rather than for just the local system. Packets addressed to other systems are passed to the monitoring packet filter but are not delivered to network protocols. The IFF_ALLMULTI flag is similar, but applies to only multicast packets; it can be used by a multicast forwarding agent. The IFF_SIMPLEX flag is set by Ethernet drivers whose hardware cannot receive packets that they send; here, the output function simulates reception of broadcast and (depending on the protocol) multicast packets that have been sent. Finally, the IFF_DEBUG flag can be set to enable any optional driver-level diagnostic tests or messages. In addition to these interface flags, three additional flags are defined for use by individual link-layer drivers (IFF_LINK0, IFF_LINK1, and IFF_LINK2). They can be used to select link-layer options, such as Ethernet medium type.

Interface addresses and flags are set with *ioctl* requests. The requests specific to a network interface pass the name of the interface as a string in the input data structure, with the string containing the name for the interface type plus the unit number. Either the SIOCSIFADDR request or the SIOCAIFADDR request is used initially to define each interface's addresses. The former sets a single address for the protocol on this interface. The latter adds an address, with an associated address mask and broadcast address. It allows an interface to support multiple addresses for the same protocol. In either case, the protocol allocates an *ifaddr* structure and sufficient space for the addresses and any private data, and links the structure onto the list of addresses for the network interface. In addition, most protocols keep a list of the addresses for the protocol. The result appears somewhat like a two-dimensional linked list, as shown in Fig. 12.5. An address can be deleted with the SIOCDIFADDR request.

The SIOCSIFFLAGS request can be used to change an interface's state and to do site-specific configuration. The destination address of a point-to-point link is set with the SIOCSIFDSTADDR request. Corresponding operations exist to read each value. Protocol families also can support operations to set and read the broadcast address. Finally, the SIOCGIFCONF request can be used to retrieve a list of interface names and protocol addresses for all interfaces and protocols configured in a running system. Similar information is returned by a newer mechanism based on the *sysctl* system call with a request in the routing protocol family (see Sections 12.5 and 14.7). These requests permit developers to construct network processes such as the routing daemon without detailed knowledge of the system's internal data structures.

Figure 12.5 Network-interface and protocol data structures. The linked list of *ifnet* structures appears on the left side of the figure. The *ifaddr* structures storing the addresses for each interface are on a linked list headed in the *ifnet* structure and shown as a horizontal list. The *ifaddr* structures for most protocols are linked together as well, shown in the vertical lists headed by *pf1_addr* and *pf2_addr*.

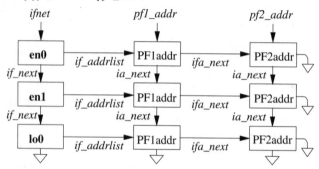

Each interface has a queue of messages to be transmitted and routines used for initialization and output. The *if_output*() routine accepts a packet for transmission, and normally handles link-layer encapsulation and queueing that are independent of the specific hardware driver in use. If the IFF_OACTIVE flag is not set, the output routine may then invoke the driver's *if_start*() function to begin transmission. The start function then sets the IFF_OACTIVE flag if it is unable to accept additional packets for transmission; the flag will be cleared when transmission completes. The *if_done*() entry point is provided as a callback function for use when the output queue is emptied. This facility is not yet used, but is intended to support *striping* of data for a single logical interface across multiple physical interfaces.

If the interface resides on a system bus, a reset routine will be invoked after a bus reset has been done, so that the driver may reinitialize the interface. (This function was used on only the VAX, and should be removed or moved to a machine-dependent data structure.) An interface may also specify a watchdog timer routine and a timer value that (if it is nonzero) the system will decrement once per second, invoking the timer routine when the value expires. The timeout mechanism is typically used by interfaces to implement watchdog schemes for unreliable hardware, and to collect statistics that reside on the hardware device.

12.2   Socket-to-Protocol Interface

The interface from the socket routines to the communication protocols is through the user request, *pr_usrreq*(), and control output, *pr_ctloutput*(), routines, which are defined in the protocol-switch table for each protocol. When the socket layer requires services of a supporting protocol, it makes a call to one of these two routines. The control-output routine implements the *getsockopt* and *setsockopt* system calls; the user-request routine is used for all other operations. Calls to *pr_usrreq*() specify one of the requests shown in Table 12.3 (on page 406). Calls to *pr_ctloutput*() specify PRCO_GETOPT to get the current value of an option, or PRCO_SETOPT to set the value of an option.

Protocol User-Request Routine

Given a pointer to a protocol-switch entry, *pr*, a call on the user-request routine is of the form

```
error = (*pr->pr_usrreq)(so, req, m, addr, control);
    struct socket *so;
    int req;
    struct mbuf *m, *addr, *control;
```

The *so* parameter specifies the socket for which the operation is requested, and *req* names the operation that is requested. The mbuf data chain *m* is supplied for

Table 12.3 *pr_usrreq* routine requests.

Request	Description
PRU_ABORT	abort connection and detach
PRU_ACCEPT	accept connection from peer
PRU_ATTACH	attach protocol to socket
PRU_BIND	bind name to socket
PRU_CONNECT	establish connection to peer
PRU_CONNECT2	connect two sockets
PRU_CONTROL	control protocol operation (*ioctl*)
PRU_DETACH	detach protocol from socket
PRU_DISCONNECT	disconnect from peer
PRU_FASTTIMO†	service 200-millisecond timeout
PRU_LISTEN	listen for connections
PRU_PEERADDR	fetch peer's address
PRU_PROTORCV†	receive from below
PRU_PROTOSEND†	send to below
PRU_RCVD	have taken data; more room now
PRU_RCVOOB	retrieve out-of-band data
PRU_SEND	send these data
PRU_SENDOOB	send out-of-band data
PRU_SENSE	sense socket status (*fstat*)
PRU_SHUTDOWN	will not send any more data
PRU_SLOWTIMO†	service 500-millisecond timeout
PRU_SOCKADDR	fetch socket's address

† Request used only internally by protocols.

output operations and for certain other operations where a result is to be returned. The *addr* parameter is supplied for address-oriented requests, such as PRU_BIND, PRU_CONNECT, and PRU_SEND (when an address is specified—e.g., the *sendto* call). The address is stored in an mbuf as a *sockaddr* structure. The *control* parameter is a pointer to an optional mbuf chain containing protocol-specific control information passed via the *sendmsg* call, such as user-specified access rights (see Section 11.6). Each protocol is responsible for disposal of the data mbuf chains on output operations. A nonzero return value from the user-request routine indicates an error number that should be passed to higher-level software. A description of each of the possible requests follows.

• **PRU_ATTACH: Attach protocol to socket**　　When a protocol is first bound to a socket (with the *socket* system call), the protocol module is called with the

PRU_ATTACH request. It is the responsibility of the protocol module to allocate any resources necessary. The *attach* request will always precede any of the other requests, and will occur only once per socket.

• **PRU_DETACH: Detach protocol from socket**   This operation is the inverse of the attach request, and is used at the time that a socket is deleted. The protocol module may deallocate any resources assigned to the socket.

• **PRU_BIND: Bind address to socket**   When a socket is initially created, it has no address bound to it. This request indicates that an address should be bound to an existing socket. The protocol module must verify that the requested address is valid and is available for use.

• **PRU_LISTEN: Listen for incoming connections**   The *listen request* indicates that the user wishes to listen for incoming connection requests on the associated socket. The protocol module should make any state changes needed to meet this request (if possible). A listen request always precedes any request to accept a connection.

• **PRU_CONNECT: Connect socket to peer**   The *connect request* indicates that the user wants to a establish an association. The *addr* parameter describes the peer to which a connection is desired. The effect of a connect request may vary depending on the protocol. Virtual-circuit protocols use this request to initiate establishment of a network connection. Datagram protocols simply record the peer's address in a private data structure. They use it as the source address of all outgoing packets and as a destination filter for incoming packets. There are no restrictions on how many times a connect request may be used after an attach, although most stream protocols allow only one connect call.

• **PRU_ACCEPT: Accept pending connection**   Following a successful listen request and the arrival of one or more connections, this request is made to indicate that the user is about to accept a socket from the queue of sockets ready to be returned. The socket supplied as a parameter is the socket that is being *accepted*; the protocol module is expected to fill in the supplied buffer with the address of the peer connected to the socket.

• **PRU_DISCONNECT: Disconnect connected socket**   This request eliminates an association created with a connect request. It is used with datagram sockets before a new association is created; it is used with connection-oriented protocols only when the socket is closed.

• **PRU_SHUTDOWN: Shut down socket data transmission**   This call indicates that no more data will be sent. The protocol may, at its discretion, deallocate any data structures related to the shutdown and may notify a connected peer of the shutdown.

• **PRU_RCVD: Data were received by user**   This request is made only if the protocol entry in the protocol-switch table includes the PR_WANTRCVD flag. When the socket layer removes data from the receive queue and passes them to the user, this request will be sent to the protocol module. This request may be used by the protocol to trigger acknowledgments, to refresh windowing information, to initiate data transfer, and so on. This request is also made when an application attempts to receive data on a socket that is in the *confirming* state, indicating that the protocol must accept the connection request before data can be received (see Section 11.5).

• **PRU_SEND: Send user data**   Each user request to send data is translated into one or more PRU_SEND requests. A protocol may indicate that a single user send request must be translated into a single PRU_SEND request by specifying the PR_ATOMIC flag in its protocol description. The data to be sent are presented to the protocol as a chain of mbufs, and an optional address is supplied in the *addr* parameter. The protocol is responsible for preserving the data in the socket's send queue if it is not able to send them immediately or if it may need them at some later time (e.g., for retransmission). The protocol must eventually pass the data to a lower level or free the mbufs.

• **PRU_ABORT: Abnormally terminate service**   This request indicates an abnormal termination of service. The protocol should delete any existing associations.

• **PRU_CONTROL: Do control operation**   The *control request* is generated when a user does an *ioctl* system call on a socket and the *ioctl* is not intercepted by the socket routines. This request allows protocol-specific operations to be provided outside the scope of the common socket interface. The *addr* parameter contains a pointer to a kernel data area where relevant information may be obtained or returned. The *m* parameter contains the actual *ioctl* request code. The *control* parameter contains a pointer to a network-interface structure if the *ioctl* operation pertains to a particular network interface. This case illustrates the most serious problem with the *pr_usrreq* entry point: for some requests, the parameters are overloaded with completely different data types.

• **PRU_SENSE: Sense socket status**   The *sense request* is generated when the user makes an *fstat* system call on a socket; it requests the status of the associated socket. This call returns a standard *stat* structure that typically contains only the optimal transfer size for the connection (based on buffer size, windowing information, and maximum packet size).

• **PRU_RCVOOB: Receive out-of-band data**   This operation requests that any *out-of-band* data now available are to be returned. An mbuf is passed to the protocol module, and the protocol should either place data in the mbuf or attach new mbufs to the one supplied if there is insufficient space in the single mbuf. An error may be returned if out-of-band data are not (yet) available or have already been consumed. The *addr* parameter contains any options, such as MSG_PEEK, that should be observed while this request is carried out.

• **PRU_SENDOOB: Send out-of-band data**   This request is like the send request, but is used for out-of-band data.

• **PRU_SOCKADDR: Retrieve local socket address**   This request indicates that the local address of the socket is to be returned, if one has been bound to the socket. The address (stored in a *sockaddr* structure in an address-family–specific format) is returned in the mbuf passed in the *addr* parameter.

• **PRU_PEERADDR: Retrieve peer socket address**   This request indicates that the address of the peer to which the socket is connected is to be returned. The socket must be in a connected state for this request to be made to the protocol. The address (stored in a *sockaddr* structure in an address-family–specific format) is returned in the mbuf pointed to by the *addr* parameter.

• **PRU_CONNECT2: Connect two sockets without binding addresses**   In this request, the protocol module is supplied two sockets, and is asked to establish a connection between the two without binding any addresses, if possible. The system uses this call in implementing the *socketpair* system call.

Internal Requests

The following requests are used internally by the protocol modules and are never generated by the socket routines. In certain instances, they are used solely for convenience in tracing a protocol's operation (e.g., the slow timeout request).

• **PRU_FASTTIMO: Service fast timeout**   A fast timeout has occurred. This request is made when a timeout occurs in the protocol's *pr_fasttimo*() routine. The *addr* parameter indicates which timer expired.

• **PRU_SLOWTIMO: Service slow timeout**   A slow timeout has occurred. This request is made when a timeout occurs in the protocol's *pr_slowtimo*() routine. The *addr* parameter indicates which timer expired.

• **PRU_PROTORCV: Receive data for protocol**   This request is used between protocols, rather than by the socket layer; it requests reception of data destined for a protocol and not for the user. No protocols currently use this facility.

• **PRU_PROTOSEND: Send data to protocol**   This request allows a protocol to send data destined for another protocol module, rather than for a user. The details of how data are marked *addressed-to-protocol* instead of *addressed-to-user* are left to the protocol modules. No protocols currently use this facility.

Protocol Control-Output Routine

A call on the control-output routine is of the form

```
error = (*pr->pr_ctloutput)(op, so, level, optname, mp);
    int op;
    struct socket *so;
    int level, optname;
    struct mbuf **mp;
```

where *op* is PRCO_SETOPT when an option's value is set, and is PRCO_GETOPT when an option's value is retrieved. The *level* parameter indicates the layer of software that should interpret the option request. A *level* of SOL_SOCKET is specified to control an option at the socket layer. When the option is to be processed by a protocol module below the socket layer, *level* is set to the appropriate protocol number (the same number used in the *socket* system call.) Each level has its own set of option names; this name is interpreted by only the targeted layer of software. The final parameter is a pointer to a pointer to an mbuf; the preexisting mbuf contains an option's new value when setting, and the pointer is used to return an mbuf that contains an option's value when getting. Mbufs passed to the control-output routine when the socket layer is setting an option value must be freed by the protocol. When the socket layer is getting an option value, mbufs used to return an option value are allocated by the protocol and are returned to the socket layer, where they are freed after data are copied to the user.

In supporting the *getsockopt* and *setsockopt* system calls, the socket layer always invokes the control-output routine of the protocol attached to the socket. To access lower-level protocols, each control-output routine must pass control-output requests that are not for itself *downward* to the next protocol in the protocol hierarchy. Chapter 13 describes some of the options provided by the protocols in the Internet communication domain.

12.3 Protocol–Protocol Interface

The interface between protocol modules uses the *pr_usrreq*(), *pr_input*(), *pr_output*(), *pr_ctlinput*(), and *pr_ctloutput*() routines. The *pr_usrreq*() and *pr_ctloutput*() routines are used by the socket layer to communicate with protocols and have standard calling conventions. The remaining routines are not normally accessed outside a protocol family, and therefore different calling conventions have evolved.

Although imposing a standard calling convention for all of a protocol's entry points might theoretically permit an arbitrary interconnection of protocol modules, it would be difficult in practice. Crossing of a protocol-family boundary would require a network address to be converted from the format of the caller's domain to the format of the receiver's domain. Consequently, connection of protocols in different communication domains is not generally supported, and calling conventions for the routines listed in the preceding paragraph are typically standardized on a per-domain basis. (However, the system does support encapsulation of packets from one protocol into packets of a protocol in another family to *tunnel* one protocol through another.)

In this section, we briefly examine the general framework and calling conventions of protocols. In Chapter 13, we examine specific protocols to see how they fit into this framework.

pr_output

The protocol output routine often uses a calling convention designed to send a single message on a connection; for example,

```
error = (*pr_output)(pcb, m);
    struct pcb *pcb;
    struct mbuf *m;
```

would send a message contained in *m* on a connection described by protocol control block *pcb*. Lower-level protocol output routines may not always have protocol control blocks, and thus may require more explicit parameters.

pr_input

Upper-level protocol input routines are usually called at software-interrupt level once the network-level protocol has located the protocol identifier. They generally have stricter conventions than do output routines because they are often called via a protocol switch. Depending on the protocol family, they may receive a pointer to a control block identifying the connection, or they may have to locate the control block from information in the received packet. A typical calling convention is

```
(void) (*pr_input)(m, hlen);
    struct mbuf *m;
    int hlen;
```

In this example, the incoming packet is passed to a transport protocol in an mbuf *m* with the network protocol header still in place for the transport protocol to use, as well as the length of the header, *hlen*, so that the header can be removed. The protocol does the connection-level demultiplexing based on information in the network and transport headers.

pr_ctlinput

This routine passes *control* information (i.e., information that might be passed to the user, but does not consist of data) *upward* from one protocol module to another. The common calling convention for this routine is

```
(void) (*pr_ctlinput)(req, addr);
    int req;
    struct sockaddr *addr;
```

The *req* parameter is one of the values shown in Table 12.4 (on page 412). The *addr* parameter is the remote address to which the condition applies. Many of the requests have been derived from the Internet Control Message Protocol (ICMP)

Table 12.4 Control-input routine requests.

Request	Description
PRC_IFDOWN	network interface transition
PRC_ROUTEDEAD	select new route if possible
PRC_MSGSIZE	message size forced packet to be dropped
PRC_HOSTDEAD	remote host is down
PRC_HOSTUNREACH	remote host is unreachable
PRC_UNREACH_NET	no route to network
PRC_UNREACH_HOST	no route to host
PRC_UNREACH_PROTOCOL	protocol not supported by destination
PRC_UNREACH_PORT	port number not in use at destination
PRC_UNREACH_NEEDFRAG	fragmentation needed but not allowed
PRC_UNREACH_SRCFAIL	source route failed
PRC_REDIRECT_NET	routing redirect for a network
PRC_REDIRECT_HOST	routing redirect for a host
PRC_REDIRECT_TOSNET	routing redirect for type of service and network
PRC_REDIRECT_TOSHOST	routing redirect for type of service and host
PRC_TIMXCEED_INTRANS	packet lifetime expired in transit
PRC_TIMXCEED_REASS	lifetime expired on reassembly queue
PRC_PARAMPROB	header-parameter problem detected

[Postel, 1981], and from error messages defined in the 1822 host/IMP convention [BBN, 1978]. Some protocols may pass additional parameters internally, such as local addresses or more specific information.

12.4 Interface between Protocol and Network Interface

The lowest layer in the set of protocols that constitutes a protocol family must interact with one or more network interfaces to transmit and receive packets. It is assumed that any routing decisions have been made before a packet is sent to a network interface; a routing decision is necessary to locate any interface at all, unless a single *hardwired* interface is used. There are two cases with which we should be concerned in the interaction between protocols and network interfaces: transmission of a packet and receipt of a packet. We shall consider each separately.

Packet Transmission

If a protocol has chosen an interface identified by *ifp*, a pointer to a network interface structure, the protocol transmits a fully formatted network-level packet with the following call:

```
error = (*ifp->if_output)(ifp, m, dst, rt);
    struct ifnet *ifp;
    struct mbuf *m;
    struct sockaddr *dst;
    struct rtentry *rt;
```

The output routine for the network interface transmits the packet *m* to the protocol address specified in *dst*, or returns an error number. In reality, transmission may not be immediate or successful; typically, the output routine validates the destination address, queues the packet on its send queue, and primes an interrupt-driven routine to transmit the packet if the interface is not busy. For unreliable media, such as the Ethernet, *successful* transmission simply means that the packet has been placed on the cable without a collision. In contrast, an *X.25* interface guarantees proper delivery or an error indication for each message transmitted. The model employed in the networking system attaches no promise of delivery to the packets presented to a network interface, and thus corresponds most closely to the Ethernet. Errors returned by the output routine are only those that can be detected immediately and are normally trivial in nature (network down, no buffer space, address format not handled, etc.). If errors are detected after the call has returned, the protocol is not notified.

When messages are transmitted, each network interface usually must formulate a link-layer address for each outgoing packet.† The interface layer must understand each protocol address format that it supports to formulate corresponding link-layer addresses. The network layer for each protocol family selects a destination address for each message, and then uses that address to select the appropriate network interface to use. This destination address is passed to the interface's output routine as a *sockaddr* structure. Presuming that the address format is supported by the interface, the interface must map the destination protocol address into an address for the link-layer protocol associated with the transmission medium that the interface supports. This mapping may be a simple algorithm, it may require a table lookup, or it may require more involved techniques, such as use of the Address Resolution Protocol described in Section 12.8.

Packet Reception

Network interfaces receive packets, and dispatch packets to the appropriate network-layer protocol according to information encoded in the link-layer protocol header. Each protocol family must have one or more protocols that constitute the network layer described in Section 12.1. In this system, each network-layer protocol has an input-packet queue assigned to it. Incoming packets received by a network interface are queued in a protocol's input packet queue, and a software interrupt is posted to initiate network-layer processing; see Fig. 12.6 (on page 414). Similar queues are used to store packets awaiting transmission by network-interface modules.

---

†A link-layer address may not be required for a point-to-point link.

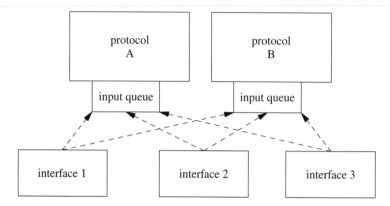

Figure 12.6 Input packets dispatched to protocol input queues.

Several macros are available for manipulating packet queues:

- **IF_ENQUEUE(ifq, m)**   Place the packet *m* at the tail of the queue *ifq*.

- **IF_DEQUEUE(ifq, m)**   Place a pointer to the packet at the head of queue *ifq* in *m*, and remove the packet from the queue; *m* will be zero if the queue is empty.

- **IF_PREPEND(ifq, m)**   Place the packet *m* at the head of the queue *ifq*.

Packet queues have a maximum length associated with them as a simple form of congestion control. The macro IF_QFULL() can be used to determine whether a queue is full; if it is, another macro, IF_DROP(), can then be used to record the event in statistics kept for the queue. For example, the following code fragment could be used in a network interface's output routine:

```
if (IF_QFULL(ifp->if_snd)) {
    IF_DROP(ifp->if_snd);
    m_freem(m);        /* discard packet */
    error = ENOBUFS;
} else
    IF_ENQUEUE(ifp->if_snd, m);
```

On receiving a packet, a network interface decodes the packet type, strips the link-layer protocol header, records the identity of the receiving interface, and then dispatches the packet to the appropriate protocol. For example, packets are enqueued for the Internet domain with

```
s = splimp();
if (IF_QFULL(&ipintrq)) {
    IF_DROP(&ipintrq);
    ifp->if_iqdrops++;
    m_freem(m);
} else {
    schednetisr(NETISR_IP);    /* schedule IP input routine */
    IF_ENQUEUE(&ipintr, m);    /* place message on IP's queue */
}
splx(s);
```

The *schednetisr*() macro marks a bit in a global status word, and then posts a software interrupt. When the software interrupt occurs, the interrupt handler scans the status word, and, for each preassigned bit that is set, invokes the associated protocol input routine. Note that multiple interfaces can place packets into the same queue, and thus interrupts from other interfaces must be blocked. Bits in the status word are assigned according to the value of their protocol-family identifiers, shown in Table 12.5.

Entries on a protocol's input queue are mbuf chains with a valid packet header containing the packet's length and a pointer to the network interface on which the packet was received. The pointer to the interface has many potential uses, such as deciding when to generate routing redirect messages. Input-handling routines that run at software-interrupt level are typically of the form

```
for (;;) {
    s = splimp();            /* block network from queue */
    IF_DEQUEUE(&xxintrq, m);
    splx(s);
    if (m == 0)  /* all packets processed */
        break;
    /* process packet and determine receiving protocol */
    (*pr_input)(m, hlen);    /* invoke protocol */
}
```

Table 12.5 Network-interrupt status-word bit assignments.

Status bit	Value	Input queue	Use
NETISR_IP	PF_INET	*ipintrq*	Internet IP protocol input
NETISR_NS	PF_NS	*nsintrq*	Xerox NS protocol input
NETISR_ISO	PF_ISO	*clnlintrq*	ISO/OSI connectionless network
NETISR_CCITT	PF_CCITT	*llcintrq*	X.25 packet level
NETISR_ARP	PF_ARP	*arpintrq*	ARP input

While an entry is dequeued from an input queue, a protocol blocks all network-interface input handling by raising the processor's priority level with *splimp*() to ensure that pointers in the queue data structure are not altered. Once a message is dequeued, it is processed; if there is information in the packet for a higher-level protocol, the message is passed upward.

12.5 Routing

The networking system was designed for an internetwork environment in which a collection of local-area networks is connected at one or more points through network nodes with multiple network interfaces, as shown in the example in Fig. 12.7. Nodes with multiple network interfaces—one on each local-area or long-haul network—may act as routers.† In such an environment, issues related to gatewaying and packet routing are important. Certain of these issues, such as congestion control, are handled simplistically in 4.4BSD (see Section 12.6). For others, the network system provides simple mechanisms on which more involved policies can be implemented. These mechanisms ensure that, as these problems become better understood, their solutions can be incorporated into the system.

This section describes the facilities provided for packet routing. The routing facilities were designed for use by singly connected and multiply connected hosts, as well as for routers. There are several components involved in routing, illustrated in Fig. 12.8. The design of the routing system places some components within the operating system and others at user level. The routing facilities included in the kernel do not impose *routing policies*, but instead support a *routing mechanism* by which externally defined policies can be implemented. By a *routing mechanism*, we mean a table lookup that provides a first-hop route (a specific network interface and immediate destination) for each destination. Routing policies include all the components involved in choosing the first-hop routes, such as discovery of the local network topology, implementation of various routing protocols, and configuration information specifying local policies. The routing design places enough information in the kernel for packets to be sent on their way without external help; all other components are outside the kernel. User-level processes can be used to implement policies ranging from simple static routing to complex dynamic algorithms. These processes communicate with the kernel via a routing socket to manipulate the kernel routing table and to listen for internal routing events. Each of these components is described in this section. Although there is nothing in the system that prevents protocols from managing their own routing information, the facilities described here were designed to support most needs.

---

†At the time of the original design of this part of the system, a network node that forwarded network-level packets was generally known as a *gateway*. The current Internet term is *router*. We use both terms interchangeably, in part because the system data structures continue to use the name *gateway*.

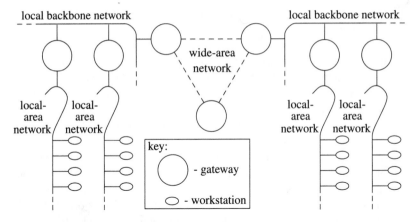

Figure 12.7 Example of the topology for which routing facilities were designed.

Kernel Routing Tables

The kernel routing mechanism implements a routing table for looking up first-hop routes (or next hop, when forwarding packets). It includes two distinct portions: a data structure describing each specific route (a routing entry) and a lookup algorithm to find the correct route for each possible destination. This subsection describes the entries in the routing table, and the next subsection explains the lookup algorithm. A destination is described by a *sockaddr* structure with an address family, a length, and a value. Routes are typed in two ways: as either *host* or *network* routes, and as either *direct* or *indirect*. The host–network distinction determines whether the route applies to a specific host, or to a group of hosts with a portion of their addresses in common—usually a prefix of the address. For host routes, the destination address of a route must exactly match the desired destination; the address family, length, and bit pattern of the destination must match those

Figure 12.8 Routing design.

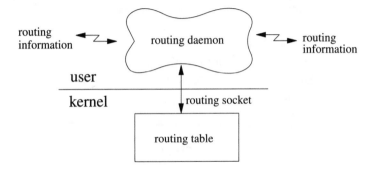

in the route. For network routes, the destination address in the route is paired with a mask. The route matches any address that contains the same bits as the destination in the positions indicated by bits set in the mask. A host route is a special case of a network route, in which the mask bits are set for the whole address, and thus no bits are ignored in the comparison. Another special case is a *wildcard route*: a network route with an empty mask. Such a route matches every destination and serves as a default route for destinations not otherwise known. This fall-back network route can be pointed to an *intelligent gateway* that can then make more informed routing decisions.

The other major distinction between types of routes is either direct or indirect. A *direct* route is one that leads directly to the destination: The first hop of the path is the entire path, and the destination is on a network shared with the source. Most routes are *indirect*: The route specifies a gateway on a local network that is the first-hop destination for the route. Much of the literature (especially for Internet protocols) refers to a *local–remote* decision, where an implementation checks first whether a destination is local to an attached network or is remote; in the first case, a packet is sent locally (via the link layer) to the destination; in the latter case, it is sent locally to the gateway to the destination. In the implementation, the *local–remote* decision is made as part of the routing lookup. If the best route is *direct*, then the destination is local. Otherwise, the route is *indirect*, the destination is remote, and the route entry specifies the gateway to the destination. In either case, the route specifies a first-hop route: a link-level interface to be used in sending packets, and the destination for the packets in this hop if different from the final destination. This information allows a packet to be sent via a local interface to a destination directly reachable via that interface–either the final destination or a router on the path to the destination. This distinction is needed when the

---

Table 12.6 Elements of a routing-table entry (*rtentry*) structure.

Element	Description
rt_nodes[2]	internal and leaf radix nodes
	(with references to destination and mask)
rt_gateway	reference to gateway address
rt_flags	flags; see Table 12.7
rt_refcnt	reference count
rt_ifp	reference to interface, *ifnet*
rt_ifa	reference to interface address, *ifaddr*
rt_genmask	mask for cloning
rt_llinfo	pointer to link-layer private data
rt_rmx	route metrics (e.g. MTU)
rt_gwroute	if indirect, route to gateway

link-layer encapsulation is done. If a packet is destined for a peer at a host or
network that is not directly connected to the source, the internetwork packet
header will contain the address of the eventual destination, whereas the link-layer
protocol header will address the intervening gateway.

The network system maintains a set of routing tables that is used by protocols
in selecting a network interface to use in delivering a packet to its destination.
These tables are composed of entries of the form shown in Table 12.6.

Routing entries are stored in an *rtentry* structure, which contains a reference
to the destination address and mask (unless the route is to a host, in which case the
mask is implicit). The destination address, the address mask, and the gateway
address are variable in size, and thus are placed in separately allocated memory.
Routing entries also contain a reference to a network interface, a set of flags that
characterize the route, and optionally a gateway address. The flags indicate a
route's type (host or network, direct or indirect) and the other attributes shown in
Table 12.7. The route entry also contains a count of the number of packets sent
via the route, a field for use by the link-layer driver, and a set of metrics. The
RTF_HOST flag in a routing-table entry indicates that the route applies to a single
host, using an implicit mask containing all the bits of the address. The
RTF_GATEWAY flag in a routing-table entry indicates that the route is to an *indirect* gateway agent, and that the link-layer header should be filled in from the
rt_gateway field, instead of from the final internetwork destination address. The
route entry contains a field that can be used by the link layer to cache a reference

---

Table 12.7 Route entry flags.

Flag	Description
RTF_UP	route is valid
RTF_GATEWAY	destination is a gateway
RTF_HOST	host entry (net otherwise)
RTF_REJECT	host or net unreachable
RTF_DYNAMIC	created dynamically (by redirect)
RTF_MODIFIED	modified dynamically (by redirect)
RTF_DONE	message confirmed
RTF_MASK	subnet mask present
RTF_CLONING	generate new routes on use
RTF_XRESOLVE	external daemon resolves name
RTF_LLINFO	generated by link layer
RTF_STATIC	manually added by administrator
RTF_BLACKHOLE	just discard packets (during updates)
RTF_PROTO2	protocol-specific routing flag
RTF_PROTO1	protocol-specific routing flag

to the *direct* route for the gateway. The RTF_UP flag is set when a route is installed. When a route is removed, the RTF_UP flag is cleared, but the route entry is not freed until all users of the route have noticed the failure and have released their references. The route entry contains a reference count because it is allocated dynamically and cannot be freed until all references have been released. The RTF_CLONING flag indicates that a route is a generic route that must be *cloned* and made more specific before use. This flag is usually used for link-layer routes that apply to a directly attached network, and the cloned routes are generally host routes for hosts on that network that contain some link-level information about that host. When a route is cloned, an external agent may be invoked to complete the link-layer information needed for a destination. Other flags (RTF_REJECT and RTF_BLACKHOLE) mark the destination of the route as being unreachable, causing either an error or a silent failure when an attempt is made to send to the destination. Reject routes are useful when a router receives packets for a cluster of addresses from the outside, but may not have routes for all hosts or networks in the cluster at all times. It is undesirable for packets with unreachable destinations to be sent outside the cluster via a default route, because the default router would send back such packets for delivery within the cluster. Black-hole routes are used during routing transients when a new route may become available shortly.

Network protocols often send to the same destination repeatedly and may desire information about the path. Some of this information can be estimated dynamically for each connection, such as the round-trip time. It is useful to cache such information so that the estimation does not need to begin anew for each connection. The routing entry contains a set of *route metrics* stored in a *rt_metrics* structure that may be set externally, or may be determined dynamically by the protocols. These metrics include the maximum packet size for the path, called the *maximum transmission unit* (*MTU*); the hop count; the round-trip time and variance; the send and receive buffering requirements implied by the bandwidth–delay product; and congestion-avoidance parameters. Individual metrics can be locked, in which case they cannot be updated with dynamic estimates.

When a route is added or created by cloning, and when a route is deleted, the link layer is called via the *ifa_rtrequest* entry point stored in the *ifaddr* structure for this interface address. The link layer can allocate private storage associated with the route entry. This feature is used with *direct* routes to networks that are marked as cloning routes; the link layer can use this mechanism to manage link-layer address-translation information for each host. The address translation can be arranged within the system—for example, with a dynamic mechanism—or it can be handled outside the kernel when the RTF_XRESOLVE flag is set.

Routing Lookup

Given a set of routing entries describing various destinations, from specific hosts to a wildcard route, a routing lookup algorithm is required. Earlier versions of the system used a hash lookup in a pair of routing tables: one for host routes and one for network routes. However, this algorithm required the ability to determine the network part of each address to be looked up, which could be expensive or impossible. Not all protocols encode the address with a network part and a host part, and many protocols use multilevel addressing hierarchies. It is useful to create routes at any level of a hierarchy, allowing aggregation of the largest group of hosts for which the next-hop route is the same. Therefore, a new routing lookup algorithm was needed. The lookup algorithm in 4.4BSD uses a modification of the *radix search trie* [Sedgewick, 1990]. (The initial design was to use a PATRICIA search, also described in [Sedgewick, 1990], which differs only in the details of storage management.) The radix search algorithm provides a way to find a bit string, such as a network address, in a set of known strings. Although the modified search was implemented for routing lookups, the radix code is implemented in a more general way so that it can be used for other purposes. For example, the filesystem code uses a radix tree to manage information about clients to which filesystems can be exported. Each kernel route entry begins with the data structures for the radix tree, including an internal radix node and a leaf node that refers to the destination address and mask.

The radix search algorithm uses a binary tree of nodes beginning with a root node for each address family. Fig. 12.9 shows an example radix tree. A search begins at the root node, and descends through some number of internal nodes until a leaf node is found. Each internal node requires a test of a specific bit in the string, and the search descends in one of two directions depending on the value of that bit. The internal nodes contain an index of the bit to be tested, as well as a

Figure 12.9 Example radix tree. This simplified example of a radix tree contains routes for one protocol family using 32-bit addresses. The circles represent internal nodes, beginning with the head of the tree at the top. The bit position to be tested is shown within the circle. Leaf nodes are shown as rectangles containing a key (a destination address, listed as four decimal bytes separated by dots) and the corresponding mask (in hexadecimal). Some interior nodes are associated with masks found lower in the tree, as indicated by dashed arrows.

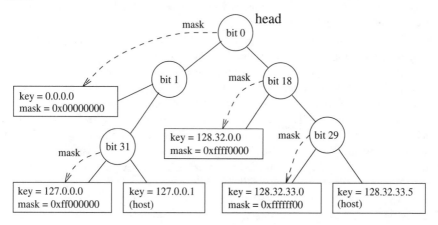

precomputed byte index and mask for use in the test. A leaf node is marked with a bit index of −1, which terminates the search. For example, a search for the address 127.0.0.1 with the tree in Fig. 12.9 would start at the head, and would branch left when testing bit 0, right at the node for bit 1, and right on testing bit 31. This search leads to the leaf node containing a host route specific to that host; such a route does not contain a mask, but uses an implicit mask with all bits set.

This lookup technique tests the minimum number of bits required to distinguish among a set of bit strings. Once a leaf node is found, either it specifies the specific bit string in question, or that bit string is not present in the table. This algorithm allows a minimal number of bits to be tested in a string to look up an unknown, such as a host route; however, it does not provide for partial matching as required by a routing lookup for a network route. Thus, the routing lookup uses a modified radix search, in which each network route includes a mask, and nodes are inserted into the tree such that longer masks are found later in the search [Sklower, 1991]. Interior nodes for subtrees with a common prefix are marked with a mask for that prefix. (Masks generally select a prefix from an address, although the mask does not need to specify a contiguous portion of the address.) As the routing lookup proceeds, the internal nodes that are passed are associated with masks that increase in specificity. If the route that is found at the leaf after the lookup is a network route, the destination is masked before comparison with the key, thus matching any destination on that network. If the leaf node does not match the destination, one of the interior nodes visited during the route lookup should refer to the best match. After a lookup that does not find a match at the leaf node, the lookup procedure iterates backward through the tree, using a parent pointer in each node. At each interior node that contains a mask, a search is made for the part of the destination under that mask from that point. For example, a search for the address 128.32.33.7 in the table in Fig. 12.9 would test bits 0, 18, and 29 before arriving at the host route on the right (128.32.33.5). Because this address is not a match, the search moves up one level, where a mask is found. The mask is a 24-bit prefix, and is associated with the route to 128.32.33.0, which is the best match. If the mask was not a prefix (in the code, a route with a mask specifying a prefix is called a *normal* route), a search would have been required for the value 128.32.33.0 starting from this point.

The first match found is the best match for the destination; that is, it has the longest mask for any matching route. Matches are thus found by a combination of a radix search, testing 1 bit per node on the way down the tree, plus a full comparison under a mask at the leaf node. If the leaf node (either host or network) does not match, the search backtracks up the tree, checking each parent with a mask until a match is found. This algorithm avoids a complete comparison at each step when searching down the tree, which would eliminate the efficiency of the radix search algorithm. It is optimized for matches to routes with longer masks, and performs least efficiently when the best match is the default route (the route with the shortest mask).

Another complication of using a radix search is that a radix tree does not allow duplicated keys. There are two possible reasons for a key to be duplicated in the routing table: either multiple routes exist to the same destination or the same key is present with different masks. The latter case is not a complete duplicate, but the two routes would occupy the same location in the tree. The routing code does not support completely duplicate routes, but it supports multiple routes that differ in only the mask. When the addition of a route causes a key to be duplicated, the affected routes are chained together from a single leaf node. The routes are chained in order of mask significance, most specific mask first. If the masks are contiguous, longer masks are considered to be more specific (with a host route considered to have the longest possible mask). If a routing lookup visits a node with a duplicated key when doing a masked comparison (either at the leaf node, or while moving back up the tree), the comparison is repeated for each duplicate node on the chain, with the first successful comparison producing the best match.

As we noted, 4.4BSD does not support multiple routes to the same destination (identical key and mask). The main reason to support multiple paths would be to allow the load to be split among the paths. However, most network protocols in 4.4BSD cache a reference to a route, using it as long as the destination is the same and the route is valid. Similarly, when acting as a router, a network protocol may cache references to routes. In either case, interleaving of traffic across the available paths would often be suboptimal. A better design would be to add a pointer to an output function in each route. Most routes would copy the output pointer for the interface used by the route. Routes for which multiple paths were available would be represented by a virtual route containing references to the individual routes, which would not be placed in the radix tree. The virtual route would interpose an intermediate output function that would distribute packets to the output functions for the individual routes. This scheme would allow good packet interleaving even when a path was used by a single connection.

Routing Redirects

A *routing redirect* is a control request from a protocol to the routing system to modify an existing routing-table entry or to create a new routing-table entry. Protocols usually generate such requests in response to routing-redirect messages that they receive from routers. Routers generate routing-redirect messages when they recognize that a better route exists for a packet that they have been asked to forward. For example, if two hosts A and B are on the same network, and host A sends a packet to host B via a router C, then C will send a routing-redirect message to A indicating that A should send packets to B directly.

On hosts where exhaustive routing information is too expensive to maintain (e.g., small workstations), the combination of wildcard routing entries and routing-redirect messages can be used to provide a simple routing-management scheme without the use of a higher-level policy process. Current connections can be rerouted after notification of the protocols by the protocols' *pr_ctlinput*() entries. Statistics are kept by the routing-table routines on the use of routing-redirect messages and on the latter's effect on the routing tables. A redirect causes the gateway for a route to be changed if the redirect applies to all destinations to which the route applies; otherwise a new, more specific route is added.

Routing-Table Interface

A protocol accesses the routing tables through three routines: one to allocate a route, one to free a route, and one to process a routing-redirect control message. The routine *rtalloc()* allocates a route; it is called with a pointer to a *route* structure, which contains the desired destination, as shown in Fig. 12.10, and a pointer that will be set to reference the routing entry that is the best match for the destination. The destination is recorded so that subsequent output operations can check whether the new destination is the same as the previous one, allowing the same route to be used. The route returned is assumed to be *held* by the caller until released with a call to *rtfree()*. Protocols that implement virtual circuits, such as the Transmission Control Protocol (TCP), hold onto routes for the duration of the circuit's lifetime; connectionless protocols, such as the User Datagram Protocol (UDP), allocate and free routes whenever the routes' destination address changes. The *rtalloc()* routine simply checks whether the route already contains a reference to a valid route. If no route is referenced or the route is no longer valid, *rtalloc()* calls the *rtalloc1()* routine to look up a routing entry for the destination, passing a flag indicating whether the route will be used or is simply being checked. If packets will be sent, the route is created by cloning if necessary.

The *rtredirect()* routine is called to process a routing-redirect control message. It is called with a destination address and mask, the new gateway to that destination, and the source of the redirect. Redirects are accepted from only the current router for the destination. If a nonwildcard route exists to the destination, the gateway entry in the route is modified to point at the new gateway supplied. Otherwise, a new routing-table entry is inserted that reflects the information supplied. Routes to interfaces and routes to gateways that are not directly accessible from the host are ignored.

Figure 12.10 Data structures used in route allocation.

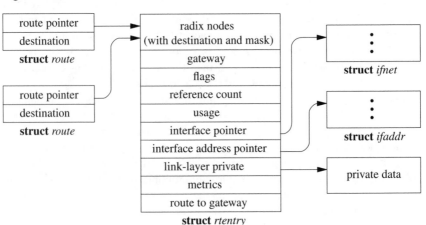

User-Level Routing Policies

The kernel routing facilities deliberately refrain from making policy decisions. Instead, routing policies are determined by user processes, which then add, delete, or change entries in the kernel routing tables. The decision to place policy decisions in a user process implies that routing-table updates may lag a bit behind the identification of new routes, or the failure of existing routes. This period of instability is normally short if the routing process is implemented properly. Internet-specific advisory information, such as ICMP error messages and IMP diagnostic messages, may also be read from raw sockets (described in Section 12.7).

Several routing-policy processes have been implemented. The system standard *routing daemon*, *routed* (8), uses a variant of the Xerox NS Routing Information Protocol [Xerox, 1981] to maintain up-to-date routing tables in a local environment. This protocol has become known as the Routing Information Protocol (RIP) [Hedrick, 1988]. Many sites that require the use of other routing protocols or more configuration options than are provided by *routed* (8) use a multiprotocol routing process called *gated* [Hallgren & Honig, 1993].

User-Level Routing Interface: Routing Socket

User-level processes that implement routing policy and protocols require an interface to the kernel routing table so that they can add, delete, and change kernel routes. In older versions of the system, route addition and deletion were implemented as *ioctl* commands that passed a kernel route entry as data. In those versions of the system, the route entry contained fixed-sized *sockaddr* structures for the destination and gateway values. However, it is no longer possible to use fixed-sized structures, and changes to the routing entry may require other components such as a mask for network routes, a mask for cloning operations, or an identification of the interface to be used by the route. A new interface was designed to accommodate these changes. Another design goal was to allow a routing process such as *gated* to learn of routing changes due to redirects, and of changes made by other processes.

The interface to the kernel routing layer in 4.4BSD uses a socket in a new protocol family to communicate with the kernel routing layer. A privileged process creates a raw socket in the routing protocol family, and then passes messages to and from the kernel routing layer. This socket operates like a normal datagram socket, including queueing of messages received at the socket, except that communication takes place between a user process and the kernel. Messages include a header with a message type identifying the action, as listed in Table 12.8 (on page 426). Messages to the kernel are requests to add, modify, or delete a route, or are requests for information about the route to a specific destination. The kernel sends a message in reply with the original request, an indication that the message is a reply, and an error number in case of failure. Because routing sockets are raw sockets, each open routing socket receives a copy of the reply. The message header includes a process ID and a sequence number so that each process can determine whether this message is a reply to its own request and can match replies

Table 12.8 Routing message types.

Message type	Description
RTM_ADD	add route
RTM_DELETE	delete route
RTM_CHANGE	change metrics or flags
RTM_GET	report route and metrics
RTM_LOSING	kernel suspects partitioning
RTM_REDIRECT	told to use different route
RTM_MISS	lookup failed on this address
RTM_LOCK	lock specified metrics
RTM_OLDADD	caused by SIOCADDRT
RTM_OLDDEL	caused by SIOCDELRT
RTM_RESOLVE	request to resolve link address
RTM_NEWADDR	address added to interface
RTM_DELADDR	address removed from interface
RTM_IFINFO	interface going up or down

with requests. The kernel also sends messages as indications of asynchronous events, such as redirects and changes in local interface state. These messages allow a daemon to monitor changes in the routing table made by other processes, events detected by the kernel, and changes to the local interface addresses and state. The routing socket is also used to deliver requests for external resolution of a link-layer route when the RTF_XRESOLVE flag is set on a route entry.

Requests to add or change a route include all the information needed for the route. The header has a field for the route flags listed in Table 12.7, and contains a *rt_metrics* structure of metrics that may be set or locked. The header also carries a bit vector that describes the set of addresses carried in the message; the addresses follow the header as an array of variable-sized *sockaddr* structures. A destination address is required, as is a mask for network routes. A gateway address is generally required as well. The system normally determines the interface to be used by the route from the gateway address, using the interface shared with that gateway. By convention, *direct* routes contain the local address of the interface to be used. In some cases, the gateway address is not sufficient to determine the interface, and an interface address can be passed as well, generally using a *sockaddr_dl* structure containing the interface name or index (see Section 12.1).

12.6   Buffering and Congestion Control

A major factor affecting the performance of a protocol is the buffering policy. Lack of a proper buffering policy can force packets to be dropped, cause false windowing information to be emitted by protocols, fragment host memory, and degrade the overall host performance. Because of problems such as these, most systems allocate a fixed pool of memory to the networking system and impose a policy optimized for *normal* network operation.

The 4.4BSD networking system is not dramatically different in this respect. Mbuf structures are allocated as needed via the general allocator *malloc*() up to the per-type limit for the network, and are eventually freed for reuse. At boot time, a small, fixed amount of memory is allocated by the networking system for mbuf clusters. At later times, more system memory may be requested for mbuf clusters as the need arises, up to a preconfigured limit; at no time, however, is this memory ever returned to the system. It would be possible to reclaim memory from the network. In the environments where the system has been used, storage use has not been an issue, and thus storage reclamation has been left unimplemented.

Protocol Buffering Policies

When a socket is created, the protocol reserves some amount of buffer space for send and receive queues. These amounts define the high watermarks used by the socket routines in deciding when to block and unblock a process. The reservation of space does not currently result in any action by the memory-management routines.

Protocols that provide connection-level flow control base their decisions on the amount of space in the associated socket queues. That is, windows sent to peers are calculated based on the amount of free space in the socket's receive queue, whereas utilization of the send window received from a peer is dependent on the high watermark of the send queue.

Queue Limiting

Incoming packets from the network are always received unless memory allocation fails. However, each network-layer protocol input queue has an upper bound on the queue's length, and any packets exceeding that bound are discarded. It is possible for a host to be overwhelmed by excessive network traffic (e.g., if the host is acting as a gateway from a high-bandwidth network to a low-bandwidth network). As a *defense mechanism*, the queue limits can be adjusted to throttle network-traffic load on a host. Discarding packets is not always a satisfactory solution to a problem such as this (simply dropping packets is likely to increase the load on a network); the queue lengths were incorporated mainly as a safeguard mechanism. On the other hand, limiting *output* queue lengths can be valuable on hosts that gateway traffic from a high-bandwidth network to a low-bandwidth network. The queue limit should be sufficiently high that transient overload can be handled by buffering, but allowing the queue to be too large causes network delays to increase to unacceptable levels.

12.7 Raw Sockets

A *raw socket* allows privileged users direct access to a protocol other than those normally used for transport of user data—for example, network-level protocols. Raw sockets are intended for knowledgeable processes that wish to take advantage of some protocol feature not directly accessible through the normal interface, or for the development of protocols built atop existing protocols. For example, the *ping* (8) program is implemented using a raw ICMP socket (see Section 13.8). The raw IP socket interface attempts to provide an identical interface to the one a protocol would have if it were resident in the kernel.

The raw socket support is built around a generic raw socket interface, possibly augmented by protocol-specific processing routines. This section describes only the core of the raw socket interface; details specific to particular protocols are not discussed. Some protocol families (including Internet) use private versions of the routines and data structures described here.

Control Blocks

Every raw socket has a protocol control block of the form shown in Fig. 12.11. All control blocks are kept on a doubly linked list for performing lookups during packet dispatch. Associations may be recorded in fields referenced by the control block and may be used by the output routine in preparing packets for transmission. The *rcb_proto* field contains the protocol family and protocol number with which the raw socket is associated. The protocol, family, and addresses are used to filter packets on input, as described in the next subsection.

A raw socket interface is datagram oriented: Each send or receive on the socket requires a destination address. Destination addresses may be supplied by the user, or referenced via pointers to sockaddr structures in the control block and

Figure 12.11 Raw-socket control block.

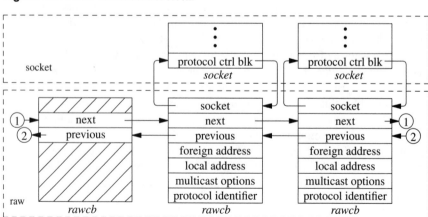

automatically installed in the outgoing packet by the output routine. If routing is necessary, it must be performed by an underlying protocol.

Input Processing

Input packets are assigned to raw sockets based on a simple pattern-matching scheme. Each protocol (and potentially some network interfaces) gives unassigned packets to the raw input routine with the call

```
raw_input(m, proto, src, dst)
    struct mbuf *m;
    struct sockproto *proto;
    struct sockaddr *src, *dst;
```

This call must be made at software-interrupt level (e.g., from a network-level protocol handler), rather than directly from hardware interrupt level. Input packets are placed into the input queues of all raw sockets that match the header according to the following rules:

1. The protocol family of the socket and header agree.

2. If the protocol number in the socket is nonzero, then it agrees with that found in the packet header.

3. If a local address is defined for the socket, the address format of the socket's local address is the same as the packet's destination address, and the two addresses agree exactly.

4. Rule 3 is applied to the socket's foreign address and the packet's source address.

A basic assumption in the pattern-matching scheme is that addresses present in the control block and packet header (as constructed by the network interface and any raw input-protocol module) are in a canonical form that can be compared on a bit-for-bit basis. If multiple sockets match the incoming packet, the packet is copied as needed.

Output Processing

On output, each send request results in a call to the raw socket's user request routine, which is specific to the protocol or protocol family. Any necessary processing is done before the packet is delivered to the appropriate network interface.

12.8   Additional Network-Subsystem Topics

In this section, we shall discuss several aspects of the network subsystem that are not easy to categorize.

Out-of-Band Data

The ability to process out-of-band data is a facility specific to the stream-socket and sequenced-packet–socket abstractions. Little agreement appears to exist on what out-of-band data's semantics should be. TCP defines a notion called *urgent data*, in which in-line data are marked for *urgent delivery*. The protocol provides a mark on the data stream delimiting urgent data from subsequent normal data. The ISO/OSI protocols [Burruss, 1980] and numerous other protocols provide a fully independent logical transmission channel along which out-of-band data are sent. In addition, the number of the data that can be sent in an out-of-band message varies from protocol to protocol, from 1 bit to 512 bytes or more.

A stream socket's notion of out-of-band data has been defined as the lowest reasonable common denominator. Out-of-band data are expected to be transmitted out of the normal sequencing and flow-control constraints of the data stream. A minimum of 1 byte of out-of-band data and one outstanding out-of-band message is expected to be provided by protocols supporting out-of-band messages. It is a protocol's prerogative to support larger-sized messages or more than one outstanding out-of-band message at a time.

Out-of-band data may be maintained by the protocol, stored separately from the socket's receive queue. They may also be prepended to the normal receive queue marked as out-of-band data. A socket-level option, SO_OOBINLINE, is provided to force all out-of-band data to be placed in the normal receive queue when urgent data are received. This option is provided because the 4.2BSD TCP implementation removed 1 byte of data from the data stream at the urgent mark for separate presentation. However, this removal caused problems when additional urgent data were sent before the first such byte was received by the application.

Placement of out-of-band data in the normal data stream can permit a protocol to hold several out-of-band messages simultaneously. This mechanism can avoid the loss of out-of-band messages caused by a process that responds slowly.

Address Resolution Protocol

The Address Resolution Protocol (ARP) is a link-level protocol that provides a dynamic address-translation mechanism for networks that support broadcast or multicast communication [Plummer, 1982]. ARP is used in 4.4BSD to map 32-bit Internet addresses to 48-bit Ethernet addresses. Although ARP is not specific either to Internet protocol addresses or to Ethernet, the 4.4BSD network subsystem supports only that combination, although it makes provision for addition combinations to be added. ARP is incorporated into the network-interface layer, although it logically sits *between* the network and network-interface layers.

The general idea of ARP is simple. A set of translations from network addresses to link-layer addresses is maintained. When an address-translation request is made to the ARP service by a network interface and the requested address is not in ARP's set of known translations, an ARP message is created that specifies the requested network address and an unknown link-layer address. This message is then broadcast by the interface in the expectation that a host attached to the network will know the translation—usually because the host is the intended target of the original message. If a response is received in a timely fashion, the ARP service uses the response to update its translation tables and to resolve the pending request, and the requesting network interface is then called to transmit the original message.

In practice, the simplicity of this algorithm is complicated by the necessity to avoid stale translation data, to minimize broadcasts when a target host is down, and to deal with failed translation requests. In addition, it is necessary to deal with packets for which transmission is attempted before the translation is completed. The ARP translation tables are implemented as a part of the routing table. The route to a local Ethernet is set up as a *cloning route* so that individual host routes will be created for each local host when referenced. When the route is cloned, the link layer creates an empty ARP entry associated with the route. Older versions of the system used a separate ARP hash table, but the use of the routing table avoids a separate lookup. The network output routine normally requires a routing lookup or a cached route, and it now passes a reference to the route to the interface output function.

A request is made to resolve an Internet address to an Ethernet address for an outgoing message by the call

```
result = arpresolve(ac, rt, m, destip, desten);
    struct arpcom *ac;
    struct rtentry *rt;
    struct mbuf *m;
    struct sockaddr *destip;
    u_char *desten;
```

ARP first checks its tables to see whether the destination address is a broadcast or multicast address, in which cases the Ethernet address can be calculated directly. Otherwise, it checks whether the route entry that was passed already contains a *complete* translation that has not timed out. If so, the *gateway* value in the route entry is a link-layer address for the destination, and its value is returned in *desten* for use as the destination address of the outgoing packet. If the link-layer address is not known or has timed out, ARP must queue the outgoing message for future transmission, and must broadcast a message requesting the Internet address translation. The time is recorded in the ARP entry when a request is broadcast, and no further broadcasts are made within the same second if additional transmissions are attempted. If another translation request is made before a reply is received, the queued message is discarded and only the newer one is saved. After some number of broadcasts without a reply (normally 5, in no less than 5 seconds), the route is changed to a *reject* route with an expiration time after 20 seconds, causing host-down errors to be returned in response to attempts to reach the host within that time.

At a later time—preferably before the timer has expired on the queued message—ARP will receive a response to its translation request. The received message is processed first by the *ether_input*() routine, as invoked from Ethernet device driver. Because the packet has a packet type of ARP, it is enqueued for the ARP software-interrupt routine, analogous to other network-level protocol input interrupts. The ARP packet is processed to locate the translation entry in the routing table. If the message completes a pending translation, the entry is updated and the original message is passed back to the network interface for transmission. This time, the resultant call to *arpresolve*() will succeed without delay.

ARP input handling must cope with requests for the host's own address, as well as responses to translation requests that the host generated. The input module also watches for responses from other hosts that advertise a translation for its own Internet address. This monitoring is done to ensure that no two hosts on the same network believe that they have the same Internet address (although this error may be detected, ARP's only recourse is to log a diagnostic message).

ARP normally times out completed translation entries in its cache after 20 minutes, and incomplete translation entries after about 5 seconds. Entries may be marked *permanent*, however, in which case they are never removed. Entries may also be marked *published*, allowing one host to act as a surrogate for other hosts that do not support ARP, or to act as a *proxy* for a host that is not on the Ethernet, but is reached via a router.

Exercises

12.1   Name two key data structures used in the networking subsystem that are important in ensuring that the socket-layer software is kept independent of the networking implementation.

12.2   Why are software interrupts used to trigger network protocol processing on receipt of data, rather than the protocol processing being encapsulated in separate processes?

12.3   Which routines in the protocol switch are called by the socket layer? Explain why each of these routines is called.

12.4   Assume that a *reliably-delivered–message socket* (SOCK_RDM) is a connectionless socket that guarantees reliable delivery of data and that preserves message boundaries. Which flags would a protocol that supported this type of socket have set in the *pr_flags* field of its protocol-switch entry?

12.5   Give an example of a network interface that is useful without an underlying hardware device.

12.6   Give two reasons why the addresses of a network interface are *not* in the network-interface data structure.

12.7   Why is the name or address of a socket kept at the network layer, rather than at the socket layer?

12.8 Why does 4.4BSD not attempt to enforce a rigid protocol–protocol interface structure?

12.9 Describe two tasks performed by a network-interface output routine.

12.10 Why is the identity of the network interface on which each message is received passed upward with the message?

12.11 Which routing *policies* are implemented in the kernel?

12.12 Describe three types of routes that can be found in the routing table that differ by the type of destination to which they apply.

12.13 What routing facility is designed mainly to support workstations?

12.14 What is a routing redirect? For what is it used?

12.15 Why do the output-packet queues for each network interface have limits on the number of packets that may be queued?

12.16 What does the SO_OOBINLINE socket option do? Why does it exist?

*12.17 Explain why it is impossible to use the raw socket interface to support parallel protocol implementations—some in the kernel and some in user mode. What modifications to the system would be necessary to support this facility?

*12.18 Why are ancillary data, such as access rights, provided to the user request routine at the same time as any associated data are provided, instead of being sent in a separate call?

*12.19 Previous versions of the system used a hashed routing lookup for a destination as a host or as a network. Name two ways in which the radix search algorithm in 4.4BSD is more capable.

References

BBN, 1978.
> BBN, "Specification for the Interconnection of Host and IMP," Technical Report 1822, Bolt, Beranek, and Newman, Cambridge, MA, May 1978.

Burruss, 1980.
> J. Burruss, "Features of the Transport and Session Protocols," Report No. ICST/HLNP-80-1, National Bureau of Standards, Washington, D.C., March 1980.

Hallgren & Honig, 1993.
> M. Hallgren & J. Honig, "GateD and the GateD Consortium," *Connexions*, vol. 7, no. 9, pp. 61–66, Interop Company, Mountain View, CA, September 1993.

Hedrick, 1988.

C. Hedrick, "Routing Information Protocol," RFC 1058, available by anonymous FTP from ds.internic.net, June 1988.

ISO, 1984.

ISO, "Open Systems Interconnection: Basic Reference Model," ISO 7498, International Organization for Standardization, 1984. available from the: American National Standards Institute, 1430 Broadway, New York, NY 10018.

Plummer, 1982.

D. Plummer, "An Ethernet Address Resolution Protocol," RFC 826, available by anonymous FTP from ds.internic.net, September 1982.

Postel, 1981.

J. Postel, "Internet Control Message Protocol," RFC 792, available by anonymous FTP from ds.internic.net, September 1981.

Sedgewick, 1990.

R. Sedgewick, *Algorithms in C,* Addison-Wesley, Reading, MA, 1990.

Sklower, 1991.

K. Sklower, "A Tree-Based Packet Routing Table for Berkeley UNIX," *USENIX Association Conference Proceedings*, pp. 93–99, January 1991.

Wright & Stevens, 1995.

G. R. Wright & W. R. Stevens, *TCP/IP Illustrated, Volume 2, The Implementation,* Addison-Wesley, Reading, MA, 1995.

Xerox, 1981.

Xerox, "Internet Transport Protocols," Xerox System Integration Standard 028112, Xerox Corporation, Stamford, CT, December 1981.

CHAPTER 13

Network Protocols

Chapter 12 presented the network-communications architecture of 4.4BSD. In this chapter, we examine the network protocols implemented within this framework. The 4.4BSD system supports four major communication domains: DARPA Internet, Xerox Network Systems (NS), ISO/OSI, and local domain (formerly known as the UNIX domain). The local domain does not include network protocols because it operates entirely within a single system. The Internet protocol suite was the first set of protocols implemented within the network architecture of 4.2BSD. Following the release of 4.2BSD, several proprietary protocol families were implemented by vendors within the network architecture. However, it was not until the addition of the Xerox NS protocols in 4.3BSD that the system's ability to support multiple network-protocol families was visibly demonstrated. Although some parts of the protocol interface were previously unused and thus unimplemented, the changes required to add a second network-protocol family did not substantially modify the network architecture. The implementation of the ISO OSI networking protocols, as well as other changing requirements, led to a further refinement of the network architecture in 4.4BSD.

In this chapter, we shall concentrate on the organization and implementation of the Internet protocols. This protocol implementation is used widely, both in 4BSD systems and in many other systems, because it was publicly available when many vendors were looking for tuned and reliable communication protocols. Developers have implemented other protocols, including Xerox NS and OSI, by following the same general framework set forth by the Internet protocol routines. After describing the overall architecture of the Internet protocols, we shall examine their operation according to the structure defined in Chapter 12. We shall also describe the significant algorithms used by the Internet protocols. We then shall discuss changes that the developers made in the system motivated by aspects of the OSI protocols and their implementation.

13.1 Internet Network Protocols

The Internet network protocols were developed under the sponsorship of DARPA, for use on the ARPANET [McQuillan & Walden, 1977; DARPA, 1983]. They are commonly known as TCP/IP, although TCP and IP are only two of the many protocols in the family. Unlike earlier protocols used within the ARPANET (the ARPANET Host-to-Host Protocol, sometimes called the Network Control Program (NCP)) [Carr et al, 1970], these protocols do not assume a reliable subnetwork that ensures delivery of data. Instead, the Internet protocols were devised for a model in which hosts were connected to networks with varying characteristics, and the networks were interconnected by routers (generally called gateways at the time). Such a model is called a *catenet* [Cerf, 1978]. The Internet protocols were designed for packet-switching networks ranging from the ARPANET or X.25, which provide reliable message delivery or notification of failure, to pure datagram networks such as Ethernet, which provide no indication of datagram delivery.

This model leads to the use of at least two protocol layers. One layer operates end to end between two hosts involved in a conversation. It is based on a lower-level protocol that operates on a hop-by-hop basis, forwarding each message through intermediate routers to the destination host. In general, there exists at least one protocol layer above the other two: it is the application layer. This three-level layering has been called the ARPANET Reference Model [Padlipsky, 1985]. The three layers correspond roughly to levels 3 (network), 4 (transport), and 7 (application) in the ISO Open Systems Interconnection reference model [ISO, 1984].

The Internet communications protocols that support this model have the layering illustrated in Fig. 13.1. The Internet Protocol (IP) is the lowest-level protocol in the ARPANET Reference Model; this level corresponds to the ISO network layer. IP operates hop by hop as a datagram is sent from the originating host to the

Figure 13.1 Internet protocol layering. TCP—Transmission Control Protocol; UDP—User Datagram Protocol; IP—Internet Protocol; ICMP—Internet Control Message Protocol.

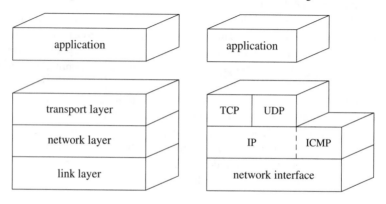

destination via any intermediate routers. It provides the network-level services of host addressing, routing, and, if necessary, packet fragmentation and reassembly if intervening networks cannot send an entire packet in one piece. All the other protocols use the services of IP. (The version of IP used in 4.4BSD is version 4. The next generation of IP, version 6, was in development about the time of the release of 4.4BSD.) The Transmission Control Protocol (TCP) and User Datagram Protocol (UDP) are transport-level protocols that provide additional facilities to IP. Each protocol adds a port identifier to IP's host address so that local and remote sockets can be identified. TCP provides reliable, unduplicated, and flow-controlled transmission of data; it supports the stream socket type in the Internet domain. UDP provides a data checksum for checking integrity in addition to a port identifier, but otherwise adds little to the services provided by IP. UDP is the protocol used by datagram sockets in the Internet domain. The Internet Control Message Protocol (ICMP) is used for error reporting and for other network-management tasks; it is logically a part of IP, but like the transport protocols is layered above IP. It is usually not accessed by users. Raw access to the IP and ICMP protocols is possible through *raw sockets*; see Section 12.7 for information on this facility.

The Internet protocols were designed to support heterogeneous host systems and architectures. These systems use a wide variety of internal data representations. Even the basic unit of data, the *byte*, was not the same on all host systems; one common type of host supported variable-sized bytes. The network protocols, however, require a standard representation. This representation is expressed in terms of the *octet*—an 8-bit byte. We shall use this term as it is used in the protocol specifications to describe network data, although we continue to use the term *byte* to refer to data or storage within the system. All fields in the Internet protocols that are larger than an octet are expressed in *network byte order*, with the most significant octet first. The 4.4BSD network implementation uses a set of routines or macros to convert 16-bit and 32-bit integer fields between host and network byte order on hosts (such as the VAX and i386-compatible systems) that have a different native ordering.

Internet Addresses

An *Internet host address* is a 32-bit number that identifies both the network on which a host is located and the host on that network. Network identifiers are assigned by a central agency, whereas host identifiers are assigned by each network's administrator. It follows that a host with network interfaces attached to multiple networks has multiple addresses. Figure 13.2 shows the original addressing scheme that was tied to the subnetwork addressing used on the ARPANET; each host was known by the number of the ARPANET IMP to which it was attached and by its host port number on that IMP (Interface Message Processor). The IMP and host numbers each occupied one octet of the address. One remaining octet was used to designate the network and the other was available for uses such as multiplexed host connections—thus the name *logical host*. This encoding of

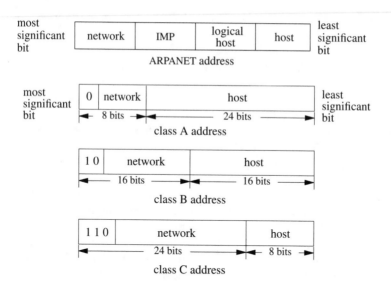

Figure 13.2 Internet addresses. IMP—Interface Message Processor.

the address limits the number of networks to 255, a number that quickly proved to be too small. Figure 13.2 shows how the network portion of the address was encoded such that it could be variable in size. The most significant bits of the network part of the address determine the class of an address. Three classes of network address are defined, A, B and C, with high-order bits of 0, 10, and 110; they use 8, 16, and 24 bits, respectively, for the network part of the address. Each class has fewer bits for the host part of each address, and thus supports fewer hosts than do the higher classes. This form of frequency encoding supports a larger number of networks of varying size, yet is compatible with the old encoding of ARPANET addresses.

Subnets

The basic Internet addressing scheme uses a 32-bit address that contains both a network and a host identifier. All interconnected networks must be known to a central collection of routing agents for full connectivity. This scheme does not handle a large number of interconnected networks well because of the excessive routing information necessary to ensure full connectivity. Furthermore, when networks are installed at a rapid pace, the administrative overhead is significant. However, many networks are installed at organizations such as universities, companies, and research centers that have many interconnected local-area networks with only a few points of attachment to external networks. To handle these problems, the notion of a *subnet* addressing scheme was added [Mogul & Postel, 1985]; it allows a collection of networks to be known by a single network number.

Subnets allow the addition of another level of hierarchy to the Internet address space. They partition a network assigned to an organization into multiple address spaces (see Fig. 13.3). This partitioning, each part of which is termed a *subnet*, is visible to only those hosts and routers on the subnetted network. To hosts that are not on the subnetted network, the subnet structure is not visible. Instead, all hosts on subnets of a particular network are perceived externally as being on a single network. The scheme allows Internet routing to be done on a site-by-site basis, as all hosts on a site's subnets appear to off-site hosts and routers to be on a single Internet network. This partitioning scheme also permits sites to have greater local autonomy over the network topology at their site.

When a subnet addressing scheme is set up at a site, a partitioning of the assigned Internet address space for that site must be chosen. Consider Fig. 13.3: If a site has a class B network address assigned to it, it has 16 bits of the address in which to encode a subnet number and the identifier of a host on that subnet. An arbitrary subdivision of the 16 bits is permitted, but sites must balance the number of subnets they will need against the number of hosts that may be addressed on each subnet. To inform the system of the desired partitioning scheme, the site administrator specifies a *network mask* for each network interface. This mask shows which bits in the Internet address specify the network part of the local address. The mask includes the normal network portion, as well as the subnet field. This mask also is used when the host part of an address is extracted. When interpreting an address that is not local, the system uses the mask corresponding to the class of the address. The mask does not need to be uniform throughout a subnetted network, although uniformity is common.

The implementation of subnets is isolated, for the most part, to the routines that manipulate Internet addresses. Each Internet address assigned to a network interface is maintained in an *in_ifaddr* structure that contains an interface address structure and additional information for use in the Internet domain (see Fig. 13.4 on page 440). When an interface's network mask is specified, it is recorded in the *ia_subnetmask* field of the address structure. The network mask, *ia_netmask*, is calculated based on the type of the network number (class A, B, or C) when the

---

Figure 13.3 Example of subnet address partitioning.

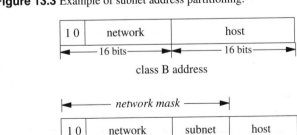

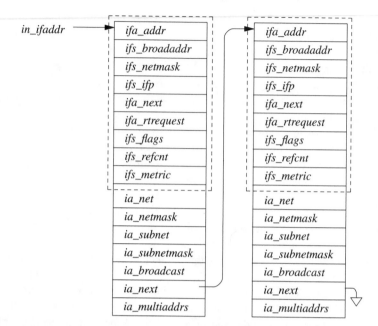

Figure 13.4 Internet interface address structure (in_ifaddr).

interface's address is assigned. For nonsubnetted networks, the two masks are identical. The system then interprets local Internet addresses using these values. An address is considered to be local to the subnet if the field under the subnetwork mask matches the subnetwork field of an interface address. The system can also determine whether an address is on the logical network using the network mask and number.

As the number of Internet networks has grown, it has become necessary to generalize the handling of Internet addresses to avoid exhausting the set of available network numbers. The new scheme is based on *Classless Inter-Domain Routing* (*CIDR*) [Fuller et al, 1993]. The allocation of network addresses does not necessarily follow the boundaries according to class (A, B or C). Instead, an organization may be assigned a contiguous group of addresses described by a single value and mask, such as a group of 16 class C networks (using a 20-bit mask), or one-half of a class C network (using a 25-bit mask). This group of addresses may in turn be subnetted within the organization. In addition, these blocks of addresses are often assigned from a larger block by an Internet service provider, allowing aggregation of routes to clients of the provider. In general, 4.4BSD handles classless addressing in the same fashion as subnets, setting the local network mask along with each address. The local network mask can be set to a value either longer or shorter than that of the mask associated with the network class (A, B, or C). When such a network is subnetted, it would sometimes be desirable to set both the network and subnet masks, although the network mask has little remaining significance. As network routes now include explicit masks (see Section 12.5), the system can route to subnets, traditional network classes, and clusters of networks using the same mechanism.

Broadcast Addresses

On networks capable of supporting broadcast datagrams, 4.2BSD used the address with a host part of zero for broadcasts. After 4.2BSD was released, the Internet broadcast address was defined as the address with a host part of all 1s [Mogul, 1984]. This change and the introduction of subnets both complicated the recognition of broadcast addresses. Hosts may use a host part of 0 or 1s to signify broadcast, and some may understand the presence of subnets, whereas others may not. For these reasons, 4.3BSD and later systems set the broadcast address for each interface to be the host value of all 1s, but allows the alternate address to be set for backward compatibility. If the network is subnetted, the subnet field of the broadcast address contains the normal subnet number. The *logical* broadcast address for the network also is calculated when the address is set; this address would be the standard broadcast address if subnets were not in use. This address is needed by the IP input routine to filter input packets. On input, 4.4BSD recognizes and accepts subnet and network broadcast addresses with host parts of 0s or 1s, as well as the address with 32 bits of 1 ("broadcast on this physical network").

Internet Multicast

Many link-layer networks, such as the Ethernet, provide a multicast capability that can address groups of hosts, but is more selective than broadcast because it provides a number of different multicast group addresses. IP provides a similar facility at the network-protocol level, using link-layer multicast where available [Deering, 1989]. IP multicasts are sent using class D destination addresses with high-order bits 1110. Unlike host addresses in classes A, B, and C, class D addresses do not contain network and host portions; instead, the entire address names a group, such as a group of hosts using a particular service. These groups can be created dynamically, and the members of the group can change over time. IP multicast addresses map directly to physical multicast addresses on networks such as the Ethernet, using the low 24 bits of the IP address along with a constant 24-bit prefix to form a 48-bit link-layer address.

For a socket to use multicast, it must join a multicast group using the *setsockopt* system call. This call informs the link layer that it should receive multicasts for the corresponding link-layer address, and also sends a multicast membership report using the Internet Group Management Protocol (IGMP). Multicast agents on the network can thus keep track of the members of each group. Multicast agents receive all multicast packets from directly attached networks and forward multicast datagrams as needed to group members on networks. This function is similar to the role of routers that forward normal (unicast) packets, but the criteria for packet forwarding are different, and a packet can be forwarded to multiple neighboring networks.

Internet Ports and Associations

At the IP level, packets are addressed to a host, rather than to a process or communications port. However, each packet contains an 8-bit protocol number that identifies the next protocol that should receive the packet. Internet transport protocols use an additional identifier to designate the connection or communications port on the host. Most protocols (including TCP and UDP) use a 16-bit port number for this purpose. Each protocol maintains its own mapping of port numbers to processes or descriptors. Thus, an *association*, such as a connection, is fully specified by the tuple <source address, destination address, protocol number, source port, destination port>. Connection-oriented protocols, such as TCP, must enforce the uniqueness of associations; other protocols generally do so as well. When the local part of the address is set before the remote part, it is necessary to choose a unique port number to prevent collisions when the remote part is specified.

Protocol Control Blocks

For each TCP- or UDP-based socket, an *Internet protocol control block* (an *inpcb* structure) is created to hold Internet network addresses, port numbers, routing information, and pointers to any auxiliary data structures. TCP, in addition,

Figure 13.5 Internet Protocol data structures.

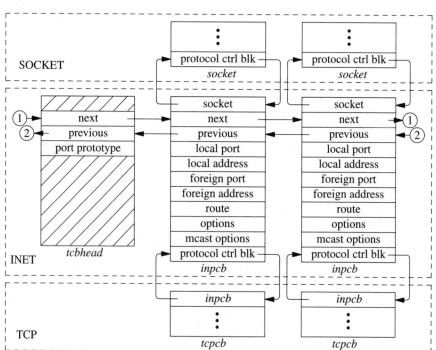

creates a *TCP control block* (a *tcpcb* structure) to hold the wealth of protocol state information necessary for its implementation. Internet control blocks for use with TCP are maintained on a doubly linked list private to the TCP protocol module. Internet control blocks for use with UDP are kept on a similar list private to the UDP protocol module. Two separate lists are needed because each protocol in the Internet domain has a distinct space of port identifiers. Common routines are used by the individual protocols to add new control blocks to a list, to fix the local and remote parts of an association, to locate a control block by association, and to delete control blocks. IP demultiplexes message traffic based on the protocol identifier specified in its protocol header, and each higher-level protocol is then responsible for checking its list of Internet control blocks to direct a message to the appropriate socket. Figure 13.5 shows the linkage between the socket data structure and these protocol-specific data structures.

The implementation of the Internet protocols is rather tightly coupled, as befits the strong intertwining of the protocols. For example, the transport protocols send and receive packets including not only their own header, but also an IP pseudoheader containing the source and destination address, the protocol identifier, and a packet length. This pseudoheader is included in the transport-level packet checksum.

We are now ready to examine the operation of the Internet protocols. We begin with UDP, as it is far simpler than TCP.

13.2   User Datagram Protocol (UDP)

The *User Datagram Protocol* (*UDP*) [Postel, 1980] is a simple unreliable datagram protocol that provides only peer-to-peer addressing and optional data checksums.† Its protocol headers are extremely simple, containing only the source and destination port numbers, the datagram length, and the data checksum. The host addresses for a datagram are provided by the IP pseudoheader.

Initialization

When a new datagram socket is created in the Internet domain, the socket layer locates the protocol-switch entry for UDP and calls the *udp_usrreq*() routine PRU_ATTACH entry with the socket as a parameter. UDP uses *in_pcballoc*() to create a new protocol control block on its list of current sockets. It also sets the default limits for the socket send and receive buffers. Although datagrams are never placed in the send buffer, the limit is set as an upper limit on datagram size; the UDP protocol-switch entry contains the flag PR_ATOMIC, requiring that all data in a send operation be presented to the protocol at one time.

---

†In 4.4BSD, checksums are enabled or disabled on a system-wide basis and cannot be enabled or disabled on individual sockets.

If the application program wishes to bind a port number—for example, the well-known port for some datagram service—it calls the *bind* system call. This request reaches UDP as the PRU_BIND request to *udp_usrreq*( ). The binding may also specify a specific host address, which must be an address of an interface on this host. Otherwise, the address will be left unspecified, matching any local address on input, and with an address chosen as appropriate on each output operation. The binding is done by *in_pcbbind*( ), which verifies that the chosen port number (or address and port) is not in use, then records the local part of the association.

To send datagrams, the system must know the remote part of an association. A program can specify this address and port with each send operation using *sendto* or *sendmsg*, or can do the specification ahead of time with the *connect* system call. In either case, UDP uses the *in_pcbconnect*( ) function to record the destination address and port. If the local address was not bound, and if a route for the destination is found, the address of the outgoing interface is used as the local address. If no local port number was bound, one is chosen at this time.

Output

A system call that sends data reaches UDP as a call to *udp_usrreq*( ) with the PRU_SEND request and a chain of mbufs containing the data for the datagram. If the call provided a destination address, the address is passed as well; otherwise, the address from a prior *connect* call is used. The actual output operation is done by *udp_output*( ),

```
error = udp_output(inp, m, addr, control);
    struct inpcb *inp;
    struct mbuf *m;
    struct mbuf *addr;
    struct mbuf *control;
```

where *inp* is an Internet protocol control block, *m* is an mbuf chain that contains the data to be sent, and *addr* is an optional mbuf containing the destination address. Any ancillary data in *control* are discarded. The destination address could have been prespecified with a *connect* call; otherwise, it must be provided in the send call. UDP simply prepends its own header, fills in the UDP header fields and those of a prototype IP header, and calculates a checksum before passing the packet on to the IP module for output:

```
error = ip_output(m, opt, ro, flags, imo);
    struct mbuf *m, *opt;
    struct route *ro;
    int flags;
    struct ip_moptions *imo;
```

The call to IP's output routine is more complicated than is that to UDP's because the IP routine cannot depend on having a protocol control block that contains information about the current sender and destination. The *m* parameter indicates the data to be sent, and the *opt* parameter may specify a list of IP options that should be placed in the IP packet header. For multicast destinations, the *imo* parameter may reference multicast options, such as the choice of interface and hop count for multicast packets. IP options may be set for a socket with the *setsockopt* system call specifying the IP protocol level and option IP_OPTIONS. These options are stored in a separate mbuf, and a pointer to this mbuf is stored in the protocol control block for a socket; the pointer is passed to *ip_output*() with each packet sent. The *ro* parameter is optional; UDP passes a pointer to the route structure in the protocol control block for the socket. IP will determine a route and leave it in the control block, so that it can be reused on later calls. The *flags* parameter indicates whether the user is allowed to transmit a broadcast message, and whether routing is to be bypassed for the message being sent (see Section 13.3). The broadcast flag may be inconsequential if the underlying hardware does not support broadcast transmissions. The flags also indicate whether the packet includes an IP pseudoheader or a completely initialized IP header, as when Ip forwards packets.

Input

All Internet transport protocols that are layered directly on top of IP use the following calling convention when receiving input packets from IP:

```
(void) (*pr_input)(m, hlen);
    struct mbuf *m;
    int hlen;
```

Each mbuf chain passed is a single packet to be processed by the protocol module. The packet includes the IP header in lieu of a pseudoheader, and the IP header length is passed as the second parameter. The UDP input routine *udp_input*() is typical of protocol input routines. It first verifies that the length of the packet is at least as long as the IP plus UDP headers, and it uses *m_pullup*() to make the header contiguous. It then checks that the packet is the correct length and checksums the data if a checksum is present. If any of these tests fail, the packet is simply discarded. Finally, the protocol control block for the socket that is to receive the data is located by *in_pcblookup*() from the addresses and port numbers in the packet. There might be multiple control blocks with the same local port number, but different local or remote addresses; if so, the control block with the best match is selected. An exact association matches best; but if none exists, a socket with the correct local port number but unspecified local address, remote port number, or remote address will match. A control block with unspecified local or remote addresses thus acts as a *wildcard* that receives packets for its port if no exact match is found. If a control block is located, the data and the address from which the packet was received are placed in the receive buffer of the indicated socket with *sbappendaddr()*. If the destination address is a multicast address, copies of the packet are delivered to each socket with matching addresses. Otherwise, if no receiver is found and if the packet was not addressed to a broadcast or multicast address, an ICMP *port unreachable* error message is sent to the originator of the datagram.†

Control Operations

UDP supports few control operations. It supports no options in 4.4BSD, and passes calls to its *pr_ctloutput()* entry directly to IP. It has a simple *pr_ctlinput()* routine that receives notification of any asynchronous errors. Some errors simply cause cached routes to be flushed. Other errors are passed to any datagram socket with the indicated destination; only sockets with a destination fixed by a *connect* call may be notified of errors asynchronously. Such errors are simply noted in the appropriate socket, and socket wakeups are issued in case the process is selecting or sleeping while waiting for input.

When a UDP datagram socket is closed, the *udp_usrreq()* is called with the PRU_DETACH request. The protocol control block and its contents are simply deleted with *in_pcbdetach()*; no other processing is required.

13.3   Internet Protocol (IP)

Having examined the operation of a simple transport protocol, we continue with a discussion of the network-layer protocol [Postel, 1981a; Postel et al, 1981]. The *Internet Protocol* (IP) is the level responsible for host-to-host addressing and routing, packet forwarding, and packet fragmentation and reassembly. Unlike the transport protocols, it does not always operate on behalf of a socket on the local host; it may forward packets, receive packets for which there is no local socket, or generate error packets in response to these situations.

The functions done by IP are illustrated by the contents of its packet header, shown in Fig. 13.6. The header identifies source and destination hosts and the destination protocol, and contains header and packet lengths. The identification and fragment fields are used when a packet or fragment must be broken into smaller sections for transmission on its next hop, and to reassemble the fragments when they arrive at the destination. The fragmentation flags are *Don't Fragment* and *More Fragments*; the latter flag plus the offset are sufficient to assemble the fragments of the original packet at the destination.

---

†This error message normally has no effect, as the sender typically connects to this destination only temporarily, and destroys the association before new input is processed. However, if the sender still has a fully specified association, it may receive notification of the error. The host-name lookup routine in 4.4BSD uses this mechanism to detect the absence of a nameserver at boot time, allowing the lookup routine to fall back to the local host file.

0	3 4	7 8	15 16	31
version	IHL	type of service	total length	
ID			fragment flags and offset	
time to live		protocol	header checksum	
source address				
destination address				
options				

Figure 13.6 Internet Protocol header. IHL is the Internet header length specified in units of four octets. Options are delimited by IHL.

IP options are present in an IP packet if the header length field has a value larger than the minimum. The *no-operation* option and the *end-of-option-list* option are each one octet in length. All other options are self-encoding, with a type and length preceding any additional data. Hosts and routers are thus able to skip over options that they do not implement. Examples of existing options are the *timestamp* and *record-route* options, which are updated by each router that forwards a packet, and the *source-route* options, which supply a complete or partial route to the destination.

Output

We have already seen the calling convention for the IP output routine, which is

```
error = ip_output(m, opt, ro, flags, imo);
    struct mbuf *m, *opt;
    struct route *ro;
    int flags;
    struct ip_moptions *imo;
```

As described in the subsection on output in the previous section, the parameter *m* is an mbuf chain containing the packet to be sent, including a skeletal IP header; *opt* is an optional mbuf containing IP options to be inserted after the header. If the route *ro* is given, it may contain a reference to a routing entry (*rtentry* structure), which specifies a route to the destination from a previous call, and in which any new route will be left for future use. The *flags* may allow the use of broadcast or may indicate that the routing tables should be bypassed. If present, *imo* includes options for multicast transmissions.

The outline of the work done by *ip_output*( ) is as follows:

• Insert any IP options.

• Fill in the remaining header fields (IP version, zero offset, header length, and a new packet identification) if the packet contains an IP pseudoheader.

- Determine the route (i.e., outgoing interface and next-hop destination).

- Check whether the destination is a multicast address. If it is, determine the outgoing interface and hop count.

- Check whether the destination is a broadcast address; if it is, check whether broadcast is permitted.

- If the packet size is no larger than the maximum packet size for the outgoing interface, compute the checksum and call the interface output routine.

- If the packet size is larger than the maximum packet size for the outgoing interface, break the packet into fragments and send each in turn.

We shall examine the routing step in more detail. First, if no route reference is passed as a parameter, an internal routing reference structure is used temporarily. A route structure that is passed from the caller is checked to see that it is a route to the same destination, and that it is still valid. If either test fails, the old route is freed. After these checks, if there is no route, *rtalloc*() is called to allocate a route. The route returned includes a pointer to the outgoing interface information. This information includes the maximum packet size, flags including broadcast and multicast capability, and the output routine. If the route is marked with the RTF_GATEWAY flag, the address of the next-hop gateway (router) is given by the route; otherwise, the packet's destination is the next-hop destination. If routing is to be bypassed because of a MSG_DONTROUTE option (see Section 11.1) or a SO_DONTROUTE option, a directly attached network shared with the destination is found; if there is no directly attached network, an error is returned. Once the outgoing interface and next-hop destination are found, enough information is available to send the packet.

As described in Chapter 12, the interface output routine normally validates the destination address and places the packet on its output queue, returning errors only if the interface is down, the output queue is full, or the destination address is not understood.

Input

In Chapter 12, we described the reception of a packet by a network interface, and the packet's placement on the input queue for the appropriate protocol. The network-interface handler then schedules the protocol to run by setting a corresponding bit in the network status word and scheduling a *software interrupt*. The IP input routine is invoked via this software interrupt when network interfaces receive messages for an Internet protocol; consequently, it is called without any parameters. The input routine, *ipintr*(), removes packets from its input queue one at a time and processes them to completion. A packet's processing is completed in one of four ways: it is passed as input to a higher-level protocol, it encounters an error that is reported back to the source, it is dropped because of an error, or it is forwarded along the path to its destination. In outline form, the steps in the processing of an IP packet on input are as follows:

1. Verify that the packet is at least as long as an IP header, and ensure that the header is contiguous.

2. Checksum the header of the packet, and discard the packet if there is an error.

3. Verify that the packet is at least as long as the header indicates, and drop the packet if it is not. Trim any padding from the end of the packet.

4. Process any IP options in the header.

5. Check whether the packet is for this host. If it is, continue processing the packet. If it is not, and if doing IP packet forwarding, try to forward the packet. Otherwise, drop the packet.

6. If the packet has been fragmented, keep it until all its fragments are received and reassembled, or until it is too old to keep.

7. Pass the packet to the input routine of the next-higher-level protocol.

When the incoming packet is removed from the input queue, it is accompanied by an indication of the interface on which the packet was received. This information is passed to the next protocol, to the forwarding function, or to the error-reporting function. If any error is detected and is reported to the packet's originator, the source address of the error message will be set according to the packet's destination and the incoming interface.

The decision whether to accept a received packet for local processing by a higher-level protocol is not as simple as we might think. If a host has multiple addresses, the packet is accepted if its destination matches one of those addresses. If any of the attached networks support broadcast and the destination is a broadcast address, the packet is also accepted. (For reasons that are given in Section 13.1, there may be as many as five possible broadcast addresses for a given network.)

The IP input routine uses a simple and efficient scheme for locating the input routine for the receiving protocol of an incoming packet. The protocol field in the IP packet is 8 bits long; thus, there are 256 possible protocols. Fewer than 256 protocols are defined or implemented, and the Internet protocol switch has far fewer than 256 entries. Therefore, IP input uses a 256-element mapping array to map from the protocol number to the protocol-switch entry of the receiving protocol. Each entry in the array is initially set to the index of a raw IP entry in the protocol switch. Then, for each protocol with a separate implementation in the system, the corresponding map entry is set to the index of the protocol in the IP protocol switch. When a packet is received, IP simply uses the protocol field to index into the mapping array, and uses the value at that location as the index into the protocol-switch table for the receiving protocol.

Forwarding

Implementations of IP traditionally have been designed for use by either hosts or routers, rather than by both. That is, a system was either an endpoint for IP packets (as source or destination) or a router (which forwards packets between hosts on different networks, but only uses upper-level protocols for maintenance functions). Traditional host systems do not incorporate packet-forwarding functions; instead, if they receive packets not addressed to them, they simply drop the packets. 4.2BSD was the first common IP implementation that attempted to provide both host and router services in normal operation. This approach had advantages and disadvantages. It meant that 4.2BSD hosts connected to multiple networks could serve as routers as well as hosts, reducing the requirement for dedicated router machines. Early routers were neither inexpensive nor especially powerful. On the other hand, the existence of router-function support in ordinary hosts made it more likely for misconfiguration errors to result in problems on the attached networks. The most serious problem had to do with forwarding of a broadcast packet because of a misunderstanding by either the sender or the receiver of the packet's destination. The packet-forwarding router functions are disabled by default in 4.4BSD. They may be enabled when a kernel binary is configured, and can be enabled at run time with the *sysctl* call. Hosts not configured as routers never attempt to forward packets or to return error messages in response to misdirected packets. As a result, far fewer misconfiguration problems are capable of causing synchronized or repetitive broadcasts on a local network, called *broadcast storms*.

The procedure for forwarding IP packets received at a router but destined for another host is the following:

1. Check that forwarding is enabled. If it is not, drop the packet.

2. Check that the destination address is one that allows forwarding. Packets destined for network 0, network 127 (the official loopback network), or illegal network addresses cannot be forwarded.

3. Save at most 64 octets of the received message, in case an error message must be generated in response.

4. Determine the route to be used in forwarding the packet.

5. If the outgoing route uses the same interface as that on which the packet was received, and if the originating host is on that network, send an ICMP redirect message to the originating host. (ICMP is described in Section 13.8.)

6. Call *ip_output()* to send the packet to its destination or to the next-hop gateway.

7. If an error is detected, send an ICMP error message to the source host.

Multicast transmissions are handled separately from other packets. Systems may be configured as multicast agents independently from other routing functions. Multicast agents receive all incoming multicast packets, and forward those packets to local receivers and group members on other networks according to group memberships and the remaining hop count of incoming packets.

13.4   Transmission Control Protocol (TCP)

The major protocol of the Internet protocol suite is the *Transmission Control Protocol* (*TCP*) [Postel, 1981b; Cerf & Kahn, 1974]. TCP is the reliable connection-oriented stream transport protocol on which most application protocols are based. It includes several features not found in the other transport and network protocols described so far:

• Explicit and acknowledged connection initiation and termination

• Reliable, in-order, unduplicated delivery of data

• Flow control

• Out-of-band indication of urgent data

• Congestion avoidance

   Because of these features, the TCP implementation is much more complicated than are those of UDP and IP. These complications, along with the prevalence of the use of TCP, make the details of TCP's implementation both more critical and more interesting than are the implementations of the simpler protocols. We shall begin with an examination of the TCP itself, then continue with a description of its implementation in 4.4BSD.

   A TCP connection may be viewed as a bidirectional, sequenced stream of data octets transferred between two peers. The data may be sent in packets of varying sizes and at varying intervals—for example, when they are used to support a login session over the network. The stream initiation and termination are explicit events at the start and end of the stream, and they occupy positions in the *sequence space* of the stream so that they can be acknowledged in the same manner as data are. Sequence numbers are 32-bit numbers from a circular space; that is, comparisons are made modulo 2^{32}, so that zero is the next sequence number after $2^{32} - 1$. The sequence numbers for each direction start with an arbitrary value, called the *initial sequence number*, sent in the initial packet for a connection. In accordance with the TCP specification, the TCP implementation selects the initial sequence number by sampling a software counter that increments at about 250 Kbyte per second, then incrementing the counter so that later connections choose a different starting point, reducing the chance that an old duplicate packet will match the sequence space of a current connection. 4.4BSD includes a random component in the counter value so that the initial sequence number is somewhat less predictable, making it harder to "spoof" a network connection. Each packet of a TCP connection carries the sequence number of its first datum and (except during connection establishment) an acknowledgment of all contiguous data received. A TCP packet is known as a *segment* because it begins at a specific location in the sequence space and has a specific length. Acknowledgments are specified as the sequence number of the next sequence number not yet received. Acknowledgments are cumulative, and thus may acknowledge data received in more than one (or part of one) packet. A packet may or may not contain data, but always contains the sequence number of the next datum to be sent.

Flow control in TCP is done with a *sliding-window scheme*. Each packet with an acknowledgment contains a window, which is the number of octets of data that the receiver is prepared to accept, beginning with the sequence number in the acknowledgment. The window is a 16-bit field, limiting the window to 65535 octets by default; however, the use of a larger window may be negotiated (see the next subsection). Urgent data are handled similarly; if the flag indicating urgent data is set, the urgent-data pointer is used as a positive offset from the sequence number of the packet to indicate the extent of urgent data. Thus, TCP can send notification of urgent data without sending all intervening data, even if the flow-control window would not allow the intervening data to be sent.

The complete header for a TCP packet is shown in Fig. 13.7. The flags include SYN and FIN, denoting the initiation (synchronization) and completion of a connection. Each of these flags occupies a sequence space of one. A complete connection thus consists of a SYN, zero or more octets of data, and a FIN sent from each peer and acknowledged by the other peer. Additional flags indicate whether the acknowledgment field (ACK) and urgent fields (URG) are valid, and include a connection-abort signal (RST). The header includes a header-length field so that the header can be extended with optional fields. Options are encoded in the same way as are IP options: the *no-operation* and *end-of-options* options are single octets, and all other options include a type and a length. The only option in the initial specification of TCP indicates the maximum segment (packet) size that a correspondent is willing to accept; this option is used only during initial connection establishment. Several other options have been defined. To avoid confusion,

Figure 13.7 TCP packet header.

0								15 16		31
source port								destination port		
sequence number										
acknowledgment number										
data offset	reserved	U R G	A C K	P S H	R S T	S Y N	F I N	window		
checksum								urgent pointer		
options									padding	
data										

the protocol standard allows these options to be used in data packets only if both endpoints include them during establishment of the connection.

TCP Connection States

The connection-establishment and connection-completion mechanisms of TCP are designed for robustness. They serve to frame the data that are transferred during a connection, so that not only the data but also their extent are communicated reliably. In addition, the procedure is designed to discover old connections that have not terminated correctly because of a crash of one peer or loss of network connectivity. If such a half-open connection is discovered, it is aborted. Hosts choose new initial sequence numbers for each connection to lessen the chances that an old packet may be confused with a current connection.

The normal connection-establishment procedure is known as a *three-way handshake*. Each peer sends a SYN to the other, and each in turn acknowledges the other's SYN with an ACK. In practice, a connection is normally initiated by one of the two (the client) attempting to connect to the other (a server listening on a well-known port). The client chooses a port number and initial sequence number and uses these selections in the initial packet with a SYN. The server creates a new connection block for the pending connection and sends a packet with its initial sequence number, a SYN, and an ACK of the client's SYN. The client responds with an ACK of the server's SYN, completing connection establishment. As the ACK of the first SYN is piggybacked on the second SYN, this procedure requires three packets, leading to the term *three-way handshake*. (The protocol still operates correctly if both peers initiate the connection simultaneously, although it requires four packets in that case.)

4.4BSD includes three options along with SYN when initiating a connection. One contains the maximum segment size that the system is willing to accept. The other two options are more recent additions [Jacobson et al, 1992]. The first of these options specifies a window-scaling value expressed as a binary shift value, allowing the window to exceed 65535 octets. If both peers include this option during the three-way handshake, both scaling values take effect; otherwise, the window value remains in octets. The third option is a timestamp option. If this option is sent in both directions during connection establishment, it will also be sent in each packet during data transfer. The data field of the timestamp option includes a timestamp associated with the current sequence number, and also echoes a timestamp associated with the current acknowledgment. Like the sequence space, the timestamp uses a 32-bit field and modular arithmetic. The unit of the timestamp field is not defined, although it must fall between 1 millisecond and 1 second. The value sent by each system must be monotonically nondecreasing during a connection. 4.4BSD uses the value of a counter that is incremented twice per second. These timestamps can be used to implement round-trip timing. They also serve as an extension of the sequence space to prevent old duplicate packets from being accepted; this extension is valuable when a large window or a fast path is used.

After a connection is established, each peer includes an acknowledgment and window information in each packet. Each may send data according to the window

Table 13.1 TCP connection states.

State	Description
States involved while a connection becomes established	
CLOSED	closed
LISTEN	listening for connection
SYN SENT	active, have sent SYN
SYN RECEIVED	have sent and received SYN
State during an established connection	
ESTABLISHED	established
States involved when the remote end initiates a connection shutdown	
CLOSE WAIT	have received FIN, waiting for close
LAST ACK	have received FIN and close; awaiting FIN ACK
CLOSED	closed
States involved when the local end initiates a connection shutdown	
FIN WAIT 1	have closed, sent FIN
CLOSING	closed, exchanged FIN; awaiting FIN ACK
FIN WAIT 2	have closed, FIN is acknowledged; awaiting FIN
TIME WAIT	in 2MSL† quiet wait after close
CLOSED	closed

† 2MSL—twice maximum segment lifetime.

that it receives from its peer. As data are sent by one end, the window becomes filled. As data are received by the peer, acknowledgments may be sent so that the sender can discard the data from its send queue. If the receiver is prepared to accept additional data, perhaps because the receiving process has consumed the previous data, it will also advance the flow-control window. Data, acknowledgments, and window updates may all be combined in a single message.

If a sender does not receive an acknowledgment within some reasonable time, it retransmits data that it presumes were lost. Duplicate data are discarded by the receiver but are acknowledged again in case the retransmission was caused by loss of the acknowledgment. If the data are received out of order, the receiver generally retains the out-of-order data for use when the missing segment is received. Out-of-order data cannot be acknowledged, because acknowledgments are cumulative.†

Each peer may terminate data transmission at any time by sending a packet with the FIN bit. A FIN represents the end of the data (like an end-of-file indication). The FIN is acknowledged, advancing the sequence number by 1. The connection may continue to carry data in the other direction until a FIN is sent in that

---

†A selective acknowledgment mechanism was introduced in [Jacobson et al, 1992], but is not implemented in 4.4BSD.

direction. The acknowledgment of that FIN terminates the connection. To guarantee synchronization at the conclusion of the connection, the peer sending the last ACK of a FIN must retain state long enough that any retransmitted FIN packets would have reached it or have been discarded; otherwise, if the ACK were lost and a retransmitted FIN were received, the receiver would be unable to repeat the acknowledgment. This interval is arbitrarily set to twice the maximum expected segment lifetime (known as 2MSL).

The TCP input-processing module and timer modules must maintain the state of a connection throughout that connection's lifetime. Thus, in addition to processing data received on the connection, the input module must process SYN and FIN flags and other state transitions. The list of states for one end of a TCP connection is given in Table 13.1. Figure 13.8 shows the finite-state machine made up by these states, the events that cause transitions, and the actions during the transitions. An earlier version of the TCP implementation was implemented as an explicit state machine.

If a connection is lost because of a crash or timeout on one peer, but is still considered established by the other, then any data sent on the connection and

Figure 13.8 TCP state diagram. TCB—TCP control block; 2MSL—twice maximum segment lifetime.

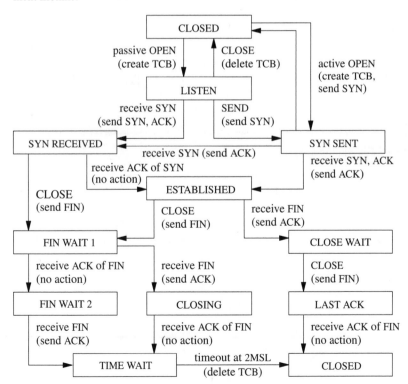

received at the other end will cause the half-open connection to be discovered. When a half-open connection is detected, the receiving peer sends a packet with the RST flag and a sequence number derived from the incoming packet to signify that the connection is no longer in existence.

Sequence Variables

Each TCP connection maintains a large set of state variables in the TCP control block. This information includes the connection state, timers, options and state flags, a queue that holds data received out of order, and several sequence number variables. The sequence variables are used to define the send and receive sequence space, including the current *window* for each. The window is the range of data sequence numbers that are currently allowed to be sent, from the first octet of data not yet acknowledged up to the end of the range that has been offered in the window field of a header. The variables used to define the windows in 4.4BSD are a superset of those used in the protocol specification [Postel, 1981b]. The send and receive windows are shown in Fig. 13.9. The meanings of the sequence variables are listed in Table 13.2.

The area between *snd_una* and *snd_una* + *snd_wnd* is known as the *send window*. Data for the range *snd_una* to *snd_max* have been sent but not yet acknowledged, and are kept in the socket send buffer along with data not yet transmitted. The *snd_nxt* field indicates the next sequence number to be sent, and is incremented as data are transmitted. The area from *snd_nxt* to *snd_una* + *snd_wnd* is the remaining usable portion of the window, and its size determines whether additional data may be sent. The *snd_nxt* and *snd_max* values are normally maintained together except when TCP is retransmitting.

The area between *rcv_nxt* and *rcv_nxt* + *rcv_wnd* is known as the *receive window*. These variables are used in the output module to decide whether data can be

---

Figure 13.9 TCP sequence space.

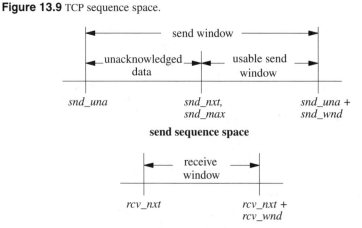

send sequence space

receive sequence space

Table 13.2 TCP sequence variables.

Variable	Description
snd_una	lowest send sequence number not yet acknowledged
snd_nxt	next data sequence to be sent
snd_wnd	number of data octets peer will receive, starting with *snd_una*
snd_max	highest sequence number sent
rcv_nxt	next receive sequence number expected
rcv_wnd	number of octets past *rcv_nxt* that may be accepted
rcv_adv	last octet of receive window advertised to peer
ts_recent	most recent timestamp received from peer
ts_recentage	time when *ts_recent* was received

sent, and in the input module to decide whether data that are received can be accepted. When the receiver detects that a packet is not acceptable because the data are all outside the window, it drops the packet, but sends a copy of its most recent acknowledgment. If the packet contained old data, the first acknowledgment may have been lost, and thus it must be repeated. The acknowledgment also includes a window update, synchronizing the sender's state with the receiver's state.

If the TCP timestamp option is in use for the connection, the tests to see whether an incoming packet is acceptable are augmented with checks on the timestamp. Each time that an incoming packet is accepted as the next expected packet, its timestamp is recorded in the *ts_recent* field in the TCP protocol control block. If an incoming packet includes a timestamp, the timestamp is compared to the most recently received timestamp. If the timestamp is less than the previous value, the packet is discarded as being an old duplicate and a current acknowledgment is sent in response. In this way, the timestamp serves as an extension to the sequence number, avoiding accidental acceptance of an old duplicate when the window is large or sequence numbers can be reused quickly. However, because of the granularity of the timestamp value, a timestamp received more than 24 days ago cannot be compared to a new value, and this test is bypassed. The current time is recorded when *ts_recent* is updated from an incoming timestamp to make this test. Of course, connections are seldom idle for longer than 24 days.

13.5 TCP Algorithms

Now that we have introduced TCP, its state machine, and its sequence space, we can begin to examine the implementation of the protocol in 4.4BSD. Several aspects of the protocol implementation depend on the overall state of a connection. The TCP connection state, output state, and state changes depend on external events and timers. TCP processing occurs in response to one of three events:

1. A request from the user, such as sending data, removing data from the socket receive buffer, or opening or closing a connection

2. The receipt of a packet for the connection

3. The expiration of a timer

These events are handled in the routines *tcp_usrreq*(), *tcp_input*(), and *tcp_timers*(), respectively. Each routine processes the current event and makes any required changes in the connection state. Then, for any transition that may require output, the *tcp_output*() routine is called to do any output that is necessary.

The criteria for sending a packet with data or control information are complicated, and therefore the TCP send policy is the most interesting and important part of the protocol implementation. For example, depending on the state- and flow-control parameters for a connection, any of the following may allow to be sent data that could not be sent previously:

• A user send call that places new data in the send queue

• The receipt of a window update from the peer TCP

• The expiration of the retransmission timer

• The expiration of the window-update (persist) timer

In addition, the *tcp_output*() routine may decide to send a packet with control information, even if no data may be sent, for any of these reasons:

• A change in connection state (e.g., open request, close request)

• Receipt of data that must be acknowledged

• A change in the receive window because of removal of data from the receive queue

• A send request with urgent data

• A connection abort

We shall consider most of these decisions in greater detail after we have described the states and timers involved. We begin with algorithms used for timing, connection setup, and shutdown; they are distributed through several parts of the code. We continue with the processing of new input and an overview of output processing and algorithms.

Timers

Unlike a UDP socket, a TCP connection maintains a significant amount of state information, and, because of that state, some operations must be done asynchronously. For example, data might not be sent immediately when a process presents them, because of flow control. The requirement for reliable delivery implies that data must be retained after they are first transmitted so that they can be retransmitted if necessary. To prevent the protocol from hanging if packets are lost, each connection maintains a set of timers used to recover from losses or failures of the peer TCP. These timers are stored in the protocol control block for a connection. Whenever they are set, they are decremented every 500 milliseconds by the *tcp_slowtimo*() routine (called as the TCP protocol switch *pr_slowtimo* routine) until they expire, triggering a call to *tcp_timers*().

Two timers are used for output processing. One is the *retransmit timer* (TCPT_REXMT). Whenever data are sent on a connection, the retransmit timer is started, unless it is already running. When all outstanding data are acknowledged, the timer is stopped. If the timer expires, the oldest unacknowledged data are resent (at most one full-sized packet) and the timer is restarted with a longer value. The rate at which the timer value is increased (the *timer backoff*) is determined by a table of multipliers that provides an exponential increase in timeout values up to a ceiling.

The other timer used for maintaining output flow is the *persist timer* (TCPT_PERSIST). This timer protects against the other type of packet loss that could cause a connection to constipate: the loss of a window update that would allow more data to be sent. Whenever data are ready to be sent, but the send window is too small to bother sending (zero, or less than a reasonable amount), and no data are already outstanding (the retransmit timer is not set), the persist timer is started. If no window update is received before the timer expires, the output routine sends as large a segment as the window allows. If that size is zero, it sends a *window probe* (a single octet of data) and restarts the persist timer. If a window update was lost in the network, or if the receiver neglected to send a window update, the acknowledgment will contain current window information. On the other hand, if the receiver is still unable to accept additional data, it should send an acknowledgment for previous data with a still-closed window. The closed window might persist indefinitely; for example, the receiver might be a network-login client, and the user might stop terminal output and leave for lunch (or vacation).

The third timer used by TCP is a *keepalive timer* (TCPT_KEEP). The keepalive timer has two different purposes at different phases of a connection. During connection establishment, this timer limits the time for the three-way handshake to complete. If it expires, the connection is timed out. Once the connection completes, the keepalive timer monitors idle connections that might no longer exist on the correspondent TCP because of timeout or a crash. If a socket-level option is set and the connection has been idle since the most recent keepalive timeout, the timer routine will send a *keepalive packet* designed to produce either an acknowledgment or a reset (RST) from the peer TCP. If a reset is received, the connection will be closed; if no response is received after several attempts, the connection will be dropped. This facility is designed so that network servers can avoid languishing forever if the client disappears without closing. Keepalive packets are not an explicit feature of the TCP protocol. The packets used for this purpose by 4.4BSD set the sequence number to 1 less than *snd_una*, which should elicit an acknowledgment from the correspondent TCP if the connection still exists.†

The final TCP timer is known as the *2MSL timer* (TCPT_2MSL; "twice the maximum segment lifetime"). TCP starts this timer when a connection is completed by sending an acknowledgment for a FIN (from FIN_WAIT_2 or CLOSING states, where the send side is already closed). Under these circumstances, the sender does not know whether the acknowledgment was received. If the FIN is retransmitted, it is desirable that enough state remain that the acknowledgment can be repeated. Therefore, when a TCP connection enters the TIME_WAIT state, the 2MSL timer is started; when the timer expires, the control block is deleted. If a retransmitted FIN is received, the timer is restarted. To prevent this delay from blocking a process closing the connection, any process close request is returned successfully without the process waiting for the timer. Thus, a protocol control block may continue its existence even after the socket descriptor has been closed. In addition, 4.4BSD starts the 2MSL timer when FIN_WAIT_2 state is entered after the user has closed; if the connection is idle until the timer expires, it will be closed. Because the user has already closed, new data cannot be accepted on such a connection in any case. This timer is set because certain other TCP implementations (incorrectly) fail to send a FIN on a receive-only connection. Connections to such hosts would remain in FIN_WAIT_2 state forever if the system did not have a timeout.

In addition to the four timers implemented by the TCP *tcp_slowtimo*() routine, TCP uses the protocol switch *pr_fasttimo* entry. The *tcp_fasttimo*() routine, called every 200 milliseconds, processes delayed acknowledgment requests. These functions will be described in Section 13.6.

Estimation of Round-Trip Time

When connections must traverse slow networks that lose packets, an important decision determining connection throughput is the value to be used when the retransmission timer is set. If this value is too large, data flow will stop on the connection for an unnecessarily long time before the dropped packet is resent. Another round-trip time interval is required for the sender to receive an acknowledgment of the missing segment and a window update, allowing it to send new data. (With luck, only one segment will have been lost, and the acknowledgment

---

†In 4.4BSD, the keepalive packet contains no data unless the system is configured with a kernel option for compatibility with 4.2BSD, in which case a single null octet is sent. A bug prevented 4.2BSD from responding to a keepalive packet unless the packet contained data. This option should no longer be necessary.

will include the other segments that had been sent.) If the timeout value is too small, however, packets will be retransmitted needlessly. If the cause of the network slowness or packet loss is congestion, then unnecessary retransmission only exacerbates the problem. The traditional solution to this problem in TCP is for the sender to estimate the round-trip time (*rtt*) for the connection path by measuring the time required to receive acknowledgments for individual segments. The system maintains an estimate of the round-trip time as a smoothed moving average, *srtt* [Postel, 1981b], using

$$srtt = (ALPHA \times srtt) + ((1 - ALPHA) \times rtt).$$

Older versions of the system set the initial retransmission timeout to a constant multiple (BETA) of the current smoothed round-trip time, with a smoothing factor ALPHA of 0.9 (retaining 90 percent of the previous average) and a variance factor BETA of 2. BSD versions, beginning with the 4.3BSD Tahoe release, use a more sophisticated algorithm. In addition to a smoothed estimate of the round-trip time, TCP keeps a smoothed variance (estimated as mean difference, to avoid square-root calculations in the kernel). It employs an ALPHA value of 0.875 for the round-trip time and a corresponding smoothing factor of 0.75 for the variance. These values were chosen in part so that the system could compute the smoothed averages using shift operations on fixed-point values, instead of using floating-point values, as the earlier system did. (On many hardware architectures, it is expensive to use floating-point arithmetic in interrupt routines, because doing so forces floating-point registers and status to be saved and restored.) The initial retransmission timeout is then set to the current smoothed round-trip time plus four times the smoothed variance. This algorithm is substantially more efficient on long-delay paths with little variance in delay, such as satellite links, because it computes the BETA factor dynamically [Jacobson, 1988].

For simplicity, the variables in the TCP protocol control block allow measurement of the round-trip time for only one sequence value at a time. This restriction prevents accurate time estimation when the window is large; only one packet per window can be timed. However, if the TCP timestamps option is supported by both peers, a timestamp is sent with each data packet and is returned with each acknowledgment. In this case, estimates of round-trip time can be obtained with each new acknowledgment; the quality of the smoothed average and variance is thus improved, and the system can respond more quickly to changes in network conditions.

Connection Establishment

There are two ways in which a new TCP connection can be established. An active connection is initiated by a *connect* call, whereas a passive connection is created when a listening socket receives a connection request. We consider each in turn.

The initial steps of an active connection attempt are similar to the actions taken during the creation of a UDP socket. The process creates a new socket, resulting in a call to *tcp_usrreq()* with the PRU_ATTACH request. TCP creates an *inpcb* protocol control block just as does UDP, then creates an additional control block (a *tcpcb* structure), as described in Section 13.1. Some of the flow-control parameters in the *tcpcb* are initialized at this time. If the process explicitly binds an address or port number to the connection, the actions are identical to those for a UDP socket. Then, a *connect* call initiates the actual connection. The first step is to set up the association with *in_pcbconnect*( ), again identically to this step in UDP. A packet-header template is created for use in construction of each output packet. An initial sequence number is chosen from a sequence-number prototype, which is then advanced by a substantial amount. The socket is then marked with *soisconnecting*( ), the TCP connection state is set to TCPS_SYN_SENT, the keepalive timer is set (to 75 seconds) to limit the duration of the connection attempt, and *tcp_output*( ) is called for the first time.

The output-processing module *tcp_output*( ) uses an array of packet control flags indexed by the connection state to determine which control flags should be sent in each state. In the TCPS_SYN_SENT state, the SYN flag is sent. Because it has a control flag to send, the system sends a packet immediately using the proto-type just constructed and including the current flow-control parameters. The packet normally contains three option fields: a maximum-segment-size option, a window-scale option and a timestamps option (see Section 13.4). The maximum-segment-size option communicates the largest segment size that TCP is willing to accept. To compute this value, the system locates a route to the destination. If the route specifies a maximum transmission unit (MTU), the system uses that value after allowing for packet headers. If the connection is to a destination on a local network (or a subnet of a local network—see Section 13.1), the maximum trans-mission unit of the outgoing network interface is used, possibly rounding down to a multiple of the mbuf cluster size for efficiency of buffering. If the destination is not local, nothing is known about the intervening path,† and the default segment size (512 octets) is used. The retransmit timer is set to the default value (6 sec-onds), because no round-trip time information is available yet.

With a bit of luck, a responding packet will be received from the target of the connection before the retransmit timer expires. If not, the packet is retransmitted and the retransmit timer is restarted with a greater value. If no response is received before the keepalive timer expires, the connection attempt is aborted with a "Connection timed out" error. If a response is received, however, it is checked for agreement with the outgoing request. It should acknowledge the SYN that was sent, and should include a SYN. If it does both, the receive sequence variables are initialized, and the connection state is advanced to TCPS_ESTABLISHED. If a maximum-segment-size option is present in the response, the maximum segment size for the connection is set to the minimum of the offered size and the maximum transmission unit of the outgoing interface; if the option is not present, the default size (512 data bytes) is recorded. The flag TF_ACKNOW is set in the TCP control block before the output routine is called, so that the SYN will be acknowledged immediately. The connection is now ready to transfer data.

---

†TCP should use Path MTU Discovery as described in [Mogul & Deering, 1990]. However, this fea-ture is not implemented in 4.4BSD.

The events that occur when a connection is created by a passive open are different. A socket is created and its address is bound as before. The socket is then marked by the *listen* call as willing to accept connections. When a packet arrives for a TCP socket in TCPS_LISTEN state, a new socket is created with *sonewconn*(), which calls the TCP PRU_ATTACH request to create the protocol control blocks for the new socket. The new socket is placed on the queue of partial connections headed by the listening socket. If the packet contains a SYN and is otherwise acceptable, the association of the new socket is bound, both the send and the receive sequence numbers are initialized, and the connection state is advanced to TCPS_SYN_RECEIVED. The keepalive timer is set as before, and the output routine is called after TF_ACKNOW has been set to force the SYN to be acknowledged; an outgoing SYN is sent as well. If this SYN is acknowledged properly, the new socket is moved from the queue of partial connections to the queue of completed connections. If the owner of the listening socket is sleeping in an *accept* call or does a *select*, the socket will indicate that a new connection is available. Again, the socket is finally ready to send data. Up to one window of data may have already been received and acknowledged by the time that the *accept* call completes.

Connection Shutdown

A TCP connection is symmetrical and full-duplex, so either side may initiate disconnection independently. As long as one direction of the connection can carry data, the connection remains open. A socket may indicate that it has completed sending data with the *shutdown* system call, which results in a call to the *tcp_usrreq*() routine with request PRU_SHUTDOWN. The response to this request is that the state of the connection is advanced; from the ESTABLISHED state, the state becomes FIN_WAIT_1. The ensuing output call will send a FIN, indicating an end-of-file. The receiving socket will advance to CLOSE_WAIT, but may continue to send. The procedure may be different if the process simply closes the socket; in that case, a FIN is sent immediately, but if new data are received, they cannot be delivered. Normally, higher-level protocols conclude their own transactions such that both sides know when to close. If they do not, however, TCP must refuse new data; it does so by sending a packet with RST set if new data are received after the user has closed. If data remain in the send buffer of the socket when the *close* is done, TCP will normally attempt to deliver them. If the socket option SO_LINGER was set with a linger time of zero, the send buffer is simply flushed; otherwise, the user process is allowed to continue, and the protocol waits for delivery to conclude. Under these circumstances, the socket is marked with the state bit SS_NOFDREF (no file-descriptor reference). The completion of data transfer and the final close can take place an arbitrary amount of time later. When TCP finally completes the connection (or gives up because of timeout or other failure), it calls *tcp_close*(). The protocol control blocks and other dynamically allocated structures are freed at this time. The socket also is freed if the SS_NOFDREF flag has been set. Thus, the socket remains in existence as long as either a file descriptor or a protocol control block refers to it.

13.6 TCP Input Processing

Although TCP input processing is considerably more complicated than is UDP input handling, the preceding sections have provided the background that we need to examine the actual operation. As always, the input routine is called with parameters

```
(void) tcp_input(m, hlen);
    struct mbuf *m;
    int hlen;
```

The first few steps probably are beginning to sound familiar:

1. Locate the TCP header in the received IP datagram. Make sure that the packet is at least as long as a TCP header, and use *m_pullup*() if necessary to make it contiguous.

2. Compute the packet length, set up the IP pseudoheader, and checksum the TCP header and data. Discard the packet if the checksum is bad.

3. Check the TCP header length; if it is larger than a minimal header, make sure that the whole header is contiguous.

4. Locate the protocol control block for the connection with the port number specified. If none exists, send a packet containing the reset flag RST and drop the packet.

5. Check whether the socket is listening for connections; if it is, follow the procedure described for passive connection establishment.

6. Process any TCP options from the packet header.

7. Clear the idle time for the connection, and set the keepalive timer to its normal value.

At this point, the normal checks have been made, and we are prepared to deal with data and control flags in the received packet. There are still many consistency checks that must be made during normal processing; for example, the SYN flag must be present if we are still establishing a connection, and must not be present if the connection has been established. We shall omit most of these checks from our discussion, but the tests are important to prevent wayward packets from causing confusion and possible data corruption.

The next step in checking a TCP packet is to see whether the packet is acceptable according to the receive window. It is important that this step be done before control flags—in particular RST—are examined, because old or extraneous packets should not affect the current connection unless they are clearly relevant in the current context. A segment is acceptable if the receive window has nonzero size, and if at least some of the sequence space occupied by the packet falls within the receive window. If the packet contains data, some of the data must fall within the window; portions of the data that precede the window are trimmed, as they have already been received, and portions that exceed the window also are discarded, as they have been sent prematurely. If the receive window is closed (*rcv_wnd* is zero), then only segments with no data and with a sequence number equal to *rcv_nxt* are acceptable. If an incoming segment is not acceptable, it is dropped after an acknowledgment is sent.

The processing of incoming TCP packets must be fully general, taking into account all the possible incoming packets and possible states of receiving endpoints. However, the bulk of the packets processed falls into two general categories. Typical packets contain either the next expected data segment for an existing connection or an acknowledgment plus a window update for one or more data segments, with no additional flags or state indications. Rather than considering each incoming segment based on first principles, *tcp_input()* checks first for these common cases. This algorithm is known as *header prediction*. If the incoming segment matches a connection in the ESTABLISHED state, if it contains the ACK flag but no other flags, if the sequence number is the next value expected (and the timestamp, if any, is nondecreasing), if the window field is the same as in the previous segment, and if the connection is not in a retransmission state, then the incoming segment is one of the two common types. The system processes any timestamp option that the segment contains, recording the value received to be included in the next acknowledgment. If the segment contains no data, it is a *pure acknowledgment* with a window update. In the usual case, round-trip–timing information is sampled if it is available, acknowledged data are dropped from the socket send buffer, and the sequence values are updated. The packet is discarded once the header values have been checked. The retransmit timer is canceled if all pending data have been acknowledged; otherwise, it is restarted. The socket layer is notified if any process might be waiting to do output. Finally, *tcp_output()* is called because the window has moved forward, and that operation completes the handling of a pure acknowledgment.

If a packet meeting the tests for header prediction contains the next expected data, if no out-of-order data are queued for the connection, and if the socket receive buffer has space for the incoming data, then this packet is a pure in-sequence data segment. The sequencing variables are updated, the packet headers are removed from the packet, and the remaining data are appended to the socket receive buffer. The socket layer is notified so that it can notify any interested process, and the control block is marked with a flag indicating that an acknowledgment is needed. No additional processing is required for a pure data packet.

For packets that are not handled by the header-prediction algorithm, the processing steps are as follows:

1. Process the timestamp option if it is present, rejecting any packets for which the timestamp has decreased, first sending a current acknowledgment.

2. Check whether the packet begins before *rcv_nxt*. If it does, ignore any SYN in the packet, and trim any data that fall before *rcv_nxt*. If no data remain, send a current acknowledgment and drop the packet. (The packet is presumed to be a duplicate transmission.)

3. If the packet still contains data after trimming, and the process that created the socket has already closed the socket, send a reset (RST) and drop the connection. This reset is necessary to abort connections that cannot complete; it typically is sent when a remote-login client disconnects while data are being received.

4. If the end of the segment falls after the window, trim any data beyond the window. If the window was closed and the packet sequence number is *rcv_nxt*, the packet is treated as a window probe; TF_ACKNOW is set to send a current acknowledgment and window update, and the remainder of the packet is processed. If SYN is set and the connection was in TIME_WAIT state, this packet is really a new connection request, and the old connection is dropped; this procedure is called *rapid connection reuse*. Otherwise, if no data remain, send an acknowledgment and drop the packet.

The remaining steps of TCP input processing check the following flags and fields and take the appropriate actions: RST, ACK, window, URG, data, and FIN. Because the packet has already been confirmed to be acceptable, these actions can be done in a straightforward way:

5. If a timestamp option is present, and the packet includes the next sequence number expected, record the value received to be included in the next acknowledgment.

6. If RST is set, close the connection and drop the packet.

7. If ACK is not set, drop the packet.

8. If the acknowledgment-field value is higher than that of previous acknowledgments, new data have been acknowledged. If the connection was in SYN_RECEIVED state and the packet acknowledges the SYN sent for this connection, enter ESTABLISHED state. If the packet includes a timestamp option, use it to compute a round-trip time sample; otherwise, if the sequence range that was newly acknowledged includes the sequence number for which the round-trip time was being measured, this packet provides a sample. Average the time sample into the smoothed round-trip time estimate for the connection. If all outstanding data have been acknowledged, stop the retransmission timer; otherwise, set it back to the current timeout value. Finally, drop from the send queue in the socket the data that were acknowledged. If a FIN has been sent and was acknowledged, advance the state machine.

9. Check the window field to see whether it advances the known send window. First, check whether this packet is a new window update. If the sequence number of the packet is greater than that of the previous window update, or the sequence number is the same but the acknowledgment-field value is higher, or

if both sequence and acknowledgment are the same but the window is larger, record the new window.

10. If the urgent-data flag URG is set, compare the urgent pointer in the packet to the last-received urgent pointer. If it is different, new urgent data have been sent. Use the urgent pointer to compute *so_oobmark*, the offset from the beginning of the socket receive buffer to the urgent mark (Section 11.6), and notify the socket with *sohasoutofband( )*. If the urgent pointer is less than the packet length, the urgent data have all been received. TCP normally removes the final data octet sent in urgent mode (the last octet before the urgent pointer), and places that octet in the protocol control block until it is requested with a PRU_RCVOOB request. (The end of the urgent data is a subject of disagreement; the BSD interpretation follows the original TCP specification.) A socket option, SO_OOBINLINE, may request that urgent data be left in the queue with the normal data, although the mark on the data stream is still maintained.

11. At long last, examine the data field in the received packet. If the data begin with *rcv_nxt*, then they can be placed directly into the socket receive buffer with *sbappend( )*. The flag TF_DELACK is set in the protocol control block to indicate that an acknowledgment is needed, but the latter is not sent immediately in hope that it can be piggybacked on any packets sent soon (presumably in response to the incoming data) or combined with acknowledgment of other data received soon; see the subsection on delayed acknowledgments and window updates in Section 13.7. If no activity causes a packet to be returned before the next time that the *tcp_fasttimo( )* routine runs, it will change the flag to TF_ACKNOW and call the *tcp_output( )* routine to send the acknowledgment. Acknowledgments can thus be delayed by no more than 200 milliseconds. If the data do not begin with *rcv_nxt*, the packet is retained in a per-connection queue until the intervening data arrive, and an acknowledgment is sent immediately.

12. As the final step in processing a received packet, check for the FIN flag. If it is present, the connection state machine may have to be advanced, and the socket is marked with *socantrcvmore( )* to convey the end-of-file indication. If the send side has already closed (a FIN was sent and acknowledged), the socket is now considered closed, and it is so marked with *soisdisconnected( )*. The TF_ACKNOW flag is set to force immediate acknowledgment.

Step 10 completes the actions taken when a new packet is received by *tcp_input( )*. However, as noted earlier in this section, receipt of input may require new output. In particular, acknowledgment of all outstanding data or a new window update requires either new output or a state change by the output module. Also, several special conditions set the TF_ACKNOW flag. In these cases, *tcp_output( )* is called at the conclusion of input processing.

13.7   TCP Output Processing

We are finally ready to investigate the most interesting part of the TCP implementation—the send policy. As we saw earlier, a TCP packet contains an acknowledgment and a window field as well as data, and a single packet may be sent if any of these three fields change. A naive TCP send policy might send many more packets than necessary. For example, consider what happens when a user types one character to a remote-terminal connection that uses remote echo. The server-side TCP receives a single-character packet. It might send an immediate acknowledgment of the character. Then, milliseconds later, the login server would read the character, removing the character from the receive buffer; the TCP might immediately send a window update noting that one additional octet of send window was available. After another millisecond or so, the login server would send an echoed character back to the client, necessitating a third packet sent in response to the single character of input. It is obvious that all three responses (the acknowledgment, the window update, and the data returns) could be sent in a single packet. However, if the server were not echoing input data, the acknowledgment could not be withheld for too long a time or the client-side TCP would begin to retransmit. The algorithms used in the send policy to minimize network traffic yet to maximize throughput are the most subtle part of a TCP implementation. The send policy used in 4.4BSD includes several standard algorithms, as well as a few approaches suggested by the network research community. We shall examine each part of the send policy.

As we saw in the previous section, there are several different events that may trigger the sending of data on a connection; in addition, packets must be sent to communicate acknowledgments and window updates (consider a one-way connection!).

Sending of Data

The most obvious reason that the tcp output module *tcp_output*() is called is that the user has written new data to the socket. Write operations are done with a call to *tcp_usrreq*() with the PRU_SEND request. (Recall that *sosend*() waits for enough space in the socket send buffer if necessary, then copies the user's data into a chain of mbufs that is passed to the protocol with the PRU_SEND request.) The action in *tcp_usrreq*() is simply to place the new output data in the socket's send buffer with *sbappend*(), and to call *tcp_output*(). If flow control permits, *tcp_output*() will send the data immediately.

The actual send operation is not substantially different from one for a UDP datagram socket. The differences are that the header is more complicated, and additional fields must be initialized, and that the data sent are simply a copy of the user's data.† A copy must be retained in the socket's send buffer in case retransmission is required. Also, if the number of data octets is larger than the size of a

---

†However, for send operations large enough for *sosend*() to place the data in external mbuf clusters, the copy is done by creation of a new reference to the data cluster.

single maximum-sized segment, multiple packets will be constructed and sent in a single call.

The *tcp_output*( ) routine allocates an mbuf to contain the output packet header, and copies the contents of the header template into that mbuf. If the data to be sent (if any) fit into the same mbuf as the header, *tcp_output*( ) copies them into place from the socket send buffer using the *m_copydata*( ) routine. Otherwise, *tcp_output*( ) adds the data to be sent as a separate chain of mbufs obtained with an *m_copy*( ) operation from the appropriate part of the send buffer. The sequence number for the packet is set from *snd_nxt*, and the acknowledgment is set from *rcv_nxt*. The flags are obtained from an array containing the flags to be sent in each connection state. The window to be advertised is computed from the amount of space remaining in the socket's receive buffer; however, if that amount is small (less than one-fourth of the buffer and less than one segment), it is set to zero. The window is never allowed to end at a smaller sequence number than the one in which it ended in the previous packet. If urgent data have been sent, the urgent pointer and flag are set accordingly. One other flag must be set: The PUSH flag on a packet indicates that data should be passed to the user; it is like a buffer-flush request. This flag is generally considered obsolete, but is set whenever all the data in the send buffer have been sent; 4.4BSD ignores this flag on input. Once the header is filled in, the packet is checksummed. The remaining parts of the IP header are initialized, including the type-of-service and time-to-live fields, and the packet is sent with *ip_output*( ). The retransmission timer is started if it it is not already running, and the *snd_nxt* and *snd_max* values for the connection are updated.

Avoidance of the Silly-Window Syndrome

Silly-window syndrome is the name given to a potential problem in a window-based flow-control scheme in which a system sends several small packets, rather than waiting for a reasonable-sized window to become available [Clark, 1982]. For example, if a network-login client program has a total receive buffer size of 4096 octets, and the user stops terminal output during a large printout, the buffer will become nearly full as new full-sized segments are received. If the remaining buffer space dropped to 10 bytes, it would not be useful for the receiver to volunteer to receive an additional 10 octets. If the user then allowed a few characters to print and stopped output again, it still would not be useful for the receiving TCP to send a window update allowing another 14 octets. Instead, it is desirable to wait until a reasonably large packet can be sent, as the receive buffer already contains enough data for the next several pages of output. Avoidance of the silly-window syndrome is desirable in both the receiver and the sender of a flow-controlled connection, as either end can prevent silly small windows from being used. We described receiver avoidance of the silly-window syndrome in the previous subsection; when a packet is sent, the receive window is advertised as zero if it is less than one packet and less than one-fourth of the receive buffer. For sender avoidance of the silly-window syndrome, an output operation is delayed if at least a full packet of data is ready to be sent, but less than one full packet can be sent because of the size of the send window. Instead of sending, *tcp_output*() sets the output state to persist state by starting the persist timer. If no window update has been received by the time that the timer expires, the allowable data are sent in the hope that the acknowledgment will include a larger window. If it does not, the connection stays in persist state, sending a window probe periodically until the window is opened.

An initial implementation of sender avoidance of the silly-window syndrome produced large delays and low throughput over connections to hosts using TCP implementations with tiny buffers. Unfortunately, those implementations *always* advertised receive windows less than the maximum segment size, which behavior was considered silly by this implementation. As a result of this problem, the 4.4BSD TCP keeps a record of the largest receive window offered by a peer in the protocol-control-block variable *max_sndwnd*. When at least one-half of *max_sndwnd* may be sent, a new segment is sent. This technique improved performance when a system was communicating with these primitive hosts.

Avoidance of Small Packets

Network traffic exhibits a bimodal distribution of sizes. Bulk data transfers tend to use the largest possible packets for maximum throughput. Network-login services tend to use small packets, however, often containing only a single data character. On a fast local-area network, such as an Ethernet, the use of single-character packets generally is not a problem, as the network bandwidth usually is not saturated. On long-haul networks interconnected by slow or congested links, it is desirable to collect input over some period and then to send it in a single network packet. Various schemes have been devised for collecting input over a fixed time—usually about 50 to 100 milliseconds—and then sending it in a single packet. These schemes noticeably slow character echo times on fast networks, however, and often save few packets on slow networks. In contrast, a simple and elegant scheme for reducing small-packet traffic was suggested by Nagle [Nagle, 1984]. This scheme allows the first octet output to be sent alone in a packet with no delay. Until this packet is acknowledged, however, no new small packets may be sent. If enough new data arrive to fill a maximum-sized packet, another packet is sent. As soon as the outstanding data are acknowledged, the input that was queued while waiting for the first packet may be sent. Only one small packet may ever be outstanding on a connection at one time. The net result is that data from small output operations are queued during one round-trip time. If the round-trip time is less than the intercharacter arrival time, as it is in a remote-terminal session on a local-area network, transmissions are never delayed, and response time remains low. When a slow network intervenes, input after the first character is queued, and the next packet contains the input received during the preceding round-trip time. This algorithm is attractive both because of its simplicity and because of its self-tuning nature.

Eventually, people discovered that this algorithm did not work well for certain classes of network clients that sent streams of small requests that could not be batched. One such client was the network-based X Window System [Scheifler &

Gettys, 1986], which required immediate delivery of small messages to get real-time feedback for user interfaces such as rubber-banding to sweep out a new window. Hence, the developers added an option to TCP, TCP_NODELAY, to defeat this algorithm on a connection. This option can be set with a *setsockopt* call, which reaches TCP via the *tcp_ctloutput*() routine.†

Delayed Acknowledgments and Window Updates

TCP packets must be sent for reasons other than data transmission. On a one-way connection, the receiving TCP must still send packets to acknowledge received data and to advance the sender's send window. The mechanism for delaying acknowledgments in hope of piggybacking or coalescing them with data or window updates was described in Section 13.6. In a bulk data transfer, the time at which window updates are sent is a determining factor for network throughput. For example, if the receiver simply set the TF_DELACK flag each time that data were received on a bulk-data connection, acknowledgments would be sent every 200 milliseconds. If 8192-octet windows are used on a 10-Mbit/s Ethernet, this algorithm will result in a maximum throughput of 320 Kbit/s, or 3.2 percent of the physical network bandwidth. Clearly, once the sender has filled the send window that it has been given, it must stop until the receiver acknowledges the old data (allowing them to be removed from the send buffer and new data to replace them) and provides a window update (allowing the new data to be sent).

Because TCP's window-based flow control is limited by the space in the socket receive buffer, TCP has the PR_RCVD flag set in its protocol-switch entry so that the protocol will be called (via the PRU_RCVD request of *tcp_usrreq*()) when the user has done a receive call that has removed data from the receive buffer. The PRU_RCVD entry simply calls *tcp_output*(). Whenever *tcp_output*() determines that a window update sent under the current circumstances would provide new send window to the sender large enough to be worthwhile, it sends an acknowledgment and window update. If the receiver waited until the window was full, the sender would already have been idle for some time when it finally received a window update. Furthermore, if the send buffer on the sending system was smaller than the receiver's buffer, and thus the than receiver's window, the sender would be unable to fill the receiver's window without receiving an acknowledgment. Therefore, the window-update strategy in 4.4BSD is based on only the maximum segment size. Whenever a new window update would move the window forward by at least two full-sized segments, the window update is sent. This window-update strategy produces a two-fold reduction in acknowledgment traffic and a two-fold reduction in input processing for the sender. However, updates are sent often enough to give the sender feedback on the progress of the connection and to allow the sender to continue sending additional segments.

Note that TCP is called at two different stages of processing on the receiving side of a bulk data transfer: It is called on packet reception to process input, and it

---

†Unfortunately, the X Window System library sets the TCP_NODELAY flag always, rather than only when the client is using mouse-driven positioning.

is called after each receive operation removing data from the input buffer. At the first call, an acknowledgment could be sent, but no window update could be sent. After the receive operation, a window update also is possible. Thus, it is important that the algorithm for updates run in the second half of this cycle.

Retransmit State

When the retransmit timer expires while a sender is awaiting acknowledgment of transmitted data, *tcp_output*() is called to retransmit. The retransmit timer is first set to the next multiple of the round-trip time in the backoff series. The variable *snd_nxt* is moved back from its current sequence number to *snd_una*. A single packet is then sent containing the oldest data in the transmit queue. Unlike some other systems, 4.4BSD does not keep copies of the packets that have been sent on a connection; it retains only the data. Thus, although only a single packet is retransmitted, that packet may contain more data than does the oldest outstanding packet. On a slow connection with small send operations, such as a remote login, this algorithm may cause a single-octet packet that is lost to be retransmitted with all the data queued since the initial octet was first transmitted.

If a single packet was lost in the network, the retransmitted packet will elicit an acknowledgment of all data transmitted thus far. If more than one packet was lost, the next acknowledgment will include the retransmitted packet and possibly some of the intervening data. It may also include a new window update. Thus, when an acknowledgment is received after a retransmit timeout, any old data that were not acknowledged will be resent as though they had not yet been sent, and some new data may be sent as well.

Slow Start

Many TCP connections traverse several networks between source and destination. When some of the networks are slower than others, the entry router to the slowest network often is presented with more traffic than it can handle. It may buffer some input packets to avoid dropping packets because of sudden changes in flow, but eventually its buffers will fill and it must begin dropping packets. When a TCP connection first starts sending data across a fast network to a router forwarding via a slower network, it may find that the router's queues are already nearly full. In the original send policy used in BSD, a bulk-data transfer would start out by sending a full window of packets once the connection was established. These packets could be sent at the full speed of the network to the bottleneck router, but that router could transmit them at only a much slower rate. As a result, the initial burst of packets was highly likely to overflow the router's queue, and some of the packets would be lost. If such a connection used an expanded window size in an attempt to gain performance—for example, when traversing a satellite-based network with a long round-trip time—this problem would be even more severe. However, if the connection could once reach steady state, a full window of data often could be accommodated by the network if the packets were spread evenly throughout the path. At steady state, new packets would be injected into the network only when previous packets were acknowledged, and the number of packets in the network would be constant. In addition, even if packets arrived at the outgoing router in a cluster, they would be spread out when the network was traversed by at least their transmission times in the slowest network. If the receiver sent acknowledgments when each packet was received, the acknowledgments would return to the sender with approximately the correct spacing. The sender would then have a self-clocking means for transmitting at the correct rate for the network without sending bursts of packets that the bottleneck could not buffer.

An algorithm named *slow start* brings a TCP connection to this steady state [Jacobson, 1988]. It is called slow start because it is necessary to start data transmission slowly when traversing a slow network. The scheme is simple: A connection starts out with a limit of just one outstanding packet. Each time that an acknowledgment is received, the limit is increased by one packet. If the acknowledgment also carries a window update, two packets can be sent in response. This process continues until the window is fully open. During the slow-start phase of the connection, if each packet was acknowledged separately, the limit would be doubled during each exchange, resulting in an exponential opening of the window. Delayed acknowledgments might cause acknowledgments to be coalesced if more than one packet could arrive at the receiver within 200 milliseconds, slowing the window opening slightly. However, the sender never sends bursts of more than two or three packets during the opening phase, and sends only one or two packets at a time once the window has opened.

The implementation of the slow-start algorithm uses a second window, like the send window but maintained separately, called the *congestion window* (*snd_cwnd*). The congestion window is maintained according to an estimate of the data that the network is currently able to buffer for this connection. The send policy is modified so that new data are sent only if allowed by both the normal and congestion send windows. The congestion window is initialized to the size of one packet, causing a connection to begin with a slow start. It is set to one packet whenever transmission stops because of a timeout. Otherwise, once a dropped packet was acknowledged, the resulting window update might allow a full window of data to be sent, which would once again overrun intervening routers. This slow start after a retransmission timeout eliminates the need for a test in the output routine to limit output to one packet on the initial timeout. In addition, the timeout may indicate that the network has become slower because of congestion, and temporary reduction of the window may help the network to recover from its condition. The connection is forced to reestablish its clock of acknowledgments after the connection has come to a halt, and the slow start has this effect as well. A slow start is also forced if a connection begins to transmit after an idle period of at least the current retransmission value (a function of the smoothed round-trip time and variance estimates).

Source-Quench Processing

If a router along the route used by a connection receives more packets than it can send along this path, it will eventually be forced to drop packets. When packets are dropped, the router may send an ICMP *source quench* error message to hosts whose packets have been dropped, to indicate that the senders should slow their transmissions. Although this message indicates that some change should be made, it provides no information on how much of a change must be made or for how long the change should take effect. In addition, not all routers send source-quench messages for each packet dropped. The use of the slow-start algorithm after retransmission timeouts allows a connection to respond correctly to a dropped packet, whether or not a source quench is received to indicate the loss. The action on receipt of a source quench for a TCP connection is simply to anticipate the timeout because of the dropped packet, setting the congestion window to one packet. This action prevents new packets from being sent until the dropped packet is resent at the next timeout. At that time, the slow start will begin again.

Buffer and Window Sizing

The performance of a TCP connection is obviously limited by the bandwidth of the path that the connection must transit. The performance is also affected by the round-trip time for the path. For example, paths that traverse satellite links have a long intrinsic delay, even though the bandwidth may be high, but the throughput is limited to one window of data per round-trip time. After filling the receiver's window, the sender must wait for at least one round-trip time for an acknowledgment and window update to arrive. To take advantage of the full bandwidth of a path, both the sender and receiver must use buffers at least as large as the bandwidth-delay product to allow the sender to transmit during the entire round-trip time. In steady state, this buffering allows the sender, receiver, and intervening parts of the network to keep the pipeline filled at each stage. For some paths, using slow start and a large window can lead to much better performance than could be achieved previously.

The round-trip time for a network path includes two components: transit time and queuing time. The transit time comprises the propagation, switching, and forwarding time in the physical layers of the network, including the time to transmit packets bit by bit after each store-and-forward hop. Ideally, queuing time would be negligible, with packets arriving at each node of the network just in time to be sent after the preceding packet. This ideal flow is possible when a single connection using a suitable window size is synchronized with the network. However, as additional traffic is injected into the network by other sources, queues build up in routers, especially at the entrance to the slower links in the path. Although queuing delay is part of the round-trip time observed by each network connection that is using a path, it is not useful to increase the operating window size for a connection to a value larger than the product of the limiting bandwidth for the path times the transit delay. Sending additional data beyond that limit causes the additional data to be queued, increasing queuing delay without increasing throughput.

Avoidance of Congestion with Slow Start

The addition of the slow-start algorithm to TCP allows a connection to send packets at a rate that the network can tolerate, reaching a steady state at which packets are sent only when another packet has exited the network. A single connection may reasonably use a large window without flooding the entry router to the slow network on startup. As a connection opens the window during a slow start, it injects packets into the network until the network links are kept busy. During this phase, it may send packets at up to twice the rate at which the network can deliver data, because of the exponential opening of the window. If the window is chosen appropriately for the path, the connection will reach steady state without flooding the network. However, with multiple connections sharing a path, the bandwidth available to each connection is reduced. If each connection uses a window equal to the bandwidth-delay product, the additional packets in transit must be queued, increasing delay. If the total offered load is too high, routers must drop packets rather than increasing the queue sizes and delay. Thus, the appropriate window size for a TCP connection depends not only on the path, but also on competing traffic. A window size large enough to give good performance when a long-delay link is in the path will overrun the network when most of the round-trip time is in queuing delays. It is highly desirable for a TCP connection to be self-tuning, as the characteristics of the path are seldom known at the endpoints and may change with time. If a connection expands its window to a value too large for a path, or if additional load on the network collectively exceeds the capacity, router queues will build until packets must be dropped. At this point, the connection will close the congestion window to one packet and will initiate a slow start. If the window is simply too large for the path, however, this process will repeat each time that the window is opened too far.

The connection can learn from this problem, and can adjust its behavior accordingly with another algorithm associated with the slow-start algorithm. This algorithm keeps a new state variable for each connection, $t\_ssthresh$ (slow-start threshold), which is an estimate of the usable window for the path. When a packet is dropped, as evidenced by a retransmission timeout, this window estimate is set to one-half the number of the outstanding data octets. The current window is obviously too large at the moment, and the decrease in window utilization must be large enough that congestion will decrease rather than stabilizing. At the same time, the slow-start window (snd_cwnd) is set to one segment to restart. The connection starts up as before, opening the window exponentially until it reaches the $t\_ssthresh$ limit. At this point, the connection is near the estimated usable window for the path. It enters steady state, sending data packets as allowed by window updates. To test for improvement in the network, it continues to expand the window slowly; as long as this expansion succeeds, the connection can continue to take advantage of reduced network load. The expansion of the window in this phase is linear, with one additional full-sized segment being added to the current window for each full window of data transmitted. This slow increase allows the connection to discover when it is safe to resume use of a larger window while reducing the loss in throughput because of the wait after the loss of a packet before transmission can resume. Note that the increase in window size during this phase of the connection is linear as long as no packets are lost, but the decrease in window size when signs of congestion appear is exponential (it is divided by 2 on each timeout). With the use of this dynamic window-sizing algorithm, it is possible to use larger default window sizes for connection to all destinations without overrunning networks that cannot support them.

Fast Retransmission

Packets can be lost in the network for two reasons: congestion and corruption. In either case, TCP detects lost packets by a timeout causing a retransmission. When a packet is lost, the flow of packets on a connection comes to a halt while waiting for the timeout. Depending on the round-trip time and variance, this timeout can result in a substantial period during which the connection makes no progress. Once the timeout occurs, a single packet is retransmitted as the first phase of a slow start, and the slow-start threshold is set to one-half previous operating window. If later packets are not lost, the connection goes through a slow start up to the new threshold, and it then gradually opens the window to probe whether any congestion has disappeared. Each of these phases lowers the effective throughput for the connection. The result is decreased performance, even though congestion may have been brief.

When a connection reaches steady state, it sends a continuous stream of data packets in response to a stream of acknowledgments with window updates. If a single packet is lost, the receiver sees packets arriving out of order. Most TCP receivers, including 4.4BSD, respond to an out-of-order segment with a repeated acknowledgment for the in-order data. If one packet is lost while enough packets to fill the window are sent, each packet after the lost packet will provoke a duplicate acknowledgment with no data, window update, or other new information. The receiver can infer the out-of-order arrival of packets from these duplicate acknowledgments. Given sufficient evidence of reordering, the receiver can assume that a packet has been lost. The 4.4BSD TCP implements *fast retransmission* based on this signal. After detecting four identical acknowledgments, the *tcp_input*() function saves the current connection parameters, simulates a retransmission timeout to resend one segment of the oldest data in the send queue, and then restores the current transmit state. Because this indication of a lost packet is a congestion signal, the estimate of the network buffering limit, *t_ssthresh*, is set to one-half of the current window. However, because the stream of acknowledgments has not stopped, a slow start is not needed. If a single packet has been lost, doing fast retransmission fills in the gap more quickly than would waiting for the retransmission timeout. An acknowledgment for the missing segment, plus all out-of-order segments queued before the retransmission, will then be received, and the connection can continue normally.

Even with fast retransmission, it is likely that a TCP connection that suffers a lost segment will reach the end of the send window and be forced to stop transmission while awaiting an acknowledgment for the lost segment. However, after the fast retransmission, duplicate acknowledgments are received for each additional packet received by the peer after the lost packet. These duplicate acknowledgments imply that a packet has left the network and is now queued by the receiver. In that case, the packet does not need to be considered as within the network congestion window, possibly allowing additional data to be sent if the receiver's window is large enough. Each duplicate acknowledgment after a fast retransmission thus causes the congestion window to be moved forward artificially by the segment size. If the receiver's window is large enough, it allows the connection to make forward progress during a larger part of the time that it awaits an acknowledgment for the retransmitted segment. For this algorithm to have effect, the sender and receiver must have additional buffering beyond the normal bandwidth-delay product; twice that amount is needed for the algorithm to have full effect.

13.8   Internet Control Message Protocol (ICMP)

The *Internet Control Message Protocol (ICMP)* [Postel, 1981c] is the control- and error-message protocol for IP. Although it is layered above IP for input and output operations, much like in UDP, it is really an integral part of IP. Unlike those of UDP, most ICMP messages are received and implemented by the kernel. ICMP messages may also be sent and received via a raw IP socket (see Section 12.7).

ICMP messages fall into three general classes. One class includes various errors that may occur somewhere in the network and that may be reported back to the originator of the packet provoking the error. Such errors include routing failures (network or host unreachable), expiration of the time-to-live field in a packet, or a report by the destination host that the target protocol or port number is not available. Error packets include the IP header plus at least eight additional octets of the packet that encountered the error. The second message class may be considered as router-to-host control messages. The two instances of such messages are the *source-quench message*, which reports excessive output and packet loss, and the *routing redirect*, which informs a host that a better route is available for a host or network via a different router. The final message class includes network management, testing, and measurement packets. These packets include a network-address request and reply, a network-mask request and reply, an echo request and reply, and a timestamp request and reply.

All the actions and replies required by an incoming ICMP message are done by the kernel ICMP layer. ICMP packets are received from IP via the normal protocol-input entry point because ICMP has its own IP protocol number. The ICMP input routine formulates responses to any requests and passes the reply to *ip_output()* to be returned to the sender. When error indications or source quenches are received, a generic address is constructed in a *sockaddr* structure. The address and error code are reported to each network protocol's control-input entry, *pr_ctlinput()*, by *pfctlinput()*, which is passed a pointer to the returned IP header in case additional information is needed about the source or destination associated with the error. For example, an ICMP *port unreachable* message causes errors for only those connections with the indicated remote port and protocol.

Routing changes indicated by redirect messages are processed by the *rtredirect*() routine. It verifies that the router from which the message was received was the next-hop gateway in use for the destination, and it checks that the new gateway is on a directly attached network. If these tests succeed, the kernel routing tables are modified accordingly. If the new route is of equivalent scope to the previous route (e.g., both are for the destination network), the gateway in the route is changed to the new gateway. If the scope of the new route is smaller than that of the original route (either a host redirect is received when a network route was used, or the old route used a wildcard route), a new route is created in the kernel table. Routes that are created or modified by redirects are marked with the flags RTF_DYNAMIC and RTF_MODIFIED, respectively. Once the routing tables are updated, the protocols are notified by *pfctlinput*(), using a redirect code, rather than an error code. TCP and UDP simply flush any cached route from the protocol control block when a redirect is received. The next packet sent on the socket will thus reallocate a route, choosing the new route if that one is now the best route.

Once an incoming ICMP message has been processed by the kernel, it is passed to *rip_input*() for reception by any ICMP raw sockets. The raw sockets can also be used to send ICMP messages. The low-level network test program **ping** works by sending ICMP echo requests on a raw socket and listening for corresponding replies.

ICMP is also used by other Internet network protocols to generate error messages. UDP sends only ICMP *port unreachable* error messages, and TCP uses other means to report such errors. However, many different errors may be detected by IP, especially on systems used as IP gateways. The *icmp_error*() function constructs an error message of a specified type in response to an IP packet. Most error messages include a portion of the original packet that caused the error, as well as the type and code for the error. The source address for the error packet is selected according to the context. If the original packet was sent to a local system address, that address is used as the source. Otherwise, an address is used that is associated with the interface on which the packet was received, as when forwarding is done; the source address of the error message can then be set to the address of the router on the network closest to (or shared with) the originating host. Also, when IP forwards a packet via the same network interface on which that packet was received, it may send a redirect message to the originating host if that host is on the same network. The *icmp_error*() routine accepts an additional parameter for redirect messages: the address of the new router to be used by the host.

13.9   OSI Implementation Issues

4.4BSD includes an ISO networking domain that contains implementations of several of the ISO OSI protocols. The domain supports the Connectionless Network Protocol (CLNP), class 4 of the Transport Protocol (TP-4), the Connectionless Transport Protocol (CLTP), and several supporting protocols. A description of these protocols is given in [Rose, 1990]. It also supports the Connection-Oriented Network Service (CONS) over X.25. Despite support for these OSI protocols in 4.4BSD and the earlier 4.3BSD Reno release, OSI networking has not become popular, and these implementations have not seen much use.

Although the OSI protocols have not been used widely, their implementation in BSD drove several changes in the networking framework. This section summarizes features of the OSI protocols that required these changes, as well as discussing the changes in the socket interface and framework.

The OSI networking protocols were designed with a layering similar to other protocols already running in the BSD network, and thus they generally fit into the existing framework. The following features of the OSI protocols, in contrast, did *not* fit easily into the existing (4.3BSD) framework:

• Long addresses (network addresses of 20 octets)

• Multilevel routing hierarchy

• Server confirmation of incoming connections

• Receipt of protocol information with connections

• Record marks

We discuss each of these features in turn, along with changes made to the socket interface and layering designed to accommodate them.

At the network level, ISO addresses can be as long as 20 octets. Transport-level selectors, analogous to TCP ports during connection establishment, can be up to 64 octets long. The *sockaddr* structure in 4.3BSD allowed only 14 bytes for network and transport addresses. The socket system-call interface allows variable-sized addresses to be passed to and from the kernel, but internal data structures, such as routing entries and interface addresses, did not allow longer addresses. The fixed-sized *sockaddr* structure was also used in system-management interfaces, such as the *ioctl* to set a route.

The problems with longer addresses led to a change in the *sockaddr* structure in 4.4BSD. The developers divided the *sa_family* field in the *sockaddr* to make space for a new *sa_len* field containing the total length of the *sockaddr*, which is now truly variable. Within the kernel, storage for *sockaddr* structures is allocated dynamically, except within a protocol family within which the structures are known to be fixed in size. This change was not necessary outside of the kernel, because the basic socket system calls convey the length of each sockaddr passed with a system call, but the new structure is more convenient within the kernel and in the more complicated interfaces, such as the routing socket (see Section 12.5).

Network addresses in ISO are variable in size, up to 20 octets. The first few octets specify the addressing authority and address format. The interpretation of the remainder of the address depends on the authority. The routing tables in 4.3BSD supported a two-level routing hierarchy, with network routes and host routes. However, ISO addresses are not divided into network and host parts in any standard way, and it is not simple to determine the longest prefix of an address for which a route might exist. These problems were the initial motivation for the redesign of the routing table and lookup algorithm to use a radix tree, described in Section 12.5. These changes have since proved to be useful with IP as well, especially when using addressing based on CIDR (see Section 13.1).

The ISO transport service uses a notion of connection establishment for servers that was somewhat different from the model used in the socket interface and implementation in 4.3BSD. The major difference is that the ISO service definition specifies a *connection indication* to the server, possibly including data associated with the connection request; the server can then choose whether to accept or reject the request.

The biggest obstacle to graceful implementation of this connection paradigm in BSD is the name of the *accept* system call, which waits for a new connection on a listening socket, then returns another socket associated with the new connection. This call has been redefined in 4.4BSD to allow the returned socket to be associated either with a connection indication or with a fully established connection. Protocols such as TCP continue to complete connections before they are returned via *accept*, but the ISO transport allows connections to be returned immediately on receipt of a connection request. The server receiving the request can confirm or reject the connection explicitly. If the server begins normal input or output operations without confirming the connection, the connection is confirmed automatically.

The final two items on the list of problems posed by the OSI protocols are receipt of protocol data with connections and record marks; they were both addressed with the same mechanism. The *recvmsg* system call was changed to allow receipt of protocol-specific data, including data from a connection request, as well as new flags describing any data returned. The *msghdr* structure used by *recvmsg* has a new field that supplies a buffer for *ancillary data*, which can include connection data or other protocol-dependent information associated with received data (see section Section 11.1). The *msghdr* structure also contains new flags, including a flag to indicate the end of a record. This flag supports the use of arbitrarily long records for protocols such as ISO transport. Internally, records are delimited with the new M_EOR flag on *mbuf* structures in the socket receive buffer (described in section Section 11.6).

The developers made the changes described in this section motivated initially by requirements of the OSI protocol implementations. The changes are not specific to OSI, however; they generalize the socket interface and internal framework to allow support for a wider variety of protocols. Several of the changes are useful with Internet protocols, as well as with OSI and other protocols.

13.10 Summary of Networking and Interprocess Communication

In this section, we shall tie together much of the material presented in the Chapters 11 through 13. For this purpose, we shall describe the operation of the socket and network layers during normal use.

There are three stages in the lifetime of a socket. Initially, the socket is created and is associated with a communication domain. During its lifetime, data passes through it to one or more other sockets. When the socket is no longer needed, it must go through an orderly shutdown process in which its resources are freed.

Creation of a Communication Channel

Sockets are created by users with the *socket* system call and internally with the *socreate*() routine. To create a socket, the user must supply a communication domain and socket type, and also may request a specific communication protocol within that domain. The socket routines first locate the domain structure for the communication domain from a global list initialized at boot time for each configured domain. The table of those protocols that constitute the domain's protocol family is located in the domain structure. This table of protocol-switch entries is then scanned for an appropriate protocol to support the type of socket being created (or for a specific protocol, if one was specified). The socket routine does this search by examining the *pr_type* field, which contains a possible socket type (e.g., SOCK_STREAM), and the *pr_protocol* field, which contains the protocol number of the protocol—normally a well-known value. If a suitable protocol is found, a reference to the protocol's protocol-switch entry is then recorded in the socket's *so_proto* field, and all requests for network services are made through the appropriate procedure identified in the structure.

After locating a handle on a protocol, *socreate*() allocates space for the socket data structure and initializes the socket for the initial state. To complete the creation process, *socreate*() makes a PRU_ATTACH request to the protocol's user request routine so that the protocol can *attach* itself to the new socket.

Next, an address may be bound to a socket. Binding of an address is done internally by *sobind*(), which makes a PRU_BIND request to the socket's supporting protocol. Each domain provides a routine that manages its address space. Addresses in the local (UNIX) domain are names in the filesystem name space, and consequently name requests go through the filesystem name-lookup routine, *namei*().

For a socket to be ready to accept connections, the socket layer must inform the protocols with a PRU_LISTEN request. This request obviously has no meaning for connectionless protocols such as UDP. For connection-oriented protocols such as TCP, however, a listen request causes a protocol state transition. Before effecting this state change, protocols verify that the socket has an address bound to it; if there is no address bound, the protocol module chooses one for the socket.

In the local domain, a listen request causes no state change, but a check is made to ensure that the socket has a name. Unlike the other protocols, however, the local domain will not select a name for the socket.

Soconnect() is invoked to establish a connection, generating a PRU_CONNECT request to the protocol. For connectionless protocols, the address is recorded as a default address to be used when data are sent on the socket (i.e., the process does a *write* or *send*, instead of a *sendto*). Setting the address does not require any peer communication, and the protocol module returns immediately.

For a connection-based protocol, the peer's address is verified, and a local address is assigned for unbound sockets. Instead of the socket entering a *connected* state immediately, it is marked as *connecting* with *soisconnecting*(). The protocol then initiates a handshake with the peer by transmitting a connection-request message. When a connection request of this sort is completed—usually, on receipt of a message by the protocol input routine—the socket's state is changed with a call to *soisconnected*().

From a user's perspective, all connection requests appear synchronous because the *connect* system call invokes *soconnect*() to initiate a connection, and then, at the socket level, puts the calling process to sleep if the connection request has not been completed. Alternatively, if the socket has been made nonblocking with *fcntl*, *connect* returns the error EINPROGRESS once the connection has been initiated successfully. The caller may test the completion of the connection with a *select* call testing for ability to write to the socket.

For connection-based communication, a process must accept an incoming connection request on a listening socket by calling *accept*, which in turn calls *soaccept*(). This call returns the next completed connection from the socket receive queue.

Sending and Receiving of Data

Once a socket has been created, data can begin to flow through it. A typical TCP/IP connection is shown in Fig. 13.10. The *sosend*() routine is responsible for copying data from the sending process's address space into mbufs. It then presents the data to the network layer with one or more calls to the protocol's PRU_SEND request. The network may choose to send the data immediately, or to wait until a more auspicious time. If the protocol delays, or if it must retain a copy of the data for possible retransmission, it may store the data in the socket's send buffer. Eventually, the data are passed down through TCP and IP as one or more packets to the interface driver selected by a routing lookup; at each layer, an appropriate header is added. Each packet is sent out over the network to its destination machine.

On receipt at the destination machine, the interface driver's receiver-interrupt handler verifies and removes its own header, and places the packet onto an appropriate network-protocol input queue. Later, the network-level input-processing module (e.g., IP) is invoked by a software interrupt; it runs at a lower interrupt-priority level than that of the hardware network-interface interrupt. In this example, the packets on the input queue are processed first by IP and then by TCP, each of which verifies and removes its own header. If they are received in order, the data are then placed on the appropriate socket's input queue, ready to be copied out by *soreceive*() on receipt of a *read* request.

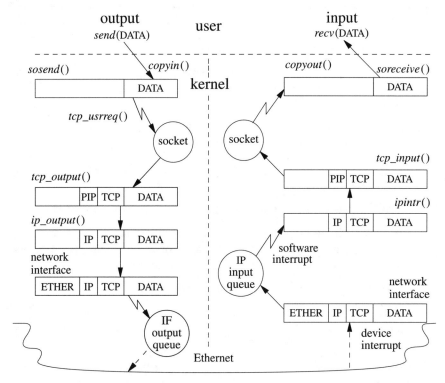

Figure 13.10 Data flow through a TCP/IP connection over an Ethernet. ETHER—Ethernet header; PIP—pseudo IP header; IP—IP header; TCP—TCP header; IF—interface.

Termination of Data Transmission or Reception

The *soshutdown()* routine stops data flow at a socket. Shutting down a socket for reading is a simple matter of flushing the receive queue and marking the socket as unable to receive more data; this action is done with a call to *sorflush()*, which in turn invokes *socantrcvmore()* to change the socket state, and then releases any resources associated with the receive queue. Shutting down a socket for writing, however, involves notifying the protocol with a PRU_SHUTDOWN request. For reliable connections, any data remaining in the send queue must be drained before the connection can finish shutting down. If a protocol supports the notion of a unidirectional connection (i.e., a connection in which unidirectional data flow is possible), the socket may continue to be usable; otherwise, the protocol may start a disconnect sequence. Once a socket has been shut down in both directions, the protocol starts a disconnect sequence. When the disconnect completes, first the resources associated with the protocol, and then those associated with the socket, are freed.

Exercises

13.1   Is TCP a transport-, network-, or link-layer protocol?

13.2   How does IP identify the next-higher-level protocol that should process an incoming message? How might this dispatching differ in other networking architectures?

13.3   How many hosts can exist on a class C Internet network? Is it possible to use subnet addressing with a class C network? Explain your answer.

13.4   What is a broadcast message? How are IP broadcast messages identified in the Internet?

13.5   Why are TCP and UDP protocol control blocks kept on separate lists?

13.6   Why does the IP output routine, rather than the socket-layer send routine (*sosend*()), check the destination address of an outgoing packet to see whether the destination address is a broadcast address?

13.7   Why does 4.4BSD not forward broadcast messages?

13.8   Why does the TCP header include a header-length field even though it is always encapsulated in an IP packet that contains the length of the TCP message?

13.9   What is the flow-control mechanism used by TCP to limit the rate at which data are transmitted?

13.10 How does TCP recognize messages from a host that are directed to a connection that existed previously, but that has since been shut down (such as after a machine is rebooted)?

13.11 When is the size of the TCP receive window for a connection not equal to the amount of space available in the associated socket's receive buffer? Why are these values not equal at that time?

13.12 What are keepalive messages? For what does TCP use them? Why are keepalive messages implemented in the kernel rather than, say, in each application that wants this facility?

13.13 Why is calculating a *smoothed* round-trip time important, rather than, for example, just averaging calculated round-trip times?

13.14 Why does TCP delay acknowledgments for received data? What is the maximum time that TCP will delay an acknowledgment?

13.15 Explain what the silly-window syndrome is. Give an example in which its avoidance is important to good protocol performance. Explain how the 4.4BSD TCP avoids this problem.

13.16 What is meant by *small-packet avoidance*? Why is small-packet avoidance bad for clients (e.g., the X Window System) that exhibit one-way data flow and that require low latency for good interactive performance?

*13.17 A *directed broadcast* is a message that is to be broadcast on a network one or more hops away from the sender. Describe a scheme for supporting directed-broadcast messages in the Internet domain.

*13.18 Why is the initial sequence number for a TCP connection selected at random, rather than being, say, always set to zero?

*13.19 In the TCP protocol, why do the SYN and FIN flags occupy space in the sequence-number space?

*13.20 Describe a typical TCP packet exchange during connection setup. Assume that an active client initiated the connection to a passive server. How would this scenario change if the passive server tried simultaneously to initiate a connection to the client?

*13.21 Sketch the TCP state transitions that would take place if a server process accepted a connection and then immediately closed that connection before receiving any data. How would this scenario be altered if 4.4BSD TCP supported a mechanism whereby a server could refuse a connection request before the system completed the connection?

*13.22 At one time, the 4BSD TCP used a strict exponential backoff strategy for transmission. Explain how this nonadaptive algorithm can adversely affect performance across networks that are very *lossy*, but that have high bandwidth (e.g., some networks that use satellite connections).

*13.23 Why does UDP match the completely specified destination addresses of incoming messages to sockets with incomplete local and remote destination addresses?

*13.24 Why might a sender set the *Don't Fragment* flag in the header of an IP packet?

*13.25 The *maximum segment lifetime* (MSL) is the maximum time that a message may exist in a network—that is, the maximum time that a message may be in transit on some hardware medium, or queued in a gateway. What does TCP do to ensure that TCP messages have a limited MSL? What does IP do to enforce a limited MSL? See [Fletcher & Watson, 1978] for another approach to this issue.

**13.26 Why does TCP use the timestamp option, in addition to the sequence number, in detecting old duplicate packets? Under what circumstances is this detection most desirable?

**13.27 Describe a protocol for calculating a bound on the maximum segment lifetime of messages in an internet environment. How might TCP use a bound on the MSL (see Exercise 12.25) for a message to minimize the overhead associated with shutting down a TCP connection?

References

Carr et al, 1970.
> S. Carr, S. Crocker, & V. Cerf, "Host–Host Communication Protocol in the ARPA Network," *Proceedings of the AFIPS Spring Joint Computer Conference*, pp. 589–597, 1970.

Cerf, 1978.
> V. Cerf, "The Catenet Model for Internetworking," Technical Report IEN 48, SRI Network Information Center, Menlo Park, CA, July 1978.

Cerf & Kahn, 1974.
> V. Cerf & R. Kahn, "A Protocol for Packet Network Intercommunication," *IEEE Transactions on Communications*, vol. 22, no. 5, pp. 637–648, May 1974.

Clark, 1982.
> D. D. Clark, "Window and Acknowledgment Strategy in TCP," RFC 813, available by anonymous FTP from ds.internic.net, July 1982.

DARPA, 1983.
> DARPA, "A History of the ARPANET: The First Decade," Technical Report, Bolt, Beranek, and Newman, Cambridge, MA, April 1983.

Deering, 1989.
> S. Deering, "Host Extensions for IP Multicasting," RFC 1112, available by anonymous FTP from ds.internic.net, August 1989.

Fletcher & Watson, 1978.
> J. Fletcher & R. Watson, "Mechanisms for a Reliable Timer-Based Protocol," in *Computer Networks 2*, pp. 271–290, North-Holland, Amsterdam, The Netherlands, 1978.

Fuller et al, 1993.
> V. Fuller, T. Li, J. Yu, & K. Varadhan, "Classless Inter-Domain Routing (CIDR): An Address Assignment and Aggregation Strategy," RFC 1519, available by anonymous FTP from ds.internic.net, September 1993.

ISO, 1984.
> ISO, "Open Systems Interconnection: Basic Reference Model," ISO 7498, International Organization for Standardization, 1984. available from the: American National Standards Institute, 1430 Broadway, New York, NY 10018.

Jacobson, 1988.
> V. Jacobson, "Congestion Avoidance and Control," *Proceedings of the ACM SIGCOMM Conference*, pp. 314–329, August 1988.

Jacobson et al, 1992.
> V. Jacobson, R. Braden, & D. Borman, "TCP Extensions for High Performance," RFC 1323, available by anonymous FTP from ds.internic.net, May 1992.

McQuillan & Walden, 1977.
> J. M. McQuillan & D. C. Walden, "The ARPA Network Design Decisions," *Computer Networks*, vol. 1, no. 5, pp. 243–289, 1977.

Mogul, 1984.
> J. Mogul, "Broadcasting Internet Datagrams," RFC 919, available by anonymous FTP from ds.internic.net, October 1984.

Mogul & Deering, 1990.
> J. Mogul & S. Deering, "Path MTU Discovery," RFC 1191, available by anonymous FTP from ds.internic.net, November 1990.

Mogul & Postel, 1985.
> J. Mogul & J. Postel, "Internet Standard Subnetting Procedure," RFC 950, available by anonymous FTP from ds.internic.net, August 1985.

Nagle, 1984.
> J. Nagle, "Congestion Control in IP/TCP Internetworks," RFC 896, available by anonymous FTP from ds.internic.net, January 1984.

Padlipsky, 1985.
> M. A. Padlipsky, *The Elements of Networking Style,* Prentice-Hall, Englewood Cliffs, NJ, 1985.

Postel, 1980.
> J. Postel, "User Datagram Protocol," RFC 768, available by anonymous FTP from ds.internic.net, August 1980.

Postel, 1981a.
> J. Postel, "Internet Protocol," RFC 791, available by anonymous FTP from ds.internic.net, September 1981.

Postel, 1981b.
> J. Postel, "Transmission Control Protocol," RFC 793, available by anonymous FTP from ds.internic.net, September 1981.

Postel, 1981c.
> J. Postel, "Internet Control Message Protocol," RFC 792, available by anonymous FTP from ds.internic.net, September 1981.

Postel et al, 1981.
> J. Postel, C. Sunshine, & D. Cohen, "The ARPA Internet Protocol," *Computer Networks*, vol. 5, no. 4, pp. 261–271, July 1981.

Rose, 1990.
> M. Rose, *The Open Book: A Practical Perspective on OSI,* Prentice-Hall, Englewood Cliffs, NJ, 1990.

Scheifler & Gettys, 1986.
> R. W. Scheifler & J. Gettys, "The X Window System," *ACM Transactions on Graphics*, vol. 5, no. 2, pp. 79–109, April 1986.

PART 5

System Operation

CHAPTER 14

System Startup

When a computer is powered on, there is nothing running on the CPU. For a program to be set running, the binary image of the program must first be loaded into memory from a storage device. Many microprocessor systems automatically start programs that reside in nonvolatile storage devices such as programmable read-only memories (PROMs). Once the image of the program is loaded, the CPU must be directed to start execution at the first memory location of the loaded program. This process of *bootstrapping* a program into execution starts a program running on a CPU.

In this chapter, we examine how the 4.4BSD kernel, or any other similar program, is bootstrapped. We then study the operation of the system during the initialization phase, which takes the system from a *cold start* to the point at which user-mode programs can be run. A final section examines topics that are related to the startup procedure. These topics include configuring the kernel load image, shutting down a running system, and debugging system failures.

14.1 Overview

The 4.4BSD kernel is only a program, albeit a complex one. Like any 4.4BSD program, its binary image resides in a file on a filesystem until it is loaded and set running. 4.4BSD presumes that the executable image of the kernel resides in a file named **/vmunix** on a filesystem that is designated as the *root filesystem*. The initial bootstrap mechanism is machine dependent. In many cases, a small bootstrap program is placed in a reserved area near the start of the primary disk. Often, this program is limited to a small area—as little as one 512-byte disk sector—and simply loads a larger program from the following area of the disk. This program, or some other mechanism, is usually used to load and run a special program, named **boot**. The **boot** program's task is to load and initialize the executable image of a program and to start that program running. **Boot** may come from the same storage device as the file that it bootstraps, or it may be loaded from a storage device supported by the machine's console processor specifically for bootstrapping purposes.

The **boot** program reads the binary image of a program to be bootstrapped into main memory, and then initializes the CPU so that the loaded program can be started. Programs loaded by **boot** are set running with virtual-address translation and hardware interrupts disabled. The loaded program is responsible for enabling these facilities and any additional hardware, such as I/O devices, that it intends to use.

When the 4.4BSD kernel is loaded by the **boot** program, the kernel goes through several stages of hardware and software initialization in preparation for normal system operation. The first stage is responsible for initializing the state of the CPU, including the run-time stack and virtual-memory mapping. Memory mapping, including virtual-address translation, is enabled early in the startup procedure to minimize the amount of special-purpose assembly-language code that those porting the kernel must write. Once virtual-memory mapping is enabled, the system does machine-dependent initializations, and then machine-independent initializations. The machine-dependent operations include setting up virtual-memory page tables and configuring I/O devices; the machine-independent actions include mounting the root filesystem and initializing the myriad system data structures. This order is necessary because many of the machine-independent initializations depend on the I/O devices being initialized properly.

Following the setup of the machine-independent portions of the kernel, the system is in operational status. System processes are created and made runnable, and user-level programs are brought in from the filesystems to execute. At this point, the system is ready to run normal applications.

14.2 Bootstrapping

Bootstrapping a program is a machine-dependent operation. On most machines, this operation is supported either by a secondary processor termed the *console processor*, or by a *console monitor*. The console-monitor program is resident in nonvolatile storage and is invoked automatically when the CPU is reset. The console facilities are expected to support the bootstrap of standalone programs. Most console processors and monitors also execute diagnostic operations when a machine is reset to ensure that the hardware is functioning properly.

The boot Program

The console processor or console monitor usually does not understand the format of the 4.4BSD filesystem. Instead, the startup procedure interprets a vendor's proprietary filesystem format, or reads a program from a reserved area of the boot disk. This procedure ultimately results in the execution of the 4.4BSD **boot** program. This program is a general-purpose standalone program that the system can use to load and execute other standalone programs. A *standalone program* is a program that is capable of operating without the assistance of the 4.4BSD kernel.

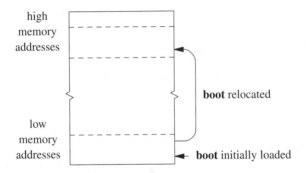

Figure 14.1 Placement of the **boot** program in memory.

Standalone programs usually are linked with the *standalone I/O library*, a library that supports a 4.4BSD-like I/O interface on a variety of hardware devices. The standalone I/O library provides these facilities through a collection of *standalone device drivers* and a library of routines that support reading of files from 4.4BSD filesystems that reside on the devices. The **boot** program is stored in a location accessible to the console monitor. This location may be the first few sectors of a system disk or a PROM managed by the console processor.

Once the **boot** program has been loaded and started, it must load the file containing the executable image of the program to be bootstrapped, and then must start the loaded program running. To load the appropriate file, **boot** must know the pathname of the file to be loaded and the hardware device on which the file resides. The boot program usually has a default device and program name from which it tries to load. Often, this default is stored in the console processor PROM. The console processor communicates the bootstrapping information to the **boot** program by initializing the run-time stack, and then placing the parameters on the stack in the same way that the 4.4BSD kernel passes arguments to programs. Alternatively, a user may type in the device and program name to be used.

Boot always loads programs at memory location 0. Since **boot** is initially loaded in memory at location 0, it must copy its own image to another place in memory to avoid loading on top of itself the image of the program that it bootstraps (see Fig. 14.1). This *relocation* implies that the **boot** program must be created with its starting address set to the memory location at which it will be copied; otherwise, references to data structures in the **boot** program will access the wrong memory locations after **boot** is copied (remember that **boot** operates with virtual-address translation disabled).

14.3 Kernel Initialization

When the 4.4BSD kernel is started by the **boot** program, it does an initialization in preparation for the execution of application programs. The initialization process is roughly divided into three stages. The first stage is written entirely in assembly language and does the work necessary for non–assembly-language code to operate. The second stage does machine-dependent operations, including the configuration and initialization of the I/O devices on the machine. The third stage does machine-independent operations, completing its work by starting up the system-resident processes that compose the foundation for the normal 4.4BSD runtime environment.

Assembly-Language Startup

The first steps taken by the system during initialization are carried out by assembly-language code. This work is highly machine dependent; it includes

- Setting up the run-time stack
- Identifying the type of CPU on which the system is executing
- Calculating the amount of physical memory on the machine
- Enabling the virtual-address–translation hardware
- Initializing the memory-management hardware
- Crafting the hardware context for process 0
- Invoking the initial C-based entry point of the system

Although the details of these steps vary from architecture to architecture, the broad outline described here is applicable to any machine on which 4.4BSD runs.

When the **boot** program starts the 4.4BSD kernel running, it sets up only two components of the machine state:

1. The interrupt priority is set at its highest level so that all hardware interrupts are blocked.

2. The hardware address-translation facility is disabled so that all memory references are to physical memory locations.

The **boot** program also passes to the kernel the identity of the boot device and a set of boot flags. The 4.4BSD kernel presumes nothing else about the state of the machine on which it is running.

The kernel is loaded into physical memory at a known location—often, at the lowest physical address. In normal operation, the address-translation hardware is enabled, and the kernel image is mapped into virtual memory starting at an address near the top of the address space. Before the address translation has been enabled, the assembly-language startup code must convert all absolute addresses from their virtual-memory location to their physical-memory location. The kernel is usually loaded into contiguous physical memory, so the translation is simply a constant offset that can be saved in an index register.

A second task of the startup code is to identify the type of CPU on which the system is executing. Often, older versions of the CPU support only a subset of the complete instruction set. For these machines, the kernel must *emulate* the missing hardware instructions in software. For most architectures, 4.4BSD can be configured such that a single kernel load image can support all the models in an architecture family. The startup code may also call machine-dependent code to initialize the CPU or virtual-memory subsystem. Most architectures have a *pmap_bootstrap()* function that is called at this time.

Machine-Dependent Initialization

After the assembly-language code has completed its work, it calls the first machine-independent kernel routine written in C, the *main()* routine. One parameter is passed to this routine: a typeless pointer intended for use in setting up an initial stack frame. The *main()* routine initializes several subsystems, beginning with the console and virtual-memory system. It then calls the *cpu_startup()* routine to do machine-dependent initializations. The tasks of the *cpu_startup()* routine include

• Initialization of the *error-message buffer*

• Allocation of memory for system data structures

• Initialization of the kernel's memory allocator

• Autoconfiguration and initialization of I/O devices

A few other hardware-specific parts of the machine are initialized after the call to *cpu_startup()* returns; these operations are described later, in our discussion of the machine-independent startup code.

Message Buffer

The *message buffer* is a 4-Kbyte circular buffer located at the top of physical memory. Diagnostic messages displayed on the console with the *printf()* routine (or with one of its variants) are kept in this buffer as an aid in tracking problems. Before 4.3BSD, the message buffer was accessible only through the **/dev/kmem** special device. Furthermore, utilities such as the **dmesg** program that read the message buffer and copy the buffer's contents to an administrative log file were unable to synchronize their activities properly with the generation of new diagnostic messages. For these reasons, 4.3BSD added a special device, **/dev/log**. This device provides a read-only interface to the message buffer that supports the *select* system call. In addition, most system diagnostics are now generated in a format that is interpreted by the **syslogd** program. These changes ensure that system diagnostics are saved reliably in log files.

    Initialization of the message buffer is straightforward. First, the system allocates memory for the buffer by deducting the size of the message buffer from the size of physical memory. Then, this page is mapped into the kernel address space, and *msgbufp* is initialized to reference the memory just allocated.

System Data Structures

Allocation of memory for the system data structures is easy at this point in the startup procedure. The identity of the first available page of physical memory that follows the resident kernel, *firstaddr*, is known. The starting virtual address for the kernel also is known. Thus, to allocate space for contiguous data structures, the system simply assigns the virtual address of the next available block of physical memory to each data structure:

```
base = VM_MIN_KERNEL_ADDRESS | (firstaddr * NBPG)
```

it then increments the value of *firstaddr* by the size of the data structure. Memory allocated to data structures in this way is not necessarily initialized to zero; initialization routines called from *main*() ensure that the contents of each data structure are set up properly.

The technique just described allocates memory for each contiguous system data structure. Most of these data structures are sized at the time that the system is configured, with the sizes based on the peak number of users expected. The buffer cache and *vm_page* structures, however, are sized according to the amount of physical memory available on the machine. The buffer-cache size is calculated as 10 percent of the first 2 Mbyte of physical memory plus 5 percent of the remaining memory. The system ensures that there is a minimum of 16 buffers, although this lower limit should never be a problem unless the system is configured with very large filesystem block sizes. In addition to the buffers dedicated to the buffer cache, the system must also allocate buffer headers for raw I/O and swapping operations: one-half of the number of file I/O buffer headers is allocated for use in raw I/O, swap, and paging operations. The system must calculate the number of *vm_page* structures after allocating the buffer cache and static data structures, because that value maps all the physical memory not otherwise allocated to the system. Once the *vm_page* structures and system-memory allocator have been initialized (described in Section 14.5), the normal system memory-allocation mechanisms must be used.

14.4 Autoconfiguration

Autoconfiguration is the procedure carried out by the system to recognize and enable the hardware devices present in a system. Autoconfiguration works by systematically probing the possible I/O buses on the machine. Depending on the architecture, these buses may include proprietary buses, such as the SPARC-based SBUS, or industry-standard buses, such as SCSI, EISA, and PCI. For each I/O bus that is found, the type of device attached to it is interpreted and, depending on this type, the necessary actions are taken to initialize and configure the device.

4.4BSD includes a new implementation of autoconfiguration. Only the SPARC version of the system uses the new scheme; other architectures continue to use the old version. The newer version includes machine-independent routines and data structures for use by machine-dependent layers, and provides a framework for dynamic allocation of data structures for each device. The older version is implemented entirely in machine-dependent functions, although there is substantial similarity in the functions for various architectures.

Some hardware devices, such as the interface to the console terminal, are required for system operation. Other devices, however, may not be needed, and their inclusion in the system may needlessly waste system resources. Devices that might be present in different numbers, at different addresses, or in different combinations are difficult to configure in advance, however, and the system must support them if they are present, and must fail gracefully if they are not present. To address these problems, 4.4BSD supports both a static *configuration procedure* that is done when a bootable system image is created and a dynamic *autoconfiguration phase* that is done when the system is bootstrapped.

The static configuration procedure is done by the **/usr/sbin/config** program. A configuration file is created by the system administrator that defines the set of hardware devices that might be present on a machine. This file identifies not only the types of devices, but also where each device might be located on the machine. For example, a system might be configured with two SCSI host adapters (controllers) and four disk drives that are connected in any of the configurations shown in Fig. 14.2. The configuration procedure generates several files that define the

Figure 14.2 Alternative drive configurations.

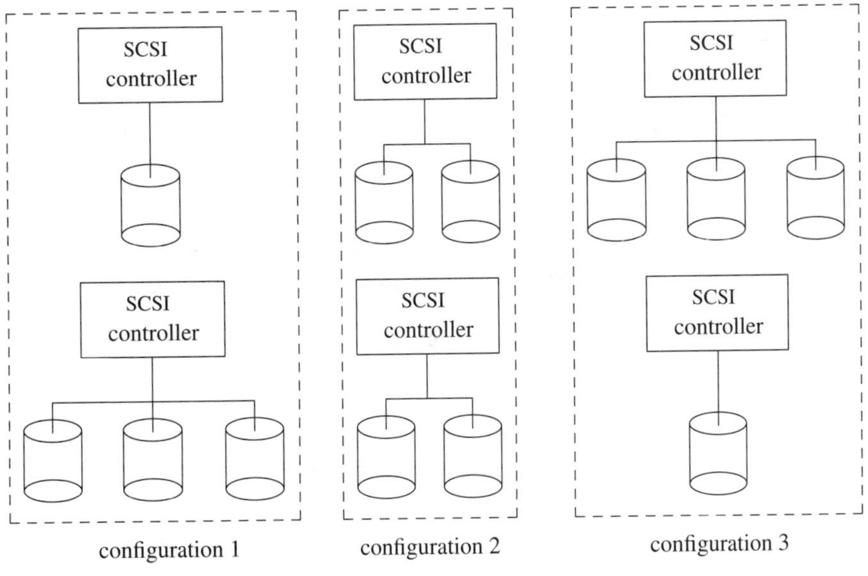

configuration 1   configuration 2   configuration 3

hardware topology. These files are compiled into the system for use in the autoconfiguration phase.

The autoconfiguration phase is done during system initialization to identify the set of configured devices that are present on a machine. In general, autoconfiguration recurses through a tree of device interconnections, such as buses and controllers to which other devices attach. Autoconfiguration works in one of two ways at each level in the tree: by *probing* for configured devices at each of the possible locations where the device might be attached or by checking each possible location to see what type of device (if any) is present. The second mechanism can be used only when a fixed number of locations are possible and when devices at those locations are self-identifying. Devices that are recognized during the autoconfiguration phase are *attached* and are made available for use. Devices that are present but not recognized remain unavailable until the system is rebooted. The *attach* function for a bus or controller must initiate a probe for devices that might be attached at that location.

Although this scheme requires that all the device drivers for hardware devices that might potentially be present on a machine be configured into a system, it permits device drivers to allocate system resources for only those devices that are present in a running system. It allows the physical device topology to be changed without requiring the system load image to be regenerated. It also prevents crashes resulting from attempts to access a nonexistent device. In the remainder of this section, we consider the autoconfiguration facilities from the perspective of the device-driver writer. We examine the device-driver support required to identify hardware devices that are present on a machine, and the steps needed to *attach* a device once its presence has been noted. The available facilities depend on the version of autoconfiguration in use, on the hardware architecture, and on the layer in the device hierarchy.

Device Probing

During the autoconfiguration phase, a device-driver *probe routine* is called for each configured hardware device controller. The description of a controller location depends on the I/O bus; it might include details such as I/O register location, memory location, and interrupt vectors. The system passes to the probe routine a description of the controller's location, and expects the routine both to verify that the device is present and, if possible, to force the device to interrupt the host to identify the controller's interrupt vector. If the probe routine is successful in forcing an interrupt, then the system will trap the interrupt, and will use the value of the vector to initialize the appropriate entries in the interrupt-vector table, so that the interrupt service routines for the device driver will be invoked on later interrupts. For some hardware devices, it is impossible to force an interrupt reliably. In these instances, the system allows the probe routine to force a device to be configured by returning a known interrupt vector. If no interrupt is received and none is returned, the system assumes that the controller is not present at the supplied location.

In addition to probing for device controllers, a device driver may also be asked to probe for devices that may be attached to a controller. For example, the system will first probe to see whether a SCSI host adapter is present. For each adapter found, the system will then probe for each possible target that might be attached, such as disk drives. The mechanism for this probe depends on whether the new or old autoconfiguration mechanism is in use, as well as on what type of controller is used. In the old mechanism, devices attached to a controller are termed *slave devices*. Disk drives and tape transports are two possible types of slave devices. Bus controllers that may have slave devices attached to them must provide a *slave routine* to probe for slave devices. The slave routine does not have to force an interrupt for each slave device; it needs only to indicate whether the slave device is present. The new autoconfiguration mechanism provides greater flexibility, allowing a controller to determine the appropriate manner in which to probe for additional devices attached to the controller.

Device Attachment

Once a device is found by a probe, the autoconfiguration code must *attach* it. Attaching a device is separated from probing so that the system can initialize data structures used by the bus-controller routines. Most device drivers use the attach routine to initialize the hardware device and any software state. For disk devices, for example, the attach routine identifies the geometry of the disk drive and may initialize the partition table that defines the placement of filesystems on the drive.

New Autoconfiguration Data Structures

The new version of autoconfiguration in 4.4BSD includes machine-independent data structures and support routines. The previous autoconfiguration data structures were machine dependent, and often were bus dependent as well. This machine dependency presented a design challenge. The new data structures allow machine- and bus-dependent information to be stored in a general way, and allow the autoconfiguration process to be driven by the configuration data, rather than by compiled-in rules. The new version of the **/usr/sbin/config** program constructs many of the tables from information in the kernel-configuration file and from a machine-description file. The new **config** program is thus data driven as well, and contains no machine-dependent code. Figure 14.3 shows the data structures introduced with this version of autoconfiguration, which we describe in this subsection. The data structures fall into three categories, shown in the figure separated by dashed lines: those generated by the **config** program are shown in the left-hand section, those statically initialized in each driver are shown in the center, and those allocated dynamically by the autoconfiguration routines are shown on the right.

The major data structure used during autoconfiguration is the *cfdata* structure. The **config** program constructs a *cfdata* structure for each possible device attachment in the kernel-configuration file. Because the addressing information depends on the type of bus and system, location information is stored in a variable-length array of integers called a *locator*. The machine-description file controls the

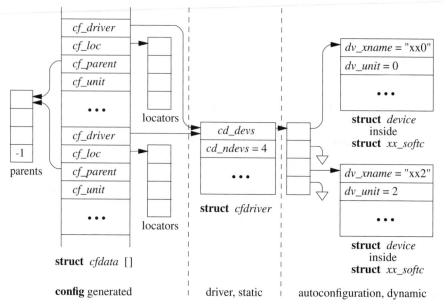

Figure 14.3 New autoconfiguration data structures.

mapping from location keywords, such as *slot* or *port*, to indices in the locator used by each type of bus. The *cfdata* structure contains a reference to a *cfdriver* structure, which the driver initializes and exports, and which has references to the driver entry points for autoconfiguration. The *cfdata* structure also contains a pointer to a list of possible parent devices and a unit number, which can be a wild-card value to allow *cloning* of the entry to match multiple units.

The new autoconfiguration scheme introduces another new data structure, which is now the central data structure for most device drivers. The *device* structure contains the basic description of a specific device. This structure includes the name, unit number, and class of a device, as well as a pointer to the configuration data (*cfdata*) for the device and a pointer to the parent device. The device structure is allocated dynamically, when the device is found during autoconfiguration. When the structure for each unit is created, its location is recorded in a dynamically allocated array referenced by the *cfdriver* structure. The *cfdriver* structure also contains the size of this array. This arrangement allows the kernel to find the device structure for a unit by checking the array size, then indexing into the array if the unit number is within range.

Most drivers require additional information for each unit: thus, the *cfdriver* structure specifies the amount of storage to be allocated. For example, Figure 14.3 shows an *xx_softc* structure containing the information about each *xx* unit. The *device* structure is placed first in this area. In fact, the *device* structure is the description of a *base class*, and the larger driver data structure describes a *derived class* that inherits from the base class. Some drivers use multiple levels of inheritance—for example, a SCSI disk device that is based on a disk device, which in turn is based on a generic device.

New Autoconfiguration Functions

The new autoconfiguration data structures make it possible to implement machine-independent support routines for much of the autoconfiguration process. Location of the primary bus (the device or devices at the root of the device tree) is machine dependent. Once this device is identified, it is attached, and its *attach* function is called. Like *attach* functions for other buses or controllers, this function must initiate a probe for devices on that bus. Generic functions are provided for the two primary methods of autoconfiguration described in the previous subsection. If it is possible to scan the bus, searching for devices and identifying them, the bus *attach* function will call the *config_found()* routine with a description of each device that it finds. The *config_found()* routine looks for a matching device-configuration entry (*cfdata* structure), and attaches the device if an entry is found. On a bus or controller for which it is not reasonable to search for all possible devices, another mechanism is available. The *config_search()* function will search for all devices that might be attached to this parent device, and will call the *probe* function for each of them. If the probe is successful, the device is then attached. The *config_attach()* routine is responsible for allocation and initialization of the device structure, recording the pointer to the device structure for this unit via the *cfdriver* structure, and then calling the driver's attach function to allow the driver to initialize its portion of the device structure.

Device Naming

The autoconfiguration facilities support flexible placement of hardware on a machine by imposing a level of indirection in the naming of devices. Applications reference devices through block and character special files placed in the filesystem. The inode associated with a special file contains the major and minor device numbers of the associated hardware device. The major device number identifies the type of the device, whereas the minor device number identifies a *logical device unit*. For example, suppose that the file **/dev/sd1a** was created with the command

> **/sbin/mknod /dev/sd1a** b 2 8

This file would refer to a block device with major device number 2 and minor device number of 8. Internally, the major device number would indicate a disk drive supported by the *sd* device driver. The minor device number would be passed to the device driver, where it would be interpreted according to the formula

$$minor = (8 \times logical\ unit) + logical\ partition$$

or, in this instance, partition 0 on logical unit (drive) 1. The *logical unit* for each device is assigned during the autoconfiguration phase and is distinct from hardware unit numbers used to identify devices. That is, whereas a tape unit or disk drive might have a hardware unit plug that identifies the device as physical unit x on a controller, to the system that device would be identified by a possibly different logical unit *y*. A logical unit may refer to different hardware devices each time that a system is initialized, or, more interesting, a specific hardware device may map to the same logical unit no matter where it is placed on the machine. This logical-to-physical mapping of device names within the system permits, for example, a disk drive to be shifted from one disk controller to another without rebuilding of the operating system. Flexibility in device naming is important in simplifying system maintenance in environments where redundant hardware is maintained for reliability. It also allows logical numbering to span controllers: There may be more than one hardware unit 0, whereas there can be only one logical unit 0.

Although some versions of UNIX can load device drivers after the system is completely booted, 4.4BSD cannot load device drivers because

- The 4.4BSD kernel does not have the ability to load modules dynamically.

- The 4.4BSD device-driver data structures are not all dynamically extensible

- A new device might interrupt at the same location as an existing device, leading to confusion

These problems are all well understood and are easy to fix. However, allowing code to be loaded dynamically into the kernel raises many security problems. Code running outside the kernel is limited in the damage that it can do because it does not run in privileged mode, so cannot directly access the hardware. The kernel runs with full privilege and access to the hardware. Thus, if it loads a module that contains a virus, it can inflict wide-ranging damage within the system. Kernels can be loaded across the network from a central server; if the kernel allowed dynamic loading of modules, they too could come across the network, so there are numerous added points for malfeasance. An important goal of adding dynamic-loading functionality to 4.4BSD is to develop a scheme to verify the source of and lack of corruption in any code before that code is permitted to be loaded and used.

14.5 Machine-Independent Initialization

With the static system data structures allocated and the I/O devices configured and initialized, the system is ready to complete the initialization procedure and to start up the first few processes. The first action of the *main*( ) routine on return from *cpu_startup*( ) is to set up the context for process 0; the process that will eventually implement the swapping policy of the virtual-memory system. A process entry is declared statically for process 0, and the process is marked runnable and is installed as the currently running process (see Chapter 4). The user structure, run-time stack, and process control block for this process were initialized in the assembly-language startup code, so only minor work is required to complete the initialization. On architectures that support read-only kernel memory, the final page of the run-time stack is marked read-only to act as a *red zone*; this unwritable page ensures that the process will not expand its stack beyond the fixed space allocated to it without causing a system trap. The substructures associated with the process entry are also declared statically and are linked into the process 0 entry. The system default parameters in the process entry that are inherited across a *fork* system call are established. The latter include the resource limits, the file-creation mask, and the group-identifier array.

When process 0 has been crafted, various routines are called to initialize each system data structure:

- The *vm_mem_init*( ) routine sets up the parameters used by the paging system. These parameters are dependent on the amount of available physical memory. The resource limits on a process's stack and data segments, as well as on the resident-set size, are installed in the limits substructure of process 0. These limits will then be inherited automatically by all other processes because the latter are descendents of process 0.

- The *vfsinit*( ) routine allocates the global filesystem structures, such as the vnode- and name-cache–management structures. Next, it builds the operation vectors for each of the filesystem types that is configured in the kernel. Finally, it calls the filesystem-specific initialization routine for each of configured filesystems. Typically, these initialization routines allocate hash tables and other data structures that the filesystem will need to operate.

- The real-time clock is started through a call to *initclocks*( ). This routine primes the necessary hardware that supplies regular interrupts to the system. It also starts any other clocks that the system uses, such as a profiling or statistics-gathering clock. The clock rate, if programmable, is set according to the *hz* variable that is defined at the time the system is configured. By default, 4.4BSD runs with a 100-hertz real-time clock. This value can be altered, but selecting a frequency of less than 50 hertz degrades the system's response time to I/O devices that are polled. For some hardware terminal multiplexers, lowering the clock frequency can permit high data-flow rates to swamp input buffers. A poorly chosen clock frequency can also cause roundoff errors in certain calculations. For example, with a 60-hertz clock rate, integer calculations involving the clock frequency will skew. A final consideration in choosing a clock frequency is that the frequency defines the minimal observable time interval in the system. This interval is important for statistical calculations, such as for program profiling and accounting, where *entire* clock ticks are charged to a process- or program-counter value at the time that a real-time clock interrupt is serviced. In general, the clock frequency should be selected to be as high as possible without too much system overhead being incurred.

Following the initialization of the clock, the network memory-management system is initialized with a call to *mbinit*( ) (see Section 11.3). The character-list data structures used by the terminal I/O facilities are set up through a call to *clist_init*( ), and later calls are then made to initialize

- The communication domains and network-communication protocols

- The process-management–data structures

- The swap-space management data structures

Before the system can reach single-user operation, it must still mount the root filesystem, and create process 1 (the process that executes **/sbin/init**) and process 2 (the process that selects pages of memory to be replaced, copying to secondary storage if needed, in support of the virtual-memory system). The root filesystem may be supplied by any filesystem type that provides a *mountroot* function. The default is to use the 4.4BSD filesystem, but the kernel can be configured to give the user a list of choices. For example, a diskless machine can choose to use an NFS filesystem as its root. If a local filesystem is selected, its identity is defined by the value of the *rootdev* variable. This value is initially defined at configuration time, although users may change it at boot time by bootstrapping the system from a device other than the configured one (see the discussion of autoconfiguration in Section 14.4).

The root inode of the mounted root filesystem is needed to initialize the current working directory and root directory for process 0. In addition, the kernel may use the most recent modification date in the superblock of the root filesystem to initialize the system's time of day. The timestamp from the superblock is compared to any current value for the time of day available in hardware, and the current time of day is constrained to be within 6 months of the time in the filesystem (unless the filesystem time is completely unbelievable). This consistency check ensures that the system will be bootstrapped with a reasonably accurate time of day. User-level facilities—such as *timed* or *ntpd*—support time synchronization and recalibration in a network environment.

Finally, the system is ready to execute user-mode programs. Process 1 is created with a call to *fork*(), then the kernel calls the *start_init*() function to start the **init** process. *Start_init*() creates the argument vector for **init**, then internally calls the standard system *exec*() function. If the *exec*() fails, it tries several backup locations for **init** until it finds one that works, or until the list is exhausted. Finding an operational **init** program is critical to operation: If **init** does not run correctly, if it is not there, or if the parts of the filesystem necessary to reach it are damaged, the system cannot be booted from that filesystem. This error is more serious than is an incorrect **/vmunix**, because the bootstrap allows naming of a different object file for the kernel, but there is no direct way to specify a different **init** program without recompiling the kernel with additions to the list of possible names and locations. The best protection against losing a critical binary such as **init** is to keep a copy of the root filesystem in a spare disk partition.

The second process to be started is the *pagedaemon*, with process identifier 2. This process executes entirely in kernel mode by invoking the *vm_pageout*() routine—a procedure that never returns. Like process 0, the *pagedaemon* marks its process structure to ensure that that structure will not be removed from memory. The *pagedaemon* also expands its data segment to provide itself room to map the pages of memory that it will be writing to secondary storage (see Section 5.12).

The final action of *main*() is to call the *scheduler*() routine within process 0. Like the *pagedaemon*, this process executes entirely in kernel mode, and the call to *scheduler*() never returns. The *scheduler*() routine implements the scheduling policy of the system; it is described in Section 4.4.

14.6   User-Level Initialization

With the start of process 1, most of the system is operating and functional. There are several additional steps taken between this point and the time a user sees a prompt to sign on to the system. All these actions are done by user-level programs that use the standard 4.4BSD system-call interface that has been described in previous chapters. We shall briefly examine the steps that take place in a typical system.

/sbin/init

The **/sbin/init** program is invoked as the final step in the bootstrapping procedure. The parameters specified at the time 4.4BSD was boostrapped are passed to **init** in a machine-dependent fashion. **Init** uses the values of these flags to determine whether it should bring up the system to single-user or to multiuser operation. In single-user operation, **init** forks a process that invokes the standard shell, **/bin/sh**. The standard input, output, and error descriptors of the process are directed to the system's console terminal, **/dev/console**. This shell then operates normally, but with superuser privileges, until it terminates.

In multiuser operation, **init** first spawns a shell to interpret the commands in the file **/etc/rc**. These commands do filesystem-consistency checks, start up system processes, and initialize database files, such as the name-list cache used by **ps**. If the **/etc/rc** script completes successfully, **init** then forks a copy of itself for each terminal device that is marked for use in the file **/etc/ttys**. These copies of **init** invoke other system programs, such as **/usr/libexec/getty**, to manage the standard sign on procedure. Process 1 always acts as the master coordinating process for system operation. It is responsible for spawning new processes as terminal sessions are terminated, and for managing the shutdown of a running system.

/etc/rc

The **/etc/rc** command script first checks the integrity of the filesystems. This check is necessary to ensure that any damage that might have occurred from a previous system failure is repaired. The filesystem support within the kernel is concerned solely with reading and writing existing filesystems. Any inconsistencies in a filesystem are repaired by user-level programs.

The program **/sbin/fsck** is the major tool used in checking filesystem consistency and in repairing damaged filesystems. Normally, **fsck** is invoked from the **/etc/rc** script to examine and repair each filesystem before the latter is mounted. When the system is initially booted, the root filesystem is mounted read-only. If the root filesystem requires repairs, 4.4BSD does a variant of the *mount* system call that requests the kernel to reload all its root-filesystem data structures. Reloading ensures consistency between the data in the kernel memory and any data in the filesystem that were modified by **fsck**. Having the root filesystem mounted read-only ensures that the kernel will not have any modified data in memory that cannot be reloaded.

Following the filesystem checks, the filesystems are mounted, the root filesystem is updated to be writable, and any devices that are to be used for swapping and paging are enabled. Disk quotas are then checked and enabled, and the system starts the background processes that implement various system services. These processes include **/usr/sbin/update**, the program that flushes the disk writes from the buffer cache every 30 seconds; **/usr/sbin/cron**, the program that executes commands at periodic intervals; **/usr/sbin/accton**, the program that enables system accounting; and **/usr/sbin/syslogd**, the system error-logging process. Some of these processes are started from the command script **/etc/rc.local**. The commands in **/etc/rc.local** are tailored according to the needs of each host, whereas the commands in **/etc/rc** are common to all hosts. For example, processes that provide nonstandard services are typically started up from the **/etc/rc.local** command file [Nemeth et al, 1995].

/usr/libexec/getty

The **/usr/libexec/getty** program is spawned by **init** for each hardware terminal line on a system. This program is responsible for opening and initializing the terminal line. As a precaution against another process opening the line and snooping on the user's input, **getty** uses the *revoke* system call to revoke access to any open descriptors on the line (see Section 6.6). It then creates a new session for the line and requests that the terminal be made the controlling terminal for the session. The **getty** program sets the initial parameters for a terminal line and establishes the type of terminal attached to the line. For lines attached to a modem, **getty** can be directed to accept connections at a variety of baud rates. **Getty** selects this baud rate by changing the speed of the terminal line in response to a break character or a framing error, typically generated as a result of the user hitting a break key. A user can hit successive break keys to cycle through several line speeds until the proper one is found. **Getty**'s actions are driven by a terminal-configuration database that is located in the file **/etc/gettytab**.

Getty finally reads a login name and invokes the **/usr/bin/login** program to complete a login sequence.

/usr/bin/login

The **login** program is responsible for signing a user onto the system; it is usually invoked by **/usr/libexec/getty** with the name of the user who wishes to log into the system. **Login** prompts the user for a password (after turning off terminal echoing if possible). If the password supplied by the user encrypts to the same value as that stored in the master password file **/etc/master.passwd**, **login** writes a record of the sign on in various accounting files, initializes the user and group identifiers to those specified in the password and **/etc/group** files, and changes to the user's login directory. The user's login name is stored in the session structure using the *setlogin* system call, so that it can be obtained reliably via the *getlogin* system call by programs that want to know the login name associated with a given process. Finally, **login** uses *exec* to overlay itself with the user's shell.

The **login** program is also invoked when a user enters the system through a network connection. **Getty** and **init** are bypassed for such connections; their functionality is subsumed by the daemon spawned when the network connection is established.

14.7 System-Startup Topics

In this section, we consider topics that are related to the system-startup procedure.

Kernel Configuration

The software that makes up a 4.4BSD kernel is defined by a *configuration file* that is interpreted by the **/usr/sbin/config** program. Configuration files specify the hardware and software components that should be supported by a kernel. The configuration file is used by **config** to generate several output files, some of which are compiled, and are linked into the kernel's load image:

- A file that describes the hardware-device topology and the devices that might be present on the machine

- A file that includes assembly-language routines that connect the hardware interrupt-vector entry points to the device-driver interrupt handlers specified in the configuration file

- A file that defines the devices to use for the root filesystem and for swapping and paging

- Several small header files that control conditional compilations of source code

- A file for the *make* program that compiles and links the kernel load image

A complete description of the configuration process and of **config** is given in [Leffler & Karels, 1994].

System Shutdown and Autoreboot

4.4BSD provides several utility programs to halt or reboot a system, or to bring a system from multiuser to single-user operation. Safe halting and rebooting of a system require support from the kernel. This support is provided by a *reboot* system call.

The *reboot* system call is a privileged call. A single parameter specifies how the system should be shut down and rebooted. This parameter is a superset of the flags passed by the **boot** program to the system when the latter is initially bootstrapped. A system can be brought to a halt (typically by its being forced to execute an infinite loop), or it can be rebooted to single-user or multiuser operation. There are additional controls that can be used to force a crash dump before rebooting (see the next subsection for information about crash dumps) and to disable the writing of data that are in the buffer cache to disk (in case the information in the buffer cache is wrong).

On most hardware, rebooting requires support from the console processor or monitor. Typically, a reboot operation is started by a command being passed to the console processor. This command causes the system to be rebooted as though someone had typed the appropriate commands on the console terminal. Automatic rebooting is also commonly done by the console processor when a catastrophic failure is recognized. The system will reboot itself automatically if it recognizes an unrecoverable failure during normal operation. Failures of this sort, termed *panics*, are all handled by the *panic()* subroutine. 4.1BSD was among the first UNIX systems to be able to recover *automatically* from catastrophic failures by rebooting, repairing any filesystem damage, and then restarting normal operation. Facilities to *checkpoint* the state of active processes and automatically to resume the processes' execution after a system reboot have been added by certain vendors, such as by Cray Research.

System Debugging

4.4BSD provides several facilities for debugging system failures. The most commonly used facility is the *crash dump*; a copy of memory that is saved on secondary storage by the kernel when a catastrophic failure occurs. Crash dumps are created by the *doadump()* routine. They occur if a reboot system call is made in which the RB_DUMP flag is specified, or if the system encounters an unrecoverable—and unexpected—error.

The *doadump()* routine disables virtual-address translation, raises the processor priority level to the highest value to block out all device interrupts, and then invokes the *dumpsys()* routine to write the contents of physical memory to secondary storage. The precise location of a crash dump is configurable; most systems place the information at the end of the primary swap partition. The device driver's dump entry point does this operation.

A crash dump is retrieved from its location on disk after the system is rebooted and the filesystems have been checked. The **/sbin/savecore** program exists solely for this purpose. It creates a file into which the crash-dump image is copied. **Savecore** also makes a copy of the initial kernel load image, **/vmunix**, for use in debugging. The system administrator can examine crash dumps with the standard 4.4BSD debugging program, **gdb**. The kernel is also set up so that a **gdb** debugger running on one machine can attach itself across a serial line to a kernel running on another machine. Once attached, it can set breakpoints, examine and modify kernel data structures, and invoke kernel routines on the machine being debugged.

Passage of Information To and From the Kernel

In 4.3BSD and earlier systems, utilities that needed to get information from the kernel would open the special device **/dev/kmem**, which gave access to the kernel's memory. Using the name list from the kernel binary, the utility would seek to the address of the symbol being sought and would read the value at that location. Utilities with superuser privilege could also use this technique to modify kernel variables. Although this approach worked, it had four problems:

1. Applications did not have a way to find the binary for the currently running kernel reliably. Using an incorrect binary would result in looking at the wrong location in **/dev/kmem**, resulting in turn in wildly incorrect output. For programs that modified the kernel, using the wrong binary would usually result in crashing the system by trashing some unrelated data structure.

2. Reading and interpreting the kernel name list is time consuming. Thus, applications that had to read kernel data structures ran slowly.

3. Applications given access to the kernel memory could read the entire kernel memory. Malicious programs could snoop the terminal or network input queues looking for users who were typing sensitive information such as passwords.

4. As more of the kernel data structures became dynamically allocated, it became difficult to extract the desired information reliably. For example, in 4.3BSD, the process structures were all contained in a single statically allocated table that could be read in a single operation. In 4.4BSD, process structures are allocated dynamically and are referenced through a linked list. Thus, they can be read out only one process entry at a time. Because a process entry is subdivided into many separate pieces, each of which resides in a different part of the kernel memory, every process entry takes several seeks and reads to extract through **/dev/kmem**.

To resolve these problems, 4.4BSD introduced the *sysctl* system call. This extensible kernel interface allows controlled access to kernel data structures. The problems enumerated previously are resolved as follows:

1. Applications do not need to know which kernel binary they are running. The running kernel responds to their request and knows where its data structures are stored. Thus, the correct data structure is always returned or modified.

2. No time is spent reading or interpreting name lists. Accessing kernel data structures takes only a few system calls.

3. Sensitive data structures cannot be accessed. The kernel controls the set of data structures that it will return. Nothing else in the kernel is accessible. The kernel can impose its own set of access restrictions on a data-structure–by–data-structure basis.

4. The kernel can use its standard mechanisms for ensuring consistent access to distributed data structures. When requesting process entries, the kernel can collect the relevant information without blocking, to ensure that no intervening operations can be done that would modify the process state.

Additional benefits of the interface include these:

• Values to be changed can be validated before the data structure is updated. If modification of the data structure requires exclusive access, an appropriate lock can be obtained before the update is done. Thus, an element can be added to a linked list without danger of another process traversing the list while the update is in progress.

• Information can be computed only on demand. Infrequently requested information can be computed only when it is requested, rather than being computed continually. For example, many of the virtual-memory statistics are computed only when a system-monitoring program requests them.

• The interface allows the superuser to change kernel parameters even when the system is running in secure mode (secure mode is described in Section 7.6). To prevent malfeasance, the kernel does not allow **/dev/kmem** to be opened for writing while the system is running in secure mode. Even when the system running in secure mode, the *sysctl* interface will still allow a superuser to modify kernel data structures that do not affect security.

The *sysctl* system call describes the kernel name space using a management information base (MIB). An MIB is a hierarchical name space much like the filesystem name space, except that each component is described with an integer value, rather than with a string name. A hierarchical name space has several benefits:

• New subtrees can be added without existing applications being affected.

• If the kernel omits support for a subsystem, the *sysctl* information for that part of the system can be omitted.

• Each kernel subsystem can define its own naming conventions. Thus, the network can be divided into protocol families. Each protocol family can be divided into protocol specific information, and so on.

• The name space can be divided into those parts that are machine independent and are available on every architecture, and those parts that are machine dependent and are defined on an architecture-by-architecture basis.

The use of the MIB interface should allow *sysctl* to be integrated easily into the emerging network-management protocols.

Exercises

14.1   What is the purpose of the **boot** program?

14.2   What is the job of the machine-language startup? Why is this program written in machine language?

14.3   What is the purpose of the kernel's message buffer?

14.4   What are the first three processes started when the system is booted?

14.5   Assume that **/boot** is read in from the console media. Name the three other files that must be present for the system to boot to single-user mode.

14.6   The *reboot* system call causes the system to halt or reboot. Give two reasons why this system call is useful.

*14.7 Suppose that a machine does not have a battery-backup time-of-day clock. Propose a method for determining that the time-of-day clock is incorrect. Describe a way to initialize the clock's time of day. What are the limitations of your method?

References

Leffler & Karels, 1994.
    S. J. Leffler & M. J. Karels, "Building 4.4BSD Kernels with Config," in *4.4BSD System Manager's Manual*, pp. 2:1–24, O'Reilly & Associates, Inc., Sebastopol, CA, 1994.

Nemeth et al, 1995.
    E. Nemeth, G. Snyder, S. Seebass, & T. Hein, *UNIX System Administration Handbook*, Prentice-Hall, Englewood Cliffs, NJ, 1995.

Glossary

absolute pathname See *pathname*.

access rights In an operating system, the rights of processes to access system-maintained objects. For example, the ability to write data into a file. Rights are recognized and enforced by the system, and typically are associated with capabilities. The passing of access rights in messages is supported by the 4.4BSD interprocess-communication facilities. For example, the local communication domain supports the transmission of file descriptors and their associated access rights.

address family A collection of related address formats, as found in a communication domain.

address format A set of rules used in creating network addresses of a particular format. For example, in the Internet communication domain, a version 4 IP host address is a 32-bit value that is encoded with one of four rules, according to the type of network on which the host resides.

Address Resolution Protocol (ARP) A communication protocol used to map one network address to another dynamically. For example, ARP is used in 4.4BSD to map Internet addresses into Ethernet addresses dynamically.

address translation A mechanism, typically implemented in hardware, that translates memory addresses supplied by a program into physical memory addresses. This facility is important in supporting multiprogramming because it allows an operating system to load programs into different areas of memory, and yet to have each program execute as though it were loaded at a single, fixed memory location.

advisory lock A lock that is enforced only when a process explicitly requests its enforcement. An advisory lock is contrasted with a mandatory lock, which is always enforced. See also *mandatory lock*.

AGE buffer list A list in the filesystem buffer cache. This list holds buffers whose contents have not yet proved useful—for example, read-ahead blocks. See also *buffer cache; least recently used.*

ancillary data Specially interpreted data sent on a network connection. Ancillary data may include protocol-specific data, such as addressing or options, and also specially interpreted data, called access rights.

anonymous object An anonymous object represents a region of transient backing storage. Pages of an anonymous object are zero-filled on first reference, and modified pages will be stored in the swap area if memory becomes tight. The object is destroyed when no references remain.

ARP See *Address Resolution Protocol.*

association In the interprocess-communication facilities, a logical binding between two communication endpoints that must be established before communication can take place. Associations may be long lived, such as in virtual-circuit–based communication, or short lived, such as in a datagram-based communication paradigm.

AST See *asynchronous system trap.*

asynchronous system trap (AST) A software-initiated interrupt to a service routine. ASTs enable a process to be notified of the occurrence of a specific event asynchronously with respect to its execution. In 4.4BSD, ASTs are used to initiate process rescheduling.

autoconfiguration phase A phase of operation that the system goes through when bootstrapping itself into operation. In the autoconfiguration phase, the system probes for hardware devices that might be present in the machine and attaches each device that it locates. See also *attach routine; probe routine; slave routine.*

background process In job-control–oriented process-management systems, a process whose process group is different from that of its controlling terminal; thus, this process is currently blocked from most terminal access. Otherwise, a background process is one for which the command interpreter is not waiting; that is, the process was set running with the "&" operator. The opposite of a background process is a *foreground process.*

backing storage Storage that is used to hold objects that are removed from main memory during paging and swapping operations. See also *secondary storage.*

block In the filesystem, a unit of allocation. The filesystem allocates space in block-size units, or in fragments of block-size units.

block accounting The process of maintaining a count of the number of disk blocks available for writing in the Log-Structured Filesystem or for the storage of new data in either the Fast Filesystem or the Log-Structured Filesystem.

block device A random-access mass-storage device that supports a block-oriented interface—for example, a disk drive. See also *character device.*

block-device interface The conventions established for accessing block devices within the kernel. These conventions include the set of procedures that can be called to do I/O operations, as well as the parameters that must be passed in each call. See also *character device interface*.

block-device table A table within the kernel in which the device-driver routines that support the block-device interface for each device are recorded. The ordering of entries in the block-device table is important, because it defines the major-device number for block devices. See also *character-device table*.

block I/O I/O to a block device.

block size The natural unit of space allocated to a file (*filesystem block size*), or the smallest unit of I/O that a block device can do (for disk devices, usually the sector size). In 4.4BSD, the filesystem block size is a parameter of the filesystem that is fixed at the time that the filesystem is created.

bootstrapping The task of bringing a system up into an operational state. When a machine is first powered on, it is typically not running any program. Bootstrapping initializes the machine, loads a program from secondary storage into main memory, and sets that program running.

bottom half With regard to system operation, the collection of routines in the kernel that is invoked as a result of interrupts. These routines cannot depend on any per-process state, and, as a result, cannot block by calling the *sleep()* routine. See also *top half*.

breakpoint fault A hardware trap that is generated when a process executes a breakpoint instruction.

broadcast A transmission to all parties. In a network, a *broadcast message* is transmitted to all stations attached to a common communication medium.

bss segment The portion of a program that is to be initialized to zero at the time the program is loaded into memory. The name *bss* is an abbreviation for "block started by symbol." See also *data segment; stack segment; text segment*.

buffer cache A cache of recently used disk blocks. In 4.4BSD, approximately 10 percent of the main memory on the machine is used for the buffer cache. Most cache entries are maintained on a least-recently used list; some are kept on a separate AGE buffer list. See also *AGE buffer list; least recently used*.

buffered As in "buffered I/O"; a technique whereby data are held, or buffered, to minimize the number of I/O operations that are done. For example, the standard I/O library buffers output to files by accumulating data to be written until there is a full filesystem block to write, or until the application requests that the data be flushed to disk.

bus A standardized electrical and mechanical interconnection for components of a computer.

byte A unit of measure applied to data. A byte is almost always 8 bits. See also *octet*.

callback A scheme where a server keeps track of all the objects that each of its clients has cached. When a cached object is held by two or more clients and one of them modifies it, the server sends an eviction notice to all the other clients holding that object so that they can purge it from their cache. See also *eviction notice; lease.*

canonical mode A terminal mode. Characters input from a terminal or a pseudo-terminal that is running in canonical mode are processed to provide standard line-oriented editing functions, and input is presented to a process on a line-by-line basis. When the terminal is processing in noncanonical mode, input is passed through to the reading process immediately and without interpretation. Canonical mode is also known as *cooked mode*, and noncanonical mode is also known as *raw mode. Cbreak mode* is similar to raw mode, although some input processing is done.

capability Data presented by a process to gain access to an object. See also *access rights.*

catenet A network in which hosts are connected to networks with varying characteristics, and the networks are interconnected by gateways. The Internet is an example of a catenet.

cathode ray tube (CRT) A screen-display device commonly used in computer terminals. A terminal that includes a CRT is often called a CRT.

caught signal A signal the delivery of which to a process results in a signal-handler procedure being invoked. A signal handler is installed by a process with the *sigaction* system call.

C-block The buffer that holds the actual data in a C-list data structure.

cbreak mode A mode of operation for a terminal device whereby processes reading from the terminal receive input immediately as it is typed. This mode differs from raw mode in that certain input processing, such as interpreting the interrupt character, is still performed by the system. See also *canonical mode.*

central processing unit (CPU) The primary computational unit in a computer. The CPU is the processing unit that executes applications. Additional processing units may be present in a computer—for example, for handling I/O.

character A datum that represents a single printable or control symbol. Characters are usually 8 or 16 bits long. See also *byte; octet.*

character device A device that provides either a character-stream oriented I/O interface or, alternatively, an unstructured (raw) interface. For example, a terminal multiplexer is a character device that exhibits a character-oriented I/O interface, whereas all magnetic-tape devices support a character-device interface that provides a raw interface to the hardware. Devices that are not character devices are usually block devices. See also *block device.*

character-device interface The conventions established for accessing character-oriented devices within the kernel. These conventions include the set of procedures that can be called to do I/O operations, as well as the parameters that must be passed in each call. See also *block-device interface.*

character-device table A table within the kernel in which the device-driver routines that support the character-device interface for each device are recorded. The ordering of entries in the character-device table is important because it defines the major-device number for character devices. See also *block-device table*.

checkpoint The task of writing all modified information stored in volatile memory to stable storage. A filesystem does a checkpoint by writing all modified information in main memory to disk so that the filesystem data structures are consistent.

checksum The value of a mathematical function computed for a block of data; used to detect corruption of the data block.

child process A process that is a direct descendent of another process as a result of being created with a *fork* system call.

cleaning The process of garbage collection used by the Log-Structured Filesystem to reclaim space. Logical file blocks that were written to disk but have been deleted or superseded are periodically reclaimed and used for future filesystem writes.

client process In the client–server model of communication, a process that contacts a server process to request services. A client process is usually unrelated to a server process; the client process's only association with the server process is through a communication channel. See also *server process*.

C-list A linked-list data structure, used by the system in supporting serial line I/O.

cloning route A routing entry that is not used directly, but that causes a new instance of a route to be created. For example, the route to a local Ethernet is set up as a cloning route so that individual host routes will be created for each local host when referenced.

cluster The logical grouping of contiguous physical pages of memory. In 4.4BSD, this grouping is used by the virtual-memory system to simulate memory pages with sizes larger than the physical page size supported by the hardware.

cold start The initial phase of a bootstrap procedure. The term is derived from the fact that the software assumes nothing about the state of the machine—as though the machine had just been turned on and were cold.

communication domain An abstraction used by the interprocess-communication facilities to organize the properties of a communication network or similar facility. A communication domain includes a set of protocols, termed the *protocol family*; rules for manipulating and interpreting names; the *address family*; and, possibly, other intrinsic properties, such as the ability to transmit access rights. The facilities provided by the system for interprocess communication are defined such that they are independent of the communication domains supported by the system. This design makes it possible for applications to be written in a communication-domain–independent manner.

communication protocol A set of conventions and rules used by two communicating processes.

configuration file A file that contains parameters for the system-configuration program **/usr/sbin/config**. This file describes the hardware devices and topology that the system should be able to support, as well as miscellaneous parameters, such as the maximum number of users that are expected to use the system simultaneously.

configuration procedure The procedure followed by a system administrator in configuring a kernel for a machine, or for a collection of machines. The configuration procedure requires a configuration file, which is then supplied to the **/usr/sbin/config** program to create the necessary data files for building a kernel.

connect request A request passed to the user-request routine of a communication-protocol module as a result of a process making a *connect* system call on a socket. The request causes the system to attempt to establish an association between a local and a remote socket.

console monitor The terminal attached to a console-terminal interface.

console processor An auxiliary processor to the main CPU that allows an operator to start and stop the system, to monitor system operation, and to run hardware diagnostics.

context switching The action of interrupting the currently running process and of switching to another process. Context switching occurs as one process after another is scheduled for execution. An interrupted process's context is saved in that process's process control block, and another process's context is loaded.

continue signal Signal 19 (SIGCONT). A signal that, when delivered to a stopped or sleeping process, causes that process to resume execution.

controlling process The session leader that established the connection to the controlling terminal. See also *session leader*.

controlling terminal The terminal device associated with a process's session from which keyboard-related signals may be generated. The controlling terminal for a process is normally inherited from the process's parent.

control request A request passed to the user-request routine of a communication-protocol module as a result of a process making an *ioctl* or *setsockopt* system call on a socket.

cooked mode See *canonical mode*.

copy-on-write A technique whereby multiple references to a common object are maintained until the object is modified (written). Before the object is written, a copy is made; the modification is made to the copy, rather than to the original. In virtual-memory management, copy-on-write is a common scheme that the kernel uses to manage pages shared by multiple processes. All the page-table entries mapping a shared page are set such that the first write reference to the page causes a page fault. When the page fault is serviced, the faulted page is replaced with a private copy, which is writable.

core file A file (named **core**) that is created by the system when certain signals are delivered to a process. The file contains a record of the state of the process at the time the signal occurred. This record includes the contents of the process's virtual address space and, on most systems, the user structure.

CPU See *central processing unit.*

crash Among computer scientists, an unexpected system failure.

crash dump A record of the state of a machine at the time of a crash. This record is usually written to a place on secondary storage that is thought to be safe, so that it can be saved until the information can be recovered.

CRT See *cathode ray tube.*

current working directory The directory from which relative pathnames are interpreted for a process. The current working directory for a process is set with the *chdir* or *fchdir* system call.

cylinder The tracks of a disk that are accessible from one position of the head assembly.

cylinder group In the Fast Filesystem, a collection of cylinders on a disk drive that is grouped together for the purpose of localizing information. That is, the filesystem allocates inodes and data blocks on a per–cylinder-group basis.

daemon A long-lived process that provides a system-related service. There are daemon processes that execute in kernel mode (e.g., the *pagedaemon*), and daemon processes that execute in user mode (e.g., the *routing daemon*). The old English term, *daemon*, means "a deified being," as distinguished from the term, *demon*, which means an "evil spirit."

DARPA Defense Advanced Research Projects Agency. An agency of the U.S. Department of Defense that is responsible for managing defense-sponsored research in the United States.

datagram socket A type of socket that models potentially unreliable connectionless packet communication.

data segment The segment of a process's address space that contains the initialized and uninitialized data portions of a program. See also *bss segment; stack segment; text segment.*

decapsulation In network communication, the removal of the outermost header information on a message. The inverse of encapsulation.

demand paging A memory-management technique in which memory is divided into pages and the pages are provided to processes as needed—that is, *on demand.* See also *pure demand paging.*

demon See *daemon.*

descriptor An integer assigned by the system when a file is referenced by the *open* system call, or when a socket is created with the *socket*, *pipe*, or *socketpair* system calls. The integer uniquely identifies an access path to the file or socket from a given process, or from any of that process's children. Descriptors can also be duplicated with the *dup* and *fcntl* system calls.

descriptor table A per-process table that holds references to objects on which I/O may be done. I/O descriptors are indices into this table.

device In UNIX, a peripheral connected to the CPU.

device driver A software module that is part of the kernel and that supports access to a peripheral device.

device flags Data specified in a system configuration file and passed to a device driver. The use of these flags varies across device drivers. Device drivers for terminal devices use the flags to indicate the terminal lines on which the driver should ignore modem-control signals on input.

device number A number that uniquely identifies a device within the block- or character-device classes. A device number comprises two parts: a major-device number and a minor-device number.

device special file A file through which processes can access hardware devices on a machine. For example, a tape drive is accessed through such a file.

directed broadcast A message that is to be broadcast on a network to which the sender is not connected directly.

direct memory access (DMA) A facility whereby a peripheral device can access main memory without the assistance of the CPU. DMA is typically used to transfer contiguous blocks of data between main memory and a peripheral device.

directory In UNIX, a special type of file that contains entries that are references to other files. By convention, a directory contains at least two entries: dot (.) and dot-dot (..). Dot refers to the directory itself; dot-dot refers to the parent directory.

directory entry An entry that is represented by a variable-length record structure in the directory file. Each structure holds an ASCII string that represents the filename, the number of bytes of space provided for the string, the number of bytes of space provided for the entry, the type of the file referenced by the entry, and the number of the inode associated with the filename. By convention, a directory entry with a zero inode number is treated as unallocated, and the space held by the entry is available for use.

dirty In computer systems, modified. A system usually tracks whether or not an object has been modified—is dirty—because it needs to save the object's contents before reusing the space held by the object. For example, in the filesystem, a buffer in the buffer cache is dirty if its contents have been modified. Dirty buffers must be written back to the disk before they are reused.

disk partition A contiguous region of a disk drive that is used as a swap area or to hold a filesystem.

distributed program A program that is partitioned among multiple processes, possibly spread across multiple machines.

DMA   See *direct memory access.*

double indirect block   See *indirect block.*

effective GID   See *effective group identifier.*

effective group identifier (effective GID)   The first entry in the groups array. The effective GID, along with the other GIDs in the groups array, is used by the filesystem to check group access permission. The effective GID is set when a set-group-identifier program is executed. See also *group identifier; real group identifier; saved group identifier.*

effective UID   See *effective user identifier.*

effective user identifier (effective UID)   The UID that the system uses to check many user permissions. For example, the effective UID is used by the filesystem to check owner access permission on files. The effective UID is set when a set-user-identifier program is executed. See also *user identifier; real user identifier; saved user identifier.*

elevator sorting algorithm   An algorithm used by the device drivers for I/O requests for moving head disks. The algorithm sorts requests into a cyclic ascending order based on the cylinder number of the request. The name is derived from the fact that the algorithm orders disk requests in a manner similar to the way ride requests for an elevator would be handled most efficiently.

emulate   To simulate. Many ports of 4.4BSD can emulate the system-call interface of the UNIX operating system provided by the hardware vendor. For example, the HP300 version of 4.4BSD can run binaries compiled for HP-UX.

encapsulation   In network communication, the procedure by which a message is created that has an existing message enclosed in it as data. A protocol normally encapsulates a message by crafting a leading protocol header that indicates that the original message is to be treated as data. The inverse of decapsulation.

erase character   The character that is recognized by the terminal handler, when the latter is running in canonical mode, to mean "delete the last character in the line of input." Each terminal session can have a different erase character, and that erase character can be changed at any time with a *tcsetattr* system call. The terminal handler does not recognize the erase character on terminals that are in noncanonical mode. See also *word-erase character; kill character.*

errno   The global variable in C programs that holds an error code that indicates why a system call failed. The value to be placed in *errno* is returned by the kernel in the standard return register; it is moved from this return register to *errno* by code in the C run-time library.

error-message buffer   See *message buffer.*

eviction notice   A call-back message from a server to a client notifying the client that its lease for an object is being terminated. A lease is usually terminated because another client wants to modify the object that the lease represents. See also *callback; lease.*

fault rate   The rate at which a process generates page faults. For a reference string, the fault rate is defined to be time independent by its being specified as the number of page faults divided by the length of the reference string.

fetch policy   The policy used by a demand-paged virtual-memory–management system in processing page faults. Fetch policies differ primarily in the way that they handle prepaging of data.

FIFO file   In the filesystem, a type of file that can be used for interprocess communication. Data written by one process to a FIFO are read by another in the order in which they were sent. The name refers to the fact that data are transferred in a first-in, first-out fashion.

file   An object in the filesystem that is treated as a linear array of bytes. A file has at least one name, and it exists until all its names are deleted explicitly.

file handle   A globally unique token created by an NFS server and passed back to an NFS client. The client can then use the file handle to refer to the associated file on the server. A handle is created when a file is first opened; it is passed to the server by the client in later operations, such as read and write, that reference the open file.

filename   A string of ASCII characters that is used to name an ordinary file, special file, or directory. The characters in a filename cannot include null (0) or the ASCII code for slash ('/').

file offset   A byte offset associated with an open file descriptor. The file offset for a file descriptor is set explicitly with the *lseek* system call, or implicitly as a result of a *read* or *write* system call.

file structure   The data structure used by the kernel to hold the information associated with one or more open file descriptors that reference a file. In most cases, each open file descriptor references a unique file structure. File structures may be shared, however, when open descriptors are duplicated with the *dup* and *dup2* system calls, inherited across a *fork* system call, or received in a message through the interprocess-communication facilities.

filesystem   A collection of files. The UNIX filesystem is hierarchical, with files organized into directories, and filesystems, in most cases, restricted to a single physical hardware device, such as a disk drive. Filesystems typically include facilities for naming files and for controlling access to files.

fill-on-demand page fault   The first page fault for an individual page; it must be resolved by retrieval of data from the filesystem or by allocation of a zero-filled page.

first-level bootstrap   The initial code that is executed in a multilevel bootstrapping operation. Usually, the first-level bootstrap is limited in size and does little more than bootstrap into operation a larger, more intelligent, program. Typically, the first-level bootstrap loads the **/boot** program, so that **/boot** can, in turn, bootstrap the kernel.

foreground process   In job-control–oriented process-management systems, a process whose process group is the same as that of its controlling terminal; thus, the process is allowed to read from and to write to the terminal. Otherwise, a foreground process is one for which the command interpreter is currently waiting. The opposite of a foreground process is a *background process*.

forward-mapped page table A large contiguous array indexed by the virtual address that contains one element, or page-table entry, for each virtual page in the address space. This element contains the physical page to which the virtual page is mapped, as well as access permissions and status bits telling whether the page has been referenced or modified, and a bit indicating whether the entry contains valid information. Most current memory-management–unit designs use some variant of a forward-mapped page table. See also *inverted page table*.

fragment In the filesystem, a part of a block. The filesystem allocates new disk space to a file as a full block or as one or more fragments of a block. The filesystem uses fragments, rather than allocating space in only full block-size units, to reduce wasted space when the size of a full block is large.

fragment-descriptor table A data structure in the Fast Filesystem that describes the fragments that are free in an entry of the allocation map. The filesystem uses the fragment-descriptor table by taking a byte in the allocation map and using the byte to index into the fragment-descriptor table. The value in the fragment-descriptor table indicates how many fragments of a particular size are available in the entry of the allocation map. By doing a logical AND with the bit corresponding to the desired fragment size, the system can determine quickly whether a desired fragment is contained within the allocation-map entry.

free list In the memory-management system, the list of available clusters of physical memory (also called the *memory free list*). There is a similar free list in the system for dynamically allocated kernel memory. Many kernel data structures are dynamically allocated, including vnodes, file-table entries, and disk-quota structures.

free-space reserve A percentage of space in a filesystem that is held in reserve to ensure that certain allocation algorithms used by the filesystem will work well. By default, 10 percent of the available space in the Fast Filesystem and 2 clean segments in the Log-Structured Filesystem, are held in reserve.

garbage collection A memory-management facility in which unused portions of memory are reclaimed without an application having to release them explicitly.

gateway See *router*.

generation number The number assigned to an inode each time that the latter is allocated to represent a new file. Each generation number is used only once. Most NFS implementations use a random-number generator to select a new generation number; the 4.4BSD implementation selects a generation number that is approximately equal to the creation time of the file.

GID See *group identifier*.

global page-replacement algorithm   An algorithm that does page replacement according to systemwide criteria. A global-page-replacement strategy tends to make the most efficient use of the system memory. However, a single process can thrash the entire system by trying to use all the available memory.

group identifier (GID)   An integer value that uniquely identifies a collection of users. GIDs are used in the access-control facilities provided by the filesystem. See also *effective group identifier; real group identifier; saved group identifier; set-group-identifier program.*

half-open connection   A connection that is thought to be open by only one of the two endpoints. For example, a connection that is lost because of a crash or timeout on one peer, but is still considered established by the other, is half-open.

handler   A procedure that is invoked in response to an event such as a signal.

hard limit   A limit that cannot be exceeded. See also *soft limit.*

hard link   A directory entry that directly references an inode. If there are multiple hard links to a single inode and if one of the links is deleted, the remaining links still reference the inode. By contrast, a symbolic link is a file that holds a pathname that is used to reference a file.

header prediction   A heuristic used by TCP on incoming packets to detect two common cases: the next expected data segment for an existing connection, or an acknowledgment plus a window update for one or more data segments. When one of these two cases arise, and the packet has no additional flags or state indications, the fully general TCP input processing is skipped.

heap   The region of a process that can be expanded dynamically with the *sbrk* system call (or *malloc* C library call). The name is derived from the disorderly fashion in which data are placed in the region.

high watermark   An upper bound on the number of data that may be buffered. In the interprocess-communication facilities, each socket's data buffer has a high watermark that specifies the maximum number of data that may be queued in the data buffer before a request to send data will block the process (or will return an error if nonblocking I/O is being used). See also *low watermark.*

hole   In a file, a region that is part of the file, but that has no associated data blocks. The filesystem returns zero-valued data when a process reads from a hole in a file. A hole is created in a file when a process positions the file pointer past the current end-of-file, writes some data, and then closes the file. The hole appears between the previous end-of-file and the beginning of the newly written data.

home directory   The current working directory that is set for a user's shell when the user logs into a system. This directory is usually private to the user. The home directory for a user is specified in a field in the password-file entry for the user.

host-unreachable message   An ICMP message that indicates that the host to which a previous message was directed is unavailable because there is no known path to the desired host.

ICMP   See *Internet Control Message Protocol.*

idempotent   An operation that can be repeated several times without changing the final result or causing an error. For example, writing the same data to the same offset in a file is idempotent, because it will yield the same result whether it is done once or many times. However, trying to remove the same file more than once is nonidempotent because the file will no longer exist after the first try.

idle loop   The block of code inside the kernel that is executed when there is nothing else to run. In 4.4BSD, the idle loop waits for a process to be added to the run queue.

index file   The Log-Structured Filesystem read-only file, visible in the filesystem, that contains segment-usage information and the inode number to disk-block address mapping. By convention, the index file is named *ifile*.

indirect block   In the filesystem, an auxilliary data block that holds the number of a data block. The first 12 blocks of a file are pointed to directly by the inode. Additional data blocks are described with a pointer from the inode to an *indirect data block*; the system must first fetch the indirect block that holds the number of the data block. In 4.4BSD, the kernel may have to fetch as many as three indirect blocks to locate the desired data block. An indirect block that contains data-block numbers is termed a *single-level indirect block*; an indirect block that contains block numbers of single-level indirect blocks is called a *double-level indirect block*; an indirect block that contains block numbers of double-level indirect blocks is called a *triple-level indirect block*.

init   The first user program (**/sbin/init**) that runs when the system is booted.

initial sequence number   See *sequence space.*

inode   A data structure used by the filesystem to describe a file. The contents of an inode include the file's type, the UID of the file's owner, and a list of the disk blocks and fragments that make up the file. Note that inodes do not have names; directory entries are used to associate a name with an inode.

input/output (I/O)   The transfer of data between the computer and its peripheral devices.

intelligent gateway   A gateway machine that is capable of making intelligent decisions about routing network data. Such machines usually participate in a scheme whereby routing information is updated dynamically to reflect changes in network topology. An intelligent gateway is also expected to respond with routing redirect messages to hosts that make poor routing decisions.

interactive program   A program that must periodically obtain user input to do its work. A screen-oriented text editor is an example of an interactive program.

Internet Control Message Protocol (ICMP) A host-to-host communication protocol used in the Internet for reporting errors and controlling the operation of IP.

Internet domain A communication domain in the interprocess-communication facilities that supports the Internet architecture. This architecture supports both stream- and datagram-oriented styles of communication between processes on machines on an Internet.

Internet host address In the Internet, a number that identifies both the network on which a host is located and the host on that network. For version 4 of IP, the address is 32 bits.

Internet Protocol (IP) The network-layer communication protocol used in the Internet. IP is responsible for host-to-host addressing and routing, packet forwarding, and packet fragmentation and reassembly.

interpreter A program that parses and executes a descriptive language in a single step, rather than using the more common two-stage process of compiling the language and executing the resulting binary. The shell is an example of an interpreter; it parses and executes a shell script, rather than first compiling it.

interprocess communication (IPC) The transfer of data between processes. Most facilities for interprocess communication are designed such that data are transferred between objects other than processes. An interprocess-communication model that is not directly process oriented is advantageous because it is possible to model scenarios in which communication endpoints are location independent and, possibly, are migrated dynamically. For example, in 4.4BSD, communication is between sockets, rather than between processes.

interrupt In computer systems, an event external to the currently executing process that causes a change in the normal flow of instruction execution. Interrupts usually are generated by hardware devices that are external to the CPU.

interrupt priority level The priority that is associated with a device interrupt. This value is usually defined by switches or jumpers located on a device controller and transmitted with each interrupt request made by the hardware device. See also *processor priority level*.

interrupt stack A run-time stack that is used by procedures that are invoked to respond to interrupts and traps. On most architectures, a systemwide interrupt stack is provided that is independent of the normal kernel run-time stack located in the user structure of each process.

inverted page table (reverse-mapped page table) A hardware-maintained memory-resident table that contains one entry per physical page, and that is indexed by physical address instead of by virtual address. An entry contains the virtual address to which the physical page is currently mapped; the entry also includes protection and status attributes. The hardware does virtual-to-physical address translation by computing a hash function on the virtual address to select an entry in the table. The hardware handles collisions by linking together table entries, and making a linear search of this chain until it finds the matching virtual address. See also *forward-mapped page table*.

I/O   See *input/output*.

I/O redirection   The redirection of an I/O stream from the default assignment. For example, all the standard shells permit users to redirect the standard output stream to a file or process.

I/O stream   A stream of data directed to, or generated from, a process. Most I/O streams in UNIX have a single common data format that permits users to write programs in a tool-oriented fashion, and to combine these programs in pipelines by directing the standard output stream of one program to the standard input stream of another.

iovec   A data structure used to specify user I/O requests made to the kernel. Each structure holds the address of a data buffer and the number of bytes of data to be read or written. Arrays of such structures are passed to the kernel in *readv* and *writev* system calls.

I/O vector   See *iovec*.

IP   See *Internet Protocol*.

IPC   See *interprocess communication*.

job   In UNIX, a set of processes that all have the same process-group identifier. Jobs that have multiple processes are normally created with a pipeline. A job is the fundamental object that is manipulated with job control.

job control   A facility for managing jobs. With job control, a job may be started, stopped, and killed, as well as moved between the foreground and the background. The terminal handler provides facilities for automatically stopping a background job that tries to access the controlling terminal, and for notifying a job's controlling process when such an event occurs.

keepalive packet   A type of packet used by TCP to maintain information about whether or not a destination host is up. Keepalive packets are sent to a remote host, which, if it is up, must respond. If a response is not received in a reasonable time to any of several keepalive packets, then the connection is terminated. Keepalive packets are used on only those TCP connections that have been created for sockets that have the SO_KEEPALIVE option set on them.

keepalive timer   A timer used by the TCP protocol in conjunction with keepalive packets. The timer is set when a keepalive packet is transmitted. If a response to the packet is not received before the timer expires several times, then the connection is shut down.

kernel   The central controlling program that provides basic system facilities. The 4.4BSD kernel creates and manages processes, provides functions to access the filesystem, and supplies communication facilities. The 4.4BSD kernel is the only part of 4.4BSD that a user cannot replace.

kernel mode   The most privileged processor-access mode. The 4.4BSD kernel operates in kernel mode.

kernel process A process that executes with the processor in kernel mode. The *pagedaemon* and *swapper* processes are examples of kernel processes.

kernel state The run-time execution state for the kernel. This state, which includes the program counter, general-purpose registers, and run-time stack, must be saved and restored on each context switch.

kill character The character that is recognized by the terminal handler in canonical mode to mean "delete everything typed on this terminal after the most recent end-of-line character." Each terminal session can have a different kill character, and the user can change that kill character at any time with an *tcsetattr* system call. The terminal handler does not recognize the kill character on terminals that are in noncanonical mode. See also *erase character; word-erase character*.

lease A ticket permitting an activity that is valid until a specified expiration time. In the NQNFS protocol, a client gets a lease from its server to read, write, or read and write a file. As long the client holds a valid lease, it knows that the server will notify it if the file status changes. Once the lease has expired, the client must contact the server to request a new lease before using any data that it has cached for the file. See also *callback; eviction notice*.

least recently used (LRU) A policy of reuse whereby the least recently used items are reused first. For example, in the filesystem, there is a fixed number of data buffers available for doing I/O. Buffers that hold valid data are reallocated in an LRU order on the LRU buffer list, in the hope that the data held in the buffer may be reused by a subsequent read request. See also *AGE buffer list; buffer cache*.

line discipline A processing module in the kernel that provides semantics for an asynchronous serial interface or for a software emulation of such an interface. Line disciplines are described by a procedural interface whose entry points are stored in the *linesw* data structure.

line mode See *canonical mode*.

link layer Layer 2 in the ISO Open Systems Interconnection Reference Model. In this model, the link layer is responsible for the (possibly unreliable) delivery of messages within a single physical network. The link layer corresponds most closely to the network-interface layer of the 4.4BSD network subsystem.

listen request A request passed to the user-request routine of a communication-protocol module as a result of a process making a *listen* system call on a socket. This request indicates that the system should listen for requests to establish a connection to the socket. Otherwise, the system will reject any connection requests that it receives for the socket.

load average A measure of the CPU load on the system. The load average in 4.4BSD is defined as an average of the number of processes ready to run or waiting for disk I/O to complete, as sampled over the previous 1-minute interval of system operation.

local domain   A communication domain in the interprocess-communication facilities that supports stream- and datagram-oriented styles of communication between processes on a single machine.

locality of reference   A phenomenon whereby memory references of a running program are localized within the virtual address space over short periods. Most programs tend to exhibit some degree of locality of reference. This locality of reference makes it worthwhile for the system to prefetch pages that are adjacent to a page that is faulted, to reduce the fault rate of a running program.

local page-replacement algorithm   An algorithm for page replacement that first chooses a process from which to replace a page, and then chose a page within that process based on per-process criteria. Usually, a process is given a fixed number of pages, and must then select from among its own pages when it needs a new page.

log   An append-only file. A file where existing data are never overwritten; the kernel thus modifies the file only by appending new data. The Log-Structured Filesystem implements an abstraction of a log on the disk. See also *no-overwrite policy*.

logical block   A block defined by dividing a file's linear extent by the underlying filesystem block size. Each logical block of a file is mapped into a physical block. This additional level of mapping permits physical blocks to be placed on disk without concern for the linear organization of the logical blocks in a file.

logical drive partitions   A software scheme that divides a disk drive into one or more linear extents or partitions.

logical unit   An integer that specifies the unit number of a hardware device. The hardware device and unit number are specified in terms of logical devices and units as discovered by the system during the autoconfiguration phase of its bootstrap sequence. For example, a reference to "partition 1 on disk drive 2" typically refers to partition 1 on the third disk drive identified at boot time (devices are numbered starting at 0). The actual mapping between logical unit numbers and physical devices is defined by the configuration file that is used to build a kernel. For flexibility, most systems are configured to support a reasonably dynamic mapping between physical and logical devices. This dynamic mapping permits, for example, system administrators to move a disk drive from one controller to another without having to reconfigure a new kernel or to reconstruct the associated special files for the device.

long-term–scheduling algorithm   See *short-term–scheduling algorithm*.

lossy   A communication medium that has a high rate of data loss.

low watermark   A lower bound that specifies the minimum number of data that must be present before an action can be taken. In the interprocess-communication facilities, each socket's data buffer has a low watermark that specifies the minimum number of data that must be present in the data buffer before a reception request will be satisfied. See also *high watermark*.

LRU See *least recently used.*

machine check An exceptional machine condition that indicates that the CPU detected an error in its operation. For example, a machine check is generated if a parity error is detected in a cache memory.

magic number The number located in the first few bytes of an executable file that specifies the type of the executable file.

main memory The primary memory system on a machine.

major-device number An integer number that uniquely identifies the type of a device. This number is defined as the index into the array of device-driver entry points for the device. It is used, for example, when a user creates a device special file with the *mknod* system call.

mandatory lock A lock that cannot be ignored or avoided. A mandatory lock is contrasted with an advisory lock, which is enforced only when a process explicitly requests its enforcement. See also *advisory lock.*

mapped object An object whose pages are mapped into a process address space. Processes map objects into their virtual address space using the *mmap* system call.

mapping structure The machine-dependent state required to describe the translation and access rights of a single page. See also *page-table entry.*

mark and sweep algorithm A garbage-collection algorithm that works by sweeping through the set of collectable objects, marking each object that is referenced. If, after this marking phase, there are any objects that are unmarked, they are reclaimed.

marshalling Preparing a set of parameters to be sent across a network. Marshalling includes replacing pointers by the data to which they point, and converting binary data to the canonical network byte order. See also *remote procedure call.*

masked signal A signal blocked in a *sigprocmask* system call. When a signal is masked, its delivery is delayed until it is unmasked. In addition, in 4.4BSD, the system automatically masks a caught signal while that signal is being handled.

master device See *slave device.*

maximum segment lifetime (MSL) The maximum time that a segment of data may exist in the network. See also *2MSL timer.*

mbuf A data structure that describes a block of data; mbufs are used in the interprocess-communication facilities. "Mbuf" is shorthand for "memory buffer."

memory address A number that specifies a memory location. Memory addresses are often categorized as *physical* or *virtual* according to whether they reference physical or virtual memory.

memory free list See *free list.*

memory-management system The part of the operating system that is responsible for the management of memory resources available on a machine.

memory-management unit A hardware device that implements memory-management–related tasks, such as address translation and memory protection. Most contemporary memory-management units also provide support for demand-paged virtual-memory management.

message buffer A circular buffer in which the system records all kernel messages directed to the console terminal. The device **/dev/klog** can be used by a user program to read data from this buffer in a manner that ensures that no data will be lost. On most systems, the message buffer is allocated early in the bootstrapping of the system; it is placed in high memory so that it can be located after a reboot, allowing messages printed out just before a crash to be saved.

minor-device number An integer number that uniquely identifies a subunit of a device. For example, the minor-device number for a disk device specifies a subunit termed a *partition*, whereas the minor-device number for a terminal multiplexer identifies a specific terminal line. The minor-device number is interpreted on a per-device basis and is used, for example, when a user creates a device special file with the *mknod* system call.

modem control For data-communication equipment, the support of a set of signals used to ensure reliable initiation and termination of connections over asynchronous serial lines, defined by the RS-232 standard. Support for modem control is normally important for only serial lines that are accessed via dialup modems.

MSL See *maximum segment lifetime*.

multilevel feedback queue A queueing scheme in which requests are partitioned into multiple prioritized subqueues, with requests moving between subqueues based on dynamically varying criteria. The 4.4BSD kernel uses a multilevel-feedback-queueing scheme for scheduling the execution of processes.

multiplexed file A type of file used for interprocess communication that was supported in the Seventh Edition UNIX system.

network address A number that specifies a host machine.

network architecture The collection of protocols, facilities, and conventions (such as the format of a network address) that define a network. Like machine architectures, network architectures may be realized in different ways. For example, some network architectures are specifically designed to permit their implementation in hardware devices.

network byte order The order defined by a network for the transmission of protocol fields that are larger than one octet. In the Internet protocols, this order is "most significant octet first."

network-interface layer The layer of software in the 4.4BSD network subsystem that is responsible for transporting messages between hosts connected to a common transmission medium. This layer is mainly concerned with driving the transmission media involved, and with doing any necessary link-level protocol encapsulation and decapsulation.

network layer   The layer of software in the 4.4BSD network subsystem that is responsible for the delivery of data destined for remote transport or network-layer protocols.

network mask   A value that is used in the subnet addressing scheme of the Internet. A network mask specifies which bits in a local Internet address the system should include when extracting a network identifier from a local address.

network virtual terminal   A terminal device that receives and transmits data across a network connection.

nice   A user-controllable process-scheduling parameter. The value of a process's *nice* variable is used in calculating that process's scheduling priority. Positive values of *nice* mean that the process is willing to receive less than its share of the processor. Negative values of *nice* mean that the process requests more than its share of the processor.

nonblocking I/O   A mode in which a descriptor may be placed, whereby the system will return an error if any I/O operation on the descriptor would cause the process to block. For example, if a *read* system call is done on a descriptor that is in nonblocking I/O mode, and no data are available, the system will return the error code EWOULDBLOCK, rather than block the process until data arrive. See also *polling I/O; signal-driven I/O*.

noncanonical mode   See *canonical mode*.

nonlocal goto   A transfer in control that circumvents the normal flow of execution in a program across routine boundaries. For example, if procedure A calls procedure B, and B calls C, then a direct transfer of control from C back to A (bypassing B) would be a nonlocal goto.

nonresident object   An object that is not present in main memory. For example, a page in the virtual address space of a process may be nonresident if it has never been referenced.

no-overwrite policy   A policy such that, when existing data are modified, new copies of the data are created, rather than the data being overwritten in place. The Log-Structured Filesystem implements a no-overwrite policy for files. See also *log*.

object   See *virtual-memory object*.

object cache   A cache in the virtual-memory system for inactive objects. Inactive file objects are retained in a least-recently-used cache so that future uses of the associated file can reuse the object and that object's associated cached physical pages.

octet   A basic unit of data representation; an 8-bit byte. The term *octet* is used instead of *byte* in the definition of many network protocols because some machines use other byte sizes.

optimal replacement policy   A replacement policy that optimizes the performance of a demand-paging virtual-memory system. In this book, a policy whereby the full reference string of a program is known in advance, and pages are selected such that the number of page faults is minimized.

orphaned process group A process group in which the parent of every member is either itself a member of the group or is not a member of the group's session. Such a parent would normally be a job-control shell capable of resuming stopped child processes.

out-of-band data Data transmitted and received out of the normal flow of data. Stream sockets support a logically separate out-of-band data channel through which at least one message of at least 1 octet of data may be sent. The system immediately notifies a receiving process of the presence of out-of-band data, and out-of-band data may be retrieved out of received order.

overlay In computer systems, a region of code or data that may be replaced with other such regions on demand. Overlays are usually loaded into a process's address space on demand, possibly on top of another overlay. Overlays are a commonly used scheme for programs that are too large to fit in the address space of a machine that does not support virtual memory.

page In memory management, the fixed-sized unit of measure used to divide a physical or virtual address space. See also *demand paging*.

pagedaemon In 4.4BSD, the name of the kernel process that is responsible for writing parts of the address space of a process to secondary storage, to support the paging facilities of the virtual-memory system. See also *swapper*.

page fault An exception generated by a process's reference to a page of that process's virtual address space that is not marked as resident in memory.

pagein An operation done by the virtual-memory system in which the contents of a page are read from secondary storage.

pageout An operation done by the virtual-memory system in which the contents of a page are written to secondary storage.

page push A pageout of a dirty page.

pager A kernel module responsible for providing the data to fill a page, and for providing a place to store that page when it has been modified and the memory associated with it is needed for another purpose.

page reclaim A page fault, where the page that was faulted is located in memory, usually on the inactive list.

page-table entry (PTE) The machine-dependent data structure that identifies the location and status of a page of a virtual address space. When a virtual page is in memory, the PTE contains the page-frame number that the hardware needs to map the virtual page to a physical page.

page-table pages The second level of a three-level hierarchy of data structures used by a forward-mapped page-table algorithm to describe the virtual address space of a process. Page-table pages are pointed to by entries in the top-level segment table; each entry in a page-table page points to a page of bottom-level page-table entries. See also *forward-mapped page table; page-table entry; segment table*.

paging   The actions of bringing pages of an executing process into main memory when they are referenced, and of removing them from memory when they are replaced. When a process executes, all its pages are said to reside in virtual memory. Only the actively used pages, however, need to reside in main memory. The remaining pages can reside on disk until they are needed.

panic   In UNIX, an unrecoverable system failure detected by the kernel. 4.4BSD automatically recovers from a panic by rebooting the machine, repairing any filesystem damage, and then restarting normal operation. See also *crash dump*.

parent process   A process that is a direct relative of another process as a result of a *fork* system call.

partition   See *disk partition*.

pathname   A null-terminated character string starting with an optional slash ("/"), followed by zero or more directory names separated by slashes, and optionally followed by a filename. If a pathname begins with a slash, it is said to be an *absolute pathname*, and the path search begins at the root directory. Otherwise, the pathname is said to be a *relative pathname*, and the path search begins at the current working directory of the process. A slash by itself names the root directory. A null pathname refers to the current working directory.

PCB   See *process control block*.

persist timer   A timer used by TCP for maintaining output flow on a connection. This timer is started whenever data are ready to be sent, but the send window is too small to bother sending and no data are already outstanding. If no window update is received before the timer expires, a window probe is sent.

physical block   One or more contiguous disk sectors to which the system maps a logical block.

physical mapping (pmap)   The software state, also referred to as the *pmap* structure, needed to manage the machine-dependent translation and access tables that are used either directly or indirectly by the memory-management hardware. This mapping state includes information about access rights, in addition to address translation.

PID   See *process identifier*.

pipe   An interprocess-communication facility that supports the unidirectional flow of data between related processes. Data transfer is stream-oriented, reliable, and flow controlled. A pipe is specified to the shell with the "|" symbol. For example, to connect the standard output of program **a** to the standard input of program **b**, the user would type the command "a | b".

pipeline   A collection of processes in which the standard output of one process is connected to the standard input of the next with a pipe.

placement policy   The policy used by the virtual-memory system to place pages in main memory when servicing a page fault.

pmap   See *physical mapping*.

polling I/O The normal mode for a descriptor whereby the system will block if a read request has no data available or a write request has no buffering available. A process can determine whether an I/O operation will block by polling the kernel using the *select* system call. The *select* system call can be requested to return immediately with the information or to block until at least one of the requested I/O operations can be completed. See also *nonblocking I/O; signal-driven I/O*.

POSIX The standards group for P1003, the portable operating-system interfaces established by the IEEE. Its first established standard was the kernel interface, 1003.1, which was ratified in 1988.

prefetching The retrieval of data before they are needed. Many machines prefetch machine instructions so that they can overlap the time spent fetching instructions from memory with the time spent decoding instructions.

prepaging The prefetching of pages of memory. Prepaging is a technique used by virtual-memory systems to reduce the number of page faults.

probing The operation of checking to see whether a hardware device is present on a machine. Each different type of hardware device usually requires its own technique for probing.

process In operating systems, a task or thread of execution. In UNIX, user processes are created with the *fork* system call.

process control block (PCB) A data structure used to hold process context. The hardware-defined PCB contains the hardware portion of this context. The software PCB contains the software portion, and is located in memory immediately after the hardware PCB.

process group A collection of processes on a single machine that all have the same process-group identifier. The kernel uses this grouping to arbitrate among multiple jobs contending for the same terminal.

process-group identifier A positive integer used to identify uniquely each active process group in the system. Process-group identifiers are typically defined to be the PID of the process-group leader. Process-group identifiers are used by command interpreters in implementing job control, when the command interpreter is broadcasting signals with the *killpg* system call, and when the command interpreter is altering the scheduling priority of all processes in a process group with the *setpriority* system call.

process-group leader The process in a process group whose PID is used as the process-group identifier. This process is typically the first process in a pipeline.

process identifier (PID) A nonnegative integer used to identify uniquely each active process in the system.

process open-file table See *descriptor table*.

processor priority level A priority that the kernel uses to control the delivery of interrupts to the CPU. Most machines support multiple priority levels at which the processor may execute. Similarly, interrupts also occur at multiple levels. When an interrupt is posted to the processor, if the priority level of the interrupt is greater than that of the processor, then the interrupt is recognized by the processor and execution is diverted to service the interrupt. Otherwise, the interrupt is not acknowledged by the CPU and is held pending until the processor priority drops to a level that permits the interrupt to be acknowledged. Changing the processor priority level is usually a privileged operation that can be done only when the processor is executing in kernel mode.

process priority A parameter used by the kernel to schedule the execution of processes. The priority for a process changes dynamically according to the operation of the process. In addition, the *nice* parameter can be set for a process to weight the overall scheduling priority for the process.

process structure A data structure maintained by the kernel for each active process in the system. The process structure for a process is always resident in main memory, as opposed to the user structure, which is moved to secondary storage when the process is swapped out.

/proc filesystem A filesystem-based interface to active processes that provides process-debugging facilities. Each process is represented by a directory entry in a pseudodirectory named **/proc**. Applications access the virtual address space of a process by opening the file in **/proc** that is associated with the process, and then using the *read* and *write* system calls as though the process were a regular file.

programmed I/O Input or output to a device that is unable to do direct-memory access. Each character must be loaded into the device's output-character register for transmission. Depending on the device, the CPU may then have to wait after each character for the transmit-complete interrupt before sending the next character.

protocol family A collection of communication protocols, the members of which are related by being part of a single network architecture. For example, the TCP, UDP, IP, and ICMP protocols are part of the protocol family for the Internet.

protocol switch structure A data structure that holds all the entry points for a communication protocol supported by the kernel.

PTE See *page-table entry*.

pure demand paging Demand paging without prepaging.

race condition A condition in which two or more actions for an operation occur in an undefined order. Trouble arises if there exists a possible order that results in an incorrect outcome.

raw-device interface The character-device interface for block-oriented devices such as disks and tapes. This interface provides raw access to the underlying device, arranging for direct I/O between a process and the device.

raw mode   See *canonical mode.*

raw socket   A socket that provides direct access to a lower-level communication protocol.

real GID   See *real group identifier.*

real group identifier (real GID)   The GID that is recorded in the accounting record when a process terminates. The real GID for a process is initially set at the time that a user logs into a system, and is then inherited by child processes across subsequent *fork* and *execve* system calls (irrespective of whether or not a program is set-group-identifier). See also *effective group identifier; set-group-identifier program; saved group identifier.*

real UID   See *real user identifier.*

real user identifier (real UID)   With respect to a process, the true identity of the user that is running the process. The real UID for a process is initially set at the time a user logs into a system, and is then inherited by child processes across subsequent *fork* and *execve* system calls (irrespective of whether or not a program is set-user-identifier). The real UID is recorded in the accounting record when a process terminates. See also *effective user identifier; set-user-identifier program; saved user identifier.*

receive window   In TCP, the range of sequence numbers that defines the data that the system will accept for a connection. Any data with sequence numbers outside this range that are received are dropped. See also *sliding-window scheme.*

reclaim   See *page reclaim.*

reclaim from inactive   A page reclaim from the inactive list. A page can be reclaimed from the inactive list if that page is freed by the page-replacement algorithm, but the page is not reassigned before a process faults on it.

record   In networking, a message that is delimited from other messages on a communication channel. The message boundaries are created by the sender, and are communicated to the receiver. A write or read operation transfers data from a single record, but certain protocols allow a record to be transferred via multiple write or read operations.

recovery storm   A failure condition that can occur when a server is congested on returning to service after a period of being unavailable. If there is heavy pent-up demand for the server, it may be with requests. If the server simply ignores requests that it cannot handle, the clients will quickly resend them. So, the server typically replies "try again later" to the requests that it is not yet ready to service. Clients receiving such a response will wait considerably longer than a typical timeout period before resending their request.

red zone   A read-only region of memory immediately below the last page of the per-process kernel-mode run-time stack. The red zone is set up by the system so that a fault will occur if a process overflows the space allocated for its kernel stack.

referenced page In the virtual-memory system, a page that is read or written.

reference string A dataset that describes the pages referenced by a process over the time of the process's execution. This description represents the memory-related behavior of the process at discrete times during that process's lifetime.

region A range of memory that is being treated in the same way. For example, the text of a program is a region that is read-only and is demand paged from the file on disk that contains it.

relative pathname See *pathname*.

reliably-delivered–message socket A type of socket that guarantees reliable data delivery and preservation of message boundaries, and that is not connection based.

relocation The copying of a program's contents from one place in an address space to another. This copying may be accompanied by modifications to the image of the program, so that memory references encoded in the program remain correct after that program is copied. Code that is not bound to a particular starting memory address is said to be *relocatable*.

remote procedure call (RPC) A procedure call made from a client process to a subroutine running in a different server process. Typically, the client and server processes are running on different machines. A remote procedure call operates much like a local procedure call: the client makes a procedure call, then waits for the result while the procedure executes. See also *marshalling*.

replacement policy The policy that a demand-paged virtual-memory–management system uses to select pages for reuse when memory is otherwise unavailable.

resident object An object that is present in main memory. For example, a page in the virtual address space of a process is resident if its contents are present in main memory.

resident-set size The number of pages of physical memory held by a process. In a well-tuned system, the resident-set size of a process will be that process's working set. Usually, the precise working set cannot be calculated, so a process will have additional pages beyond that needed for its working set.

resource map A data structure used by the system to manage the allocation of a resource that can be described by a set of linear extents.

retransmit timer A timer used by TCP to trigger the retransmission of data. This timer is set each time that data are transmitted to a remote host. It is set to a value that is expected to be greater than the time that it will take the receiving host to receive the data and return an acknowledgment.

reverse-mapped page table See *inverted page table*.

roll forward The double act of reading a log of committed operations, beginning at a checkpoint, and of reapplying any operations that are not reflected in the underlying storage system.

root directory The directory that the kernel uses in resolving absolute pathnames. Each process has a root directory that can be set with the *chroot* system call, and the system has a unique root directory, the identity of which is set at the time that the system is bootstrapped.

root filesystem The filesystem containing the root directory that is considered the root of all filesystems on a machine. The identity of a default root filesystem is compiled into a kernel, although the actual root filesystem used by a system may be set to some other filesystem at the time that a system is bootstrapped.

rotational-layout table A Fast Filesystem data structure that describes the rotational position of blocks in the filesystem. The Fast Filesystem uses the rotational-layout table in selecting rotationally optimal blocks for allocation to a file.

round robin In queueing, an algorithm in which each requester is serviced for a fixed time in a first-come first-served order; requests are placed at the end of the queue if they are incomplete after service.

route In packet-switched–network communication, a route to a destination specifies the host or hosts through which data must be transmitted to reach the destination.

router A machine, also known as a gateway, that has two or more network interfaces, and that forwards packets between the networks to which it has access. Typically, a router runs a routing process that gathers information on the network topology; it uses that information to devise a set of next-hop routes that it installs in the kernel's routing table. See also *routing mechanism; routing policy.*

routing daemon The process in 4.4BSD that provides a routing-management service for the system. This service uses a protocol that implements a distributed database of routing information that is updated dynamically to reflect changes in topological connectivity.

routing mechanism The routing facilities included in the kernel that implement externally defined policies. The routing mechanism uses a lookup mechanism that provides a first-hop route (a specific network interface and immediate destination) for each destination. See also *router; routing policies.*

routing policies The routing facilities provided in a user-level process that define external policies. Routing policies include all the components that the routing daemon uses in choosing the first-hop routes, such as discovery of the local network topology, implementation of various routing protocols, and configuration information specifying local policies. See also *router; routing mechanism.*

routing redirect message A message generated by a gateway when the latter recognizes that a message that it has received can be delivered via a more direct route.

RPC See *remote procedure call*.

run queue The queue of those processes that are ready to execute.

saved GID A mechanism that records the identity of a setgid program by copying the value of the effective GID at the time that the program is *exec*'ed. During its execution, the program may temporarily revoke its setgid privilege by setting is effective GID to its real GID. It can later recover its setgid privilege by setting its effective GID back to its saved GID. See also *effective group identifier*.

saved UID A mechanism that records the identity of a setuid program by copying the value of the effective UID at the time that the program is *exec*'ed. During its execution, the program may temporarily revoke its setuid privilege by setting is effective UID to its real UID. It can later recover its setuid privilege by setting its effective UID back to its saved UID. See also *effective user identifier*.

scheduling In operating systems, the planning used to share a resource. For example, process scheduling is used to share the CPU and main memory.

scheduling priority A per-process parameter maintained by the kernel that specifies the priority with which the latter will schedule the execution of a process. When a process is executing in user mode, the system periodically calculates the scheduling priority, using the process priority and the *nice* parameter.

secondary storage Storage that is used to hold data that do not fit in main memory. Secondary storage is usually located on rotating magnetic media, such as disk drives. See also *backing storage*.

sector The smallest contiguous region on a disk that can be accessed with a single I/O operation.

segment A contiguous range of data defined by a base and an extent. In memory management, a segment describes a region of a process's address space. In communication protocols, a segment is defined by a contiguous range of sequence numbers for which there are associated data. In the Log-Structured Filesystem, a segment is the logical unit of cleaning.

segment table The top level of a three-level hierarchy of data structures used by a forward-mapped page-table algorithm to describe the virtual address space of a process. Each entry in a segment-table points to a page of middle-level page-table pages. A three-level mapping hierarchy is used on the PC and Motorola 68000 architectures. See also *forward-mapped page table; page-table entry; page-table pages*.

send window In TCP, the range of sequence numbers that defines the data that the system can transmit on a connection and be assured that the receiving party has space to hold the data on receipt. Any data with sequence numbers prior to the start of the send window have already been sent and acknowledged. Any data with sequence numbers after the end of the window will not be sent until the send window changes to include them. See also *sliding-window scheme*.

sense request A request passed to the user-request routine of a communication-protocol module as a result of a process making a *stat* system call on a socket.

sequenced-packet socket A type of socket that models sequenced, reliable, unduplicated, connection-based communication that preserves message boundaries.

sequence space The range of sequence numbers that are assigned to data transmitted over a TCP connection. In TCP, sequence numbers are taken from a 32-bit circular space that starts with an arbitrary value called the *initial sequence number*.

serial-line IP (SLIP) An encapsulation used to transfer IP datagrams over asynchronous serial lines. Also, the line discipline that implements this encapsulation.

server process A process that provides services to client processes via an interprocess-communication facility. See also *client process*.

session A collection of process groups established for job control purposes. Normally, a session is created for each login shell. All processes started by that login shell are part of its session.

session leader A process that has created a session. The session leader is the controlling process for the session and is permitted to allocate and assign the controlling terminal for the session. Normally, a session is created for each login shell. All processes started by that login shell are part of its session.

set-group-identifier program A program that runs with an additional group privilege. Set-group-identifier programs are indicated by a bit in the inode of the file. When a process specifies such a file in an *execve* system call, the GID of the file is made the effective GID of the process.

set-priority-level (SPL) A request that sets the current *processor priority level*. In 4.4BSD, all such requests are made with calls to routines that have a name with the prefix "spl." For example, to set the processor priority level high enough to block interrupts that cause terminal processing, the kernel would call the *spltty()* routine. See also *processor priority level*.

set-user-identifier program A program that runs with an UID different from that of the process that started it running. Set-user-identifier programs are indicated by a bit in the inode of the file. When a process specifies such a file in an *execve* system call, the UID of the file is made the effective UID of the process.

shadow object An anonymous object that is interposed between a process and an underlying object to prevent changes made by the process from being reflected back to the underlying object. A shadow object is used when a process makes a private mapping of a file, so that changes made by the process are not reflected in the file.

shell A program that interprets and executes user commands. When a user logs into a UNIX system, a shell process is normally created with its standard input, standard output, and standard error descriptors directed to the terminal or network virtual terminal on which the user logged in.

short-term–scheduling algorithm The algorithm used by the system to select the next process to run from among the set of processes that are deemed runnable. The *long-term–scheduling algorithm*, on the other hand, can influence the set of runnable processes by swapping processes in and out of main memory (and thus in and out of the set of runnable processes).

signal In UNIX, a software event. In 4.4BSD, this event is modeled after a hardware interrupt.

signal-driven I/O A mode in which a descriptor can be placed, whereby the system will deliver a SIGIO signal to a process whenever I/O is possible on the descriptor. See also *nonblocking I/O; polling I/O*.

signal handler A procedure that is invoked in response to a signal.

signal post A notification to a process that a signal is pending for that process. Since most of the actions associated with a signal are done by the receiving process, a process that is posting a signal usually does little more than to record the pending signal in the receiving process's process structure and to arrange for the receiving process to be run.

signal-trampoline code A piece of code that is used to invoke a signal handler. The signal-trampoline code contains instructions that set up parameters for calling a signal handler, do the actual call to the signal handler, and, on return, do a *sigreturn* system call to reset kernel state and resume execution of the process after the signal is handled.

silly-window syndrome A condition observed in window-based flow-control schemes in which a receiver sends several small (i.e., silly) window allocations, rather than waiting for a reasonable-sized window to become available.

single indirect block See *indirect block*.

slave device A hardware device that is controlled by a *master device*. For example, a disk drive is a slave device to a SCSI bus controller. The distinction between master and slave devices is used by the autoconfiguration system. A slave device is assumed to be accessible only if its corresponding master device is present.

slave routine A device-driver routine that is responsible for deciding whether or not a slave device is present on a machine. Slave routines are never called unless the master device for the slave has been probed successfully.

sleep queue The queue of those processes that are blocked awaiting an event. The name is derived from the *sleep*() routine that places processes on this queue.

sliding-window scheme A flow-control scheme in which the receiver limits the number of data that it is willing to receive. This limit is expressed as a contiguous range of sequence numbers termed the *receive window*. It is periodically communicated to the sender, who is expected to transmit only those data that are within the window. As data are received and acknowledged, the window *slides* forward in the sequence space. See also *sequence space; receive window; send window*.

SLIP See *serial-line IP*.

small-packet avoidance In networking, avoiding the transmission of a packet so small that its transmission would be inefficient.

socket In the 4.4BSD interprocess-communication model, an endpoint of communication. Also, the data structure that is used to implement the socket abstraction, and the system call that is used to create a socket.

soft limit A limit that may be temporarily exceeded, or exceeded a limited number of times. A soft limit is typically used in conjunction with a hard limit. See also *hard limit*.

soft link See *symbolic link*.

software interrupt A software-initiated interrupt. It is requested with an asynchronous system trap.

software-interrupt process A process that is set running in response to a software interrupt. In 4.4BSD, input processing for each transport-layer communication protocol is embodied in a software-interrupt process.

special file See *device special file*.

spin loop A sequence of instructions that causes the processor to do a specific operation repeatedly. Standalone device drivers use spin loops to implement real-time delays.

SPL See *set-priority-level*.

stack An area of memory set aside for temporary storage, or for procedure and interrupt-service linkages. A stack uses the last-in, first-out (LIFO) concept. On most architectures, the stack grows from high memory addresses to low memory addresses. As items are added to (pushed onto) the stack, the stack pointer decrements; as items are retrieved from (popped off) the stack, the stack pointer increments.

stack segment A segment that holds a stack. See also *bss segment; data segment; text segment*.

stale translation A translation or mapping that was true previously, but that is no longer valid. For example, on machines that have a translation lookaside buffer, if a page-table entry in memory is changed to alter the mapping, any address translation for that page that is present in the translation lookaside buffer must be flushed to avoid a stale translation.

standalone Software that can run without the support of an operating system.

standalone device driver A device driver that is used in a standalone program. A standalone device driver usually differs from a device driver used in an operating system in that it does not have interrupt services, memory management, or full support for virtual-memory mapping. In the 4.4BSD standalone I/O library, for example, a standalone device driver polls a device to decide when an operation has completed, and is responsible for setting up its own memory mapping when doing transfers between the device and main memory.

standalone I/O library A library of software that is used in writing standalone programs. This library includes standalone device drivers that are used to do I/O.

standard error The I/O stream on which error messages are conventionally placed. This stream is usually associated with descriptor 2 in a process.

standard input The I/O stream on which input is conventionally received. This stream is usually associated with descriptor 0 in a process.

standard output The I/O stream to which output is conventionally directed. This stream is usually associated with descriptor 1 in a process.

start routine A device-driver routine that is responsible for starting a device operation after the system has acquired all the resources that are required for the operation.

stateless server A server that does not need to maintain any information about which clients it is serving or which data have been passed to them. Every request that is received by such a server must be completely self-contained, providing all information needed to fulfill it.

sticky bit The bit in an inode representing a directory that indicates that an unprivileged user may not delete or rename files of other users in that directory. The sticky bit may be set by any user on a directory that the user owns or for which she has appropriate permissions. Historically, the bit in an inode that indicated that the text segment of the program was to be shared and kept memory or swap-space resident because of expected future use. That bit is no longer needed for this purpose because the virtual-memory system tracks recently used executables.

stream I/O system A facility in System V Release 4 that permits the flexible configuration of processing for streams of data. In this system, it is possible to connect kernel-resident modules dynamically in a stack-oriented fashion, and to have these modules process data sent and received on an I/O stream.

stream socket A type of socket that models a reliable, connection-based, byte stream that can support out-of-band data transmission.

subnetwork A physical network that is a part of a larger logical network with a single shared network address. The subnet is assigned a subset of the logical network's address space.

superblock A data structure in the on-disk filesystem that specifies the basic parameters of the filesystem.

superuser The user whose UID is 0. Processes owned by the superuser are granted special privileges by UNIX. The superuser's login name is usually *root*.

swap area A region on secondary storage that is used for swapping and paging.

swap device A device on which a swap area resides.

swapper In 4.4BSD, the name of the kernel process that implements the swapping portion of the memory-management facilities. Historically, the swapper is process 0. See also *pagedaemon*.

swapping A memory-management algorithm in which entire processes are moved to and from secondary storage when main memory is in short supply.

swap space   See *swap area*.

symbolic link   A file whose contents are interpreted as a pathname when it is supplied as a component of a pathname. Also called a *soft link*.

synchronous   Synchronized with the currently running process. For example, in UNIX, all I/O operations appear to be synchronous: The *read* and *write* system calls do not return until the operation has been completed. (For a *write*, however, the data may not actually be written to their final destination until some time later—for example, in writing to a disk file.)

system activity   An entry into the kernel. System activities can be categorized according to the event or action that initiates them: system calls, hardware interrupts, hardware traps, and software-initiated traps or interrupts.

system call   In operating systems, a request to the system for service; also called a *system service request*.

system clock   The device that is used to maintain the system's notion of time of day. On most systems, this device is an interval timer that periodically interrupts the CPU. The system uses these interrupts to maintain the current time of day, as well as to do periodic functions such as process scheduling.

system mode   See *kernel mode*.

TCP   See *Transmission Control Protocol*.

terminal   In computer systems, a device used to enter and receive data interactively from a computer. Most terminals include a CRT, which displays data that are received from a computer. In the Electrical Industry Association (EIA) standard RS-232-C for connecting computers and data-terminal equipment (DTE), a terminal is a device that is placed at the other end of a wire that is connected to data-communications equipment (DCE). In this standard, a terminal might be any kind of device, rather than only a device on which people type.

terminal multiplexer   A hardware device that connects multiple serial lines to a computer. These serial lines can be used to connect terminals, modems, printers, and similar devices.

termios structure   The structure used to describe terminal state. Terminal state includes special characters, such as the erase, kill, and word-erase characters; modes of operation, such as canonical or noncanonical; and hardware serial-line parameters, such as parity and baud rate.

text segment   The segment of a program that holds machine instructions. The system usually makes a program's text segment read-only and shareable by multiple processes when the program image is loaded into memory. See also *bss segment; data segment; stack segment*.

thrashing   A condition where requested memory utilization far exceeds the memory availability. When a machine is thrashing, it usually spends more time doing system-related tasks than executing application code in user mode.

thread The unit of execution of a process. A thread requires an address space and other resources, but it can shared many of those resources with other threads. Threads sharing an address space and other resources are scheduled independently, and can all do system calls simultaneously.

three-level mapping hierarchy See *segment table*.

tick An interrupt by the system clock.

time quantum In a timesharing environment, the period of time that the process scheduler gives a process to run before it preempts that process so that another process can execute. Also called a *time slice*.

timer backoff The rate at which a timer value is increased. For example, in TCP, the value of the retransmit timer is determined by a table of multipliers that provide a near-exponential increase in timeout values.

time slice See *time quantum*.

time-stable identifier An identifier that refers uniquely to some entity both while it exists and for a long time after it is deleted. A time-stable identifier allows a system to remember an identity across transient failures, and to detect and report errors for attempts to access deleted entities.

TLB See *translation lookaside buffer*.

top half With regard to system operation, the routines in the kernel that are invoked synchronously as a result of a system call or trap. These routines depend on per-process state and can block by calling *sleep( )*. See also *bottom half*.

trace trap A trap used by the system to implement single-stepping in program debuggers. On architectures that provide trace-bit support, the kernel sets the hardware-defined trace bit in the context of the process being debugged, and places the process on the run queue. When the process next runs, the trace bit causes a trap to be generated after the process executes one instruction. This trap is fielded by the kernel, which stops the process and returns control to the debugging process.

track In computer systems, the sectors of a disk that are accessible by one head at one of its seek positions.

track cache When the kernel is reading from a disk, memory associated with the disk that holds data that are passing under the disk heads regardless of whether they have been requested explicitly. When the kernel is writing to a disk, memory associated with the disk in which data are stored until the disk heads reach the correct position for writing them.

translation lookaside buffer (TLB) A processor cache containing translations for recently used virtual addresses.

Transmission Control Protocol (TCP) A connection-oriented transport protocol used in the Internet. TCP provides for the reliable transfer of data, as well as for the out-of-band indication of urgent data.

transport layer The layer of software in the network subsystem that provides the addressing structure required for communication between sockets, as well as any protocol mechanisms necessary for socket semantics such as reliable data delivery.

triple indirect block   See *indirect block*.

tty driver   The software module that implements the semantics associated with a terminal device. See also *line discipline*.

2MSL timer   A timer used by the TCP protocol during connection shutdown. The name refers to the fact that the timer is set for twice the maximum time that a segment may exist in the network. This value is chosen to ensure that future shutdown actions on the connection are done only after all segments associated with the connection no longer exist. See also *maximum segment lifetime*.

type-ahead   Transmission of data to a system, usually by a user typing at a keyboard, before the data are requested by a process.

u-dot   See *user structure*.

UDP   See *User Datagram Protocol*.

UID   See *user identifier*.

uio   A data structure used by the system to describe an I/O operation. This structure contains an array of *iovec* structures; the file offset at which the operation should start; the sum of the lengths of the I/O vectors; a flag showing whether the operation is a read or a write; and a flag showing whether the source and destination are both in the kernel's address space, or whether the source and destination are split between user and kernel address spaces.

urgent data   In TCP, data that are marked for urgent delivery.

user area   See *user structure*.

User Datagram Protocol (UDP)   A simple, unreliable, datagram protocol used in the Internet. UDP provides only peer-to-peer addressing and optional data checksums.

user identifier (UID)   A nonnegative integer that identifies a user uniquely. UIDs are used in the access-control facilities provided by the filesystem. See also *effective user identifier; real user identifier; saved user identifier; set-user-identifier program*.

user mode   The least privileged processor-access mode. User processes run in user mode.

user-request routine   A routine provided by each communication protocol that directly supports a socket (a protocol that indirectly supports a socket is layered underneath a protocol that directly supports a socket). This routine serves as the main interface between the layer of software that implements sockets and the communication protocol. The interprocess-communication facilities make calls to the user-request routine for most socket-related system calls. See also *connect request; control request; listen request; sense request*.

user structure   A data structure maintained by the kernel for each active process in the system. The user structure contains the process control block, process statistics, signal actions, and kernel-mode run-time stack. Unlike the process structure, the user structure for a process is moved to secondary storage if the process is swapped out. Also referred to as the *u-dot area* and *user area*.

virtual address An address that references a location in a *virtual address space*.

virtual-address aliasing Two or more processes mapping the same physical page at different virtual addresses. When using an inverted page table, there can only be one virtual address mapping any given physical page at any one time. Here, the kernel must invalidate the page-table entry for the aliased page whenever it switches between the processes with the conflicting virtual addresses for that page. See also *inverted page table*.

virtual address space A contiguous range of virtual-memory locations.

virtual machine A machine whose architecture is emulated in software.

virtual memory A facility whereby the effective range of addressable memory locations provided to a process is independent of the size of main memory; that is, the virtual address space of a process is independent of the physical address space of the CPU.

virtual-memory object A kernel data structure that represents a repository of data—for example, a file. An object contains a pager to get and put the data from and to secondary storage, and a list of physical pages that cache pieces of the repository in memory.

vnode An extensible object-oriented interface containing generic information about a file. Each active file in the system is represented by a vnode, plus filesystem-specific information associated with the vnode by the filesystem containing the file. The kernel maintains a single systemwide table of vnodes that is always resident in main memory. Inactive entries in the table are reused on a least-recently used basis.

wait The system call that is used to wait for the termination of a descendent process.

wait channel A value used to identify an event for which a process is waiting. In most situations, a wait channel is defined as the address of a data structure related to the event for which a process is waiting. For example, if a process is waiting for the completion of a disk read, the wait channel is specified as the address of the buffer data structure supplied to the block I/O system.

wildcard route A route that is used if there is no explicit route to a destination.

window probe In TCP, a message that is transmitted when data are queued for transmission, the send window is too small for TCP to bother sending data, and no message containing an update for the send window has been received in a long time. A window-probe message contains a single octet of data.

wired page Memory that is not subject to replacement by the pageout daemon. A nonpageable range of virtual addresses has physical memory assigned when the addresses are allocated. Wired pages must never cause a page fault that might result in a blocking operation. Wired pages are typically used in the kernel's address space.

word-erase character   The character that is recognized by the terminal handler in canonical mode to mean "delete the most recently typed word on this terminal." By default, preceding whitespace and then a maximal sequence of non-whitespace characters are erased. Alternatively, an alternate erase algorithm tuned to deleting pathname components may be specified. Each terminal session can have a different word-erase character, and the user can change that character at any time with an *tcsetattr* system call. The terminal handler does not recognize the word-erase character on terminals that are in noncanonical mode. See also *erase character; kill character.*

working directory   See *current working directory.*

working set   The set of pages in a process's virtual address space to which memory references have been made over the most recent few seconds. Most processes exhibit some locality of reference, and the size of their working set is typically less than one-half of their total virtual-memory size.

zombie process   A process that has terminated, but whose exit status has not yet been received by its parent process (or by **init**).

Index

Index   **573**

Index   **573**

setsid, 109
setsockopt, 367, 391, 405, 410, 441, 445, 471, 518
settimeofday, 63
shutdown, 367, 386, 463
sigaction, 102–104, 106, 516
sigaltstack, 102, 104
sigpause, 89
sigpending, 104
sigprocmask, 102, 530
sigreturn, 103, 107, 542
sigsuspend, 102
socket, 11, 16, 32, 34, 43, 364–365, 374, 380, 406, 410, 481, 519
socketpair, 367, 409, 519
stat, 232, 249, 262, 408, 541
statfs, 223
symlink, 295
sync, 197, 220, 239, 274, 291
sysctl, 399, 404, 450, 509–510
tcsetattr, 521, 528, 549
truncate, 39, 262
undelete, 236
unlink, 38
unmount, 232
vfork, 98, 108, 146, 149–150, 188
wait, 27, 69, 77, 82, 89, 108, 149, 155–156
wait4, 27, 99–100, 112
write, 25, 32, 35–36, 43, 113, 145, 206, 213, 217, 254, 274, 297, 321, 326–327, 340, 349, 366–367, 377, 382, 481, 522, 536, 545
writev, 35–36, 216, 366, 527
system debugging, 508
system entry, 50
system performance, 14, 53, 56, 58, 60, 62, 64, 78, 97, 384, 503
system processes initialization, 502–504
system shutdown, 507–508
system startup, 491–492
    initial state, 494
system statistics, 58

T

table, forward-mapped page, 173, 523
TCP. See *Transmission Control Protocol*
tcp_close(), 463
tcp_ctloutput(), 471

tcp_fasttimo(), 460, 467
tcp_input(), 458, 465, 467, 476
    operation of, 464–467
tcp_output(), 458, 462, 465, 467–472
    operation of, 469
tcp_slowtimo(), 459–460
tcp_timers(), 458–459
tcp_usrreq(), 458, 461, 463, 468, 471
tcsetattr system call, 521, 528, 549
tcsetpgrp(), 110
telldir(), 248
TENEX operating system, 10
Tenth Edition UNIX, 7
terminal, 42–43, 545
    buffering, 344–346
    multiplexer, 194, 337, 545
    operations, 347–355
terminal driver, 204, 339–340, 547
    bottom half of, 340
    close(), 355
    data queues, 343–346, 348–350, 352–353
    hardware state, 342–343
    input, 351–353
    input, bottom half of, 351–352
    input silo, 351
    input, top half of, 352–353
    ioctl(), 340–342, 353–354
    modem control, 346–347
    modem transitions, 354–355
    modes, 338–339, 343, 351–352
    open(), 347
    output, 349–350
    output, bottom half of, 350
    output, *stop*(), 353
    output, top half of, 349–350
    software state, 343
    special characters, 338, 343
    start(), 349
    *tc**(), 340–342
    top half of, 339
    user interface, 10, 340–342
    window size, 343, 347
terminal process group, 110, 343–344, 352, 355
termios, 15
    structure, 340, 545
text segment, 29, 60–61, 545. See also *shared text segment*
Thompson, Ken, 3, 7, 10, 22
thrashing, 79–80, 545

UNIX and Open Systems Series

Series Editors
  Marshall Kirk McKusick
  John S. Quarterman

Programming under Mach	Joseph Boykin David Kirschen Alan Langerman Susan LoVerso
Practical Internetworking with *TCP/IP and UNIX*	Smoot Carl-Mitchell John S. Quarterman
Frontiers of Electronic Commerce	Ravi Kalakota Andrew Whinston
Network Management: A Practical *Perspective, Second Edition*	Allan Leinwand Karen Fang Conroy
The Internet Connection: System *Connectivity and Configuration*	John S. Quarterman Smoot Carl-Mitchell
UNIX, POSIX, and Open Systems: *The Open Standards Puzzle*	John S. Quarterman Susanne Wilhelm
A Quarter Century of UNIX	Peter H. Salus
Casting the Net: From ARPANET *to Internet and Beyond*	Peter H. Salus
Network Programming in Windows NT	Alok Sinha

Other Titles of Interest

UNIX for the Impatient, Second Edition	Paul W. Abrahams
	Bruce R. Larson
Distributed Systems: Concepts and Design, Second Edition	George Coulouris
	Jean Dollimore
	Tim Kindberg
Operating System Concepts, Fourth Edition	Abraham Silberschatz
	Peter Galvin
A Practical Guide to the UNIX System, Third Edition	Mark G. Sobell
BUGS in Writing	Lyn Dupré